CONSUMER GUIDE®

BASEBALL CARD PRICE GUIDE 1994

C0-AZO-329

All rights reserved under International and Pan American copyright conventions. Copyright © 1994 Publications International, Ltd. This publication may not be reproduced or quoted in whole or in part by mimeograph or any other printed or electronic means, or for presentation on radio, television, videotape, or film without written permission from Louis Weber, C.E.O. of Publications International, Ltd., 7373 North Cicero Ave., Lincolnwood, Illinois 60646. Permission is never granted for commercial purposes. Printed in U.S.A.

Contributing writer: Jeff Kurowski
Photography: Sam Griffith Studio, Inc.
Special thanks to: AU Sports Memorabilia, Skokie, Illinois

Jeff Kurowski is a professional baseball card price guide coordinator and former editor of *Sports Card Price Guide Monthly* and *Sports Collector's Digest Baseball Card Price Guide*. He also served as the editor of *The Standard Catalogue of Baseball Cards*.

Contents

Contents

INTRODUCTION

Now, more than ever, is the time to read the *Baseball Card Price Guide*. Card companies keep challenging the interests (and bank accounts) of collectors with a ceaseless flow of new products. And it's no secret that uncertain economic times force hobbyists to ponder the future of baseball cards—along with other collectibles—as sure-fire investments.

While it's true that not every baseball card skyrocketed in value during 1993, don't start a cardboard bonfire just yet. The wisest card veterans know that a buyer's market has prevailed during the past year, when temporary downswings in price created some short-term bargains.

You've taken a first step toward a healthy hobby future. This publication reviews all major card sets and offers values for selected cards that have been issued during the last 45 years, from 1948 Bowman through 1993 Upper Deck. Individual values are given for all major sets and for various series within sets.

Along with listings for stars, rookies, and other notables, you'll find introductory paragraphs offering background notes on each year's edition. You'll also see listings for many cards of secondary players: These are cards—known as "commons"—that hold somewhat less interest for fans and collectors. In all, more than 35,000 cards have been individually selected for listing in this book.

Unlike other price guides, the *Baseball Card Price Guide* does more than simply list prices. Much more. Some 800 photos illustrate important cards from every set. This provides the opportunity to examine the details of valuable cards up close, and at the same time you can learn to identify each set at a glance. Best of all, this book displays cards the way they were meant to be, in full color and close to life size.

Count on the *Baseball Card Price Guide* for an advance look at 1994's Hottest Cards. This section offers a look at two dozen new cards of baseball's brightest newcomers. Along with an identifying checklist, value predictions are included for these potential stars.

Throughout these pages you'll find some Best Buy suggestions indicated by a bullet symbol (•) following the card number. In past editions, a few of the player types highlighted include rising stars, reborn sluggers, and future Hall of Famers. Even sets from the 1950s and 1960s can provide surprises. For example, Steve Carlton or Mike Schmidt will be up for Hall of Fame induction soon, and prices for their cards should shoot way up. Sometimes prices will rise up to 50 percent if a player gets inducted.

Selections for Best Buys and other prices were established after a thorough analysis of previous card prices. Feedback from a number of card dealers and collectors helped shape the price estimates that follow.

Note that this volume does not include checklists for every card issued by the major companies. That's because many of these past sets, such as the infamous 1982 Topps KMart set, have become hobby nightmares. Overproduced editions have glutted the hobby and confused newcomers. Some beginners quit collecting out of frustration, unable to find, much less afford, every card issued by even one manufacturer.

The prices listed in this book are estimated retail values. Hobbyists planning to sell their cards should expect dealers to pay anywhere from 50 to 60 percent of the prices specified for star cards. Commons of poorer quality could be sold for about ten percent of these prices.

To make the most of the *Baseball Card Price Guide,* it's important to note that some names appear in italic type, and several abbreviations are used.

Names in *italics:* Rookie cards. A rookie card is defined as a card issue for the first appearance made by a player for any card company *during his rookie season.* However, a player who is shuttled between the majors and minors may not appear on a card for years. In that case he might not have a rookie card at all, though he would eventually have a First Card (FC) (see below). A rookie card may be part of a specially designated rookie issue shared by other players, or it may be an ordinary card.

In addition, fall extension sets like Fleer Update and Topps Traded have muddled the definition of rookie cards. Because they have not been sold individually through any sources outside of the hobby in the past, cards from fall-issued sets are not recognized by the *Baseball Card Price Guide* as genuine rookie cards. Topps and Donruss have sold complete sets of these late issues on a sporadic basis through toy stores and by mail order. Upper Deck, however, has been the only company through 1992 willing to include special updated cards mixed in individual packages with its other standard-issue cards. When collectors have unlimited access to all the fall-issued cards (without being forced to rely on hobby dealers) then rookie card definitions can be reconsidered.

(DK): Diamond Kings. This refers to a yearly card set of painted portraits of one selected player from each team—part of the Donruss sets from 1982 through 1991. These cards became bonus-card inserts separate from the regular set beginning in 1992.

(FC): First cards. This means that a listed card marks a player's *first appearance for a certain card company.* When it comes to rookie cards, don't believe everything card companies claim. A special designation seen on the card, such as the Donruss "Rated Rookie" label, doesn't mean you're seeing the first-ever card of that player. Todd Van Poppel is a 1992 "Rated Rookie," yet he appears in many 1991 sets. And when Reds manager Lou Piniella began his playing career in the 1960s, Topps pictured him on different "Rookie" cards in consecutive years—as a Cleveland Indian (1968) and a Seattle Pilot (1969). Actually, he made his debut with the Baltimore Orioles back in 1964.

FS: Future Stars. A number of cards for promising young players carry this designation.

IA: In-Action cards. On several occasions Topps has produced both standard cards and action-photo cards of selected popular players.

(RR): "Rated Rookies." These are specially marked Donruss cards honoring promising newcomers.

(DP): Double-Printed cards. When Topps expanded its set size to more than 600 cards, uneven numbers neutralized the usual 132-card printing sheets. To compensate, the company printed certain cards twice on each sheet. The supply of some cards doubled as a result. When star cards were involved, this increase in supply lessened demand and lowered the value. Common cards of average players take drastic price drops when double-printing occurs.

In addition to these abbreviations, it is worth noting that some set profiles mention high-number and low-number cards. Before 1974, Topps issued cards throughout each summer in several series of approximately 110 cards each. Typically, the last 100-odd cards from such a set are in shorter supply than other series. This occurred because some retailers overstocked baseball cards early in the summer when demand was high. When the baseball season was winding down, the cards issued later in the season—those with higher numbers—were harder to find. Since fewer were sold in the past, fewer are available today. The result of this process is that such high-numbered cards are scarce and as a consequence tend to be more valuable.

Condition, however, is even more important than supply and demand when determining card values. The prices listed in this *Guide* are for cards in top condition—for all sets issued prior to 1980 that means Near Mint, and for all sets since 1980 that means Mint. Obviously, cards in poorer condition will command lower prices. This makes proper grading of your cards of critical importance. The following guidelines on condition will be helpful in grading and thus estimating the value of your cards.

Introduction

Mint cards are perfect, well-centered cards showing absolutely no wear, fading, scratches, printing flaws, loss of luster, or other imperfections. True Mint cards prior to 1980 may command values that are 40 to 50 percent higher than the Near Mint price listed. But it would be a mistake to assume that cards found in factory-collated sets or freshly removed from packs will always be graded as Mint. Cards with printing flaws, uneven borders, or gum stains can be discounted by as much as 20 percent.

Near Mint cards are nearly perfect, with only a very minor flaw preventing a grade of full Mint. Such cards may be slightly off-center or have one corner that is less than perfect. Near Mint cards issued since 1980 may be worth 70 to 80 percent of the Mint value listed.

Excellent cards may have lost some original surface gloss, but they will display very little wear, have no serious defects, and still have sharp corners. Excellent cards may be off-center, but will have no creases or stains from gum or wax. Cards in Excellent condition are worth approximately 40 to 60 percent of the Mint or Near Mint values listed.

Very Good cards will display some wear and have slightly rounded corners, minor creases, or stains. They will usually be valued at about 25 to 30 percent of the Mint or Near Mint values listed.

Good cards show a great deal of handling and perhaps even some abuse. They may have softened corners, major creases, and other defects, but all parts of the card will still be intact, without being defaced by holes, tears, tape or writing. This is generally the poorest condition that most collectors would even consider. Cards in Good condition are worth approximately 10 to 15 percent of the Mint or Near Mint values listed.

Fair and *Poor* cards show excessive wear or damage and are generally not considered collectible.

Remember that geographical demand can influence card prices almost as much as condition or scarcity. Early in the 1993 season John Olerud and Andres Galarraga were pushing the magical .400 mark. Card values in Toronto and Colorado soared as locals snapped up those cards.

While reading the *Baseball Card Price Guide,* understand that it should be used only as a general aid in determining the value of baseball cards. Changes in methods of printing or distribution by card companies and successes (or failures) by teams and players themselves can cause quick fluctuations in card values. If a team does surprisingly well in a season, collectors may often go after cards of players from that team, just because they have had extra media attention.

Finally, this publication does not represent an offer by the publishers or any other party to buy or sell cards. Reputable hobby dealers remain the best source for collectors. Check card shops, hobby conventions, advertisements in collector publications, or the telephone book business directory under "baseball cards." While every effort has been made to provide a high level of accuracy in the price estimates contained within this book, the publishers cannot assume any responsibility for errors that may occur.

The *Baseball Card Price Guide* is for your use and enjoyment. But don't forget that the actual paper and ink used for each card has a minimal intrinsic value. The unpredictable and sometimes amazing prices realized from sets and singles come from the ever-changing interests and loyalties shown by you. As a fan, collector, and consumer, you can help determine the fate of a hobby and an industry.

1948 BOWMAN

The Philadelphia-based Bowman Company entered the baseball card market in 1948 with this set of 48 cards. Featuring black-and-white photos of players on the front (with stadium backgrounds) and black printing on gray cardboard on the back, these 2¹⁄₁₆- by 2½-inch cards took Bowman to market dominance in a single year. The white-bordered cards were sold with a package of gum, one card per pack. A total of 12 cards were short-printed (numbers 7, 8, 13, 16, 20, 22, 24, 26, 28, 29, 30, and 34). With the exception of Phil Rizzuto (number 8) all short-prints are lesser-known players today. Eight Hall of Famers are included: Berra, Feller, Kiner, Mize, Musial, Schoendienst, Slaughter, and Spahn.

	NR MT
Complete set	$3800.00
Commons (1-36)	22.00
Commons (37-48)	32.00

36 Stan Musial

1	*Bob Elliott*	$95.00
2	*Ewell (The Whip) Blackwell*	50.00
3	*Ralph Kiner*	200.00
4	Johnny Mize	100.00
5	Bob Feller	250.00
6	*Larry (Yogi) Berra*	600.00
7	Pete (Pistol Pete) Reiser	65.00
8	Phil (Scooter) Rizzuto	275.00
9	Walker Cooper	25.00
10	Buddy Rosar	22.00
12	*Johnny Sain*	60.00
13	Willard Marshall	30.00
14	*Allie Reynolds*	55.00
16	Jack Lohrke	32.00
17	Enos (Country) Slaughter	100.00
18	*Warren Spahn*	290.00
19	Tommy Henrich	30.00
20	Buddy Kerr	30.00
22	Floyd (Bill) Bevins	30.00
24	Emil (Dutch) Leonard	30.00
25	Barney McCoskey	22.00
26	Frank Shea	30.00
28	Emil (The Antelope) Verban	30.00
29	*Joe Page*	50.00
30	"Whitey" Lockman	45.00
34	Sheldon (Available) Jones	30.00
35	George (Snuffy) Stirnweiss	22.00
36	*Stan Musial*	900.00
38	Al "Red" Schoendienst	175.00
40	*Marty Marion*	80.00
41	*Rex Barney*	35.00
42	Ray Poat	32.00
43	Bruce Edwards	32.00
44	Johnny Wyrostek	32.00
45	Hank Sauer	40.00
46	Herman Wehmeier	32.00
47	*Bobby Thomson*	80.00
48	*George "Dave" Koslo*	60.00

1949 BOWMAN

Bowman's sophomore series of 240 cards for 1949 was probably the most complete set that year. The 2¹⁄₁₆- by 2½-inch cards feature colorized photo portraits with white borders on solid color backgrounds. The backs are cream-colored with red-and-blue printing. Rookie cards for Hall of Famers Robin Roberts and Duke Snider are included, and the great Satchel Paige makes a rare set appearance. An unusual error occurs on card number 240: It was supposed to show Babe Young, but somehow Bobby Young's photo was printed instead. Also, cards #1-3 and 5-73 can be found with white or gray backs.

84 Roy Campanella

		NR MT
Complete set		$17,000.00
Commons (1-36)		18.00
Commons (37-73)		20.00
Commons (74-144)		15.00
Commons (145-240)		75.00

1	Vernon Bickford	$80.00
2	Carroll "Whitey" Lockman	20.00
3	Bob Porterfield	22.00
4	Jerry Priddy (no name on front)	18.00
4	Jerry Priddy (name on front)	35.00
5	Hank Sauer	25.00
6	Phil Cavarretta	23.00

7	Joe Dobson	18.00
8	Murray Dickson	18.00
9	Ferris Fain	18.00
11	Lou Boudreau	70.00
14	Curt Simmons	30.00
15	Ned Garver	18.00
18	Bobby Thomson	35.00
19	Bobby Brown	60.00
20	Gene Hermanski	18.00
23	Bobby Doerr	75.00
24	Stan Musial	575.00
26	George Kell	60.00
27	Bob Feller	165.00
29	Ralph Kiner	110.00
32	Eddie Yost	20.00
33	Warren Spahn	175.00
35	Vic Raschi	50.00
36	Harold "Peewee" Reese	220.00

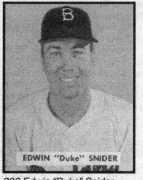

EDWIN "Duke" SNIDER

226 Edwin "Duke" Snider

224 Leroy "Satchell" Paige

37	John Wyrostek	15.00
38	Emil "The Antelope" Verban	15.00
39	Bill Goodman	15.00
40	George "Red"Munger	15.00
41	Lou Brissie	15.00
42	Walter "Hoot" Evers	15.00
43	Dale Mitchell	15.00
44	Dave Philley	15.00
45	Wally Westlake	15.00
46	Robin Roberts	275.00
47	Johnny Sain	30.00
48	Willard Marshall	15.00
49	Frank Shea	22.00
50	Jackie Robinson	900.00
51	Herman Wehmeier	15.00
52	Johnny Schmitz	15.00
53	Jack Kramer	15.00
54	Marty "Slats" Marion	30.00
55	Eddie Joost	15.00
56	Pat Mullin	15.00
57	Gene Bearden	15.00
58	Bob Elliott	15.00
59	Jack "Lucky" Lohrke	15.00
60	Larry "Yogi" Berra	350.00
61	Rex Barney	20.00
62	Grady Hatton	15.00
63	Andy Pafko	20.00
64	Dom "The Little Professor" DiMaggio	30.00
65	Enos "Country" Slaughter	90.00
66	Elmer Valo	25.00
67	Alvin Dark	30.00
70	*Carl Furillo*	75.00
78	Sam Zoldak (no name on front)	15.00
78	Sam Zoldak (name on front)	30.00
82	Joe Page	25.00
83	Bob Scheffing (no name on front)	15.00
83	Bob Scheffing (name on front)	30.00
84	*Roy Campanella*	1000.00
85	Johnny "Big John" Mize (no name on front)	80.00
85	Johnny "Big John" Mize (name on front)	150.00
86	Johnny Pesky	25.00
88	Bill Salkeld (no name on front)	15.00
88	Bill Salkeld (name on front)	30.00
98	Phil Rizzuto (no name on front)	110.00
98	Phil Rizzuto (name on front)	225.00
100	*Gil Hodges*	250.00
101	Sid Gordon	15.00
110	*Early Wynn*	125.00
111	Al "Red" Schoendienst	75.00
112	Sam Chapman	15.00
113	Ray LaManno	15.00
114	Allie Reynolds	35.00
145	Sylvester "Blix" Donnelly	75.00
146	Myron "Mike" McCormick	75.00
147	Elmer "Bert" Singleton	75.00
148	Bob Swift	75.00
149	Roy Partee	75.00
150	Alfred "Allie" Clark	75.00
151	Maurice "Mickey" Harris	75.00
152	Clarence Maddern	75.00
153	Phil Masi	75.00
154	Clint Hartung	75.00
155	Fermin "Mickey" Guerra	75.00

156	Al "Zeke" Zarilla	75.00
157	Walt Masterson	75.00
158	Harry "The Cat" Brecheen	100.00
159	Glen Moulder	75.00
160	Jim Blackburn	75.00
161	John "Jocko" Thompson	75.00
162	*Elwin "Preacher" Roe*	150.00
163	Clyde McCullough	75.00
164	*Vic Wertz*	100.00
165	George "Snuffy" Stirnweiss	80.00
166	Mike Tresh	75.00
167	Boris "Babe" Martin	75.00
168	Doyle Lade	75.00
169	Jeff Heath	75.00
170	Bill Rigney	77.00
171	Dick Fowler	75.00
172	Eddie Pellagrini	75.00
173	Eddie Stewart	75.00
174	*Terry Moore*	125.00
175	Luke Appling	150.00
176	Ken Raffensberger	75.00
177	Stan Lopata	80.00
178	Tommy Brown	75.00
179	Hugh Casey	80.00
180	Connie Berry	75.00
181	Gus Niarhos	70.00
182	Hal Peck	70.00
183	Lou Stringer	70.00
184	Bob Chipman	70.00
185	Pete Reiser	100.00
186	John "Buddy" Kerr	70.00
187	Phil Marchildon	70.00
188	Karl Drews	70.00
189	Earl Wooten	70.00
190	Jim Hearn	70.00
191	Joe Haynes	70.00
192	Harry Gumbert	70.00
193	Ken Trinkle	70.00
194	*Ralph Branca*	110.00
195	Eddie Bockman	75.00
196	Fred Hutchinson	100.00
197	Johnny Lindell	75.00
198	Steve Gromek	75.00
199	Cecil "Tex" Hughson	70.00
200	Jess Dobernic	70.00

214 Richie Ashburn

201	Sibby Sisti	70.00
202	Larry Jansen	90.00
203	Barney McCosky	70.00
204	Bob Savage	70.00
205	Dick Sisler	70.00
206	Bruce Edwards	70.00
207	Johnny "Hippity" Hopp	70.00
208	Paul "Dizzy" Trout	75.00
209	Charlie "King Kong" Keller	100.00
210	Joe "Flash" Gordon	85.00
211	Dave "Boo" Ferriss	70.00
212	Ralph Hamner	70.00
213	Charles "Red" Barrett	70.00
214	*Richie Ashburn*	535.00
215	Kirby Higbe	70.00
216	Lynwood "Schoolboy" Rowe	70.00
217	Marino Pieretti	70.00
218	Dick Kryhoski	60.00
219	Virgil "Fire" Trucks	80.00
220	Johnny McCarthy	70.00
221	Bob Muncrief	70.00
222	Alex Kellner	70.00
223	Bob Hoffman	70.00
224	*Leroy "Satchell" Paige*	1300.00
225	Gerry Coleman	100.00
226	*Edwin "Duke" Snider*	1200.00
227	Fritz Ostermueller	70.00
228	Jackie Mayo	70.00

229	*Ed Lopat*	150.00
230	Augie Galan	70.00
231	Earl Johnson	70.00
232	George McQuinn	70.00
233	*Larry Doby*	150.00
234	Truett "Rip" Sewell	80.00
235	Jim Russell	70.00
236	Fred Sanford	70.00
237	Monte Kennedy	70.00
238	*Bob Lemon*	275.00
239	Frank McCormick	70.00
240	Norman "Babe" Young (photo actually Bobby Young)	125.00

1950 BOWMAN

In its third year Bowman increased its set size to 252 cards. No double printing was necessary, since 36 cards of 2¹⁄₁₆ by 2½ inches fit on each printer's sheet, making an even series of seven sheets. Instead of using actual photographs, Bowman introduced paintings based on photographs, which have become well known. The backs have red-and-black print on a cream-colored background. Ted Williams made his Bowman debut, while Luke Appling made his farewell card appearance. Although no rookies of note are featured, Bowman started something big by featuring non-playing managers Leo Durocher, Frank Frisch, and Casey Stengel.

	NR MT
Complete set	**$9750.00**
Commons (1-72)	**55.00**
Commons (73-252)	**17.00**

1	*Mel Parnell*	$175.00
2	Vern Stephens	35.00
3	Dom DiMaggio	70.00
4	*Gus Zernial*	65.00
5	Bob Kuzava	55.00
6	Bob Feller	200.00
7	Jim Hegan	55.00
8	George Kell	100.00
9	Vic Wertz	55.00
10	Tommy Henrich	70.00
11	Phil Rizzuto	190.00
12	Joe Page	70.00
13	Ferris Fain	60.00
14	Alex Kellner	55.00
15	Al Kozar	55.00
16	*Roy Sievers*	65.00
17	Sid Hudson	55.00
18	Eddie Robinson	55.00

98 Ted Williams

19	Warren Spahn	225.00
20	Bob Elliott	55.00
21	Harold Reese	225.00
22	Jackie Robinson	750.00
23	*Don Newcombe*	155.00
24	Johnny Schmitz	55.00

25	Hank Sauer	55.00
26	Grady Hatton	55.00
27	Herman Wehmeier	55.00
28	Bobby Thomson	70.00
29	Ed Stanky	60.00
30	Eddie Waitkus	55.00
31	Del Ennis	55.00
32	Robin Roberts	165.00
33	Ralph Kiner	125.00
34	Murry Dickson	55.00
35	Enos Slaughter	125.00
36	Eddie Kazak	55.00
37	Luke Appling	75.00
38	Bill Wight	55.00
39	Larry Doby	70.00
40	Bob Lemon	100.00
41	Walter "Hoot" Evers	55.00
42	Art Houtteman	55.00
43	Bobby Doerr	100.00
44	Joe Dobson	55.00
45	Al "Zeke" Zarilla	55.00
46	Larry "Yogi" Berra	400.00
47	Jerry Coleman	60.00
48	Leland "Lou" Brissie	55.00
49	Elmer Valo	55.00
50	Dick Kokos	55.00
51	Ned Garver	55.00
52	Sam Mele	55.00
53	Clyde Vollmer	55.00
54	Gil Coan	55.00
55	John "Buddy" Kerr	55.00
56	*Del Crandell*	65.00
57	Vernon Bickford	55.00
58	Carl Furillo	75.00
59	Ralph Branca	65.00
60	Andy Pafko	57.00
61	Bob Rush	55.00
62	Ted Kluszewski	100.00
63	Ewell Blackwell	65.00
64	Alvin Dark	70.00
65	Dave Koslo	55.00
66	Larry Jansen	57.00
67	Willie Jones	60.00
68	Curt Simmons	57.00
69	Wally Westlake	55.00
70	Bob Chesnes	55.00
71	Al Schoendienst	100.00
72	Howie Pollet	55.00
73	Willard Marshall	17.00

22 Jackie Robinson

74	*Johnny Antonelli*	35.00
75	Roy Campanella	350.00
76	Rex Barney	20.00
77	Edwin "Duke" Snider	325.00
78	Mickey Owen	17.00
79	Johnny Vander Meer	20.00
80	Howard Fox	17.00
81	Ron Northey	17.00
82	Carroll Lockman	17.00
83	Sheldon Jones	17.00
84	Richie Ashburn	110.00
85	Ken Heintzelman	17.00
86	Stan Rojek	17.00
87	Bill Werle	17.00
88	Marty Marion	30.00
89	George Munger	17.00
90	Harry Brecheen	21.00
91	Cass Michaels	17.00
92	Hank Majeski	17.00
93	Gene Bearden	17.00
94	Lou Boudreau	55.00
95	Aaron Robinson	17.00
96	Virgil "Fire" Trucks	20.00
97	Maurice McDermott	17.00
98	Ted Williams	850.00
99	Billy Goodman	17.00
100	Vic Raschi	35.00
101	Bobby Brown	35.00
102	Billy Johnson	17.00
103	Eddie Joost	17.00
104	Sam Chapman	17.00

21 Harold Reese

105	Bob Dillinger	17.00
106	Cliff Fannin	17.00
107	Sam Dente	17.00
108	Rae Scarborough	17.00
109	Sid Gordon	17.00
110	Tommy Holmes	17.00
111	Walker Cooper	17.00
112	Gil Hodges	100.00
113	Gene Hermanski	17.00
114	*Wayne Terwilliger*	17.00
115	Roy Smalley	17.00
116	Virgil "Red" Stallcup	17.00
117	Bill Rigney	20.00
118	Clint Hartung	17.00
119	Dick Sisler	17.00
120	John Thompson	17.00
121	Andy Seminick	17.00
122	Johnny Hopp	17.00
123	Dino Restelli	17.00
124	Clyde McCullough	17.00
125	Del Rice	17.00
126	Al Brazle	17.00
127	Dave Philley	17.00
128	Phil Masi	17.00
129	Joe "Flash" Gordon	18.00
130	Dale Mitchell	17.00
131	Steve Gromek	17.00
132	James Vernon	18.00
133	Don Kolloway	17.00
134	Paul "Dizzy" Trout	18.00
135	Pat Mullin	17.00
136	Warren Rosar	17.00

137	Johnny Pesky	21.00
138	Allie Reynolds	37.00
139	Johnny Mize	75.00
140	Pete Suder	17.00
141	Joe Coleman	17.00
142	*Sherman Lollar*	20.00
143	Eddie Stewart	17.00
144	Al Evans	17.00
145	Jack Graham	17.00
146	Floyd Baker	17.00
147	*Mike Garcia*	22.00
148	Early Wynn	70.00
149	Bob Swift	17.00
150	George Vico	17.00
151	Fred Hutchinson	24.00
152	Ellis Kinder	17.00
153	Walt Masterson	17.00
154	Gus Niarhos	17.00
155	Frank "Spec" Shea	17.00
156	Fred Sanford	17.00
157	Mike Guerra	17.00
158	Paul Lehner	17.00
159	Joe Tipton	17.00
160	Mickey Harris	17.00
161	Sherry Robertson	17.00
162	Eddie Yost	17.00
164	Sibby Sisti	17.00
165	Bruce Edwards	17.00
166	Joe Hatten	17.00
167	Elwin Roe	35.00
172	Peanuts Lowery	17.00
180	Harry Walker	18.00

33 Ralph Kiner

186	Ken Keltner	18.00	
193	Harold "Pete" Reiser	24.00	
194	Billy Cox	24.00	
195	Phil Cavaretta	24.00	
203	Danny Murtaugh	22.00	
212	Gerry Priddy	17.00	
214	Dick Fowler	17.00	
215	Ed Lopat	35.00	
216	Bob Porterfield	17.00	
217	Casey Stengel	150.00	
218	Cliff Mapes	17.00	
219	*Hank Bauer*	85.00	
220	Leo Durocher	70.00	
222	Bobby Morgan	17.00	
223	Jimmy Russell	17.00	
224	Jack Banta	17.00	
225	Eddie Sawyer	20.00	
226	*Jim Konstanty*	40.00	
229	Frank Frisch	45.00	
232	*Al "Flip" Rosen*	60.00	
233	Allie Clark	17.00	
234	*Bobby Shantz*	30.00	
246	*Walt Dropo*	30.00	
248	*Sam Jethroe*	25.00	
251	John Lester Moss	18.00	
252	*Billy DeMars*	65.00	

1951 BOWMAN

At 324 cards, Bowman's 1951 baseball card set was the most complete issue up to that time. In addition to making the set larger for 1951, Bowman made the individual cards larger. The 2⅛- by 3⅛-inch size would be maintained for two years. Each card displays the player name in a horizontal black box. Card backs use red-and-blue printing on gray cardboard, but no statistics are provided. Few changes were made from the 1950 Bowman edition. In fact, some of the same color paintings of the players from the 1950 issue were used in an enlarged version for 1951. Bowman started a trend for the 1950s by issuing a card for each major league skipper. The rising value of the 1951 Bowman set comes largely from a high-number series that includes the prized rookie cards of Willie Mays and Mickey Mantle.

NR MT

Complete set	**$22,000.00**	
Commons (1-36)	**20.00**	
Commons (37-252)	**15.00**	
Commons (253-324)	**55.00**	

1	*Ed "Whitey" Ford*	$1250.00
2	Larry "Yogi" Berra	450.00
3	Robin Roberts	85.00
4	Del Ennis	20.00
5	Dale Mitchell	20.00
6	Don Newcombe	45.00
7	Gil Hodges	85.00
8	Paul Lehner	20.00
9	Sam Chapman	20.00
10	Al "Red" Schoendienst	80.00
11	George "Red" Munger	20.00
12	Hank Majeski	20.00
13	Ed Stanky	22.00
14	Alvin Dark	25.00
15	Johnny Pesky	22.00
16	Maurice McDermott	20.00
17	Pete Castiglione	20.00
18	Gil Coan	20.00
19	Sid Gordon	20.00
20	Del Crandall	22.00
21	George "Snuffy" Stirnweiss	20.00
22	Hank Sauer	22.00

1 Ed "Whitey" Ford

23	Walter "Hoot" Evers.....	20.00
24	Ewell Blackwell............	22.00
25	Vic Raschi	30.00
26	Phil Rizzuto	115.00
27	Jim Konstanty..............	25.00
28	Eddie Waitkus	20.00
29	Allie Clark	20.00
30	Bob Feller....................	135.00
31	Roy Campanella........	325.00
32	Duke Snider	275.00
33	Bob Hooper.................	20.00
34	Marty Marion	25.00
35	Al Zarilla	20.00
36	Joe Dobson	20.00
37	Whitey Lockman..........	15.00
40	*Dave "Gus" Bell*...........	25.00
41	Eddie Yost...................	15.00
46	George Kell	55.00
49	Jerry Coleman	22.00
50	Johnny Mize	65.00
51	Andy Seminick	15.00
52	Dick Sisler	15.00
53	Bob Lemon..................	50.00
54	Ray Boone	17.00
55	Gene Hermanski	16.00
56	Ralph Branca	30.00
58	Enos Slaughter............	50.00

62	Lou Boudreau..............	50.00
65	Mickey Vernon	16.00
67	Roy Sievers.................	17.00
73	Tommy Byrne..............	16.00
76	Stan Lopata.................	15.00
78	Early Wynn	55.00
80	Harold "Peewee" Reese	150.00
81	Carl Furillo..................	35.00
86	Harry Brecheen	16.00
92	Vern "Junior" Stephens	16.00
100	Sherman Lollar............	16.00
103	Andy Pafko.................	16.00
104	Virgil "Fire" Trucks.......	16.00
109	Allie Reynolds	30.00
110	• Bobby Brown	25.00
111	Curt Simmons	15.00
113	Bill "Swish" Nicholson..	15.00
114	Sam Zoldak	15.00
115	Steve Gromek	15.00
117	Eddie Miksis	15.00
118	Preacher Roe	30.00
119	Eddie Joost	15.00
120	Joe Coleman	15.00
121	Gerry Staley	15.00
122	*Joe Garagiola*............	150.00
123	Howie Judson..............	15.00
125	Bill Rigney	16.00
126	Bobby Thomson	30.00
127	*Sal Maglie*	50.00
128	Ellis Kinder	15.00
129	Matt Batts	15.00
131	Cliff Chambers	15.00
132	Cass Michaels.............	15.00
133	Sam Dente	15.00
134	Warren Spahn	125.00
135	Walker Cooper	15.00
136	Ray Coleman	15.00
138	Phil Cavarretta	17.00
140	Eddie Lake	15.00
141	Fred Hutchinson	17.00
142	Aaron Robinson	15.00
143	Ted Kluszewski	40.00
144	Herman Wehmeier	15.00
147	Ken Heintzelman..........	15.00
148	Granny Hamner	16.00
149	Emory "Bubba" Church	15.00
150	Mike Garcia	17.00
151	Larry Doby...................	35.00

305 Willie Mays

152	Cal Abrams	15.00
153	Rex Barney	17.00
154	Pete Suder	15.00
155	Lou Brissie	15.00
156	Del Rice	15.00
157	Al Brazle	15.00
159	Eddie Stewart	15.00
160	Phil Masi	15.00
161	*Wes Westrum*	16.00
162	Larry Jansen	15.00
163	Monte Kennedy	15.00
165	Ted Williams	**750.00**
166	Stan Rojek	15.00
167	Murry Dickson	15.00
170	Sibby Sisti	15.00
171	Buddy Kerr	15.00
172	Ned Garver	15.00
174	Mickey Owen	15.00
175	Wayne Terwilliger	15.00
176	Vic Wertz	17.00
177	Charlie Keller	17.00
179	Danny Litwhiler	15.00
180	Howie Fox	15.00
181	Casey Stengel	**100.00**
182	Tom Ferrick	15.00
183	Hank Bauer	30.00
184	Eddie Sawyer	15.00
185	Jimmy Bloodworth	15.00
186	Richie Ashburn	65.00
187	Al "Flip" Rosen	30.00
188	*Roberto Avila*	20.00
189	Erv Palica	15.00
190	Joe Hatten	15.00
195	Paul Richards	20.00
196	*Bill Pierce*	30.00
198	*Monte Irvin*	100.00
203	*Vernon Law*	25.00
207	Billy Southworth	15.00
217	Joe Page	20.00
218	Ed Lopat	30.00
219	*Gene Woodling*	40.00
223	Johnny Vander Meer	25.00
224	Billy Cox	17.00
225	Dan Bankhead	17.00
226	Jimmy Dykes	17.00
227	Bobby Schantz	17.00
228	Cloyd Boyer	15.00
230	Max Lanier	15.00
232	*Nelson Fox*	150.00
233	● Leo Durocher	50.00
234	Clint Hartung	15.00
238	Pete Reiser	18.00
242	Sam Jethroe	17.00
243	John Antonelli	17.00
245	*John Berardino*	25.00
248	Johnny Klippstein	15.00
253	*Mickey Mantle*	8800.00
254	*Jackie Jensen*	150.00
255	Milo Candini	67.00
256	Ken Silvestri	67.00
257	Birdie Tebbetts	67.00
258	*Luke Easter*	65.00
259	Charlie Dressen	75.00
260	*Carl Erskine*	125.00
261	Wally Moses	67.00
262	Gus Zernial	67.00

253 Mickey Mantle

263	Howie Pollett	67.00	294	Jocko Thompson	67.00
264	Don Richmond	67.00	295	Al Lopez	120.00
265	Steve Bilko	67.00	296	Bob Kennedy	67.00
266	Harry Dorish	67.00	297	Dave Philley	67.00
267	Ken Holcombe	67.00	298	Joe Astroth	67.00
268	Don Mueller	67.00	299	Clyde King	67.00
269	Ray Noble	67.00	300	Hal Rice	67.00
270	Willard Nixon	67.00	301	Tommy Glaviano	67.00
271	Tommy Wright	67.00	302	Jim Busby	67.00
272	Billy Meyer	67.00	303	Marv Rotblatt	67.00
273	Danny Murtaugh	70.00	304	Allen Gettel	67.00
274	George Metkovich	67.00	305	*Willie Mays*	4000.00
275	Bucky Harris	75.00	306	*Jim Piersall*	125.00
276	Frank Quinn	67.00	307	Walt Masterson	67.00
277	Roy Hartsfield	67.00	308	Ted Beard	67.00
278	Norman Roy	67.00	309	Mel Queen	67.00
279	Jim Delsing	67.00	310	Erv Dusak	67.00
280	Frank Overmire	67.00	311	Mickey Harris	67.00
281	Al Widmar	67.00	312	*Gene Mauch*	75.00
282	Frank Frisch	100.00	313	Ray Mueller	67.00
283	Walt Dubiel	67.00	314	Johnny Sain	80.00
284	Gene Bearden	67.00	315	Zack Taylor	67.00
285	Johnny Lipon	67.00	316	Duane Pillette	67.00
286	Bob Usher	67.00	317	*Forrest Burgess*	85.00
287	Jim Blackburn	67.00	318	Warren Hacker	67.00
288	Bobby Adams	67.00	319	Red Rolfe	67.00
289	Cliff Mapes	67.00	320	Hal White	67.00
290	Bill Dickey	180.00	321	Earl Johnson	67.00
291	Tommy Henrich	80.00	322	Luke Sewell	67.00
292	Eddie Pellagrini	67.00	323	*Joe Adcock*	110.00
293	Ken Johnson	67.00	324	*Johnny Pramesa*	125.00

1951 TOPPS BLUE BACKS

In addition to the designations for series A and B on the card fronts, the only differences between the Topps Blue Back and Red Back sets are secondary border colors on the cards and scarcity in distribution. Both 52-card issues were sold at approximately the same time and packaged with two cards and a piece of candy for a penny. A large supply of Red Backs was discovered in a Philadelphia warehouse in the 1980s, but the Blue Backs are tougher to find. Fortunately, the cards were printed on heavy cardboard and are found in top condition today. Each round-cornered card measures 2 by 2⅝ inches. On each card is a baseball situation making it possible to play a game with the cards from this year.

		NR MT
Complete set		**$2000.00**
Commons		**30.00**

1	Eddie Yost	$45.00
2	Hank Majeski	30.00
3	Richie Ashburn	165.00
4	Del Ennis	40.00
5	Johnny Pesky	45.00
6	Albert (Red) Schoendienst	125.00
7	Gerald Staley	30.00
8	Dick Sisler	30.00
9	Johnny Sain	45.00
10	Joe Page	40.00
12	Sam Jethroe	32.00
13	James (Mickey) Vernon	40.00
15	Eddie Joost	30.00
16	Murry Dickson	30.00
17	Roy Smalley	30.00
18	Ned Garver	30.00
20	Ralph Branca	42.00
21	Billy Johnson	30.00
23	Paul (Dizzy) Trout	30.00
24	Sherman Lollar	40.00
25	Sam Mele	30.00
26	*Chico Carrasquel*	35.00
27	Andy Pafko	40.00
28	Harry (The Cat) Brecheen	40.00
29	Granville Hamner	30.00

50 Johnny Mize

30	Enos (Country) Slaughter	125.00
32	Bob Elliott	30.00
35	Tommy Byrne	30.00
36	Cliff Fannin	30.00
37	Bobby Doerr	110.00
39	Ed Lopat	50.00
40	Vic Wertz	40.00
41	Johnny Schmitz	30.00
43	Willie (Puddin' Head) Jones	32.00
45	*Bill Pierce*	50.00
48	Billy Cox	40.00
49	Henry (Hank) Sauer	40.00
50	Johnny Mize	150.00

1951 TOPPS RED BACKS

Although recognized as the first widespread baseball offering of the company, the 1951 Topps Red Backs set is one of the least appreciated of the early sets. The 52-card set was designed like a deck of playing cards (to be used in playing a basic baseball game) because Bowman, at that time, held an exclusive contract to produce bubble gum cards. In addition to a black-and-white player photo set in a baseball diamond in the card center, each round-cornered card features the player name, a short biography, and a number.

38 Ed (Duke) Snider

		NR MT
Complete set		**$725.00**
Commons		**8.00**

1	Larry (Yogi) Berra....	$125.00
3	Ferris Fain	8.00
4	Verne Stephens (Vern)	8.00
5	Phil Rizzuto	35.00
6	Allie Reynolds	10.00
7	Howie Pollet	5.00
8	Early Wynn	20.00
9	Roy Sievers	6.00
10	Mel Parnell	6.00
12	Jim Hegan	5.00
13	Dale Mitchell	5.00
15	Ralph Kiner	30.00
16	Preacher Roe	10.00
17	*Dave Bell*	9.00
18	Gerry Coleman	9.00
20	Dominick DiMaggio	14.00
22	Bob Feller	55.00
23	*Ray Boone*	9.00
24	Hank Bauer	15.00
26	*Luke Easter*	11.00
29	Bob Kennedy	5.00
30	Warren Spahn	55.00
31	Gil Hodges	35.00
34	Grady Hatton	5.00
35	Al Rosen	12.00
36	Gus Zernial (Chicago in bio)	30.00
36	Gus Zernial (Philadelphia in bio)	20.00
37	Wes Westrum	6.00
38	Ed (Duke) Snider	75.00
39	Ted Kluszewski	20.00
40	Mike Garcia	9.00
41	Whitey Lockman	5.00
42	Ray Scarborough	5.00
43	Maurice McDermott	5.00
45	Andy Seminick	5.00
48	Eddie Stanky	7.00
50	*Monte Irvin*	50.00
51	Eddie Robinson	5.00
52	Tommy Holmes (Boston in bio)	30.00
52	Tommy Holmes (Hartford in bio)	24.00

1952 BOWMAN

The 1952 Bowman set follows a format similar to the 1951 issue. Players on the card fronts are depicted in paintings made from photographs. Unlike 1951, however, each player name appears as a facsimile autograph on card fronts. Backs show black printing on gray cardboard but maintain the 1951 format of the player name and vital data along with a brief biography. Some cards advertise a mail-in offer, which provided a baseball cap for five wrappers and 50 cents. Despite the reduced number of cards (just 252, compared to 324 in 1951), the 1952 Bowman set has enjoyed non-stop popularity because of its simple design and striking paintings. Collectors forgave Bowman for the unrealistic autographs on some cards, such as the misspelling of Willie Mays (card 218). Artwork for 15 cards never issued was discovered several years ago, and a reprint set was produced including these cards.

	NR MT
Complete set	$9750.00
Commons (1-36)	20.00
Commons (37-72)	16.00
Commons (73-144)	15.00
Commons (145-216)	13.00
Commons (217-252)	30.00

1 Larry "Yogi" Berra

1	Larry "Yogi" Berra....	$600.00
2	Bobby Thomson	35.00
3	Fred Hutchinson	25.00
4	Robin Roberts	70.00
5	*Orestes Minoso*	110.00
6	Virgil "Red" Stallcup	17.00
7	Mike Garcia	18.00
8	Harold "Pee Wee" Reese	125.00
9	Vern Stephens	17.00
10	Bob Hooper	17.00
11	Ralph Kiner	70.00
12	Max Surkont	17.00
13	Cliff Mapes	17.00
14	Cliff Chambers	17.00
15	Sam Mele	17.00
16	Omar Lown	17.00
17	Ed Lopat	35.00
18	Don Mueller	17.00
19	Bob Cain	17.00
20	Willie Jones	17.00
21	Nelson Fox	50.00
22	Willard Ramsell	17.00
23	Bob Lemon	55.00
24	Carl Furillo	35.00
25	Maurice McDermott	17.00
26	Eddie Joost	17.00
27	Joe Garagiola	70.00
28	Roy Hartsfield	17.00
29	Ned Garver	17.00
30	Al "Red" Schoendienst	70.00
31	Eddie Yost	17.00
32	Eddie Miksis	17.00
33	*Gil McDougald*	70.00
34	Al Dark	20.00

1952 Bowman

116 Duke Snider

35	Gran Hamner	17.00
36	Cass Michaels	17.00
37	Vic Raschi	25.00
38	Whitey Lockman	16.00
39	Vic Wertz	18.00
40	Emory Church	16.00
41	Chico Carrasquel	16.00
43	Bob Feller	125.00
44	Roy Campanella	250.00
45	Johnny Pesky	21.00
48	Vern Bickford	16.00
49	Jim Hearn	16.00
50	Gerry Staley	16.00
51	Gil Coan	16.00
52	Phil Rizzuto	90.00
53	Richie Ashburn	60.00
54	Billy Pierce	20.00
56	Clyde King	16.00
58	Hank Majeski	16.00
59	Murray Dickson	16.00
60	Sid Gordon	16.00
61	Tommy Byrne	16.00
64	Roy Smalley	16.00
65	Hank Bauer	30.00
66	Sal Maglie	25.00
69	Joe Adcock	25.00
70	Carl Erskine	25.00
71	Vernon Law	20.00

73	Jerry Coleman	16.00
74	Wes Westrum	16.00
75	George Kell	45.00
76	Del Ennis	17.00
80	Gil Hodges	75.00
82	Gus Zernial	16.00
84	Sam Jethroe	16.00
85	Marty Marion	17.00
86	Cal Abrams	17.00
87	Mickey Vernon	17.00
93	Paul Richards	18.00
95	Luke Easter	18.00
96	Ralph Branca	19.00
98	Jimmy Dykes	18.00
100	Sibby Sisti	17.00
101	Mickey Mantle	2800.00
102	Peanuts Lowrey	17.00
104	Hal Jeffcoat	17.00
105	Bobby Brown	21.00
107	Del Rice	13.00
109	Tom Morgan	13.00
110	Max Lanier	13.00
111	Walter "Hoot" Evers	13.00
112	Forrest "Smokey" Burgess	14.00
113	Al Zarilla	13.00
115	Larry Doby	30.00

101 Mickey Mantle

116	Duke Snider	200.00
120	Chet Nichols	13.00
126	Phil Cavarretta	16.00
127	Dick Sisler	13.00
128	Don Newcombe	35.00
134	Al Brazle	13.00
139	Jerry Priddy	13.00
142	Early Wynn	50.00
145	Johnny Mize	60.00
146	● Leo Durocher	40.00
151	Al "Flip" Rosen	25.00
152	Billy Cox	17.00
154	Ferris Fain	13.00
156	Warren Spahn	100.00
158	Bucky Harris	25.00
159	Dutch Leonard	12.00
160	Eddie Stanky	13.00
161	Jackie Jensen	30.00
162	Monte Irvin	45.00
164	Connie Ryan	12.00
165	Saul Rogovin	12.00
166	Bobby Adams	12.00
167	Bob Avila	12.00
168	Preacher Roe	25.00
169	Walt Dropo	12.00
170	Joe Astroth	12.00
171	Mel Queen	12.00

44 Roy Campanella

173	Gene Bearden	12.00
174	Mickey Grasso	12.00
175	Ransom Jackson	12.00
176	Harry Brecheen	15.00
177	Gene Woodling	17.00
178	Dave Williams	12.00
179	Pete Suder	12.00
181	*Joe Collins*	17.00
184	Curt Simmons	12.00
188	Charlie Dressen	15.00
189	Jim Piersall	17.00
191	*Bob Friend*	25.00
196	Stan Musial	600.00
197	*Charlie Silvera*	15.00
198	Chuck Diering	12.00
199	Ted Gray	12.00
203	Steve Gromek	12.00
204	Andy Pafko	16.00
206	Elmer Valo	12.00
207	George Strickland	12.00
213	Monte Kennedy	12.00
214	Ray Boone	13.00
217	Casey Stengel	190.00
218	Willie Mays	1500.00
219	Neil Berry	28.00
220	Russ Meyer	28.00
221	Lou Kretlow	28.00
222	Homer "Dixie" Howell	28.00

218 Willie Mays

223	Harry Simpson	28.00	240	*Billy Loes*	40.00
224	Johnny Schmitz	28.00	241	Mel Parnell	30.00
225	Del Wilber	28.00	242	Everett Kell	28.00
226	Alex Kellner	28.00	243	George "Red" Munger	28.00
232	Enos Slaughter	100.00	244	Lew Burdette	60.00
233	Bob Kuzava	28.00	245	George Schmees	28.00
230	Frank Shea	28.00	246	Jerry Snyder	28.00
234	Fred Fitzsimmons	28.00	247	John Pramesa	28.00
235	Steve Souchock	28.00	248	Bill Werle	28.00
236	Tommy Brown	28.00	249	Henry Thompson	28.00
237	Sherman Lollar	30.00	250	Ivan Delock	28.00
238	*Roy McMillan*	35.00	251	Jack Lohrke	28.00
239	Dale Mitchell	28.00	252	Frank Crosetti	160.00

1952 TOPPS

By far the most valuable *set* of baseball cards of the post-World War II period, the marvelous 1952 Topps edition also contains the single most expensive *card* of that time: Number 311, showing the great Mickey Mantle, is currently valued at a phenomenal $30,000. Both in terms of size (2⅝ by 3¼ inches) and number of cards (407), the Topps set was the biggest baseball product of 1952. The cards offer colorized photos along with the player name, facsimile autograph, and team logo on a movie marquee card front. The backs, for the first time, include both 1951 and lifetime statistics. The final series of cards (311-407) is extremely rare and commands premium prices. How popular is the 1952 Topps set? Even the reprinted edition, issued by Topps in 1983, has grown in price from $40 to as much as $200 today.

	NR MT		
Complete set	**$67,000.00**	7 Wayne Terwilliger	57.00
Commons (1-80)	**55.00**	8 Fred Marsh	55.00
Commons (81-250)	**30.00**	9 Bobby Hogue	55.00
Commons (251-280)	**50.00**	10 Al Rosen	80.00
Commons (281-300)	**55.00**	11 Phil Rizzuto	175.00
Commons (301-310)	**50.00**	12 Monty Basgall	55.00
Commons (311-407)	**215.00**	13 Johnny Wyrostek	55.00
		14 Bob Elliott	55.00
1 Andy Pafko	$1300.00	15 Johnny Pesky	65.00
2 *James E. Runnells*	60.00	16 Gene Hermanski	55.00
3 Hank Thompson	60.00	17 Jim Hegan	55.00
4 Don Lenhardt	55.00	18 Merrill Combs	55.00
5 Larry Jansen	60.00	19 Johnny Bucha	55.00
6 Grady Hatton	55.00	20 *Billy Loes*	110.00
		21 Ferris Fain	60.00
		22 Dom DiMaggio	100.00
		23 Billy Goodman	55.00

24 Luke Easter................ **60.00**
25 Johnny Groth **55.00**
26 Monte Irvin **110.00**
27 Sam Jethroe **55.00**
28 Jerry Priddy **55.00**
29 Ted Kluszewski......... **100.00**
30 Mel Parnell **60.00**
31 Gus Zernial **70.00**
32 Eddie Robinson **55.00**
33 Warren Spahn........... **250.00**
34 Elmer Valo **55.00**
35 Hank Sauer................ **65.00**
36 Gil Hodges **175.00**
37 Duke Snider **300.00**
38 Wally Westlake **55.00**
39 "Dizzy" Trout **60.00**
40 Irv Noren **55.00**
41 Bob Wellman **55.00**
42 Lou Kretlow **55.00**
43 Ray Scarborough........ **55.00**
44 Con Dempsey **55.00**
45 Eddie Joost **55.00**
46 Gordon Goldsberry **55.00**
47 Willie Jones................ **60.00**
48 Joe Page
      (Johnny Sain bio)..... **300.00**
48 Joe Page (correct bio) **80.00**
49 Johnny Sain
      (Joe Page bio) **325.00**
49 Johnny Sain
      (correct bio)............... **100.00**
50 Marv Rickert................ **55.00**
51 Jim Russell **55.00**
52 Don Mueller................ **55.00**
53 Chris Van Cuyk........... **55.00**
54 Leo Kiely **55.00**
55 Ray Boone **60.00**
56 Tommy Glaviano......... **57.00**
57 Ed Lopat **100.00**
58 Bob Mahoney.............. **55.00**
59 Robin Roberts........... **165.00**
60 Sid Hudson **55.00**
61 "Tookie" Gilbert **55.00**
62 Chuck Stobbs **55.00**
63 Howie Pollet................ **60.00**
64 Roy Sievers **65.00**
65 Enos Slaughter **150.00**
66 "Preacher" Roe **110.00**
67 Allie Reynolds **110.00**

311 Mickey Mantle

68 Cliff Chambers **55.00**
69 Virgil Stallcup **55.00**
70 Al Zarilla..................... **55.00**
71 Tom Upton **55.00**
72 Karl Olson **55.00**
73 William Werle.............. **55.00**
74 Andy Hansen **55.00**
75 Wes Westrum **60.00**
76 Eddie Stanky.............. **65.00**
77 Bob Kennedy **55.00**
78 Ellis Kinder **55.00**
79 Gerald Staley **55.00**
80 Herman Wehmeier...... **55.00**
81 Vernon Law................. **30.00**
88 Bob Feller **175.00**
91 Al Schoendienst.......... **90.00**
98 Bill Pierce **30.00**
99 Gene Woodling **50.00**
106 Mickey Vernon **30.00**
108 Jim Konstanty **30.00**
117 Sherman Lollar **30.00**
122 Jack Jensen **70.00**
123 Eddie Yost **27.00**
125 Bill Rigney.................. **27.00**
126 Fred Hutchinson **30.00**
129 Johnny Mize................ **90.00**
140 John Antonelli **30.00**
162 Del Crandall **30.00**

407 Ed Mathews

175	*Billy Martin*	350.00
180	*Charley Maxwell*	30.00
189	Pete Reiser	30.00
191	Yogi Berra	375.00
195	*Orestes Minoso*	125.00
200	*Ralph Houk*	70.00
203	Curt Simmons	27.00
215	Hank Bauer	50.00
216	Richie Ashburn	110.00
219	Bobby Shantz	35.00
223	Del Ennis	30.00
226	Dave Philley	27.00
227	Joe Garagiola	125.00
229	Gene Bearden	27.00
232	Billy Cox	30.00
233	*Bob Friend*	30.00
235	Walt Dropo	30.00
237	Jerry Coleman	30.00
239	Rocky Bridges	27.00
243	Larry Doby	45.00
244	Vic Wertz	30.00
246	George Kell	75.00
247	Randy Gumpert	25.00
250	Carl Erskine	65.00
251	Chico Carrasquel	47.00
252	Vern Bickford	45.00
253	*Johnny Berardino*	55.00
254	Joe Dobson	45.00
255	Clyde Vollmer	45.00
256	Pete Suder	45.00
257	Bobby Avila	47.00
258	Steve Gromek	45.00
259	Bob Addis	45.00
260	Pete Castiglione	45.00
261	Willie Mays	3000.00
262	Virgil Trucks	50.00
263	Harry Brecheen	50.00
264	Roy Hartsfield	45.00
265	Chuck Diering	45.00
266	Murry Dickson	45.00
267	Sid Gordon	45.00
268	Bob Lemon	175.00
269	Willard Nixon	45.00
270	Lou Brissie	45.00
271	Jim Delsing	45.00
272	Mike Garcia	47.00
273	Erv Palica	45.00
274	Ralph Branca	80.00
275	Pat Mullin	45.00
276	Jim Wilson	45.00
277	Early Wynn	175.00
278	Al Clark	45.00
279	Ed Stewart	45.00
280	Cloyd Boyer	47.00
281	Tommy Brown	55.00
282	Birdie Tebbetts	58.00
283	Phil Masi	55.00
284	Hank Arft	55.00
285	Cliff Fannin	55.00
286	Joe DeMaestri	55.00
287	Steve Bilko	55.00
288	Chet Nichols	55.00
289	Tommy Holmes	60.00
290	Joe Astroth	55.00
291	Gil Coan	55.00
292	Floyd Baker	55.00
293	Sibby Sisti	55.00
294	Walker Cooper	55.00
295	Phil Cavarretta	65.00
296	"Red" Rolfe	55.00
297	Andy Seminick	60.00
298	Bob Ross	55.00
299	Ray Murray	55.00
300	Barney McCosky	55.00
301	Bob Porterfield	45.00
302	Max Surkont	45.00
303	Harry Dorish	45.00
304	Sam Dente	45.00

305	Paul Richards	50.00
306	Lou Sleator	45.00
307	Frank Campos	45.00
308	Luis Aloma	45.00
309	Jim Busby	45.00
310	George Metkovich	45.00
311	Mickey Mantle	30,000.00
312	Jackie Robinson	1400.00
313	Bobby Thomson	225.00
314	Roy Campanella	2200.00
315	Leo Durocher	350.00
316	*Davey Williams*	250.00
317	Connie Marrero	175.00
318	Hal Gregg	175.00
319	Al Walker	175.00
320	*John Rutherford*	225.00
321	*Joe Black*	250.00
322	Randy Jackson	175.00
323	Bubba Church	175.00
324	Warren Hacker	175.00
325	Bill Serena	175.00
326	*George Shuba*	250.00
327	Archie Wilson	175.00
328	Bob Borkowski	175.00
329	Ivan Delock	175.00
330	Turk Lown	175.00
331	Tom Morgan	175.00
332	Tony Bartirome	175.00
333	Pee Wee Reese	1200.00
334	Wilmer Mizell	225.00
335	Ted Lepcio	175.00
336	Dave Koslo	175.00
337	Jim Hearn	175.00
338	Sal Yvars	175.00
339	Russ Meyer	175.00
340	Bob Hooper	175.00
341	Hal Jeffcoat	175.00
342	*Clem Labine*	250.00
343	Dick Gernert	175.00
344	Ewell Blackwell	230.00
345	Sam White	175.00
346	George Spencer	175.00
347	Joe Adcock	250.00
348	Bob Kelly	175.00
349	Bob Cain	175.00
350	Cal Abrams	175.00
351	Al Dark	250.00
352	Karl Drews	220.00
353	Bob Del Greco	175.00

333 Pee Wee Reese

354	Fred Hatfield	175.00
355	Bobby Morgan	175.00
356	Toby Atwell	175.00
357	Smoky Burgess	250.00
358	John Kucab	175.00
359	Dee Fondy	175.00
360	*George Crowe*	225.00
361	Bill Posedel	175.00
362	Ken Heintzelman	175.00
363	Dick Rozek	175.00
364	Clyde Sukeforth	175.00
365	"Cookie" Lavagetto	190.00
366	Dave Madison	175.00
367	Bob Thorpe	175.00
368	Ed Wright	175.00
369	*Dick Groat*	350.00
370	Billy Hoeft	220.00
371	Bob Hofman	175.00
372	*Gil McDougald*	350.00
373	Jim Turner	175.00
374	Al Benton	175.00
375	Jack Merson	175.00
376	Faye Throneberry	175.00
377	Chuck Dressen	225.00
378	Les Fusselman	175.00
379	Joe Rossi	175.00
380	Clem Koshorek	175.00
381	Milton Stock	175.00
382	Sam Jones	175.00

383	Del Wilber	175.00
384	Frank Crosetti	250.00
385	*Herman Franks*	225.00
386	Eddie Yuhas	175.00
387	Billy Meyer	175.00
388	Bob Chipman	175.00
389	Ben Wade	175.00
390	Glen Nelson	175.00
391	Ben Chapman (photo is Sam Chapman)	175.00
392	*Hoyt Wilhelm*	700.00
393	Ebba St. Claire	175.00
394	Billy Herman	275.00
395	Jake Pitler	175.00
396	*Dick Williams*	250.00
397	Forrest Main	175.00
398	Hal Rice	175.00
399	Jim Fridley	175.00
400	Bill Dickey	700.00
401	Bob Schultz	175.00
402	Earl Harrist	175.00
403	Bill Miller	175.00
404	Dick Brodowski	175.00
405	Eddie Pellagrini	175.00
406	*Joe Nuxhall*	250.00
407	*Ed Mathews*	3200.00

1953 BOWMAN B&W

The 1953 Bowman black-and-white set was a separate issue from the Bowman color cards of the same year. The black-and-white cards came in a different wrapper and are numbered 1 through 64. In format, however, the sets are identical. Each one measures 2½ by 3¾ inches, with a full photo surrounded by a black line and a white border. Card backs show a bio, stats for 1952, and lifetime stats. A blank line to write in numbers for the current year was included; thankfully, few youngsters took advantage of the opportunity. As a result, nearly all cards found today are free of any writing.

		NR MT
Complete set		**$2550.00**
Commons		**33.00**

1	Gus Bell	$110.00
2	Willard Nixon	33.00
3	Bill Rigney	35.00
4	Pat Mullin	33.00
5	Dee Fondy	33.00
6	Ray Murray	33.00
7	Andy Seminick	33.00
8	Pete Suder	33.00
9	Walt Masterson	33.00
10	Dick Sisler	33.00
11	Dick Gernert	33.00
12	Randy Jackson	33.00
13	Joe Tipton	33.00
14	Bill Nicholson	33.00
15	Johnny Mize	125.00
16	*Stu Miller*	45.00
17	Virgil Trucks	40.00
18	Billy Hoeft	33.00
19	Paul LaPalme	33.00
20	Eddie Robinson	33.00
25	John Sain	50.00
26	Preacher Roe	50.00
27	Bob Lemon	125.00
28	Hoyt Wilhelm	125.00
29	Sid Hudson	33.00
30	Walker Cooper	33.00
31	Gene Woodling	50.00
32	Rocky Bridges	33.00
33	Bob Kuzava	33.00
36	Jim Piersall	50.00
37	Hal Jeffcoat	33.00

38	Dave Cole	33.00
39	Casey Stengel	310.00
40	Larry Jensen	33.00
41	Bob Ramazotti	33.00
42	Howie Judson	33.00
44	Jim Delsing	33.00
45	Irv Noren	33.00
46	Bucky Harris	55.00
47	Jack Lohrke	33.00
48	Steve Ridzik	33.00
49	Floyd Baker	33.00
50	Dutch Leonard	33.00
51	Lou Burdette	50.00
52	Ralph Branca	40.00
53	Morris Martin	33.00
54	Bill Miller	33.00
56	Roy Smalley	33.00
57	Andy Pafko	40.00
58	Jim Konstanty	40.00
59	Duane Pillette	33.00
60	Billy Cox	40.00
61	Tom Gorman	33.00
62	Keith Thomas	33.00

39 Casey Stengel

63	Steve Gromek	33.00
64	Andy Hansen	45.00

1953 BOWMAN COLOR

Many collectors consider Bowman's 1953 set of 160 cards—the first ever to make use of color photography (as opposed to colorized black-and-white photos)—to be the most beautiful ever created. The jump in technology was due to competition from Topps, which also encouraged Bowman to increase card size (2½ by 3¾ inches) and to include stats on the card backs (which are cream-colored white red-and-black print). The splendid photographs are presented with a simple white border. Stan Musial made his farewell Bowman appearance in this set, while multiple player photos—a first in this century—include one card of Martin and Rizzuto; another of Mantle, Berra, and Bauer.

	NR MT
Complete set	**$11,500.00**
Commons (1-112)	**30.00**
Commons (113-128)	**55.00**
Commons (129-160)	**45.00**

1	Davey Williams	$100.00
2	Vic Wertz	33.00
3	Sam Jethroe	30.00
8	Al Rosen	50.00
9	Phil Rizzuto	110.00
10	Richie Ashburn	90.00
11	Bobby Shantz	35.00

59 Mickey Mantle

12	Carl Erskine	45.00
14	Billy Loes	33.00
16	Bob Friend	33.00
18	Nelson Fox	70.00
19	Al Dark	35.00
21	Joe Garagiola	80.00
22	Bob Porterfield	30.00
23	Herman Wehmeier	30.00
24	Jackie Jensen	40.00
27	Vic Raschi	45.00
28	Forrest "Smoky" Burgess	33.00
30	Phil Cavarretta	33.00
31	Jimmy Dykes	33.00
32	Stan Musial	600.00
33	Harold "Peewee" Reese	550.00
36	Orestes Minoso	60.00
39	Paul Richards	27.00
40	Larry Doby	50.00
43	Mike Garcia	27.00
44	Hank Bauer, Yogi Berra, Mickey Mantle	500.00
46	Roy Campanella	300.00
48	Hank Sauer	35.00
49	Eddie Stanky	35.00
51	Monte Irvin	60.00
52	Marty Marion	40.00
55	Leo Durocher	75.00
57	Lou Boudreau	50.00
59	Mickey Mantle	2750.00
60	Granny Hamner	30.00
61	George Kell	65.00
62	Ted Kluszewski	65.00
63	Gil McDougald	65.00
65	Robin Roberts	80.00
68	Allie Reynolds	50.00
69	Charlie Grimm	35.00
70	Clint Courtney	25.00
73	Billy Pierce	33.00
78	Carl Furillo	50.00
79	Ray Boone	33.00
80	Ralph Kiner	80.00
81	Enos Slaughter	80.00
84	Hank Bauer	50.00
85	Solly Hemus	30.00
90	Joe Nuxhall	33.00
92	Gil Hodges	135.00
93	Billy Martin, Phil Rizzuto	250.00
96	Sal Maglie	45.00
97	Eddie Mathews	200.00
98	Hector Rodriquez	30.00
99	Warren Spahn	200.00
101	Al "Red" Schoendienst	90.00
102	Jim Hegan	30.00
103	Del Ennis	30.00
104	Luke Easter	30.00
105	Eddie Joost	30.00
106	Ken Raffensberger	30.00
107	Alex Kellner	30.00
111	Jim Dyck	30.00
112	Toby Atwell	30.00
113	Karl Drews	45.00
114	Bob Feller	350.00
115	Cloyd Boyer	45.00
116	Eddie Yost	45.00
117	Duke Snider	600.00
118	Billy Martin	325.00
119	Dale Mitchell	45.00
120	Marlin Stuart	45.00
121	Yogi Berra	625.00
122	Bill Serena	45.00
123	Johnny Lipon	45.00
124	Charlie Dressen	60.00
125	Fred Hatfield	45.00
126	Al Corwin	45.00
127	Dick Kryhoski	45.00

128	Whitey Lockman	45.00
129	Russ Meyer	40.00
130	Cass Michaels	40.00
131	Connie Ryan	40.00
132	Fred Hutchinson	45.00
133	Willie Jones	40.00
134	Johnny Pesky	45.00
135	Bobby Morgan	40.00
136	Jim Brideweser	40.00
137	Sam Dente	40.00
138	Bubba Church	40.00
139	Pete Runnels	45.00
140	Alpha Brazle	40.00
141	Frank "Spec" Shea	40.00
142	Larry Miggins	40.00
143	Al Lopez	75.00
144	Warren Hacker	40.00
145	George Shuba	50.00
146	Early Wynn	110.00
148	Billy Goodman	40.00
149	Al Corwin	40.00
150	Carl Scheib	40.00
151	Joe Adcock	50.00
152	Clyde Vollmer	40.00
153	Ed "Whitey" Ford	525.00
154	Omar "Turk" Lown	40.00
155	Allie Clark	40.00
156	Max Surkont	40.00
157	Sherman Lollar	50.00
158	Howard Fox	40.00
159	Mickey Vernon (photo is Floyd Baker)	55.00

1953 TOPPS

Topps' second set was reduced to 274 cards because of disputes with Bowman over player contracts. Cards are numbered to 280, but due to last-minute legal considerations, six are missing (numbers 253, 261, 267, 268, 271, and 275). With no checklists to guide them, frustrated collectors pursued these non-existent cards in vain. Measuring 2⅝ by 3¾ inches, the fronts feature a color painting, a team logo, and a panel for player identification. Backs are red and black printed on gray cardboard, with the first of Topps' popular Dugout Quiz series. Although the Mick's card is the most expensive, Willie Mays' is scarcer, as is a mint Jackie Robinson. Numbers 221-280 command premium value if the player's personal stats in the upper red panel are listed in black instead of white.

NR MT

Complete set	**$14,000.00**
Commons (1-165) single-print	**30.00**
Commons (1-165) double-print	**25.00**
Commons (166-220)	**22.00**
Commons (221-280) single-print	**90.00**
Commons (221-280) double-print	**48.00**

1	Jackie Robinson	$600.00
2	Luke Easter	20.00
3	George Crowe	27.00
4	Ben Wade	25.00
5	Joe Dobson	25.00
6	Sam Jones	25.00
9	Joe Collins	32.00
10	Smoky Burgess	35.00
11	Sal Yvars	25.00
14	Clem Labine	27.00
15	Bobo Newsom	27.00
17	Billy Hitchcock	25.00
20	Hank Thompson	27.00
21	Billy Johnson	25.00

1 Jackie Robinson

22	Howie Fox	25.00
24	Ferris Fain	27.00
25	Ray Boone	27.00
27	Roy Campanella	275.00
28	Eddie Pellagrini	25.00
29	Hal Jeffcoat	25.00
30	Willard Nixon	25.00
31	Ewell Blackwell	45.00
32	Clyde Vollmer	25.00
34	George Shuba	25.00
35	Irv Noren	20.00
37	Ed Mathews	115.00
39	Eddie Miksis	25.00
40	John Lipon	25.00
41	Enos Slaughter	90.00
42	Gus Zernial	25.00
43	Gil McDougald	45.00
44	Ellis Kinder	30.00
47	Bubba Church	20.00
50	Chuck Dressen	30.00
54	Bob Feller	110.00
57	Carl Scheib	25.00
58	George Metkovich	22.00
61	Early Wynn	100.00
62	Monte Irvin	45.00
64	Dave Philley	24.00
65	Earl Harrist	22.00
66	Orestes Minoso	50.00
67	Roy Sievers	27.00
68	Del Rice	25.00
69	Dick Brodowski	25.00
70	Ed Yuhas	25.00
71	Tony Bartirome	25.00
72	Fred Hutchinson	35.00
73	Eddie Robinson	25.00
74	Joe Rossi	25.00
75	Mike Garcia	27.00
76	Pee Wee Reese	175.00
77	John Mize	75.00
78	Al Schoendienst	70.00
79	Johnny Wyrostek	25.00
80	Jim Hegan	25.00
81	Joe Black	70.00
82	Mickey Mantle	3500.00
83	Howie Pollet	26.00
85	Bobby Morgan	25.00
86	Billy Martin	150.00
87	Ed Lopat	40.00
96	Virgil Trucks	25.00
99	Dave Madison	25.00
100	Bill Miller	25.00
101	Ted Wilks	25.00
102	Connie Ryan	17.00
103	Joe Astroth	17.00
104	Yogi Berra	275.00
105	Joe Nuxhall	25.00
106	Johnny Antonelli	25.00
109	Alvin Dark	30.00
110	Herman Wehmeier	25.00
111	Hank Sauer	20.00
112	Ned Garver	20.00
113	Jerry Priddy	25.00
114	Phil Rizzuto	120.00
118	Gus Bell	20.00
119	John Sain	45.00
121	Walt Dropo	25.00
122	Elmer Valo	25.00
123	Tommy Byrne	25.00
124	Sibby Sisti	25.00
125	Dick Williams	23.00
126	Bill Connelly	25.00
127	Clint Courtney	25.00
128	Wilmer Mizell	22.00
129	Keith Thomas	25.00
130	Turk Lown	20.00
131	Harry Byrd	25.00
132	Tom Morgan	22.00

133	Gil Coan	25.00
134	Rube Walker	20.00
135	Al Rosen	30.00
136	Ken Heintzelman	20.00
137	John Rutherford	20.00
138	George Kell	50.00
139	Sammy White	20.00
140	Tommy Glaviano	20.00
141	Allie Reynolds	35.00
142	Vic Wertz	25.00
143	Billy Pierce	30.00
144	Bob Schultz	20.00
145	Harry Dorish	20.00
146	Granville Hamner	20.00
147	Warren Spahn	150.00
148	Mickey Grasso	20.00
149	Dom DiMaggio	32.00
150	Harry Simpson	20.00
151	Hoyt Wilhelm	75.00
152	Bob Adams	20.00
153	Andy Seminick	20.00
154	Dick Groat	40.00
155	Dutch Leonard	20.00
156	Jim Rivera	20.00
157	Bob Addis	20.00
158	*John Logan*	30.00
159	Wayne Terwilliger	21.00
160	Bob Young	20.00
161	Vern Bickford	20.00
162	Ted Kluszewski	50.00
163	Fred Hatfield	25.00
164	Frank Shea	25.00
165	Billy Hoeft	25.00
167	Art Schult	22.00
174	Billy Loes	22.00
183	*Stu Miller*	22.00
188	*Andy Carey*	30.00
191	Ralph Kiner	65.00
197	Del Crandall	25.00
207	Whitey Ford	160.00
210	*Bob Cerv*	25.00
214	*Bill Bruton*	25.00
215	*Gene Conley*	25.00
216	Jim Hughes	22.00
218	Les Fusselman	20.00
219	Pete Runnels (photo is Don Johnson)	22.00
220	Satchell Paige (Satchel)	500.00

82 Mickey Mantle

221	Bob Milliken	48.00
222	*Vic Janowicz*	48.00
223	John O'Brien	48.00
224	Lou Sleater	48.00
225	Bobby Shantz	100.00
226	Ed Erautt	48.00
227	Morris Martin	48.00
228	Hal Newhouser	150.00
229	Rocky Krsnich	48.00
230	Johnny Lindell	48.00
231	Solly Hemus	48.00
232	Dick Kokos	48.00
233	Al Aber	48.00
234	Ray Murray	48.00
235	John Hetki	48.00
236	Harry Perkowski	48.00
237	Clarence Podbielan	48.00
238	Cal Hogue	48.00
239	Jim Delsing	48.00
240	Freddie Marsh	48.00
241	Al Sima	48.00
242	Charlie Silvera	95.00
243	Carlos Bernier	48.00
244	Willie Mays	2800.00
245	Bill Norman	48.00
246	*Roy Face*	90.00
247	Mike Sandlock	48.00
248	Gene Stephens	48.00

249	Ed O'Brien	48.00
250	Bob Wilson	48.00
251	Sid Hudson	48.00
252	Henry Foiles	48.00
254	Preacher Roe	85.00
255	Dixie Howell	48.00
256	Les Peden	48.00
257	Bob Boyd	48.00
258	*Jim Gilliam*	275.00
259	Roy McMillan	48.00
260	Sam Calderone	48.00
262	Bob Oldis	48.00
263	*John Podres*	275.00
264	Gene Woodling	75.00
265	Jackie Jensen	115.00
266	Bob Cain	48.00
269	Duane Pillette	48.00
270	Vern Stephens	48.00
272	Bill Antonello	48.00
273	Harvey Haddix	125.00
274	John Riddle	48.00
276	Ken Raffensberger	48.00
277	Don Lund	48.00
278	Willie Miranda	48.00
279	Joe Coleman	48.00
280	Milt Bolling	350.00

1954 BOWMAN

Following the splendid 1953 set, Bowman's efforts in 1954 seem lackluster in comparison. The 224 cards (measuring 2½ by 3¾ inches) again use colorized photographs. A pastel rectangle at the bottom contains a facsimile autograph of each depicted player. The 1954 Bowman set is best known for having two number 66 cards: The common number 66 is of Jimmy Piersall; the scarce version is of Ted Williams, who appeared in a Topps set for the first time in 1954. It is believed that his contract with Topps prevented Bowman from using his image, and Williams' card was later pulled from circulation. Note that the complete set price does not include #66 Williams card.

	NR MT
Complete set	**$4500.00**
Commons (1-112)	**9.00**
Commons (113-224)	**14.00**

1	Phil Rizzuto	$125.00
2	Jack Jensen	13.00
4	Bob Hooper	9.00
6	Nelson Fox	25.00
7	Walt Dropo	9.00
8	James F. Busby	9.00
9	Dave Williams	9.00
10	Carl Daniel Erskine	15.00
11	Sid Gordon	9.00
12	Roy McMillan	9.00
14	Gerald Staley	9.00
15	Richie Ashburn	35.00
17	Tom Gorman	9.00
18	Walter "Hoot" Evers	9.00
19	Bobby Shantz	12.00
20	Artie Houtteman	9.00
21	Victor Wertz	11.00
22	Sam Mele	9.00
23	*Harvey Kuenn*	35.00
24	Bob Porterfield	9.00
25	Wes Westrum	9.00
26	Billy Cox	12.00
28	Jim Greengrass	9.00
29	Johnny Klippstein	9.00
30	Delbert Rice Jr.	9.00
31	"Smoky" Burgess	11.00
32	Del Crandall	11.00
33	Victor Raschi (with traded line)	35.00
35	Eddie Joost	9.00
36	George Strickland	9.00
37	Dick Kokos	9.00

38	Orestes Minoso	17.00
39	Ned Garver	9.00
45	Ralph Kiner	45.00
50	George Kell	30.00
57	Hoyt Wilhelm	30.00
58	"Pee Wee" Reese	75.00
62	Enos Slaughter	50.00
64	Ed Mathews	70.00
65	Mickey Mantle	1000.00
66	Ted Williams	5200.00
66	Jimmy Piersall	90.00
67	Carl Scheib	9.00
68	Bob Avila	9.00
72	Ed Yost	9.00
74	James Gilliam	18.00
75	Max Surkont	9.00
76	Joe Nuxhall	11.00
79	Curt Simmons	9.00
81	Jerry Coleman	9.00
82	Bill Goodman	10.00
84	Larry Doby	17.00
89	Willie May (Mays)	450.00
90	Roy Campanella	175.00
91	Cal Abrams	9.00
93	Bill Serena	9.00
94	Solly Hemus	9.00
95	Robin Roberts	40.00
96	Joe Adcock	14.00
97	Gil McDougald	18.00
99	Pete Suder	9.00
101	*Don James Larsen*	40.00
102	Bill Pierce	11.00
103	Stephen Souchock	9.00
104	Frank Spec Shea	9.00
105	Sal Maglie	12.00
106	"Clem" Labine	11.00
107	Paul E. LaPalme	9.00
108	Bobby Adams	9.00
109	Roy Smalley	9.00
110	Al Schoendienst	40.00
112	Andy Pafko	9.00
113	Allie Reynolds	17.00
114	Willard Nixon	14.00
115	Don Bollweg	14.00
117	Dick Kryhoski	14.00
119	Fred Hatfield	14.00
121	Ray Katt	14.00
122	Carl Furillo	20.00
123	Toby Atwell	14.00

89 Willie May (Mays)

124	Gus Bell	12.00
127	Del Ennis	11.00
129	Hank Bauer	24.00
130	Milt Bolling	14.00
131	Joe Astroth	14.00
132	Bob Feller	100.00
134	Luis Aloma	14.00
135	Johnny Pesky	14.00
136	Clyde Vollmer	14.00
138	Gil Hodges	75.00
139	Preston Ward	14.00
140	Saul Rogovin	14.00
141	Joe Garagiola	50.00
142	Al Brazle	14.00
144	*Ernie Johnson*	14.00
145	Billy Martin	70.00
146	Dick Gernert	14.00
147	Joe DeMaestri	14.00
148	Dale Mitchell	14.00
149	Bob Young	14.00
151	Patrick J. Mullin	14.00
152	Mickey Vernon	16.00
153	Whitey Lockman	16.00
154	Don Newcombe	20.00
155	*Frank Thomas*	12.00
156	Everett Lamar Bridges	11.00
157	Omar Lown	14.00
158	Stu Miller	12.00

66 Ted Williams

159	John Lindell	14.00
161	Yogi Berra	175.00
162	Ted Lepcio	14.00
163	Dave Philley (157 games with traded line)	15.00
163	Dave Philley (152 games w/o traded line)	13.00
164	Early "Gus" Wynn	45.00
165	Johnny Groth	14.00
170	Edwin D. Snider	150.00
174	Peter Paul Castiglione	14.00
177	Edward Ford	100.00
179	Morris Martin	14.00
180	Joe Tipton	14.00
182	Sherman Lollar	17.00
183	Matt Batts	14.00
184	Mickey Grasso	14.00
185	Daryl Spencer	14.00
186	Russell Meyer	14.00
187	Verne Law (Vern)	13.00
188	Frank Smith	13.00
190	Joe Presko	14.00
191	Karl A. Drews	14.00
192	• Selva L. Burdette	17.00
193	Eddie Robinson	14.00
194	Sid Hudson	12.00
195	Bob Cain	12.00
196	Bob Lemon	35.00
197	Lou Kretlow	14.00
198	Virgil Trucks	16.00
199	Steve Gromek	14.00
200	C. Marrero	14.00
201	Bob Thomson	15.00
202	George Shuba	12.00
203	Vic Janowicz	12.00
204	Jack Collum	14.00
205	Hal Jeffcoat	12.00
206	Steve Bilko	12.00
207	Stan Lopata	14.00
208	Johnny Antonelli	12.00
209	Gene Woodling (photo reversed)	15.00
210	Jimmy Piersall	15.00
212	Owen L. Friend	14.00
213	Dick Littlefield	12.00
214	Ferris Fain	14.00
215	Johnny Bucha	14.00
216	Jerry Snyder	14.00
217	Henry Thompson	15.00
218	Preacher Roe	15.00
219	Hal Rice	14.00
220	Hobie Landrith	14.00
221	Frank Baumholtz	14.00
222	Memo Luna	14.00
223	Steve Ridzik	14.00
224	William Bruton	40.00

65 Mickey Mantle

1954 TOPPS

Topps came up with a number of innovations for its 250-card set in 1954, including the introduction of coach cards. This year marked Topps' first use of more than one player to a card and the first-ever instance of two distinct photographic images: These 2⅝- by 3¾-inch cards feature both a colorized portrait and a posed black-and-white photo on the front. The backs have green, red, and black printing on white cardboard. Ted Williams appears twice to honor his exclusive new contract with Topps. Rookies include Hank Aaron, Ernie Banks, Al Kaline, and Tommy Lasorda. This is Lasorda's only card appearance as a major league player.

	NR MT
Complete set	**$8500.00**
Commons (1-50)	**15.00**
Commons (51-75)	**32.00**
Commons (76-250)	**15.00**

10 Jackie Robinson

1 Ted Williams	$625.00
2 Gus Zernial	17.00
3 Monte Irvin	35.00
4 Hank Sauer	15.00
5 Ed Lopat	25.00
7 Ted Kluszewski	30.00
9 Harvey Haddix	17.00
10 Jackie Robinson	310.00
12 Del Crandall	17.00
13 Billy Martin	100.00
14 Preacher Roe	25.00
15 Al Rosen	25.00
17 Phil Rizzuto	75.00
20 Warren Spahn	110.00
21 Bobby Shantz	20.00
25 *Harvey Kuenn*	40.00
30 Ed Mathews	100.00
32 Duke Snider	150.00
35 Junior Gilliam	30.00
36 Hoyt Wilhelm	50.00
37 Whitey Ford	110.00
43 Dick Groat	20.00
45 Richie Ashburn	50.00
50 Yogi Berra	250.00
51 Johnny Lindell	32.00
52 *Vic Power*	35.00
53 Jack Dittmer	32.00
54 Vern Stephens	32.00

55 Phil Cavarretta	40.00
56 Willie Miranda	32.00
57 Luis Aloma	32.00
58 Bob Wilson	32.00
59 Gene Conley	35.00
60 Frank Baumholtz	32.00
61 Bob Cain	32.00
62 Eddie Robinson	32.00
63 Johnny Pesky	40.00
64 Hank Thompson	37.00
65 Bob Swift	32.00
66 Ted Lepcio	32.00
67 Jim Willis	32.00
68 Sammy Calderone	32.00

201 Al Kaline

69	Bud Podbielan	32.00
70	Larry Doby	70.00
71	Frank Smith	32.00
72	Preston Ward	32.00
73	Wayne Terwilliger	32.00
74	Bill Taylor	32.00
75	Fred Haney	32.00
77	Ray Boone	15.00
79	Andy Pakfo	15.00
80	Jackie Jensen	24.00
81	Dave Hoskins	15.00
82	Milt Bolling	15.00
83	Joe Collins	18.00
84	Dick Cole	15.00
85	*Bob Turley*	30.00
86	Billy Herman	27.00
87	Roy Face	20.00
88	Matt Batts	15.00
89	Howie Pollet	15.00
90	Willie Mays	600.00
91	Bob Oldis	15.00
92	Wally Westlake	15.00
93	Sid Hudson	15.00
94	Ernie Banks	825.00
95	Hal Rice	15.00
96	Charlie Silvera	15.00
97	Jerry Lane	15.00
98	Joe Black	17.00

100	Bob Keegan	15.00
102	Gil Hodges	75.00
103	*Jim Lemon*	17.00
104	Mike Sandlock	15.00
105	Andy Carey	15.00
106	Dick Kokos	15.00
107	Duane Pillette	15.00
108	Thornton Kipper	15.00
109	Bill Bruton	15.00
110	Harry Dorish	15.00
112	Bill Renna	15.00
113	Bob Boyd	15.00
114	Dean Stone	15.00
115	"Rip" Repulski	15.00
117	Solly Hemus	15.00
118	Carl Scheib	12.00
119	Johnny Antonelli	15.00
120	Roy McMillan	15.00
121	Clem Labine	18.00
122	Johnny Logan	17.00
126	Ben Wade	15.00
127	Steve O'Neill	15.00
128	*Henry Aaron*	2000.00
129	Forrest Jacobs	15.00
130	Hank Bauer	35.00
131	Reno Bertoia	15.00
132	Tom Lasorda	175.00
133	Del Baker	15.00

128 Henry Aaron

134	Cal Hogue	15.00
135	Joe Presko	15.00
136	Connie Ryan	15.00
137	*Wally Moon*	25.00
138	Bob Borkowski	15.00
139	Ed & Johnny O'Brien	30.00
140	Tom Wright	15.00
141	*Joe Jay*	18.00
142	Tom Poholsky	15.00
143	Rollie Hemsley	15.00
144	Bill Werle	12.00
145	Elmer Valo	12.00
146	Don Johnson	12.00
149	Jim Robertson	12.00
151	Alex Grammas	12.00
153	"Rube" Walker	12.00
154	Mike Fornieles	12.00
155	Bob Kennedy	12.00
156	Joe Coleman	12.00
158	"Peanuts" Lowrey	12.00
159	Dave Philley	12.00
160	"Red" Kress	12.00
162	Herman Wehmeier	12.00
165	Jim Pendleton	12.00
166	Johnny Podres	27.00
170	*Jim Rhodes*	18.00
171	Leo Kiely	12.00
172	Hal Brown	12.00

250 Ted Williams

94 Ernie Banks

173	Jack Harshman	12.00
174	Tom Qualters	12.00
175	*Frank Leja*	18.00
177	Bob Milliken	12.00
180	Wes Westrum	13.00
181	Mel Roach	12.00
182	Chuck Harmon	12.00
183	*Earle Combs*	25.00
184	Ed Bailey	15.00
185	Chuck Stobbs	15.00
187	"Heinie" Manush	30.00
191	*Dick Schofield*	17.00
192	"Cot" Deal	15.00
193	Johnny Hopp	15.00
194	Bill Sarni	15.00
195	*Bill Consolo*	15.00
196	Stan Jok	15.00
197	"Schoolboy" Rowe	15.00
198	Carl Sawatski	15.00
200	Larry Jansen	15.00
201	*Al Kaline*	850.00
205	Johnny Sain	27.00
209	Charlie Thompson	15.00
210	*Bob Buhl*	17.00
211	Don Hoak	15.00
213	John Fitzpatrick	15.00
215	Ed McGhee	15.00
216	Al Sima	15.00
217	Paul Schreiber	15.00

218	Fred Marsh	15.00	234	*Jerry Lynch*	17.00
219	Chuck Kress	15.00	235	Vern Law	17.00
220	Ruben Gomez	15.00	237	Mike Ryba	15.00
221	Dick Brodowski	15.00	238	Al Aber	15.00
222	Bill Wilson	15.00	239	*Bill Skowron*	75.00
223	Joe Haynes	15.00	240	Sam Mele	15.00
224	Dick Weik	15.00	241	Bob Miller	15.00
225	Don Liddle	15.00	242	Curt Roberts	15.00
226	Jehosie Heard	15.00	243	Ray Blades	15.00
227	Buster Mills	15.00	245	Roy Sievers	16.00
228	Gene Hermanski	15.00	246	Howie Fox	15.00
229	Bob Talbot	15.00	247	Eddie Mayo	15.00
230	Bob Kuzava	15.00	248	*Al Smith*	16.00
233	Augie Galan	15.00	250	Ted Williams	750.00

1955 BOWMAN

Both color and baseball were relatively new to television in 1955 when Bowman came out with its television set of cards, the last set issued by Bowman before the company was bought out by Topps. The front of each 2½- by 3¾-inch card features a color photo framed to look as if the player were on TV. The 320-card set has red-and-black printing on gray cardboard backs. In addition to the first umpire cards of the century, manager and coach cards were also released. Lots of superstars appear as well: Whitey Ford, Ralph Kiner, The Mick, and Pee Wee Reese.

		NR MT			
Complete set		**$5250.00**	14	Gus Keriazakos	6.00
Commons (1-224)		**6.00**	15	Frank Sullivan	6.00
Commons (225-320)		**15.00**	16	Jim Piersall	12.00
			17	Del Ennis	6.00
1	Hoyt Wilhelm	$100.00	18	Stan Lopata	6.00
2	Al Dark	14.00	19	Bobby Avila	6.00
3	Joe Coleman	6.00	20	Al Smith	6.00
4	Eddie Waitkus	6.00	21	Don Hoak	8.00
5	Jim Robertson	6.00	22	Roy Campanella	150.00
6	Pete Suder	6.00	23	Al Kaline	150.00
7	Gene Baker	6.00	24	Al Aber	6.00
8	Warren Hacker	6.00	25	Orestes Minnie Minoso	15.00
9	Gil McDougald	20.00	26	Virgil Trucks	8.00
10	Phil Rizzuto	55.00	27	Preston Ward	6.00
11	Billy Bruton	6.00	28	Dick Cole	6.00
12	Andy Pafko	7.00	29	Al "Red" Schoendienst	30.00
13	Clyde Vollmer	6.00	30	Bill Sarni	6.00
			31	*Johnny Temple*	9.00
			32	Wally Post	9.00

184 Willie Mays

33	Nelson Fox	**25.00**
34	Clint Courtney	**6.00**
35	Bill Tuttle	**6.00**
36	Wayne Belardi	**6.00**
37	Harold "Pee Wee" Reese	**80.00**
38	Early Wynn	**30.00**
39	Bob Darnell	**6.00**
40	Vic Wertz	**6.00**
41	Mel Clark	**6.00**
42	Bob Greenwood	**6.00**
43	Bob Buhl	**6.00**
44	Danny O'Connell	**6.00**
45	Tom Umphlett	**6.00**
46	Mickey Vernon	**6.00**
47	Sammy White	**6.00**
48	Milt Bolling (Frank Bolling on back)	**7.00**
48	Milt Bolling (Milt Bolling on back)	**18.00**
49	Jim Greengrass	**6.00**
50	Hobie Landrith	**6.00**
51	Elvin Tappe	**6.00**
52	Hal Rice	**6.00**
53	Alex Kellner	**6.00**
54	Don Bollweg	**6.00**
55	Cal Abrams	**6.00**
56	Billy Cox	**6.00**
57	Bob Friend	**6.00**
58	Frank Thomas	**8.00**
59	Ed "Whitey" Ford	**75.00**
60	Enos Slaughter	**30.00**
61	Paul LaPalme	**6.00**
62	Royce Lint	**6.00**
63	Irv Noren	**7.00**
64	Curt Simmons	**7.00**
65	*Don Zimmer*	**30.00**
66	George Shuba	**8.00**
67	Don Larsen	**17.00**
68	*Elston Howard*	**75.00**
69	Bill Hunter	**7.00**
70	● Lou Burdette	**9.00**
71	Dave Jolly	**6.00**
72	Chet Nichols	**6.00**
73	Eddie Yost	**6.00**
74	Jerry Snyder	**6.00**
75	*Brooks Lawrence*	**7.00**
76	Tom Poholsky	**6.00**
77	Jim McDonald	**6.00**
78	Gil Coan	**6.00**
79	Willie Miranda	**6.00**
80	Lou Limmer	**6.00**
81	Bob Morgan	**6.00**
82	Lee Walls	**6.00**
83	Max Surkont	**6.00**
84	George Freese	**6.00**
85	Cass Michaels	**6.00**
86	Ted Gray	**6.00**
87	Randy Jackson	**6.00**
88	Steve Bilko	**6.00**
89	Lou Boudreau	**24.00**
90	Art Ditmar	**6.00**
91	Dick Marlowe	**6.00**
92	George Zuverink	**6.00**
93	Andy Seminick	**6.00**
94	Hank Thompson	**6.00**

202 Mickey Mantle

95	Sal Maglie	11.00
96	*Ray Narleski*	8.00
97	John Podres	17.00
98	James "Junior" Gilliam	15.00
99	Jerry Coleman	7.00
100	Tom Morgan	8.00
101	Don Johnson (Braves' Ernie Johnson on front)	7.00
101	Don Johnson (Orioles' Don Johnson on front)	16.00
102	Bobby Thomson	11.00
103	Eddie Mathews	50.00
104	Bob Porterfield	6.00
105	Johnny Schmitz	6.00
106	Del Rice	6.00
107	Soliy Hemus	6.00
108	Lou Kretlow	6.00
109	Vern Stephens	6.00
110	Bob Miller	6.00
111	Steve Ridzik	6.00
112	Gran Hamner	6.00
113	Bob Hall	6.00
114	Vic Janowicz	6.00
115	Roger Bowman	6.00
117	Johnny Groth	6.00
118	Bobby Adams	6.00
121	Rufus Crawford	6.00
126	Billy Goodman	6.00
130	Richie Ashburn	25.00
132	• Harvey Kueen (incorrect spelling on back)	11.00
132	Harvey Kuenn (correct spelling on back)	30.00
134	Bob Feller	75.00
143	Don Newcombe	15.00
145	Bob Nieman	6.00
146	Don Liddle	6.00
150	Billy Klaus	6.00
152	Johnny Klippstein	6.00
153	Eddie Robinson	6.00
155	Jerry Staley	6.00
156	Jim Hughes	6.00
157	Ernie Johnson (Braves' Ernie Johnson on front)	15.00
158	Gil Hodges	40.00
160	Bill Skowron	25.00
168	Larry "Yogi" Berra	110.00
169	Carl Furillo	17.00
170	Carl Erskine	17.00
171	Robin Roberts	27.00
179	Hank Aaron	275.00
184	Willie Mays	275.00
191	Bob Lemon	25.00
195	Erv Palica (traded line on back)	25.00
197	Ralph Kiner	35.00
201	Allie Reynolds	17.00
202	Mickey Mantle	625.00
204	*Frank Bolling* (Frank Bolling on back)	20.00
213	George Kell	25.00
225	Paul Richards	17.00
226	W.F. McKinley (umpire)	23.00
227	Frank Baumholtz	15.00
228	John M. Phillips	15.00
229	*Jim Brosnan*	20.00

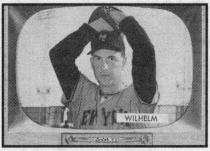

1 Hoyt Wilhelm

230	Al Brazle	15.00		
231	Jim Konstanty	20.00		
232	Birdie Tebbetts	15.00		
233	Bill Serena	15.00		
234	Dick Bartell	17.00		
235	J.A. Paparella (umpire)	23.00		

230 Al Brazle 15.00
231 Jim Konstanty 20.00
232 Birdie Tebbetts 15.00
233 Bill Serena 15.00
234 Dick Bartell 17.00
235 J.A. Paparella
(umpire) 23.00
236 Murray Dickson
(Murry) 15.00
237 Johnny Wyrostek 15.00
238 Eddie Stanky 17.00
239 Edwin A. Rommel
(umpire) 23.00
240 Billy Loes 17.00
241 John Pesky 17.00
242 Ernie Banks 450.00
243 Gus Bell 16.00
244 Duane Pillette 15.00
245 Bill Miller 15.00
246 Hank Bauer 35.00
247 Dutch Leonard 15.00
248 Harry Dorish 15.00
249 Billy Gardner 15.00
250 Larry Napp (umpire) 23.00
251 Stan Jok 15.00
252 Roy Smalley 15.00
253 Jim Wilson 15.00
254 Bennett Flowers 15.00
255 Pete Runnels 17.00
256 Owen Friend 15.00
257 Tom Alston 15.00
258 John W. Stevens
(umpire) 23.00
259 *Don Mossi* 20.00

260 Edwin H. Hurley
(umpire) 23.00
261 Walt Moryn 17.00
262 Jim Lemon 17.00
263 Eddie Joost 15.00
264 Bill Henry 15.00
265 *Albert J. Barlick*
(umpire) 80.00
266 Mike Fornieles 15.00
267 *George "Jim" Honochick*
(umpire) 75.00
268 Roy Lee Hawes 15.00
269 *Joe Amalfitano* 18.00
270 Chico Fernandez 17.00
271 Bob Hooper 15.00
272 John Flaherty
(umpire) 23.00
273 *Emory "Bubba" Church* 16.00
274 Jim Delsing 16.00
275 William T. Grieve
(umpire) 23.00
276 Ivan Delock 16.00
277 Ed Runge
(umpire) 25.00
278 *Charles Neal* 25.00
279 Hank Soar (umpire) 23.00
280 Clyde McCullough 16.00
281 Charles Berry
(umpire) 23.00
282 Phil Cavarretta 18.00
283 Nestor Chylak
(umpire) 25.00
284 William A. Jackowski
(umpire) 23.00

22 Roy Campanella

285	Walt Dropo	**18.00**
286	Frank E. Secory (umpire)	**23.00**
287	Ron Mrozinski	**16.00**
288	Dick Smith	**16.00**
289	Arthur J. Gore (umpire)	**23.00**
290	Hershell Freeman	**16.00**
291	Frank Dascoli (umpire)	**23.00**
292	Marv Blaylock	**18.00**
293	Thomas D. Gorman (umpire)	**25.00**
294	Wally Moses	**17.00**
295	E. Lee Ballanfant (umpire)	**23.00**
296	*Bill Virdon*	**35.00**
297	L.R. "Dusty" Boggess (umpire)	**23.00**
298	Charlie Grimm	**18.00**
299	Lonnie Warneke (umpire)	**23.00**
300	Tommy Byrne	**19.00**
301	William R. Engeln (umpire)	**23.00**
302	*Frank Malzone*	**20.00**
303	J.B. "Jocko" Conlan (umpire)	**100.00**
304	Harry Chiti	**16.00**
305	Frank Umont (umpire)	**23.00**
306	Bob Cerv	**22.00**
307	R.A. "Babe" Pinelli (umpire)	**23.00**

242 Ernie Banks

308	Al Lopez	50.00	314	Dale Mitchell ... 16.00
309	Hal H. Dixon (umpire)	23.00	315	*Cal Hubbard* (umpire) ... 100.00
310	Ken Lehman	17.00	316	Marion Fricano ... 16.00
311	Lawrence J. Goetz (umpire)	23.00	317	Wm. R. Summers (umpire) ... 23.00
312	Bill Wight	16.00	318	Sid Hudson ... 16.00
313	*A.J. Donatelli* (umpire)	30.00	319	Albert B. Schroll ... 16.00
			320	*George D. Susce, Jr.* ... 50.00

1955 TOPPS

Topps' first cards with a horizontal or landscape format again make use of a combination of protraits and full-figure photos. Both images on the 3¾- by 2⅝-inch fronts are colorized, with a horizontal bottom strip for player identification, a team logo in the upper right, and a facsimile autograph below. Unfortunately, many of the 206 portraits (Topps' smallest run ever) are reruns from the company's 1954 set. The backs feature red, black, and green printing on a white background. Rookies include Roberto Clemente, Harmon Killebrew, and Sandy Koufax. This was scheduled to be a 210-card set, but #175, 186, 203, and 209 were never issued.

	NR MT
Complete set	**$7500.00**
Commons (1-150)	**9.00**
Commons (151-160)	**18.00**
Commons (161-210)	**27.00**

1	"Dusty" Rhodes	$45.00
2	Ted Williams	425.00
3	Art Fowler	9.00
4	Al Kaline	235.00
5	Jim Gilliam	12.00
6	Stan Hack	9.00
7	Jim Hegan	9.00
9	Bob Miller	9.00
10	Bob Keegan	9.00
11	Ferris Fain	9.00
12	"Jake" Thies	9.00
14	Jim Finigan	9.00
16	Roy Sievers	10.00
18	Russ Kemmerer	9.00
19	Billy Herman	15.00

20	Andy Carey	12.00
21	Alex Grammas	9.00
22	Bill Skowron	20.00
24	Hal Newhouser	20.00
25	Johnny Podres	20.00
26	Dick Groat	10.00
27	Billy Gardner	9.00
28	Ernie Banks	225.00
29	Herman Wehmeier	9.00
30	Vic Power	9.00
31	Warren Spahn	90.00
32	Ed McGhee	9.00
33	Tom Qualters	9.00
34	Wayne Terwilliger	9.00
35	Dave Jolly	9.00
36	Leo Kiely	9.00
37	*Joe Cunningham*	11.00
38	Bob Turley	13.00
39	Bill Glynn	9.00
40	Don Hoak	9.00
42	"Windy" McCall	9.00
43	Harvey Haddix	11.00

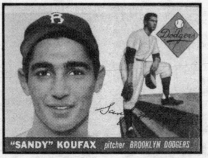

123 "Sandy" Koufax

44 "Corky" Valentine	....	**9.00**
45 Hank Sauer	....	**9.00**
46 Ted Kazanski	....	**9.00**
47 Hank Aaron	....	**400.00**
48 Bob Kennedy	....	**9.00**
49 J.W. Porter	....	**9.00**
50 Jackie Robinson	....	**250.00**
51 Jim Hughes	....	**9.00**
53 Bill Taylor	....	**9.00**
54 Lou Limmer	....	**9.00**
55 "Rip" Repulski	....	**9.00**
57 Billy O'Dell	....	**9.00**
58 Jim Rivera	....	**9.00**
59 Gair Allie	....	**9.00**
61 "Spook" Jacobs	....	**9.00**
63 Joe Collins	....	**9.00**
64 *Gus Triandos*	....	**15.00**
65 Ray Boone	....	**9.00**
67 Wally Moon	....	**9.00**
70 Al Rosen	....	**15.00**
75 *Sandy Amoros*	....	**25.00**
80 *Bob Grim*	....	**12.00**
81 Gene Conley	....	**9.00**
84 *Camilo Pascual*	....	**15.00**
85 *Don Mossi*	....	**12.00**
88 *Bob Skinner*	....	**15.00**
90 *Karl Spooner*	....	**15.00**
92 *Don Zimmer*	....	**40.00**
99 Frank Leja	....	**10.00**
100 Monte Irvin	....	**27.00**
106 Frank Sullivan	....	**9.00**
108 "Rube" Walker	....	**9.00**
109 Ed Lopat	....	**13.00**
110 Gus Zernial	....	**10.00**

111 Bob Milliken	....	**9.00**
113 Harry Brecheen	....	**11.00**
120 Ted Kluszewski	....	**25.00**
123 *"Sandy" Koufax*	....	**1300.00**
124 *Harmon Killebrew*	......	**350.00**
125 *Ken Boyer*	....	**75.00**
126 Dick Hall	....	**9.00**
127 *Dale Long*	....	**10.00**
133 Dave Hoskins	....	**9.00**
139 Steve Kraly	....	**9.00**
140 Mel Parnell	....	**9.00**
146 *Dick Donovan*	....	**10.00**
151 "Red" Kress	....	**18.00**
152 *Harry Agganis*	....	**80.00**
153 "Bud" Podbielan	....	**18.00**
154 Willie Miranda	....	**18.00**
155 Ed Mathews	....	**110.00**
156 Joe Black	....	**30.00**
157 Bob Miller	....	**18.00**
158 Tom Carroll	....	**18.00**
159 Johnny Schmitz	....	**18.00**
160 *Ray Narleski*	....	**20.00**
161 *Chuck Tanner*	....	**30.00**
162 Joe Coleman	....	**27.00**
163 Faye Throneberry	....	**27.00**
164 *Roberto Clemente*	...	**2000.00**
165 Don Johnson	....	**26.00**
166 Hank Bauer	....	**45.00**
167 Tom Cassagrande	....	**27.00**
168 Duane Pillette	....	**27.00**
169 Bob Oldis	....	**27.00**
170 Jim Pearce	....	**27.00**
171 Dick Brodowski	....	**27.00**
172 Frank Baumholtz	....	**27.00**

173	Bob Kline	27.00
174	Rudy Minarcin	27.00
175	Not Issued	
176	Norm Zauchin	27.00
177	Jim Robertson	27.00
178	Bobby Adams	27.00
179	Jim Bolger	27.00
180	Clem Labine	30.00
181	Roy McMillan	27.00
182	Humberto Robinson	27.00
183	Tony Jacobs	27.00
184	Harry Perkowski	27.00
185	Don Ferrarese	27.00
186	Not Issued	
187	Gil Hodges	150.00
188	Charlie Silvera	27.00
189	Phil Rizzuto	150.00
190	Gene Woodling	30.00
191	Ed Stanky	30.00
192	Jim Delsing	27.00
193	Johnny Sain	35.00
194	Willie Mays	550.00
195	*Ed Roebuck*	25.00
196	Gale Wade	27.00
197	Al Smith	30.00
198	Yogi Berra	250.00
199	Bert Hamric	27.00
200	Jack Jensen	50.00
201	Sherm Lollar	30.00
202	Jim Owens	27.00
203	Not Issued	
204	Frank Smith	27.00
205	*Gene Freese*	27.00
206	Pete Daley	27.00
207	Bill Consolo	27.00
208	Ray Moore	27.00
209	Not Issued	
210	Duke Snider	550.00

1956 TOPPS

Topps continued to improve upon its double-photo format by superimposing a colorized portrait over an action shot. A facsimile autograph is displayed on these horizontal 3¾- by 2⅝-inch cards, which have red, green, and black print on backs that are either white or gray. Three new types of cards were introduced in this 340-card set: teams, checklists, and league presidents. Of these, checklists are the most difficult to find today, although when issued they were thought of as disposable, of no value, and not tradable. Card backs feature humorous illustrations showing highlights from the player's career.

		NR MT
Complete set (without		
checklists)		**$7750.00**
Commons (1-100)		**8.00**
Commons (101-180)		**11.00**
Commons (181-260)		**17.00**
Commons (261-340)		**12.00**
1	William Harridge	$125.00
2	Warren Giles	20.00
5	Ted Williams	325.00
6	Ray Boone	9.00
8	Walter Alston	47.00
10	Warren Spahn	80.00
11a	Cubs Team (with date)	50.00
11b	Cubs Team (no date, name centered)	18.00
11c	Cubs Team (no date, name at left)	18.00
12	Andy Carey	10.00
13	Roy Face	10.00
14	Ken Boyer	17.00
15	Ernie Banks	100.00

33 Roberto Clemente

16	*Hector Lopez*	10.00
17	Gene Conley	9.00
20	Al Kaline	125.00
21	Joe Collins	10.00
24	Dick Groat	10.00
25	Ted Kluszewski	22.00
30	Jackie Robinson	150.00
31	Hank Aaron	275.00
33	Roberto Clemente	425.00
35	Al Rosen	13.00
39	Don Mossi	9.00
40	Bob Turley	15.00
42	Sandy Amoros	9.00
45	Gus Zernial	9.00
49	*Pedro Ramos*	9.00
50	"Dusty" Rhodes	9.00
52	Bob Grim	20.00
55	Wally Moon	9.00
56	Dale Long	9.00
58	Ed Roebuck	9.00
61	Bill Skowron	17.00
63	*Roger Craig*	30.00
64	Luis Arroyo	7.00
69	Chuck Tanner	10.00
72a	Phillies Team (with date)	50.00
72b	Phillies Team (no date, name centered)	15.00
72c	Phillies Team (no date, name at left)	15.00
75	Roy Sievers	9.00
77	Harvey Haddix	9.00
79	Sandy Koufax	425.00
80	Gus Triandos	9.00
83	Karl Spooner	9.00
85a	Indians Team (with date)	50.00
85b	Indians Team (no date, name centered)	15.00
85c	Indians Team (no date, name at left)	15.00
88	Johnny Kucks	10.00
90a	Redlegs Team (with date)	50.00
90b	Redlegs Team (no date, name centered)	15.00
90c	Redlegs Team (no date, name at left)	15.00
95a	Braves Team (with date)	50.00
95b	Braves Team (no date, name centered)	15.00
95c	Braves Team (no date, name at left)	15.00
99	Don Zimmer	15.00
100a	Orioles Team (with date)	40.00
100b	Orioles Team (no date, name centered)	15.00
100c	Orioles Team (no date, name at left)	15.00
101	Roy Campanella	150.00
102	Jim Davis	11.00
103	Willie Miranda	11.00
105	Al Smith	11.00
106	Joe Astroth	11.00
107	Ed Mathews	65.00
109	Enos Slaughter	35.00
110	Yogi Berra	150.00
111	Red Sox Team	14.00

135 Mickey Mantle

112	Dee Fondy	11.00
113	Phil Rizzuto	60.00
115	Jackie Jensen	15.00
116	Eddie O'Brien	11.00
117	Virgil Trucks	12.00
118	"Nellie" Fox	35.00
119	*Larry Jackson*	13.00
120	Richie Ashburn	35.00
121	Pirates Team	14.00
122	Willard Nixon	11.00
123	Roy McMillan	11.00
124	Don Kaiser	11.00
125	"Minnie" Minoso	22.00
127	Willie Jones	11.00
128	Eddie Yost	11.00
129	"Jake" Martin	11.00
130	Willie Mays	400.00
131	Bob Roselli	11.00
132	Bobby Avila	11.00
133	Ray Narleski	11.00
134	Cardinals Team	14.00
135	Mickey Mantle	1250.00
136	Johnny Logan	11.00
137	Al Silvera	11.00
138	Johnny Antonelli	11.00
140	*Herb Score*	30.00
141	Joe Frazier	11.00
142	Gene Baker	11.00
143	Jim Piersall	14.00
145	Gil Hodges	55.00
146	Senators Team	14.00
147	Earl Torgeson	11.00
148	Alvin Dark	14.00
149	"Dixie" Howell	11.00
150	"Duke" Snider	150.00
151	"Spook" Jacobs	11.00
152	Billy Hoeft	11.00
153	Frank Thomas	11.00
155	Harvey Kuenn	15.00
156	Wes Westrum	11.00
157	Dick Brodowski	11.00
158	Wally Post	11.00
159	Clint Courtney	11.00
160	Billy Pierce	14.00
161	Joe DeMaestri	11.00
162	"Gus" Bell	13.00
163	Gene Woodling	13.00
164	Harmon Killebrew	150.00
165	"Red" Schoendienst	37.00
166	Dodgers Team	200.00
170	Bill Virdon	14.00
172	*Frank Torre*	13.00
173	Johnny Podres	17.00
175	Del Crandall	13.00
177	Hank Bauer	22.00
178	Joe Black	13.00
180	Robin Roberts	40.00
181	Billy Martin	90.00
182	Paul Minner	17.00
183	Stan Lopata	17.00
184	Don Bessent	17.00
185	Bill Bruton	17.00
186	Ron Jackson	17.00
187	Early Wynn	40.00
188	White Sox Team	20.00
189	Ned Garver	17.00
190	Carl Furillo	25.00
191	Frank Lary	17.00
192	"Smoky" Burgess	17.00
193	Wilmer Mizell	17.00

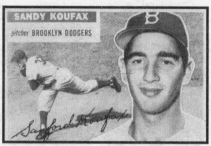

79 Sandy Koufax

194 Monte Irvin	35.00	
195 George Kell	32.00	
196 Tom Poholsky	17.00	
197 Granny Hamner	17.00	
198 Ed Fitzgerald (Fitz Gerald)	17.00	
199 Hank Thompson	20.00	
200 Bob Feller	125.00	
201 "Rip" Repulski	17.00	
202 Jim Hearn	17.00	
203 Bill Tuttle	17.00	
204 Art Swanson	17.00	
205 "Whitey" Lockman	17.00	
206 Erv Palica	17.00	
207 Jim Small	17.00	
208 Elston Howard	60.00	
209 Max Surkont	17.00	
210 Mike Garcia	18.00	
211 Murry Dickson	17.00	
212 Johnny Temple	17.00	
213 Tigers Team	60.00	
214 Bob Rush	17.00	
215 Tommy Byrne	17.00	
216 Jerry Schoonmaker	17.00	
217 Billy Klaus	17.00	
218 Joe Nuxall (Nuxhall)	18.00	
219 • Lew Burdette	20.00	
220 Del Ennis	17.00	
221 Bob Friend	17.00	
222 Dave Philley	17.00	
223 Randy Jackson	17.00	
224 "Bud" Podbielan	17.00	
225 Gil McDougald	30.00	
226 Giants Team	80.00	
227 Russ Meyer	17.00	
228 "Mickey" Vernon	19.00	
229 Harry Brecheen	20.00	
230 "Chico" Carrasquel	18.00	
231 Bob Hale	17.00	
232 "Toby" Atwell	17.00	
233 Carl Erskine	22.00	
234 "Pete" Runnels	18.00	
235 Don Newcombe	50.00	
236 Athletics Team	25.00	
237 Jose Valdivielso	17.00	
238 Walt Dropo	19.00	
239 Harry Simpson	17.00	
240 "Whitey" Ford	150.00	
241 Don Mueller	18.00	
242 Hershell Freeman	17.00	
243 Sherm Lollar	18.00	
244 Bob Buhl	17.00	
245 Billy Goodman	17.00	
246 Tom Gorman	17.00	
247 Bill Sarni	17.00	
248 Bob Porterfield	17.00	
249 Johnny Klippstein	17.00	
250 Larry Doby	30.00	
251 Yankees Team	200.00	
252 Vernon Law	19.00	
253 Irv Noren	17.00	
254 George Crowe	17.00	
255 Bob Lemon	35.00	
256 Tom Hurd	17.00	
257 Bobby Thomson	22.00	
258 Art Ditmar	17.00	
259 Sam Jones	17.00	
260 "Pee Wee" Reese	150.00	
268 Dale Mitchell	15.00	
270 Billy Loes	13.00	

280	Jim Gilliam	13.00
288	Bob Cerv	15.00
290	Curt Simmons	13.00
292	*Luis Aparicio*	150.00
293	Stu Miller	13.00
294	Ernie Johnson	13.00
295	Clem Labine	15.00
296	Andy Seminick	13.00
297	Bob Skinner	13.00
298	Johnny Schmitz	13.00
299	Charley Neal	30.00
300	Vic Wertz	13.00
301	Marv Grissom	13.00
302	Eddie Robinson	13.00
304	Frank Malzone	18.00
305	Brooks Lawrence	13.00
306	Curt Roberts	13.00
307	Hoyt Wilhelm	35.00
309	*Don Blasingame*	15.00
312	Andy Pafko	13.00
316	Jerry Coleman	15.00
320	Joe Adcock	15.00
321	Jim Konstanty	15.00
328	Preston Ward	12.00
332	Don Larsen	45.00
340	Mickey McDermott	45.00
—	Checklist 1/3 (unnumbered)	300.00
—	Checklist 2/4 (unnumbered)	300.00

1957 TOPPS

The Topps set was modernized in a number of ways for 1957. The cards were scaled down to a vertical 2½ by 3½ inches, the standard for today's sets. This edition also saw the first appearance of actual color photos in place of the colorized photos used earlier. While card fronts maintain simple designs, the backs are more sophisticated: Instead of giving statistics for only the previous season, complete year-by-year statistics for each player are now included. Hot rookies in this edition include Don Drysdale, Tony Kubek, and Brooks Robinson. Advanced collectors may want to pursue the four valuable checklist series cards, scarce survivors from 1957. Multi-player cards were introduced in this set, for example #400 Dodgers' Sluggers.

NR MT

Complete set (without checklists) $7500.00
Commons (1-264) 7.00
Commons (265-352) 20.00
Commons (353-407) 7.00

1	Ted Williams	$450.00
2	Yogi Berra	135.00
3	Dale Long	6.00
4	Johnny Logan	6.00
5	Sal Maglie	11.00
6	Hector Lopez	6.00
7	Luis Aparicio	50.00
8	Don Mossi	6.00
9	Johnny Temple	9.00
10	Willie Mays	250.00
11	George Zuverink	6.00
12	Dick Groat	10.00
13	Wally Burnette	6.00
14	Bob Nieman	6.00
15	Robin Roberts	25.00
16	Walt Moryn	6.00
18	*Don Drysdale*	275.00
19	Bob Wilson	6.00
20	Hank Aaron (photo reversed)	260.00
21	Frank Sullivan	6.00
22	Jerry Snyder (photo is Ed Fitz Gerald)	6.00
23	Sherm Lollar	6.00
24	*Bill Mazeroski*	65.00

95 Mickey Mantle

25	Whitey Ford	65.00
26	Bob Boyd	6.00
27	Ted Kazanski	6.00
28	Gene Conley	6.00
29	*Whitey Herzog*	35.00
30	Pee Wee Reese	70.00
31	Ron Northey	6.00
33	Jim Small	6.00
34	Tom Sturdivant	6.00
35	*Frank Robinson*	300.00
36	Bob Grim	6.00
37	Frank Torre	6.00
38	Nellie Fox	25.00
39	Al Worthington	6.00
40	Early Wynn	22.00
41	Hal Smith	6.00
42	Dee Fondy	6.00
43	Connie Johnson	6.00
44	Joe DeMaestri	6.00
45	Carl Furillo	15.00
46	Bob Miller	6.00
47	Don Blasingame	6.00
48	Bill Bruton	6.00
49	Daryl Spencer	6.00
50	Herb Score	8.00
51	Clint Courtney	6.00
53	Clem Labine	10.00
54	Elmer Valo	6.00
55	Ernie Banks	110.00

56	Dave Sisler	6.00
57	Jim Lemon	6.00
58	Ruben Gomez	6.00
59	Dick Williams	11.00
60	Billy Hoeft	6.00
61	Dusty Rhodes	6.00
62	Billy Martin	50.00
63	Ike Delock	6.00
64	Pete Runnels	7.00
65	Wally Moon	6.00
66	Brooks Lawrence	6.00
67	Chico Carrasquel	6.00
69	Roy McMillan	6.00
70	Richie Ashburn	25.00
71	Murry Dickson	7.00
72	Bill Tuttle	7.00
73	George Crowe	7.00
74	Vito Valentinetti	6.00
75	Jim Piersall	12.00
76	Bob Clemente	250.00
77	Paul Foytack	6.00
78	Vic Wertz	10.00
79	*Lindy McDaniel*	12.00
80	Gil Hodges	50.00
81	Herm Wehmeier	6.00
82	Elston Howard	20.00
83	Lou Skizas	6.00
84	Moe Drabowsky	6.00
85	Larry Doby	12.00
86	Bill Sarni	6.00
88	Harvey Kuenn	12.00
89	Roy Sievers	7.00
90	Warren Spahn	75.00
91	Mack Burk	6.00
92	Mickey Vernon	7.00
93	Hal Jeffcoat	6.00
94	Bobby Del Greco	6.00
95	Mickey Mantle	1200.00
96	*Hank Aguirre*	7.00
97	Yankees Team	60.00
98	Al Dark	8.00
99	Bob Keegan	6.00
100	League Presidents (Warren Giles, William Harridge)	10.00
101	Chuck Stobbs	6.00
102	Ray Boone	6.00
103	Joe Nuxhall	8.00
104	Hank Foiles	6.00

105	Johnny Antonelli	6.00
106	Ray Moore	6.00
107	Jim Rivera	6.00
108	Tommy Byrne	6.00
109	Hank Thompson	6.00
110	Bill Virdon	8.00
113	Wilmer Mizell	6.00
114	Braves Team	20.00
115	Jim Gilliam	12.00
116	Mike Fornieles	6.00
117	Joe Adcock	8.00
118	Bob Porterfield	6.00
119	Stan Lopata	7.00
120	Bob Lemon	225.00
121	*Cletis Boyer*	25.00
122	Ken Boyer	15.00
123	Steve Ridzik	6.00
124	Dave Philley	6.00
125	Al Kaline	100.00
126	Bob Wiesler	6.00
127	Bob Buhl	6.00
129	Saul Rogovin	6.00
130	Don Newcombe	15.00
131	Milt Bolling	6.00
132	Art Ditmar	6.00
133	Del Crandall	8.00
134	Don Kaiser	6.00
135	Bill Skowron	15.00
136	Jim Hegan	6.00
137	Bob Rush	6.00
138	• Minnie Minoso	15.00
139	Lou Kretlow	6.00
140	Frank Thomas	6.00
141	Al Aber	6.00
142	Charley Thompson	6.00
143	Andy Pafko	8.00
144	Ray Narleski	6.00
146	Don Ferrarese	6.00
147	Al Walker	6.00
148	Don Mueller	6.00
149	Bob Kennedy	6.00
150	Bob Friend	8.00
151	Willie Miranda	8.00
152	Jack Harshman	7.00
153	Karl Olson	7.00
154	Red Schoendienst	25.00
155	Jim Bronsnan	9.00
156	Gus Triandos	6.00
157	Wally Post	6.00

1 Ted Williams

158	Curt Simmons	6.00
160	Billy Pierce	10.00
161	Pirates Team	18.00
162	Jack Meyer	8.00
164	Tommy Carroll	8.00
165	Ted Kluszewski	40.00
166	Roy Face	9.00
167	Vic Power	7.00
168	Frank Lary	9.00
169	Herb Plews	7.00
170	Duke Snider	115.00
171	Red Sox Team	18.00
172	Gene Woodling	8.00
173	Roger Craig	15.00
174	Willie Jones	6.00
175	Don Larsen	18.00
176	Gene Baker	6.00
177	Eddie Yost	6.00
178	Don Bessent	6.00
180	Gus Bell	7.00
181	Dick Donovan	6.00
182	Hobie Landrith	6.00
183	Cubs Team	13.00
184	*Tito Francona*	8.00
185	Johnny Kucks	7.00
187	Virgil Trucks	8.00
188	Felix Mantilla	7.00
189	Willard Nixon	7.00
190	Randy Jackson	7.00

407 Yankees' Power Hitters

191	Joe Margoneri	7.00
192	Jerry Coleman	8.00
193	Del Rice	7.00
194	Hal Brown	7.00
195	Bobby Avila	7.00
196	Larry Jackson	7.00
199	Vern Law	7.00
200	Gil McDougald	15.00
203	Hoyt Wilhelm	20.00
210	Roy Campanella	115.00
212	*Rocco Colavito*	150.00
215	Enos Slaughter	24.00
230	George Kell	22.00
240	Hank Bauer	13.00
250	Ed Mathews	45.00
252	Carl Erskine	11.00
265	Harvey Haddix	22.00
266	Ken Kuhn	18.00
267	Danny Kravitz	18.00
268	Jackie Collum	18.00
269	Bob Cerv	18.00
270	Senators Team	50.00
271	Danny O'Connell	18.00
272	Bobby Shantz	30.00
273	Jim Davis	18.00
274	Don Hoak	20.00
275	Indians Team	50.00
276	Jim Pyburn	18.00
277	Johnny Podres	60.00
278	Fred Hatfield	18.00
279	Bob Thurman	18.00
280	Alex Kellner	18.00
281	Gail Harris	18.00
282	Jack Dittmer	18.00
283	*Wes Covington*	21.00
284	Don Zimmer	27.00
285	Ned Garver	18.00
286	*Bobby Richardson*	125.00
287	Sam Jones	18.00
288	Ted Lepcio	18.00
289	Jim Bolger	18.00
290	Andy Carey	20.00
291	Windy McCall	18.00
292	Billy Klaus	18.00
293	Ted Abernathy	18.00
294	Rocky Bridges	18.00
295	Joe Collins	20.00
296	Johnny Klippstein	18.00
297	Jack Crimian	18.00
298	Irv Noren	18.00
299	Chuck Harmon	18.00
300	Mike Garcia	21.00
301	Sam Esposito	18.00
302	Sandy Koufax	375.00
303	Billy Goodman	18.00
304	Joe Cunningham	21.00
305	Chico Fernandez	18.00
306	Darrell Johnson	20.00
307	Jack Phillips	18.00
308	Dick Hall	18.00
309	Jim Busby	18.00
310	Max Surkont	18.00
311	Al Pilarcik	18.00
312	*Tony Kubek*	100.00
313	Mel Parnell	20.00
314	Ed Bouchee	18.00
315	Lou Berberet	18.00
316	Billy O'Dell	18.00
317	Giants Team	60.00
318	Mickey McDermott	18.00
319	Gino Cimoli	18.00
320	Neil Chrisley	18.00
321	Red Murff	18.00
322	Redlegs Team	60.00
323	Wes Westrum	19.00
324	Dodgers Team	125.00
325	Frank Bolling	18.00
326	Pedro Ramos	18.00

327	Jim Pendleton	18.00	345	Paul Smith	18.00
328	*Brooks Robinson*	400.00	346	Dick Littlefield	18.00
329	White Sox Team	50.00	347	Hal Naragon	18.00
330	Jim Wilson	18.00	348	Jim Hearn	18.00
331	Ray Katt	18.00	349	Nelson King	18.00
332	Bob Bowman	18.00	350	Eddie Miksis	18.00
333	Ernie Johnson	18.00	351	Dave Hillman	18.00
334	Jerry Schoonmaker	18.00	352	Ellis Kinder	18.00
335	Granny Hamner	18.00	391	*Ralph Terry*	10.00
336	*Haywood Sullivan*	25.00	400	Dodgers' Sluggers	
337	Rene Valdes	18.00		(Campanella, Furillo,	
338	*Jim Bunning*	150.00		Hodges, Snider)	225.00
339	Bob Speake	18.00	407	Yankees' Power Hitters	
340	Bill Wight	18.00		(Berra, Mantle)	400.00
341	Don Gross	18.00	—	Checklist Series 1/2	250.00
342	Gene Mauch	30.00	—	Checklist Series 2/3	400.00
343	Taylor Phillips	18.00	—	Checklist Series 3/4	750.00
344	Paul LaPalme	18.00	—	Checklist Series 4/5	875.00

1958 TOPPS

Topps stretched its 1958 set to 494 cards, providing a vivid contrast to the mild-mannered issue of the previous year. The 2½- by 3½-inch vertical cards for 1958 show portraits or posed-action photos set against plain but brightly colored backgrounds. Team cards include set checklists on the card backs. Interestingly, 33 cards (dispersed randomly between numbers 2 and 108) are famous as yellow-letter variations. Either the player name or the team name on the card front is printed in yellow. This is indicated in the following list with (YP) or (YT), respectively, following the name. The more common style, with ordinary white printing, is marked (WP) or (WT). One of the most popular subsets in the 1958 edition consists of the 20 cards of All-Star players selected by *Sport* magazine (shown below with AS following the name). An additional All-Star card shows the two 1957 World Series managers, Fred Haney and Casey Stengel.

	NR MT
Complete set	**$5500.00**
Commons (1-110)	**8.00**
Commons (111-440)	**5.00**
Commons (441-494)	**5.00**

1	Ted Williams	$400.00
2	Bob Lemon (YT)	50.00
2	Bob Lemon (WT)	20.00
3	Alex Kellner	8.00
4	Hank Foiles	8.00
5	Willie Mays	200.00
6	George Zuverink	7.00
7	Dale Long	7.00
8	Eddie Kasko (YP)	30.00
8	Eddie Kasko (WP)	8.00
9	Hank Bauer	12.00
10	Lou Burdette	10.00
11	Jim Rivera (YT)	30.00
11	Jim Rivera (WT)	8.00
12	George Crowe	12.00

30 Hank Aaron

13	Billy Hoeft (YP)	30.00
13	Billy Hoeft (WP)	8.00
14	Rip Repulski	8.00
15	Jim Lemon	8.00
16	Charlie Neal	11.00
17	Felix Mantilla	18.00
18	Frank Sullivan	19.00
19	Giants Team/ Checklist 1-88	35.00
20	Gil McDougald (YP)	45.00
20	Gil McDougald (WP)	15.00
21	Curt Barclay	8.00
22	Hal Naragon	8.00
23	Bill Tuttle (YP)	30.00
23	Bill Tuttle (WP)	8.00
24	Hobie Landrith (YP)	30.00
24	Hobie Landrith (WP)	8.00
25	Don Drysdale	80.00
27	Bud Freeman	8.00
28	Jim Busby	8.00
30	Hank Aaron (YP)	400.00
30	Hank Aaron (WP)	200.00
31	Tex Clevenger	8.00
32	J.W. Porter (YP)	30.00
32	J.W. Porter (WP)	8.00
33	Cal Neeman (YT)	30.00
33	Cal Neeman (WT)	8.00
34	Bob Thurman	8.00
35	Don Mossi (YT)	30.00
35	Don Mossi (WT)	8.00
36	Ted Kazanski	8.00
37	*Mike McCormick* (photo is Ray Monzant)	9.00
38	Dick Gernert	9.00
40	George Kell	16.00
41	Dave Hillman	8.00
42	*John Roseboro*	15.00
43	Sal Maglie	10.00
44	Senators Team/ Checklist 1-88	14.00
45	Dick Groat	10.00
46	Lou Sleater (WP)	8.00
47	*Roger Maris*	525.00
48	Chuck Harmon	8.00
49	Smoky Burgess	10.00
50	Billy Pierce (YT)	27.00
50	Billy Pierce (WT)	9.00
51	Del Rice	7.00
52	Bob Clemente (YT)	400.00
52	Bob Clemente (WT)	200.00
53	Morrie Martin (YP)	20.00
53	Morrie Martin (WP)	10.00
54	*Norm Siebern*	10.00
55	Chico Carrasquel	6.00
57	Tim Thompson (YP)	30.00
57	Tim Thompson (WP)	8.00
58	Art Schult (YT)	30.00
58	Art Schult (WT)	8.00
59	Dave Sisler	9.00
60	Del Ennis (YP)	35.00
60	Del Ennis (WP)	9.00
61	Darrell Johnson (YP)	17.00
61	Darrell Johnson (WP)	8.00
62	Joe DeMaestri	8.00
63	Joe Nuxhall	9.00
64	Joe Lonnett	8.00
65	Von McDaniel (YP)	40.00
65	Von McDaniel (WP)	10.00
66	Lee Walls	8.00
67	Joe Ginsberg	8.00
69	Wally Burnette	8.00
70	Al Kaline (WP)	90.00
70	Al Kaline (YP)	175.00
71	Dodgers Team/ Checklist 1-88	55.00
72	Bud Byerly	8.00
73	Pete Daley	8.00

74	*Roy Face*	9.00
75	Gus Bell	8.00
76	Dick Farrell (YT)	18.00
76	Dick Farrell (WT)	12.00
77	Don Zimmer (YT)	40.00
77	Don Zimmer (WT)	11.00
78	Ernie Johnson (YP)	35.00
78	Ernie Johnson (WP)	10.00
79	Dick Williams (YT)	40.00
79	Dick Williams (WT)	10.00
80	Dick Drott	8.00
81	*Steve Boros* (YT)	30.00
81	*Steve Boros* (WT)	8.00
82	Ronnie Kline	8.00
83	Bob Hazle	8.00
84	Billy O'Dell	8.00
85	Luis Aparicio (YT)	60.00
85	Luis Aparicio (WT)	25.00
87	Johnny Kucks	9.00
88	Duke Snider	75.00
89	Billy Klaus	8.00
90	Robin Roberts	24.00
91	Chuck Tanner	9.00
92	Clint Courtney (YP)	35.00
92	Clint Courtney (WP)	8.00
93	Sandy Amoros	10.00
94	Bob Skinner	8.00
95	Frank Bolling	8.00
96	Joe Durham	8.00
97	Larry Jackson (YP)	30.00
97	Larry Jackson (WP)	8.00
98	Billy Hunter (YP)	30.00
98	Billy Hunter (WP)	8.00
99	Bobby Adams	8.00
100	Early Wynn (YT)	60.00
100	Early Wynn (WT)	20.00
101	Bobby Richardson (YP)	50.00
101	Bobby Richardson (WP)	20.00
102	George Strickland	8.00
103	Jerry Lynch	8.00
104	Jim Pendleton	8.00
105	Billy Gardner	8.00
106	Dick Schofield	8.00
107	Ossie Virgil	8.00
108	Jim Landis (YT)	30.00
108	Jim Landis (WT)	8.00
109	Herb Plews	8.00

70 Al Kaline

110	Johnny Logan	9.00
111	Stu Miller	5.00
112	Gus Zernial	5.00
113	Jerry Walker	5.00
114	Irv Noren	5.00
115	Jim Bunning	25.00
116	Dave Philley	5.00
117	Frank Torre	5.00
118	Harvey Haddix	5.00
119	Harry Chiti	5.00
120	Johnny Podres	8.00
121	Eddie Miksis	5.00
122	Walt Moryn	5.00
125	Al Dark	6.00
127	Tom Sturdivant	5.00
128	*Willie Kirkland*	5.00
129	Jim Derrington	5.00
130	Jackie Jensen	9.00
131	Bob Henrich	5.00
132	Vernon Law	6.00
133	Russ Nixon	5.00
134	Phillies Team/ Checklist 89-176	14.00
135	Mike Drabowsky	5.00
137	Russ Kemmerer	5.00
138	Earl Torgeson	5.00
139	George Brunet	5.00
140	Wes Covington	6.00

1958 Topps

150 Mickey Mantle

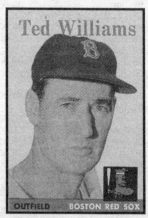

1 Ted Williams

199	Don Blasingame	5.00
200	Bob Keegan	5.00
201	Jim Bolger	5.00
202	*Woody Held*	5.00
203	Al Walker	5.00
204	Leo Kiely	5.00
205	Johnny Temple	5.00
206	Bob Shaw	6.00
207	Solly Hemus	5.00
208	Cal McLish	5.00
209	Bob Anderson	5.00
210	Wally Moon	5.00
211	Pete Burnside	5.00
212	Bubba Phillips	5.00
213	Red Wilson	5.00
214	Willard Schmidt	5.00
215	Jim Gilliam	9.00
216	Cardinals Team/ Checklist 177-264	15.00
217	Jack Harshman	5.00
218	Dick Rand	5.00
219	Camilo Pascual	6.00
220	Tom Brewer	5.00
221	Jerry Kindall	5.00
222	Bud Daley	5.00
223	Andy Pafko	6.00
224	Bob Grim	6.00
225	Billy Goodman	6.00
226	Bob Smith (photo is Bobby Gene Smith)	5.00
227	Gene Stephens	5.00
228	Duke Maas	5.00
229	Frank Zupo	5.00
230	Richie Ashburn	20.00
231	Lloyd Merritt	5.00
232	Reno Bertoia	5.00
233	Mickey Vernon	5.00
234	Carl Sawatski	5.00
235	Tom Gorman	5.00
236	Ed Fitz Gerald	5.00
237	Bill Wight	5.00
238	Bill Mazeroski	15.00
239	Chuck Stobbs	5.00
240	Moose Skowron	13.00
241	Dick Littlefield	5.00
242	Johnny Klippstein	5.00
243	Larry Raines	5.00
244	*Don Demeter*	5.00
245	*Frank Lary*	5.00

47 Roger Maris

246	Yankees Team/ Checklist 177-264	50.00
247	Casey Wise	5.00
248	Herm Wehmeier	5.00
249	Ray Moore	5.00
250	Roy Sievers	5.00
251	Warren Hacker	5.00
252	Bob Trowbridge	5.00
253	Don Mueller	5.00
254	Alex Grammas	5.00
255	Bob Turley	10.00
256	White Sox Team/ Checklist 265-352	12.00
257	Hal Smith	5.00
258	Carl Erskine	10.00
259	Al Pilarcik	5.00
260	Frank Malzone	5.00
261	Turk Lown	5.00
262	Johnny Groth	5.00
263	Eddie Bressoud	5.00
264	Jack Sanford	5.00
265	Pete Runnels	5.00
266	Connie Johnson	5.00
267	Sherm Lollar	5.00
268	Granny Hamner	5.00
269	Paul Smith	5.00
270	Warren Spahn	60.00
271	Billy Martin	20.00

418 World Series Batting Foes

272	Ray Crone	5.00
273	Hal Smith	5.00
274	Rocky Bridges	5.00
275	• Elston Howard	15.00
276	Bobby Avila	5.00
277	Virgil Trucks	5.00
278	Mack Burk	5.00
279	Bob Boyd	5.00
280	Jim Piersall	7.00
281	Sam Taylor	5.00
282	Paul Foytack	5.00
283	Ray Shearer	5.00
284	Ray Katt	5.00
285	Frank Robinson	100.00
286	Gino Cimoli	2.50
287	Sam Jones	2.50
288	Harmon Killebrew	100.00
295	Minnie Minoso	7.00
296	*Ryne Duren*	15.00
304	Tigers' Big Bats (Al Kaline, Harvey Kuenn)	20.00
307	Brooks Robinson	125.00
310	Ernie Banks	110.00
312	Red Sox Team/ Checklist 353-440	15.00
314	Dodgers' Boss and Power (Walt Alston, Duke Snider)	25.00

320	Whitey Ford	40.00
321	Sluggers' Supreme (Ted Kluszewski, Ted Williams)	40.00
324	Hoyt Wilhelm	20.00
340	Don Newcombe	11.00
343	*Orlando Cepeda*	90.00
351	Braves' Fence Busters (Hank Aaron, Joe Adcock, Del Crandall, Ed Mathews)	35.00
368	Rocky Colavito	30.00
370	Yogi Berra	110.00
375	Pee Wee Reese	60.00
377	Braves Team (numerical checklist)	85.00
386	Birdie's Young Sluggers (Ed Bailey, Frank Robinson, Birdie Tebbetts)	10.00
393	Tony Kubek	20.00
397	Tigers Team (numerical checklist)	80.00
400	Nellie Fox	14.00
408	Orioles Team (numerical checklist)	80.00
417	Carl Furillo	9.00
418	World Series Batting Foes (Mickey Mantle, Hank Aaron)	200.00
420	*Vada Pinson*	30.00
424	Larry Doby	7.00
428	Redlegs Team (numerical checklist)	80.00
436	Rival Fence Busters (Willie Mays, Duke Snider)	60.00
438	Whitey Herzog	8.00
440	Ed Mathews	40.00
448	Charlie Lau	5.00
450	Preston Ward	5.00
457	Milt Pappas	5.00
462	Gary Geiger	7.00
464	*Curt Flood*	25.00
475	AS Managers (Fred Haney, Casey Stengel)	20.00
476	Stan Musial AS	40.00
479	Nellie Fox AS	9.00
480	Eddie Mathews AS	15.00
482	Ernie Banks AS	25.00

483 Luis Aparicio AS	14.00	**488** Hank Aaron AS	50.00
484 Frank Robinson AS	25.00	**494** Warren Spahn AS	20.00
485 Ted Williams AS	75.00	**495** Herb Score AS	15.00
486 Willie Mays AS	50.00	— Contest Card	15.00
487 Mickey Mantle AS	125.00	— Felt Emblems Insert	

1959 TOPPS

Topps closed out the 1950s with a 572-card set, the largest of the decade, and added many specialty subsets to the regular player cards. Normal cards feature a nearly round color photo on a solid-color background outside the circle and a white outer border. A facsimile autograph appears across the photo. Card backs have year-by-year stats, a cartoon, and a short player biography. One specialty group is a ten-card subset highlighting events from the 1958 season. Other subsets include 31 Rookie Stars and 22 All-Star selections. Card number 550, titled Symbol of Courage, portrays Roy Campanella in his wheelchair following a near-fatal car accident. Card number 440 shows Lou Burdette posing as a lefty pitcher, tricking the photographer. Included in this set is a card of commissioner Ford Frick. Also, cards #199-286 can be found with white or gray backgrounds, though gray is more common.

	NR MT
Complete set	**$5000.00**
Commons (1-110)	7.00
Commons (111-506)	3.00
Commons (507-572)	16.00

1	Ford Frick	$85.00
2	Eddie Yost	7.00
3	Don McMahon	6.00
4	Albie Pearson	6.00
5	Dick Donovan	6.00
7	Al Pilarcik	6.00
8	Phillies Team/ Checklist 1-88	40.00
10	Mickey Mantle	525.00
11	Billy Hunter	6.00
12	Vern Law	7.00
15	Dick Drott	6.00
17	Danny's All Stars (Ted Kluszewski, Danny Murtaugh, Frank Thomas)	7.00

561 Hank Aaron AS

18	Jack Urban	6.00
19	Ed Bressoud	6.00
20	Duke Snider	70.00

202 Roger Maris

21	Connie Johnson	6.00
22	Al Smith	6.00
23	Murry Dickson	7.00
24	Red Wilson	6.00
25	Don Hoak	6.00
26	Chuck Stobbs	6.00
27	Andy Pafko	7.00
28	Red Worthington	6.00
29	Jim Bolger	6.00
30	Nellie Fox	15.00
31	Ken Lehman	6.00
32	Don Buddin	6.00
33	Ed Fitz Gerald	6.00
34	Pitchers Beware (Al Kaline, Charlie Maxwell)	15.00
35	Ted Kluszewski	10.00
36	Hank Aguirre	6.00
37	Gene Green	6.00
38	Morrie Martin	6.00
39	Ed Bouchee	6.00
40	Warren Spahn	60.00
41	Bob Martyn	6.00
42	Murray Wall	6.00
43	Steve Bilko	6.00
44	Vito Valentinetti	6.00
45	Andy Carey	7.00
46	Bill Henry	6.00
47	Jim Finigan	6.00
48	Orioles Team/ Checklist 1-88	20.00
49	Bill Hall	6.00
50	Willie Mays	175.00
51	Rip Coleman	6.00
52	Coot Veal	6.00
53	Stan Williams	6.00
54	Mel Roach	6.00
55	Tom Brewer	6.00
56	Carl Sawatski	6.00
57	Al Cicotte	6.00
58	Eddie Miksis	6.00
59	Irv Noren	6.00
60	Bob Turley	6.00
61	Dick Brown	6.00
62	Tony Taylor	6.00
63	Jim Hearn	6.00
64	Joe DeMaestri	6.00
65	Frank Torre	6.00
66	Joe Ginsberg	6.00
67	Brooks Lawrence	6.00
68	Dick Schofield	6.00
69	Giants Team/ Checklist 89-176	20.00
70	Harvey Kuenn	9.00
71	Don Bessent	6.00
72	Bill Renna	6.00
73	Ron Jackson	6.00
74	Directing the Power (Cookie Lavagetto, Jim Lemon, Roy Sievers)	7.00
75	Sam Jones	6.00
76	Bobby Richardson	20.00
77	John Goryl	6.00
78	Pedro Ramos	6.00
79	Harry Chiti	6.00
80	Minnie Minoso	7.00
81	Hal Jeffcoat	6.00
82	Bob Boyd	6.00
83	Bob Smith	6.00
84	Reno Bertoia	6.00
85	Harry Anderson	6.00
86	Bob Keegan	6.00
87	Danny O'Connell	6.00
88	Herb Score	8.00
89	Billy Gardner	6.00
90	Bill Skowron	15.00

91	Herb Moford	6.00
92	Dave Philley	6.00
93	Julio Becquer	6.00
94	White Sox Team/ Checklist 89–176	25.00
95	Carl Willey	6.00
96	Lou Berberet	6.00
97	Jerry Lynch	6.00
98	Arnie Portocarrero	6.00
99	Ted Kazanski	6.00
100	Bob Cerv	6.00
101	Alex Kellner	6.00
102	*Felipe Alou*	25.00
103	Billy Goodman	6.00
104	Del Rice	6.00
105	Lee Walls	6.00
106	Hal Woodeshick	6.00
107	Norm Larker	6.00
108	Zack Monroe	6.00
109	Bob Schmidt	6.00
110	George Witt	6.00
111	Redlegs Team/ Checklist 89–176	13.00
112	Billy Consolo	3.00
113	Taylor Phillips	3.00
114	Earl Battey	3.00
115	Mickey Vernon	4.00
116	*Bob Allison*	10.00
117	*John Blanchard*	7.00
118	John Buzhardt	3.00
119	*John Callison*	7.00
120	Chuck Coles	3.00
121	Bob Conley	3.00
122	Bennie Daniels	3.00
123	Don Dillard	3.00
125	*Ron Fairly*	7.00
131	*Deron Johnson*	6.00
133	Bob Lillis	3.00
134	Jim McDaniel	3.00
135	Gene Oliver	3.00
136	Jim O'Toole	3.00
137	Dick Ricketts	3.00
138	John Romano	3.00
139	Ed Sadowski	3.00
140	Charlie Secrest	3.00
142	Dick Stigman	3.00
143	Willie Tasby	3.00
144	Jerry Walker	3.00
146	Jerry Zimmerman	3.00

10 Mickey Mantle

147	Cubs' Clubbers (Ernie Banks, Dale Long, Walt Moryn)	14.00
148	Mike McCormick	3.00
149	Jim Bunning	12.00
150	Stan Musial	175.00
151	Bob Malkmus	3.00
152	Johnny Klippstein	3.00
153	Jim Marshall	3.00
155	Enos Slaughter	20.00
156	Ace Hurlers (Billy Pierce, Robin Roberts)	6.00
157	Felix Mantilla	3.00
158	Walt Dropo	3.00
159	Bob Shaw	3.00
160	Dick Groat	5.00
161	Frank Baumann	3.00
163	Sandy Koufax	175.00
164	Johnny Groth	3.00
165	Bill Bruton	3.00
166	• Destruction Crew (Rocky Colavito, Larry Doby, Minnie Minoso)	7.00
167	Duke Maas	3.00
169	Ted Abernathy	3.00
170	Gene Woodling	5.00
171	Willard Schmidt	3.00

150 Stan Musial

172	A's Team/Checklist 177-242	13.00
173	Bill Monbouquette	3.00
176	Preston Ward	3.00
177	Johnny Briggs	3.00
178	*Ruben Amaro*	3.00
179	Don Rudolph	3.00
180	Yogi Berra	85.00
181	Bob Porterfield	3.00
183	Stu Miller	3.00
184	Harvey Haddix	4.00
185	Jim Busby	3.00
186	Mudcat Grant	3.00
187	Bubba Phillips	3.00
188	Juan Pizarro	3.00
190	Bill Virdon	5.00
191	Russ Kemmerer	3.00
192	Charley Beamon	3.00
194	Jim Brosnan	4.00
196	Billy Moran	3.00
197	Ray Semproch	3.00
198	Jim Davenport	3.00
199	Leo Kiely	3.00
200	• Warren Giles	5.00
202	Roger Maris	150.00
203	Ozze Virgil	3.00
204	Casey Wise	3.00
205	Don Larsen	7.00
206	Carl Furillo	7.00
207	George Strickland	3.00
208	Willie Jones	3.00
211	Bob Blaylock	3.00
212	Fence Busters (Hank Aaron, Eddie Mathews)	60.00
213	Jim Rivera	3.00
214	Marcelino Solis	3.00
216	Andre Rodgers	3.00
217	Carl Erskine	5.00
218	Roman Mejias	3.00
219	George Zuverink	3.00
220	Frank Malzone	3.00
221	Bob Bowman	3.00
222	Bobby Shantz	4.00
223	Cards Team/ Checklist 265-352	14.00
224	Claude Osteen	4.00
225	Johnny Logan	3.00
226	Art Ceccarelli	3.00
227	Hal Smith	3.00
228	Don Gross	3.00
229	Vic Power	3.00
230	Bill Fischer	3.00
231	Ellis Burton	3.00
232	Eddie Kasko	3.00
233	Paul Foytack	3.00
234	Chuck Tanner	4.00
237	• Run Preventers (Gil McDougald, Bobby Richardson, Bob Turley)	10.00
238	Gene Baker	3.00
239	Bob Trowbridge	3.00
240	Hank Bauer	7.50
241	Billy Muffett	3.00
243	Marv Grissom	3.00
244	Dick Gray	3.00
245	Ned Garver	3.00
246	J.W. Porter	3.00
247	Don Ferrarese	3.00
248	Red Sox Team/ Checklist 177-264	13.00
249	Bobby Adams	3.00
251	Cletis Boyer	4.00
252	Ray Boone	3.00
253	Seth Morehead	3.00
254	Zeke Bella	3.00

255 Del Ennis 3.00
256 Jerry Davie 3.00
257 *Leon Wagner*................. 4.00
259 Jim Pisoni 3.00
260 Early Wynn..................... 15.00
261 Gene Stephens 3.00
262 ● Hitters' Foes
    (Don Drysdale,
    Clem Labine,
    Johnny Podres) 10.00
263 Buddy Daley.................. 3.00
264 Chico Carrasquel 3.00
267 John Romonosky 3.00
268 Tito Francona 3.00
269 Jack Meyer..................... 3.00
270 Gil Hodges 20.00
271 Orlando Pena 3.00
272 Jerry Lumpe 3.25
273 Joe Jay........................... 3.00
274 Jerry Kindall 3.00
275 Jack Sanford 3.00
277 Turk Lown 3.00
278 Chuck Essegian 3.00
279 Ernie Johnson 3.00
280 Frank Bolling 3.00
284 Steve Korcheck 3.00
285 Joe Cunningham 4.00
286 Dean Stone 3.00
287 Don Zimmer 4.00
288 Dutch Dotterer............... 3.00
289 Johnny Kucks................ 3.00
290 Wes Covington.............. 4.00
291 Pitching Partners
    (Camilo Pascual,
    Pedro Ramos) 3.00
292 Dick Williams................. 3.00
294 Hank Foiles 3.00
295 Billy Martin.................... 15.00
296 Ernie Broglio.................. 3.00
297 Jackie Brandt 3.00
298 Tex Clevenger............... 3.00
299 Billy Klaus..................... 3.00
300 Richie Ashburn............. 15.00
302 Don Mossi 3.00
303 Marty Keough 3.00
304 Cubs Team/
    Checklist 265-352 .... 13.00
305 Curt Raydon 3.00
306 Jim Gilliam..................... 7.00

50 Willie Mays

307 Curt Barclay 3.00
308 Norm Siebern 3.00
309 Sal Maglie 4.00
310 Luis Aparicio................ 20.00
311 Norm Zauchin................ 3.00
312 Don Newcombe............. 5.00
315 Joe Adcock.................... 5.00
316 Ralph Lumenti (with
    option statement) 3.00
316 Ralph Lumenti
    (w/o option statement). 90.00
317 NL Hitting Kings (Richie
    Ashburn, Willie Mays) . 30.00
318 Rocky Bridges 3.00
320 Bob Skinner................... 3.00
321 Bob Giallombardo
    (with option statement).. 3.00
321 Bob Giallombardo (w/o
    option statement) 80.00
322 Harry Hanebrink (with
    trade statement) 3.00
322 Harry Hanebrink (w/o
    trade statement) 80.00
325 Ken Boyer 9.00
326 Marv Throneberry.......... 5.00
327 Gary Bell 3.00
329 Tigers Team/
    Checklist 353-429 .... 9.00

514 Bob Gibson

519 Infield Power (Dick
  Gernert, Frank Malzone,
  Pete Runnels) **16.00**
520 Don Elston................... **15.00**
521 Gary Geiger................. **15.00**
522 Gene Snyder............... **15.00**
523 Harry Bright............... **15.00**
524 Larry Osborne **15.00**
525 Jim Coates **15.00**
528 Pirates Team/
  Checklist 496-572 .... **50.00**
529 George Bamberger **16.00**
530 Wally Moon **16.00**
531 Ray Webster **15.00**
532 Mark Freeman............ **15.00**
533 Darrell Johnson **15.00**
534 Faye Throneberry........ **15.00**
535 Ruben Gomez **15.00**
536 Dan Kravitz................. **15.00**
537 Rudolfo Arias.............. **15.00**
538 Chick King **15.00**
539 Gary Blaylock **15.00**
540 Willy Miranda **15.00**
541 Bob Thurman **15.00**
542 *Jim Perry* **25.00**
543 Corsair Outfield Trio
  (Bob Clemente, Bob
  Skinner, Bill Virdon)..... **70.00**
544 Lee Tate **15.00**
545 Tom Morgan............... **15.00**
546 Al Schroll **15.00**
547 Jim Baxes.................. **15.00**
548 Elmer Singleton........... **15.00**
549 Howie Nunn................ **15.00**
550 Roy Campanella
  (Symbol of Courage) . **210.00**
551 Fred Haney AS............ **17.00**
552 Casey Stengel AS **40.00**
553 Orlando Cepeda AS **25.00**
554 Bill Skowron AS........... **25.00**
555 Bill Mazeroski AS **20.00**
556 Nellie Fox AS **25.00**
557 Ken Boyer AS............. **25.00**
558 Frank Malzone AS....... **18.00**
559 Ernie Banks AS **65.00**
560 Luis Aparicio AS.......... **35.00**
561 Hank Aaron AS **135.00**
562 Al Kaline AS **60.00**
563 Willie Mays AS **135.00**

550 Roy Campanella

564 Mickey Mantle AS **300.00**
565 Wes Covington AS **16.00**
566 Roy Sievers AS **16.00**
567 Del Crandall AS........... **16.00**
568 Gus Triandos AS......... **16.00**
569 Bob Friend AS............. **18.00**
570 Bob Turley AS............. **20.00**
571 Warren Spahn AS **40.00**
572 Billy Pierce AS............. **25.00**

515 Harmon Killebrew

1960 TOPPS

In this 572-card set Topps revived the horizontal format used in 1955 and 1956. Color photos were used alongside smaller black-and-white photos on card fronts. The horizontal format and use of two photos, however, detract from the visual appeal of the cards. The backs, in contrast, are simpler than usual, with black-and-gold printing on gray or white cardboard. Card numbers 375-440 are slightly rarer in the white cardboard variety. For the first time, the 1960 set contained World Series highlight cards from the previous year. Hot cards include rookies Carl Yastrzemski, Willie McCovey, and Jim Kaat, along with superstars Bob Clemente, Mickey Mantle, and Roger Maris.

	NR MT
Complete set	$4000.00
Commons (1-286)	3.00
Commons (287-440)	4.00
Commons (441-506)	6.00
Commons (507-572)	12.00

1	Early Wynn	$40.00
2	Roman Mejias	2.00
3	Joe Adcock	4.00
5	Wally Moon	2.00
6	Lou Berberet	2.00
7	Master & Mentor (Willie Mays, Bill Rigney)	20.00
9	Faye Throneberry	2.00
10	Ernie Banks	55.00
11	Norm Siebern	2.00
12	Milt Pappas	2.00
13	Wally Post	2.00
14	Jim Grant	2.00
15	Pete Runnels	2.00
16	Ernie Broglio	2.00
17	Johnny Callison	2.00
18	Dodgers Team/ Checklist 1-88	25.00
19	Felix Mantilla	2.00
20	Roy Face	4.00
21	Dutch Dotterer	2.00
22	Rocky Bridges	2.00
25	Roy Sievers	5.00
26	Wayne Terwilliger	2.00
27	Dick Drott	2.00
28	Brooks Robinson	55.00
29	Clem Labine	4.00
30	Tito Francona	2.00
31	Sammy Esposito	2.00
32	Sophomore Stalwarts (Jim O'Toole, Vada Pinson)	5.00
33	Tom Morgan	2.25
34	George Anderson	15.00
35	Whitey Ford	45.00
36	Russ Nixon	2.00
37	Bill Bruton	2.00
38	Jerry Casale	2.00
40	Joe Cunningham	3.00
41	Barry Latman	2.00
42	Hobie Landrith	2.00
43	Senators Team/ Checklist 1-88	10.00
44	Bobby Locke	2.00
45	Roy McMillan	2.00
47	Don Zimmer	3.00
48	Hal Smith	2.00
50	Al Kaline	55.00
52	Dave Philley	2.00
53	Jackie Brandt	2.00
54	Mike Fornieles	2.00
55	● Bill Mazeroski	7.00
56	Steve Korcheck	2.00
57	Win Savers (Turk Lown, Gerry Staley)	2.00
58	Gino Cimoli	2.00
59	Juan Pizarro	2.00
60	Gus Triandos	2.00
61	Eddie Kasko	2.00
63	George Strickland	2.00
64	Jack Meyer	2.00

350 Mickey Mantle

65	Elston Howard	7.00
67	*Jose Pagan*	2.00
70	Lou Burdette	6.00
71	Marty Keough	2.00
72	Tigers Team/Checklist 89-176	8.00
73	Bob Gibson	70.00
74	Walt Moryn	2.00
75	Vic Power	2.00
77	Hank Foiles	2.00
78	Bob Grim	2.00
79	Walt Dropo	2.00
80	Johnny Antonelli	4.00
82	Ruben Gomez	2.00
83	Tony Kubek	8.00
84	Hal Smith	2.00
85	Frank Lary	2.00
87	John Romonosky	2.00
88	John Roseboro	2.00
89	Hal Brown	2.00
90	Bobby Avila	2.00
91	Bennie Daniels	2.00
92	Whitey Herzog	6.00
93	Art Schult	2.00
94	Leo Kiely	2.00
95	Frank Thomas	2.00
96	Ralph Terry	3.00
97	Ted Lepcio	2.00
99	Lenny Green	2.00
100	Nellie Fox	10.00
101	Bob Miller	2.00
109	Cletis Boyer	6.00
111	Vic Wertz	4.00
114	Ken Aspromonte	2.00
115	Fork & Knuckler (Roy Face, Hoyt Wilhelm)	6.00
119	*Chico Cardenas*	2.00
125	Dick Ellsworth	2.00
126	Chuck Estrada	2.00
132	*Frank Howard*	15.00
134	*Deron Johnson*	4.00
136	*Jim Kaat*	40.00
138	*Art Mahaffey*	4.00
148	*Carl Yastrzemski*	225.00
150	Billy Pierce	4.00
151	Giants Team/Checklist 177-264	9.00
153	Bobby Thomson	5.00
159	Jim Piersall	5.00
160	Rival All Stars (Ken Boyer, Mickey Mantle)	55.00
164	Reds Team/Checklist 89-176	9.00
168	Alex Grammas	2.00
169	Jake Striker	2.00
170	Del Crandall	4.00
171	Johnny Groth	2.00
172	Willie Kirkland	2.00
173	Billy Martin	12.00
174	Indians Team/Checklist 89-176	8.00
176	Vada Pinson	6.00
177	Johnny Kucks	2.00
178	Woody Held	2.00

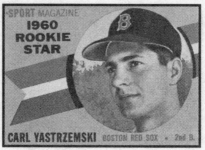

148 Carl Yastrzemski

181	Billy Loes	2.00
183	Eli Grba	2.00
188	Dick Williams	3.50
190	Gene Woodling	4.00
196	Andy Carey	2.00
200	Willie Mays	135.00
208	White Sox Team/ Checklist 177-264	8.00
210	Harmon Killebrew	30.00
212	Walt Alston	12.00
213	Chuck Dressen	4.00
216	Joe Gordon	5.00
217	Charley Grimm	6.00
219	Fred Hutchinson	5.00
221	Cookie Lavagetto	4.00
222	Al Lopez	7.00
223	Danny Murtaugh	5.00
224	Paul Richards	4.00
225	Bill Rigney	4.00
227	Casey Stengel	20.00
230	Mound Magicians (Bob Buhl, Lou Burdette, Warren Spahn)	7.00
235	Gus Bell	2.00
237	Elmer Valo	2.00
240	Luis Aparicio	15.00
241	Albie Pearson	1.50
242	Cards Team/ Checklist 265-352	9.00
245	Eddie Yost	2.00
247	Gil McDougald	6.00
249	*Earl Wilson*	2.00
250	Stan Musial	110.00
255	Jim Gilliam	6.00
258	Dick Groat	7.00
260	Power Plus (Rocky Colavito, Tito Francona)	6.00
262	Hank Bauer	5.00
264	Robin Roberts	15.00
270	Bob Turley	5.00
275	Curt Flood	6.00
279	Chuck Tanner	3.50
281	Ray Boone	3.50
282	Joe Nuxhall	3.50
283	John Blanchard	5.00
287	Felipe Alou	6.00
290	Jerry Lumpe	4.00
292	Dodger Backstops (Joe Pignatano, John Roseboro)	4.00
295	Gil Hodges	20.00
300	Hank Aaron	125.00
302	Phillies Team/ Checklist 353-429	9.00
305	Richie Ashburn	11.00
310	Frank Malzone	4.00
312	Charlie Lau	4.00
315	Bobby Shantz	5.00
316	*Willie McCovey*	225.00
317	Pumpsie Green	2.00
318	Jim Baxes	2.00
319	Joe Koppe	2.00
320	Bob Allison	3.00
321	Ron Fairly	3.00

200 Willie Mays

324	Jim Perry	**5.00**
326	Bob Clemente	**125.00**
327	Ray Sadecki	**2.00**
328	Earl Battey	**2.00**
329	Zack Monroe	**2.00**
330	Harvey Kuenn	**5.00**
331	Henry Mason	**2.00**
332	Yankees Team/	
	Checklist 265-352	**25.00**
335	Red Schoendienst	**12.00**
340	Harvey Haddix	**3.00**
341	Carroll Hardy	**3.00**
343	Sandy Koufax	**125.00**
349	Moe Drabowsky	**4.00**
350	Mickey Mantle	**425.00**
351	Don Nottebart	**3.00**
352	Cincy Clouters (Gus	
	Bell, Jerry Lynch,	
	Frank Robinson)	**6.00**
353	Don Larsen	**5.00**
354	Bob Lillis	**3.00**
355	● Bill White	**7.00**
356	Joe Amalfitano	**3.00**
357	Al Schroll	**3.00**
358	Joe DeMaestri	**3.00**
359	Buddy Gilbert	**3.00**
360	Herb Score	**3.00**
361	Bob Oldis	**3.00**
362	Russ Kemmerer	**3.00**
363	Gene Stephens	**3.00**
364	Paul Foytack	**3.00**
365	Minnie Minoso	**5.00**
366	*Dallas Green*	**12.00**
367	Bill Tuttle	**3.00**
368	Daryl Spencer	**3.00**
369	Billy Hoeft	**3.00**
370	Bill Skowron	**7.00**
371	Bud Byerly	**3.00**
373	Don Hoak	**5.00**
374	Bob Buhl	**5.00**
375	Dale Long	**3.00**
376	Johnny Briggs	**3.00**
377	Roger Maris	**125.00**
378	Stu Miller	**3.00**
379	Red Wilson	**3.00**
380	Bob Shaw	**3.00**
381	Braves Team/	
	Checklist 353-429	**9.00**
382	Ted Bowsfield	**3.00**
383	Leon Wagner	**3.00**
384	Don Cardwell	**3.00**
385	World Series Game 1	
	(Neal Steals Second)	**5.00**
386	World Series Game 2	
	(Neal Belts 2nd	
	Homer)	**5.00**
387	World Series Game 3	
	(Furillo Breaks Up	
	Game)	**6.00**
388	World Series Game 4	
	(Hodges' Winning	
	Homer)	**9.00**
389	World Series Game 5	
	(Luis Swipes Base)	**9.00**
390	World Series Game 6	
	(Scrambling After Ball)	**5.00**

377 Roger Maris

391	World Series Summary (The Champs Celebrate)	5.00
392	Tex Clevenger	3.00
393	Smoky Burgess	3.00
394	Norm Larker	3.00
395	Hoyt Wilhelm	12.00
396	Steve Bilko	3.00
397	Don Blasingame	3.00
398	Mike Cuellar	5.00
399	Young Hill Stars (Jack Fisher, Milt Pappas, Jerry Walker)	3.00
400	Rocky Colavito	12.00
401	Bob Duliba	3.00
402	Dick Stuart	5.00
403	Ed Sadowski	3.00
404	Bob Rush	3.00
405	Bobby Richardson	8.00
406	Billy Klaus	3.00
407	*Gary Peters* (color photo is J.C. Martin)	5.00
408	Carl Furillo	5.00
409	Ron Samford	3.00
410	Sam Jones	3.00
411	Ed Bailey	3.00
412	Bob Anderson	3.00
413	A's Team/ Checklist 430-495	9.00
414	Don Williams	3.00
415	Bob Cerv	3.00
416	Humberto Robinson	3.00
417	Chuck Cottier	3.00
418	Don Mossi	3.00
419	George Crowe	3.00
420	Ed Mathews	35.00
421	Duke Maas	3.00
422	Johnny Powers	3.00
423	Ed Fitz Gerald	3.00
424	Pete Whisenant	3.00
425	Johnny Podres	3.00
426	Ron Jackson	3.00
427	Al Grunwald	3.00
428	Al Smith	3.00
429	AL Kings (Nellie Fox, Harvey Kuenn)	6.00
430	Art Ditmar	3.00
431	Andre Rodgers	3.00
432	Chuck Stobbs	3.00
433	Irv Noren	3.00
434	Brooks Lawrence	3.00
435	Gene Freese	3.00
436	Marv Throneberry	5.00
437	Bob Friend	5.00
438	Jim Coker	3.00
439	Tom Brewer	3.00
440	Jim Lemon	3.00
441	Gary Bell	4.00
442	Joe Pignatano	4.00
443	Charlie Maxwell	4.00
444	Jerry Kindall	4.00
445	Warren Spahn	50.00
446	Ellis Burton	4.00
447	Ray Moore	4.00

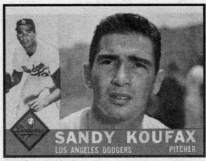

343 Sandy Koufax

448	*Jim Gentile*	**12.00**
449	Jim Brosnan	**4.00**
450	Orlando Cepeda	**20.00**
451	Curt Simmons	**4.00**
452	Ray Webster	**4.00**
453	Vern Law	**9.00**
454	Hal Woodeshick	**4.00**
455	Orioles Coaches (Harry Brecheen, Lum Harris, Eddie Robinson)............	**8.00**
456	Red Sox Coaches (Del Baker, Billy Herman, Sal Maglie, Rudy York)	**9.00**
457	Cubs Coaches (Lou Klein, Charlie Root, Elvin Tappe)	**7.00**
458	White Sox Coaches (Ray Berres, Johnny Cooney, Tony Cuccinello, Don Gutteridge.............	**7.00**
459	Reds Coaches (Cot Deal, Wally Moses, Reggie Otero)...............	**7.00**
460	Indians Coaches (Mel Harder, Red Kress, Bob Lemon, Jo-Jo White)	**9.00**
461	Tigers Coaches (Luke Appling, Tom Ferrick, Billy Hitchcock)	**9.00**
462	A's Coaches (Walker Cooper, Fred Fitzsimmons, Don Heffner).................	**7.00**
463	Dodgers Coaches (Joe Becker, Bobby Bragan, Greg Mulleavy, Pete Reiser)	**8.00**
464	Braves Coaches (George Myatt, Andy Pafko, Bob Scheffing, Whitlow Wyatt)	**8.00**
465	Yankees Coaches (Frank Crosetti, Bill Dickey, Ralph Houk, Ed Lopat).....................	**15.00**
466	Phillies Coaches (Dick Carter, Andy Cohen, Ken Silvestri)	**7.00**
467	Pirates Coaches (Bill Burwell, Sam Narron, Frank Oceak, Mickey Vernon)	**7.00**
468	Cardinals Coaches (Ray Katt, Johnny Keane, Howie Pollet, Harry Walker)	**9.00**

250 Stan Musial

469	Giants Coaches (Salty Parker, Bill Posedel, Wes Westrum)	7.00
470	Senators Coaches (Ellis Clary, Sam Mele, Bob Swift)	7.00
471	Ned Garver	4.00
472	Al Dark	7.00
473	Al Cicotte	4.00
474	Haywood Sullivan	4.00
475	Don Drysdale	60.00
476	Lou Johnson	4.00
477	Don Ferrarese	4.00
478	Frank Torre	4.00
480	Yogi Berra	80.00
481	Wes Stock	4.00
482	Frank Bolling	4.00
483	Camilo Pascual	4.00
484	Pirates Team/ Checklist 430-495	30.00
485	Ken Boyer	4.00
486	Bobby Del Greco	4.00
487	Tom Sturdivant	4.00
488	Norm Cash	12.00
489	Steve Ridzik	4.00
490	Frank Robinson	65.00
491	Mel Roach	4.00
492	Larry Jackson	4.00
493	Duke Snider	65.00
494	Orioles Team/ Checklist 496-572	15.00
495	Sherm Lollar	7.00
496	Bill Virdon	7.00

498	Al Pilarcik	4.00
499	Johnny James	4.00
500	Johnny Temple	4.00
501	Bob Schmidt	4.00
502	Jim Bunning	12.00
503	Don Lee	4.00
504	Seth Morehead	4.00
505	Ted Kluszewski	15.00
506	Lee Walls	4.00
507	Dick Stigman	12.00
508	Billy Consolo	12.00
509	*Tommy Davis*	27.00
510	Jerry Staley	12.00
511	Ken Walters	12.00
512	Joe Gibbon	12.00
513	Cubs Team/ Checklist 496-572	35.00
514	*Steve Barber*	15.00
515	*Stan Lopata*	12.00
516	Marty Kutyna	12.00
517	Charley James	12.00
518	*Tony Gonzalez*	13.00
519	Ed Roebuck	12.00
520	Don Buddin	12.00
521	Mike Lee	12.00
522	Ken Hunt	12.00
523	*Clay Dalrymple*	13.00
524	Bill Henry	12.00
525	Marv Breeding	12.00
526	Paul Giel	12.00
527	Jose Valdivielso	12.00
528	Ben Johnson	12.00
529	Norm Sherry	12.00

300 Hank Aaron

530	Mike McCormick..........	**12.00**
531	Sandy Amoros.............	**13.00**
532	Mike Garcia	**13.00**
533	Lu Clinton	**12.00**
534	Ken MacKenzie	**12.00**
535	Whitey Lockman..........	**12.00**
536	Wynn Hawkins	**12.00**
537	Red Sox Team/	
	Checklist 496-572	**37.00**
538	Frank Barnes...............	**12.00**
539	Gene Baker	**12.00**
540	Jerry Walker	**12.00**
541	Tony Curry	**12.00**
542	Ken Hamlin..................	**12.00**
543	Elio Chacon	**12.00**
544	Bill Monbouquette	**12.00**
545	Carl Sawatski	**12.00**
546	Hank Aguirre	**12.00**
547	*Bob Aspromonte*	**13.00**
548	*Don Mincher*................	**14.00**
549	John Buzhardt.............	**12.00**
550	Jim Landis	**12.00**
551	Ed Rakow	**12.00**
552	Walt Bond...................	**12.00**
553	Bill Skowron AS...........	**18.00**
554	Willie McCovey AS......	**70.00**
555	Nellie Fox AS	**20.00**
556	Charlie Neal AS...........	**15.00**
557	Frank Malzone AS........	**15.00**
558	Eddie Mathews AS......	**35.00**
559	Luis Aparicio AS..........	**25.00**
560	Ernie Banks AS...........	**60.00**

316 Willie McCovey

561	Al Kaline AS	**60.00**
562	Joe Cunningham AS ...	**15.00**
563	Mickey Mantle AS	**300.00**
564	Willie Mays AS	**125.00**
565	Roger Maris AS	**120.00**
566	Hank Aaron AS	**125.00**
567	Sherm Lollar AS	**15.00**
568	Del Crandall AS...........	**15.00**
569	Camilo Pascual AS	**12.00**
570	Don Drysdale AS.........	**40.00**
571	Billy Pierce AS	**15.00**
572	Johnny Antonelli AS	**25.00**

1961 TOPPS

Topps returned to a vertical format in 1961 and issued a standard-sized edition of 589 cards. Two cards in the All-Star subset were never issued (numbers 587 and 588), but many of the released all-star cards are currently among the most valuable in the set. On the whole, the set is simple, yet attractive. A large color photo is accented by a two-part horizontal rectangle below the photo for the player name, position, and team. Card backs again contain statistics by year and utilize black-and-green/gold printing on gray cardboard. The 1961 set features a unique 16-card subset honoring each MVP Award winner since 1951. Card numbers 523 through 589 are among the scarcest high numbers ever produced by Topps. In error, two #463 cards exist—Jack Fisher and Braves team card.

		NR MT
Complete set		**$5800.00**
Commons (1-370)		**3.00**
Commons (371-522)		**5.00**
Commons (523-589)		**35.00**

1	Dick Groat	**$21.00**
2	Roger Maris...............	**175.00**
3	John Buzzhardt	**2.00**
4	Lenny Green	**2.00**
5	Johnny Romano	**2.00**
6	Ed Roebuck.................	**2.00**
7	White Sox Team............	**4.00**
8	Dick Williams	**2.00**
9	Bob Purkey...................	**2.00**
10	Brooks Robinson	**35.00**
11	Curt Simmons	**2.00**
12	Moe Thacker	**2.00**
14	Don Mossi	**2.00**
16	Willie Kirkland..............	**2.00**
17	Checklist 1-88	**6.00**
19	Cletis Boyer	**5.00**
20	Robin Roberts	**12.00**
21	*Zorro Versalles (Zoilo)*...	**6.00**
22	Clem Labine	**2.00**
23	Don Demeter	**2.00**
25	Red's Heavy Artillery (Gus Bell, Vada Pinson, Frank Robinson)............	**8.00**
28	Hector Lopez	**2.00**
29	Don Nottebart	**2.00**
30	Nellie Fox	**7.00**
32	Ray Sadecki	**2.00**
35	*Ron Santo*	**55.00**
36	Jack Kralick	**2.00**
37	Charlie Maxwell.............	**2.00**
40	Bob Turley	**4.00**
41	NL Batting Ldrs (Bob Clemente, Dick Groat, Norm Larker, Willie Mays).....	**10.00**
42	AL Batting Ldrs (Minnie Minoso, Pete Runnels, Bill Skowron, Al Smith) ..	**6.00**
43	NL HR Ldrs (Hank Aaron, Ernie Banks, Ken Boyer, Eddie Mathews)	**12.00**

44 AL HR Ldrs (Rocky Colavito,
Jim Lemon, Mickey
Mantle, Roger Maris)... **45.00**
45 NL ERA Ldrs
(Ernie Broglio, Don
Drysdale, Bob Friend,
Mike McCormick, Stan
Williams) **6.00**
46 AL ERA Ldrs
(Frank Baumann, Hal
Brown, Jim Bunning,
Art Ditmar) **6.00**
47 NL Pitching Ldrs
(Ernie Broglio,Lou
Burdette, Vern Law,
Warren Spahn) **7.00**
48 AL Pitching Ldrs
(Bud Daley, Art Ditmar,
Chuck Estrada, Frank
Lary, Milt Pappas,
Jim Perry) **6.00**
49 NL SO Ldrs
(Ernie Broglio, Don
Drysdale, Sam Jones,
Sandy Koufax) **6.00**
50 AL SO Ldrs (Jim Bunning,
Frank Lary, Pedro Ramos,
Early Wynn) **6.00**
51 Tigers Team **6.00**
53 Russ Nixon **2.00**
55 Jim Davenport **2.00**
56 Russ Kemmerer **2.00**
57 Marv Throneberry **4.00**
58 Joe Schaffernoth **2.00**
59 Jim Woods **2.00**
60 Woodie Held.................. **2.00**
62 Al Pilarcik **2.00**
63 Jim Kaat **9.00**
65 Ted Kluszewski **6.00**
68 Deron Johnson **2.00**
69 Earl Wilson **2.00**
70 Bill Virdon **4.00**
71 Jerry Adair **2.00**
74 Joe Pignatano **2.00**
75 Lindy Shows Larry
(Larry Jackson,
Lindy McDaniel) **2.00**
80 Harmon Killebrew **20.00**
81 Tracy Stallard **2.00**

2 Roger Maris

82 Joe Christopher **2.00**
86 Dodgers Team **8.00**
88 Richie Ashburn **9.00**
89 Billy Martin **9.00**
90 Jerry Staley **2.00**
91 Walt Moryn **2.00**
92 Hal Naragon **2.00**
93 Tony Gonzalez **2.00**
94 Johnny Kucks **2.00**
95 Norm Cash **6.00**
98 Checklist 89-176
("Checklist" in red
on front) **7.00**
98 Checklist 89-176
("Checklist" in yellow,
"98" in black on back).... **5.00**
98 Checklist 89-176
("Checklist" in yellow,
"98" in white on back).... **7.00**
100 Harvey Haddix **2.00**
101 Bubba Phillips **2.00**
102 Gene Stephens **2.00**
103 Ruben Amaro **2.00**
104 John Blanchard **2.00**
106 Whitey Herzog **4.00**
109 Johnny Podres **4.00**
110 Vada Pinson **5.00**
111 Jack Meyer **2.00**

300 Mickey Mantle

112	Chico Fernandez	2.00
114	Hobie Landrith	2.00
115	Johnny Antonelli	2.00
116	Joe DeMaestri	2.00
117	Dale Long	2.00
119	A's Big Armor (Hank Bauer, Jerry Lumpe, Norm Siebern)	4.00
120	Ed Mathews	30.00
122	Cubs Team	7.00
124	J.C. Martin	2.00
125	Steve Barber	2.00
126	Dick Stuart	2.00
127	Ron Kline	2.00
128	Rip Repulski	2.00
131	Paul Richards	2.00
132	Al Lopez	5.00
133	Ralph Houk	5.00
136	Walt Alston	6.00
141	*Billy Williams*	110.00
142	Luis Arroyo	2.00
143	Russ Snyder	2.00
147	Ed Rakow	2.00
149	Julian Javier	2.00
150	Willie Mays	135.00
159	Orioles Team	6.00
160	Whitey Ford	40.00
167	Giants Team	7.00
168	Tommy Davis	5.00
173	Beantown Bombers (Jackie Jensen, Frank Malzone, Vic Wertz)	4.00
180	Bobby Richardson	7.50
184	Steve Bilko	2.00
185	Herb Score	4.00
186	Elmer Valo	2.00
189	Checklist 177-264	5.00
200	Warren Spahn	35.00
205	Bill Pierce	2.00
207	Dodger Southpaws (Sandy Koufax, Johnny Podres)	21.00
211	Bob Gibson	45.00
213	*Bill Stafford*	2.00
215	Gus Bell	2.00
219	Gene Mauch	4.00
220	Al Dark	2.00
222	Jimmie Dykes	4.00
223	Bob Scheffing	2.00
224	Joe Gordon	4.00
225	Bill Rigney	2.00
226	Harry Lavagetto	2.00
227	Juan Pizzaro	2.00
228	Yankees Team	35.00
230	Don Hoak	2.00
232	Bill White	5.00
238	Jim Gilliam	4.00
245	Joe Adcock	4.00
249	Reds Team	2.00
250	• Buc Hill Aces (Roy Face, Vern Law)	4.00
251	Bill Bruton	2.00
260	Don Drysdale	30.00
261	Charlie Lau	2.00
265	Tony Kubek	9.00
273	Checklist 265-352	5.00
275	Gene Woodling	4.00
280	Frank Howard	5.00
281	Frank Sullivan	2.00
282	Faye Throneberry	2.00
284	Dick Gernert	2.00
285	Sherm Lollar	2.00
287	Carl Yastrzemski	125.00
290	Stan Musial	110.00
295	Milt Pappas	2.00

297	Athletics Team	5.00
300	Mickey Mantle	**435.00**
306	World Series Game 1 (Virdon Saves Game)	7.00
307	World Series Game 2 (Mantle Slams 2 Homers)	**45.00**
308	World Series Game 3 (Richardson Is Hero)	8.00
309	World Series Game 4 (Cimoli Is Safe In Crucial Play)	7.00
310	World Series Game 5 (Face Saves the Day)	7.00
311	World Series Game 6 (Ford Pitches Second Shutout)	10.00
312	World Series Game 7 (Mazeroski's Homer Wins It!)	**12.00**
313	World Series Summary (The Winners Celebrate)	7.00
318	Danny O'Connell	2.00
319	Valmy Thomas	2.00
320	Lou Burdette	4.00
321	Marv Breeding	2.00
323	Sammy Esposito	2.00
324	Hank Aguirre	2.00
325	Wally Moon	2.00
327	*Matty Alou*	7.00
328	Jim O'Toole	2.00
329	Julio Becquer	2.00
330	Rocky Colavito	12.00
337	• Al's Aces (Al Lopez, Herb Score, Early Wynn)	5.00
340	Vic Wertz	2.00
344	Sandy Koufax	110.00
345	Jim Piersall	4.00
347	Cardinals Team	6.00
349	Danny McDevitt	2.00
350	Ernie Banks	45.00
355	Bob Allison	3.00
359	Dallas Green	4.00
360	Frank Robinson	45.00
361	Checklist 353-429 ("Topps Baseball" in black on front)	5.00

589 Warren Spahn AS

361	Checklist 353-429 ("Topps Baseball" in yellow on front)	6.00
365	Jerry Lumpe	2.00
369	Dave Philley	2.00
370	Roy Face	4.00
371	Bill Skowron	35.00
372	Bob Hendley	3.00
373	Red Sox Team	9.00
374	Paul Giel	3.00
375	Ken Boyer	8.00
376	Mike Roarke	3.00
377	Ruben Gomez	3.00
378	Wally Post	3.00
379	Bobby Shantz	6.00
380	• Minnie Minoso	7.00
381	Dave Wickersham	3.00
382	Frank Thomas	3.00
383	Frisco First Liners (Mike McCormick, Billy O'Dell, Jack Sanford)	3.00
384	Chuck Essegian	3.00
385	Jim Perry	6.00
386	Joe Hicks	3.00
387	Duke Maas	3.00
388	Bob Clemente	115.00
389	Ralph Terry	6.00
390	Del Crandall	6.00

417 Juan Marichal

391	Winston Brown	3.00
392	Reno Bertoia	3.00
393	Batter Bafflers (Don Cardwell, Glen Hobbie)	3.00
394	Ken Walters	3.00
395	Chuck Estrada	3.00
396	Bob Aspromonte	3.00
397	Hal Woodeshick	3.00
398	Hank Bauer	7.00
399	Cliff Cook	3.00
400	Vern Law	7.00
401	Babe Ruth Hits 60th Homer	30.00
402	Larsen Pitches Perfect Game	20.00
403	Brooklyn-Boston Play 26-Inning Tie	7.00
404	Hornsby Tops NL With .424 Average	10.00
405	Gehrig Benched After 2,130 Games	25.00
406	Mantle Blasts 565 Ft. HR	50.00
407	Jack Chesbro Wins 41st Game	7.00
408	Mathewson Strikes Out 267 Batters	7.00

409	Johnson Hurls 3rd Shutout in 4 Days	7.00
410	Haddix Pitches 12 Perfect Innings	7.00
411	Tony Taylor	3.00
412	Larry Sherry	3.00
413	Eddie Yost	3.00
414	Dick Donovan	3.00
415	Hank Aaron	135.00
416	*Dick Howser*	9.00
417	*Juan Marichal*	135.00
418	Ed Bailey	3.00
419	Tom Borland	3.00
420	Ernie Broglio	3.00
421	Ty Cline	3.00
422	Bud Daley	3.00
423	Charlie Neal	3.00
424	Turk Lown	3.00
425	Yogi Berra	75.00
426	Not Issued	
427	Dick Ellsworth	3.00
428	Ray Barker	3.00
429	Al Kaline	50.00
430	Bill Mazeroski	35.00
431	Chuck Stobbs	3.00
432	Coot Veal	3.00
433	Art Mahaffey	3.00
434	Tom Brewer	3.00
435	Orlando Cepeda	13.00
436	*Jim Maloney*	12.00
437	Checklist 430-506	8.00
438	Curt Flood	8.00
439	*Phil Regan*	7.00
440	Luis Aparicio	15.00
441	Dick Bertell	3.00
442	Gordon Jones	3.00
443	Duke Snider	40.00
444	Joe Nuxhall	3.00
445	Frank Malzone	3.00
446	Bob "Hawk" Taylor	3.00
447	Harry Bright	3.00
448	Del Rice	3.00
449	*Bobby Bolin*	3.00
450	Jim Lemon	3.00
451	Power for Ernie (Ernie Broglio, Daryl Spencer, Bill White)	3.00
452	Bob Allen	3.00
453	Dick Schofield	3.00

454	Pumpsie Green	3.00
455	Early Wynn	15.00
456	Hal Bevan	3.00
457	Johnny James	3.00
458	Willie Tasby	3.00
459	Terry Fox	3.00
460	Gil Hodges	15.00
461	Smoky Burgess	3.00
462	Lou Klimchock	3.00
463	Braves Team (should be card 426)	8.00
463	Jack Fisher	3.00
464	*Leroy Thomas*	3.00
465	Roy McMillan	3.00
466	Ron Moeller	3.00
467	Indians Team	8.00
468	Johnny Callison	3.00
469	Ralph Lumenti	3.00
470	Roy Sievers	3.00
471	Phil Rizzuto MVP	17.00
472	Yogi Berra MVP	60.00
473	Bobby Shantz MVP	8.00
474	Al Rosen MVP	9.00
475	Mickey Mantle MVP	150.00
476	Jackie Jensen MVP	8.00
477	Nellie Fox MVP	8.00
478	Roger Maris MVP	50.00
479	Jim Konstanty MVP	8.00
480	Roy Campanella MVP	35.00
481	Hank Sauer MVP	8.00
482	Willie Mays MVP	50.00
483	Don Newcombe MVP	8.00
484	Hank Aaron MVP	50.00
485	Ernie Banks MVP	30.00
486	Dick Groat MVP	8.00
487	Gene Oliver	3.00
488	Joe McClain	3.00
489	Walt Dropo	3.00
490	Jim Bunning	10.00
491	Phillies Team	8.00
492	Ron Fairly	7.00
493	Don Zimmer	6.00
494	Tom Cheney	3.00
495	Elston Howard	10.00
496	Ken MacKenzie	3.00
497	Willie Jones	3.00
498	Ray Herbert	3.00
499	Chuck Schilling	3.00
500	Harvey Kuenn	7.00

287 Carl Yastrzemski

501	John DeMerit	3.00
502	Clarence Coleman	3.00
503	Tito Francona	3.00
504	Billy Consolo	3.00
505	Red Schoendienst	16.00
506	*Willie Davis*	17.00
507	Pete Burnside	3.00
508	Rocky Bridges	3.00
509	Camilo Carreon	3.00
510	Art Ditmar	3.00
511	Joe Morgan	3.00
512	Bob Will	3.00
513	Jim Brosnan	5.50
514	Jake Wood	3.00
515	Jackie Brandt	3.00
516	Checklist 507-587	8.00
517	Willie McCovey	60.00
518	Andy Carey	3.00
519	Jim Pagliaroni	3.00
520	Joe Cunningham	3.00
521	Brother Battery (Larry Sherry, Norm Sherry)	7.00
522	Dick Farrell	3.00
523	Joe Gibbon	30.00
524	Johnny Logan	30.00
525	Ron Perranoski	30.00
526	R.C. Stevens	30.00
527	Gene Leek	30.00

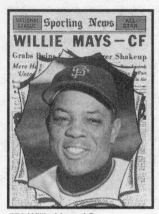

579 Willie Mays AS

528	Pedro Ramos	**30.00**
529	Bob Roselli	**30.00**
530	Bobby Malkmus	**30.00**
531	Jim Coates	**30.00**
532	Bob Hale	**30.00**
533	Jack Curtis	**30.00**
534	Eddie Kasko	**30.00**
535	Larry Jackson	**30.00**
536	Bill Tuttle	**30.00**
537	Bobby Locke	**30.00**
538	Chuck Hiller	**30.00**
539	Johnny Klippstein	**30.00**
540	Jackie Jensen	**40.00**
541	Roland Sheldon	**30.00**
542	Twins Team	**70.00**
543	Roger Craig	**40.00**
544	George Thomas	**30.00**
545	Hoyt Wilhelm	**70.00**
546	Marty Kutyna	**30.00**
547	Leon Wagner	**30.00**
548	Ted Wills	**30.00**
549	Hal R. Smith	**30.00**
550	Frank Baumann	**30.00**
551	George Altman	**30.00**
552	Jim Archer	**30.00**
553	Bill Fischer	**30.00**
554	Pirates Team	**70.00**
555	Sam Jones	**30.00**

556	Ken R. Hunt	**30.00**
557	Jose Valdivielso	**30.00**
558	Don Ferrarese	**30.00**
559	Jim Gentile	**30.00**
560	Barry Latman	**30.00**
561	Charley James	**30.00**
562	Bill Monbouquette	**30.00**
563	Bob Cerv	**30.00**
564	Don Cardwell	**30.00**
565	Felipe Alou	**50.00**
566	Paul Richards AS	**30.00**
567	Danny Murtaugh AS	**30.00**
568	Bill Skowron AS	**40.00**
569	Frank Herrera AS	**35.00**
570	Nellie Fox AS	**45.00**
571	Bill Mazeroski AS	**40.00**
572	Brooks Robinson AS	**100.00**
573	Ken Boyer AS	**40.00**
574	Luis Aparicio AS	**50.00**
575	Ernie Banks AS	**100.00**
576	Roger Maris AS	**175.00**
577	Hank Aaron AS	**175.00**
578	Mickey Mantle AS	**450.00**
579	Willie Mays AS	**175.00**
580	Al Kaline AS	**100.00**
581	Frank Robinson AS	**100.00**
582	Earl Battey AS	**35.00**
583	Del Crandall AS	**35.00**

577 Hank Aaron AS

584	Jim Perry AS	38.00	586	Whitey Ford AS	100.00
585	Bob Friend AS	35.00	589	Warren Spahn AS	150.00

1962 TOPPS

Topps used a woodgrain border design in 1962 that resurfaced in 1987. At 598 cards, the 1962 set was larger than any previous edition. A ten-card subset highlighting the career of Babe Ruth is included, although the cards are surprisingly undervalued. One of the most notable features of the set is the first use of multiplayer photos for rookie cards, grouping four or five players together by position. Many challenges are posed for collectors of this set, with both a rare final series (cards 523-598) and several photo changes in later printings. All photo variations are found in cards 129-190. Note, complete set price does not include variations.

	NR MT
Complete set	**$5500.00**
Commons (1-370)	**3.50**
Commons (371-522)	**5.00**
Commons (523-598)	**15.00**

1	Roger Maris	$250.00
2	Jim Brosnan	4.00
3	Pete Runnels	2.00
4	John DeMerit	2.00
5	Sandy Koufax	125.00
6	Marv Breeding	2.00
7	Frank Thomas	2.00
10	Bob Clemente	125.00
11	Tom Morgan	2.00
13	Dick Howser	2.00
14	• Bill White	5.00
17	Johnny Callison	2.00
18	Managers' Dream (Mickey Mantle, Willie Mays)	150.00
19	*Ray Washburn*	2.00
20	Rocky Colavito	10.00
21	Jim Kaat	6.00
22	Checklist 1-88 (numbers 33-88 on back)	6.00
22	Checklist 1-88 (numbers 121-176 on back)	5.00

23	Norm Larker	2.00
24	Tigers Team	7.00
25	Ernie Banks	45.00
26	Chris Cannizzaro	2.00
27	Chuck Cottier	2.00
28	Minnie Minoso	5.00
29	Casey Stengel	20.00
30	Ed Mathews	20.00
31	*Tom Tresh*	18.00
32	John Roseboro	2.00
33	Don Larsen	5.00
34	Johnny Temple	2.00
35	*Don Schwall*	2.00
36	Don Leppert	2.00
37	Tribe Hill Trio (Barry Latman, Jim Perry, Dick Stigman)	2.00
40	Orlando Cepeda	9.00
43	Dodgers Team	8.00
44	Don Taussig	2.00
45	Brooks Robinson	35.00
46	*Jack Baldschun*	2.00
47	Bob Will	2.00
48	Ralph Terry	5.00
49	Hal Jones	2.00
50	Stan Musial	110.00
51	AL Batting Ldrs (Norm Cash, Elston Howard, Al Kaline, Jim Piersall)	6.00

320 Hank Aaron

52	NL Batting Ldrs (Ken Boyer, Bob Clemente, Wally Moon, Vada Pinson)	8.00
53	AL HR Ldrs (Jim Gentile, Harmon Killebrew, Mickey Mantle, Roger Maris)	60.00
54	NL HR Ldrs (Orlando Cepeda, Willie Mays, Frank Robinson)	9.00
55	AL ERA Ldrs (Dick Donovan, Don Mossi, Milt Pappas, Bill Stafford)	5.00
56	NL ERA Ldrs (Mike McCormick, Jim O'Toole, Curt Simmons, Warren Spahn)	6.00
57	AL Win Ldrs (Steve Barber, Jim Bunning, Whitey Ford, Frank Lary)	6.00
58	NL Win Ldrs (Joe Jay, Jim O'Toole, Warren Spahn)	7.00
59	AL SO Ldrs (Jim Bunning, Whitey Ford, Camilo Pascual, Juan Pizarro)	6.00
60	NL SO Ldrs (Don Drysdale, Sandy Koufax, Jim O'Toole, Stan Williams)	9.00
61	Cardinals Team	9.00
62	Steve Boros	2.00
63	*Tony Cloninger*	4.00
64	Russ Snyder	2.00
65	Bobby Richardson	7.00
66	Cuno Barragon (Barragan)	2.00
67	Harvey Haddix	3.00
69	Phil Ortega	2.00
70	Harmon Killebrew	20.00
71	Dick LeMay	2.00
72	Bob's Pupils (Steve Boros, Bob Scheffing, Jake Wood)	2.00
73	Nellie Fox	7.00
74	Bob Lillis	2.00
75	Milt Pappas	2.00
78	Gene Green	2.00
79	Ed Hobaugh	2.00
80	• Vada Pinson	5.00
81	Jim Pagliaroni	2.00
84	Lenny Green	2.00
85	Gil Hodges	17.00
86	*Donn Clendenon*	4.00
87	Mike Roarke	2.00
88	Ralph Houk	4.00
89	Barney Schultz	2.00
90	Jim Piersall	3.00
93	John Blanchard	2.00
94	Jay Hook	2.00
95	Don Hoak	2.00
96	Eli Grba	2.00
97	Tito Francona	2.00
98	Checklist 89-176	4.00
99	*John Powell*	20.00
100	Warren Spahn	30.00
103	Don Blasingame	2.00
105	Don Mossi	2.00
108	Willie Davis	3.00
109	Bob Shaw	2.00
110	Bill Skowron	5.00
111	Dallas Green	4.00
112	Hank Foiles	2.00
113	White Sox Team	7.00
116	Herb Score	4.00
117	Gary Geiger	2.00
118	Julian Javier	2.00
121	Billy Hitchcock	2.00
123	Mike de la Hoz	2.00

125	Gene Woodling	4.00
126	Al Cicotte	2.00
127	Pride of the A's (Hank Bauer, Jerry Lumpe, Norm Siebern)	2.00
128	Art Fowler	2.00
129	Lee Walls (facing left)	12.00
129	Lee Walls (facing right)	4.00
130	Frank Bolling	2.00
131	*Pete Richert*	2.00
132	Angels Team (with inset photos)	15.00
132	Angels Team (w/o inset photos)	8.00
133	Felipe Alou	4.00
134	Billy Hoeft (green sky)	12.00
134	Billy Hoeft (blue sky)	4.00
135	Babe as a Boy	13.00
136	Babe Joins Yanks	13.00
137	Babe and Mgr. Huggins	13.00
138	The Famous Slugger	13.00
139	Hal Reniff (pitching)	50.00
139	Hal Reniff (portrait)	12.00
139	Babe Hits 60	25.00
140	Gehrig and Ruth	25.00
141	Twilight Years	15.00
142	Coaching for the Dodgers	13.00
143	Greatest Sports Hero	13.00
144	Farewell Speech	13.00
147	Bill Kunkel (pitching)	12.00
147	Bill Kunkel (portrait)	2.00
148	Wally Post	2.00
150	Al Kaline	35.00
151	Johnny Klippstein	2.00
152	Mickey Vernon	2.00
153	Pumpsie Green	2.00
157	Wes Covington	2.00
158	Braves Team	9.00
159	*Hal Reniff*	2.00
162	Sammy Drake	2.00
163	Hot Corner Guardians (Cletis Boyer, Billy Gardner)	4.00
167	*Tim McCarver*	35.00
168	Leo Posada	2.00
169	Bob Cerv	2.00
170	Ron Santo	12.00

360 Yogi Berra

171	Dave Sisler	2.00
173	Chico Fernandez	2.00
174	Carl Willey (with cap)	12.00
174	Carl Willey (w/o cap)	2.00
175	Frank Howard	5.00
176	Eddie Yost (batting)	12.00
176	Eddie Yost (portrait)	3.00
177	Bobby Shantz	4.00
180	Bob Allison	4.00
183	Roger Craig	5.00
184	Haywood Sullivan	2.00
185	Roland Sheldon	2.00
186	*Mack Jones*	2.00
189	Dick Hall	2.00
190	Wally Moon (with cap)	15.00
190	Wally Moon (w/o cap)	4.00
192	Checklist 177-264	5.00
193	Eddie Kasko	2.00
194	*Dean Chance*	5.00
195	Joe Cunningham	2.00
199	*Gaylord Perry*	125.00
200	Mickey Mantle	600.00
208	Billy Martin	9.00
209	*Jim Fregosi*	8.00
213	Richie Ashburn	10.00
217	Walt Alston	5.00
218	*Joe Torre*	30.00
219	*Al Downing*	5.00

387 Lou Brock

243	Robin Roberts	13.00
251	Yankees Team	30.00
288	Billy Williams	40.00
300	Willie Mays	150.00
310	Whitey Ford	40.00
312	Spahn Shows No-Hit Form	10.00
313	Maris Blasts 61st	25.00
315	Ford Tosses A Curve	10.00
316	Killebrew Sends One Into Orbit	10.00
317	Musial Plays 21st Season	20.00
318	The Switch-Hitter Connects (Mickey Mantle)	75.00
320	Hank Aaron	150.00
325	Luis Aparicio	15.00
340	Don Drysdale	50.00
350	Frank Robinson	50.00
360	Yogi Berra	75.00
371	Earl Battey	5.00
372	Jack Curtis	5.00
373	Al Heist	5.00
374	Gene Mauch	5.00
375	Ron Fairly	5.00
376	Bud Daley	5.00
377	Johnny Orsino	5.00
378	Bennie Daniels	5.00
379	Chuck Essegian	5.00
380	• Lou Burdette	7.00
381	Chico Cardenas	5.00
382	Dick Williams	6.00
383	Ray Sadecki	5.00
384	Athletics Team	15.00
385	Early Wynn	20.00
386	Don Mincher	5.00
387	Lou Brock	250.00
388	Ryne Duren	5.50
389	Smoky Burgess	5.00
390	Orlando Cepeda AS	7.50
391	Bill Mazeroski AS	6.00
392	Ken Boyer AS	7.00
393	Roy McMillan AS	6.00
394	Hank Aaron AS	50.00
395	Willie Mays AS	50.00
396	Frank Robinson AS	18.00
397	John Roseboro AS	6.00
398	Don Drysdale AS	18.00
399	Warren Spahn AS	15.00
400	Elston Howard	10.00
401	AL & NL Homer Kings (Orlando Cepeda, Roger Maris)	40.00
402	Gino Cimoli	5.00
403	Chet Nichols	5.00
404	Tim Harkness	5.00
405	Jim Perry	5.50
406	Bob Taylor	5.00
407	Hank Aguirre	5.00
408	Gus Bell	6.00
409	Pirates Team	15.00
410	Al Smith	5.00
411	Danny O'Connell	5.00
412	Charlie James	5.00
413	Matty Alou	7.00
414	Joe Gaines	5.00
415	Bill Virdon	6.00
416	Bob Scheffing	5.00
417	Joe Azcue	5.00
418	Andy Carey	5.00
419	Bob Bruce	5.00
420	Gus Triandos	5.00
421	Ken MacKenzie	5.00
422	Steve Bilko	5.00
423	Rival League Relief Aces (Roy Face, Hoyt Wilhelm)	7.00

424	Al McBean	5.00
425	Carl Yastrzemski	200.00
426	Bob Farley	5.00
427	Jake Wood	5.00
428	Joe Hicks	5.00
429	Bill O'Dell	5.00
430	Tony Kubek	9.00
431	*Bob Rodgers*	10.00
432	Jim Pendleton	5.00
433	Jim Archer	5.00
434	Clay Dalrymple	5.00
435	Larry Sherry	5.00
436	Felix Mantilla	5.00
437	Ray Moore	5.00
438	Dick Brown	5.00
439	Jerry Buchek	5.00
440	Joe Jay	5.00
441	Checklist 430-506	5.00
442	Wes Stock	5.00
444	Ted Wills	5.00
445	Vic Power	5.00
446	Don Elston	5.00
447	Willie Kirkland	5.00
448	Joe Gibbon	5.00
449	Jerry Adair	5.00
450	Jim O'Toole	5.00
451	*Jose Tartabull*	5.00
452	Earl Averill	5.00
453	Cal McLish	5.00
454	Floyd Robinson	5.00
455	Luis Arroyo	5.00
456	Joe Amalfitano	5.00
457	Lou Clinton	5.00
458	Bob Buhl ("M" on cap)	5.00
458	Bob Buhl (plain cap)	65.00
459	Ed Bailey	5.00
460	Jim Bunning	13.00
461	*Ken Hubbs*	25.00
462	Willie Tasby ("W" on cap)	5.00
462	Willie Tasby (plain cap)	65.00
463	Hank Bauer	6.00
464	*Al Jackson*	6.00
465	Reds Team	15.00
466	Norm Cash AS	8.00
467	Chuck Schilling AS	6.00
468	Brooks Robinson AS	18.00
469	Luis Aparicio AS	12.00

425 Carl Yastrzemski

470	Al Kaline AS	20.00
471	Mickey Mantle AS	165.00
472	Rocky Colavito AS	10.00
473	Elston Howard AS	10.00
474	Frank Lary AS	7.00
475	Whitey Ford AS	15.00
476	Orioles Team	15.00
477	Andre Rodgers	5.00
478	Don Zimmer	6.00
479	*Joel Horlen*	5.00
480	Harvey Kuenn	7.00
481	Vic Wertz	5.00
482	Sam Mele	5.00
483	Don McMahon	5.00
484	Dick Schofield	5.00
485	Pedro Ramos	5.00
486	Jim Gilliam	6.00
487	Jerry Lynch	5.00
488	Hal Brown	5.00
489	Julio Gotay	5.00
490	Clete Boyer	6.00
491	Leon Wagner	5.00
492	Hal Smith	5.00
493	Danny McDevitt	5.00
494	Sammy White	5.00
495	Don Cardwell	5.00
496	Wayne Causey	5.00
497	Ed Bouchee	5.00

5 Sandy Koufax

498	Jim Donohue	**5.00**
499	Zoilo Versalles	**5.00**
500	Duke Snider	**50.00**
501	Claude Osteen	**5.00**
502	Hector Lopez	**5.00**
503	Danny Murtaugh	**5.00**
504	Eddie Bressoud	**5.00**
505	Juan Marichal	**40.00**
506	Charlie Maxwell	**5.00**
507	Ernie Broglio	**5.00**
508	Gordy Coleman	**5.00**
509	*Dave Giusti*	**8.00**
510	Jim Lemon	**5.00**
511	Bubba Phillips	**5.00**
512	Mike Fornieles	**5.00**
513	Whitey Herzog	**9.00**
514	Sherm Lollar	**5.00**
515	Stan Williams	**5.00**
516	Checklist 507-598	**15.00**
517	Dave Wickersham	**5.00**
518	Lee Maye	**5.00**
519	Bob Johnson	**5.00**
520	Bob Friend	**6.00**
521	Jacke Davis	**5.00**
523	Russ Nixon	**14.00**
524	Howie Nunn	**14.00**
525	George Thomas	**14.00**
526	Hal Woodeshick	**14.00**

527	*Dick McAuliffe*	**18.00**
528	Turk Lown	**14.00**
529	John Schaive	**14.00**
530	Bob Gibson	**180.00**
531	Bobby G. Smith	**14.00**
532	Dick Stigman	**14.00**
533	Charley Lau	**16.00**
534	Tony Gonzalez	**14.00**
535	Ed Roebuck	**14.00**
536	Dick Gernert	**14.00**
537	Indians Team	**50.00**
538	Jack Sanford	**14.00**
539	Billy Moran	**14.00**
540	Jim Landis	**14.00**
541	Don Nottebart	**14.00**
542	Dave Philley	**14.00**
543	Bob Allen	**14.00**
544	Willie McCovey	**150.00**
545	Hoyt Wilhelm	**55.00**
546	Moe Thacker	**14.00**
547	Don Ferrarese	**14.00**
548	Bobby Del Greco	**14.00**
549	Bill Rigney	**14.00**
550	Art Mahaffey	**14.00**
551	Harry Bright	**14.00**
552	Cubs Team	**50.00**
553	Jim Coates	**14.00**
554	Bubba Morton	**14.00**

530 Bob Gibson

555	John Buzhardt	14.00
556	Al Spangler	14.00
557	Bob Anderson	14.00
558	John Goryl	14.00
559	Mike Higgins	14.00
560	Chuck Estrada	14.00
561	Gene Oliver	14.00
562	Bill Henry	14.00
563	Ken Aspromonte	14.00
564	Bob Grim	14.00
565	Jose Pagan	14.00
566	Marty Kutyna	14.00
567	Tracy Stallard	14.00
568	Jim Golden	14.00
569	Ed Sadowski	14.00
570	Bill Stafford	14.00
571	Billy Klaus	14.00
572	Bob Miller	14.00
573	Johnny Logan	16.00
574	Dean Stone	14.00
575	Red Schoendienst	55.00
576	Russ Kemmerer	14.00
577	Dave Nicholson	14.00
578	Jim Duffalo	14.00
579	Jim Schaffer	14.00
580	Bill Monbouquette	14.00
581	Mel Roach	14.00
582	Ron Piche	14.00

1 Roger Maris

583	Larry Osborne	14.00
584	Twins Team	14.00
585	Glen Hobbie	14.00
586	Sammy Esposito	14.00
587	Frank Funk	14.00
588	Birdie Tebbets	14.00
589	Bob Turley	18.00
590	Curt Flood	20.00
591	Rookie Parade Pitchers (*Sam McDowell,* Ron Mischwitz, Art Quirk, *Dick Radatz, Ron Taylor*)	60.00
592	Rookie Parade Pitchers (*Bo Belinsky,* Joe Bonikowski, *Jim Bouton,* Dan Pfister, Dave Stenhouse)	70.00
593	Rookie Parade Pitchers (Craig Anderson, *Jack Hamilton,* Jack Lamabe, Bob Moorhead, *Bob Veale*)	25.00
594	Rookie Parade Catchers (Doug Camilli, *Doc Edwards,* Don Pavletich, Ken Retzer, *Bob Uecker*)	80.00

200 Mickey Mantle

595	Rookie Parade Infielders (*Ed Charles,* Marlin Coughtry, Bob Sadowski, Felix Torres) 25.00		597	Rookie Parade Infielders (Rod Kanehl, Jim McKnight, *Denis Menke,* Amado Samuel) 35.00
596	Rookie Parade Infielders (*Bernie Allen, Phil Linz, Joe Pepitone, Rich Rollins*) 60.00		598	Rookie Parade Outfielders (Howie Goss, *Jim Hickman,* Manny Jimenez, Al Luplow, Ed Olivares) 75.00

1963 FLEER

Over three decades after its quiet debut, the 1963 Fleer set is finally gaining recognition from the collecting world. In 1963, Fleer challenged Topps in the "confectionery" department by issuing its cards not with gum but with a cookie. Topps responded by hauling Fleer into court. No one knew whether or not the Philadelphia-based Fleer would have added to the 66-card issue in the absence of legal roadblocks. In any case, Fleer topped Topps by providing the first nationally distributed card of Maury Wills, the base-stealing star of the LA Dodgers. Wills, still upset that Topps had neglected him in his rookie days, seemed to enjoy sharing his fame with a rival company. Other stars in the set include Roberto Clemente, Bob Gibson, Sandy Koufax, Willie Mays, Brooks Robinson, Warren Spahn, and Carl Yastrzemski. However, the rarest cards in the set are for Joe Adcock, number 46, and an unnumbered checklist. The scarcity is supposedly due to short-printing of these two cards.

	NR MT
Complete set	$1500.00
Commons	12.00

1	Steve Barber	$20.00
2	Ron Hansen	12.00
3	Milt Pappas	15.00
4	Brooks Robinson	70.00
5	Willie Mays	200.00
6	Lou Clinton	12.00
7	Bill Monbouquette	12.00
8	Carl Yastrzemski	100.00
9	Ray Herbert................	12.00
10	Jim Landis	12.00
11	Dick Donovan	12.00
12	Tito Francona	12.00

14	Frank Lary	12.00
15	Dick Howser	15.00
16	Jerry Lumpe	12.00
17	Norm Siebern	12.00
18	Don Lee........................	12.00
19	Albie Pearson.............	15.00
20	Bob Rodgers	12.00
21	Leon Wagner	12.00
22	Jim Kaat	18.00
23	Vic Power	15.00
25	Bobby Richardson	18.00
26	Ralph Terry	14.00
29	Jimmy Piersall	15.00
32	Ron Santo	18.00
34	Vada Pinson................	16.00
40	Tommy Davis	15.00
41	Don Drysdale	60.00

42	Sandy Koufax	175.00
43	*Maury Wills*	85.00
44	Frank Bolling	12.00
45	Warren Spahn	55.00
46	Joe Adcock	175.00
47	Roger Craig	15.00
50	Ruben Amaro	12.00
51	John Callison	12.00
52	Clay Dalrymple	12.00
53	Don Demeter	12.00
54	Art Mahaffey	12.00
55	"Smoky" Burgess	12.00
56	Roberto Clemente	175.00
57	Elroy Face	15.00
58	Vernon Law	15.00
59	Bill Mazeroski	18.00
60	Ken Boyer	18.00
61	Bob Gibson	60.00
62	Gene Oliver	12.00
63	Bill White	20.00
64	Orlando Cepeda	25.00
65	Jimmy Davenport	14.00

46 Joe Adcock

66	Billy O'Dell	18.00
—	Checklist 1-66	425.00

1963 TOPPS

This set of 576 cards is most remembered as the one in which Pete Rose made his premiere. His rookie card is far from glamorous: It is shared with three other players, and only their heads are shown, reduced to the size of postage stamps. Yet it is one of the most valuable cards of the decade. Aside from the rookie cards, the only specialty subsets in 1963 honor league leaders (the first 10 cards) and the 1962 World Series. The 1963 Topps set also features an ultrascarce series, from 447 to 506, which commands a premium.

	NR MT
Complete set	**$5500.00**
Commons 1-283	**3.00**
Commons 284-446	**4.00**
Commons 447-506	**15.00**
Commons 507-576	**10.00**

1 NL Batting Ldrs
(Hank Aaron, Tommy Davis, Stan Musial, Frank Robinson, Bill White $40.00

2 AL Batting Ldrs
(Chuck Hinton, Mickey Mantle, Floyd Robinson, Pete Runnels, Norm Siebern) 25.00

390 Hank Aaron

3 NL HR Ldrs (Hank Aaron,
Ernie Banks, Orlando
Cepeda, Willie Mays,
Frank Robinson)...........**25.00**
4 AL HR Ldrs
(Norm Cash, Rocky
Colavito, Jim Gentile,
Harmon Killebrew,
Roger Maris,
Leon Wagner) **9.00**
5 NL ERA Ldrs
(Don Drysdale,
Bob Gibson, Sandy
Koufax, Bob Purkey,
Bob Shaw)....................**10.00**
6 AL ERA Ldrs (Hank
Aguirre, Dean Chance,
Eddie Fisher, Whitey Ford,
Robin Roberts) **6.00**
7 NL Pitching Ldrs
(Don Drysdale,
Joe Jay, Art Mahaffey,
Billy O'Dell, Bob
Purkey, Jack Sanford) ... **6.00**
8 AL Pitching Ldrs (Jim
Bunning, Dick Donovan,
Ray Herbert, Camilo
Pascual, Ralph Terry) ... **6.00**

9 NL SO Ldrs
(Don Drysdale, Dick
Farrell, Bob Gibson,
Sandy Koufax,
Billy O'Dell)................. **10.00**
10 AL SO Ldrs
(Jim Bunning, Jim Kaat,
Camilo Pascual,
Juan Pizarro,
Ralph Terry)................... **5.00**
13 Phillies Team................. **5.00**
14 Pedro Ramos **2.00**
15 Ken Hubbs **5.00**
17 Ryne Duren **3.50**
18 Bucs Blasters (Smoky
Burgess, Bob Clemente,
Bob Skinner, Dick
Stuart) **12.00**
19 Pete Burnside................. **2.00**
20 Tony Kubek **6.00**
22 Curt Simmons **2.00**
23 Ed Lopat **3.50**
25 Al Kaline **35.00**
27 Choo Choo Coleman..... **3.50**
28 Mike Fornieles **2.00**
29 1962 Rookie Stars
(John Boozer,
*Ray Culp, Sammy
Ellis,* Jesse Gonder) **6.00**

540 Bob Clemente

29 1963 Rookie Stars
(John Boozer,
*Ray Culp, Sammy
Ellis*, Jesse Gonder) **2.00**
30 Harvey Kuenn **3.50**
33 Bob Belinsky **2.00**
34 Dick Schofield **2.00**
39 Angels Team **5.00**
40 Vic Power **2.00**
41 Charlie Lau **2.00**
42 Stan Williams **2.00**
43 Veteran Masters
(Casey Stengel,
Gene Woodling) **5.00**
45 Bob Aspromonte **2.00**
46 *Tommie Aaron*............... **4.00**
48 Birdie Tebbetts **2.00**
49 *Dal Maxvill*..................... **4.00**
50 Bill Pierce **2.00**
54 1962 Rookie Stars (Jack
Cullen, *Dave DeBuschere,*
Harry Fanok, Nelson
Mathews).................... **14.00**
54 1963 Rookie Stars (Jack
Cullen, *Dave DeBuschere,*
Harry Fanok, Nelson
Mathews)...................... **6.00**
55 Bill Virdon **3.50**
59 Craig Anderson **2.00**
60 Elston Howard............... **6.00**
63 Reds Team.................... **5.00**
64 Dick McAuliffe **2.00**
67 Ed Charles **2.00**
68 Friendly Foes (Gil Hodges,
Duke Snider) **15.00**
69 Bud Zipfel **2.00**
70 Jim O'Toole **2.00**
71 *Bobby Wine*................... **2.00**
72 Johnny Romano **2.00**
73 Bobby Bragan **2.00**
74 *Denver LeMaster*........... **2.00**
75 Bob Allison **3.50**
76 Earl Wilson **2.00**
78 Marv Throneberry.......... **5.00**
79 Checklist 1-88 .... **3.00**
80 Jim Gilliam.................... **4.00**
85 Tom Haller..................... **2.00**
87 Bob Veale..................... **2.00**
88 Ron Hansen **2.00**

300 Willie Mays

89 Dick Stigman **2.00**
91 Dallas Green **4.00**
92 Hector Lopez **2.00**
93 Galen Cisco................... **2.00**
94 Bob Schmidt.................. **2.00**
97 Bob Duliba..................... **2.00**
99 Jim Umbricht **2.00**
100 Joe Cunningham **2.00**
101 Checklist 89-176
("Checklist" in red on
front)........................... **3.00**
101 Checklist 89-176
("Checklist" in white on
front)........................... **8.00**
103 Chuck Essegian **2.00**
104 Lew Krause **2.00**
105 Ron Fairly..................... **2.00**
107 Jim Hickman.................. **2.00**
108 Hoyt Wilhelm **11.00**
109 Lee Maye **2.00**
111 Al Jackson.................... **2.00**
113 Don Landrum (photo is Ron
Santo).......................... **3.50**
115 Carl Yastrzemski **65.00**
116 Jim Brosnan **2.00**
118 Sherm Lollar.................. **2.00**
120 Roger Maris................ **60.00**
121 Jim Hannan................... **2.00**

200 Mickey Mantle

221	Cookie Rojas	3.00
222	Cubs Team	6.00
226	Julian Javier	2.00
228	1963 Rookie Stars (Max Alvis, Bob Bailey, Ed Kranepool, Pedro Oliva)	50.00
229	Willie Davis	3.50
230	Pete Runnels	2.00
231	Eli Grba (photo is Ryne Duren)	2.00
232	Frank Malzone	2.00
233	Casey Stengel	18.00
239	Harvey Haddix	2.25
240	Rocky Colavito	9.00
242	Power Plus (Hank Aaron, Ernie Banks)	40.00
245	Gil Hodges	20.00
247	Yankees Team	20.00
250	Stan Musial	135.00
252	Ron Santo	7.5.00
275	Ed Mathews	22.00
300	Willie Mays	200.00
301	Bill Fischer	2.00
302	Whitey Herzog	5.00
303	Earl Francis	3.00
312	Colt .45s Team	15.00
313	Ernie Broglio	3.00
317	Sam McDowell	4.00
318	Gene Mauch	3.00
320	Warren Spahn	45.00
324	1963 Rookie Stars (Vic Davalillo, Phil Roof, Pete Ward, George Williams)	6.00
335	Leon Wagner	5.00
337	Dodgers Team	12.00
340	Yogi Berra	80.00
347	Joe Torre	9.00
348	Billy Williams	45.00
353	Billy Williams	27.00
360	Don Drysdale	45.00
363	Dick Radatz	3.00
364	Howie Goss	3.00
365	Jim Bunning	8.00
366	Tony Taylor	3.00
367	Tony Cloninger	3.00
368	Ed Bailey	3.00
369	Jim Lemon	3.00
370	Dick Donovan	3.00

210 Sandy Koufax

371	Ron Kanehl	3.00
372	Don Lee	3.00
373	Jim Campbell	3.00
374	Claude Osteen	3.00
375	Ken Boyer	8.00
376	Johnnie Wyatt	3.00
377	Orioles Team	7.00
378	Bill Henry	3.00
379	Bob Anderson	3.00
380	Ernie Banks	70.00
381	Frank Baumann	3.00
382	Ralph Houk	7.00
385	Art Mahaffey	3.00
386	1963 Rookie Stars (John Bateman, Larry Bearnarth, Ed Kirkpatrick, Garry Roggenburk)	5.00
387	Al McBean	3.00
388	Jim Davenport	3.00
389	Frank Sullivan	3.00
390	Hank Aaron	175.00
391	Bill Dailey	3.00
392	Tribe Thumpers (Tito Francona, Johnny Romano)	3.00
393	Ken MacKenzie	3.00
394	Tim McCarver	15.00
395	Don MacMahon	3.00

173 Bomber's Best

396	Joe Koppe	3.00
397	Athletics Team	8.00
398	• Boog Powell	25.00
399	Dick Ellsworth	3.00
400	Frank Robinson	50.00
401	Jim Bouton	9.00
402	Mickey Vernon	3.00
403	Ron Perranoski	3.00
407	1976 Rookie Stars (Larry Elliot, Frank Kostro, Chico Ruiz, Dick Simpson)	3.00
408	Billy Gardner	3.00
409	Roy Face	4.00
410	Earl Battey	3.00
412	Dodgers' Big Three (Don Drysdale, Sandy Koufax, Johnny Podres)	40.00
415	Bob Gibson	50.00
416	Alex Grammas	3.00
417	Giants Team	8.00
418	Johnny Orsino	3.00
419	Tracy Stallard	3.00
420	Bobby Richardson	9.00
422	Fred Hutchinson	5.00
425	Smoky Burgess	3.00
429	Lou Burdette	5.00
430	Norm Siebern	3.00

431	Checklist 430-506 ("Checklist" in black on front)	8.00
432	Checklist 430-506 ("Checklist" in white on front)	5.00
433	Denis Menke	3.00
434	Johnny Callison	4.50
437	Bill Bruton	3.00
439	Don Zimmer	6.00
440	Juan Marichal	30.00
443	Jim Piersall	3.50
444	Jim Maloney	3.00
445	Norm Cash	6.00
446	Whitey Ford	42.00
447	Felix Mantilla	10.00
448	Jack Kralick	10.00
449	Jose Tartabull	10.00
450	Bob Friend	15.00
451	Indians Team	25.00
452	Barney Schultz	10.00
453	Jake Wood	10.00
454	Art Fowler	10.00
455	Ruben Amaro	10.00
456	Jim Coker	10.00
457	Tex Clevenger	10.00
458	Al Lopez	20.00

490 Willie McCovey

459	Dick LeMay	10.00
460	Del Crandall	18.00
461	Norm Bass	10.00
462	Wally Post	10.00
463	Joe Schaffernoth	10.00
464	Ken Aspromonte	10.00
465	Chuck Estrada	10.00
466	1963 Rookie Stars (*Bill Freehan,* Tony Martinez, Nate Oliver, Jerry Robinson)	50.00
467	Phil Ortega	10.00
469	Jay Hook	10.00
470	Tom Tresh	50.00
471	Ken Retzer	10.00
472	Lou Brock	150.00
473	Mets Team	125.00
474	Jack Fisher	10.00
475	Gus Triandos	10.00
476	Frank Funk	10.00
477	Donn Clendenon	16.00
478	Paul Brown	10.00
479	Ed Brinkman	16.00
480	Bill Monbouquette	10.00
481	Bob Taylor	10.00
482	Felix Torres	10.00
483	Jim Owens	10.00

500 Harmon Killebrew

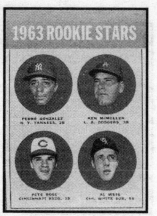

537 1963 Rookie Stars

484	Dale Long	16.00
485	Jim Landis	10.00
486	Ray Sadecki	10.00
487	John Roseboro	16.00
488	Jerry Adair	10.00
489	Paul Toth	10.00
490	Willie McCovey	150.00
491	Harry Craft	10.00
492	Dave Wickersham	10.00
493	Walt Bond	10.00
494	Phil Regan	10.00
495	Frank Thomas	16.00
496	1963 Rookie Stars (Carl Bouldin, *Steve Dalkowski, Fred Newman,* Jack Smith)	16.00
497	Bennie Daniels	10.00
498	Eddie Kasko	10.00
499	J.C. Martin	10.00
500	Harmon Killebrew	125.00
501	Joe Azcue	10.00
502	Daryl Spencer	10.00
503	Braves Team	10.00
504	Bob Johnson	10.00
505	Curt Flood	12.00
506	Gene Green	11.00
507	Rolando Sheldon	8.00
508	Ted Savage	7.00

250 Stan Musial

509a	Checklist 509-576 (copyright centered)	**15.00**
509b	Checklist 509-576 (copyright to right)	**12.00**
510	Ken McBride	**7.00**
511	Charlie Neal	**7.50**
512	Cal McLish	**7.00**
513	Gary Geiger	**7.00**
514	Larry Osborne	**7.00**
515	Don Elston	**7.00**
516	Purnal Goldy	**7.00**
517	Hal Woodeshick	**7.00**
518	Don Blasingame	**7.00**
519	Claude Raymond	**7.00**
520	Orlando Cepeda	**25.00**
521	Dan Pfister	**7.00**
522	1963 Rookie Stars (Mel Nelson, Gary Peters, Art Quirk, Jim Roland)	**7.50**
523	Bill Kunkel	**12.00**
524	Cardinals Team	**10.00**
525	Nellie Fox	**12.00**
526	Dick Hall	**7.00**
527	Ed Sadowski	**7.00**
528	Carl Willey	**7.50**
529	Wes Covington	**7.00**
530	Don Mossi	**7.50**
531	Sam Mele	**7.00**
532	Steve Boros	**7.00**
533	Bobby Shantz	**8.00**
534	Ken Walters	**7.00**
535	Jim Perry	**11.00**
536	Norm Larker	**7.00**
537	1963 Rookie Stars (Pedro Gonzalez, *Ken McMullen, Pete Rose, Al Weis*)	**1000.00**
538	George Brunet	**7.00**
539	Wayne Causey	**7.00**
540	Bob Clemente	**250.00**
541	Ron Moeller	**7.00**
542	Lou Klimchock	**7.00**
543	Russ Snyder	**7.00**
544	1963 Rookie Stars (Duke Carmel, Bill Haas, Dick Phillips, *Rusty Staub*)	**30.00**
545	Jose Pagan	**7.00**
546	Hal Reniff	**8.00**
547	Gus Bell	**7.50**
548	Tom Satriano	**7.00**
549	1963 Rookie Stars (*Marcelino Lopez,* Pete Lovrich, Elmo Plaskett, Paul Ratliff)	**7.50**
550	Duke Snider	**80.00**
551	Billy Klaus	**7.00**

553 1963 Rookie Stars

552	Tigers Team	15.00
553	1963 Rookie Stars (Brock Davis, Jim Gosger, John Herrnstein, *Willie Stargell*)	250.00
554	Hank Fischer	7.00
555	John Blanchard	8.00
556	Al Worthington	7.00
557	Cuno Barragan	7.00
558	1963 Rookie Stars (Bill Faul, *Ron Hunt*, Bob Lipski, Al Moran)	12.00
559	Danny Murtaugh	11.00
560	Ray Herbert	7.00
561	Mike de la Hoz	7.00
562	1963 Rookie Stars (Randy Cardinal, *Dave McNally*, Don Rowe, Ken Rowe)	15.00
563	Mike McCormick	7.50
564	George Banks	7.00
565	Larry Sherry	7.00
566	Cliff Cook	7.50
567	Jim Duffalo	7.00
568	Bob Sadowski	7.00
569	Luis Arroyo	8.00
570	Frank Bolling	7.00
571	Johnny Klippstein	7.00
572	Jack Spring	7.00
573	Coot Veal	7.00
574	Hal Kolstad	7.00
575	Don Cardwell	7.50
576	Johnny Temple	15.00

1964 TOPPS

A simple yet striking format highlights Topps' 1964 set of 587 cards. Close-up poses and a lack of clutter make the cards especially attractive. For the first time ever, Topps grouped rookies together by team, with two players per card. Rickie Allen, Tommy John, Phil Niekro, and Lou Piniella are the most recognizable names found in the first-year cards, while Mickey Mantle and Pete Rose are the set's most valuable cards of individual players. One of the most unusual cards is an In Memoriam card for Chicago Cubs second baseman Ken Hubbs, who was killed in a plane crash. On many card backs, a baseball quiz could be answered by rubbing the question box with a coin.

	NR MT
Complete set	**$3500.00**
Commons (1-196)	**2.25**
Commons (197-370)	**3.00**
Commons (371-522)	**5.00**
Commons (523-587)	**10.00**

1	NL ERA Ldrs (Dick Ellsworth, Bob Friend, Sandy Koufax)	$20.00
2	AL ERA Ldrs (Camilo Pascual, Gary Peters, Juan Pizarro)	3.00
3	NL Pitching Ldrs (Sandy Koufax, Jim Maloney, Juan Marichal, Warren Spahn)	15.00
4	AL Pitching Ldrs (Jim Bouton, Whitey Ford, Camilo Pascual)	3.50
5	NL SO Ldrs (Don Drysdale, Sandy Koufax, Jim Maloney)	10.00
6	AL SO Ldrs (Jim Bunning, Camilo Pascual, Dick Stigman)	3.00

440 Bob Clemente

7	NL Batting Ldrs (Hank Aaron, Bob Clemente, Tommy Davis, Dick Groat)	8.00
8	AL Batting Ldrs (Al Kaline, Rich Rollins, Carl Yastrzemski)	8.00
9	NL HR Ldrs (Hank Aaron, Orlando Cepeda, Willie Mays, Willie McCovey)	20.00
10	AL HR Ldrs (Bob Allison, Harmon Killebrew, Dick Stuart)	4.00
11	NL RBI Ldrs (Hank Aaron, Ken Boyer, Bill White)	7.00
12	AL RBI Ldrs (Al Kaline, Harmon Killebrew, Dick Stuart)	4.00
13	Hoyt Wilhelm	8.00
14	Dodgers Rookies (Dick Nen, Nick Willhite)	1.00
15	Zoilo Versalles	1.00
16	John Boozer	1.00
17	Willie Kirkland	1.00
20	Bob Friend	2.50
21	Yogi Berra	45.00
22	Jerry Adair	1.00
23	Chris Zachary	1.00
25	Bill Monbouquette	1.00
26	Gino Cimoli	1.00
27	Mets Team	6.00
28	Claude Osteen	150.00
29	Lou Brock	40.00
30	Ron Perranoski	1.00
32	Dean Chance	3.00
33	Reds Rookies (Sammy Ellis, Mel Queen)	1.00
34	Jim Perry	2.75
35	Ed Mathews	22.00
36	Hal Reniff	1.00
37	Smoky Burgess	2.50
38	*Jim Wynn*	7.00
39	Hank Aguirre	1.00
40	Dick Groat	2.75
41	Friendly Foes (Willie McCovey, Leon Wagner)	6.00
42	Moe Drabowsky	1.00
43	Roy Sievers	1.00
44	Duke Carmel	1.00
45	Milt Pappas	1.00
46	Ed Brinkman	1.00
47	Giants Rookies (*Jesus Alou,* Ron Herbel)	3.00
50	Mickey Mantle	300.00
54	Sam Mele	1.00
55	Ernie Banks	30.00
58	Don Demeter	1.00
59	Ernie Broglio	1.00
60	Frank Malzone	1.00
61	Angel Backstops (Bob Rodgers, Ed Sadowski)	3.00
63	Johnny Orsino	1.00
64	Ted Abernathy	1.00
65	Felipe Alou	2.50
66	Eddie Fisher	1.00
67	Tigers Team	4.00
68	Willie Davis	2.75
69	Clete Boyer	3.00
70	Joe Torre	4.00

72	Chico Cardenas	1.00
73	*Jimmie Hall*	1.00
76	Checklist 1-88	4.00
77	Jerry Walker	1.00
79	Bob Heffner	1.00
80	Vada Pinson	4.00
81	All-Star Vets (Nellie Fox, Harmon Killebrew)	6.00
83	Gus Triandos	1.00
85	Pete Ward	1.00
86	Al Downing	1.50
87	Cardinals Team	5.00
88	John Roseboro	1.00
89	Boog Powell	5.00
90	Earl Battey	1.00
91	Bob Bailey	1.00
92	Steve Ridzik	1.00
93	Gary Geiger	1.00
95	George Altman	1.00
96	Bob Buhl	1.00
97	Jim Fregosi	2.50
98	Bill Bruton	1.00
100	Elston Howard	5.00
101	Walt Alston	4.00
102	Checklist 89-176	4.00
103	• Curt Flood	3.00
104	Art Mahaffey	1.00
105	Woody Held	1.00
106	Joe Nuxhall	1.00
109	Rusty Staub	8.00
110	Albie Pearson	1.00
111	Don Elston	1.00
116	Twins Rookies (Tony Oliva, Jay Ward)	16.00
118	John Blanchard	1.00
120	Don Drysdale	25.00
121	Pete Runnels	1.00
123	Jose Pagan	1.00
125	Pete Rose	170.00
128	• *Mickey Lolich*	17.50
132	Braves Team	4.00
134	Don Zimmer	3.00
135	John Callison	3.00
136	World Series Game 1 (Koufax Strikes Out 15)	10.00
137	World Series Game 2 (Davis Sparks Rally)	4.00

200 Sandy Koufax

138	World Series Game 3 (L.A. Takes 3rd Straight)	4.00
139	World Series Game 4 (Sealing Yanks' Doom)	4.00
140	World Series Summary (The Dodgers Celebrate)	4.00
141	Danny Murtaugh	1.00
145	Norm Siebern	1.00
146	Indians Rookies (*Tommy John*, Bob Chance)	65.00
150	Willie Mays	110.00
151	Athletics Team	4.00
153	Dick Williams	2.00
155	Duke Snider	30.00
157	Gene Mauch	2.75
160	Ken Boyer	5.00
161	Dave McNally	3.00
167	Senators Rookies (Mike Brumley, *Lou Piniella*)	35.00
169	Del Crandall	3.00
172	Indians Team	4.00
175	Billy Williams	20.00
180	Tommy Davis	2.75

300 Hank Aaron

182	Sox Sockers (Chuck Schilling, Carl Yastrzemski)	12.00
188	Checklist 177-264	4.00
190	Bobby Richardson	5.50
200	Sandy Koufax	110.00
201	Orioles Rookies (Sam Bowens, *Wally Bunker*)	3.00
204	Matty Alou	3.00
205	Nellie Fox	6.00
207	Fred Hutchinson	3.00
210	Carl Yastrzemski	65.00
213	Angels Team	6.00
219	Young Aces (Jim Bouton, Al Downing)	5.00
222	Bill Pierce	2.00
225	Roger Maris	65.00
226	Colts Rookies (*Gerald Grote*, Larry Yellen)	5.00
230	Brooks Robinson	35.00
232	Al Lopez	5.00
235	Ron Hunt	2.00
237	Cubs Team	6.00
240	• Bill White	4.00
242	• Harvey Kuenn	2.00
243	Phillies Rookies (*Richie Allen*, John Herrnstein)	25.00
244	*Tony LaRussa*	14.00
246	Manny Mota	4.00
247	• Dave DeBusschere	4.00
250	Al Kaline	30.00
251	Choo Choo Coleman	2.00
257	Giants Team	7.00
260	Frank Robinson	30.00
262	Cardinals Rookies (Harry Fanok, *Mike Shannon*)	6.00
265	Jim Bunning	5.00
267	*Wilbur Wood*	5.00
274	Checklist 265-352	4.00
280	Juan Marichal	15.00
281	Yankees Rookies (Jake Gibbs, Tom Metcalf)	2.00
283	*Tommy McGraw*	4.00
285	Robin Roberts	12.00
287	Red Sox Rookies (*Tony Conigliaro*, Bill Spanswick)	35.00
290	Bob Allison	2.00
293	Phillies Team	6.00
295	Roger Craig	4.00
300	Hank Aaron	120.00
306	Giant Gunners (Orlando Cepeda, Willie Mays)	30.00
310	Jim Gilliam	4.50
318	Twins Team	4.00
320	Rocky Colavito	8.00
324	Casey Stengel	17.00
331	AL Bombers (Norm Cash, Al Kaline, Mickey Mantle, Roger Maris)	125.00
342	Willie Stargell	50.00
343	Senators Team	5.00
350	Willie McCovey	25.00
353	Wally Moon	2.00
354	Dave Giusti	2.00
355	Vic Power	2.00
358	Ron Kline	2.00
359	Jim Schaffer	2.00

360 Joe Pepitone 2.00
362 Checklist 353-429 .... 4.00
363 Dick McAuliffe 2.00
365 Cal McLish 2.00
367 Fred Whitfield 2.00
368 White Sox Rookies
    (Fritz Ackley,
    Don Buford) 2.00
369 Jerry Zimmerman 2.00
370 Hal Woodeshick 2.00
371 Frank Howard 6.00
372 Howie Koplitz 3.00
373 Pirates Team 8.00
374 Bobby Bolin 3.00
375 Ron Santo 8.00
376 Dave Morehead............. 6.00
377 Bob Skinner................... 3.00
378 Braves Rookies
    (Jack Smith,
    Woody Woodward)........ 3.25
379 Tony Gonzalez 3.00
380 Whitey Ford................. 30.00
381 Bob Taylor..................... 3.00
382 Wes Stock 3.00
383 Bill Rigney 3.00
384 Ron Hansen 3.00
385 Curt Simmons 3.00
386 Lenny Green 3.00
387 Terry Fox....................... 3.00
388 Athletics Rookies
    (John O'Donoghue,
    George Williams) 3.00
389 Jim Umbricht 3.00
390 Orlando Cepeda............ 8.00
391 Sam McDowell 3.00
392 Jim Pagliaroni................ 3.00
393 Casey Teaches
    (Ed Kranepool,
    Casey Stengel).............. 6.00
394 Bob Miller 3.00
395 Tom Tresh...................... 6.00
396 Dennis Bennett.............. 3.00
397 Chuck Cottier 3.00
398 Mets Rookies
    (Bill Haas,
    Dick Smith).................... 3.00
399 Jackie Brandt 3.00
400 Warren Spahn 40.00
401 Charlie Maxwell............. 3.00

50 Mickey Mantle

402 Tom Sturdivant.............. 3.00
403 Reds Team................... 10.00
404 Tony Martinez 3.00
405 Ken McBride.................. 3.00
406 Al Spangler................... 3.00
407 Bill Freehan 6.00
408 Cubs Rookies (Fred
    Burdette, Jim Stewart)... 3.00
409 Bill Fischer.................... 3.00
410 Dick Stuart.................... 3.00
411 Lee Walls 3.00
412 Ray Culp 3.00
413 Johnny Keane 6.00
414 Jack Sanford 3.00
415 Tony Kubek 7.00
416 Lee Maye 3.00
417 Don Cardwell................. 3.00
418 Orioles Rookies (*Darold
    Knowles*, Les Narum).... 3.00
419 *Ken Harrelson* 8.00
420 Jim Maloney 3.00
421 Camilo Carreon 3.00
422 Jack Fisher................... 3.00
423 Topps in NL (Hank Aaron,
    Willie Mays).............. 125.00
424 Dick Bertell 3.00
425 Norm Cash 7.00
426 Bob Rodgers 3.00

105

125 Pete Rose

428	Red Sox Rookies (Archie Skeen, Pete Smith)	3.00
429	Tim McCarver	9.00
430	Juan Pizarro	3.00
431	George Alusik	3.00
432	Ruben Amaro	3.00
433	Yankees Team	18.00
434	Don Nottebart	3.00
435	Vic Davalillo	3.00
436	Charlie Neal	3.00
437	Ed Bailey	3.00
438	Checklist 430-506	5.00
439	Harvey Haddix	3.00
440	Bob Clemente	150.00
441	Bob Duliba	3.00
442	Pumpsie Green	3.00
443	Chuck Dressen	3.00
444	Larry Jackson	3.00
445	Bill Skowron	6.00
446	Julian Javier	3.00
447	Ted Bowsfield	3.00
448	Cookie Rojas	3.00
449	Deron Johnson	3.00
450	Steve Barber	3.00
452	Giants Rookies (Gil Garrido, *Jim Hart*)	7.00
454	Tommie Aaron	3.00
455	Bernie Allen	3.00
456	Dodgers Rookies (*Wes Parker,* John Werhas)	7.00
457	Jesse Gonder	3.00
458	Ralph Terry	4.00
459	Red Sox Rookies (Pete Charton, Dalton Jones)	3.50
460	Bob Gibson	40.00
461	George Thomas	3.00
462	Birdie Tebbetts	3.00
463	Don Leppert	3.00
464	Dallas Green	3.00
465	Mike Hershberger	3.00
466	Athletics Rookies (*Dick Green,* Aurelio Monteagudo)	3.00
467	Bob Aspromonte	3.00
468	Gaylord Perry	50.00
469	Cubs Rookies (Fred Norman, Sterling Slaughter)	3.00
470	Jim Bouton	6.00
471	*Gates Brown*	6.00
472	Vern Law	6.00
473	Orioles Team	10.00
474	Larry Sherry	3.00
475	Ed Charles	3.00
476	Braves Rookies (*Rico Carty,* Dick Kelley)	10.00
477	Mike Joyce	3.00
478	Dick Howser	6.00
479	Cardinals Rookies (Dave Bakenhaster, Johnny Lewis)	3.00
481	Chuck Schilling	3.00
482	Phillies Rookies (*Danny Cater, John Briggs*)	3.00
483	Fred Valentine	3.00
484	Bill Pleis	3.00
485	Tom Haller	3.00
486	Bob Kennedy	3.00
487	Mike McCormick	3.00
488	Yankees Rookies (Bob Meyer, Pete Mikkelsen)	3.00

489 Julio Navarro 3.00
490 Ron Fairly 6.00
491 Ed Rakow 3.00
492 Colts Rookies
(Jim Beauchamp,
Mike White) 3.00
493 Don Lee 3.00
494 Al Jackson 3.00
495 Bill Virdon 6.00
496 White Sox Team 6.00
497 Jeoff Long 3.00
498 Dave Stenhouse 3.00
499 Indians Rookies
(Chico Salmon, Gordon
Seyfried) 3.00
500 Camilo Pascual 6.00
501 Bob Veale 6.00
502 Angels Rookies (*Bobby
Knoop*, Bob Lee) 6.00
503 Earl Wilson 3.00
504 Claude Raymond 3.00
505 Stan Williams 6.00
506 Bobby Bragan 3.00
507 John Edwards 3.00
508 Diego Segui 3.00
509 Pirates Rookies
(*Gene Alley*, Orlando
McFarlane) ..:............... 8.00
510 Lindy McDaniel 3.00
511 Lou Jackson 3.00
512 Tigers Rookies
(Willie Horton,
Joe Sparma) 12.00
513 Don Larsen 6.00
514 Jim Hickman 6.00
515 Johnny Romano 3.00
516 Twins Rookies
(Jerry Arrigo,
Dwight Siebler) 3.00
517 Checklist 507-587 .... 5.00
518 Carl Bouldin 3.00
519 Charlie Smith 3.00
520 Jack Baldschun 3.00
522 Bobby Tiefenauer 3.00
523 Lou Burdette 10.00
524 Reds Rookies
(Jim Dickson,
Bobby Klaus) 8.00
527 Larry Bearnarth 8.00

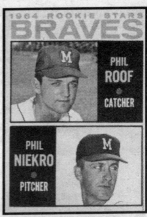

541 Braves Rookies

528 Athletics Rookies
(*Dave Duncan,*
Tom Reynolds) 12.00
529 Al Dark 12.00
530 Leon Wagner 12.00
531 Dodgers Team 25.00
532 Twins Rookies
(Bud Bloomfield,
Joe Nossek) 8.00
533 Johnny Klippstein 8.00
534 Gus Bell 8.00
535 Phil Regan 8.00
536 Mets Rookies
(Larry Elliot,
John Stephenson) 8.00
537 Dan Osinski 8.00
538 Minnie Minoso 12.00
539 Roy Face 12.00
540 Luis Aparicio 20.00
541 Braves Rookies
(*Phil Niekro,*
Phil Roof) 200.00
542 Don Mincher 8.00
543 Bob Uecker 50.00
544 Colts Rookies
(Steve Hertz,
Joe Hoerner) 8.00
545 Max Alvis 8.00

546	Joe Christopher	8.00
547	Gil Hodges	15.00
548	NL Rookies (Wayne Schurr, Paul Speckenbach)	8.00
549	Joe Moeller	8.00
550	Ken Hubbs	25.00
551	Billy Hoeft	8.00
552	Indians Rookies (Tom Kelley, *Sonny Siebert*)	8.00
553	Jim Brewer	8.00
556	Mets Rookies (Steve Dillon, Ron Locke)	8.00
561	Phillies Rookies (Dave Bennett, *Rick Wise*)	12.00
562	Pedro Ramos	8.00
563	Dal Maxvill	12.00
564	AL Rookies (Joe McCabe, Jerry McNertney)	8.00
565	Stu Miller	8.00
566	Ed Kranepool	10.00
567	Jim Kaat	14.00
568	NL Rookies (Phil Gagliano, Cap Peterson)	8.00
569	Fred Newman	8.00
570	Bill Mazeroski	12.00
571	Gene Conley	8.00
572	AL Rookies (Dick Egan, Dave Gray)	8.00
573	Jim Duffalo	8.00
574	Manny Jimenez	8.00
575	Tony Cloninger	8.00
576	Mets Rookies (Jerry Hinsley, Bill Wakefield)	8.00
577	Gordy Coleman	8.00
578	Glen Hobbie	8.00
579	Red Sox Team	20.00
580	Johnny Podres	11.00
581	Yankees Rookies (Pedro Gonzalez, Archie Moore)	12.00
582	Rod Kanehl	8.00
583	Tito Francona	8.00
586	Jim Piersall	12.00
587	Bennie Daniels	12.00

1965 TOPPS

Team logos returned to the front of the 1965 Topps set of 598 cards. Each 2½- by 3½-inch card also has a team pennant. Cartoons and year-by-year stats are the main elements of card backs. A number of first-class players have rookie cards in the 1965 set: The most valuable are for Steve Carlton, Jim Hunter, Joe Morgan, and Tony Perez. For the first time since 1957, no multi-player feature cards are included except rookie and league-leader cards. An eight-card subset highlights the Cardinals World Series win over the Yankees. Noted baseball funnyman Bob Uecker (card number 519), a catcher who hit right-handed, tricked the photographer and posed as if a left-handed batter. The higher prices of some last series cards is due to their limited inclusion on printing sheets, explaining the scarcity.

	NR MT		
Complete set	$3800.00	**Commons (371-446)**	6.00
Commons (1-198)	2.00	**Commons (447-522)**	7.00
Commons (199-370)	2.50	**Commons (523-598)**	7.50

1 AL Batting Ldrs (Elston Howard, Tony Oliva, Brooks Robinson)...... **$16.00**
2 NL Batting Ldrs (Hank Aaron, Rico Carty, Bob Clemente **10.00**
3 AL HR Ldrs (Harmon Killebrew, Mickey Mantle, Boog Powell) **25.00**
4 NL HR Ldrs (Johnny Callison, Orlando Cepeda, Jim Hart, Willie Mays, Billy Williams) **7.00**
5 AL RBI Ldrs (Harmon Killebrew, Mickey Mantle, Brooks Robinson, Dick Stuart) **25.00**
6 NL RBI Ldrs (Ken Boyer, Willie Mays, Ron Santo) **5.00**
7 AL ERA Ldrs (Dean Chance, Joel Horlen) **3.00**
8 NL ERA Ldrs (Don Drysdale, Sandy Koufax) **12.00**
9 AL Pitching Ldrs (Wally Bunker, Dean Chance, Gary Peters, Juan Pizarro, Dave Wickersham) **4.00**
10 NL Pitching Ldrs (Larry Jackson, Juan Marichal, Ray Sadecki) **3.50**
11 AL SO Ldrs (Dean Chance, Al Downing, Camilo Pascual) **3.00**
12 NL SO Ldrs (Don Drysdale, Bob Gibson, Bob Veale) **4.00**
13 Pedro Ramos **1.00**
15 Robin Roberts **9.00**
16 Houston Rookies (*Sonny Jackson, Joe Morgan*) **190.00**

250 Willie Mays

20 • Jim Bunning................ **4.00**
24 Twins Team.................... **4.00**
30 Jim Bouton **4.00**
49 Orioles Rookies (*Curt Blefary,* John Miller) **1.00**
50 Juan Marichal............... **12.00**
55 Tony Conigliaro **9.00**
57 Cardinals Team............. **6.00**
62 • Jim Katt (Kaat) **5.00**
65 Tony Kubek **4.00**
67 Harvey Haddix............... **2.50**
68 Del Crandall **2.50**
69 Bill Virdon **2.50**
70 Bill Skowron **2.50**
74 Red Sox Rookies (*Rico Petrocelli,* Jerry Stephenson).................. **6.00**
79 Checklist 1-88 .... **5.00**
91 Cubs Team.................... **3.00**
92 Dick Howser.................. **2.50**
95 Bill Mazeroski **3.00**
97 Pedro Gonzalez **1.00**
99 Gil Hodges **7.00**
100 Ken Boyer **3.00**
104 Checklist 89-176 .... **5.00**
107 Phillies Rookies (*Pat Corrales,* Costen Shockley) **3.00**

207 Pete Rose

110	Ron Santo	4.00
115	Bobby Richardson	4.50
116	Cardinals Rookies (Dave Dowling, *Bob Tolan*)	3.00
118	*Hal Lanier*	3.00
120	Frank Robinson	30.00
126	Dodgers Team	4.00
130	Al Kaline	30.00
131	Johnny Keane	2.75
132	World Series Game 1 (Cards Take Opener)	3.50
133	World Series Game 2 (Stottlemyre Wins)	4.00
134	World Series Game 3 (Mantle's Clutch HR)	45.00
135	World Series Game 4 (Boyer's Grand Slam)	5.00
136	World Series Game 5 (10th Inning Triumph)	4.00
137	World Series Game 6 (Bouton Wins Again)	4.00
138	World Series Game 7 (Gibson Wins Finale)	7.50
139	World Series Summary (The Cards Celebrate)	4.00
144	Ed Kranepool	2.00
145	• *Luis Tiant*	15.00
150	Brooks Robinson	30.00
151	Athletics Team	3.00
153	Norm Cash	4.00
155	Roger Maris	70.00
157	Zoilo Versalles	2.00
160	Bob Clemente	85.00
166	Indians Rookies (*Tommie Agee*, George Culver)	2.50
170	Hank Aaron	100.00
172	Jim Piersall	2.00
173	Tigers Team	3.25
176	Willie McCovey	20.00
180	Bob Allison	2.75
187	Casey Stengel	15.00
189	Checklist 177-264	3.00
193	Gaylord Perry	18.00
200	Joe Torre	4.00
201	Twins Rookies (*Cesar Tovar*, Sandy Valdespino)	3.00
203	Dallas Green	3.00
205	Warren Spahn	30.00
206	Willie Horton	3.00
207	Pete Rose	200.00
208	• Tommy John	14.00
209	Pirates Team	4.00
210	Jim Fregosi	3.50
217	Walt Alston	4.50
218	Dick Schofield	3.00
220	Billy Williams	14.00
224	Bob Chance	2.50
225	Bob Belinsky	2.50
226	Yankees Rookies (Jake Gibbs, Elvio Jimenez)	2.50
227	Bobby Klaus	2.50
230	Ray Sadecki	2.50
231	Jerry Adair	2.50
232	*Steve Blass*	3.00
233	Don Zimmer	3.50
234	White Sox Team	4.00
235	Chuck Hinton	2.50
236	*Dennis McLain*	25.00
237	Bernie Allen	2.50
239	Doc Edwards	2.50
242	George Brunet	2.50
243	Reds Rookies (*Tommy Helms*, Ted Davidson)	2.50

244	Lindy McDaniel	2.50
245	Joe Pepitone	3.00
247	Wally Moon	2.50
248	Gus Triandos	2.50
249	Dave McNally	3.00
250	Willie Mays	110.00
251	Billy Herman	3.00
252	Pete Richert	2.50
253	Danny Cater	2.50
254	Roland Sheldon	2.50
255	Camilo Pascual	2.50
256	Tito Francona	2.50
257	• Jim Wynn	2.75
258	Larry Bearnarth	2.50
259	Tigers Rookies (*Jim Northrup, Ray Oyler*)	4.00
260	Don Drysdale	25.00
261	Duke Carmel	2.50
264	Bob Buhl	2.50
266	*Bert Campaneris*	7.00
267	Senators Team	5.00
268	Ken McBride	2.50
269	Frank Bolling	2.50
270	Milt Pappas	2.50
273	Checklist 265-352	3.50
275	Dick Groat	2.75
276	Hoyt Wilhelm	8.00
277	Johnny Lewis	2.50
280	Dick Stuart	2.75
281	Bill Stafford	2.50
282	Giants Rookies (Dick Estelle, *Masanori Murakami*)	4.00
284	Nick Willhite	2.50
285	Ron Hunt	2.50
286	Athletics Rookies (Jim Dickson, Aurelio Monteagudo)	2.50
290	Wally Bunker	2.50
291	Jerry Lynch	2.50
292	Larry Yellen	2.50
293	Angels Team	4.00
294	Tim McCarver	5.00
295	Dick Radatz	2.75
296	Tony Taylor	2.75
297	• Dave DeBusschere	4.00
298	Jim Stewart	2.50
299	Jerry Zimmerman	2.50

300 Sandy Koufax

300	Sandy Koufax	125.00
301	Birdie Tebbetts	2.50
302	Al Stanek	2.50
303	Johnny Orsino	2.50
304	Dave Stenhouse	2.50
305	Rico Carty	4.00
306	Bubba Phillips	2.50
308	Mets Rookies (*Cleon Jones, Tom Parsons*)	5.00
309	Steve Hamilton	2.50
310	Johnny Callison	2.50
312	Joe Nuxhall	2.50
314	Sterling Slaughter	2.25
315	Frank Malzone	2.75
316	Reds Team	6.00
318	Matty Alou	2.75
319	Ken McMullen	2.50
320	Bob Gibson	35.00
321	Rusty Staub	5.00
322	Rick Wise	2.50
323	Hank Bauer	2.50
325	Donn Clendenon	2.50
330	Whitey Ford	30.00
331	Dodgers Rookies (Al Ferrara, John Purdin)	2.50
335	Mickey Lolich	5.00

350 Mickey Mantle

336	Woody Held	2.50
337	Mike Cuellar	3.00
338	Phillies Team	6.00
339	Ryne Duren	2.50
340	Tony Oliva	15.00
342	Bob Rodgers	2.50
343	Mike McCormick	2.50
344	Wes Parker	2.50
346	Bobby Bragan	2.50
347	Roy Face	2.50
350	Mickey Mantle	500.00
351	Jim Perry	2.50
352	*Alex Johnson*	2.50
353	Jerry Lumpe	2.50
355	Vada Pinson	4.00
358	Albie Pearson	2.50
360	Orlando Cepeda	8.00
361	Checklist 353-429	4.00
363	Bob Johnson	2.50
364	Galen Cisco	2.50
365	Jim Gentile	2.50
367	Leon Wagner	2.50
368	White Sox Rookies (*Ken Berry, Joel Gibson*)	2.50
369	Phil Linz	2.50
370	Tommy Davis	3.00
372	Clay Dalrymple	4.00
373	Curt Simmons	4.00
374	Angels Rookies (*Jose Cardenal, Dick Simpson*)	8.00
377	Willie Stargell	30.00
379	Giants Team	9.00
380	Rocky Colavito	9.00
381	Al Jackson	4.00
383	Felipe Alou	7.00
384	Johnny Klippstein	4.00
385	Carl Yastrzemski	75.00
387	Johnny Podres	8.00
388	John Blanchard	4.00
389	Don Larsen	8.00
390	Bill Freehan	8.00
392	Bob Friend	4.00
395	Jim Hart	4.00
400	Harmon Killebrew	35.00
401	Carl Willey	4.00
402	Joe Amalfitano	4.00
403	Red Sox Team	9.00
405	John Roseboro	9.00
406	Ralph Terry	4.00
410	Luis Aparicio	11.00
411	Roger Craig	7.00
413	Hal Reniff	4.00
414	Al Lopez	8.00
415	Curt Flood	9.00
417	Ed Brinkman	4.00
419	Ruben Amaro	4.00
426	Braves Team	8.00
429	Don Demeter	4.00
430	Gary Peters	4.00
431	Cardinals Rookies (*Nelson Briles, Wayne Spiezio*)	9.00
435	Willie Davis	7.00
436	Don Elston	4.00
437	Chico Cardenas	4.00
438	Harry Walker	4.00
439	Moe Drabowsky	4.00
440	Tom Tresh	8.00
442	Vic Power	7.00
443	Checklist 430-506	8.00
446	Art Mahaffey	4.00
447	Julian Javier	5.00
448	Lee Stange	5.00
449	Mets Rookies (Jerry Hinsley, Gary Kroll)	5.00

450	Elston Howard	9.00
451	Jim Owens	5.00
452	Gary Geiger	5.00
453	Dodgers Rookies (*Willie Crawford,* John Werhas)	5.00
454	Ed Rakow	5.00
455	Norm Siebern	5.00
456	Bill Henry	5.00
457	Bob Kennedy	5.00
458	John Buzhardt	5.00
459	Frank Kostro	5.00
460	Richie Allen	24.00
461	Braves Rookies (Phil Niekro, *Clay Carroll*)	60.00
462	Lew Krausse (photo is Pete Lovrich)	5.00
463	Manny Mota	5.00
464	Ron Piche	5.00
465	Tom Haller	5.00
466	Senators Rookies (Pete Craig, Dick Nen)	5.00
467	Ray Washburn	5.00
468	Larry Brown	5.00
469	Don Nottebart	5.00
470	Yogi Berra	65.00
471	Billy Hoeft	5.00
472	Don Pavletich	5.00
473	Orioles Rookies (*Dave Johnson, Paul Blair*)	12.00
474	Cookie Rojas	5.00
475	Clete Boyer	9.00
477	Cardinals Rookies (Fritz Ackley, *Steve Carlton*)	525.00
478	Wilbur Wood	5.00
479	Ken Harrelson	9.00
480	Joel Horlen	5.00
481	Indians Team	10.00
482	Bob Priddy	5.00
483	George Smith	5.00
484	Ron Perranoski	5.00
485	Nellie Fox	11.00
486	Angels Rookies (Tom Egan, Pat Rogan)	5.00
487	Woody Woodward	5.00
488	Ted Wills	5.00
489	Gene Mauch	5.00

526 Athletics Rookies

490	Earl Battey	5.00
491	Tracy Stallard	5.00
492	Gene Freese	5.00
493	Tigers Rookies (Bruce Brubaker, Bill Roman)	5.00
494	Jay Ritchie	5.00
495	Joe Christopher	5.00
496	Joe Cunningham	7.50
497	Giants Rookies (*Ken Henderson,* Jack Hiatt)	5.00
498	Gene Stephens	5.00
499	Stu Miller	5.00
500	Ed Mathews	35.00
501	Indians Rookies (Ralph Gagliano, Jim Rittwage)	5.00
502	Don Cardwell	5.00
503	Phil Gagliano	5.00
504	Jerry Grote	5.00
505	Ray Culp	5.00
506	Sam Mele	5.00
507	Sammy Ellis	5.00
508	Checklist 507-598	10.00
509	Red Sox Rookies (Bob Guindon, Gerry Vezendy)	5.00
510	Ernie Banks	80.00
511	Ron Locke	5.00
512	Cap Peterson	5.00

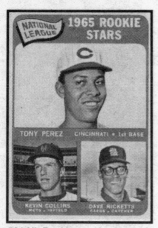

581 NL Rookies

513	Yankees Team	15.00
514	Joe Azcue	5.00
515	Vern Law	8.00
516	Al Weis	5.00
517	Angels Rookies (Paul Schaal, Jack Warner)	5.00
518	Ken Rowe	5.00
519	Bob Uecker	50.00
520	Tony Cloninger	5.00
523	Mike Brumley	7.50
524	Dave Giusti	7.50
525	Eddie Bressoud	7.50
526	Athletics Rookies (*Jim Hunter, Rene Lachemann, Skip Lockwood, Johnny Odom*)	125.00
527	Jeff Torborg	15.00
528	George Altman	7.50
529	Jerry Fosnow	7.50
530	Jim Maloney	8.00
531	Chuck Hiller	7.50
532	Hector Lopez	8.00
533	Mets Rookies (Jim Bethke, Tug McGraw, Dan Napolean, *Ron Swoboda*)	35.00
534	John Herrnstein	7.50

535	Jack Kralick	7.50
536	Andre Rodgers	7.50
537	Angels Rookies (Marcelino Lopez, *Rudy May*, Phil Roof)	8.00
538	Chuck Dressen	7.50
539	Herm Starrette	7.50
540	Lou Brock	60.00
541	White Sox Rookies (Greg Bollo, Bob Locker)	7.50
542	Lou Klimchock	7.50
543	Ed Connolly	7.50
544	Howie Reed	7.50
545	Jesus Alou	8.00
546	Indians Rookies (Ray Barker, Bill Davis, Mike Hedlund, Floyd Weaver)	8.00
547	Jake Wood	7.50
548	Dick Stigman	7.50
549	Cubs Rookies (*Glenn Beckert*, Roberto Pena)	18.00
550	*Mel Stottlemyre*	32.00
551	Mets Team	35.00
552	Julio Gotay	5.50
553	Astros Rookies (Dan Coombs, Jack McClure, Gene Ratliff)	5.50
554	Chico Ruiz	5.50
555	Jack Baldschun	5.50
556	Red Schoendienst	20.00
557	Jose Santiago	5.50
558	Tommie Sisk	5.50
559	Ed Bailey	5.50
560	Boog Powell	20.00
561	● Dodgers Rookies (Dennis Daboll, *Mike Kekich, Jim Lefebvre,* Hector Valle)	12.00
562	Billy Moran	5.50
563	Julio Navarro	5.50
564	Mel Nelson	5.50
565	Ernie Broglio	5.50
566	Yankees Rookies (Gil Blanco, Art Lopez, Ross Moschitto)	8.00
567	Tommie Aaron	8.00
568	Ron Taylor	5.50

569	Gino Cimoli	5.50
570	Claude Osteen	8.00
571	Ossie Virgil	5.50
572	Orioles Team	30.00
573	Red Sox Rookies (*Jim Lonborg,* Gerry Moses, Mike Ryan, Bill Schlesinger)	25.00
574	Roy Sievers	8.00
575	Jose Pagan	5.50
576	Terry Fox	5.50
577	AL Rookies (Jim Buschhorn, Darold Knowles, Richie Scheinblum)	5.50
578	Camilo Carreon	5.50
579	Dick Smith	5.50
580	Jimmie Hall	5.50
581	NL Rookies (Kevin Collins, *Tony Perez,* Dave Ricketts)	125.00
582	Bob Schmidt	5.50
583	Wes Covington	5.50
584	Harry Bright	5.50
585	Hank Fischer	5.50
586	Tommy McGraw	5.50
587	Joe Sparma	5.50
588	Lenny Green	5.50
589	Giants Rookies (Frank Linzy, Bob Schroeder)	5.50
590	Johnnie Wyatt	5.50
591	Bob Skinner	5.50
592	Frank Bork	5.50
593	Tigers Rookies (Jackie Moore, John Sullivan)	5.50
594	Joe Gaines	5.50
595	Don Lee	5.50
596	Don Landrum	5.50
597	Twins Rookies (Joe Nossek, Dick Reese, John Sevcik)	8.00
598	Al Downing	15.00

1966 TOPPS

Multi-player cards reappeared in 1966, but no surprises were unveiled in this 298-card set. Well-known rookies who made their debuts in the 1966 Topps offering include Ferguson Jenkins, Bobby Murcer, Jim Palmer, George "Boomer" Scott, and Don Sutton. The set features two series that are tough to locate today: Cards numbering 447 to 522 are somewhat hard to find, while the high numbers from 523 through 598 constitute one of the scarcest series of the 1960s. Short supply and his election to the Hall of Fame explain the $265 value placed Gaylord Perry's card, number 598.

	NR MT
Complete set	**$4500.00**
Commons (1-110)	**1.50**
Commons (111-370)	**2.00**
Commons (371-445)	**4.00**
Commons (447-522)	**7.50**
Commons (523-598)	**16.00**

1	Willie Mays	$150.00
28	Phil Niekro	20.00
30	Pete Rose	60.00
36	Jim Hunter	30.00
37	Billy Herman	2.00
50	Mickey Mantle	210.00
62	Merritt Ranew (with sold statement)	1.00
62	Merritt Ranew (w/o sold statement)	25.00
70	Carl Yastrzemski	40.00
72	Tony Perez	30.00
76	Red Schoendienst	4.00
90	Luis Aparicio	9.00

50 Mickey Mantle

91	Bob Uecker (with trade statement)	**18.00**
91	Bob Uecker (w/o trade statement)	**55.00**
92	Yankees Team	**4.00**
99	Buc Belters (Donn Clendenon, Willie Stargell)	**3.50**
100	Sandy Koufax	**100.00**
101	Checklist 89-176 (115 is Spahn)	**12.00**
101	Checklist 89-176 (115 is Henry)	**7.00**
103	Dick Groat (with trade statement)	**1.50**
103	Dick Groat (w/o trade statement)	**25.00**
104	Alex Johnson (with trade statement)	**1.00**
104	Alex Johnson (w/o trade statement)	**20.00**
110	Ernie Banks	**25.00**
111	Gary Peters	**1.00**
112	Manny Mota	**1.00**
113	Hank Aguirre	**1.00**
116	Walt Alston	**3.00**
117	Jake Gibbs	**1.00**
118	Mike McCormick	**1.00**
119	Art Shamsky	**1.00**
120	Harmon Killebrew	**21.00**
122	Joe Gaines	**1.00**
123	Pirates Rookies (Frank Bork, Jerry May)	**1.00**
124	Tug McGraw	**5.00**
125	Lou Brock	**25.00**
126	*Jim Palmer*	**200.00**
128	Jim Landis	**1.00**
129	Jack Kralick	**1.00**
130	Joe Torre	**4.00**
131	Angels Team	**3.00**
132	Orlando Cepeda	**5.00**
134	Wes Parker	**1.00**
135	Dave Morehead	**1.00**
136	Woody Held	**1.00**
137	Pat Corrales	**1.00**
138	Roger Repoz	**1.00**
139	Cubs Rookies (Byron Browne, Don Young)	**1.00**
143	Jose Tartabull	**1.00**
144	Don Schwall	**1.00**
145	Bill Freehan	**1.00**
146	George Altman	**1.00**
147	Lum Harris	**1.00**
148	Bob Johnson	**1.00**
150	Rocky Colavito	**5.00**
151	Gary Wagner	**1.00**
152	Frank Malzone	**1.00**
153	Rico Carty	**2.00**
154	Chuck Hiller	**1.00**
155	Marcelino Lopez	**1.00**
156	DP Combo (Hal Lanier, Dick Schofield)	**1.00**
157	Rene Lachemann	**1.00**
158	Jim Brewer	**1.00**
159	Chico Ruiz	**1.00**
160	Whitey Ford	**22.00**
161	Jerry Lumpe	**1.00**
162	Lee Maye	**1.00**
163	Tito Francona	**1.00**
164	White Sox Rookies (Tommie Agee, Marv Staehle)	**1.00**
165	Don Lock	**1.00**
167	Boog Powell	**4.00**
170	Cookie Rojas	**1.00**
171	Nick Willhite	**1.00**
172	Mets Team	**3.00**

173	Al Spangler	1.00
175	Bert Campaneris	2.00
176	Jim Davenport	1.00
177	Hector Lopez	1.00
178	Bob Tillman	1.00
179	Cardinals Rookies (Dennis Aust, Bob Tolan)	1.00
180	Vada Pinson	3.00
181	Al Worthington	1.00
182	Jerry Lynch	1.00
183	Checklist 177-264	4.00
184	Denis Menke	1.00
185	Bob Buhl	1.00
186	Ruben Amaro	1.00
187	Chuck Dressen	1.00
188	Al Luplow	1.00
189	John Roseboro	1.00
191	Darrell Sutherland	1.00
193	Dave McNally	2.00
194	Senators Team	3.00
195	Joe Morgan	40.00
197	Sonny Siebert	2.00
198	*Mickey Stanley*	3.00
199	Chisox Clubbers (Floyd Robinson, Johnny Romano, Bill Skowron)	2.00
200	Ed Mathews	13.00
202	Clay Dalrymple	2.00
203	Jose Santiago	2.00
204	Cubs Team	3.00
205	Tom Tresh	3.00
209	Tigers Rookies (Fritz Fisher, *John Hiller*)	3.00
210	Bill Mazeroski	3.50
211	Frank Kreutzer	2.00
212	Ed Kranepool	2.00
213	Fred Newman	2.00
214	Tommy Harper	2.00
215	NL Batting Ldrs (Hank Aaron, Bob Clemente, Willie Mays)	30.00
216	AL Batting Ldrs (Vic Davalillo, Tony Oliva, Carl Yastrzemski)	6.00

500 Hank Aaron

217	NL HR Ldrs (Willie Mays, Willie McCovey, Billy William)	15.00
218	AL HR Ldrs (Norm Cash, Tony Conigliaro, Willie Horton)	3.50
219	NL RBI Ldrs (Deron Johnson, Willie Mays, Frank Robinson)	6.00
220	AL RBI Ldrs (Rocky Colavito, Willie Horton, Tony Oliva)	3.50
221	NL ERA Ldrs (Sandy Koufax, Vern Law, Juan Marichal)	5.50
222	AL ERA Ldrs (Eddie Fisher, Sam McDowell, Sonny Siebert)	3.50
223	NL Pitching Ldrs (Tony Cloninger, Don Drysdale, Sandy Koufax)	5.00

598 Gaylord Perry

330 Ron Fairly 2.00
333 Senators Rookies
(*Joe Coleman*,
Jim French) 2.00
338 Dal Maxvill 2.00
339 Del Crandall 2.25
341 Wes Westrum 2.00
344 Steve Blass 2.00
345 Bob Allison 2.00
348 Orioles Team.................. 4.00
350 Mel Stottlemyre 4.00
354 Smoky Burgess 2.00
355 Wade Blasingame 2.00
356 Red Sox Rookies
(Owen Johnson,
Ken Sanders) 2.00
359 Johnny Briggs 2.00
360 Ron Hunt 2.00
361 Tom Satriano 2.00
362 Gates Brown 2.00
363 Checklist 353-429 .... 5.00
364 Nate Oliver 2.00
365 Roger Maris................. 70.00
366 Wayne Causey 2.00
367 Mel Nelson 2.00
368 Charlie Lau.................... 2.25
370 Chico Cardenas 2.00
371 Lee Stange 3.00
372 • Harvey Kuenn 5.00
373 Giants Rookies
(Dick Estelle,
Jack Hiatt) 3.00
374 Bob Locker 3.00
375 Donn Clendenon 3.00
377 Turk Farrell 3.00
379 Cardinals Team............. 8.00
380 Tony Conigliaro 8.00
382 Phil Roof....................... 3.00
384 Al Downing 4.50
385 Ken Boyer 5.00
386 Gil Hodges 8.00
388 Don Mincher 3.00
390 Brooks Robinson 30.00
391 Chuck Hinton.................. 3.00
392 Cubs Rookies
(*Bill Hands*,
Randy Hundley) 5.00
393 George Brunet............... 3.00
395 Len Gabrielson.............. 3.00

1 Willie Mays

397 Bill White 5.00
398 Danny Cater 3.00
400 Zoilo Versalles............... 3.00
401 Ken McMullen 3.00
402 Jim Hickman.................. 3.00
404 Pirates Team................. 7.00
405 • Elston Howard 7.00
406 Joe Jay 3.00
409 Billy Hoeft 3.00
410 Al Kaline 30.00
411 Gene Mauch................... 3.00
413 John Romano 3.00
414 Dan Coombs 3.00
416 Phil Ortega 3.00
417 Angels Rookies
(Jim McGlothlin,
Ed Sukla)...................... 3.00
420 Juan Marichal.............. 13.00
421 Roy McMillan 3.00
422 Ed Charles 3.00
423 Ernie Broglio................. 3.00
424 Reds Rookies
(*Lee May*,
Darrell Osteen) 7.00
425 Bob Veale 3.00
426 White Sox Team............. 8.00
428 Sandy Alomar................ 3.00
429 Bill Monbouquette 3.00

126 Jim Palmer

430	Don Drysdale	25.00
433	Alvin Dark	3.00
434	Willie Kirkland	3.00
435	Jim Bunning	7.00
436	Julian Javier	3.00
437	Al Stanek	3.00
439	Pedro Ramos	3.00
440	Deron Johnson	3.00
442	Orioles Rookies (Ed Barnowski, Eddie Watt)	3.00
444	Checklist 430-506	7.00
445	• Jim Kaat	7.00
446	Mack Jones	3.00
447	Dick Ellsworth (photo is Ken Hubbs)	9.00
448	Eddie Stanky	6.00
449	Joe Moeller	6.00
450	Tony Oliva	10.00
451	Barry Latman	6.00
452	Joe Azcue	6.00
453	Ron Kline	6.00
454	Jerry Buchek	6.00
455	Mickey Lolich	10.00
456	Red Sox Rookies (Darrell Brandón, Joe Foy)	6.00
457	Joe Gibbon	6.00
458	Manny Jiminez (Jimenez)	6.00
459	Bill McCool	6.00
460	Curt Blefary	6.00
461	Roy Face	9.00
462	Bob Rodgers	6.00
463	Phillies Team	12.00
464	Larry Bearnarth	6.00
465	Don Buford	6.00
466	Ken Johnson	6.00
467	Vic Roznovsky	6.00
468	Johnny Podres	9.00
469	Yankees Rookies (*Bobby Murcer*, Dooley Womack)	25.00
470	Sam McDowell	9.00
471	Bob Skinner	6.00
472	Terry Fox	6.00
473	Rich Rollins	6.00
474	Dick Schofield	6.00
475	Dick Radatz	6.00
476	Bobby Bragan	6.00
477	Steve Barber	6.00
478	Tony Gonzalez	6.00
479	Jim Hannan	6.00
480	Dick Stuart	6.00
481	Bob Lee	6.00
482	Cubs Rookies (John Boccabella, Dave Dowling)	6.00
483	Joe Nuxhall	6.00
484	Wes Covington	8.00
486	Tommy John	16.00
487	Al Ferrara	8.00
489	Curt Simmons	8.00
490	Bobby Richardson	13.00
492	Athletics Team	13.00
493	Johnny Klippstein	6.00
494	Gordon Coleman	6.00
495	Dick McAuliffe	6.00
496	Lindy McDaniel	6.00
497	Chris Cannizzaro	6.00
498	Pirates Rookies (*Woody Fryman*, *Luke Walker*)	9.00
500	Hank Aaron	125.00
503	Steve Hamilton	6.00
504	Grady Hatton	6.00
505	Jose Cardenal	6.00

506	Bo Belinsky	6.00
508	*Steve Hargan*	6.00
509	Jake Wood	6.00
510	Hoyt Wilhelm	**17.00**
511	Giants Rookies (Bob Barton, *Tito Fuentes*)	**9.00**
512	Dick Stigman	6.00
513	Camilo Carreon	6.00
514	Hal Woodeshick	6.00
515	Frank Howard	**9.00**
517	Checklist 507-598	**12.00**
518	Braves Rookies (Herb Hippauf, Arnie Umbach)	6.00
520	Jim Wynn	**9.00**
523	Bob Sadowski	**16.00**
524	Giants Rookies (Ollie Brown, Don Mason)	**18.00**
525	Gary Bell	**16.00**
526	Twins Team	**70.00**
527	Julio Navarro	**16.00**
528	Jesse Gonder	**21.00**
529	White Sox Rookies (*Lee Elia,* Dennis Higgins, Bill Voss)	**19.00**
530	Robin Roberts	**48.00**
531	Joe Cunningham	**17.00**
532	Aurelio Monteagudo	**16.00**
533	Jerry Adair	**16.00**
534	Mets Rookies (Dave Eilers, Rob Gardner)	**19.00**
535	Willie Davis	**50.00**
536	Dick Egan	**16.00**
537	Herman Franks	**18.00**
538	Bob Allen	**16.00**
539	Astros Rookies (Bill Heath, Carroll Sembera)	**16.00**
540	Denny McLain	**70.00**
541	Gene Oliver	**16.00**
542	George Smith	**16.00**
543	Roger Craig	**35.00**
544	Cardinals Rookies (Joe Hoerner, George Kernek, Jimmy Williams)	**35.00**

550 Willie McCovey

545	Dick Green	**21.00**
546	Dwight Siebler	**16.00**
547	*Horace Clarke*	**50.00**
548	Gary Kroll	**21.00**
549	Senators Rookies (Al Closter, Casey Cox)	**16.00**
550	Willie McCovey	**125.00**
551	Bob Purkey	**23.00**
552	Birdie Tebbetts	**23.00**
553	Major League Rookies (Pat Garrett, Jackie Warner)	**16.00**
554	Jim Northrup	**24.00**
555	Ron Perranoski	**24.00**
556	Mel Queen	**22.00**
557	Felix Mantilla	**16.00**
558	Red Sox Rookies (Guido Grilli, Pete Magrini, *George Scott*)	**27.00**
559	Roberto Pena	**16.00**
560	Joel Horlen	**16.00**
561	Choo Choo Coleman	**45.00**
562	Russ Snyder	**16.00**
563	Twins Rookies (Pete Cimino, Cesar Tovar)	**19.00**

564	Bob Chance	**16.00**
565	Jimmy Piersall	**35.00**
566	Mike Cuellar	**30.00**
567	Dick Howser	**30.00**
568	Athletics Rookies (Paul Lindblad, Ron Stone)	**16.00**
569	Orlando McFarlane	**16.00**
570	Art Mahaffey	**22.00**
571	Dave Roberts	**16.00**
572	Bob Priddy	**16.00**
573	Derrell Griffith	**16.00**
574	Mets Rookies (Bill Hepler, Bill Murphy)	**19.00**
575	Earl Wilson	**16.00**
576	Dave Nicholson	**21.00**
577	Jack Lamabe	**16.00**
578	Chi Chi Olivo	**16.00**
579	Orioles Rookies (Frank Bertaina, Gene Brabender, Dave Johnson)	**20.00**
580	Billy Williams	**100.00**
581	Tony Martinez	**16.00**
582	Garry Roggenburk	**16.00**
583	Tigers Team	**150.00**
584	Yankees Rookies (Frank Fernandez, *Fritz Peterson*)	**19.00**
586	Claude Raymond	**16.00**
587	Dick Bertell	**16.00**
588	Athletics Rookies (Chuck Dobson, Ken Suarez)	**16.00**
590	Bill Skowron	**40.00**
591	NL Rookies (*Grant Jackson*, Bart Shirley)	**45.00**
592	Andre Rodgers	**16.00**
593	Doug Camilli	**21.00**
594	Chico Salmon	**16.00**
595	Larry Jackson	**16.00**
596	Astros Rookies (*Nate Colbert*, Greg Sims)	**19.00**
597	John Sullivan	**16.00**
598	Gaylord Perry	**265.00**

1967 TOPPS

Scarcity and attractiveness make the 1967 Topps set one of the hottest collectibles of the 1960s. The 609 cards in the set made it the largest produced by Topps at the time of issue. The standard-sized cards feature large color photos with facsimile autographs (except for Milt Pappas, number 254, which lacks an autograph). Card backs are the first ever from Topps to utilize vertical backs. The set is highlighted by a 12-card subset of 1966 league leaders and a five-card series honoring the previous World Series. An ultrarare final series, from 534 through 609, makes completing the set a real challenge, especially since four key cards in the series (Tommy John, Brooks Robinson, and rookie cards of Rod Carew and Tom Seaver) together are valued at over $2000. Also please note that 542, 550, and 569 are double prints.

	NR MT		
Complete set	**$5000.00**	**Commons (371-457)**	**3.00**
Commons (1-110)	**1.50**	**Commons (458-533)**	**4.00**
Commons (111-370)	**2.00**	**Commons (534-609)**	**18.00**

150 Mickey Mantle

1967 Topps

250 Hank Aaron

151 World Series Game 1
(Moe Mows Down 11) ... 4.00
152 World Series Game 2
(Palmer Blanks
Dodgers) 6.00
153 World Series Game 3
(Blair's Homer Defeats
L.A.) 4.00
154 World Series Game 4
(Orioles Win 4th
Straight) 4.00
155 World Series Summary
(The Winners
Celebrate) 4.00
160 Willie Davis 2.25
161 Dick Williams 2.25
166 Ed Mathews 12.00
167 Senators Rookies
(Joe Coleman,
Tim Cullen) 2.00
169 Horace Clarke 2.00
170 Dick McAuliffe 2.00
173 Cardinals Team 4.00
174 Dick Radatz 2.00
177 Tito Fuentes 2.00
179 Braves Rookies
(Cecil Upshaw,
Chas. Vaughn) 2.00

185 *Ken Holtzman* 4.50
186 Mets Maulers
(Ed Kranepool,
Ron Swoboda) 2.00
188 Ken Harrelson 2.00
191 Checklist 197-283
(Willie Mays)
(214 is Dick Kelley) 7.00
191 Checklist 197-283
(Willie Mays)
(214 is Tom Kelley) 6.00
193 Jose Cardenal 1.50
194 Bob Allison 2.00
197 Ron Perranoski 2.00
198 Chuck Hiller 2.00
200 Willie Mays 100.00
201 Hal Reniff 2.00
204 Orioles Rookies
(Tom Phoebus,
Mike Epstein) 2.00
205 Dick Groat 2.25
210 Bob Gibson 20.00
211 Twins Team 4.00
213 ● Jay Johnstone 3.00
215 Ernie Banks 20.00
216 Bengal Belters
(Norm Cash,
Al Kaline) 7.50
217 Rob Gardner 2.00
218 Wes Parker 2.00
219 Clay Carroll 2.00
220 Jim Hart 2.00
221 Woody Fryman 2.00
222 Reds Rookies
(Lee May,
Darrell Osteen) 3.00
225 Mel Stottlemyre 3.00
226 Julian Javier 2.00
228 Gil Hodges 5.00
230 Boog Powell 3.50
232 Don Buford 2.00
233 AL ERA Ldrs
(Steve Hargan,
Joel Horlen, Gary
Peters) 3.50
234 NL ERA Ldrs
(Mike Cuellar,
Sandy Koufax, Juan
Marichal) 10.00

235 AL Pitching Ldrs
(Jim Kaat,
Denny McLain, Earl
Wilson) 3.00
236 NL Pitching Ldrs
(Bob Gibson,
Sandy Koufax,
Juan Marichal, Gaylord
Perry) 18.00
237 AL SO Ldrs
(Jim Kaat,
Sam McDowell, Earl
Wilson) 3.00
238 NL SO Ldrs
(Jim Bunning,
Sandy Koufax, Bob
Veale) 5.00
239 AL Batting Ldrs
(Al Kaline,
Tony Oliva, Frank
Robinson)..................... 5.00
240 NL Batting Ldrs
(Felipe Alou,
Matty Alou, Rico
Carty) 3.00
241 AL RBI Ldrs
(Harmon Killebrew,
Boog Powell,
Frank Robinson)........... 5.00
242 NL RBI Ldrs
(Hank Aaron,
Richie Allen, Bob
Clemente)................... 12.00
243 AL HR Ldrs
(Harmon
Killebrew, Boog Powell,
Frank Robinson)........... 6.00
244 NL HR Ldrs
(Hank Aaron,
Richie Allen, Willie
Mays) 12.00
245 Curt Flood 3.00
246 Jim Perry 2.25
247 Jerry Lumpe 2.00
248 Gene Mauch................. 2.00
250 Hank Aaron 100.00
253 Indians Rookies
(Bill Davis,
Gus Gil) 2.00

146 Steve Carlton

254 Milt Pappas 2.00
255 Frank Howard................ 3.00
257 Charley Smith............... 2.00
260 Jim Lefevbre................. 2.50
262 Athletics Team 4.00
264 Ron Swoboda................ 2.00
265 Lou Burdette................. 2.50
266 Pitt Power (Donn
Clendenon, Willie
Stargell)........................ 4.00
270 Zoilo Versalles.............. 2.00
272 Cubs Rookies
(Bill Connors,
Dave Dowling)............... 2.00
278 Checklist 284-370
(Jim Kaat)..................... 6.00
280 Tony Conigliaro 6.00
282 Johnny Odom................ 2.00
283 Gene Alley.................... 2.00
284 Johnny Podres 3.25
285 Lou Brock 25.00
287 Mets Rookies
(Greg Goossen,
Bart Shirley) 2.00
289 Tom Tresh..................... 4.00
290 ● Bill White................... 4.00
294 Walt Alston................... 4.00
295 Sam McDowell 2.00

475 Jim Palmer

296	Glenn Beckert	2.00
299	Norm Siebern	2.00
300	• Jim Kaat	4.00
302	Orioles Team	4.00
306	*Bud Harrelson*	4.00
308	Al Downing	2.00
309	Hurlers Beware (Richie Allen, Johnny Callison)	3.50
310	Gary Peters	2.00
314	Red Sox Rookies (*Mike Andrews, Reggie Smith*)	8.00
315	• Billy Williams	12.00
326	Bob Uecker	15.00
327	Angels Team	4.00
332	Jesus Alou	2.00
334	• Twin Terrors (Bob Allison, Harmon Killebrew)	4.00
337	Joe Morgan	25.00
340	Joe Pepitone	2.25
348	Tug McGraw	4.00
350	Joe Torre	4.00
351	Vern Law	3.00
354	Cubs Team	4.00
355	Carl Yastrzemski	75.00
357	Bill Skowron	3.00

361	Checklist 371-457 (Bob Clemente)	7.00
363	Dave Johnson	3.00
369	Jim Hunter	18.00
371	Jim Lonborg	3.50
372	Mike de la Hoz	3.00
373	White Sox Rookies (Duane Josephson, Fred Klages)	3.00
374	Mel Queen	3.00
375	Jake Gibbs	3.00
376	Don Lock	3.00
377	Luis Tiant	5.00
378	Tigers Team	6.00
379	Jerry May	3.00
380	Dean Chance	3.00
381	Dick Schofield	3.00
382	Dave McNally	3.50
383	Ken Henderson	3.00
384	Cardinals Rookies (Jim Cosman, Dick Hughes)	3.00
385	Jim Fregosi	3.00
386	Dick Selma	3.00
387	Cap Peterson	3.00
388	Arnold Earley	3.00
389	Al Dark	3.00
390	Jim Wynn	3.50
391	Wilbur Wood	3.00
392	Tommy Harper	3.00
393	Jim Bouton	4.50
394	Jake Wood	3.00
395	Chris Short	3.00
396	Atlanta Aces Tony Cloninger, Denis Menke)	3.00
397	Willie Smith	3.00
398	Jeff Torborg	3.25
399	Al Worthington	3.00
400	Bob Clemente	75.00
401	Jim Coates	3.00
402	Phillies Rookies (Grant Jackson, Billy Wilson)	3.00
403	Dick Nen	3.00
404	Nelson Briles	3.00
405	Russ Snyder	3.00
406	Lee Elia	3.00
407	Reds Team	6.00

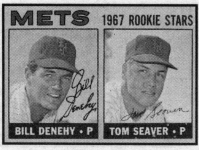

581 Mets Rookies

408	Jim Northrup	3.00
409	Ray Sadecki	3.00
410	Lou Johnson	3.00
411	Dick Howser	3.50
412	Astros Rookies (Norm Miller, *Doug Rader*)	4.00
413	Jerry Grote	3.00
417	Bob Bruce	3.00
418	Sam Mele	3.00
419	Don Kessinger	3.00
420	Denny McLain	6.00
421	Dal Maxvill	3.00
422	Hoyt Wilhelm	9.00
423	Fence Busters (Willie Mays, Willie McCovey)	25.00
424	Pedro Gonzalez	3.00
425	Pete Mikkelsen	3.00
426	Lou Clinton	3.00
427	Ruben Gomez	3.00
428	Dodgers Rookies (Tom Hutton, *Gene Michael*)	3.00
429	Gary Roggenburk	3.00
430	Pete Rose	80.00
431	Ted Uhlaender	3.00
432	Jimmie Hall	3.00
437	Senators Team	6.00
441	Jim Davenport	3.00
442	Yankees Rookies (*Bill Robinson*, Joe Verbanic)	5.00
443	Tito Francona	3.00

445	Don Sutton	35.00
450	Richie Allen	6.00
452	Ed Kranepool	3.25
454	Checklist 458-533 (Juan Marichal)	6.00
456	Phil Niekro	15.00
458	Lee Thomas	4.25
459	Senators Rookies (*Dick Bosman*, Pete Craig)	7.50
460	Harmon Killebrew	60.00
461	Bob Miller	4.00
462	Bob Barton	4.00
463	Tribe Hill Aces (Sam McDowell, Sonny Siebert)	5.00
464	Dan Coombs	4.00
465	Willie Horton	5.00
466	Bobby Wine	4.00
467	Jim O'Toole	4.00
468	Ralph Houk	5.00
469	Len Gabrielson	4.00
470	Bob Shaw	4.00
471	Rene Lachemann	4.00
472	Pirates Rookies (John Gelnar, George Spriggs)	4.00
473	Jose Santiago	4.00
474	Bob Tolan	4.50
475	Jim Palmer	110.00
476	Tony Perez	75.00
477	Braves Team	15.00
478	Bob Humphreys	4.00
479	Gary Bell	4.00

569 AL Rookies

480	Willie McCovey	**35.00**
481	Leo Durocher	**12.00**
482	Bill Monbouquette	**4.25**
483	Jim Landis	**4.00**
484	Jerry Adair	**4.00**
485	Tim McCarver	**25.00**
486	Twins Rookies (Rich Reese, Bill Whitby)	**4.00**
488	Gerry Arrigo	**4.00**
489	Doug Clemens	**4.00**
490	Tony Cloninger	**4.50**
491	Sam Bowens	**4.00**
492	Pirates Team	**15.00**
493	Phil Ortega	**4.00**
494	Bill Rigney	**4.50**
495	Fritz Peterson	**4.25**
497	Ron Campbell	**4.00**
498	Larry Dierker	**4.50**
499	Indians Rookies (George Culver, Jose Vidal)	**4.00**
500	Juan Marichal	**25.00**
501	Jerry Zimmerman	**4.00**
502	Derrell Griffith	**4.00**
503	Dodgers Team	**15.00**
504	Orlando Martinez	**4.00**
505	Tommy Helms	**4.00**
506	Smoky Burgess	**4.00**
507	Orioles Rookies (Ed Barnowski, Larry Haney)	**4.50**
508	Dick Hall	**4.00**
509	Jim King'	**4.00**
510	Bill Mazeroski	**12.00**
512	Red Schoendienst	**13.00**
515	Bert Campaneris	**7.00**
516	Giants Team	**15.00**
519	Ted Davidson	**4.00**
521	Bird Bombers (Curt Blefary, Boog Powell)	**6.00**
526	Tigers Rookies (*Pat Dobson,* George Korince)	**5.00**
527	Dennis Ribant	**4.00**
528	Rico Petrocelli	**9.00**
530	Felipe Alou	**4.00**
531	Checklist 534-609 (Brooks Robinson)	**12.00**
534	Hank Bauer	**21.00**
535	Donn Clendenon	**21.00**
536	Cubs Rookies (*Joe Niekro,* Paul Popovich)	**40.00**
537	Chuck Estrada	**21.00**
538	J.C. Martin	**21.00**
539	Dick Egan	**21.00**
540	Norm Cash	**50.00**
541	Joe Gibbon	**21.00**
542	Athletics Rookies (*Rick Monday,* Tony Pierce)	**13.00**
543	Dan Schneider	**21.00**
544	Indians Team	**30.00**
545	Jim Grant	**21.00**
546	Woody Woodward	**21.00**
547	Red Sox Rookies (Russ Gibson, Bill Rohr)	**21.00**

604 Red Sox Team

548	Tony Gonzalez	21.00
549	Jack Sanford	20.00
550	Vada Pinson	12.00
551	Doug Camili	21.00
552	Ted Savage	21.00
553	Yankees Rookies (Mike Hegan, Thad Tillotson)	30.00
554	Andre Rodgers	21.00
555	Don Cardwell	21.00
556	Al Weis	21.00
557	Al Ferrara	20.00
558	Orioles Rookies (*Mark Belanger,* Bill Dillman)	50.00
559	Dick Tracewski	21.00
560	Jim Bunning	55.00
561	Sandy Alomar	21.00
562	Steve Blass	20.00
563	Joe Adcock	20.00
564	Astros Rookies (Alonzo Harris, Aaron Pointer)	21.00
565	Lew Krausse	21.00
566	Gary Geiger	21.00
567	Steve Hamilton	20.00
568	John Sullivan	21.00
569	AL Rookies (Hank Allen, *Rod Carew*)	425.00
570	Maury Wills	80.00
571	Larry Sherry	20.00
572	Don Demeter	20.00
573	White Sox Team	30.00
574	Jerry Buchek	20.00
575	*Dave Boswell*	20.00
576	NL Rookies (Norm Gigon, Ramon Hernandez)	25.00
577	Bill Short	21.00
578	John Boccabella	21.00
579	Bill Henry	21.00
580	Rocky Colavito	75.00
581	Mets Rookies (Bill Denehy, *Tom Seaver*)	1250.00
582	Jim Owens	21.00
583	Ray Barker	21.00
584	Jim Piersall	30.00
585	Wally Bunker	21.00
586	Manny Jimenez	21.00
587	NL Rookies (Don Shaw, Gary Sutherland)	21.00
588	Johnny Klippstein	21.00
589	Dave Ricketts	21.00
590	Pete Richert	21.00
591	Ty Cline	21.00
592	NL Rookies (Jim Shellenback, Ron Willis)	25.00
595	Cookie Rojas	21.00
596	Galen Cisco	21.00
597	Ted Abernathy	21.00
598	White Sox Rookies (Ed Stroud, Walt Williams)	22.00
599	Bob Duliba	21.00
600	Brooks Robinson	275.00
601	Bill Bryan	6.00
602	Juan Pizarro	21.00
603	Athletics Rookies (Tim Talton, Ramon Webster)	21.00

604	Red Sox Team	**125.00**
605	Mike Shannon	**45.00**
606	Ron Taylor	**21.00**
607	Mickey Stanley	**35.00**

608	Cubs Rookies (Rich Nye, John Upham)	**24.00**
609	Tommy John	**135.00**

1968 TOPPS

Collectors think of the 1968 Topps issue of 598 cards as the "burlap sack" issue. That's because the photos appear on backgrounds of brown mesh. Card backs are still in a vertical format, but the cartoon now appears at the bottom, with year-by-year statistics in the middle. An All-Star subseries returned in 1968 that featured 20 players chosen by *The Sporting News*. Topps continued the practice of placing a small mug shot of a star like Orlando Cepeda or Juan Marichal on the usually bland checklists. Rookie cards of Johnny Bench and Nolan Ryan are by far the most valuable in the set, while Roger Maris and Eddie Mathews made the last card appearances of their careers in 1968.

	NR MT
Complete set	**$3500.00**
Commons (1-457)	**1.50**
Commons (458-533)	**2.50**
Commons (534-598)	**3.00**

1	NL Batting Ldrs (Matty Alou, Bob Clemente, Tony Gonzalez)	**$18.00**
2	AL Batting Ldrs (Al Kaline, Frank Robinson, Carl Yastrzemski)	**13.00**
3	NL RBI Ldrs (Hank Aaron, Orlando Cepeda, Bob Clemente)	**6.00**
4	AL RBI Ldrs (Harmon Killebrew, Frank Robinson, Carl Yastrzemski)	**8.00**
5	NL HR Ldrs (Hank Aaron, Willie McCovey, Ron Santo, Jim Wynn)	**5.00**
6	AL HR Ldrs (Frank Howard, Harmon Killebrew, Carl Yastrzemski)	**8.00**
7	NL ERA Ldrs (Jim Bunning, Phil Niekro, Chris Short)	**3.00**
8	AL ERA Ldrs (Joe Horlen, Gary Peters, Sonny Siebert)	**2.00**
9	NL Pitching Ldrs (Jim Bunning, Ferguson Jenkins, Mike McCormick, Claude Osteen)	**3.00**
10	AL Pitching Ldrs (Dean Chance, Jim Lonborg, Earl Wilson) ("Lonberg" on back)	**3.50**
10	AL Pitching Ldrs (Dean Chance, Jim Lonborg, Earl Wilson) ("Lonborg" on back)	**2.00**

247 Reds Rookies

11	NL SO Ldrs (Jim Bunning, Ferguson Jenkins, Gaylord Perry)	4.00
12	AL SO Ldrs (Dean Chance, Jim Lonborg, Sam McDowell)	3.00
14	Jerry McNertney	1.50
15	Ron Hunt	1.50
16	• Indians Rookies (Lou Piniella, Richie Scheinblum)	5.00
18	Mike Hershberger	1.50
19	Juan Pizarro	1.50
20	Brooks Robinson	25.00
21	Ron Davis	1.50
22	Pat Dobson	1.50
23	Chico Cardenas	1.50
25	Julian Javier	1.50
26	Darrell Brandon	1.50
27	Gil Hodges	7.00
28	Ted Uhlaender	1.50
29	Joe Verbanic	1.50
30	Joe Torre	3.00
31	Ed Stroud	1.50
32	Joe Gibbon	1.50
33	Pete Ward	1.50
35	Steve Hargan	1.50
36	Pirates Rookies (Bob Moose, *Bob Robertson*)	2.00
37	Billy Williams	12.00
38	Tony Pierce	1.50
39	Cookie Rojas	1.50
40	Denny McLain	10.00
41	Julio Gotay	1.50
42	Larry Haney	1.50
43	Gary Bell	1.50
45	Tom Seaver	200.00
46	Dave Ricketts	1.50
47	Ralph Houk	2.50
48	Ted Davidson	1.50
49	Ed Brinkman (yellow team letters)	50.00
49	Ed Brinkman (white team letters)	1.50
50	Willie Mays	80.00
51	Bob Locker	1.50
52	Hawk Taylor	1.50
53	Gene Alley	1.50
54	Stan Williams	1.50
55	Felipe Alou	1.75
56	Orioles Rookies (Dave Leonhard, Dave May)	1.50
57	Dan Schneider	1.50
58	Ed Mathews	12.00
59	Don Lock	1.50
60	Ken Holtzman	1.75
61	Reggie Smith	2.50
62	Chuck Dobson	1.50
65	John Roseboro	1.50
66	Casey Cox (yellow team letters)	50.00

80 Rod Carew

177 Mets Rookies

149	Bob Saverine	1.50
150	Bob Clemente	57.00
151	World Series Game 1 (Brock Socks 4 Hits in Opener)	6.00
152	World Series Game 2 (Yaz Smashes 2 Homers)	8.00
153	World Series Game 3 (Briles Cools Off Boston)	3.00
154	World Series Game 4 (Gibson Hurls Shutout!)	5.00
155	World Series Game 5 (Lonborg Wins Again!)	4.00
156	World Series Game 6 (Petrocelli Socks Two Homers)	4.00
157	World Series Game 7 (St. Louis Wins It!)	4.00
158	World Series Summary (The Cardinals Celebrate)	3.00
159	Don Kessinger	1.50
160	Earl Wilson	1.50
162	Cardinals Rookies (Hal Gilson, *Mike Torrez*)	2.00
163	Gene Brabender	1.50
165	Tony Oliva	4.00
166	Claude Raymond	1.50
167	Elston Howard	3.00
168	Dodgers Team	3.00
170	Jim Fregosi	2.00
175	Maury Wills	4.00
177	Mets Rookies (*Jerry Koosman, Nolan Ryan*)	1600.00
180	Curt Flood	2.00
190	• Bill White	2.00
192	Checklist 197-283 (Carl Yastrzemski)	4.00
195	Joe Pepitone	2.00
198	Roy Face	1.75
199	A's Rookies (Darrell Osteen, Roberto Rodriguez)	1.50
200	Orlando Cepeda	5.00
201	*Mike Marshall*	3.00
205	Juan Marichal	9.00
208	Willie Davis	1.50
210	Gary Peters	1.50
215	Jim Bunning	5.00
220	Harmon Killebrew	15.00
225	Richie Allen	4.50
228	Dodgers Rookies (*Jack Billingham,* Jim Fairey)	1.50
230	Pete Rose	45.00
233	George Scott	1.50
235	Ron Santo	3.50
236	Tug McGraw	3.00
237	Alvin Dark	1.50
240	Al Kaline	25.00
241	Felix Millan	1.50
247	Reds Rookies (*Johnny Bench,* Ron Tompkins)	250.00
250	Carl Yastrzemski	40.00

45 Tom Seaver

257	Phil Niekro	7.50
280	Mickey Mantle	250.00
290	Willie McCovey	12.00
300	Rusty Staub	3.00
310	Luis Aparicio	6.00
321	• Leo Durocher	3.00
330	Roger Maris	40.00
334	Orioles Team	3.00
350	Hoyt Wilhelm	7.00
351	Bob Barton	1.50
352	Jackie Hernandez	1.50
354	Pete Richert	1.50
355	Ernie Banks	25.00
356	Checklist 371-457 (Ken Holtzman)	4.00
357	Len Gabrielson	1.50
358	Mike Epstein	1.50
360	Willie Horton	1.50
361	Harmon Killebrew AS	8.00
362	Orlando Cepeda AS	3.00
363	Rod Carew AS	12.00
364	Joe Morgan AS	9.00
365	Brooks Robinson AS	9.00
366	Ron Santo AS	2.50
367	Jim Fregosi AS	2.00
368	Gene Alley AS	2.00
369	Carl Yastrzemski AS	10.00
370	Hank Aaron AS	15.00
371	Tony Oliva AS	3.00
372	Lou Brock AS	10.00
373	Frank Robinson AS	10.00
374	Bob Clemente AS	15.00
375	Bill Freehan AS	2.00
376	Tim McCarver AS	2.50
377	Joe Horlen AS	1.50
378	Bob Gibson AS	10.00
379	Gary Peters AS	1.50
380	Ken Holtzman AS	1.50
381	Boog Powell	3.00
382	Ramon Hernandez	1.50
383	Steve Whitaker	1.50
384	• Reds Rookies (Bill Henry, *Hal McRae*)	15.00
385	Jim Hunter	12.00
386	Greg Goossen	1.50
387	Joe Foy	1.50
388	Ray Washburn	1.50
389	• Jay Johnstone	1.50
390	Bill Mazeroski	3.00
391	Bob Priddy	1.50
392	Grady Hatton	1.50
393	Jim Perry	2.00
394	Tommie Aaron	1.50
395	Camilo Pascual	1.50
396	Bobby Wine	1.50
397	Vic Davalillo	1.50
400	Mike McCormick	1.50
401	Mets Team	6.00
402	Mike Hegan	1.75
403	John Buzhardt	1.50
404	Floyd Robinson	1.50
405	Tommy Helms	1.50
406	Dick Ellsworth	1.50
408	Steve Carlton	60.00
409	Orioles Rookies (Frank Peters, Ron Stone)	1.50
410	Ferguson Jenkins	20.00
412	Clay Carroll	1.50
413	Tommy McCraw	1.50
414	Mickey Lolich	4.50
415	Johnny Callison	1.75
416	Bill Rigney	1.50
417	Willie Crawford	1.50
419	Jack Hiatt	1.50
420	Cesar Tovar	1.50
421	Ron Taylor	1.50
422	Rene Lachemann	1.50

490 Super Stars

424	White Sox Team	**3.00**
425	Jim Maloney	**1.50**
426	Hank Allen	**1.50**
429	Tommie Sisk	**1.50**
430	Rico Petrocelli	**1.50**
431	Dooley Womack	**1.50**
432	Indians Rookies (Bill Davis, Jose Vidal)	**1.50**
433	Bob Rodgers	**1.50**
434	Ricardo Joseph	**1.50**
435	Ron Perranoski	**1.50**
436	Hal Lanier	**1.50**
437	Don Cardwell	**1.50**
438	Lee Thomas	**1.50**
440	Claude Osteen	**1.50**
441	Alex Johnson	**1.50**
444	Jack Fisher	**1.50**
445	Mike Shannon	**1.50**
446	Ron Kline	**1.50**
447	Tigers Rookies (George Korince, Fred Lasher)	**1.50**
449	Gene Oliver	**1.50**
450	Jim Kaat	**4.00**
451	Al Spangler	**1.50**
452	Jesus Alou	**1.50**
453	Sammy Ellis	**1.50**
454	Checklist 458-533 (Frank Robinson)	**7.00**
455	Rico Carty	**1.50**
456	John O'Donoghue	**1.50**
457	• Jim Lefevbre	**2.50**
458	Lew Krausse	**2.50**
460	Jim Lonborg	**2.75**
461	Chuck Hiller	**2.50**
463	Jimmie Schaffer	**2.50**
464	Don McMahon	**2.50**
465	Tommie Agee	**2.50**
467	Dick Howser	**2.00**
468	Larry Sherry	**2.50**
470	Bill Freehan	**4.50**
471	Orlando Pena	**2.50**
472	Walt Alston	**4.50**
473	Al Worthington	**2.50**
474	Paul Schaal	**2.50**
475	Joe Niekro	**4.50**
476	Woody Woodward	**2.50**
477	Phillies Team	**3.00**
478	Dave McNally	**2.50**
480	Manager's Dream (Chico Cardenas, Bob Clemente, Tony Oliva)	**40.00**
482	Jose Pagan	**2.50**
483	Darold Knowles	**2.50**
484	Phil Roof	**2.50**
485	Ken Berry	**2.50**
487	Lee May	**4.00**
488	Dick Tracewski	**2.50**
490	Super Stars (Harmon Killebrew, Willie Mays, Mickey Mantle)	**125.00**
491	Denny LeMaster	**2.50**
492	Jeff Torborg	**2.50**
494	Ray Sadecki	**2.50**
495	Leon Wagner	**2.50**
496	Steve Hamilton	**2.50**
497	Cards Team	**6.00**

280 Mickey Mantle

579	NL Rookies (*Larry Hisle, Mike Lum*) 5.00		**589**	Twins Rookies (Ron Clark, Moe Ogier) 3.00
580	Bob Bailey 3.00		**590**	Tommy Harper 3.25
581	Garry Roggenburk.......... 3.00		**591**	Dick Nen........................ 3.00
582	Jerry Grote 3.25		**592**	John Bateman 3.00
583	Gates Brown 3.25		**593**	Lee Stange..................... 3.00
584	Larry Shepard 3.00		**594**	Phil Linz 3.00
585	Wilbur Wood.................. 3.25		**595**	Phil Ortega 3.00
586	Jim Pagliaroni................ 3.00		**596**	Charlie Smith................. 3.00
587	Roger Repoz 3.00		**597**	Bill McCool 3.00
588	Dick Schofield 3.00		**598**	Jerry May 5.00

1969 TOPPS

Topps reached another record in terms of quantity with the release of its 664-card 1969 set. No team cards are included, however, and multi-player feature cards appear for the last time. Other subsets include league stat leaders, World Series cards, a *Sporting News* All-Star group, and rookie cards for Rollie Fingers, Reggie Jackson, and others. The 2½- by 3½-inch cards feature color photos on the front with the player name and position in a circle in the upper corner, printed in a variety of color combinations. Cards with white letters occur in the range of 440 through 511. They are scarce, expensive, and not included in the full set price. Card backs, now in a horizontal format, have black-and-pink printing on white cardboard, and feature lifetime stats, a brief bio, and a cartoon.

	NR MT
Complete set	**$2500.00**
Commons (1-218)	**1.50**
Commons (219-327)	**2.25**
Commons (328-512)	**1.50**
Commons (513-664)	**2.00**

1	AL Batting Ldrs (Danny Cater, Tony Oliva, Carl Yastrzemski)...... $11.00		**4**	NL RBI Ldrs (Willie McCovey, Ron Santo, Billy Williams) 4.00
2	NL Batting Ldrs (Felipe Alou, Matty Alou, Pete Rose) 7.00		**5**	AL HR Ldrs (Ken Harrelson, Willie Horton, Frank Howard) 3.00
3	AL RBI Ldrs (Ken Harrelson, Frank Howard, Jim Northrup) 3.00		**6**	NL HR Ldrs (Richie Allen, Ernie Banks, Willie McCovey) 3.50
			7	AL ERA Ldrs (Sam McDowell, Dave McNally, Luis Tiant) 3.00
			8	NL ERA Ldrs (Bobby Bolin, Bob Gibson, Bob Veale) 3.00

95 Johnny Bench

9	AL Pitching Ldrs (Denny McLain, Dave McNally, Mel Stottlemyre, Luis Tiant)	3.00
10	NL Pitching Ldrs (Bob Gibson, Fergie Jenkins, Juan Marichal)	6.00
11	AL SO Ldrs (Sam McDowell, Denny McLain, Luis Tiant)	3.00
12	NL SO Ldrs (Bob Gibson, Fergie Jenkins, Bill Singer)	4.00
13	Mickey Stanley	1.00
14	Al McBean	1.00
15	Boog Powell	3.00
16	Giants Rookies (Cesar Gutierrez, Rich Robertson)	1.00
17	Mike Marshall	1.50
18	Dick Schofield	1.00
19	Ken Suarez	1.00
20	Ernie Banks	20.00
21	Jose Santiago	1.00
22	Jesus Alou	1.00
23	Lew Krausse	1.00
24	Walt Alston	3.00
25	Roy White	1.50
26	Clay Carroll	1.00
28	Mike Ryan	1.00
29	Dave Morehead	1.00
30	Bob Allison	1.75
31	Mets Rookies (*Gary Gentry, Amos Otis*)	3.00
34	Gary Peters	1.00
35	Joe Morgan	12.00
36	Luke Walker	1.00
38	Zoilo Versalles	1.00
40	Mayo Smith	1.00
41	Bob Barton	1.00
42	Tommy Harper	2.00
43	Joe Niekro	2.00
44	Danny Cater	1.00
45	Maury Wills	3.00
46	Fritz Peterson	1.00
47	Paul Popovich (with helmet logo)	4.00
47	Paul Popovich (w/o helmet logo)	1.00
49	Royals Rookies (Steve Jones, Eliseo Rodriquez) ("Rodriquez" on front)	6.00
49	Royals Rookies (Steve Jones, Eliseo Rodriguez) ("Rodriguez" on front)	.40
50	Bob Clemente	50.00
51	Woody Fryman	1.00
54	Cisco Carlos	1.00
55	Jerry Grote	1.25
57	Checklist 1-109 (Denny McLain)	3.00
59	• Jay Johnstone	1.00
60	Nelson Briles	1.00
62	Chico Salmon	1.00
63	Jim Hickman	1.00
64	Bill Monbouquette	1.00
65	Willie Davis	1.75
66	Orioles Rookies (Mike Adamson, *Merv Rettenmund*)	2.00
69	Steve Hamilton	1.00
70	Tommy Helms	1.00

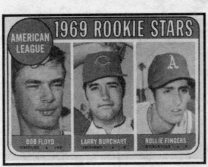

597 AL Rookies

71 Steve Whitaker **1.00**	**103** Roger Repoz **1.00**
73 Johnny Briggs **1.00**	**104** Steve Blass **1.00**
74 Preston Gomez **1.00**	**105** Rick Monday **1.00**
75 Luis Aparicio.................. **6.00**	**106** Jim Hannan **1.00**
76 Norm Miller.................... **1.00**	**107** Checklist 110-218 (Bob Gibson) (161 is Jim Purdin)............................ **4.00**
77 Ron Perranoski (with "LA" on cap) **5.00**	
77 Ron Perranoski (w/o "LA" on cap) **1.00**	**107** Checklist 110-218 (Bob Gibson) (161 is John Purdin)............................ **7.00**
79 Milt Pappas **1.00**	
80 Norm Cash **2.50**	**109** Jim Lonborg **1.75**
82 Pirates Rookies (*Rich Hebner, Al Oliver*)........ **12.00**	**110** Mike Shannon **1.00**
	111 Johnny Morris................ **1.00**
83 Mike Ferraro **1.00**	**112** J.C. Martin..................... **1.00**
85 Lou Brock **25.00**	**114** Yankees Rookies (Alan Closter, John Cumberland) **1.00**
86 Pete Richert **1.00**	
87 Horace Clarke **1.00**	
90 Jerry Koosman **5.00**	**118** Stan Williams **1.00**
91 Al Dark **1.00**	**119** Doug Rader................... **1.00**
92 Jack Billingham **1.00**	**120** Pete Rose **40.00**
94 Hank Aguirre **1.00**	**122** Ron Fairly..................... **1.00**
95 Johnny Bench **125.00**	**123** Wilbur Wood.................. **1.25**
97 Buddy Bradford **1.00**	**125** Ray Sadecki **1.00**
98 Dave Giusti.................... **1.00**	**127** Kevin Collins **1.00**
99 Twins Rookies (Danny Morris, *Craig Nettles*) (with black loop above "Twins") **25.00**	**128** Tommie Aaron............... **1.25**
	129 Bill McCool **1.00**
	130 Carl Yastrzemski **30.00**
	131 Chris Cannizzaro........... **1.00**
99 Twins Rookies (Danny Morris, *Craig Nettles*) (w/o black loop above "Twins") **15.00**	**132** Dave Baldwin **1.00**
	133 Johnny Callison............. **1.25**
	135 Tommy Davis **1.50**
100 Hank Aaron **75.00**	**136** Cards Rookies (Steve Huntz, Mike Torrez)....... **1.00**

260 Reggie Jackson

140	• Jim Lefevbre	1.00
142	Woody Woodward	1.00
144	Bob Hendley	1.00
145	Max Alvis	1.00
146	Jim Perry	1.50
147	• Leo Durocher	2.50
150	Denny McLain	5.00
151	Clay Dalrymple (Phillies)	7.00
151	Clay Dalrymple (Orioles)	1.00
153	Ed Brinkman	1.00
156	Astros Rookies (Hal Gilson, Leon McFadden)	1.00
157	Bob Rodgers	1.00
160	Vada Pinson	2.50
162	World Series Game 1 (Gibson Fans 17; Sets New Record)	5.00
163	World Series Game 2 (Tiger Homers Deck the Cards)	3.50
164	World Series Game 3 (McCarver's Homer Puts St. Louis Ahead)	5.00
165	World Series Game 4 (Brock's Leadoff Homer Starts Cards' Romp)	5.00
166	World Series Game 5 (Kaline's Key Hit Sparks Tigers Rally)	6.00
167	World Series Game 6 (Tiger 10-Run Inning Ties Mark)	3.50
168	World Series Game 7 (Lolich Series Hero, Outduels Gibson)	5.00
169	World Series Summary (Tigers Celebrate Their Victory)	3.50
170	Frank Howard	2.25
175	• Jim Bunning	4.00
190	Willie Mays	70.00
200	Bob Gibson	15.00
208	Donn Clendenon (Expos)	7.00
208	Donn Clendenon (Houston)	1.00
214	Checklist 219-327	3.00
216	Don Sutton	9.00
235	Jim Hunter	15.00
250	Frank Robinson	30.00
255	Steve Carlton	60.00
260	*Reggie Jackson*	750.00
270	Mickey Lolich	4.00
271	Larry Stahl	1.75
272	Ed Stroud	1.75
273	Ron Willis	1.75
274	Clyde King	1.75
275	Vic Davalillo	1.75
276	Gary Wagner	1.75
277	*Rod Hendricks*	1.75
278	Gary Geiger	1.75
279	Roger Nelson	1.75
280	Alex Johnson	1.75
281	Ted Kubiak	1.75
282	Pat Jarvis	1.75
283	Sandy Alomar	1.75
284	Expos Rookies (Jerry Robertson, Mike Wegener)	1.75
285	Don Mincher	3.00
286	*Dock Ellis*	3.50
287	Jose Tartabull	1.75
288	Ken Holtzman	3.00
289	Bart Shirley	1.75
290	Jim Kaat	4.50

295	Tony Perez	15.00
296	*Andy Messersmith*	4.00
297	Deron Johnson	1.75
298	Dave Nicholson	1.75
299	Mark Belanger	1.75
300	Felipe Alou	1.75
311	*Sparky Lyle*	15.00
320	Dal Maxvill	1.50
321	Jim McAndrew	1.50
322	Jose Vidal	1.50
325	Jose Cardenal	1.50
330	Tony Conigliaro	3.50
355	Phil Niekro	8.00
370	Juan Marichal	8.00
375	Harmon Killebrew	20.00
376	Royals Rookies (Mike Fiore, *Jim Rooker*)	3.00
377	Gary Bell	1.00
379	• Ken Boyer	3.50
380	Stan Bahnsen	1.75
381	Ed Kranepool	1.75
382	Pat Corrales	1.75
383	Casey Cox	1.00
385	Orlando Cepeda	3.50
388	Tom McCraw	1.00
390	Bill Freehan	1.00
393	Gene Brabender	1.00
394	• Pilots Rookies (Lou Piniella, Marv Staehle)	4.00
400	Don Drysdale	15.00
410	Al Kaline	20.00
411	Larry Dierker	1.00
412	Checklist 426-512 (Mickey Mantle)	7.00
413	Roland Sheldon	1.00
414	Duke Sims	1.00
416	Willie McCovey AS	6.50
417	Ken Harrelson AS	1.50
418	Tommy Helms AS	1.00
419	Rod Carew AS	10.00
420	Ron Santo AS	2.75
421	Brooks Robinson AS	7.00
422	Don Kessinger AS	2.00
423	Bert Campaneris AS	2.00
424	Pete Rose AS	13.00
425	Carl Yastrzemski AS	13.00
426	• Curt Flood AS	1.25
427	Tony Oliva AS	2.00
428	Lou Brock AS	7.00

500 Mickey Mantle

429	Willie Horton AS	2.00
430	Johnny Bench AS	14.00
431	Bill Freehan AS	2.00
432	Bob Gibson AS	5.00
433	Denny McLain AS	2.00
434	Jerry Koosman AS	1.50
435	Sam McDowell AS	1.50
436	Gene Alley	1.50
439	White Sox Rookies (Ed Herrmann, Dan Lazar)	1.00
440	Willie McCovey (last name in white)	100.00
440	Willie McCovey (last name in yellow)	20.00
441	Dennis Higgins (last name in white)	12.00
441	Dennis Higgins (last name in yellow)	1.00
444	Joe Moeller (last name in white)	12.00
444	Joe Moeller (last name in yellow)	1.00
446	Claude Raymond	1.00
447	Ralph Houk (last name in white)	15.00
447	Ralph Houk (last name in yellow)	1.50

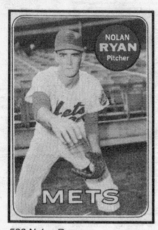

533 Nolan Ryan

448	Bob Tolan	**1.00**
450	Billy Williams	**7.00**
451	Rich Rollins (first name in white)	**18.00**
451	Rich Rollins (first name in yellow)	**1.00**
452	Al Ferrera (first name in white)	**18.00**
452	Al Ferrera (first name in yellow)	**1.00**
453	Mike Cuellar	**2.00**
454	Phillies Rookies (Larry Colton, *Don Money*) (names in white)	**18.00**
454	Phillies Rookies (Larry Colton, *Don Money*) (names in yellow)	**1.00**
456	Bud Harrelson	**2.00**
460	Joe Torre	**3.00**
461	Mike Epstein (last name in white)	**18.00**
461	Mike Epstein (last name in yellow)	**1.00**
462	Red Schoendienst	**3.00**
464	Dave Marshall (last name in white)	**18.00**
464	Dave Marshall (last name in yellow)	**1.00**
468	Pirates Rookies (Bruce Dal Canton, Bob Robertson) (names in white)	**18.00**
468	Pirates Rookies (Bruce Dal Canton, Bob Robertson) (names in yellow)	**1.00**
470	Mel Stottlemyre (last name in white)	**25.00**
470	Mel Stottlemyre (last name in yellow)	**2.00**
471	Ted Savage (last name in white)	**18.00**
471	Ted Savage (last name in yellow)	**1.00**
473	Jose Arcia (first name in white)	**18.00**
473	Jose Arcia (first name in yellow)	**1.00**
474	Tom Murphy	**1.00**
475	Tim McCarver	**2.50**
476	Red Sox Rookies (*Ken Brett,* Gerry Moses) (names in white)	**23.00**
476	Red Sox Rookies (*Ken Brett,* Gerry Moses) (names in yellow)	**2.00**
478	Don Buford	**1.00**
480	Tom Seaver	**135.00**
481	*Bill Melton*	**1.50**
482	Jim Gosger (first name in white)	**18.00**
482	Jim Gosger (first name in yellow)	**1.00**
483	Ted Abernathy	**1.00**
484	Joe Gordon	**1.00**
485	Gaylord Perry (last name in white)	**75.00**
485	Gaylord Perry (last name in yellow)	**10.00**
486	Paul Casanova (last name in white)	**18.00**
486	Paul Casanova (last name in yellow)	**1.00**
489	Clete Boyer	**1.50**

7 AL ERA Leaders

490	Matty Alou	**1.50**
491	Twins Rookies (Jerry Crider, George Mitterwald) (names in white)	**18.00**
491	Twins Rookies (Jerry Crider, George Mitterwald) (names in yellow)	**1.00**
492	Tony Cloninger	**1.00**
493	Wes Parker (last name in white)	**18.00**
493	Wes Parker (last name in yellow)	**1.50**
495	Bert Campaneris	**2.00**
497	Julian Javier	**1.00**
498	Juan Pizarro	**1.00**
500	Mickey Mantle (last name in white)	**700.00**
500	Mickey Mantle (last name in yellow)	**300.00**
501	Tony Gonzalez (first name in white)	**18.00**
501	Tony Gonzalez (first name in yellow)	**1.00**
504	Checklist 513-588 (Brooks Robinson)	**8.00**
505	Bobby Bolin (last name in white)	**18.00**
505	Bobby Bolin (last name in yellow)	**1.00**
506	Paul Blair	**1.00**
507	Cookie Rojas	**1.00**
508	Moe Drabowsky	**1.00**
509	Manny Sanguillen	**1.00**
510	Rod Carew	**75.00**
511	Diego Segui (first name in white)	**18.00**
511	Diego Segui (first name in yellow)	**1.00**
512	Cleon Jones	**1.00**
513	Camilo Pascual	**1.50**
514	Mike Lum	**1.50**
515	Dick Green	**1.50**
516	Earl Weaver	**12.00**
517	Mike McCormick	**1.00**
518	Fred Whitfield	**1.00**
519	Yankees Rookies (Len Boehmer, Gerry Kenney)	**1.50**
520	Bob Veale	**1.00**
521	George Thomas	**1.00**
523	Bob Chance	**1.00**
524	Expos Rookies (Jose Laboy, Floyd Wicker)	**1.50**
525	Earl Wilson	**1.50**
526	Hector Torres	**1.50**
527	Al Lopez	**3.00**
528	Claude Osteen	**1.75**
529	Ed Kirkpatrick	**1.75**
530	Cesar Tovar	**1.75**
531	Dick Farrell	**1.75**
532	Bird Hill Aces (Mike Cuellar, Jim Hardin, Dave McNally, Tom Phoebus)	**2.00**
533	Nolan Ryan	**600.00**
534	Jerry McNertney	**1.50**
535	Phil Regan	**1.50**

480 Tom Seaver

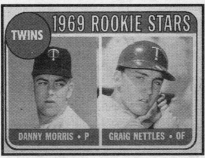

99 Twins Rookies

594	Dooley Womack	1.50
595	Lee Maye	1.50
596	Chuck Hartenstein	1.50
597	AL Rookies (Larry Burchart, *Rollie Fingers,* Bob Floyd)	135.00
598	Ruben Amaro	1.50
599	John Boozer	1.50
600	Tony Oliva	6.00
601	Tug McGraw	4.00
602	Cubs Rookies (Alec Distaso, Jim Qualls, Don Young)	1.50
603	Joe Keough	1.50
604	Bobby Etheridge	1.50
605	Dick Ellsworth	1.50
606	Gene Mauch	1.50
607	Dick Bosman	1.50
608	Dick Simpson	1.50
609	Phil Gagliano	1.50
610	Jim Hardin	1.50
611	Braves Rookies (Bob Didier, Walt Hriniak, Gary Neibauer)	3.00
612	Jack Aker	1.50
613	Jim Beauchamp	1.50
614	Astros Rookies (Tom Griffin, Skip Guinn)	1.50
615	Len Gabrielson	1.50
616	Don McMahon	1.50
617	Jesse Gonder	1.50
618	Ramon Webster	1.50
619	Royals Rookies (Bill Butler, *Pat Kelly,* Juan Rios)	1.50
620	Dean Chance	1.50
621	Bill Voss	1.50
622	Dan Osinski	1.50
623	Hank Allen	1.50
624	NL Rookies (Darrel Chaney, Duffy Dyer, Terry Harmon)	1.50
625	Mack Jones	1.50
626	Gene Michael	1.50
627	George Stone	1.50
628	Red Sox Rookies (*Bill Conigliaro,* Syd O'Brien, Fred Wenz)	3.00
630	*Bobby Bonds*	40.00
631	John Kennedy	1.50
632	Jon Warden	1.50
633	Harry Walker	1.50
634	Andy Etchebarren	1.50
635	George Culver	1.50
636	Woodie Held	1.50
637	Padres Rookies (Jerry DaVanon, *Clay Kirby,* Frank Reberger)	1.50
638	Ed Sprague	1.50
639	Barry Moore	1.50
640	Fergie Jenkins	25.00
641	NL Rookies (Bobby Darwin, Tommy Dean, John Miller)	2.00

642	John Hiller	1.50	654	White Sox Rookies (*Carlos May,* Rich Morales, Don Secrist) 4.00
643	Billy Cowan	1.50		
644	Chuck Hinton	1.50		
645	George Brunet	1.50	657	Bobby Murcer 5.00
646	Expos Rookies (Dan McGinn, *Carl Morton*) 1.50		658	AL Rookies (Bill Burbach, Tom Hall, Jim Miles) 1.50
647	Dave Wickersham	1.50	659	Johnny Podres 3.00
648	Bobby Wine	1.50	660	Reggie Smith 4.00
649	Al Jackson	1.50	662	Royals Rookies (Dick Drago, Bob Oliver, George Spriggs) 2.00
650	• Ted Williams	12.00		
651	Gus Gil	1.50		
652	Eddie Watt	1.50	663	Dick Radatz 2.00
653	• *Aurelio Rodriguez* (photo is team batboy Leonard Garcia) 3.00		664	Ron Hunt 4.00

1970 TOPPS

Team cards returned in 1970 with Topps' largest set to date of 720 cards. Card number 1 features a team photo of the new World Champion Mets, who make additional appearances in subsets highlighting the World Series and the first League Championship Series. Statistical leaders are grouped together, as are All-Star cards, which would not appear again until 1982. Backs of the 2½- by 3½-inch cards feature blue-and-yellow printing on white cardboard with yearly stats, brief bios, and a cartoon. Fronts show crisp color photos with team names in the upper corners and player names in script in the lower gray border. This set is a popular starting point for the modern collector.

	NR MT
Complete set	$2200.00
Commons (1-459)	.75
Commons (460-548)	1.50
Commons (547-633)	3.00
Commons (634-720)	6.00

1	World Champions (Mets Team)	$12.00
2	Diego Segui	.75
3	Darrel Chaney	.75
4	Tom Egan	.75
5	Wes Parker	.75
6	Grant Jackson	.75
7	Indians Rookies (Gary Boyd, Russ Nagelson)	.75
9	Checklist 1-132	3.00
10	Carl Yastrzemski	25.00
11	Nate Colbert	.75
12	John Hiller	.75
13	Jack Hiatt	.75
14	Hank Allen	.75
15	Larry Dierker	.75
17	Hoyt Wilhelm	5.00
21	Athletics Rookies (*Vida Blue, Gene Tenace*)	8.00
22	Ray Washburn	.75
23	Bill Robinson	.75
24	Dick Selma	.75
25	Cesar Tovar	.75

26 Tug McGraw.................. 1.50
29 Sandy Alomar.................. .75
30 Matty Alou 1.00
31 Marty Pattin .... .75
32 Harry Walker .... .75
33 Don Wert .... .75
34 Willie Crawford .... .75
36 Reds Rookies (Danny
   Breeden, *Bernie Carbo*).. .75
40 Rich Allen 2.00
45 Dave Johnson 1.50
50 Tommie Agee.................. .75
53 John Kennedy .... .75
54 Jeff Torborg................... .75
55 John Odom...................... .75
56 Phillies Rookies (Joe Lis,
   Scott Reid) .... .75
57 Pat Kelly .... .75
59 Dick Ellsworth................ .75
60 • Jim Wynn...................... .75
61 NL Batting Ldrs
   (Bob Clemente,
   Cleon Jones,
   Pete Rose) 6.00
62 AL Batting Ldrs
   (Rod Carew, Tony Oliva,
   Reggie Smith) 3.00
63 NL RBI Ldrs
   (Willie McCovey,
   Tony Perez,
   Ron Santo) 3.00
64 AL RBI Ldrs
   (Reggie Jackson,
   Harmon Killebrew,
   Boog Powell) 3.50
65 NL HR Ldrs (Hank Aaron,
   Lee May, Willie
   McCovey) 3.50
66 AL HR Ldrs
   (Frank Howard,
   Reggie Jackson, Harmon
   Killebrew) 3.50
67 NL ERA Ldrs
   (Steve Carlton,
   Bob Gibson, Juan
   Marichal) 3.50
68 AL ERA Ldrs (Dick
   Bosman, Mike Cuellar,
   Jim Palmer) 2.00

660 Johnny Bench

69 NL Pitching Ldrs
   (Fergie Jenkins,
   Juan Marichal, Phil Niekro,
   Tom Seaver) 4.50
70 AL Pitching Ldrs (Dave
   Boswell, Mike Cuellar,
   Dennis McLain, Dave
   McNally, Jim Perry,
   Mel Stottlemyre) 2.50
71 NL SO Ldrs (Bob Gibson,
   Fergie Jenkins, Bill
   Singer)........................... 3.00
72 AL SO Ldrs (Mickey Lolich,
   Sam McDowell, Andy
   Messersmith)................. 2.00
73 Wayne Granger............... .75
74 Angels Rookies
   (Greg Washburn,
   Wally Wolf) .... .75
75 Jim Kaat 2.50
80 Don Kessinger................. .75
82 Frank Fernandez............. .75
88 Pilots Rookies (Dick Baney,
   Miguel Fuentes) .... .75
90 Tim McCarver................. 1.50
94 Fred Patek....................... .75
96 Cards Rookies (Leron Lee,
   Jerry Reuss) 3.00

502 Rollie Fingers

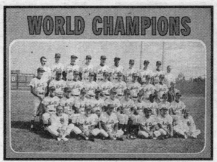

1 World Champions (Mets Team)

300 Tom Seaver

366	Barry Moore	.75
367	Mike Lum	.75
368	Ed Herrmann	.75
370	Tommy Harper	.75
373	Roy White	1.00
375	Johnny Callison	.90
380	Tony Perez	9.00
387	Orioles Team	1.50
394	Gil Hodges	4.00
403	Jim Bunning	3.25
407	Bob Watson	.75
409	Bob Tolan	.75
410	Boog Powell	3.00
411	Dodgers Team	1.50
416	Joe Verbanic	.75
418	John Donaldson	.75
420	Ken McMullen	.75
421	Pat Dobson	.75
422	Royals Team	1.25
427	Fred Norman	.75
430	Andy Messersmith	1.00
449	Jim Palmer	25.00
450	Willie McCovey AS	3.50
451	• Boog Powell AS	1.00
453	Rod Carew AS	6.00
454	Ron Santo AS	1.00
455	Brooks Robinson AS	4.50
458	Pete Rose AS	12.00
459	Reggie Jackson AS	25.00
460	Matty Alou AS	.75
461	Carl Yastrzemski AS	8.00
462	Hank Aaron AS	15.00
463	Frank Robinson AS	7.00
464	Johnny Bench AS	13.00
466	Juan Marichal AS	3.00
467	Denny McLain AS	.80
468	Jerry Koosman AS	.60
469	Sam McDowell AS	.60
470	Willie Stargell	10.00
471	Chris Zachary	1.50
472	Braves Team	1.25
473	Don Bryant	1.50
474	Dick Kelley	1.50
475	Dick McAuliffe	1.50
477	Orioles Rookies (Roger Freed, Al Severinsen)	1.50
479	Dick Woodson	1.50
480	Glenn Beckert	1.50
481	Jose Tartabull	1.50

600 Willie Mays

482	Tom Hilgendorf	1.50
485	• Jay Johnstone	1.50
486	Terry Harmon	1.50
487	Cisco Carlos	1.50
488	J.C. Martin	1.50
489	Eddie Kasko	1.50
490	Bill Singer	1.50
491	Graig Nettles	6.00
492	Astros Rookies (Keith Lampard, Scipio Spinks)	1.50
493	Lindy McDaniel	1.50
495	Dave Morehead	1.50
498	Al Weis	1.50
499	Skip Lockwood	1.50
500	Hank Aaron	60.00
501	White Sox Team	3.00
502	Rollie Fingers	40.00
503	Dal Maxvill	1.50
504	Don Pavletich	1.50
505	Ken Holtzman	1.50
507	Pat Corrales	1.50
508	Joe Niekro	1.50
509	Expos Team	3.00
510	• Tony Oliva	3.00
511	Joe Hoerner	1.50
513	Preston Gomez	1.50
514	Steve Hovley	1.50

140 Reggie Jackson

516	Yankees Rookies (John Ellis, Jim Lyttle)	1.50
522	Angels Team	3.00
530	Bob Gibson	15.00
534	Twins Team	5.00
537	Joe Morgan	14.00
539	● Phillies Rookies (*Larry Bowa*, Dennis Doyle)	4.00
542	Checklist 547-633	5.00
544	Reds Team	3.00
545	Ken Harrelson	1.75
546	Ron Reed	1.50
547	Rick Monday	3.00
548	Howie Reed	2.50
549	Cardinals Team	2.50
550	Frank Howard	5.00
551	Dock Ellis	2.50
552	Royals Rookies (Don O'Riley, Dennis Paepke, Fred Rico)	2.50
553	● Jim Lefebvre	2.50
560	Gaylord Perry	14.00
565	Jim Hunter	14.00
580	Pete Rose	75.00
590	Mike Cuellar	2.50
593	Cubs Team	6.00
595	Maury Wills	4.00

600	Willie Mays	**75.00**
601	Pete Richert	2.50
602	Ted Savage	2.50
603	Ray Oyler	2.50
604	Clarence Gaston	2.50
605	Rick Wise	2.50
606	Chico Ruiz	2.50
607	Gary Waslewski	2.50
608	Pirates Team	6.00
609	*Buck Martinez*	4.00
610	Jerry Koosman	4.00
611	Norm Cash	4.50
616	Jim Merritt	2.50
617	Jim French	2.50
618	Billy Wynne	2.50
619	Norm Miller	2.50
620	Jim Perry	4.00
621	Braves Rookies (*Darrell Evans*, Rick Kester, Mike McQueen)	20.00
622	Don Sutton	15.00
623	Horace Clarke	2.50
630	Ernie Banks	40.00
631	Athletics Team	6.00
633	Roger Nelson	3.00
634	Bud Harrelson	5.00
635	Bob Allison	5.00
636	Jim Stewart	4.50
637	Indians Team	12.00
638	Frank Bertaina	4.50
639	Dave Campbell	4.50
640	Al Kaline	50.00
641	Al McBean	4.50
642	Angels Rookies (Greg Garrett, Gordon Lund, Jarvis Tatum)	4.50
643	Jose Pagan	4.50
644	Gerry Nyman	4.50
645	Don Money	4.50
646	Jim Britton	4.50
647	Tom Matchick	4.50
648	Larry Haney	4.50
649	Jimmie Hall	4.50
650	Sam McDowell	7.00
651	Jim Gosger	4.50
652	Rich Rollins	4.50
653	Moe Drabowsky	4.50

654 NL Rookies (Boots Day, *Oscar Gamble*, Angel Mangual) 8.00
655 John Roseboro 4.50
656 Jim Hardin 4.50
657 Padres Team 12.00
658 Ken Tatum 4.50
659 Pete Ward 4.50
660 Johnny Bench 150.00
661 Jerry Robertson 4.50
662 Frank Lucchesi 4.50
663 Tito Francona 4.50
664 Bob Robertson 4.50
665 Jim Lonborg 6.50
666 Adolfo Phillips 4.50
667 Bob Meyer 4.50
668 Bob Tillman 4.50
669 White Sox Rookies (Bart Johnson, Dan Lazar, Mickey Scott) 4.50
670 Ron Santo 8.00
671 Jim Campanis 4.50
672 Leon McFadden 4.50
673 Ted Uhlaender 4.50
674 Dave Leonhard 4.50
675 Jose Cardenal 6.00
676 Senators Team 12.00
677 Woodie Fryman 5.00
678 Dave Duncan 4.50
679 Ray Sadecki 4.50
680 Rico Petrocelli 5.00
681 Bob Garibaldi 4.50
682 Dalton Jones 4.50
683 Reds Rookies (Vern Geishert, Hal McRae, Wayne Simpson) 9.00
684 Jack Fisher 4.50
685 Tom Haller 6.50
686 Jackie Hernandez 4.50
687 Bob Priddy 4.50
688 Ted Kubiak 4.50
689 Frank Tepedino 4.50
690 Ron Fairly 4.75
691 Joe Grzenda 4.50
692 Duffy Dyer 4.50
693 Bob Johnson 4.50
694 Gary Ross 4.50
695 Bobby Knoop 4.50

580 Pete Rose

696 Giants Team 12.00
697 Jim Hannan 4.50
698 Tom Tresh 6.00
699 Hank Aguirre 4.50
700 Frank Robinson 48.00
701 Jack Billingham 4.50
702 AL Rookies (Bob Johnson, Ron Klimkowski, Bill Zepp) 4.50
703 Lou Marone 4.50
705 Tony Cloninger 4.50
706 John McNamara 4.50
707 Kevin Collins 4.50
708 Jose Santiago 4.50
709 Mike Fiore 4.50
710 Felix Millan 4.50
711 Ed Brinkman 4.50
712 Nolan Ryan 600.00
713 Pilots Team 25.00
714 Al Spangler 4.50
715 Mickey Lolich 7.50
716 Cards Rookies (Sam Campisi, *Reggie Cleveland*, Santiago Guzman) 4.50
719 Jim Roland 4.50
720 Rick Reichardt 7.00

1971 TOPPS

Although Topps' 752-card set for 1971 makes a strong artistic statement, the black borders have proven difficult for collectors to maintain in mint condition. On the front, the team name appears in bold print across the top of the 2½- by 3½-inch cards, with the player name and position in smaller print just below. Facsimile autographs are superimposed at the bottom. Gray card backs with green-and-black printing were the first to feature player photos in a black-and-white inset. Brief player bios are rounded out with lifetime and 1970 stats, first pro and major league games, and abbreviated personal facts. Subsets include statistical leaders; league playoffs; World Series; and rookies such as Dave Concepcion, Steve Garvey, and Ted Simmons.

	NR MT
Complete set	**$2250.00**
Commons (1-523)	**1.00**
Commons (524-643)	**4.00**
Commons (644-752)	**6.00**

55 Steve Carlton

1	World Champions (Orioles Team) $12.00
2	Dock Ellis 1.00
5	Thurman Munson 40.00
9	George Scott 1.00
10	Claude Osteen 1.00
11	*Elliott Maddox*............... 1.00
12	Johnny Callison 1.00
13	White Sox Rookies (Charlie Brinkman, Dick Moloney) 1.00
14	*Dave Concepcion*........ 25.00
16	*Ken Singleton* 3.00
20	Reggie Jackson......... 150.00
26	*Bert Blyleven* 40.00
27	Pirates Rookies (Fred Cambria, Gene Clines) 1.00
30	Phil Niekro 5.00
35	Lou Piniella.................... 2.00
36	Dean Chance 1.00
38	*Jim Colborn*.................... 1.00
39	Tigers Rookies (Gene Lamont, *Lerrin LaGrow*) 1.00
45	Jim Hunter..................... 7.00
50	Willie McCovey............ 10.00
52	Braves Rookies (Oscar Brown, *Earl Williams*) 1.00
54	Checklist 1-132 .... 4.00
55	Steve Carlton 30.00
59	Gene Mauch.................. 1.00
61	AL Batting Ldrs (Alex Johnson, Tony Oliva, Carl Yastrzemski) 3.50
62	NL Batting Ldrs (Rico Carty, Manny Sanguillen, Joe Torre)...................... 2.50

63 AL RBI Ldrs
(Tony Conigliaro,
Frank Howard,
Boog Powell) **2.50**

64 NL RBI Ldrs
(Johnny Bench,
Tony Perez, Billy
Williams) **3.50**

65 AL HR Ldrs
(Frank Howard,
Harmon Killebrew, Carl
Yastrzemski) **3.50**

66 NL HR Ldrs
(Johnny Bench,
Tony Perez,
Billy Williams) **3.50**

67 AL ERA Ldrs
(Jim Palmer, Diego
Segui, Clyde Wright) **2.50**

68 NL ERA Ldrs
(Tom Seaver,
Wayne Simpson, Luke
Walker) **2.50**

69 AL Pitching Ldrs
(Mike Cuellar,
Dave McNally,
Jim Perry) **2.50**

70 NL Pitching Ldrs
(Bob Gibson,
Fergie Jenkins,
Gaylord Perry) **4.00**

71 AL SO Ldrs
(Bob Johnson,
Mickey Lolich, Sam
McDowell) **2.00**

72 NL SO Ldrs
(Bob Gibson,
Fergie Jenkins, Tom
Seaver) **4.50**

74 Twins Rookies
(Pete Hamm,
Jim Nettles) **1.00**

83 Mets Rookies
(Randy Bobb,
Tim Foli) **1.25**

91 Bob Lemon **2.00**

93 Senators Rookies (Norm
McRae, Denny
Riddleberger) **1.00**

600 Willie Mays

95 Luis Tiant **1.50**
100 Pete Rose **45.00**
102 Astros Rookies
(*Ken Forsch,*
Larry Howard) **1.00**
105 Tony Conigliaro **1.50**
110 Bill Mazeroski **1.50**
111 Yankees Rookies
(Loyd Colson,
Bobby Mitchell) **1.00**
112 Manny Mota **1.00**
117 *Ted Simmons* **25.00**
120 Willie Horton **1.00**
123 Checklist 133-263
(Card number on right) .. **3.00**
123 Checklist 133-263 (Card
number centered) **4.00**
124 *Don Gullett* **1.25**
133 Mickey Lolich **1.75**
135 Rick Monday **1.00**
138 Phillies Rookies
(Joe Lis,
Willie Montanez) **1.00**
140 Gaylord Perry **8.00**
146 Ralph Houk **1.00**
148 John Mayberry **1.00**
150 Sam McDowell **1.00**
151 Tommy Davis **1.00**

630 Roberto Clemente

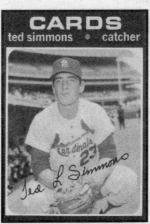

117 Ted Simmons

341 Steve Garvey

371	Jack Hiatt	1.00
372	Lew Krausse	1.00
374	Clete Boyer	1.00
375	Steve Hargan	1.00
378	Tito Fuentes	1.00
380	Ted Williams	7.00
381	Fred Gladding	1.00
382	Jake Gibbs	1.00
384	Rollie Fingers	15.00
385	Maury Wills	2.50
386	Red Sox Team	3.00
388	Al Oliver	2.50
389	Ed Brinkman	1.00
390	Glenn Beckert	1.00
393	Merv Rettenmund	1.00
394	Clay Carroll	1.00
395	Roy White	1.00
397	Alvin Dark	1.00
399	Jim French	1.00
400	Hank Aaron	60.00
401	Tom Murphy	1.00
402	Dodgers Team	3.50
403	Joe Coleman	1.00
405	Leo Cardenas	1.00
406	Ray Sadecki	1.00
407	Joe Rudi	1.00
409	Don Pavletich	1.00
410	Ken Holtzman	1.00

412	Jerry Johnson	1.00
413	Pat Kelly	1.00
414	Woodie Fryman	1.00
415	Mike Hegan	1.00
417	Dick Hall	1.00
418	Adolfo Phillips	1.00
419	Ron Hansen	1.00
420	Jim Merritt	1.00
421	John Stephenson	1.00
422	Frank Bertaina	1.00
425	Doug Rader	1.00
426	Chris Cannizzaro	1.00
427	Bernie Allen	1.00
429	Chuck Hinton	1.00
430	Wes Parker	1.00
431	Tom Burgmeier	1.00
433	Skip Lockwood	1.00
434	Gary Sutherland	1.00
435	Jose Cardenal	1.00
436	Wilbur Wood	1.00
437	Danny Murtaugh	1.00
438	Mike McCormick	1.00
439	Phillies Rookies (*Greg Luzinski,* Scott Reid)	4.00
440	Bert Campaneris	1.00
441	Milt Pappas	1.00
442	Angels Team	4.00
447	*Cesar Geronimo*	1.00
448	Dave Roberts	1.00
449	Brant Alyea	1.00
450	Bob Gibson	15.00
452	John Boccabella	1.00
453	Terry Crowley	1.00
455	Don Kessinger	1.00
456	Bob Meyer	1.00
459	• Jim Lefebvre	1.00
460	Fritz Peterson	1.00
461	Jim Hart	1.00
462	Senators Team	1.75
464	Aurelio Rodriguez	1.00
465	Tim McCarver	1.50
466	Ken Berry	1.00
467	Al Santorini	1.00
469	Bob Aspromonte	1.00
470	Bob Oliver	1.00
471	Tom Griffin	1.00
472	Ken Rudolph	1.00
475	Ron Perranoski	1.00
476	Dal Maxvill	1.00

477	Earl Weaver	3.00
478	Bernie Carbo	1.00
480	Manny Sanguillen	1.00
481	Daryl Patterson	1.00
482	Padres Team	3.50
483	Gene Michael	1.00
485	Ken McMullen	1.00
488	Jerry Stephenson	1.00
489	Luis Alvarado	1.00
492	Ken Boswell	1.00
493	Dave May	1.00
494	Braves Rookies (Ralph Garr, Rick Kester)	2.25
495	Felipe Alou	1.25
496	Woody Woodward	1.00
499	Checklist 524-643	4.00
500	Jim Perry	1.00
501	Andy Etchebarren	1.00
502	Cubs Team	3.75
503	Gates Brown	1.00
504	Ken Wright	1.00
505	Ollie Brown	1.00
507	George Stone	1.00
508	Roger Repoz	1.00
509	Jim Grant	1.00
510	Ken Harrelson	1.50
511	Chris Short	1.00
512	Red Sox Rookies (Mike Garman, Dick Mills)	1.00
513	Nolan Ryan	275.00
514	Ron Woods	1.00
515	Carl Morton	1.00
516	Ted Kubiak	1.00
517	Charlie Fox	1.00
518	Joe Grzenda	1.00
519	Willie Crawford	1.00
520	Tommy John	5.00
521	Leron Lee	1.00
522	Twins Team	4.00
523	John Odom	1.00
524	Mickey Stanley	3.00
525	Ernie Banks	50.00
526	Ray Jarvis	3.00
527	Cleon Jones	3.00
528	Wally Bunker	3.00
529	NL Rookies (Bill Buckner, Enzo Hernandez, Marty Perez)	6.00

530 Carl Yastrzemski

530	Carl Yastrzemski	45.00
531	Mike Torrez	3.00
532	Bill Rigney	3.00
533	Mike Ryan	3.00
534	Luke Walker	3.00
535	Curt Flood	5.00
536	Claude Raymond	3.00
537	Tom Egan	3.00
538	Angel Bravo	3.00
539	Larry Brown	3.00
540	Larry Dierker	3.00
541	Bob Burda	3.00
542	Bob Miller	3.00
543	Yankees Team	6.00
544	Vida Blue	6.00
545	Dick Dietz	3.00
546	John Matias	3.00
547	Pat Dobson	3.00
548	Don Mason	3.00
549	Jim Brewer	3.00
550	Harmon Killebrew	20.00
551	Frank Linzy	3.00
552	Buddy Bradford	3.00
553	Kevin Collins	3.00
554	Lowell Palmer	3.00
555	Walt Williams	3.00
556	Jim McGlothlin	3.00
557	Tom Satriano	3.00

20 Reggie Jackson

558 Hector Torres 3.00
559 AL Rookies
(Terry Cox,
Bill Gogolewski, Gary
Jones) 3.00
560 Rusty Staub 6.00
561 Syd O'Brien 3.00
562 Dave Giusti 3.00
563 Giants Team 8.00
564 Al Fitzmorris 3.00
565 Jim Wynn 4.50
566 Tim Cullen 3.00
567 Walt Alston 6.00
568 Sal Campisi 3.00
569 Ivan Murrell 3.00
570 Jim Palmer 40.00
571 Ted Sizemore 3.00
572 Jerry Kenney 3.00
573 Ed Kranepool 3.00
574 Jim Bunning 6.00
575 Bill Freehan 3.00
576 Cubs Rookies
(Brock Davis,
Adrian Garrett,
Garry Jestadt) 3.00
577 Jim Lonborg 3.00
578 Ron Hunt 3.00
579 Marty Pattin 3.00

580 Tony Perez 15.00
581 Roger Nelson 3.00
582 Dave Cash 3.00
583 Ron Cook 3.00
584 Indians Team 8.00
585 Willie Davis 5.00
586 Dick Woodson 3.00
587 Sonny Jackson 3.00
588 Tom Bradley 3.00
589 Bob Barton 3.00
590 Alex Johnson 3.00
591 Jackie Brown 3.00
592 Randy Hundley 3.00
593 Jack Aker 3.00
594 Cards Rookies
(Bob Chlupsa,
Al Hrabosky,
Bob Stinson) 6.00
595 Dave Johnson 5.00
596 Mike Jorgensen 3.00
597 Ken Suarez 3.00
598 Rick Wise 3.00
599 Norm Cash 6.00
600 Willie Mays 100.00
601 Ken Tatum 3.00
602 Mary Martinez 3.00
603 Pirates Team 8.00
604 John Gelnor 3.00
605 Orlando Cepeda 6.00
606 Chuck Taylor 3.00
607 Paul Ratliff 3.00
608 Mike Wegener 3.00
609 • Leo Durocher 6.00
610 Amos Otis 3.00
611 Tom Phoebus 3.00
612 Indians Rookies
(Lou Camilli,
Ted Ford, Steve
Mingori) 3.00
613 Pedro Borbon 3.00
614 Billy Cowan 3.00
615 Mel Stottlemyre 6.00
616 Larry Hisle 4.50
617 Clay Dalrymple 3.00
618 Tug McGraw 4.50
619 Checklist 644-752 .... 4.50
620 Frank Howard................. 4.00
621 Ron Bryant 3.00
622 Joe Lahoud 3.00

623	Pat Jarvis	3.00
624	Athletics Team	8.00
625	Lou Brock	30.00
626	Freddie Patek	3.00
627	Steve Hamilton	3.00
628	John Bateman	3.00
629	John Hiller	3.00
630	Roberto Clemente	70.00
631	Eddie Fisher	3.00
632	Darrel Chaney	3.00
633	AL Rookies (Bobby Brooks, Pete Koegel, Scott Northey)	3.00
634	Phil Regan	3.00
635	Bobby Murcer	6.00
636	Denny Lemaster	3.00
637	Dave Bristol	3.00
638	Stan Williams	3.00
639	Tom Haller	3.00
640	Frank Robinson	40.00
641	Mets Team	8.00
642	Jim Roland	3.00
643	Rick Reichardt	3.00
644	Jim Stewart	7.00
645	Jim Maloney	7.00
646	Bobby Floyd	7.00
647	Juan Pizarro	7.00
648	Mets Rookies (Rich Folkers, Ted Martinez, *Jon Matlack*)	12.00
649	Sparky Lyle	12.00
650	Rich Allen	25.00
651	Jerry Robertson	7.00
652	Braves Team	12.00
653	Russ Snyder	7.00
654	Don Shaw	7.00
655	Mike Epstein	7.00
656	Gerry Nyman	7.00
657	Jose Azcue	7.00
658	Paul Lindblad	7.00
659	Byron Browne	7.00
660	Ray Culp	7.00
661	Chuck Tanner	7.50
662	Mike Hedlund	7.00
663	Marv Staehle	7.00
664	Rookie Star Pitchers (Archie Reynolds, Bob Reynolds, Ken Reynolds)	7.00

513 Nolan Ryan

665	Ron Swoboda	7.00
666	Gene Brabender	7.00
667	Pete Ward	7.00
668	Gary Neibauer	7.00
669	Ike Brown	7.00
670	Bill Hands	7.00
671	Bill Voss	7.00
672	Ed Crosby	7.00
673	Gerry Janeski	7.00
674	Expos Team	12.00
675	Dave Boswell	7.00
676	Tommie Reynolds	7.00
677	Jack DiLauro	7.00
678	George Thomas	7.00
679	Dan O'Riley	7.00
680	Don Mincher	7.00
681	Bill Butler	7.00
682	Terry Harmon	7.00
683	Bill Burbach	7.00
684	Curt Motton	7.00
685	Moe Drabowsky	7.00
686	Chico Ruiz	7.00
687	Ron Taylor	7.00
688	• Sparky Anderson	25.00
689	Frank Baker	7.00
690	Bob Moose	7.00
691	Bob Heise	7.00

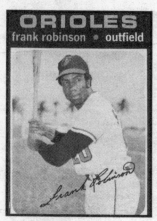

640 Frank Robinson

692	AL Rookies (Hal Haydel, Rogelio Moret, Wayne Twitchell)	7.00
693	Jose Pena	7.00
694	Rick Renick	7.00
695	Joe Niekro	7.00
696	Jerry Morales	7.00
697	Rickey Clark	7.00
698	Brewers Team	7.00
699	Jim Britton	7.00
700	Boog Powell	20.00
701	Bob Garibaldi	7.00
702	Milt Ramirez	7.00
703	Mike Kekich	7.00
704	J.C. Martin	7.00
705	Dick Selma	7.00
706	Joe Foy	7.00
707	Fred Lasher	7.00
708	Russ Nagelson	7.00
709	Rookie Star Outfielders (*Dusty Baker, Tom Paciorek, Don Baylor*)	75.00
710	Sonny Siebert	7.00
711	Larry Stahl	7.00
712	Jose Martinez	7.00
713	Mike Marshall	7.00
714	Dick Williams	7.00
715	Horace Clarke	7.00
716	Dave Leonhard	7.00
717	Tommie Aaron	7.00
718	Billy Wynne	7.00
719	Jerry May	7.00
720	Matty Alou	7.50
721	John Morris	7.00
722	Astros Team	12.00
723	Vicente Romo	7.00
724	Tom Tischinski	7.00
725	Gary Gentry	7.00
726	Paul Popovich	7.00
727	Ray Lamb	7.00
728	NL Rookies (Keith Lampard, Wayne Redmond, Bernie Williams)	7.00
729	Dick Billings	7.00
730	Jim Rooker	7.00
731	Jim Qualls	7.00
732	Bob Reed	7.00
733	Lee Maye	7.00
734	Rob Gardner	7.00
735	Mike Shannon	7.00
736	Mel Queen	7.00

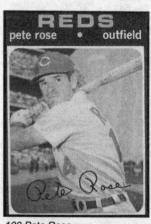

100 Pete Rose

737	Preston Gomez	7.00
738	Russ Gibson	7.00
739	Barry Lersch	7.00
740	Luis Aparicio	20.00
741	Skip Guinn	7.00
742	Royals Team	7.00
743	John O'Donoghue	7.00
744	Chuck Manuel	7.00
745	Sandy Alomar	7.00
746	Andy Kosco	7.00
747	NL Rookies (Balor Moore, Al Severinsen, Scipio Spinks)	7.00
748	John Purdin	7.00
749	Ken Szotkiewicz	7.00
750	Denny McLain	15.00
751	Al Weis	7.00
752	Dick Drago	7.00

1972 TOPPS

In 1972, Topps released a 787-card set, larger than any previous edition. Card fronts exhibit a wild design of various border colors, along with cartoonlike team headings. A number of subsets account for the increase of 35 cards over 1971. There is a seven-card series of traded players that includes Steve Carlton, Joe Morgan, and Frank Robinson. Eight cards show black-and-white boyhood photos, while thirty-four players are depicted both on standard and "in-action" cards (the latter indicated by IA" on the card list). A high-number series (657-787) is hard to locate, and the rookie card of Carlton Fisk is currently the set's second most valuable, after Nolan Ryan.

	NR MT
Complete set	**$2000.00**
Commons (1-394)	**.50**
Commons (395-525)	**1.50**
Commons (526-656)	**3.00**
Commons (657-787)	**7.00**

1	World Champions (Pirates Team)	$7.00
4	Checklist 1-132	3.00
11	Bobby Valentine	1.00
18	Juan Pizarro (green under "C" and "S")	3.50
21	Braves Team	1.00
29	Bill Bonham (green under "C" and "S")	5.00
30	Rico Petrocelli	.50
33	Billy Martin	3.50
34	Billy Martin IA	1.25
37	Carl Yastrzemski	15.00
38	Carl Yastrzemski IA	8.00
41	Tommy Davis	.90

445 Tom Seaver

559 Pete Rose

45 Glenn Beckert
(green under
"C" and "S") **5.00**
45 Glenn Beckert
(yellow under
"C" and "S") .... **.75**
49 Willie Mays **28.00**
50 Willie Mays IA **14.00**
51 Harmon Killebrew **7.00**
52 • Harmon Killebrew IA ... **3.00**
61 Cubs Rookies
(Gene Hiser,
Burt Hooton, Earl
Stephenson) **1.50**
65 Cesar Cedeno **1.25**
67 Red Schoendienst **1.25**
70 Mike Cuellar .... **.75**
71 Angels Team **2.00**
72 *Bruce Kison* .... **.80**
75 Bert Campaneris .... **.75**
79 Red Sox Rookies
(*Cecil Cooper,
Carlton Fisk,*
Mike Garman) **110.00**
80 Tony Perez **5.00**
85 NL Batting Ldrs (Glenn
Beckert, Ralph Garr,
Joe Torre) **1.50**

86 AL Batting Ldrs
(Bobby Murcer,
Tony Oliva, Merv
Rettenmund) **1.50**
87 NL RBI Ldrs
(Hank Aaron,
Willie Stargell,
Joe Torre) **3.00**
88 AL RBI Ldrs
(Harmon Killebrew,
Frank Robinson,
Reggie Smith) **3.00**
89 NL HR Ldrs
(Hank Aaron,
Lee May,
Willie Stargell) **3.00**
90 AL HR Ldrs
(Norm Cash,
Reggie Jackson,
Bill Melton) **2.00**
91 NL ERA Ldrs
(Dave Roberts,
Tom Seaver,
Don Wilson) **2.00**
92 AL ERA Ldrs (Vida
Blue, Jim Palmer,
Wilbur Wood) **1.75**
93 NL Pitching Ldrs
(Steve Carlton, Al Downing,
Fergie Jenkins, Tom
Seaver) **3.00**
94 AL Pitching Ldrs
(Vida Blue,
Mickey Lolich, Wilbur
Wood) **1.50**
95 NL SO Ldrs
(Fergie Jenkins,
Tom Seaver, Bill
Stoneman) **2.50**
96 AL SO Ldrs
(Vida Blue,
Joe Coleman, Mickey
Lolich) **1.25**
98 Chuck Tanner .... **.50**
99 Ross Grimsley .... **.60**
100 Frank Robinson **7.00**
101 Astros Rookies
(Ray Busse,
Bill Grief, *J.R. Richard*) . **1.50**

103	Checklist 133-263	3.00
104	*Toby Harrah*	1.50
106	Brewers Team	2.00
107	*Jose Cruz*	2.00
112	Greg Luzinski	1.35
114	Bill Buckner	2.00
115	Jim Fregosi	.75
117	Cleo James (green under "C" and "S")	4.00
120	Bill Freehan	.75
130	Bob Gibson	6.00
132	Joe Morgan	5.00
135	Vada Pinson	1.00
137	Dick Williams	.65
139	Tim McCarver	1.15
142	*Chris Chambliss*	3.00
147	*Dave Kingman*	6.00
150	Norm Cash	.75
154	Ted Simmons	3.00
156	Twins Team	2.00
162	Brewers Rookies (Jerry Bell, *Darrell Porter,* Bob Reynolds) (Bell & Porter photos reversed)	1.00
163	Tug McGraw	1.50
164	Tug McGraw IA	1.00
165	*Chris Speier*	1.00
166	*Chris Speier* IA	.75
169	Vida Blue	1.50
170	Vida Blue IA	1.00
171	Darrell Evans	1.75
172	Darrell Evans IA	1.00
191	*Jeff Burroughs*	1.00
192	Cubs Team	2.00
195	Orlando Cepeda	3.00
198	Dodgers Rookies (*Charlie Hough,* Bob O'Brien, Mike Strahler)	6.00
200	Lou Brock	6.00
203	*Ron Blomberg*	.50
209	Joe Rudi	.75
210	Denny McLain	1.50
216	Joe Niekro	.50
219	*Rennie Stennett*	.45
220	Jim Perry	.75

299 Hank Aaron

221	NL Playoffs (Bucs Champs!)	1.50
222	AL Playoffs (Orioles Champs!)	2.00
223	World Series Game 1	1.50
224	World Series Game 2	1.50
225	World Series Game 3	1.50
226	World Series Game 4	3.00
227	World Series Game 5	1.50
228	World Series Game 6	1.50
229	World Series Game 7	1.50
230	World Series Summary (Series Celebration)	1.25
233	• Jay Johnstone	.45
237	Yankees Team	2.25
240	Rich Allen	3.00
241	Rollie Fingers	8.00
250	Boog Powell	2.00
251	Checklist 264-394 (small print on front)	2.50
251	Checklist 264-394 (large print on front)	2.50
256	George Foster	2.00
259	Sparky Lyle	1.50
262	Padres Team	2.00
263	Felipe Alou	.65
264	Tommy John	2.75
267	Dave Concepcion	3.00

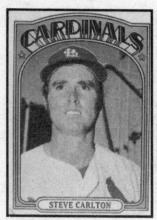

420 Steve Carlton

270	Jim Palmer	15.00
272	*Mickey Rivers*	1.00
276	Gene Mauch	.50
280	Willie McCovey	7.00
282	Astros Team	2.00
285	Gaylord Perry	7.50
291	● Hal McRae	1.50
299	Hank Aaron	35.00
300	Hank Aaron IA	17.00
303	Joe Pepitone	.50
309	Roberto Clemente	35.00
310	Roberto Clemente IA	17.00
313	Luis Aparicio	3.00
314	Luis Aparicio IA	1.50
316	Cardinals Rookies (*Jim Bibby,* Santiago Guzman, Jorge Roque)	.50
323	Earl Weaver	1.50
325	Mel Stottlemyre	1.00
327	*Steve Stone*	1.50
328	Red Sox Team	2.00
330	Jim Hunter	7.00
338	Bob Grich	1.50
340	Roy White	.75
341	Boyhood Photo (Joe Torre)	1.00
347	Boyhood Photo (Tom Seaver)	2.00
395	Matty Alou	1.80
396	Paul Lindblad	1.50
397	Phillies Team	1.90
398	Larry Hisle	1.60
399	Milt Wilcox	1.60
400	Tony Oliva	2.50
401	Jim Nash	1.50
402	Bobby Heise	1.50
403	John Cumberland	1.50
404	Jeff Torborg	1.60
405	Ron Fairly	1.75
406	*George Hendrick*	1.00
407	Chuck Taylor	1.50
408	Jim Northrup	1.60
409	Frank Baker	1.60
410	Fergie Jenkins	7.00
411	Bob Montgomery	1.50
412	Dick Kelley	1.50
413	White Sox Rookies (Don Eddy, Dave Lemonds)	1.50
414	Bob Miller	1.50
415	Cookie Rojas	1.50
416	Johnny Edwards	1.50
417	Tom Hall	1.50
418	Tom Shopay	1.50
419	Jim Spencer	1.50
420	Steve Carlton	25.00
421	Ellie Rodriguez	1.50
423	Oscar Gamble	1.60
424	Bill Gogolewski	1.50
425	Ken Singleton	1.90
426	Ken Singleton IA	1.60
427	Tito Fuentes	1.50
428	Tito Fuentes IA	1.50
429	Bob Robertson	1.50
430	Bob Robertson IA	1.50
431	Clarence Gaston	1.50
432	Clarence Gaston IA	1.50
433	Johnny Bench	35.00
434	Johnny Bench IA	18.00
435	Reggie Jackson	60.00
436	Reggie Jackson IA	30.00
437	Maury Wills	3.00
438	Maury Wills IA	2.00
439	Billy Williams	5.00
440	Billy Williams IA	2.50
441	Thurman Munson	20.00
442	Thurman Munson IA	10.00

443 Ken Henderson 1.50
444 Ken Henderson IA 1.50
445 Tom Seaver 40.00
446 Tom Seaver IA 20.00
447 Willie Stargell 5.00
448 Willie Stargell IA 2.50
449 Bob Lemon 2.00
450 Mickey Lolich 1.75
451 Tony LaRussa 2.00
452 Ed Herrmann 1.50
453 Barry Lersch 1.50
454 A's Team 3.00
455 Tommy Harper 1.60
456 Mark Belanger 1.60
457 Padres Rookies
    (Darcy Fast, Mike Ivie,
    Derrel Thomas) 1.60
458 Aurelio Monteagudo 1.50
459 Rick Renick 1.50
460 Al Downing 1.60
461 Tim Cullen 1.50
462 Rickey Clark 1.50
463 Bernie Carbo 1.50
464 Jim Roland 1.50
465 Gil Hodges 4.00
466 Norm Miller 1.50
467 Steve Kline 1.50
468 Richie Scheinblum 1.50
469 Ron Herbel 1.50
470 Ray Fosse 1.50
471 Luke Walker 1.50
472 Phil Gagliano 1.50
473 Dan McGinn 1.50
474 • Orioles Rookies
    (Don Baylor,
    Roric Harrison,
    Johnny Oates) 10.00
475 Gary Nolan 1.50
476 Lee Richard 1.50
477 Tom Phoebus 1.50
478 Checklist 526-656 .... 3.00
479 Don Shaw 1.50
480 Lee May 1.75
481 Billy Conigliaro 1.50
482 Joe Hoerner 1.50
483 Ken Suarez 1.50
484 Lum Harris 1.50
485 Phil Regan 1.50
486 John Lowenstein 1.50

435 Reggie Jackson

487 Tigers Team 2.50
488 Mike Nagy 1.50
489 Expos Rookies (Terry
    Humphrey, Keith
    Lampard) 1.50
490 Dave McNally 1.75
491 Boyhood Photo
    (Lou Piniella) 1.85
492 Boyhood Photo
    (Mel Stottlemyre) 1.60
493 Boyhood Photo
    (Bob Bailey) 1.50
494 Boyhood Photo
    (Willie Horton) 1.60
495 Boyhood Photo
    (Bill Melton) 1.50
496 Boyhood Photo
    (Bud Harrelson) 1.65
497 Boyhood Photo
    (Jim Perry) 1.60
498 Boyhood Photo
    (Brooks Robinson) 2.00
499 Vicente Romo 1.50
500 Joe Torre 2.50
501 Pete Hamm 1.50
502 Jackie Hernandez 1.50
503 Gary Peters 1.50
504 Ed Spiezio 1.50

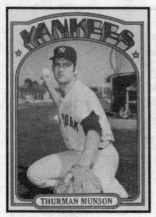

441 Thurman Munson

505	Mike Marshall	1.70
506	Indians Rookies (Terry Ley, Jim Moyer, *Dick Tidrow*)	1.80
507	Fred Gladding	1.50
508	Ellie Hendricks	1.50
509	Don McMahon	1.50
510	• Ted Williams	7.00
511	Tony Taylor	1.50
512	Paul Popovich	1.50
513	Lindy McDaniel	1.60
514	Ted Sizemore	1.50
515	Bert Blyleven	10.00
516	Oscar Brown	1.50
517	Ken Brett	1.60
518	Wayne Garrett	1.50
519	Ted Abernathy	1.50
520	Larry Bowa	2.00
521	Alan Foster	1.50
522	Dodgers Team	2.50
523	Chuck Dobson	1.50
524	Reds Rookies (Ed Armbrister, Mel Behney)	1.50
525	Carlos May	1.60
526	Bob Bailey	3.00
527	Dave Leonhard	3.00
528	Ron Stone	3.00

529	Dave Nelson	3.00
530	Don Sutton	6.00
531	Freddie Patek	4.00
532	Fred Kendall	3.00
533	Ralph Houk	4.00
534	Jim Hickman	3.00
535	Ed Brinkman	3.00
536	Doug Rader	3.00
537	Bob Locker	3.00
538	Charlie Sands	3.00
539	*Terry Forster*	4.00
540	Felix Millan	3.00
541	Roger Repoz	3.00
542	Jack Billingham	3.00
543	Duane Josephson	3.00
544	Ted Martinez	3.00
545	Wayne Granger	3.00
546	Joe Hague	3.00
547	Indians Team	6.00
548	Frank Reberger	3.00
549	Dave May	3.00
550	Brooks Robinson	25.00
551	Ollie Brown	3.00
552	Ollie Brown IA	3.00
553	Wilbur Wood	3.00
554	Wilbur Wood IA	3.00
555	Ron Santo	4.50
556	Ron Santo IA	3.50
557	John Odom	3.25
558	John Odom IA	3.00
559	Pete Rose	50.00
560	Pete Rose IA	25.00
561	Leo Cardenas	3.25
562	Leo Cardenas IA	3.00
563	Ray Sadecki	3.25
564	Ray Sadecki IA	3.00
565	Reggie Smith	3.25
566	Reggie Smith IA	3.00
567	Juan Marichal	7.00
568	Juan Marichal IA	3.50
569	Ed Kirkpatrick	3.00
570	Ed Kirkpatrick IA	3.00
571	Nate Colbert	3.00
572	Nate Colbert IA	3.00
573	Fritz Peterson	3.00
574	Fritz Peterson IA	3.00
575	Al Oliver	4.00
576	• Leo Durocher	4.00
577	Mike Paul	3.00

578	Billy Grabarkewitz	3.50
579	*Doyle Alexander*	2.50
580	Lou Piniella	5.00
581	Wade Blasingame	3.50
582	Expos Team	2.25
583	Darold Knowles	3.00
584	Jerry McNertney	3.00
585	George Scott	3.00
586	Denis Menke	3.00
587	Billy Wilson	3.00
588	Jim Holt	3.00
589	Hal Lanier	3.50
590	Graig Nettles	2.50
591	Paul Casanova	3.00
592	Lew Krausse	3.00
593	Rich Morales	3.00
594	Jim Beauchamp	3.00
595	Nolan Ryan	275.00
596	Manny Mota	3.25
597	Jim Magnuson	3.00
599	Billy Champion	3.00
600	Al Kaline	25.00
601	George Stone	3.00
602	Dave Bristol	3.00
603	Jim Ray	3.00
604	Checklist 657-787	5.00
605	Nelson Briles	3.00
606	Luis Melendez	3.00
607	Frank Duffy	3.00
608	Mike Corkins	3.00
609	Tom Grieve	3.00
610	Bill Stoneman	3.00
611	Rich Reese	3.00
612	Joe Decker	3.00
613	Mike Ferraro	3.00
614	Ted Uhlaender	3.00
615	Steve Hargan	3.00
616	*Joe Ferguson*	4.00
617	Royals Team	6.00
618	Rich Robertson	3.00
619	Rich McKinney	3.00
620	Phil Niekro	7.00
621	Commissioners Award	3.50
622	MVP Award	3.50
623	Cy Young Award	3.50
624	Minor League Player of the Year Award	3.50
625	Rookie of the Year Award	3.50

595 Nolan Ryan

626	Babe Ruth Award	3.50
627	Moe Drabowsky	3.00
628	Terry Crowley	3.00
629	Paul Doyle	3.00
630	Rich Hebner	3.00
631	John Strohmayer	3.00
632	Mike Hegan	3.00
633	Jack Hiatt	3.00
634	Dick Woodson	3.00
635	Don Money	3.00
636	Bill Lee	3.00
637	Preston Gomez	3.00
638	Ken Wright	3.00
639	J.C. Martin	3.00
640	Joe Coleman	3.00
641	Mike Lum	3.00
642	Denny Riddleberger	3.00
643	Russ Gibson	3.00
644	Bernie Allen	3.00
645	Jim Maloney	3.00
646	Chico Salmon	3.00
647	Bob Moose	3.00
648	Jim Lyttle	3.00
649	Pete Richert	3.00
650	Sal Bando	4.00
651	Reds Team	7.00
652	Marcelino Lopez	3.00
653	Jim Fairey	3.00

695 Rod Carew

654	Horacio Pina	3.00
655	Jerry Grote	3.00
657	Bobby Wine	5.00
658	Steve Dunning	5.00
659	Bob Aspromonte	5.00
660	Paul Blair	7.50
661	Bill Virdon	5.00
662	Stan Bahnsen	5.00
663	Fran Healy	5.00
664	Bobby Knoop	5.00
665	Chris Short	5.00
666	Hector Torres	5.00
667	Ray Newman	5.00
668	Rangers Team	12.00
669	Willie Crawford	7.50
670	Ken Holtzman	8.00
671	Donn Clendenon	8.00
672	Archie Reynolds	5.00
673	Dave Marshall	5.00
674	John Kennedy	5.00
675	Pat Jarvis	5.00
676	Danny Cater	5.00
677	Ivan Murrell	5.00
678	Steve Luebber	5.00
679	Astros Rookies (Bob Fenwick, Bob Stinson)	5.00
680	Dave Johnson	8.00
681	Bobby Pfeil	5.00
682	Mike McCormick	5.00
683	Steve Hovley	5.00
684	Hal Breeden	9.00
685	Joe Horlen	5.00
686	Steve Garvey	70.00
687	Del Unser	5.00
688	Cardinals Team	14.00
689	Eddie Fisher	5.00
690	Willie Montanez	5.00
691	Curt Blefary	5.00
692	Curt Blefary IA	5.00
693	Alan Gallagher	5.00
694	Alan Gallagher IA	5.00
695	Rod Carew	75.00
696	Rod Carew IA	35.00
697	Jerry Koosman	15.00
698	Jerry Koosman IA	10.00
699	Bobby Murcer	14.00
700	Bobby Murcer IA	8.00
701	Jose Pagan	5.00
702	Jose Pagan IA	5.00
703	Doug Griffin	5.00
704	Doug Griffin IA	5.00
705	Pat Corrales	5.00
706	Pat Corrales IA	5.00
707	Tim Foli	5.00
708	Tim Foli IA	5.00
709	Jim Kaat	15.00
710	Jim Kaat IA	10.00
711	Bobby Bonds	18.00
712	Bobby Bonds IA	12.00
713	Gene Michael	5.00
714	Gene Michael IA	5.00
715	Mike Epstein	5.00
716	Jesus Alou	5.00
717	Bruce Dal Canton	5.00
718	Del Rice	5.00
719	Cesar Geronimo	5.00
720	Sam McDowell	5.50
721	Eddie Leon	5.00
722	Bill Sudakis	5.00
723	Al Santorini	5.00
724	AL Rookies (John Curtis, Rich Hinton, Mickey Scott)	5.00
725	Dick McAuliffe	5.00
726	Dick Selma	5.00
727	Jose Laboy	5.00
728	Gail Hopkins	5.00

729 Bob Veale...................... **5.00**
730 Rick Monday **8.00**
731 Orioles Team................. **5.00**
732 George Culver............... **5.00**
733 Jim Hart........................ **5.00**
734 Bob Burda **5.00**
735 Diego Segui................... **5.00**
736 Bill Russell.................... **8.00**
737 *Lenny Randle*................ **5.00**
738 Jim Merritt.................... **5.00**
739 Don Mason.................... **5.00**
740 Rico Carty **8.00**
741 Major League Rookies
(Tom Hutton, *Rick Miller,*
John Milner) **10.00**
742 Jim Rooker **5.00**
743 Cesar Gutierrez............. **5.00**
744 *Jim Slaton* **5.00**
745 Julian Javier **5.00**
746 Lowell Palmer................ **5.00**
747 Jim Stewart **5.00**
748 Phil Hennigan................ **5.00**
749 Walter Alston................ **10.00**
750 Willie Horton................. **5.00**
751 Steve Carlton Traded .. **70.00**
752 Joe Morgan Traded..... **45.00**
753 Denny McLain
Traded........................ **12.00**

600 Al Kaline

433 Johnny Bench

754 Frank Robinson
Traded.......................... **35.00**
755 Jim Fregosi.................... **5.00**
756 Rick Wise Traded.......... **6.00**
757 Jose Cardenal Traded... **6.00**
758 Gil Garrido **5.00**
759 Chris Cannizzaro........... **5.00**
760 Bill Mazeroski **7.00**
761 Major League Rookies
(*Ron Cey,*
Ben Oglivie,
Bernie Williams) **28.00**
762 Wayne Simpson **5.00**
763 Ron Hansen **5.00**
764 Dusty Baker................... **9.00**
765 Ken McMullen **5.00**
766 Steve Hamilton............. **5.00**
767 Tom McCraw.................. **5.00**
768 Denny Doyle.................. **5.00**
769 Jack Aker **5.00**
770 Jim Wynn **5.50**
771 Giants Team................ **14.00**
772 Ken Tatum.................... **5.00**
773 Ron Brand **5.00**
774 Luis Alvarado **5.00**
775 Jerry Reuss **6.00**
776 Bill Voss **5.00**
777 Hoyt Wilhelm **20.00**

778	Twins Rookies Vic Albury, *Rick Dempsey,* Jim Strickland) **15.00**	**782**	Larry Stahl 5.00
779	Tony Cloninger.............. 5.00	**783**	Les Cain 5.00
780	Dick Green 5.00	**784**	Ken Aspromonte 5.00
781	Jim McAndrew............... 5.00	**785**	Vic Davalillo................... 5.00
		786	Chuck Brinkman............. 5.00
		787	Ron Reed 8.00

1973 TOPPS

Topps marked the end of an era with its 1973 edition: It was the last time a major set was issued piecemeal, one series at a time, throughout the summer. Card fronts contain a small silhouetted figure depicting each player's position—an unusual design element. Card backs have a vertical format once again and retain the basic elements of cartoons, brief biographies, and year-by-year stats. The 660-card set is noted for odd-looking manager cards. These cards include tiny black-and-white portraits of team coaches along with pictures of each team skipper. They can be found with different backgrounds surrounding the photos of the coaches, although the variations have little difference in value. Without question the most popular card in the set is number 615, titled Rookie Third Basemen, which shows future Hall of Famer Mike Schmidt along with Ron Cey. It currently fetches prices of about $500.

	NR MT
Complete set	**$1200.00**
Commons (1-396)	**.50**
Commons (397-528)	**1.00**
Commons (529-660)	**3.00**

1	All Time HR Ldrs (Babe Ruth, Hank Aaron, Willie Mays) **$30.00**	**13**	George Hendrick .... .85
2	Rich Hebner .... .55	**15**	Ralph Garr....................... .60
3	Jim Lonborg .... .60	**23**	Dave Kingman............... 1.50
5	Ed Brinkman..................... .55	**25**	Roy White .... .60
7	Rangers Team 1.50	**26**	Pirates Team 1.50
9	Johnny Oates 1.25	**28**	• Hal McRae 1.00
10	Don Sutton 3.00	**30**	Tug McGraw 1.00
11	Chris Chambliss .... .90	**31**	*Buddy Bell* 4.00
12	Padres Mgr./Coaches (Dave Garcia, Johnny Podres, Bob Skinner, Whitey Wietelmann, Don Zimmer) .... .65	**35**	Willie Davis...................... .70
		40	Reggie Smith.................. .85
		43	*Randy Moffitt*.................. .60
		44	Rick Monday.................... .65
		49	Twins Mgr./Coaches (Vern Morgan, Frank Quilici, Bob Rodgers, Ralph Rowe, Al Worthington) .... .50
		50	Roberto Clemente 35.00
		54	Checklist 1-132 .... 2.00
		55	Jon Matlack .... .60
		59	*Steve Yeager* .... .75

61 Batting Ldrs
(Rod Carew,
Billy Williams) **2.50**
62 HR Ldrs
(Dick Allen,
Johnny Bench) **2.50**
63 RBI Ldrs
(Dick Allen,
Johnny Bench) **2.50**
64 SB Ldrs
(Lou Brock, Bert
Campaneris)................. **2.00**
65 ERA Ldrs
(Steve Carlton,
Luis Tiant) **2.00**
66 Victory Ldrs
(Steve Carlton,
Gaylord Perry, Wilbur
Wood)........................... **2.00**
67 SO Ldrs
(Steve Carlton,
Nolan Ryan) **18.00**
68 Leading Firemen
(Clay Carroll,
Sparky Lyle) **1.00**
70 Milt Pappas .... **.60**
75 Vada Pinson.................. **1.00**
80 Tony Oliva **1.50**
81 Cubs Mgr./Coaches
(Hank Aguirre,
Ernie Banks, Larry
Jansen, Whitey
Lockman, Pete Reiser).... **.75**
84 Rollie Fingers **7.00**
85 Ted Simmons **2.50**
90 Brooks Robinson **7.00**
91 Dodgers Team **1.50**
100 Hank Aaron **25.00**
108 Bill Russell........................ **.65**
109 Doyle Alexander............. **.75**
115 Ron Santo **1.00**
116 Yankees Mgr./Coaches
(Jim Hegan, Ralph Houk,
Elston Howard, Dick
Howser, Jim Turner)...... **1.00**
118 John Mayberry .... **.60**
119 Larry Bowa **1.00**
125 Ron Fairly........................ **.60**
127 Brewers Team............... **1.50**

220 Nolan Ryan

129 Terry Forster .... **.60**
130 Pete Rose **18.00**
131 Red Sox Mgr./Coaches
(Doug Camilli,
Eddie Kasko,
Don Lenhardt,
Eddie Popowski,
Lee Stange)..................... **.70**
136 Orioles Mgr./Coaches
(George Bamberger,
Jim Frey,
Billy Hunter,
George Staller,
Earl Weaver) **1.50**
140 Lou Piniella.................... **1.00**
142 Thurman Munson **12.00**
145 Bobby Bonds................. **2.00**
148 *Dave Goltz* .... **.75**
150 Wilbur Wood.................... **.60**
153 Al Hrabosky..................... **.60**
155 Sal Bando........................ **.75**
158 Astros Team................. **1.50**
160 Jim Palmer **12.00**
165 Luis Aparicio................. **3.00**
167 Steve Stone..................... **.65**
170 Harmon Killebrew.......... **6.00**
174 *Rich Gossage*............. **18.00**
175 Frank Robinson............. **6.00**

1973 Topps

305 Willie Mays

193 Carlton Fisk

380 Johnny Bench

457	John Strohmayer	1.00
458	Jim Mason	1.00
459	Jimmy Howarth	1.00
460	Bill Freehan	1.25
461	Mike Corkins	1.00
462	Ron Blomberg	1.00
463	Ken Tatum	1.00
464	Cubs Team	2.00
465	Dave Giusti	1.00
466	Jose Arcia	1.00
467	Mike Ryan	1.00
468	Tom Griffin	1.00
469	Dan Monzon	1.00
470	Mike Cuellar	1.25
471	Hit Ldr (Ty Cobb)	5.00
472	Grand Slam Ldr (Lou Gehrig)	6.00
473	Total Base Ldr (Hank Aaron)	6.00
474	RBI Ldr (Babe Ruth)	10.00
475	Batting Ldr (Ty Cobb)	6.00
476	Shutout Ldr (Walter Johnson)	3.00
477	Victory Ldr (Cy Young)	3.00
478	SO Ldr (Walter Johnson)	3.00
479	Hal Lanier	1.00
480	Juan Marichal	4.00
481	White Sox Team	2.00
482	• Rick Reuschel	5.00
483	Dal Maxvill	1.00
484	Ernie McAnally	1.00
485	Norm Cash	1.50
486	Phillies Mgr./Coaches (Carroll Berringer, Billy DeMars, Danny Ozark, Ray Rippelmeyer, Bobby Wine)	1.00
487	Bruce Dal Canton	1.00
488	Dave Campbell	1.00
489	Jeff Burroughs	1.25
490	Claude Osteen	1.00
491	Bob Montgomery	1.00
492	Pedro Borbon	1.00
493	Duffy Dyer	1.00
494	Rich Morales	1.00
495	Tommy Helms	1.00
496	Ray Lamb	1.00

130 Pete Rose

497	Cardinals Mgr./Coaches (Vern Benson, George Kissell, Red Schoendienst, Barney Schultz)	1.50
498	Graig Nettles	3.00
499	Bob Moose	1.00
500	A's Team	3.00
501	Larry Gura	1.00
502	Bobby Valentine	1.50
503	• Phil Niekro	5.00
504	Earl Williams	1.00
505	Bob Bailey	1.00
506	Bart Johnson	1.00
507	Darrel Chaney	1.00
508	Gates Brown	1.00
509	Jim Nash	1.00
510	Amos Otis	1.25
511	Sam McDowell	1.25
512	Dalton Jones	1.00
513	Dave Marshall	1.00
514	Jerry Kenney	1.00
515	Andy Messersmith	1.25
516	Danny Walton	1.00
517	Pirates Mgr./Coaches (Don Leppert, Bill Mazeroski, Dave Ricketts, Bill Virdon, Mel Wright)	1.50

613 Rookie Catchers

518	Bob Veale	1.00
519	John Edwards	1.00
520	Mel Stottlemyre	1.25
521	Braves Team	2.00
522	Leo Cardenas	1.00
523	Wayne Granger	1.00
524	Gene Tenace	1.00
525	Jim Fregosi	1.25
526	Ollie Brown	1.00
527	Dan McGinn	1.00
528	Paul Blair	1.00
529	Milt May	3.00
530	Jim Kaat	4.50
531	Ron Woods	3.00
532	Steve Mingori	3.00
533	Larry Stahl	3.00
534	Dave Lemonds	3.00
535	John Callison	3.25
536	Phillies Team	6.00
537	Bill Slayback	3.00
538	Jim Hart	3.10
539	Tom Murphy	3.00
540	Cleon Jones	3.25
541	Bob Bolin	3.00
542	Pat Corrales	3.00
543	Alan Foster	3.00
544	Von Joshua	3.00
545	Orlando Cepeda	4.50
546	Jim York	3.00
547	Bobby Heise	3.00
548	Don Durham	3.00

549	Rangers Mgr./Coaches (Chuck Estrada, Whitey Herzog, Chuck Hiller, Jackie Moore)	5.00
550	Dave Johnson	4.25
551	Mike Kilkenny	3.00
552	J.C. Martin	3.00
553	Mickey Scott	3.00
554	Dave Concepcion	5.00
555	Bill Hands	3.00
556	Yankees Team	8.00
557	Bernie Williams	3.00
558	Jerry May	3.00
559	Barry Lersch	3.00
560	Frank Howard	4.00
561	Jim Geddes	3.00
562	Wayne Garrett	3.00
563	Larry Haney	3.00
564	Mike Thompson	3.00
565	Jim Hickman	3.00
567	Bob Fenwick	3.00
568	Ray Newman	3.00
569	Dodgers Mgr./Coaches (Red Adams, Walt Alston, Monty Basgall, Jim Gilliam, Tom Lasorda)	5.00
570	Bill Singer	3.00
571	Rusty Torres	3.00
572	Gary Sutherland	3.00

615 Rookie Third Basemen

573 Fred Beene 3.00
574 Bob Didier 3.00
575 Dock Ellis 3.00
576 Expos Team 6.00
577 *Eric Soderholm*.............. 3.00
578 Ken Wright 3.00
579 Tom Grieve 3.00
580 Joe Pepitone 4.00
581 Steve Kealey 3.00
582 Darrell Porter 3.50
583 Bill Greif......................... 3.00
584 Chris Arnold 3.00
585 Joe Niekro 3.50
586 Bill Sudakis................... 3.00
587 Rich McKinney 3.00
588 Checklist 529-660 .... 20.00
589 Ken Forsch 3.00
590 Deron Johnson............. 3.00
591 Mike Hedlund 3.00
592 John Boccabella........... 3.00
593 Royals Mgr./Coaches
     (Galen Cisco,
     Harry Dunlop,
     Charlie Lau, Jack
     McKeon) 3.00
594 Vic Harris...................... 3.00
595 Don Gullett 3.50
596 Red Sox Team 8.00
597 Mickey Rivers............... 3.50
598 Phil Roof....................... 3.00
599 Ed Crosby 3.00

600 Dave McNally **3.50**
601 Rookie Catchers
     (George Pena, Sergio
     Robles, Rick
     Stelmaszek) 3.00
602 Rookie Pitchers (Mel
     Behney, Ralph Garcia,
     Doug Rau)..................... 3.00
603 Rookie Third Basemen
     (Terry Hughes, Bill
     McNulty, *Ken Reitz*) 3.00
604 Rookie Pitchers
     (Jesse Jefferson,
     Dennis O'Toole,
     Bob Strampe) 3.00
605 Rookie First Basemen
     (Pat Bourque,
     Enos Cabell,
     Gonzalo Marquez)......... 3.00
606 Rookie Outfielders
     (*Gary Matthews,*
     Tom Paciorek,
     Jorge Roque) **5.00**
607 Rookie Shortstops
     (Ray Busse,
     Pepe Frias, Mario
     Guerrero)...................... 3.00
608 Rookie Pitchers
     (*Steve Busby,*
     Dick Colpaert,
     George Medich) **3.50**

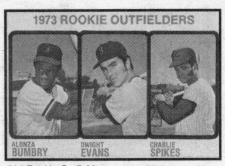

614 Rookie Outfielders

609 Rookie Second Basemen
(Larvell Blanks, Pedro
Garcia, *Dave Lopes*) **5.00**
610 Rookie Pitchers
(Jimmy Freeman,
Charlie Hough,
Hank Webb) **4.00**
611 Rookie Outfielders
(Rich Coggins,
Jim Wohlford,
Richie Zisk) **3.25**
612 Rookie Pitchers
(Steve Lawson,
Bob Reynolds,
Brent Strom) **3.00**
613 Rookie Catchers
(*Bob Boone,*
Mike Ivie, Skip
Jutze) **45.00**
614 Rookie Outfielders
(*Alonza Bumbry,*
Dwight Evans,
Charlie Spikes) **50.00**
615 Rookie Third Basemen
(Ron Cey, Dave Hilton,
Mike Schmidt) **500.00**
616 Rookie Pitchers
(Norm Angelini,
Steve Blateric,
Mike Garman) **3.00**
617 Rich Chiles **3.00**
618 Andy Etchebarren **3.00**
619 Billy Wilson **3.00**

621 Joe Ferguson **3.00**
622 Larry Hisle **3.00**
623 Steve Renko................... **3.00**
624 Astros Mgr./Coaches
(Leo Durocher, Preston
Gomez, Grady Hatton,
Hub Kittle,
Jim Owens) **5.00**
625 Angel Mangual **3.00**
627 Luis Alvarado **3.00**
628 Jim Slaton **3.00**
629 Indians Team **6.00**
630 Denny McLain **4.00**
631 Tom Matchick **3.00**
632 Dick Selma **3.00**
633 Ike Brown **3.00**
635 Gene Alley..................... **3.00**
636 Rick Clark..................... **3.00**
637 Norm Miller **3.00**
638 Ken Reynolds................. **3.00**
639 Willie Crawford **3.00**
640 Dick Bosman **3.00**
641 Reds Team..................... **8.00**
642 Jose Laboy **3.00**
643 Al Fitzmorris **3.00**
644 Jack Heidemann **3.00**
645 Bob Locker **3.00**
646 Brewers Mgr./Coaches
(Del Crandall, Harvey
Kuenn, Joe Nossek,
Bob Shaw,
Jim Walton) **3.50**
647 George Stone................. **3.00**

648	Tom Egan	3.00	658 Elliott Maddox	3.00
650	Felipe Alou	3.50	659 Jose Pagan	3.00
651	Don Carrithers	3.00	660 Fred Scherman	4.00
655	Clay Kirby	3.00	652 Ted Kubiak	3.00
656	John Ellis	3.00	653 Joe Hoerner	3.00
657	Bob Johnson	3.00	654 Twins Team	7.00

1974 TOPPS

For the first time, instead of issuing cards by series—the traditional way—Topps issued all 660 cards at one time. That allowed collectors the chance to acquire any card number at any time instead of having to wait and piece together a collection made up of separate 132-card series throughout the summer. Because everyone guessed, falsely, that the San Diego Padres would be moved to Washington, D.C., Topps changed 15 Padres cards to read "Washington, Nat'l League." When the team stayed in San Diego, Topps quickly changed the cards, but not in time to prevent the release of many that contained the error. This was also the time that Hank Aaron was just two homers short of breaking Babe Ruth's career record, and Aaron is featured on the first six cards, which are reproductions of previous cards. Dave Winfield is the top rookie featured in the set.

	NR MT
Complete set	$625.00
Commons	.45

1	Hank Aaron	$35.00
2	Aaron Special 1954-57	6.00
3	Aaron Special 1958-61	6.00
4	Aaron Special 1962-65	6.00
5	Aaron Special 1966-69	6.00
6	Aaron Special 1970-73	6.00
7	Jim Hunter	5.00
9	Mickey Lolich	.75
10	Johnny Bench	16.00
11	Jim Bibby	.50
12	Dave May	.35
15	Joe Torre	1.00
16	Orioles Team	1.00
19	Gerry Moses	.50
20	Nolan Ryan	80.00
24	John Hiller	.50
25	Ken Singleton	.50
26	*Bill Campbell*	.50

27	George Scott	.50
28	Manny Sanguillen	.50
29	Phil Niekro	4.00
30	Bobby Bonds	1.25
31	Astros Mgr./Coaches (Roger Craig, Preston Gomez, Grady Hatton, Hub Kittle, Bob Lillis)	.65
32	Johnny Grubb (Washington)	6.00
32	Johnny Grubb (San Diego)	.45
35	Gaylord Perry	4.00
36	Cardinals Team	1.00
38	Don Kessinger	.50
40	Jim Palmer	10.00
41	Bobby Floyd	.50
42	Claude Osteen	.50
43	Jim Wynn	.50
44	Mel Stottlemyre	.60
45	Dave Johnson	.90
47	*Dick Ruthven*	.50

20 Nolan Ryan

50	Rod Carew	12.00
52	Al Oliver	1.00
53	Fred Kendall (Washington)	6.00
53	Fred Kendall (San Diego)	.35
54	*Elias Sosa*	.35
55	Frank Robinson	6.00
56	Mets Team	1.75
59	Ross Grimsley	.50
60	Lou Brock	6.00
61	Luis Aparicio	3.00
65	Amos Otis	.50
66	• Sparky Lyle	.75
70	Dick Allen	.90
72	Aurelio Rodriguez	.50
73	Mike Marshall	.75
74	Twins Team	1.00
76	Mickey Rivers	.45
77	Rich Troedson (Washington)	6.00
77	Rich Troedson (San Diego)	.35
78	Giants Mgr./Coaches (Joe Amalfitano, Charlie Fox, Andy Gilbert, Don McMahon, John McNamara)	.65
79	Gene Tenace	.60
80	Tom Seaver	18.00
82	Dave Giusti	.50
83	Orlando Cepeda	1.50
84	Rick Wise	.50
85	Joe Morgan	6.00
86	Joe Ferguson	.50
87	Fergie Jenkins	4.00
88	Freddie Patek	.50
90	Bobby Murcer	.75
91	Ken Forsch	.50
92	Paul Blair	.50
93	Rod Gilbreath	.35
94	Tigers Team	1.00
95	Steve Carlton	12.00
96	*Jerry Hairston*	.35
97	Bob Bailey	.35
98	Bert Blyleven	3.00
99	Brewers Mgr./Coaches (Del Crandall, Harvey Kuenn, Joe Nossek, Jim Walton, Al Widmar)	.65
100	Willie Stargell	5.00
101	Bobby Valentine	.50
102	Bill Greif (Washington)	6.00
102	Bill Greif (San Diego)	.35
103	Sal Bando	.50
104	Ron Bryant	.35
105	Carlton Fisk	25.00
107	Alex Johnson	.35
108	Al Hrabosky	.50
109	Bob Grich	.50
110	Billy Williams	4.00
111	Clay Carroll	.50
112	Dave Lopes	.90
113	Dick Drago	.35
114	Angels Team	1.00
115	Willie Horton	.50
116	Jerry Reuss	.50
117	Ron Blomberg	.40
118	Bill Lee	.50
119	Phillies Mgr./Coaches (Carroll Beringer, Bill DeMars, Danny Ozark, Ray Ripplemeyer, Bobby Wine)	.60
120	Wilbur Wood	.50
122	Jim Holt	.35

123 Nelson Briles .... .35
125 Nate Colbert
     (Washington) 7.00
125 Nate Colbert
     (San Diego) .... .45
126 Checklist 1-132 .... 1.50
127 Tom Paciorek .... .40
128 John Ellis .... .35
129 Chris Speier .... .35
130 Reggie Jackson 40.00
131 Bob Boone 3.75
132 Felix Millan .... .40
133 *David Clyde* .... .50
134 Denis Menke .... .45
135 Roy White .... .60
136 Rick Reuschel .... .85
137 Al Bumbry .... .40
138 Ed Brinkman .... .40
139 Aurelio Monteagudo .... .35
140 Darrell Evans .... .85
141 Pat Bourque .... .35
142 Pedro Garcia .... .35
144 Dodgers Mgr./Coaches
     (Red Adams,
     Walter Alston,
     Monty Basgall,
     Jim Gilliam,
     Tom Lasorda) 2.00
145 Dock Ellis .... .40
146 Ron Fairly .... .45
147 Bart Johnson .... .35
148 Dave Hilton
     (Washington) 6.00
148 Dave Hilton
     (San Diego) .... .40
149 Mac Scarce .... .35
150 John Mayberry .... .40
151 Diego Segui .... .35
152 Oscar Gamble .... .40
153 Jon Matlack .... .40
154 Astros Team 1.00
155 Bert Campaneris .... .75
156 Randy Moffitt .... .40
158 Jack Billingham .... .40
159 Jim Ray Hart .... .40
160 Brooks Robinson 6.00
161 *Ray Burris* .... .50
162 Bill Freehan .... .50
164 Tom House .... .40

10 Johnny Bench

165 Willie Davis .... .60
166 Royals Mgr./Coaches
     (Galen Cisco,
     Harry Dunlop, Charlie
     Lau, Jack McKeon) .... .75
167 Luis Tiant .... .75
168 Danny Thompson .... .40
169 *Steve Rogers* .... .75
170 Bill Melton .... .40
172 Gene Clines .... .35
173 *Randy Jones*
     (Washington) 7.00
173 *Randy Jones*
     (San Diego) .... .60
175 Reggie Cleveland .... .35
176 John Lowenstein .... .35
178 Garry Maddox .... .50
179 Mets Mgr./Coaches
     (Yogi Berra,
     Roy McMillan,
     Joe Pignatano,
     Rube Walker,
     Eddie Yost) 2.00
180 Ken Holtzman .... .50
181 Cesar Geronimo .... .40
182 Lindy McDaniel .... .35
184 Rangers Team 1.00
185 Jose Cardenal .... .40

456 Dave Winfield

248	Tom Hall	.50
250	Willie McCovey (Washington)	30.00
250	Willie McCovey (San Diego)	7.00
251	Graig Nettles	2.00
252	*Dave Parker*	40.00
253	John Boccabella	.35
255	Larry Bowa	.90
257	Buddy Bell	1.00
259	Bob Reynolds	.50
260	Ted Simmons	2.00
261	Jerry Bell	.35
263	Checklist 133-264	2.00
264	Joe Rudi	.50
265	Tug McGraw	.75
266	Jim Northrup	.40
267	Andy Messersmith	.50
270	Ron Santo	1.00
271	Bill Hands	.35
273	Checklist 265-396	2.00
274	Fred Beene	.35
275	Ron Hunt	.35
278	Cookie Rojas	.35
279	Jim Crawford	.35
280	Carl Yastrzemski	12.00
281	Giants Team	1.00
282	Doyle Alexander	.50
283	Mike Schmidt	90.00
284	Dave Duncan	.50
285	Reggie Smith	.65
286	Tony Muser	.35
287	Clay Kirby	.35
288	*Gorman Thomas*	2.00
289	Rick Auerbach	.35
290	Vida Blue	.80
291	Don Hahn	.35
292	Chuck Seelbach	.35
293	Milt May	.35
294	Steve Foucault	.35
295	Rick Monday	.50
296	Ray Corbin	.35
297	Hal Breeden	.35
298	Roric Harrison	.35
299	Gene Michael	.55
300	Pete Rose	15.00
301	Bob Montgomery	.35
302	Rudy May	.35
303	George Hendrick	.50

280 Carl Yastrzemski

304	Don Wilson	.05
305	Tito Fuentes	.50
306	Orioles Mgr/Coaches (George Bamberger, Jim Frey, Billy Hunter, George Staller, Earl Weaver)	.90
307	Luis Melendez	.35
308	Bruce Dal Canton	.35
309	Dave Roberts (Washington)	8.00
309	Dave Roberts (San Diego)	.50
310	Terry Forster	.50
311	Jerry Grote	.50
312	Deron Johnson	.50
313	Barry Lersch	.35
314	Brewers Team	7.00
315	Ron Cey	1.00
316	Jim Perry	.60
317	Richie Zisk	.50
318	Jim Merritt	.35
319	Randy Hundley	.50
320	Dusty Baker	1.75
321	Steve Braun	.50
322	Ernie McAnally	.50
323	Richie Scheinblum	.50

250 Willie McCovey (Wash.)

40 Jim Palmer

252 Dave Parker

654 Jesus Alou (no position)

283 Mike Schmidt

1975 TOPPS

Although all 660 cards in the 1975 Topps set were issued at once, collectors found that the first 132 cards (from the first of five printing sheets) were produced in a somewhat smaller quantity. Each card front uses three colors, two for the border and one for the bold team name at the top. A large subset of 24 cards features the American and National League MVPs since 1951, pictured in miniature versions of the Topps cards from their award-winning seasons. Rookie cards show four players, grouped by position. Famous rookies include George Brett, Gary Carter, Keith Hernandez, Fred Lynn, Jim Rice, and Robin Yount. Topps also test-marketed this set in a smaller format with cards measuring 2¼ by 3⅛ inches. This mini set is a rare commodity today.

	NR MT
Complete set	**$1000.00**
Commons (1-132)	**.45**
Commons (133-660)	**.45**
Complete Mini set	**2000.00**
Mini commons	**.75**

660 Hank Aaron

1	'74 Highlights (Hank Aaron)	$30.00
2	'74 Highlights (Lou Brock)	3.50
3	'74 Highlights (Bob Gibson)	3.50
4	'74 Highlights (Al Kaline)	3.50
5	'74 Highlights (Nolan Ryan)	22.00
6	'74 Highlights (Mike Marshall)	.75
7	'74 Highlights (Dick Bosman, Steve Busby, Nolan Ryan)	3.50
8	Rogelio Moret	.40
9	Frank Tepedino	.40
10	Willie Davis	.45
11	Bill Melton	.45
12	David Clyde	.45
13	Gene Locklear	.40
14	Milt Wilcox	.45
15	Jose Cardenal	.45
16	Frank Tanana	.50
17	Dave Concepcion	2.50
18	Tigers Team (Ralph Houk)	1.00
19	Jerry Koosman	.50
20	Thurman Munson	10.00
21	Rollie Fingers	5.00
22	Dave Cash	.50
23	Bill Russell	.50
24	Al Fitzmorris	.40
25	Lee May	.50
26	Dave McNally	.50
27	Ken Reitz	.50
28	Tom Murphy	.40
29	Dave Parker	8.00

30	Bert Blyleven	2.00
31	Dave Rader	.40
32	Reggie Cleveland	.40
33	Dusty Baker	.50
34	Steve Renko	.40
35	Ron Santo	.75
36	Joe Lovitto	.40
37	Dave Freisleben	.40
38	Buddy Bell	.90
39	Andy Thornton	.75
40	Bill Singer	.40
41	Cesar Geronimo	.40
42	Joe Coleman	.40
43	Cleon Jones	.45
44	Pat Dobson	.45
45	Joe Rudi	.50
46	Phillies Team (Danny Ozark)	.90
47	Tommy John	2.00
48	Freddie Patek	.40
49	Larry Dierker	.40
50	Brooks Robinson	6.00
51	*Bob Forsch*	.90
52	Darrell Porter	.45
53	Dave Giusti	.40
54	Eric Soderholm	.40
55	Bobby Bonds	1.50
56	Rick Wise	.45
57	Dave Johnson	.90
58	Chuck Taylor	.40
59	Ken Henderson	.40
60	Fergie Jenkins	4.00
61	Dave Winfield	70.00
62	Fritz Peterson	.40
63	Steve Swisher	.40
64	Dave Chalk	.40
65	Don Gullett	.45
66	Willie Horton	.50
67	Tug McGraw	.65
68	Ron Blomberg	.40
69	John Odom	.40
70	Mike Schmidt	65.00
71	Charlie Hough	.40
72	Royals Team (Jack McKeon)	1.00
73	J.R. Richard	.50
74	Mark Belanger	.45
75	Ted Simmons	.75
76	Ed Sprague	.40

70 Mike Schmidt

77	Richie Zisk	.50
78	Ray Corbin	.40
79	Gary Matthews	.50
80	Carlton Fisk	25.00
81	Ron Reed	.40
82	Pat Kelly	.40
83	Jim Merritt	.40
84	Enzo Hernandez	.40
85	Bill Bonham	.40
86	Joe Lis	.40
87	George Foster	2.00
88	Tom Egan	.40
89	Jim Ray	.40
90	Rusty Staub	.75
91	Dick Green	.40
92	Cecil Upshaw	.45
93	Dave Lopes	.50
94	Jim Lonborg	.50
95	John Mayberry	.45
96	Mike Cosgrove	.40
97	Earl Williams	.40
98	Rich Folkers	.40
99	Mike Hegan	.40
100	Willie Stargell	4.00
101	Expos Team (Gene Mauch)	1.00
102	Joe Decker	.40
103	Rick Miller	.40

500 Nolan Ryan

199 1961—MVPs (Roger Maris, Frank Robinson)............ **4.00**
200 1962—MVPs (Mickey Mantle, Maury Wills)...... **6.00**
201 1963—MVPs (Elston Howard, Sandy Koufax) **2.00**
202 1964—MVPs (Ken Boyer, Brooks Robinson).......... **2.00**
203 1965—MVPs (Willie Mays, Zoilo Versalles) **2.00**
204 1966—MVPs (Bob Clemente, Frank Robinson) **3.00**
205 1967—MVPs (Orlando Cepeda, Carl Yastrzemski) **1.25**
206 1968—MVPs (Bob Gibson, Denny McLain) **1.25**
207 1969—MVPs (Harmon Killebrew, Willie McCovey) **1.50**
208 1970—MVPs (Johnny Bench, Boog Powell) **1.25**
209 1971—MVPs (Vida Blue, Joe Torre)...................... **1.25**
210 1972—MVPs (Rich Allen, Johnny Bench) **1.25**
211 1973—MVPs (Reggie Jackson, Pete Rose) **5.00**
212 1974—MVPs (Jeff Burroughs, Steve Garvey) **1.00**
213 Oscar Gamble .... **.40**
215 Bobby Valentine .... **.50**
216 Giants Team Wes Westrum).......................... **.40**
217 Lou Piniella...................... **.90**
220 Don Sutton **3.50**
221 Aurelio Rodriquez (Rodriguez) .... **.40**
223 *Robin Yount* **225.00**
225 Bob Grich .... **.50**
226 Bill Campbell .... **.40**
227 Bob Watson .... **.40**
228 *George Brett*............... **225.00**
230 • Jim Hunter **4.00**
236 Angels Team (Dick Williams)................. **.80**
240 Garry Maddox .... **.40**

223 Robin Yount

241 Dick Tidrow .... **.40**
242 Jay Johnstone .... **.50**
244 Bill Buckner **1.00**
245 • Mickey Lolich .... **.50**
246 • Cardinals Team (Red Schoendienst) .... **.90**
247 Enos Cabell .... **.40**
248 Randy Jones .... **.40**
249 Danny Thompson............. **.45**
250 Ken Brett .... **.40**
253 Jesus Alou....................... **.40**
254 Mike Torrez .... **.40**
255 Dwight Evans **5.00**
257 Checklist 133-264 .... **1.50**
260 Johnny Bench **15.00**
263 Jim Perry .... **.50**
266 Sandy Alomar .... **.40**
268 • Hal McRae .... **.50**
270 Ron Fairly .... **.40**
276 White Sox Team (Chuck Tanner)............................ **.80**
280 Carl Yastrzemski **9.00**
284 Ken Griffey **4.50**
290 Jon Matlack .... **.40**
291 Bill Sudakis...................... **.40**
294 *Geoff Zahn* .... **.40**
295 • Vada Pinson .... **.75**
299 Bucky Dent...................... **.50**

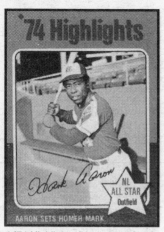

'74 Highlights

NL ALL STAR Outfield

AARON SETS HOMER MARK

1 '74 Highlights (Hank Aaron)

300	Reggie Jackson	30.00
302	*Rick Burleson*	.50
304	Pirates Team (Danny Murtaugh)	.90
306	Batting Ldrs (Rod Carew, Ralph Garr)	1.00
307	HR Ldrs (Dick Allen, Mike Schmidt)	3.00
308	RBI Ldrs (Johnny Bench, Jeff Burroughs)	1.00
309	SB Ldrs (Lou Brock, Bill North)	1.00
310	Victory Ldrs (Jim Hunter, Fergie Jenkins, Andy Messersmith, Phil Niekro)	1.25
311	ERA Ldrs (Buzz Capra, Jim Hunter)	1.00
312	SO Ldrs (Steve Carlton, Nolan Ryan)	15.00
313	Leading Firemen (Terry Forster, Mike Marshall)	1.00
315	Don Kessinger	.25
320	Pete Rose	15.00
321	Rudy May	.40
324	Ed Kranepool	.40
325	Tony Oliva	1.00
330	Mike Marshall	.45
331	Indians Team (Frank Robinson)	1.00
334	*Greg Gross*	.45
335	Jim Palmer	10.00
339	Jim Fregosi	.50
340	Paul Splittorff	.40
344	Ben Oglivie	.40
345	Clay Carroll	.40
350	Bobby Murcer	.65
351	Bob Boone	1.50
356	Rico Petrocelli	.50
357	Ken Forsch	.40
358	Al Bumbry	.40
360	George Scott	.35
361	Dodgers Team (Walter Alston)	1.00
370	Tom Seaver	20.00
375	Roy White	.50
380	Sal Bando	.50
382	Don Baylor	2.50
384	Brewers Team (Del Crandall)	.75
385	Dock Ellis	.40
386	Checklist 265-396	1.50
388	Steve Stone	.45
390	Ron Cey	1.00
392	Bruce Bochte	.40
395	Bud Harrelson	.50
397	Bill Freehan	.50
400	Dick Allen	.80
401	Mike Wallace	.35
402	Bob Tolan	.35
407	● *Herb Washington*	.40
410	Mike Cueller (Cuellar)	.40
414	Manny Mota	.40
415	John Hiller	.35
419	Dave Goltz	.35
420	Larry Bowa	.50
421	Mets Team (Yogi Berra)	1.00
422	Brian Downing	.40
426	George Medich	.35
429	*Jim Dwyer*	.35
430	● Luis Tiant	.50
437	*Al Cowens*	.40
439	Ed Brinkman	.40
440	Andy Messersmith	.40
443	Twins Team (Frank Quilici)	.80
444	Gene Garber	.40

450	Willie McCovey	**5.00**
451	Rick Dempsey	.40
453	Claude Osteen	.35
458	Ross Grimsley	.35
459	AL Championships	**1.00**
460	NL Championships	**1.00**
461	World Series Game 1	**1.50**
462	World Series Game 2	**1.00**
463	World Series Game 3	**1.00**
464	World Series Game 4	**1.00**
465	World Series Game 5	**1.00**
466	World Series Summary	**1.00**
470	Jeff Burroughs	.50
475	Darrell Evans	.75
480	Carlos May	.40
481	*Will McEnaney*	.35
482	Tom McCraw	.35
483	Steve Ontiveros	.35
484	Glenn Beckert	.40
485	Sparky Lyle	.50
487	Astros Team (Preston Gomez)	.85
488	Bill Travers	.35
489	Cecil Cooper	**1.25**
490	Reggie Smith	.60
491	Doyle Alexander	.40
492	Rich Hebner	.35
493	Don Stanhouse	.35
494	*Pete LaCock*	.35
495	Nelson Briles	.35
496	Pepe Frias	.35
497	Jim Nettles	.35
498	Al Downing	.40
499	Marty Perez	.35
500	Nolan Ryan	**75.00**
502	Pat Bourque	.35
504	Buddy Bradford	.35
505	Chris Speier	.35
506	Leron Lee	.35
507	Tom Carroll	.35
508	Bob Hansen	.35
510	Vida Blue	.75
511	Rangers Team (Billy Martin)	**1.00**
512	Larry Milbourne	.35
514	Jose Cruz	.75
515	Manny Sanguillen	.35
517	Checklist 397-528	**1.25**
518	Leo Cardenas	.35

228 George Brett

519	Jim Todd	.35
520	Amos Otis	.40
522	Gary Sutherland	.35
523	Tom Paciorek	.50
524	John Doherty	.35
525	Tom House	.35
526	Larry Hisle	.35
527	Mac Scarce	.35
529	Gary Thomasson	.35
530	Gaylord Perry	**4.00**
531	Reds Team (Sparky Anderson)	**1.00**
532	Gorman Thomas	.75
534	Alex Johnson	.40
535	Gene Tenace	.50
536	Bob Moose	.40
537	Tommy Harper	.40
538	Duffy Dyer	.40
539	Jesse Jefferson	.40
540	Lou Brock	**5.00**
541	Roger Metzger	.35
543	Larry Biittner	.35
544	Steve Mingori	.35
545	Billy Williams	**4.00**
546	John Knox	.35
547	Von Joshua	.35
548	Charlie Sands	.35
550	Ralph Garr	.40

1975 Rookie Catchers-Outfielders

GARY CARTER
c/Montreal Expos

MARC HILL
c/S.F. Giants

DANNY MEYER
of/Detroit Tigers

LEON ROBERTS
of/Detroit Tigers

620 Rookie Catchers-Outfielders

551	Larry Christensen	.35
552	Jack Brohamer	.35
553	John Boccabella	.35
554	• Rich Gossage	3.50
555	Al Oliver	.80
557	Larry Gura	1.00
558	Dave Roberts	.35
559	Bob Montgomery	.35
560	Tony Perez	.35
561	A's Team (Alvin Dark)	1.00
562	Gary Nolan	.35
564	Tommy Davis	.50
565	Joe Torre	1.00
566	Ray Burris	.35
567	*Jim Sundberg*	.90
568	Dale Murray	.35
569	Frank White	.35
570	Jim Wynn	.40
572	Roger Nelson	.35
573	Orlando Pena	.35
574	Tony Taylor	.35
575	Gene Clines	.35
578	Dave Tomlin	.35
579	Skip Pitlock	.35
580	Frank Robinson	5.00
581	Darrel Chaney	.35
583	Andy Etchebarren	.35
584	Mike Garman	.35

585	Chris Chambliss	.50
586	Tim McCarver	.80
588	Rick Auerbach	.35
589	Braves Team (Clyde King)	.50
590	Cesar Cedeno	.50
593	Gene Lamont	.35
595	Joe Niekro	.50
598	Bruce Kison	.35
599	Nate Colbert	.35
600	Rod Carew	10.00
601	Juan Beniquez	.50
602	John Vukovich	.35
603	Lew Krausse	.35
604	Oscar Zamora	.35
607	Jim Holt	.35
608	Gene Michael	.45
610	Ron Hunt	.40
611	Yankees Team (Bill Virdon)	1.50
612	Terry Hughes	.35
614	Rookie Pitchers (Jack Kucek, Dyar Miller, Vern Ruhle, Paul Siebert)	.40
615	Rookie Pitchers (Pat Darcy, *Dennis Leonard*, *Tom Underwood*, Hank Webb)	.75
616	Rookie Outfielders (Dave Augustine, Pepe Mangual, *Jim Rice*, John Scott)	22.00
617	Rookie Infielders (Mike Cubbage, *Doug DeCinces*, Reggie Sanders, Manny Trillo)	2.50
618	Rookie Pitchers (*Jamie Easterly*, Tom Johnson, *Scott McGregor*, *Rick Rhoden*)	2.25
619	Rookie Outfielders (Benny Ayala, Nyls Nyman, Tommy Smith, Jerry Turner)	.40
620	Rookie Catchers-Outfielders (*Gary Carter*, Marc Hill, Danny Meyer, Leon Roberts)	50.00

621	Rookie Pitchers (*John Denny, Rawly Eastwick, Jim Kern,* Juan Veintidos)	.75
622	Rookie Outfielders (Ed Armbrister, *Fred Lynn,* Tom Poquette, Terry Whitfield)	13.00
623	Rookie Infielders (*Phil Garner, Keith Hernandez,* Bob Sheldon, Tom Veryzer)	18.00
624	Rookie Pitchers (Doug Konieczny, *Gary Lavelle,* Jim Otten, Eddie Solomon)	.30
625	Boog Powell	.85
626	Larry Haney	.40
628	*Ron LeFlore*	.75
629	Joe Hoerner	.40
630	Greg Luzinski	.75
631	Lee Lacy	.40
632	Morris Nettles	.40
633	Paul Casanova	.40
634	Cy Acosta	.40
636	Charlie Moore	.40
638	Cubs Team (Jim Marshall)	.75
639	Steve Kline	.40
640	Harmon Killebrew	5.00
641	Jim Northrup	.35
642	Mike Phillips	.35
643	Brent Strom	.35
645	Danny Cater	.35
646	Checklist 529-660	1.50
647	*Claudell Washington*	2.00
648	Dave Pagan	.35
649	Jack Heidemann	.35
650	Dave May	.35
651	John Morlan	.35
652	Lindy McDaniel	.35
653	Lee Richards	.35
654	Jerry Terrell	.35
655	Rico Carty	.50
656	Bill Plummer	.50
657	Bob Oliver	.35
658	Vic Harris	.35
660	Hank Aaron	30.00

1976 TOPPS

Topps introduced a new design concept with its 1976 set, offering 660 cards that stress quality photos instead of gaudy borders. A large, clear photo appears on each card, complemented by just two color strips on the bottom that show the player name and team. Horizontal card backs have a simpler design and are easier to read than those of many earlier sets. One interesting subset in 1976 contains ten All-Time All-Stars selected by *The Sporting News.* Another show five players (Buddy Bell, Bob Boone, Joe Coleman, Mike Hegan, and Roy Smalley) with their fathers, who were all major-leaguers themselves in their day. Later in the season Topps issued 43 "traded" cards that show players as members of the new teams to which they had been traded. This group of cards is not considered part of the major set, however, and sells, as a subset, for $8 to $12.

	NR MT
Complete set	**$475.00**
Commons	.25

1	'75 Record Breaker (Hank Aaron)	$15.00
2	'75 Record Breaker (Bobby Bonds)	.75

316 Robin Yount

3	'75 Record Breaker (Mickey Lolich)	.50
4	'75 Record Breaker (Dave Lopes)	.50
5	'75 Record Breaker (Tom Seaver)	4.00
6	'75 Record Breaker (Rennie Stennett)	.50
10	Lou Brock	5.00
12	Richie Zisk	.30
14	Gene Garber	.30
15	George Scott	.35
17	Yankees Team (Billy Martin)	1.50
19	George Brett	60.00
20	Bob Watson	.30
22	Bill Russell	.30
23	Brian Downing	.35
24	Cesar Geronimo	.30
25	Mike Torrez	.30
26	Andy Thornton	.35
28	Dusty Baker	.35
29	Rick Burleson	.30
30	*John Montefusco*	.35
35	Tony Oliva	.75
37	John Hiller	.30
38	Garry Maddox	.30
40	Dave Kingman	.90
41	*Tippy Martinez*	.40
43	Paul Splittorff	.30
45	Boog Powell	.75
46	Dodgers Team (Walter Alston)	1.00
48	Dave Concepcion	1.00
50	Fred Lynn	2.00
55	Gaylord Perry	3.00
57	Phil Garner	.30
58	Ron Reed	.30
59	Larry Hisle	.30
60	Jerry Reuss	.30
61	Ron LeFlore	.30
64	Jerry Koosman	.30
65	Chris Chambliss	.30
66	Father & Son (Buddy Bell, Gus Bell)	.50
67	Father & Son (Bob Boone, Ray Boone)	.75
68	Father & Son (Joe Coleman, Joe Coleman, Jr.)	.30
69	Father & Son (Jim Hegan, Mike Hegan)	.30
70	Father & Son (Roy Smalley, Roy Smalley, Jr.)	.35
71	Steve Rogers	.30
72	● Hal McRae	.50
73	Orioles Team (Earl Weaver)	.80
74	Oscar Gamble	.30
75	Larry Dierker	.30
78	Cecil Cooper	1.00
80	Jim Kaat	1.00
81	Darrell Evans	.75
85	Mickey Rivers	.35
88	Duffy Dyer	.15
89	Vern Ruhle	.15
90	Sal Bando	.30
94	Jim Dwyer	.35
95	Brooks Robinson	5.00
98	*Dennis Eckersley*	60.00
100	Jim Hunter	4.00
104	Reds Team (Sparky Anderson)	1.00
110	Carlos May	.30
111	Danny Thompson	.30
112	● *Kent Tekulve*	1.75
114	Jay Johnstone	.35
115	Ken Holtzman	.35

19 George Brett

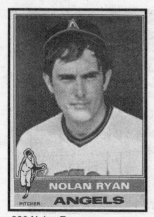

330 Nolan Ryan

334	Dennis Leonard	.35
335	Bob Grich	.35
337	Bud Harrelson	.30
339	John Denny	.35
340	• Jim Rice	6.00
341	All Time AS (Lou Gehrig)	6.00
342	All Time AS (Rogers Hornsby)	3.00
343	All Time AS (Pie Traynor)	1.25
344	All Time AS (Honus Wagner)	3.00
345	All Time AS (Babe Ruth)	10.00
346	All Time AS (Ty Cobb)	6.00
347	All Time AS (Ted Williams)	6.00
348	All Time AS (Mickey Cochrane)	1.25
349	All Time AS (Walter Johnson)	3.00
350	All Time AS (Lefty Grove)	1.00
353	Sixto Lezcano	.30
354	Ron Blomberg	.30
355	Steve Carlton	7.00
357	Ken Forsch	.30
358	Buddy Bell	.50
359	Rick Reuschel	.30
360	Jeff Burroughs	.30
361	Tigers Team (Ralph Houk)	1.00
363	Dave Collins	.60
365	Carlton Fisk	12.00
366	Bobby Valentine	.30
368	Wilbur Wood	.35
369	Frank White	.30
370	Ron Cey	.40
375	Ron Fairly	.35
376	Rich Hebner	.30
378	Steve Stone	.35
380	Bobby Bonds	.35
384	Phillies Team (Danny Ozark)	.80
385	Mickey Lolich	.40
390	Don Gullett	.30
392	Checklist 265-396	1.50
395	Jim Wynn	.30

98 Dennis Eckersley

396	Bill Lee	.30
397	Tim Foli	.15
400	Rod Carew	8.00
405	Rollie Fingers	1.25
408	Charlie Spikes	.15
410	Ralph Garr	.30
411	Bill Singer	.30
412	Toby Harrah	.35
413	Pete Varney	.15
414	Wayne Garland	.15
415	• Vada Pinson	.50
416	Tommy John	1.25
418	Jose Morales	.15
419	Reggie Cleveland	.15
420	• Joe Morgan	6.00
421	A's Team	.80
424	Phil Roof	.15
425	Rennie Stennett	.15
426	Bob Forsch	.35
427	Kurt Bevacqua	.30
429	Fred Stanley	.30
430	Jose Cardenal	.30
431	Dick Ruthven	.30
432	Tom Veryzer	.15
433	Rick Waits	.15
434	Morris Nettles	.15
435	Phil Niekro	2.00
437	Terry Forster	.35

240 Pete Rose

528	Dock Ellis	.30
529	Deron Johnson	.15
530	Don Sutton	3.00
531	Mets Team (Joe Frazier)	.90
532	Milt May	.15
533	Lee Richard	.15
534	Stan Bahnsen	.15
535	Dave Nelson	.15
536	Mike Thompson	.15
537	Tony Muser	.15
539	John Balaz	.15
540	Bill Freehan	.35
541	Steve Mingori	.15
542	Keith Hernandez	3.00
543	Wayne Twitchell	.15
544	Pepe Frias	.15
545	Sparky Lyle	.35
546	Dave Rosello	.15
547	Roric Harrison	.15
548	Manny Mota	.15
550	Hank Aaron	25.00
552	Terry Humphrey	.15
553	Randy Moffitt	.15
554	Ray Fosse	.15
556	Twins Team (Gene Mauch)	.80
557	Dan Spillner	.15
558	Clarence Gaston	.15
559	Clyde Wright	.15
560	Jorge Orta	.15
561	Tom Carroll	.15
562	Adrian Garrett	.15
564	Bubble Gum Blowing Champ (Kurt Bevacqua)	.30
565	Tug McGraw	.35
566	Ken McMullen	.15
567	George Stone	.15
568	Rob Andrews	.15
569	Nelson Briles	.15
570	George Hendrick	.30
571	Don DeMola	.15
572	Rich Coggins	.15
573	Bill Travers	.15
574	Don Kessinger	.30
575	• Dwight Evans	2.00
577	Marc Hill	.15
578	Ted Kubiak	.15
579	Clay Kirby	.15
580	Bert Campaneris	.30

550 Hank Aaron

581	• Cardinals Team (Red Schoendienst)	.80
582	Mike Kekich	.15
583	Tommy Helms	.15
585	Joe Torre	.50
589	Rookie Pitchers (Santo Alcala, *Mike Flanagan*, Joe Pactwa, Pablo Torrealba)	1.50
590	Rookie Outfielders (Henry Cruz, *Chet Lemon, Ellis Valentine,* Terry Whitfield)	1.00
592	Rookie Infielders (Dave McKay, *Willie Randolph, Jerry Royster,* Roy Staiger)	9.00
593	Rookie Pitchers (Larry Anderson, Ken Crosby, Mark Littell, *Butch Metzger*)	.40
594	Rookie Catchers and Outfielders (Andy Merchant, Ed Ott, Royle Stillman, Jerry White)	.30

596	Rookie Infielders (Lamar Johnson, *Johnny LeMaster*, Jerry Manuel, *Craig Reynolds*)	.45		

596 Rookie Infielders (Lamar Johnson, *Johnny LeMaster*, Jerry Manuel, *Craig Reynolds*) .... .45
597 Rookie Pitchers (*Don Aase*, Jack Kucek, Frank LaCorte, Mike Pazik) .... .50
598 Rookie Outfielders (Hector Cruz, *Jamie Quirk*, Jerry Turner, Joe Wallis) .... .40
599 Rookie Pitchers (Rob Dressler, *Ron Guidry*, *Bob McClure*, Pat Zachry) 8.00
600 Tom Seaver 15.00
605 Al Downing .... .30
606 Brewers Team (Alex Grammas) .... .80
620 Al Oliver 1.00
625 J.R. Richard .... .35

630 Chris Speier .... .30
631 Braves Team (Dave Bristol) .... .80
633 *John Stearns* .... .30
635 Jim Fregosi .... .35
637 Bruce Bochte .... .30
638 Doyle Alexander .... .30
640 Bill Madlock 1.00
641 Tom Paciorek .... .30
643 Checklist 529-660 .... 1.50
645 Darrell Porter .... .30
648 Al Cowens .... .30
650 Thurman Munson 8.00
651 John Odom .... .30
653 *Mike Norris* .... .30
656 White Sox Team (Chuck Tanner) .... .80
657 *Roy Smalley* .... .40
659 Ben Oglivie .... .35
660 Dave Lopes .... .90

1977 TOPPS

The 1977 Topps set of 660 cards offered superior photos, but few major surprises in subject matter were introduced. An eight-card set of league leaders opens the 1977 issue, while a smaller set acknowledges the record-setting 1976 performances of George Brett, Minnie Minoso, Jose Morales, and Nolan Ryan. A unique four-card novelty series entitled Big League Brothers is a 1977 highlight. It features Paul and Rick Reuschel (wrongly identified on their card), George and Ken Brett, Bob and Ken Forsch, and Carlos and Lee May. The hottest cards are from the multi-player rookie card subset: Jack Clark, Andre Dawson, and Dale Murphy (identified as a catcher). The set also contains the last regular-issue card of Brooks Robinson.

	NR MT
Complete set	**$450.00**
Commons	.20

1 Batting Ldrs (George Brett, Bill Madlock) $6.00
2 HR Ldrs (Graig Nettles, Mike Schmidt) 1.25
3 RBI Ldrs (George Foster, Lee May) .... .50

4 SB Ldrs (Dave Lopes, Bill North) .... .30
5 Victory Ldrs (Randy Jones, Jim Palmer) .... .80
6 SO Ldrs (Nolan Ryan, Tom Seaver) 12.00
7 ERA Ldrs (John Denny, Mark Fidrych) .... .30
8 Leading Firemen (Bill Campbell, Rawly Eastwick) .... .30

9	Doug Rader	.15
10	Reggie Jackson	20.00
11	Rob Dressler	.15
12	Larry Haney	.15
15	Don Gullett	.25
16	Bob Jones	.15
17	Steve Stone	.25
18	Indians Team (Frank Robinson)	1.00
19	John D'Acquisto	.15
20	Graig Nettles	1.00
21	Ken Forsch	.25
22	Bill Freehan	.25
23	Dan Driessen	.25
24	Carl Morton	.15
25	Dwight Evans	2.00
26	Ray Sadecki	.15
27	Bill Buckner	.35
28	Woodie Fryman	.25
29	Bucky Dent	.25
30	Greg Luzinski	.45
32	Checklist 1-132	1.25
33	Wayne Garland	.15
34	Angels Team (Norm Sherry)	.70
35	Rennie Stennett	.15
37	Steve Hargan	.15
38	Craig Kusick	.15
40	Bobby Murcer	.50
41	Jim Kern	.15
42	Jose Cruz	.35
44	Bud Harrelson	.25
45	Rawly Eastwick	.15
46	Buck Martinez	.15
47	Lynn McGlothlen	.15
48	Tom Paciorek	.15
50	Ron Cey	.50
51	Brewers Team (Alex Grammas)	.70
52	Ellis Valentine	.25
53	Paul Mitchell	.15
54	Sandy Alomar	.25
55	Jeff Burroughs	.25
56	Rudy May	.25
58	Chet Lemon	.25
59	Larry Christenson	.15
60	Jim Rice	4.00
61	Manny Sanguillen	.15
62	Eric Raich	.15

580 George Brett

63	Tito Fuentes	.15
64	Larry Biittner	.15
65	Skip Lockwood	.15
66	Roy Smalley	.15
67	*Joaquin Andujar*	.60
68	Bruce Bochte	.25
70	Johnny Bench	9.00
71	Dock Ellis	.25
72	Mike Anderson	.15
73	Charlie Williams	.15
74	A's Team (Jack McKeon)	.70
75	Dennis Leonard	.25
76	Tim Foli	.15
77	Dyar Miller	.15
78	Bob Davis	.15
79	Don Money	.15
80	Andy Messersmith	.15
81	Juan Beniquez	.25
83	Kevin Bell	.15
85	Duane Kuiper	.15
86	Pat Zachry	.15
87	Glenn Borgmann	.15
88	Stan Wall	.15
89	*Butch Hobson*	.25
90	Cesar Cedeno	.35
93	Tom Poquette	.15
94	Craig Swan	.15

10 Reggie Jackson

95	Keith Hernandez	**2.00**
96	Lou Piniella	.50
97	Dave Heaverlo	.15
98	Milt May	.15
99	Tom Hausman	.15
100	• Joe Morgan	**4.00**
104	*Omar Moreno*	.25
106	Mike Flanagan	.35
107	Bill Melton	.25
110	Steve Carlton	**7.00**
111	Rico Petrocelli	.25
113	Blue Jays Mgr./Coaches (Roy Hartsfield, Don Leppert, Bob Miller, Jackie Moore, Harry Warner)	.25
115	Rick Manning	.25
116	Joe Niekro	.30
117	• Frank White	.40
119	John Stearns	.25
120	Rod Carew	**7.00**
122	Ben Oglivie	.25
123	Fred Stanley	.15
127	Ron Fairly	.25
128	• Tommy John	**1.25**
130	Al Oliver	.60
133	Ralph Garr	.25
134	Padres Team (John McNamara)	.70
135	Mark Belanger	.25
136	*Jerry Mumphrey*	.40
140	Mike Schmidt	**20.00**
144	• *Bruce Sutter*	**7.00**
146	Dusty Baker	.25
148	Fran Healy	.25
150	Tom Seaver	**10.00**
152	• Gaylord Perry	**3.00**
155	Joe Rudi	.25
157	Ken Brett	.25
161	*Garry Templeton*	.80
162	Mike Cuellar	.25
164	Tug McGraw	.30
165	Jim Wynn	.25
170	• *Thurman Munson*	**6.00**
175	*Butch Wynegar*	.40
180	Dave Lopes	.25
183	Cardinals Team (Vern Rapp)	.70
185	Sixto Lezcano	.25
188	Bob Tolan	.25
189	Rick Dempsey	.15
193	Larry Gura	.25
194	Gary Matthews	.25
195	Ed Figueroa	.25
198	Wilbur Wood	.25
199	Pepe Frias	.15
200	Frank Tanana	.30
201	Ed Kranepool	.25
206	Boog Powell	.50
208	Checklist 133-264	**1.25**
210	Fred Lynn	**1.50**
211	Giants Team (Joe Altobelli)	.70
213	Maximino Leon	.15
214	Darrell Porter	.25
215	Butch Metzger	.15
216	Doug DeCinces	.25
217	Tom Underwood	.15
218	*John Wathan*	.60
219	Joe Coleman	.25
220	Chris Chambliss	.35
221	Bob Bailey	.15
222	Francisco Barrios	.15
224	Rusty Torres	.15
225	Bob Apodaca	.15
227	*Joe Sambito*	.25
228	Twins Team (Gene Mauch)	.80

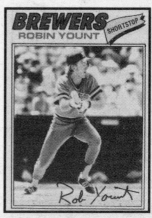

635 Robin Yount

473 Rookie Outfielders

391 Dan Warthen .... .15
392 Phil Roof .... .15
393 John Lowenstein .... .15
394 Bill Laxton .... .15
395 Manny Trillo .... .25
397 *Larry Herndon* .... .40
398 Tom Burgmeier .... .15
399 Bruce Boisclair .... .15
400 Steve Garvey 5.00
401 Mickey Scott .... .15
402 Tommy Helms .... .15
403 Tom Grieve .... .15
404 Eric Rasmussen .... .15
405 Claudell Washington .... .25
407 Dave Freisleben .... .15
408 Cesar Tovar .... .15
409 Pete Broberg .... .15
410 Willie Montanez .... .15
411 World Series Games
      1 & 2 .... 1.00
412 World Series Games
      3 & 4 .... 1.00
413 World Series Summary . 1.00
414 Tommy Harper .... .25
415 Jay Johnstone .... .25
416 Chuck Hartenstein .... .15
418 White Sox Team (Bob
      Lemon) .... .80
419 Steve Swisher .... .15
420 Rusty Staub .... .35
421 Doug Rau .... .15
422 Freddie Patek .... .15
423 Gary Lavelle .... .15
425 Joe Torre .... .40
426 Dick Drago .... .15
427 Dave Rader .... .15
428 Rangers Team (Frank
      Lucchesi) .... .80
430 Fergie Jenkins 3.00
431 Dave Collins .... .25
432 Buzz Capra .... .15
433 Turn Back The Clock
      (Nate Colbert) .... .25
434 Turn Back The Clock
      (Carl Yastrzemski) 3.00
435 Turn Back The Clock
      (Maury Wills) 1.00
436 Turn Back The Clock
      (Bob Keegan) .... .25

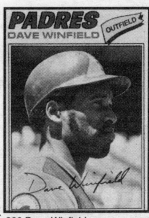

390 Dave Winfield

437 Turn Back The Clock
      (Ralph Kiner) .... .50
438 Marty Perez .... .15
439 Gorman Thomas .... .25
440 Jon Matlack .... .25
442 Braves Team
      (Dave Bristol) .... .70
443 Lamar Johnson .... .15
445 Ken Singleton .... .25
450 Pete Rose 10.00
451 Checklist 397-528 .... 1.25
455 Rick Wise .... .25
460 Willie Stargell 3.00
461 Dick Tidrow .... .25
462 Don Baylor .... .35
465 Rico Carty .... .25
467 Phillies Team
      (Danny Ozark) .... .70
470 Ted Simmons .... .90
472 Rookie Pitchers (Don
      Aase, Bob McClure,
      Gil Patterson,
      David Wehrmeister) .... .25
473 Rookie Outfielders
      (*Andre Dawson,*
      Gene Richards,
      John Scott, *Denny
      Walling*) 75.00

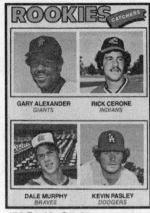

476 Rookie Catchers

541	John Denny	.25
543	Ron Blomberg	.25
545	• Bob Boone	.75
546	Orioles Team (Earl Weaver)	.80
547	• Willie McCovey	4.00
548	*Joel Youngblood*	.30
550	Randy Jones	.25
551	Bill North	.15
552	Pepe Mangual	.15
553	Jack Heidemann	.15
555	Dan Ford	.25
560	Dave Concepcion	.75
562	Checklist 529-660	1.25
564	Alan Ashby	.25
565	Mickey Lolich	.50
567	Enos Cabell	.25
568	Carlos May	.25
569	Jim Lonborg	.25
570	Bobby Bonds	.50
571	Darrell Evans	.40
574	Aurelio Rodriguez	.25
578	Bob Randall	.15
580	George Brett	35.00
585	Rick Burleson	.25
590	Buddy Bell	.30
595	John Hiller	.25
596	*Jerry Martin*	.25
597	Mariners Mgr./ Coaches (Don Bryant, Jim Busby, Darrell Johnson, Vada Pinson, Wes Stock)	.25
598	• Sparky Lyle	.35
600	• Jim Palmer	6.00
603	Willie Davis	.25
610	Jose Cardenal	.25
615	Phil Niekro	2.00
618	Pat Dobson	.25
620	Don Sutton	2.00
621	Tigers Team (Ralph Houk)	.80
622	Jim Wohlford	.15
623	Jack Kucek	.15
624	Hector Cruz	.15
625	Ken Holtzman	.25
626	Al Bumbry	.25
629	Bobby Valentine	.25
630	Bert Blyleven	.80

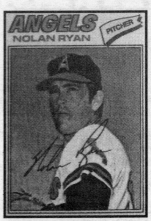

650 Nolan Ryan

631	Big League Brothers (George Brett, Ken Brett)	5.00
632	Big League Brothers (Bob Forsch, Ken Forsch)	.30
633	Big League Brothers (Carlos May, Lee May)	.30
634	Big League Brothers (Paul Reuschel, Rick Reuschel) (names reversed)	.30
635	Robin Yount	35.00
638	• Jim Kaat	.80
640	Carlton Fisk	10.00
641	Dan Larson	.15
642	Willie Crawford	.15
643	Mike Pazik	.15
644	Matt Alexander	.15
645	Jerry Reuss	.25
647	Expos Team (Dick Williams)	.80
650	Nolan Ryan	45.00
652	Tom Walker	.15
653	Diego Segui	.15
655	Tony Perez	.80
656	Ron Guidry	2.00
660	Willie Horton	.40

1978 TOPPS

The 1978 Topps set grew to 726 cards—the biggest since 1972. The simply designed cards use an extra-large photo and a minimal border. All Stars from 1977 are honored with a small red, white, and blue shield usually in the upper right-hand corner of their cards. Card backs contain a small box that features baseball situations such as a home run or ground out—this allows two people to play a simulated baseball game. Because Topps increased the set size, it needed to print 11 cards twice on each 132-card sheet. Although this increased the availability of those cards, prices for them have seen little fluctuation. Topps used six different sheets for printing, thus 66 double-printed cards exist.

	NR MT
Complete set	$350.00
Commons	.12

1	Record Breaker (Lou Brock)	$3.00
2	Record Breaker (Sparky Lyle)	.25
3	Record Breaker (Willie McCovey)	1.00
4	Record Breaker (Brooks Robinson)	1.50
5	Record Breaker (Pete Rose)	3.00
6	Record Breaker (Nolan Ryan)	12.00
7	Record Breaker (Reggie Jackson)	6.00
8	Mike Sadek	.12
9	Doug DeCinces	.25
10	Phil Niekro	2.00
12	Don Aase	.15
13	Art Howe	.12
15	Tony Perez	.75
16	Roy White	.20
17	Mike Krukow	.20
18	Bob Grich	.25
19	Darrell Porter	.20
20	Pete Rose	4.00
21	Steve Kemp	.20
22	Charlie Hough	.25
25	Jon Matlack	.20
30	George Hendrick	.20
32	Garry Templeton	.25

707 Rookie Shortstops

34	Willie McCovey	3.00
35	Sparky Lyle	.30
36	*Eddie Murray*	75.00
39	*Floyd Bannister*	.50
40	Carl Yastrzemski	5.00
41	Burt Hooton	.20
44	Toby Harrah	.20
45	Mark Fidrych	.25
48	Don Baylor	.35
49	Ed Kranepool	.20
50	Rick Reuschel	.25
52	Jim Lonborg	.20
56	Randy Jones	.20
58	Bob Forsch	.20

60	Thurman Munson	5.00
62	Jim Barr	.20
65	Ken Singleton	.25
66	White Sox Team	.50
67	Claudell Washington	.25
70	Rich Gossage	1.00
72	Andre Dawson	25.00
74	Checklist 1-121	.90
80	Ken Griffey	1.50
82	Giants Team	.50
84	Kent Tekulve	.25
85	Ron Fairly	.20
89	Ken Clay	.15
90	Larry Bowa	.30
96	Orioles Team	.50
99	*Willie Hernandez*	.65
100	George Brett	25.00
109	Joe Torre	.50
110	Richie Zisk	.20
111	Mike Tyson	.12
112	Astros Team	.50
114	Paul Blair	.20
119	Denny Martinez	.25
120	Gary Carter	5.00
122	Dennis Eckersley	10.00
123	Manny Trillo	.20
124	*Dave Rozema*	.25
125	George Scott	.20
127	Chet Lemon	.20
128	Bill Russell	.20
130	Jeff Burroughs	.20
131	Bert Blyleven	.75
132	Enos Cabell	.20
134	*Steve Henderson*	.25
135	Ron Guidry	.90
140	Rollie Fingers	.75
141	Ruppert Jones	.20
142	John Montefusco	.20
143	Keith Hernandez	1.50
145	Rick Monday	.20
146	Doyle Alexander	.30
147	Lee Mazilli	.20
148	Andre Thornton	.25
150	Bobby Bonds	.60
152	*Ivan DeJesus*	.20
153	Steve Stone	.25
154	Cecil Cooper	.20
156	Andy Messersmith	.20
158	Joaquin Andujar	.25

36 Eddie Murray

159	Lou Piniella	.35
160	Jim Palmer	5.00
161	• Bob Boone	.25
168	Reggie Smith	.25
170	Lou Brock	4.00
172	Mike Hargrove	.20
173	Robin Yount	20.00
176	Milt May	.12
179	Dick Tidrow	.20
180	Dave Concepcion	.35
181	Ken Forsch	.20
183	Doug Bird	.12
184	Checklist 122-242	.90
185	Ellis Valentine	.25
186	*Bob Stanley*	.25
188	Al Bumbry	.20
189	Tom Lasorda	.25
190	John Candelaria	.25
192	Padres Team	.50
195	Larry Dierker	.20
200	Reggie Jackson	15.00
201	Batting Ldrs (Rod Carew, Dave Parker)	1.25
202	HR Ldrs (George Foster, Jim Rice)	.25
203	RBI Ldrs (George Foster, Larry Hisle)	.25

400 Nolan Ryan

351 Jeff Torborg .... .20
352 Tony Scott .... .12
353 Doug Bair .... .12
354 Cesar Geronimo .... .20
355 Bill Travers .... .12
356 Mets Team .... .75
357 Tom Poquette .... .12
358 Mark Lemongello .... .12
359 Marc Hill .... .12
360 Mike Schmidt **18.00**
361 Chris Knapp .... .12
365 Ed Figueroa .... .20
366 Larry Milbourne .... .12
367 Rick Dempsey .... .20
368 Balor Moore .... .12
369 Tim Nordbrook .... .12
370 Rusty Staub .... .35
372 Brian Asselstine .... .12
373 Jim Willoughby .... .12
374 Jose Morales .... .12
375 Tommy John **1.00**
376 Jim Wohlford .... .12
377 Manny Sarmiento .... .12
379 Skip Lockwood .... .12
380 Ted Simmons .... .50
381 Phillies Team .... .70
382 Joe Lahoud .... .12
383 Mario Mendoza .... .12
384 Jack Clark **1.25**
385 Tito Fuentes .... .12
387 Ken Holtzman .... .25
388 Bill Fahey .... .12
389 Julio Gonzalez.................. .12
390 Oscar Gamble .... .20
391 Larry Haney...................... .12
392 Billy Almon .... .12
393 Tippy Martinez.................. .12
397 Greg Gross....................... .15
399 Pete Mackanin .... .12
400 Nolan Ryan **35.00**
401 Sparky Anderson.............. .30
402 Dave Campbell.................. .12
403 Bud Harrelson .... .20
404 Tigers Team .... .60
405 Rawly Eastwick .... .12
406 Mike Jorgensen................ .12
407 Odell Jones .... .12
409 Ron Schueler .... .12
410 Bill Madlock .... .50

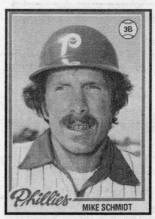

360 Mike Schmidt

411 AL Championships
    (Yankees Rally To
    Defeat Royals) **1.00**
412 NL Championships
    (Dodgers Overpower
    Phillies In Four) .... .75
413 World Series
    (Reggie & Yankees
    Reign Supreme) **4.00**
414 Darold Knowles .... .12
415 Ray Fosse .... .12
416 Jack Brohamer .... .12
417 Mike Garman..................... .12
420 Greg Luzinski .... .50
421 Junior Moore .... .12
422 Steve Braun .... .12
423 Dave Rosello .... .12
424 Red Sox Team .... .70
426 Fred Kendall..................... .12
427 *Mario Soto* .... .40
428 Joel Youngblood .... .20
429 Mike Barlow .... .12
430 Al Oliver.......................... .40
431 Butch Metzger .... .12
435 Checklist 364-484 .... .90
436 Vic Harris........................ .12
437 Bo McLaughlin .... .12
439 Ken Kravec....................... .12

530 Dave Winfield

534	Wilbur Howard	.12
535	Checklist 485-605	.90
536	Roric Harrison	.12
537	Bruce Bochte	.20
538	Johnnie LeMaster	.12
539	Vic Davalillo	.12
540	Steve Carlton	6.00
543	Larry Harlow	.12
544	Len Randle	.12
545	Bill Campbell	.12
546	Ted Martinez	.12
547	John Scott	.12
549	Joe Kerrigan	.12
550	John Mayberry	.20
551	Braves Team	.50
552	Francisco Barrios	.12
553	*Terry Puhl*	.35
554	Joe Coleman	.20
555	Butch Wynegar	.20
556	Ed Armbrister	.12
559	Phil Mankowski	.12
560	Dave Parker	3.00
561	Charlie Williams	.12
563	Dave Rader	.12
564	Mick Kelleher	.12
565	Jerry Koosman	.25
566	Merv Rettenmund	.12
567	Dick Drago	.12
568	Tom Hutton	.20
569	*Lary Sorensen*	.20
570	Dave Kingman	.90
571	Buck Martinez	.12
572	Rick Wise	.20
573	Luis Gomez	.12
574	Bob Lemon	.30
575	Pat Dobson	.20
576	Sam Mejias	.12
577	A's Team	.50
578	Buzz Capra	.12
579	*Rance Mulliniks*	.35
580	Rod Carew	6.00
581	Lynn McGlothen	.12
582	Fran Healy	.15
583	George Medich	.12
585	Woodie Fryman	.12
586	Ed Goodson	.12
587	John Urrea	.12
588	Jim Mason	.12
589	*Bob Knepper*	.25

580 Rod Carew

590	Bobby Murcer	.30
591	George Zeber	.15
592	Bob Apodaca	.12
593	Dave Skaggs	.12
594	Dave Freisleben	.12
595	Sixto Lezcano	.12
597	Steve Dillard	.12
598	Eddie Solomon	.12
599	Gary Woods	.12
600	Frank Tanana	.25
601	Gene Mauch	.25
602	Eric Soderholm	.12
605	Rick Rhoden	.25
606	Pirates Team	.50
608	Johnny Grubb	.12
609	John Denny	.12
610	Garry Maddox	.20
611	Pat Scanlon	.12
615	Clay Carroll	.20
616	Pat Kelly	.12
617	Joe Nolan	.12
618	Tommy Helms	.12
619	*Thad Bosley*	.20
620	Willie Randolph	.30
621	Craig Swan	.12
622	Champ Summers	.12
625	Jose Cruz	.25
626	Blue Jays Team	.25

708 Rookie Catchers

706 Rookie First Basemen
(Wayne Cage, Ted Cox,
*Pat Putnam, Dave
Revering*) .... .20

707 Rookie Shortstops (Mickey
Klutts, *Paul Molitor, Alan
Trammell, U.L
Washington*) **65.00**

708 Rookie Catchers (*Bo Diaz,*
Dale Murphy, *Lance Parrish,
Ernie Whitt*) **13.00**

709 Rookie Pitchers (Steve
Burke, *Matt Keough,*
Lance Rautzhan,
Dan Schatzeder) .... .25

710 Rookie Outfielders
(Dell Alston,
Rick Bosetti, *Mike
Easler,* Keith Smith) .... .50

715 Jim Kaat .... .60
716 Clarence Gaston .... .12
717 Nelson Briles .... .12
718 Ron Jackson .... .12
719 Randy Elliott .... .12
720 Fergie Jenkins 2.50
721 Billy Martin .... .70
722 Pete Broberg .... .12
723 John Wockenfuss .... .12
724 Royals Team .... .70
726 Wilbur Wood.................... .75

1979 TOPPS

Although Topps continued to supply collectors with attractive cards in
1979, few innovations were included in the 726-card set. For the first
time, rookie prospect cards are arranged by team, with each card
featuring three black-and-white photos of promising young players.
Ozzie Smith led the rookie parade in 1979, and today his card is the
most valuable of the entire set. Other rookies include Kevin Bass,
Pedro Guerrero, Carney Lansford, Lonnie Smith, and Bob Welch.

	NR MT
Complete set	**$275.00**
Commons	**.12**

1 Batting Ldrs (Rod Carew,
Dave Parker) **$3.00**

2 HR Ldrs (George Foster,
Jim Rice) .... .50

3 RBI Ldrs (George Foster,
Jim Rice) .... .50

4 SB Ldrs (Ron LeFlore,
Omar Moreno) .... .25

5 Victory Ldrs (Ron Guidry,
Gaylord Perry)................. .50

6 SO Ldrs (J.R. Richard,
Nolan Ryan) 5.00

7 ERA Ldrs (Ron Guidry,
Craig Swan) .... .25

8 Leading Firemen (Rollie
Fingers, Rich Gossage) ... .75

10 Lee May .... .20
15 Ross Grimsley.................. .20
16 Fred Stanley..................... .15
17 Donnie Moore................... .20
20 Joe Morgan .... .40
23 Terry Forster .... .20
24 Paul Molitor 22.00
25 Steve Carlton 5.00
27 Dave Goltz .... .20
30 Dave Winfield 12.00
35 Ed Figueroa..................... .20
39 Dale Murphy.................. 8.00
40 Dennis Eckersley 2.00
41 Twins Team
(Gene Mauch) .... .50
45 Al Hrabosky..................... .25
50 Steve Garvey 1.25

348 Andre Dawson

55	Willie Stargell	2.00
58	Bob Randall	.15
60	Mickey Rivers	.20
61	Bo Diaz	.20
65	Mark Belanger	.20
66	Tigers Team (Les Moss)	.60
70	John Candelaria	.25
71	Brian Downing	.20
74	*Shane Rawley*	.50
80	Jason Thompson	.20
82	Mets Team (Joe Torre)	.60
85	Gary Matthews	.20
89	Dick Tidrow	.20
90	• Bob Boone	.50
95	Robin Yount	13.00
96	Indians Team (Jeff Torborg)	.50
99	John Wathan	.20
100	Tom Seaver	4.00
107	Jesus Alou	.20
110	Vida Blue	.30
112	Phillies Team (Danny Ozark)	.50
114	Cliff Johnson	.20
115	Nolan Ryan	30.00
116	*Ozzie Smith*	75.00
118	Bud Harrelson	.20

120	Jim Sundberg	.20
121	Checklist 1–121	.25
123	Lou Whitaker	8.00
125	Rick Burleson	.20
131	Jim Clancy	.25
135	Bobby Murcer	.25
136	Jim Kaat	.60
140	Don Gullett	.20
145	Rick Rhoden	.25
151	John Hiller	.20
152	Rick Cerone	.20
155	• Dwight Evans	1.00
159	Roy White	.20
160	Mike Flanagan	.30
164	Mickey Lolich	.40
170	Don Sutton	1.50
175	George Hendrick	.20
176	Aurelio Rodriguez	.20
177	Ron Reed	.20
180	Larry Hisle	.20
183	Paul Splittorff	.20
185	Mike Torrez	.20
189	*Eddie Whitson*	.50
190	Ron Cey	.75
192	Cardinals Team (Ken Boyer)	.75
194	Randy Jones	.20
195	Bill Madlock	.40
200	Johnny Bench	3.00
201	Record Breaker (Mike Edwards)	.12
202	Record Breaker (Ron Guidry)	.50
203	Record Breaker (J.R. Richard)	.50
204	Record Breaker (Pete Rose)	3.00
205	Record Breaker (John Stearns)	.12
206	Record Breaker (Sammy Stewart)	.12
210	Larry Bowa	.50
211	Denny Martinez	.20
212	*Carney Lansford*	3.00
214	Red Sox Team (Don Zimmer)	.60
215	Willie McCovey	2.00
216	Wilbur Wood	.20
218	Dennis Leonard	.20

116 Ozzie Smith

330 George Brett

428	Bobby Valentine	.25
429	John Urrea	.12
430	Dave Parker	**2.00**
432	Dave Heaverlo	.12
433	Larry Biittner	.12
435	Gene Tenace	.20
436	Hector Cruz	.12
437	Rick Williams	.12
439	Frank White	.25
440	Rusty Staub	.30
441	Lee Lacy	.12
442	Doyle Alexander	.25
443	Bruce Bochte	.12
444	*Aurelio Lopez*	.20
445	Steve Henderson	.12
446	Jim Lonborg	.20
447	Manny Sanguillen	.12
448	Moose Haas	.12
449	Bombo Rivera	.12
450	Dave Concepcion	.65
451	Royals Team (Whitey Herzog)	.60
453	Chris Knapp	.12
454	Len Randle	.12
456	Chuck Baker	.12
457	Bruce Sutter	1.00
458	Jim Essian	.12
459	Sid Monge	.12
460	Graig Nettles	.50
461	Jim Barr	.12
462	Otto Velez	.12
464	Joe Nolan	.12
465	Reggie Smith	.25
467	Don Kessinger	.12
468	Stan Bahnsen	.12
469	Lance Parrish	1.75
470	Garry Maddox	.12
471	Joaquin Andujar	.20
472	Craig Kusick	.12
473	Dave Roberts	.12
475	Dan Driessen	.20
476	Tom Poquette	.12
477	Bob Grich	.25
478	Juan Beniquez	.15
479	Padres Team (Roger Craig)	.50
480	Fred Lynn	.75
481	Skip Lockwood	.12
483	Checklist 364-484	.25

358 Alan Trammell

484	Rick Waits	.12
485	Bucky Dent	.25
486	Bob Knepper	.20
487	Miguel Dilone	.12
488	Bob Owchinko	.12
490	Al Cowens	.12
491	Tippy Martinez	.12
492	Bob Bailor	.12
493	Larry Christenson	.12
495	Tony Perez	.90
496	Barry Bonnell	.12
497	Glenn Abbott	.12
499	Rangers Team (Pat Corrales)	.50
500	Ron Guidry	.90
501	Junior Kennedy	.12
502	Steve Braun	.12
504	*Larry McWilliams*	.20
506	John D'Acquisto	.12
507	Tony Armas	.20
508	Charlie Hough	.20
509	Mario Mendoza	.12
510	Ted Simmons	.75
511	Paul Reuschel	.12
512	Jack Clark	.80
513	Dave Johnson	.30
514	Mike Proly	.12
515	Enos Cabell	.12

95 Robin Yount

115 Nolan Ryan

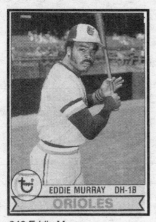

640 Eddie Murray

719 Dodgers Prospects
(Pedro Guerrero, Rudy
Law, Joe Simpson)........ 3.00

720 Expos Prospects
(Jerry Fry, Jerry Pirtle,
Scott Sanderson) .... .30

721 Mets Prospects
(*Juan Berenguer,*
Dwight Bernard,
Dan Norman)................... .30

722 Phillies Prospects
(*Jim Morrison,*
Lonnie Smith,
Jim Wright) 1.50

723 Pirates Prospects
(*Dale Berra,*
Eugenio Cotes,
Ben Wiltbank).................. .25

724 Cardinals Prospects
(Tom Bruno,
George Frazier,
Terry Kennedy) .... .60

725 Padres Prospects (Jim
Beswick, Steve Mura,
Broderick Perkins)........... .12

726 Giants Prospects (Greg
Johnston, Joe Strain, John
Tamargo)......................... .25

1980 TOPPS

Topps began the new decade with another 726-card issue. The Topps logo, which diminishes the appeal of the 1979 set, was dropped from the front of the 2½- by 3½-inch cards. Another improvement in 1980 involves the Future Stars cards (indicated with "FS" on the following list). This subset is arranged by team, with three players to a card, and unlike the preceding year, all the mug shots are in color. Some of the most important rookies in the main set were omitted from the Future Stars, including Rickey Henderson and Rick Sutcliffe.

		MINT
Complete set		**$275.00**
Commons		**.12**

1	1979 Highlights (Lou Brock, Carl Yastrzemski)	**$2.00**
2	1979 Highlights (Willie McCovey)	.80
3	1979 Highlights (Manny Mota)	.20
4	1979 Highlights (Pete Rose)	2.00
5	1979 Highlights (Garry Templeton)	.20
6	1979 Highlights (Del Unser)	.12
17	Bruce Sutter	.75
25	Lee Mazzilli	.20
30	Vida Blue	.30
31	Jay Johnstone	.20
35	Luis Tiant	.30
40	Carlton Fisk	5.00
41	Rangers Team (Pat Corrales)	.50
42	*Dave Palmer*	.40
45	Frank White	.25
46	Rico Carty	.20
50	J.R. Richard	.20
53	Ben Oglivie	.20
55	Bill Madlock	.40
56	Bobby Valentine	.20
57	Pete Vuckovich	.15
60	Bucky Dent	.25
62	Mike Ivie	.12
63	Bob Stanley	.20
65	Al Bumbry	.15
66	Royals Team (Jim Frey)	.60

235 Andre Dawson

160 Eddie Murray

580 Nolan Ryan

265 Robin Yount

482 Rickey Henderson

77 Dave Stieb

393 Ozzie Smith

1981 DONRUSS

Following a legal ruling in favor of Fleer, Donruss joined that company and Topps in the baseball card market in 1981 with a set of 605 cards. In the past, Donruss had marketed its bubble gum products only with card sets unrelated to sports. And from the looks of their initial offering, it is obvious that Donruss had little experience with baseball cards. To begin with, the set was printed on ultra-thin cardboard, which makes the cards more susceptible to damage. The color reproductions are of poor quality, and the set is filled with factual and photographic errors (38 of which were corrected). Donruss did acknowledge the popularity of superstars George Brett, Steve Garvey, Reggie Jackson, Pete Rose, and Mike Schmidt, all of whom appear more than once in the set.

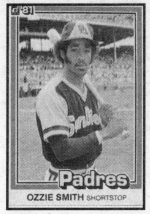

1 Ozzie Smith

156 Jeff Reardon

37	Mike Scott	.45
44	Ron Reed	.10
49	Rod Carew	2.00
50	Bert Campaneris	.10
51	Tom Donahue (incorrect spelling)	1.00
51	Tom Donohue (correct spelling)	.12
52	Dave Frost	.06
54	Dan Ford	.06
55	Garry Maddox	.12
56	Steve Garvey	.75
57	Bill Russell	.10
58	Don Sutton	.50
59	Reggie Smith	.12
60	Rick Monday	.12
61	Ray Knight	.10
62	Johnny Bench	2.00
63	Mario Soto	.10
65	George Foster	.25
66	Jeff Burroughs	.10
67	Keith Hernandez	.30
68	Tom Herr	.15
69	Bob Forsch	.10
71	Bobby Bonds	.20
72	Rennie Stennett	.12
73	Joe Strain	.06
77	Gene Garber	.06

80	Ron Hassey	.06
82	*Joe Charboneau*	.15
83	Cecil Cooper	.12
84	Sal Bando	.12
85	Moose Haas	.06
87	Larry Hisle	.12
88	Luis Gomez	.06
89	Larry Parrish	.12
90	Gary Carter	.80
91	*Bill Gullickson*	.70
94	Carl Yastrzemski	1.75
96	Dennis Eckersley	.80
97	Tom Burgmeier	.12
99	Bob Horner	.12
100	George Brett	4.00
102	Dennis Leonard	.10
103	Renie Martin	.06
104	Amos Otis	.10
105	Graig Nettles	.15
107	Tommy John	.20
109	Lou Piniella	.15
111	Bobby Murcer	.10
112	Eddie Murray	3.00
113	Rick Dempsey	.10
114	Scott McGregor	.10
115	Ken Singleton	.12
119	Rickey Henderson	12.00
120	Mike Heath	.06
121	Dave Cash	.06
122	Randy Jones	.10
127	Jack Morris	1.50
128	Dan Petry	.10
131	Pete Rose	2.00
132	Willie Stargell	.80
134	Jim Bibby	.06
135	Bert Blyleven	.25
136	Dave Parker	.50
140	J.R. Richard	.12
141	Ken Forsch	.06
142	Larry Bowa	.15
145	Buddy Bell	.12
146	Ferguson Jenkins	.45
148	John Grubb	.06
149	Alfredo Griffin	.10
151	*Paul Mirabella* (FC)	.10
152	Rick Bosetti	.06
156	● Jeff Reardon	5.00
160	Lamarr Hoyt (LaMarr)	.20
162	Thad Bosley	.06

260 Nolan Ryan

348 Reggie Jackson

374	John Candelaria	.06
376	Lee Lacy	.06
377	John Milner	.06
379	Luis Pujois (incorrect spelling)	1.00
379	Luis Pujols (correct spelling)	.12
380	Joe Niekro	.15
381	Joaquin Andujar	.12
382	*Keith Moreland*	.25
383	Jose Cruz	.12
384	Bill Virdon	.06
385	Jim Sundberg	.10
386	Doc Medich	.06
387	Al Oliver	.15
389	Bob Bailor	.06
390	Ernie Whitt	.10
392	Roy Howell	.06
393	*Bob Walk*	.20
399	Marvis Foley	.06
400	Steve Trout	.06
402	Tony Larussa (LaRussa)	.10
404	Bake McBride	.06
406	Rob Dressler	.06
408	Tom Paciorek	.06
409	Carney Lansford	.20
410	Brian Downing	.10

TIM RAINES SECOND BASE

538 Tim Raines

411	Don Aase	.06
412	Jim Barr	.06
413	Don Baylor	.12
414	Jim Fregosi	.10
415	Dallas Green	.10
416	Dave Lopes	.12
417	Jerry Reuss	.12
418	Rick Sutcliffe	.30
420	Tommy LaSorda (Lasorda)	.15
421	*Charlie Leibrandt*	1.50
422	Tom Seaver	2.00
423	Ron Oester	.06
425	Tom Seaver	2.00
426	Bobby Cox	.06
427	*Leon Durham*	.25
428	Terry Kennedy	.10
430	George Hendrick	.10
431	Red Schoendienst	.15
433	Vida Blue	.12
434	John Montefusco	.10
436	Dave Bristol	.06
437	Dale Murphy	.90
439	Jorge Orta	.06
444	Buck Martinez (photo backward)	1.00
444	Buck Martinez (photo correct)	.10

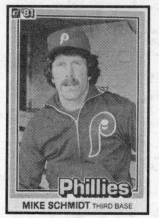

MIKE SCHMIDT THIRD BASE

11 Mike Schmidt

239

537 Best Hitters

1981 FLEER

A 1980 Pennsylvania court ruling allowed Fleer to break the virtual monopoly held by Topps and produce its own set of baseball cards. This legal victory permitted the Philadelphia company to make independent contracts with major league baseball and the Players Association—rights that had been held exclusively by Topps since 1964. The Fleer set of 660 cards is not first-rate, however, with photographic quality a notch below the standard established by Topps. It is also marred by 40 different errors, although the error cards were corrected in two subsequent press runs and aren't collected by most hobbyists, who stop with 660 cards. Graig Nettles' card, number 87, is the only notable exception. In early press runs his name appeared on the back as "Craig." The corrected version is far more common than the card with the error.

MINT

Complete set (without variations) $65.00

Commons .10

1	Pete Rose	$2.50
2	Larry Bowa	.15
5	Mike Schmidt (batting)	3.00
5	Mike Schmidt (portrait)	3.00
6	Steve Carlton ("Lefty" on front)	2.00
6	Steve Carlton ("Pitcher of the Year" on front, date "1066" on back)	2.00
6	Steve Carlton ("Pitcher of the Year" on front, date "1966" on back)	2.25
7	Tug McGraw ("Game Saver" on front)	.75
7	Tug McGraw ("Pitcher" on front)	.15
10	Greg Luzinski	.15
13	*Keith Moreland*	.25
14	*Bob Walk*	.15
15	Lonnie Smith	.20
17	Sparky Lyle	.12
19	Garry Maddox	.12
24	Kevin Saucier ("Ken Saucier" on back)	.15
24	Kevin Saucier ("Kevin Saucier" on back)	.75
27	Tim McCarver	.15
28	George Brett (batting)	4.00
28	George Brett (portrait)	4.00
29	Willie Wilson (batting)	.20
29	Willie Wilson (portrait)	.75
31	Dan Quisenberry	.50
32	Amos Otis (batting)	.50
32	Amos Otis (portrait)	.12
33	Steve Busby	.10
36	Darrell Porter	.10
41	Hal McRae	.15
42	Dennis Leonard	.10
44	Frank White	.15
46	John Wathan	.10
54	Joe Niekro	.15
56	J.R. Richard	.12
57	Nolan Ryan	9.00
59	Cesar Cedeno	.12
60	Jose Cruz	.12
63	Joaquin Andujar	.12
67	Jeff Leonard	.12
71	*Dave Smith*	.30
72	*Danny Heep*	.12
78	• Joe Morgan	.75
79	Reggie Jackson batting)	3.00
79	Reggie Jackson (portrait)	3.00
80	Bucky Dent	.12
81	Tommy John	.30
82	• Luis Tiant	.12
85	Lou Piniella	.12

481 Kirk Gibson

87	Graig Nettles ("Craig" on back)	10.00
87	Graig Nettles ("Graig" on back)	.40
88	Ron Guidry	.25
89	Rich Gossage	.20
91	Gaylord Perry	.60
93	Bob Watson	.12
94	Bobby Murcer	.12
98	Oscar Gamble	.12
109	Willie Randolph	.30
110	Steve Garvey	.80
111	Reggie Smith	.12
112	Don Sutton	.50
113	Burt Hooton	.10
114	Davy Lopes (Davey) (with fingerlike mark on back)	1.00
114	Davy Lopes (Davey) (w/o mark on back)	.12
115	Dusty Baker	.12
116	Tom Lasorda	.12
117	Bill Russell	.12
120	Robert Welch ("Bob Welch" on back)	.50
120	Robert Welch ("Robert Welch" on back)	1.00
122	Rick Monday	.12
125	Rick Sutcliffe	.30
126	Ron Cey (with fingerlike mark on back)	.85
126	Ron Cey (w/o mark on back)	.15
127	Dave Goltz	.10
128	Jay Johnstone	.10
131	*Mike Scioscia*	.60
132	Vic Davalillo	.10
135	Mickey Hatcher	.10
136	*Steve Howe*	.10
140	*Fernand Valenzuela (Fernando)*	2.50
141	Manny Mota	.10
142	Gary Carter	.95
143	Steve Rogers	.10
145	Andre Dawson	2.00
146	Larry Parrish	.12
150	*Bill Gullickson*	1.00
154	Ron LeFlore	.10
157	Bill Lee	.10
159	Woodie Fryman	.10
165	*Charlie Lea*	.10
169	Jim Palmer	1.50
171	Mike Flanagan	.10
173	Doug DeCinces	.10
174	Scott McGregor	.10
175	Mark Belanger	.10
177	Rick Dempsey (with fingerlike mark on front)	1.00
177	Rick Dempsey (w/o mark on front)	.12
178	Earl Weaver	.12
180	Dennis Martinez	.40
183	Lee May	.10
184	Eddie Murray	3.00
188	Ken Singleton	.12
195	Doug DeCinces	.10
196	Johnny Bench	2.00
197	Dave Concepcion	.15
198	Ray Knight	.12
199	Ken Griffey	.40
200	Tom Seaver	2.00
201	Dave Collins	.10
202	George Foster	.20
205	Dan Driessen	.10
208	*Charlie Leibrandt*	.70
210	*Joe Price*	.10
214	Mario Soto	.10

215	Bill Bonham (with fingerlike mark on back)	1.00
215	Bill Bonham (w/o mark on back)	.12
216	George Foster ("Slugger" on front)	.20
216	George Foster ("Outfield" on front)	.20
221	Carl Yastrzemski	1.75
222	Jim Rice	.40
223	Fred Lynn	.20
224	Carlton Fisk	2.00
225	Rick Burleson	.10
226	Dennis Eckersley	.65
232	• Dwight Evans	.40
233	Mike Torrez	.10
241	Tony Perez	.40
242	Phil Niekro	.50
243	Dale Murphy	.80
244	Bob Horner	.15
245	Jeff Burroughs	.10
251	Gary Matthews (with fingerlike mark on back)	1.00
251	Gary Matthews (w/o mark on back)	.12
252	Chris Chambliss	.10
255	Doyle Alexander	.12
260	Glenn Hubbard	.10
262	Al Hrabosky	.10
266	*Rafael Ramirez*	.20
268	• Rod Carew	1.50
269	Bobby Grich	.12
270	Carney Lansford	.15
271	Don Baylor	.12
272	Joe Rudi	.12
274	Jim Fregosi	.10
276	Frank Tanana	.12
277	Dickie Thon	.15
280	Bert Campaneris	.12
282	Brian Downing	.12
291	Dave Kingman	.15
292	Bill Buckner	.12
293	Rick Reuschel	.12
294	Bruce Sutter	.15
299	Dick Tidrow	.06
300	Randy Martz	.06

574 Rickey Henderson

301	Lenny Randle	.06
303	Cliff Johnson	.06
305	Dennis Lamp	.06
306	Bill Caudill	.06
308	Jim Tracy	.06
310	Willie Hernandez	.12
311	Mike Vail	.06
312	Mike Krukow	.12
313	Barry Foote	.06
314	Larry Biittner	.06
315	Mike Tyson	.06
316	Lee Mazzilli	.06
317	John Stearns	.06
318	Alex Trevino	.06
319	Craig Swan	.06
322	Neil Allen	.10
325	Joe Torre	.06
326	Elliott Maddox	.06
327	Pete Falcone	.06
328	Ray Burris	.06
329	Claudell Washington	.06
330	Doug Flynn	.06
332	• Bill Almon	.06
335	• *Jeff Reardon*	5.00
336	*Wally Backman*	.25
337	Dan Norman	.06
339	Ed Farmer	.06
341	Todd Cruz	.06

57 Nolan Ryan

488	Ozzie Smith	3.00
489	Gene Tenace	.10
493	Tim Flannery (negative reversed, batting right)	.15
493	Tim Flannery (correct photo, batting left)	.70
501	*Luis Salazar*	.15
502	Gary Lucas	.10
507	Gorman Thomas	.10
508	Ben Oglivie	.10
509	Larry Hisle	.10
510	Sal Bando	.10
511	Robin Yount	3.00
514	Jerry Augustine (photo is Billy Travers)	.15
514	Billy Travers (correct name and photo)	.75
515	Paul Molitor	2.00
522	Jim Gantner	.15
524	Don Money	.10
528	Ted Simmons	.20
529	Garry Templeton	.12
536	Jim Kaat	.20
537	Bob Forsch	.10
539	*Terry Landrum*	.12
540	Leon Durham	.15
541	Terry Kennedy	.10
542	George Hendrick	.10
544	Mark Littell (photo is Jeff Little)	.10
545	Keith Hernandez	.40
547	Pete Vuckovich (photo is Don Hood)	.15
547	Don Hood (correct name and photo)	.70
548	Bobby Bonds	.12
550	Tom Herr	.12
552	Jerry Koosman	.12
574	Rickey Henderson	10.00
575	Tony Armas	.12
581	Billy Martin	.20
586	*Mike Davis*	.20
590	Dwayne Murphy	.10
595	Maury Wills	.12
599	Floyd Bannister	.12
606	Steve Garvey	.65
617	Mickey Rivers	.10
619	Jim Sundberg	.10
620	Richie Zisk	.10

346 Harold Baines

621	Jon Matlack	.10
622	Ferguson Jenkins	.45
625	Buddy Bell	.12
626	Al Oliver	.15
629	Rusty Staub	.12
638	Carl Yastrzemski	2.00
639	Cecil Cooper	.12
640	Mike Schmidt	3.00
641	Checklist 1-50	.15
644	Checklist 169-220	.12
645	Triple Threat (Larry Bowa, Pete Rose, Mike Schmidt) (with number on back)	2.75
645	Triple Threat (Larry Bowa, Pete Rose, Mike Schmidt) (w/o number on back)	2.00
650	Reggie Jackson	2.75
651	Checklist 409-458	.12
652	Checklist 459-506	.12
653	Willie Wilson	.40
654	Checklist 507-550	.12
655	George Brett	4.00
656	Checklist 551-593	.12
657	Tug McGraw	.60
659	Checklist 640-660	.12
660	Steve Carlton	2.00

1981 TOPPS

The 1981 Topps set contains 726 cards, but because it was printed in six sheets of 132 cards each, 66 cards were printed twice. This happened because each sheet had one row of 11 cards that was printed a second time, making such cards twice as common as the others. Among the double-printed cards are those for Mike Schmidt and Rich Dotson. The 1981 set marks the last appearance of team cards with the manager's photo in the upper right. Once again, three Future Stars from each team share a card. At the time this set was released, and for the first time in years, Topps was facing major competition in the baseball card market.

MINT

Complete set $100.00
Commons   .08

400 Reggie Jackson

1	Batting Ldrs (George Brett, Bill Buckner)	$2.00
2	HR Ldrs (Reggie Jackson, Ben Oglivie, Mike Schmidt)	.45
3	RBI Ldrs (Cecil Cooper, Mike Schmidt)	.45
4	SB Ldrs (Rickey Henderson, Ron LeFlore)	2.00
5	Victry Ldrs (Steve Carlton, Steve Stone)	.20
6	SO Ldrs (Len Barker, Steve Carlton)	.20
7	ERA Ldrs (Rudy May, Don Sutton)	.15
8	Leading Firemen (Rollie Fingers, Tom Hume, Dan Quisenberry)	.25
9	Pete LaCock	.08
10	Mike Flanagan	.10
11	Jim Wohlford	.08
12	Mark Clear	.08
13	*Joe Charboneau*	.15
14	*John Tudor*	.50
15	Larry Parrish	.12
16	Ron Davis	.08
17	Cliff Johnson	.08
18	Glenn Adams	.08
19	Jim Clancy	.08
20	Jeff Burroughs	.10
21	Ron Oester	.08
22	Danny Darwin	.08
23	Alex Trevino	.08
24	Don Stanhouse	.08
25	Sixto Lezcano	.08
26	U.L. Washington	.08
27	Champ Summers	.08
28	Enrique Romo	.08
29	Gene Tenace	.10
30	Jack Clark	.35
31	Checklist 1-121	.10
32	Ken Oberkfell	.08
34	Aurelio Rodriguez	.08
35	Mitchell Page	.08
36	Ed Farmer	.08
37	Gary Roenicke	.08

38	Win Remmerswaal	.08
39	Tom Veryzer	.08
40	Tug McGraw	.20
41	Rangers FS (Bob Babcock, John Butcher, Jerry Don Gleaton)	.10
42	Jerry White	.08
43	Jose Morales	.08
45	Enos Cabell	.08
46	Rick Bosetti	.08
47	Ken Brett	.10
48	Dave Skaggs	.08
49	Bob Shirley	.08
50	Dave Lopes	.10
51	Bill Robinson	.08
52	Hector Cruz	.08
53	Kevin Saucier	.08
54	Ivan DeJesus	.08
55	Mike Norris	.08
56	Buck Martinez	.08
59	Dan Petry	.08
60	Willie Randolph	.25
61	Butch Wynegar	.08
62	Joe Pettini	.08
64	Brian Asselstine	.08
65	Scott McGregor	.10
67	Ken Kravec	.08
68	Matt Alexander	.08
69	Ed Halicki	.08
70	Al Oliver	.15
71	Hal Dues	.08
72	Barry Evans	.08
74	Mike Hargrove	.08
75	Reggie Smith	.15
76	Mario Mendoza	.08
77	Mike Barlow	.08
78	Steve Dillard	.08
79	Bruce Robbins	.08
80	Rusty Staub	.15
81	Dave Stapleton	.08
83	Mike Proly	.08
84	Johnnie LeMaster	.08
85	Mike Caldwell	.08
86	Wayne Gross	.08
87	Rick Camp	.08
88	Joe Lefebvre	.08
90	Bake McBride	.08
91	Tim Stoddard	.08

100 Rod Carew

94	Harry Spilman	.08
95	Jim Sundberg	.10
96	A's FS (Dave Beard, *Ernie Camacho*, Pat Dempsey)	.12
97	Chris Speier	.08
98	Clint Hurdle	.08
99	Eric Wilkins	.08
100	Rod Carew	3.00
101	Benny Ayala	.08
102	Dave Tobik	.08
103	Jerry Martin	.08
104	Terry Forster	.10
105	Jose Cruz	.15
106	Don Money	.08
107	Rich Wortham	.08
108	Bruce Benedict	.08
109	Mike Scott	.50
110	Carl Yastrzemski	2.50
111	Greg Minton	.08
113	Mike Phillips	.08
114	Tom Underwood	.08
115	Roy Smalley	.08
116	Joe Simpson	.08
117	Pete Falcone	.08
118	Kurt Bevacqua	.08
119	Tippy Martinez	.08
120	Larry Bowa	.20

261 Rickey Henderson

210	Jim Palmer	2.50
213	*Al Holland*	.10
215	Larry Hisle	.10
218	Paul Splittorff	.10
220	Tom Seaver	3.00
221	Bob Davis	.08
222	Jorge Orta	.08
223	Roy Lee Jackson	.08
225	Ruppert Jones	.08
226	Manny Sanguillen	.08
227	Fred Martinez	.08
228	Tom Paciorek	.08
229	Rollie Fingers	1.75
230	George Hendrick	.08
231	Joe Beckwith	.08
232	Mickey Klutts	.08
233	Skip Lockwood	.08
234	Lou Whitaker	.75
238	Willie Hernandez	.10
240	Nolan Ryan	12.00
242	Chet Lemon	.10
244	Cardinals FS (*Tito Landrum,* Al Olmsted, Andy Rincon)	.15
245	Ed Figueroa	.08
246	Ed Ott	.08
247	Glenn Hubbard	.08
248	Joey McLaughlin	.08
249	Larry Cox	.08
250	Ron Guidry	.50
254	Ozzie Smith	5.00
255	Mark Littell	.10
258	*Joe Price*	.10
259	● Mets FS (Juan Berenguer, *Hubie Brooks, Mookie Wilson*)	1.25
260	Ron Cey	.25
261	Rickey Henderson	14.00
263	Brian Downing	.12
265	John Candelaria	.12
266	Tom Herr	.10
270	Greg Luzinski	.12
275	Dwight Evans	.55
277	Alfredo Griffin	.10
280	Ken Griffey	.45
281	Fred Stanley	.08
283	Billy Sample	.08
284	Brian Kingman	.08
287	Lenn Sakata	.08

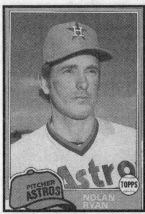

240 Nolan Ryan

289	Mickey Hatcher	.10
290	● Bob Boone	.08
293	*Charlie Lea*	.15
295	Hal McRae	.15
296	Bill Nahorodny	.08
299	Elliott Maddox	.08
300	Paul Molitor	4.00
302	Dodgers FS (Jack Perconte, *Mike Scioscia, Fernando Valenzuela*)	3.50
303	Johnny Oates	.08
306	Juan Beniquez	.08
307	Gene Garber	.08
308	Rick Manning	.08
309	*Luis Salazar*	.10
310	Vida Blue	.10
312	Rick Rhoden	.10
315	*Kirk Gibson*	5.00
321	*Leon Durham*	.20
325	Ray Knight	.12
328	Twins FS (*Dave Engle,* Greg Johnston, Gary Ward)	.12
330	Frank White	.12
335	Rick Cerone	.08
336	Eddie Whitson	.10
337	Lynn Jones	.08
338	Checklist 243-363	.08

456 Jeff Reardon

485	Garry Templeton	.10
488	*Damaso Garcia*	.12
490	Eddie Murray	3.50
493	Dan Quisenberry	.40
494	*Bob Walk*	.70
495	Dusty Baker	.10
500	Jim Rice	.50
504	Dale Murphy	1.25
515	Robin Yount	5.00
517	Richie Zisk	.10
528	Gary Matthews	.12
530	Steve Garvey	1.00
534	• *Dave Smith*	.65
540	Mike Schmidt	3.00
550	Tommy John	.40
551	• Pirates FS (*Vance Law, Tony Pena, Pascual Perez*)	1.00
554	Bert Blyleven	.50
555	Cecil Cooper	.20
560	Joe Morgan	1.15
562	Checklist 485-605	.25
563	Jim Kaat	.30
565	Burt Hooton	.10
570	Ken Singleton	.10
572	Jack Morris	2.00
573	Phil Garner	.10
575	Tony Perez	.65
577	Blue Jays FS (Luis Leal, Brian Milner, *Ken Schrom*)	.20
578	*Bill Gullickson*	1.50
580	Don Baylor	.15
582	Gaylord Perry	1.00
585	Amos Otis	.10
590	Bruce Sutter	.25
600	Johnny Bench	3.00
605	Don Sutton	.75
610	Darrell Porter	.10
615	Rick Dempsey	.10
616	Rick Wise	.10
620	Dennis Eckersley	2.25
623	Sal Bando	.10
624	Bob Welch	.55
625	Bill Buckner	.15
627	Luis Tiant	.20
629	Tony Armas	.12
630	Steve Carlton	3.00

700 George Brett

635	Bobby Bonds	.15
636	Al Hrabosky	.10
638	Checklist 606-726	.15
639	Carney Lansford	.35
640	Dave Parker	.45
641	Mark Belanger	.20
643	*Lloyd Moseby*	.20
645	Rick Reuschel	.15
648	Darrell Evans	.25
650	Bucky Dent	.12
651	Pedro Guerrero	.50
655	Dan Driessen	.10
656	Jon Matlack	.10
660	Gary Carter	1.50
661	Orioles Team (Earl Weaver)	.30
662	Red Sox Team (Ralph Houk)	.30
663	Angels Team (Jim Fregosi)	.25
664	White Sox Team (Tony LaRussa)	.25
665	Indians Team (Dave Garcia)	.25
666	Tigers Team (Sparky Anderson)	.25
667	Royals Team (Jim Frey)	.25

251

302 Dodgers Future Stars

668	Brewers Team (Bob Rodgers)	.25
669	Twins Team (John Goryl)	.25
670	Yankees Team (Gene Michael)	.25
671	A's Team (Billy Martin)	.30
672	Mariners Team (Maury Wills)	.25
673	Rangers Team (Don Zimmer)	.25
674	Blue Jays Team (Bobby Mattick)	.25
675	Braves Team (Bobby Cox)	.25
676	Cubs Team (Joe Amalfitano)	.25
677	Reds Team (John McNamara)	.25
678	Astros Team (Bill Virdon)	.25
679	Dodgers Team (Tom Lasorda)	.35
680	Expos Team (Dick Williams)	.25
681	Mets Team (Joe Torre)	.25
682	Phillies Team (Dallas Green)	.25
683	Pirates Team (Chuck Tanner)	.25
684	Cardinals Team (Whitey Herzog)	.30
685	Padres Team (Frank Howard)	.25
686	Giants Team (Dave Bristol)	.25
689	Red Sox FS (*Bruce Hurst*, Keith MacWhorter, *Reid Nichols*)	1.50
690	Bob Watson	.10
691	Dick Ruthven	.08
692	Lenny Randle	.08
693	*Steve Howe*	.30
695	Kent Tekulve	.25
696	Alan Ashby	.12
697	Rick Waits	.08
698	Mick Jorgensen	.08
699	Glenn Abbott	.08
700	George Brett	6.00
701	Joe Rudi	.12
705	Ted Simmons	.25
708	Doyle Alexander	.10
709	Alan Trammell	1.25
715	Bill Madlock	.25
719	Sparky Lyle	.12
720	Fred Lynn	.35
721	Toby Harrah	.10
722	Joe Niekro	.12
724	Lou Piniella	.20
725	Steve Rogers	.10
726	Rick Monday	.20

1981 TOPPS TRADED

Faced with its only competition in the baseball card market since 1963, Topps scrambled for an advantage over its new rivals in 1981. The company found a competitive edge in its Traded set. Unlike later years when Traded sets had a "T" designation following the card numbers and featured different color printing on the back, the 1981 Topps Traded series is a genuine extension of the 726-card regular issue. As a result, many collectors think of the extension set as the "high numbers" for 1981. Topps sold the issue in the form of a complete boxed set, and only to hobby dealers. The initial price of this 132-card edition was around nine dollars.

	MINT
Complete set	$45.00
Commons	.20

727	Danny Ainge (FC)	$6.00
728	Doyle Alexander	.20
729	Gary Alexander	.10
730	Billy Almon	.10
731	Joaquin Andujar	.25
732	Bob Bailor	.10
735	Tony Bernazard	.10
737	Doug Bird	.10
738	Bert Blyleven	1.25
740	Bobby Bonds	.30
741	Rick Bosetti	.10
742	Hubie Brooks	.90
743	Rick Burleson	.15
744	Ray Burris	.10
745	Jeff Burroughs	.15
746	Enos Cabell	.10
747	Ken Clay	.10
748	Mark Clear	.10
749	Larry Cox	.10
750	Hector Cruz	.10
751	Victor Cruz	.10
754	Brian Doyle	.10
755	Dick Drago	.10
756	Leon Durham	.25
757	Jim Dwyer	.10
758	Dave Edwards	.10
759	Jim Essian	.10

816 Tim Raines

761	Rollie Fingers	2.75
762	Carlton Fisk	7.00
763	Barry Foote	.10
764	Ken Forsch	.10
765	Kiko Garcia	.10
766	Cesar Geronimo	.10
768	Mickey Hatcher	.25
770	Marc Hill	.10
771	Butch Hobson	.10
772	Rick Honeycutt	.10
774	Mike Ivie	.10

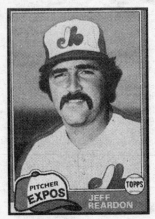

819 Jeff Reardon

776	Cliff Johnson	.10
777	Randy Jones	.25
780	Terry Kennedy	.30
781	Dave Kingman	.40
782	Bob Knepper	.10
784	Bob Lacey	.10
785	Dennis Lamp	.10
788	Carney Lansford	.75
789	Dave LaRoche	.10
791	Ron LeFlore	.25
793	Sixto Lezcano	.10
795	Mike Lum	.10
796	Greg Luzinski	.25
797	Fred Lynn	.60
800	Gary Matthews	.30
803	Rick Miller	.10
806	Jose Morales	.10
807	Joe Morgan	3.00
809	Gene Nelson (FC)	.30
811	Bob Owchinko	.10
812	Gaylord Perry	2.25
814	Darrell Porter	.25
815	Mike Proly	.10
816	Tim Raines	13.00
818	Doug Rau	.10
819	Jeff Reardon	12.00
820	Ken Reitz	.10
822	Rick Reuschel	.25

824	Dave Roberts	.10
826	Joe Rudi	.30
827	Kevin Saucier	.10
828	Tony Scott	.10
829	Bob Shirley	.10
830	Ted Simmons	.50
835	Rusty Staub	.35
836	Bill Stein	.10
837	Joe Strain	.10
838	Bruce Sutter	.50
839	Don Sutton	2.00
840	Steve Swisher	.10
841	Frank Tanana	.30
842	Gene Tenace	.10
843	Jason Thompson	.10
846	Tom Enderwood	.10
844	Dickie Thon	.10
845	Bill Travers	.10
847	John Urrea	.10
848	Mike Vail	.10
849	Ellis Valentine	.10
850	Fernando Valenzuela	3.50
851	Pete Vuckovich	.10
852	Mark Wagner	.10
853	Bob Walk	.25
854	Claudell Washington	.10
855	Dave Winfield	12.00
856	Geoff Zahn	.10
857	Richie Zisk	.15

761 Rollie Fingers

1982 DONRUSS

Donruss showed a number of improvements in its second full set of baseball cards. There were noticeable improvements in the quality of photography and reproduction, as well as statistical content. But because of a federal court ruling that Topps held the exclusive right to market baseball cards with confectionery products, the 1982 Donruss set was not distributed in gum packs. As a substitute, Donruss created a 63-piece Babe Ruth puzzle. Each wax pack contained three puzzle pieces. The new set was increased to 660 cards and contains the first series of paintings, called Diamond Kings, that portray one star from each team. These are shown in the list that follows with the abbreviation "DK" in parentheses following the player name. Rookie cards of Kent Hrbek, Cal Ripken, Jr., and Steve Sax further enrich the set.

		MINT
Complete set		**$100.00**
Commons		**.10**

1	Pete Rose (DK)	$2.00
2	Gary Carter (DK)	.50
3	Steve Garvey (DK)	.50
4	Vida Blue (DK)	.15
5	Alan Trammel (DK) (incorrect spelling)	1.25
5	Alan Trammell (DK) (correct spelling)	.40
6	Len Barker (DK)	.12
7	• Dwight Evans (DK)	.20
8	Rod Carew (DK)	.80
9	George Hendrick (DK)	.15
10	Phil Niekro (DK)	.40
11	Richie Zisk (DK)	.12
12	Dave Parker (DK)	.35
13	Nolan Ryan (DK)	3.75
14	Ivan DeJesus (DK)	.12
15	George Brett (DK)	1.50
16	Tom Seaver (DK)	1.00
17	Dave Kingman (DK)	.15
18	Dave Winfield (DK)	2.00
19	Mike Norris (DK)	.15
20	Carlton Fisk (DK)	1.00
21	Ozzie Smith (DK)	1.00
22	Roy Smalley (DK)	.08
23	Buddy Bell (DK)	.15
24	Ken Singleton (DK)	.15
25	John Mayberry (DK)	.08
26	Gorman Thomas (DK)	.15
27	Earl Weaver	.15
28	Rollie Fingers	.75
29	Sparky Anderson	.15
30	Dennis Eckersley	1.25
31	Dave Winfield	3.00
32	Burt Hooton	.12
33	Rick Waits	.08
34	George Brett	3.00
36	Steve Rogers	.12
40	George Hendrick	.12
42	Steve Carlton	1.50
46	Jack Clark	.35
47	Chris Chambliss	.12
49	Lee Mazzilli	.12
50	Julio Cruz	.08
52	Dave Stieb	.35
54	*Jorge Bell* (FC)	5.00
56	Rusty Staub	.15
58	Claudell Washington (FC)	.15
63	Larry Bowa	.15
68	Woodie Fryman	.15
70	Amos Otis	.08
72	Toby Harrah	.08
73	*Dave Righetti* (FC)	.40
74	Carl Yastrzemski	1.25
75	Bob Welch	.35
76	Alan Trammel (incorrect spelling)	1.50
76	Alan Trammell (correct spelling)	.75
77	Rick Dempsey	.08

252 Lee Smith

78	Paul Molitor	2.00
82	Carney Lansford	.20
84	Steve Garvey	.65
86	John Wathan	.12
88	Andre Dawson	2.00
90	Bobby Grich	.15
91	Bob Forsch	.08
94	Ozzie Smith	2.50
95	Dave Parker	.30
96	Doyle Alexander	.15
97	Al Hrabosky	.12
100	Floyd Bannister	.15
101	Alfredo Griffin	.12
103	Mario Soto	.12
105	Ken Singleton	.15
106	Ted Simmons	.15
107	Jack Morris	1.00
108	Bob Watson	.12
109	• Dwight Evans	.30
110	Tom Lasorda	.15
111	Bert Blyleven	.25
112	Dan Quisenberry	.15
113	Rickey Henderson	4.00
114	Gary Carter	1.00
115	Brian Downing	.15
116	Al Oliver	.15
118	Cesar Cedeno	.15
119	Keith Moreland	.12

121	Terry Kennedy	.12
124	Tony Pena (FC)	.35
127	Richie Zisk	.12
128	• Mike Scott	.15
129	Lloyd Moseby (FC)	.20
132	Gorman Thomas	.15
133	Dan Petry	.12
135	Lou Piniella	.15
136	Pedro Guerrero	.45
137	Len Barker	.12
140	*Tim Wallach* (FC)	1.00
141	Gene Mauch	.12
148	Tom Seaver	1.75
151	Leon Durham	.12
152	Gene Tenace	.12
157	Rick Reuschel	.15
158	Steve Howe	.12
162	Bill Gullickson	.25
165	Ron LeFlore	.12
167	Joe Niekro	.15
168	Pete Rose	1.75
169	Dave Collins	.12
170	Rick Wise	.12
172	Larry Herndon	.12
173	Bob Horner	.15
175	Mookie Wilson	.15
182	Dave Kingman	.15
189	• Sparky Lyle	.15
190	Whitey Herzog	.10
191	Dave Smith	.15
193	Greg Luzinski	.15
194	Bill Lee	.12
196	Hal McRae	.12
200	Jim Rice	.35
209	Bucky Dent	.15
210	Ron Cey	.15
214	Tim Raines	1.75
215	Jon Matlack	.12
216	Rod Carew	1.25
217	• Jim Kaat	.15
221	Mike Easler	.12
222	Vida Blue	.15
225	*Jody Davis* (FC)	.25
231	Jim Palmer	1.50
232	Bob Rodgers	.12
235	Mike Torrez	.12
237	*Von Hayes* (FC)	.30
239	Dwayne Murphy	.12
242	Mickey Rivers	.12

113 Rickey Henderson

419 Nolan Ryan

413	Mike Heath	.06
416	*Mike Witt* (FC)	.25
417	Bobby Molinaro	.06
418	Steve Braun	.06
419	Nolan Ryan	8.00
420	Tug McGraw	.12
421	Dave Concepcion	.12
422	Juan Eichelberger (photo is Gary Lucas)	1.25
422	Juan Eichelberger (correct photo)	.15
423	Rick Rhoden	.15
424	Frank Robinson	.25
425	Eddie Miller	.06
426	Bill Caudill	.06
427	Doug Flynn	.06
428	*Larry Anderson* (Andersen) (FC)	.25
430	Jerry Garvin	.06
431	Glenn Adams	.06
432	Barry Bonnell	.06
434	John Stearns	.06
435	Mike Tyson	.06
436	Glenn Hubbard	.06
437	Eddie Solomon	.06
438	Jeff Leonard	.15
439	Randy Bass	.06
440	Mike LaCoss	.06
441	Gary Matthews	.15
442	Mark Littell	.06
443	Don Sutton	.35
444	John Harris	.06
445	• Vada Pinson	.12
446	Elias Sosa	.06
447	Charlie Hough	.15
448	Willie Wilson	.15
449	Fred Stanley	.06
450	Tom Veryzer	.06
452	Mark Clear	.06
453	Bill Russell	.12
454	Lou Whitaker	.50
456	Reggie Cleveland	.06
457	Sammy Stewart	.06
458	Pete Vuckovich	.12
459	John Wockenfuss	.06
461	Willie Randolph	.12
462	Fernando Valenzuela (FC)	.35
463	Ron Hassey	.06

383	Terry Crowley	.06
384	Don Money	.06
385	Dan Schatzeder	.06
387	Yogi Berra	.35
388	Ken Landreaux	.06
389	Mike Hargrove	.06
390	Darryl Motley	.06
391	Dave McKay	.06
392	Stan Bahnsen	.06
393	Ken Forsch	.06
394	Mario Mendoza	.06
395	Jim Morrison	.06
396	Mike Ivie	.06
398	Darrell Evans	.15
399	Ron Reed	.12
400	Johnny Bench	1.50
401	*Steve Bedrosian* (FC)	.50
402	Bill Robinson	.06
403	Bill Buckner	.12
404	Ken Oberkfell	.06
405	*Cal Ripken, Jr.* (FC)	50.00
406	Jim Gantner	.12
407	Kirk Gibson (FC)	1.10
408	Tony Perez	.25
409	Tommy John	.20
410	*Dave Stewart* (FC)	2.75
411	Dan Spillner	.06
412	Willie Aikens	.06

464	Paul Splittorff	.06
465	Rob Picciolo	.06
466	Larry Parrish	.10
467	Johnny Grubb	.06
469	Silvio Martinez	.06
470	Kiko Garcia	.06
471	● Bob Boone	.10
472	Luis Salazar	.12
473	Randy Niemann	.06
474	Tom Griffin	.06
475	Phil Niekro	.35
476	Hubie Brooks (FC)	.40
477	Dick Tidrow	.06
479	Damaso Garcia	.06
480	Mickey Hatcher	.12
481	Joe Price	.06
482	Ed Farmer	.06
483	Eddie Murray	2.00
484	Ben Oglivie	.12
485	Kevin Saucier	.06
486	Bobby Murcer	.15
487	Bill Campbell	.06
488	Reggie Smith	.15
489	Wayne Garland	.06
490	Jim Wright	.06
491	● Billy Martin	.15
492	Jim Fanning	.06
493	Don Baylor	.12
494	Rick Honeycutt	.06
495	Carlton Fisk	1.65
496	Denny Walling	.06
497	Bake McBride	.06
498	Darrell Porter	.12
500	Ron Oester	.06
501	*Ken Dayley* (FC)	.15
503	Milt May	.06
504	Doug Bird	.06
505	Bruce Bochte	.06
506	Neil Allen	.06
507	Joey McLaughlin	.06
508	Butch Wynegar	.06
509	Gary Roenicke	.06
510	Robin Yount	2.50
511	Dave Tobik	.06
512	*Rich Gedman* (FC)	.25
513	*Gene Nelson* (FC)	.15
514	Rick Monday	.15
515	Miguel Dilone	.06
516	Clint Hurdle	.06
518	Grant Jackson	.06
519	Andy Hassler	.06
521	Greg Pryor	.06
522	Tony Scott	.06
523	Steve Mura	.06
524	Johnnie LeMaster	.06
525	Dick Ruthven	.06
528	*Johnny Ray* (FC)	.75
529	*Pat Tabler* (FC)	.25
530	Tom Herr	.15
531	San Diego Chicken (with trademark symbol on front)	1.25
531	San Diego Chicken (w/o trademark symbol)	1.25
532	Sal Butera	.06
535	Reggie Jackson	2.00
536	Ed Romero	.06
537	Derrel Thomas	.06
540	*Bob Ojeda* (FC)	.45
541	Roy Lee Jackson	.06
542	Lynn Jones	.06
543	Gaylord Perry	.45
544	Phil Garner (photo is backward)	1.25
544	Phil Garner (correct photo)	.15
545	Garry Templeton	.15
546	Rafael Ramirez (FC)	.15
547	Jeff Reardon	.20
548	Ron Guidry	.25
549	*Tim Laudner* (FC)	.15
550	John Henry Johnson	.06
551	Chris Bando	.06
554	*Scott Fletcher* (FC)	.30
555	Jerry Royster	.06
556	Shooty Babbitt	.06
557	*Kent Hrbek* (FC)	2.50
558	Yankee Winners (Ron Guidry, Tommy John)	.15
559	Mark Bomback	.06
561	Buck Martinez	.06
562	*Mike Marshall* (FC)	.40
563	Rennie Stennett	.06
564	Steve Crawford	.06
565	Bob Babcock	.06
566	Johnny Podres	.12
568	Harold Baines (FC)	1.00
570	Lee May	.12

571	Gary Ward (FC)	.10
574	*Bob Brenley* (FC)	.20
575	Bronx Bombers (Reggie Jackson, Dave Winfield)	2.00
578	Harvey Kuenn	.15
579	*Cal Ripken, Sr.*	.12
580	Juan Berenguer	.12
582	Vance Law (FC)	.15
583	*Rich Leach* (FC)	.10
585	Phillies Finest (Pete Rose, Mike Schmidt)	1.50
586	Joe Rudi	.15
588	*Luis DeLeon* (FC)	.08
592	Sal Bando	.12
593	Bert Campaneris	.15
594	Steve Kemp	.12
595	Randy Lerch (Braves)	1.25
595	Randy Lerch (Brewers)	.10
598	Mike Scioscia (FC)	.45
603	Jerry Koosman	.15
604	Dave Goltz	.12
606	• Lonnie Smith	.20
607	Joaquin Andujar	.12
622	*Luis Aguayo* (FC)	.15
624	*Steve Sax* (FC)	2.00
627	Terry Francona (FC)	.10
628	• Pride of the Reds (Johnny Bench, Tom Seaver)	1.45
634	Ken Griffey	.20
635	Bob Lemon	.15
638	• Danny Ainge	1.50
639	Willie Stargell	.50
643	Fergie Jenkins	.40
646	Jesse Orosco (FC)	.20
648	Tommy Davis	.12
650	Felipe Alou	.12
651	Harvey Haddix	.12
652	Willie Upshaw (FC)	.15
653	Bill Madlock	.15

1982 FLEER

After a triumphant debut into the baseball card world in 1981, Fleer's 1982 set of 660 cards paled in comparison. It featured many fuzzy photographs and was full of errors, only some of which were corrected. Some skeptics feel that the company purposely botched many cards just to sell more product. The hottest error card is number 576, which (due to a flipped negative) shows righty John Littlefield pitching left-handed, while Cal Ripken, Jr., is the set's biggest rookie-card draw. Due to a court ruling in favor of Topps, Fleer was prevented from issuing bubble gum in wax packs. The company distributed team logo stickers instead, which aren't considered collectible by most hobbyists.

		MINT
Complete set		**$100.00**
Commons		**.10**
1	Dusty Baker	$.15
2	Robert Castillo	.06
3	Ron Cey	.15
4	Terry Forster	.12
5	Steve Garvey	.60
6	Dave Goltz	.12
7	Pedro Guerrero (FC)	.40
8	Burt Hooton	.12
9	Steve Howe	.12
10	Jay Johnstone	.15
11	Ken Landreaux	.06
12	Davey Lopes	.15
13	*Mike Marshall* (FC)	.15
15	Rick Monday	.15
16	*Tom Niedenfuer* (FC)	.20
17	*Ted Power* (FC)	.20
18	Jerry Reuss	.15

19	Ron Roenicke	.06
20	Bill Russell	.12
21	*Steve Sax* (FC)	2.00
22	Mike Scioscia	.12
23	Reggie Smith	.10
24	*Dave Stewart* (FC)	2.50
25	Rick Sutcliffe	.20
26	Derrel Thomas	.06
27	Fernando Valenzuela	.40
28	Bob Welch	.25
31	Rick Cerone	.06
32	Ron Davis	.06
33	Bucky Dent	.10
34	Barry Foote	.06
35	George Frazier	.06
36	Oscar Gamble	.12
37	Rich Gossage	.20
38	Ron Guidry	.25
39	Reggie Jackson	2.00
40	Tommy John	.20
41	Rudy May	.06
42	Larry Milbourne	.06
43	Jerry Mumphrey	.06
44	Bobby Murcer	.15
45	*Gene Nelson*	.12
46	Graig Nettles	.15
47	Johnny Oates	.06
48	Lou Piniella	.15
49	Willie Randolph	.15
50	Rick Reuschel	.15
52	*Dave Righetti* (FC)	.40
53	Aurelio Rodriguez	.12
54	Bob Watson	.12
55	Dennis Werth	.06
56	Dave Winfield	3.00
57	Johnny Bench	1.50
58	Bruce Berenyi	.06
59	Larry Biittner	.06
61	Dave Collins	.12
62	Geoff Combe	.06
63	Dave Concepcion	.10
64	Dan Driessen	.12
65	Joe Edelen	.06
66	George Foster	.20
67	Ken Griffey	.25
68	Paul Householder	.06
70	Junior Kennedy	.06
71	Ray Knight	.15
72	Mike LaCoss	.06

92 Rickey Henderson

74	Charlie Leibrandt	.15
75	Sam Mejias	.06
76	Paul Moskau	.06
77	Joe Nolan	.06
79	Ron Oester	.06
80	Frank Pastore	.06
81	Joe Price	.06
82	Tom Seaver	1.75
83	Mario Soto	.12
84	Mike Vail	.06
85	Tony Armas	.15
86	Shooty Babitt	.06
87	Dave Beard	.06
88	Rick Bosetti	.06
89	Keith Drumright	.06
90	Wayne Gross	.06
91	Mike Heath	.06
92	Rickey Henderson	4.00
93	Cliff Johnson	.06
94	Jeff Jones	.06
95	Matt Keough	.06
96	Brian Kingman	.06
99	Steve McCatty	.06
100	Dave McKay	.06
101	Dwayne Murphy	.06
103	Mike Norris	.06
104	Bob Owchinko	.06
105	Mitchell Page	.06

229 Nolan Ryan

193 Charlie Lea .... .12
194 Bill Lee .... .12
195 Jerry Manuel .... .06
197 John Milner...................... .06
198 Rowland Office .... .06
199 David Palmer................... .06
200 Larry Parrish .... .15
201 Mike Phillips .... .06
202 Tim Raines 2.00
203 Bobby Ramos................. .06
204 Jeff Reardon 1.50
205 Steve Rogers .... .12
206 Scott Sanderson .... .06
207 Rodney Scott (photo of
    Tim Raines) .... .15
208 Elias Sosa .... .06
209 Chris Speier .... .06
210 *Tim Wallach* (FC) 1.00
211 Jerry White .... .06
212 Alan Ashby .... .06
213 Cesar Cedeno .... .12
214 Jose Cruz .... .15
215 Kiko Garcia...................... .06
217 Danny Heep .... .06
218 Art Howe .... .06
219 Bob Knepper .... .06
220 Frank LaCorte .... .06
221 Joe Niekro .... .15
223 Terry Puhl .... .06
224 Luis Pujols .... .06
226 J.R. Richard .... .15
227 Dave Roberts .... .06
228 Vern Ruhle .... .06
229 Nolan Ryan 8.00
230 Joe Sambito .... .06
231 Tony Scott....................... .06
232 Dave Smith .... .15
233 Harry Spilman .... .06
234 Don Sutton .... .45
235 Dickie Thon .... .12
236 Denny Walling.................. .12
237 Gary Woods .... .06
238 *Luis Aguayo* (FC) .... .15
239 Ramon Aviles.................. .06
240 • Bob Boone .... .15
241 Larry Bowa .... .15
242 Warren Brusstar .... .06
243 Steve Carlton 1.50
244 Larry Christenson............ .06

609 Jorge Bell

245 Dick Davis .... .06
247 Greg Gross...................... .12
248 • Sparky Lyle................... .12
249 Garry Maddox .... .12
250 Bake McBride.................. .06
251 Tug McGraw..................... .15
252 Keith Moreland .... .06
253 Dickie Noles .... .06
256 Pete Rose 1.75
257 Dick Ruthven .... .06
258 Mike Schmidt................. 2.50
259 Lonnie Smith .... .30
260 Manny Trillo .... .12
261 Del Unser .... .06
262 George Vukovich............. .06
263 Tom Brookens .... .12
264 George Capuzzello .... .06
265 Marty Castillo .... .06
266 Al Cowens .... .06
267 Kirk Gibson..................... 1.10
268 Richie Hebner .... .06
271 Steve Kemp .... .15
272 *Rick Leach* (FC) .... .15
273 Aurelio Lopez .... .06
274 Jack Morris...................... 1.00
275 Kevin Saucier .... .06
276 Lance Parrish .... .35
278 Dan Petry .... .06

603 Lee Smith

279	David Rozema	.06
280	Stan Papi	.06
281	Dan Schatzeder	.06
282	Champ Summers	.06
283	Alan Trammell	.75
284	Lou Whitaker	.40
285	Milt Wilcox	.06
286	John Wockenfuss	.06
287	Gary Allenson	.06
290	Mark Clear	.06
291	Steve Crawford	.06
292	Dennis Eckersley	1.50
293	• Dwight Evans	.25
294	*Rich Gedman* (FC)	.20
295	Garry Hancock	.06
296	Glenn Hoffman	.06
297	Bruce Hurst (FC)	.65
298	Carney Lansford	.15
301	*Bob Ojeda*	.35
302	Tony Perez	.30
303	Chuck Rainey	.06
304	Jerry Remy	.06
305	Jim Rice	.35
306	Joe Rudi	.15
307	Bob Stanley	.06
308	Dave Stapleton	.12
309	Frank Tanana	.15
310	Mike Torrez	.15

311	John Tudor (FC)	.25
312	Carl Yastrzemski	1.50
313	Buddy Bell	.12
314	Steve Comer	.06
315	Danny Darwin	.06
317	John Grubb	.06
318	Rick Honeycutt	.06
319	Charlie Hough	.15
320	Ferguson Jenkins	.45
321	John Henry Johnson	.06
323	Jon Matlack	.12
324	Doc Medich	.06
325	Mario Mendoza	.06
326	Al Oliver	.15
327	Pat Putnam	.06
328	Mickey Rivers	.12
329	Leon Roberts	.06
330	Billy Sample	.06
331	Bill Stein	.06
332	Jim Sundberg	.12
333	Mark Wagner	.06
334	Bump Wills	.06
335	Bill Almon	.06
336	Harold Baines	.80
337	Ross Baumgarten	.06
338	Tony Bernazard	.06
339	Britt Burns	.06
340	Richard Dotson	.12
341	Jim Essian	.06
342	Ed Farmer	.06
343	Carlton Fisk	1.75
344	Kevin Hickey	.06
345	Lamarr Hoyt (LaMarr)	.06
346	Lamar Johnson	.06
349	Dennis Lamp	.06
350	Ron LeFlore	.12
351	Chet Lemon	.12
352	Greg Luzinski	.15
353	Bob Molinaro	.06
355	Wayne Nordhagen	.06
356	Greg Pryor	.06
357	Mike Squires	.06
358	Steve Trout	.06
359	Alan Bannister	.06
360	Len Barker	.12
361	Bert Blyleven	.25
362	Joe Charboneau	.12
363	John Denny	.06
364	Bo Diaz	.12

367 Wayne Garland .... .06
368 Mike Hargrove .... .06
369 Toby Harrah .... .12
370 Ron Hassey .... .06
371 *Von Hayes* (FC) .... .30
373 Duane Kuiper .... .06
374 Rick Manning .... .06
375 Sid Monge .... .06
376 Jorge Orta .... .06
378 Dan Spillner .... .06
379 Mike Stanton .... .06
380 Andre Thornton .... .15
381 Tom Veryzer .... .06
382 Rick Waits .... .06
383 Doyle Alexander .... .15
384 Vida Blue .... .12
385 Fred Breining .... .06
386 Enos Cabell .... .06
387 Jack Clark .... .20
388 Darrell Evans .... .15
390 Larry Herndon .... .12
391 Al Holland .... .06
392 Gary Lavelle .... .06
393 Johnnie LeMaster .... .06
395 Milt May .... .06
396 Greg Minton .... .06
397 ● Joe Morgan .... .65
398 Joe Pettini .... .06
399 Alan Ripley .... .06
400 Billy Smith .... .06
402 Ed Whitson .... .06
404 Willie Aikens .... .06
405 George Brett 3.00
406 Ken Brett .... .12
407 Dave Chalk .... .06
408 Rich Gale .... .06
409 Cesar Geronimo .... .06
410 Larry Gura .... .06
411 Clint Hurdle .... .06
413 Dennis Leonard .... .12
415 Lee May .... .12
416 Hal McRae .... .15
419 Amos Otis .... .15
420 *Ken Phelps* (FC) .... .15
422 Dan Quisenberry .... .15
425 John Wathan .... .12
426 ● Frank White .... .15
427 Willie Wilson .... .15
436 Bob Horner .... .15

21 Steve Sax

437 Glenn Hubbard .... .12
438 Al Hrabosky
    (All Hrabosky,
    5′1″ on back) **20.00**
438 Al Hrabosky
    (Al Hrabosky,
    5′1″ on back) **1.25**
438 Al Hrabosky
    (Al Hrabosky,
    5′10″ on back) .... .35
440 *Rick Mahler* (FC) .... .15
443 Dale Murphy 1.00
444 Phil Niekro .... .45
445 Gaylord Perry .... .45
451 Don Baylor .... .15
453 Rick Burleson .... .12
454 Bert Campaneris .... .15
455 Rod Carew 1.25
457 Brian Downing .... .15
461 Bobby Grich .... .15
468 Fred Lynn .... .20
473 *Mike Witt* (FC) .... .25
484 *Vance Law* (FC) .... .15
485 Bill Madlock .... .15
489 Dave Parker .... .35
490 Tony Pena (FC) .... .25
491 Pascual Perez (FC) .... .15
492 *Johnny Ray* (FC) .... .15

176 Cal Ripken, Jr.

493	Rick Rhoden	.15
499	Willie Stargell	.70
500	Kent Tekulve	.15
504	Floyd Bannister	.15
517	Shane Rawley	.12
522	Hubie Brooks (FC)	.40
530	Dave Kingman	.15
532	Mike Marshall	.15
535	Mike Scott (FC)	.20
536	Rusty Staub	.15
542	Mookie Wilson (FC)	.15
555	Darrell Jackson (black cap on front)	1.00
555	Darrell Jackson (red cap, no emblem)	.25
555	Darrell Jackson (red cap with emblem)	.15
576	John Littlefield (pitching left-handed)	275.00
576	John Littlefield (correct photo)	.12
582	Ozzie Smith	2.50
588	Bobby Bonds	.15
592	*Jody Davis* (FC)	.20
603	*Lee Smith* (FC)	8.00
608	Danny Ainge	1.25
609	*Jorge Bell* (FC)	5.00
621	Lloyd Moseby	.12

622	Dave Stieb	.15
624	Willie Upshaw (FC)	.15
626	Ernie Whitt	.12
628	1981 AS Game	.10
629	AS Infielders (Bucky Dent, Frank White)	.15
630	Big Red Machine (Dave Concepcion, Dan Driessen, George Foster)	.15
631	Top NL Relief Pitcher (Bruce Sutter)	.15
632	Steve and Carlton (Steve Carlton, Carlton Fisk)	.95
633	3000th Game, May 25, 1981 (Carl Yastrzemski)	.75
634	Dynamic Duo (Johnny Bench, Tom Seaver)	1.50
635	West Meets East (Gary Carter, Fernando Valenzuela)	.30
636	NL SO King (Fernando Valenzuela)	.40
637	1981 HR King (Mike Schmidt)	1.50
638	NL All Stars (Gary Carter, Dave Parker)	.30
640	Pete & Re-Pete (Pete Rose, Pete Rose Jr.)	1.25
641	Phillies' Finest (Steve Carlton, Mike Schmidt, Lonnie Smith)	.75
642	Red Sox Reunion (Dwight Evans, Fred Lynn)	.15
643	1981 Most Hits, Most Runs (Rickey Henderson)	1.75
644	Most Saves 1981 AL (Rollie Fingers)	.40
645	Most 1981 Wins (Tom Seaver)	.80
646	Yankee Powerhouse (Reggie Jackson, Dave Winfield)	2.25

1982 TOPPS

In 1982, Topps increased the number of cards to 792. This expansion eliminated double-printing and allowed the new set to be produced with an equal number of cards per press sheet (in six 132-card sheets). Collectors later found that the hobby was no longer flooded with certain cards. Despite these numbers, the 1982 set has only has a mediocre design, with indistinct blue-and-green printing on card backs. Two variations in the 1982 set are hard to locate: George Foster All-Star, number 342, is found with and without the facsimile autograph, while Pascual Perez, number 383, sometimes does not have the word "Pitcher" printed in the lower left corner.

		MINT
Complete set		**$150.00**
Commons		**.08**

254 Jorge Bell

1	1981 Highlight (Steve Carlton)	$1.00
2	1981 Highlight (Ron Davis)	.08
3	1981 Highlight (Tim Raines)	.40
4	1981 Highlight (Pete Rose)	1.00
5	1981 Highlight (Nolan Ryan)	3.00
6	1981 Highlight (Fernando Valenzuela)	.20
9	Ron Guidry	.35
10	Ron Guidry IA	.15
14	Steve Howe	.10
17	Darrell Evans	.25
19	Ernie Whitt	.10
20	Garry Maddox	.10
21	Orioles FS (Bob Bonner, *Cal Ripken* (FC), Jeff Schneider)	70.00
27	Tom Herr	.10
29	Dwayne Murphy	.10
30	Tom Seaver	2.25
31	Tom Seaver IA	1.00
36	Rangers Ldrs (George Medich, Al Oliver)	.12
39	Lou Whitaker	1.00
40	Dave Parker	.40
41	Dave Parker IA	.20
47	Jeff Leonard	.15
50	Buddy Bell	.15
51	Cubs FS (*Jay Howell* (FC), Carlos Lezcano, Ty Waller)	.45
52	*Larry Andersen* (FC)	.10
55	Rick Burleson	.10
59	*Rich Gedman* (FC)	.20
60	Tony Armas	.12
63	Mario Soto	.10
65	Terry Kennedy	.10
66	Astros Ldrs (Art Howe, Nolan Ryan)	1.50
70	Tim Raines	2.00
75	Tommy John	.35

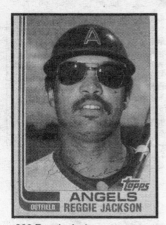

300 Reggie Jackson

90 Nolan Ryan

100 Mike Schmidt

21 Orioles Future Stars

213 Dave Stewart

395	Omar Moreno	.08
396	Twins Ldrs (Fernando Arroyo, John Castino)	.10
397	Ken Brett	.10
398	Mike Squires	.08
399	Pat Zachry	.08
400	Johnny Bench	2.00
401	Johnny Bench IA	.95
402	Bill Stein	.08
403	Jim Tracy	.08
404	Dickie Thon	.10
405	Rick Reuschel	.15
406	Al Holland	.08
407	Danny Boone	.08
408	Ed Romero	.08
410	Ron Cey	.15
411	Ron Cey IA	.10
412	Luis Leal	.08
414	Elias Sosa	.08
415	Don Baylor	.15
418	Rangers FS (John Butcher, Bobby Johnson, *Dave Schmidt* (FC))	.20
419	Steve Stone	.10
420	George Hendrick	.10
421	Mark Clear	.08

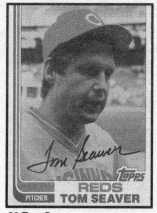

30 Tom Seaver

423	Stan Papi	.08
424	Bruce Benedict	.08
425	John Candelaria	.10
426	Orioles Ldrs (Eddie Murray, Sammy Stewart)	.30
427	Ron Oester	.08
428	Lamarr Hoyt (LaMarr)	.08
429	John Wathan	.10
430	Vida Blue	.15
431	Vida Blue IA	.10
432	Mike Scott	.25
433	Alan Ashby	.08
434	Joe Lefebvre	.08
435	Robin Yount	3.00
437	Juan Berenguer	.08
438	Pete Mackanin	.08
439	*Dave Righetti* (FC)	.70
440	Jeff Burroughs	.10
441	Astros FS (Danny Heep, Billy Smith, Bobby Sprowl)	.08
442	Bruce Kison	.08
443	Mark Wagner	.08
444	Terry Forster	.08
445	Larry Parrish	.10
446	Wayne Garland	.08
447	Darrell Porter	.10
448	Darrell Porter IA	.10

610 Rickey Henderson

449	*Luis Aguayo* (FC)	.12
450	Jack Morris	1.25
451	Ed Miller	.08
452	*Lee Smith* (FC)	12.00
453	Art Howe	.08
454	Rick Langford	.08
455	Tom Burgmeier	.08
456	Cubs Ldrs (Bill Buckner, Randy Martz)	.15
457	Tim Stoddard	.08
458	Willie Montanez	.08
459	Bruce Berenyi	.08
460	Jack Clark	.25
461	Rich Dotson	.12
464	Juan Bonilla	.08
465	Lee Mazzilli	.10
466	Randy Lerch	.08
467	Mickey Hatcher	.10
468	Floyd Bannister	.12
469	Ed Ott	.08
470	John Mayberry	.10
471	Royals FS (*Atlee Hammaker,* Mike Jones, Darryl Motley)	.15
472	Oscar Gamble	.10
473	Mike Stanton	.08
474	Ken Oberkfell	.08

475	Alan Trammell	1.45
476	Brian Kingman	.08
477	Steve Yeager	.08
480	Steve Carlton	2.00
481	Steve Carlton IA	1.00
482	Glenn Hubbard	.10
483	Gary Woods	.08
484	Ivan DeJesus	.08
485	Kent Tekulve	.10
486	Yankees Ldrs (Tommy John, Jerry Mumphrey)	.20
487	Bob McClure	.08
488	Ron Jackson	.08
489	Rick Dempsey	.10
490	Dennis Eckersley	2.50
491	Checklist 397-528	.12
492	Joe Price	.08
493	Chet Lemon	.10
494	Hubie Brooks	.45
495	Dennis Leonard	.10
496	Johnny Grubb	.08
499	Paul Mirabella	.08
500	Rod Carew	1.85
501	Rod Carew IA	.90
502	Braves FS (*Steve Bedrosian* (FC), *Brett Butler* (FC), Larry Owen)	3.50

390 Eddie Murray

503 Julio Gonzalez...............08
505 Graig Nettles 25
506 Graig Nettles IA..............12
508 *Jody Davis* (FC) 40
510 Fernando Valenzuela 40
513 Rick Rhoden...................10
515 Larry Bowa 20
516 Larry Bowa IA.................12
520 Mike Flanagan................10
526 Expos Ldrs
(Warren Cromartie,
Bill Gullickson)................10
532 Toby Harrah 10
533 Joaquin Andujar 10
535 Lance Parrish 30
536 Rafael Ramirez 10
538 Lou Piniella.....................15
540 Andre Dawson.............3.00
545 Reggie Smith..................15
546 Reggie Smith IA 10
547 Rod Carew AS 1.00
548 Willie Randolph AS 12
549 George Brett AS............1.75
550 Bucky Dent AS 12
551 Reggie Jackson AS.......1.75
552 Ken Singleton AS 12
553 Dave Winfield AS 1.75
554 Carlton Fisk AS 1.00

452 Lee Smith

555 Scott McGregor AS 12
556 Jack Morris AS................50
557 Rich Gossage AS............15
558 John Tudor 20
559 Indians Ldrs
(Bert Blyleven,
Mike Hargrove)................15
564 Doug DeCinces 15
569 Willie Randolph 20
570 Willie Randolph IA...........10
576 Giants Ldrs
(Vida Blue,
Milt May)........................15
577 Rick Monday 10
579 *Rick Mahler* (FC) 20
580 Bobby Bonds...................15
581 Ron Reed 10
585 Rollie Fingers 1.00
586 Rollie Fingers IA..............60
590 Al Oliver.........................20
591 Al Oliver IA 10
595 Dave Collins 10
600 Dave Winfield 4.00
605 Steve Rogers 10
606 Blue Jays Ldrs
(John Mayberry,
Dave Stieb) 15
607 Leon Durham 10

553 Dave Winfield AS

200 George Brett

609	Rick Sutcliffe	.35
610	Rickey Henderson	6.00
611	Joe Niekro	.20
615	• Bob Boone	.12
616	Bob Boone IA	.10
617	Scott McGregor	.10
620	Ken Griffey	.40
621	Ken Griffey IA	.20
623	Mets FS	
	(Ron Gardenhire,	
	Terry Leach (FC),	
	Tim Leary (FC))	.40
624	Fergie Jenkins	.70
625	Hal McRae	.15
626	Randy Jones	.10
630	Joe Charboneau	.20
631	Gene Tenace	.10
634	Checklist 529-660	.12
635	Ron Davis	.10
636	Phillies Ldrs	
	(Steve Carlton,	
	Pete Rose)	.50
640	Cesar Cedeno	.15
642	Mike Scioscia	.25
643	Pete Vuckovich	.10
645	Frank White	.10
646	Frank White IA	.10
650	Carl Yastrzemski	2.00

651	Carl Yastrzemski IA	1.00
653	Angels FS	
	(*Tom Brunansky* (FC),	
	Luis Sanchez,	
	Daryl Sconiers)	1.00
660	Dave Concepcion	.15
661	Dave Concepcion IA	.10
665	Jim Clancy	.10
666	Tigers Ldrs	
	(Steve Kemp,	
	Dan Petry)	.15
667	Jeff Reardon	2.50
668	Dale Murphy	1.50
670	Steve Kemp	.12
671	Mike Davis	.10
675	Cecil Cooper	.10
680	Gary Matthews	.12
681	Dodgers FS	
	(*Mike Marshall* (FC),	
	Ron Roenicke,	
	Steve Sax (FC))	3.00
683	Phil Garner	.10
684	Harold Baines	1.25
685	Bert Blyleven	.40
690	Dave Kingman	.20
696	Pirates Ldrs	
	(Bill Madlock,	
	Buddy Solomon)	.15
697	John Montefusco	.10
700	George Foster	.25
701	George Foster IA	.15
703	Brewers Ldrs	
	(Cecil Cooper,	
	Pete Vuckovich)	.15
704	Mickey Rivers	.10
705	Mickey Rivers IA	.10
710	Jerry Reuss	.10
711	Mariners FS	
	(Dave Edler,	
	Dave Henderson (FC),	
	Reggie Walton)	1.25
714	Jerry Koosman	.12
715	Willie Stargell	1.00
716	Willie Stargell IA	.45
718	Charlie Hough	.10
720	Greg Luzinski	.20
721	Greg Luzinski IA	.12
725	Amos Otis	.10
726	Amos Otis IA	.10

730	Gary Carter	1.25
740	Dave Lopes	.12
741	Dave Lopes IA	.10
744	*Mike Witt*	.25
746	Andre Thornton	.10
750	Jim Rice	.45
754	• Joe Morgan	.90
755	Joe Morgan IA	.20
756	Reds Ldrs (Ken Griffey, Tom Seaver)	.40
758	Claudell Washington	.10
760	Bill Buckner	.15
761	Dave Smith	.15
765	Gorman Thomas	.10
766	Twins FS (Lenny Faedo, *Kent Hrbek* (FC), *Tim Laudner* (FC))	3.00
769	Richie Zisk	.10
770	Rich Gossage	.35
771	Rich Gossage IA	.15
772	Bert Campaneris	.10
774	Jay Johnstone	.10
775	Bob Forsch	.10
776	Mark Belanger	.10
780	Pete Rose	2.00
781	Pete Rose IA	1.10
783	*Greg Harris* (FC)	.40
785	Dan Driessen	.10
786	Red Sox Batting and Pitching Ldrs (Carney Lansford, Mike Torrez)	.12
788	Woodie Fryman	.10
789	Checklist 661-792	.12
790	Larry Gura	.08
792	Frank Tanana	.15

1982 TOPPS TRADED

Like it or not, Topps Traded cards returned in 1982. The company found enough enthusiasm to make the "extension" set into an annual affair. In addition, the Traded set deflected criticism from Topps' failure to include rookies and traded players in the principal set of the year, which was issued earlier than ever before. Topps added a "T" suffix to each card in the alphabetized set to distinguish it from the year's earlier issue (though the "T" has been omitted from the following list). Once again, the Traded cards were available only from hobby dealers in boxed, complete sets. Noteworthy cards include the first solo Topps card of Cal Ripken, Jr., along with the first picture of Ozzie Smith in a Cardinal uniform. Unlike the 1981 Traded set, the 1982 release was numbered as a separate set.

		MINT
Complete set		$285.00
Commons		.45
1	Doyle Alexander	$ .50
2	Jesse Barfield	.70
3	Ross Baumgarten	.45
4	Steve Bedrosian	.70
5	Mark Belanger	.50
6	Kurt Bevacqua	.45
8	Vida Blue	.50
9	Bob Boone	.60
10	Larry Bowa	.50

98 Cal Ripken

13	Tom Brunansky	1.50
14	Jeff Burroughs	.45
15	Enos Cabell	.45
16	Bill Campbell	.45
17	Bobby Castillo	.45
18	Bill Caudill	.45
19	Cesar Cedeno	.50
20	Dave Collins	.45
23	Chili Davis	3.00
24	Dick Davis	.45
26	Doug DeCinces	.50
27	Ivan DeJesus	.45
28	Bob Dernier	.50
29	Bo Diaz	.45
31	Jim Essian	.45
32	Ed Farmer	.45
33	Doug Flynn	.45
34	Tim Foli	.45
35	Dan Ford	.45
36	George Foster	.55
39	Ron Gardenhire	.45
40	Ken Griffey	.75
41	Greg Harris	.45
42	Von Hayes	.60
43	Larry Herndon	.45
44	Kent Hrbek	6.00
45	Mike Ivie	.45
47	Reggie Jackson	12.00

48	Ron Jackson	.45
49	• Fergie Jenkins	2.75
50	Lamar Johnson	.45
52	Jay Johnstone	.45
53	Mick Kelleher	.45
54	Steve Kemp	.45
55	Junior Kennedy	.45
56	Jim Kern	.45
57	Ray Knight	.60
58	Wayne Krenchicki	.45
59	Mike Krukow	.45
61	Mike LaCoss	.45
62	Chet Lemon	.45
63	Sixto Lezcano	.45
64	Dave Lopes	.45
66	Renie Martin	.45
67	John Mayberry	.45
68	Lee Mazzilli	.45
69	Bake McBride	.45
72	Eddie Milner (FC)	.50
74	Jose Morales	.45
75	Keith Moreland	.45
83	Al Oliver	.60
86	Larry Parrish	.45
88	Gaylord Perry	2.50
94	Charlie Puleo (FC)	.45
95	Shane Rawley	.45
96	Johnny Ray	.45
98	Cal Ripken	250.00
101	Aurelio Rodriguez	.45
102	Joe Rudi	.50
103	Steve Sax	5.00
106	Eric Show (FC)	.50
107	Roy Smalley	.45
108	Lonnie Smith	.60
109	Ozzie Smith	20.00
110	Reggie Smith	.45
111	Lary Sorensen	.45
112	Elias Sosa	.45
113	Mike Stanton	.45
114	Steve Stroughter	.45
115	Champ Summers	.45
116	Rick Sutcliffe	1.00
117	Frank Tanana	.50
119	Garry Templeton	.45
122	Ed Vande Berg (FC)	.45
125	Bob Watson	.45
127	Eddie Whitson	.45
130	Gary Woods	.45

1983 DONRUSS

Donruss offered few innovations in its third year of baseball card production. Card backs retain the same format as the previous year, although a different yellow ink was used. Fronts again display a large photo along with a baseball bat graphic with the player name and position. A 63-piece Ty Cobb puzzle replaced the Babe Ruth puzzle of 1982, and the set was distributed in wax packs, three pieces per package. The final card of the numbered set shows the entire puzzle. For the first time Donruss sold complete boxed sets to dealers on a wholesale basis. Rookie cards of Wade Boggs, Tony Gwynn, and Ryne Sandberg are among the most popular cards in the set.

		MINT
Complete set		$125.00
Commons		.10

1	Fernando Valenzuela (DK)	$ .35
2	Rollie Fingers (DK)	.25
3	Reggie Jackson (DK)	.80
4	Jim Palmer (DK)	.55
5	Jack Morris (DK)	.35
6	George Foster (DK)	.20
7	Jim Sundberg (DK)	.12
8	Willie Stargell (DK)	.40
9	Dave Stieb (DK)	.15
10	Joe Niekro (DK)	.08
11	Rickey Henderson (DK)	1.75
12	Dale Murphy (DK)	.35
13	Toby Harrah (DK)	.12
14	Bill Buckner (DK)	.15
15	Willie Wilson (DK)	.15
16	Steve Carlton (DK)	.50
17	Ron Guidry (DK)	.25
18	Steve Rogers (DK)	.10
19	Kent Hrbek (DK)	.40
20	Keith Hernandez (DK)	.20
21	Floyd Bannister (DK)	.08
22	Johnny Bench (DK)	.50
23	Britt Burns (DK)	.10
24	Joe Morgan (DK)	.35
25	Carl Yastrzemski (DK)	.80
26	Terry Kennedy (DK)	.12
31	Ron Guidry	.25
32	Burt Hooton	.12

277 Ryne Sandberg

34	Vida Blue	.15
35	Rickey Henderson	3.50
39	Jerry Koosman	.15
40	Bruce Sutter	.25
41	Jose Cruz	.20
42	Pete Rose	1.50
43	Cesar Cedeno	.15
47	Dale Murphy	.85
49	Hubie Brooks	.15
50	Floyd Bannister	.08
53	*Gary Gaetti* (FC)	.50
56	Mookie Wilson	.12
58	Bob Horner	.15
59	Tony Pena	.15

168 Mike Schmidt

63	Garry Maddox	.12
64	Bob Forsch	.10
69	Charlie Hough	.15
70	Dan Quisenberry	.15
71	Tony Armas	.12
72	Rick Sutcliffe	.30
73	Steve Balboni (FC)	.10
77	Jim Palmer	1.00
78	Rollie Fingers	.70
83	Graig Nettles	.15
84	Ron Cey	.15
88	Byrn Smith (first name incorrect)	.20
88	Bryn Smith (correct name)	.80
90	Rod Carew	1.25
91	Lonnie Smith	.15
92	Bob Knepper	.08
97	Phil Niekro	.40
99	Bill Buckner	.15
100	*Ed VandeBerg* (Vande Berg) (FC)	.10
101	Jim Clancy	.08
104	Carlton Fisk	1.25
105	Mike Flanagan	.15
106	Cecil Cooper	.15
107	Jack Morris	.80
108	Mike Morgan (FC)	.20
110	Pedro Guerrero	.15
111	Len Barker	.10
112	Willie Wilson	.15
115	Reggie Jackson	1.75
117	Vance Law	.10
118	Nolan Ryan	7.00
119	Mike Krukow	.10
120	Ozzie Smith	1.75
122	Tom Seaver	1.35
123	Chris Chambliss	.15
126	*Mel Hall* (FC)	.80
128	*Charlie Puleo* (FC)	.10
134	Bruce Hurst (FC)	.35
136	Tom LaSorda (Lasorda)	.15
140	Al Oliver	.20
143	Harold Baines	.45
145	Garry Templeton	.12
147	Bo Diaz	.10
148	Dave Concepcion	.15
152	Keith Hernandez	.20
156	Rich Gedman	.12
157	Rich Gossage	.25
158	Jerry Reuss	.12
161	Dwayne Murphy	.10
162	Woodie Fryman	.10
168	Mike Schmidt	2.00
169	*Eddie Milner* (FC)	.10
171	Don Robinson	.12
173	Steve Bedrosian	.15
174	Willie Hernandez	.12
177	Tim Laudner	.10
179	Kent Hrbek	.75
180	Alfredo Griffin	.15
183	Jody Davis	.08
184	Glenn Hubbard	.06
189	Bob Dernier (FC)	.10
190	*Willie McGee* (FC)	2.75
191	Dickie Thon	.12
192	● Bob Boone	.15
194	Jeff Reardon	1.10
195	Jon Matlack	.10
196	*Don Slaught* (FC)	.75
199	Dave Righetti	.25
207	Alan Trammell	.55
208	Jim Rice	.35
210	Bill Russell	.15
211	Andre Thornton	.12
215	Buddy Bell	.15

586 Wade Boggs

258 Robin Yount

35 Rickey Henderson

639 Ron Jackson

279 Cal Ripken

338 George Brett

598 Tony Gwynn

490	U.L. Washington	.10
491	Steve McCatty	.10
493	Don Baylor	.15
495	Mike Squires	.10
496	Bert Roberge	.10
497	Dick Ruthven	.10
498	Tito Landrum	.10
499	Sixto Lezcano	.10
500	Johnny Bench	**1.35**
501	Larry Whisenton	.10
502	Manny Sarmiento	.10
504	Bill Campbell	.06
505	Todd Cruz	.10
507	Dave Stieb	.20
509	Dan Ford	.10
510	Gorman Thomas	.15
511	Chet Lemon	.10
512	Mike Torrez	.12
513	Shane Rawley	.10
514	Mark Belanger	.10
516	Onix Concepcion	.10
517	Mike Heath	.10
518	Andre Dawson	**1.75**
521	Rudy Law	.10
522	Ray Knight	.15
523	Joe Lefebvre	.10
524	Jim Wohlford	.10
525	*Julio Franco* (FC)	**5.00**

526	Ron Oester	.10
528	Steve Nicosia	.10
529	Junior Kennedy	.10
530	Whitey Herzog	.15
531	Don Sutton (blue frame around photo)	.60
531	Don Sutton (green frame around photo)	.50
532	Mark Brouhard	.10
533	Sparky Anderson	.15
534	Roger LaFrancois	.10
536	Tom Niedenfuer	.10
538	Lee May	.12
540	Tim Raines	.65
541	Paul Mirabella	.10
542	Luis Tiant	.15
543	Ron LeFlore	.12
544	*Dave LaPoint* (FC)	.15
549	John Candelaria	.12
550	Dave Bergman	.10
551	Bob Watson	.12
552	Pat Tabler	.10
554	Al Cowens	.10
555	Tom Brunansky (FC)	.35
556	Lloyd Moseby	.12
557	Pascual Perez (FC) (Twins)	**1.75**

115 Reggie Jackson

190 Willie McGee

382 Frank Viola

1983 FLEER

After errors and variations plagued Fleer's first two offerings, the company rebounded in 1983 with a nearly perfect set of baseball cards. The 660-card edition is arranged by team, beginning with the 1982 World Champion St. Louis Cardinals, and then alphabetically by player within each team. For the first time since the 1971 Topps set, Fleer cards feature a black-and-white shot of each player on the back of his card. The biggest sellers in this edition include rookie cards of Wade Boggs, Tony Gwynn, and Ryne Sandberg. Because Fleer flooded the market with unsold cards at season's end, this set is still plentiful today.

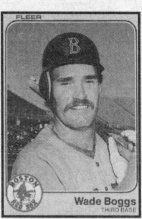

179 Wade Boggs

		MINT
Complete set		**$125.00**
Commons (1-660)		**.10**

2	Doug Bair	$ .06
3	Steve Braun	.06
5	Bob Forsch	.12
6	David Green	.06
8	Keith Hernandez	.20
9	Tom Herr	.12
10	Dane Iorg	.06
11	Jim Kaat	.20
12	Jeff Lahti	.06
14	*Dave LaPoint* (FC)	.15
15	*Willie McGee* (FC)	2.50
16	Steve Mura	.06
18	Darrell Porter	.12
19	Mike Ramsey	.06
20	Gene Roof	.06
21	Lonnie Smith	.12
22	Ozzie Smith	1.75
23	John Stuper	.06
24	Bruce Sutter	.20
25	Gene Tenace	.10
26	Jerry Augustine	.06
29	Mike Caldwell	.06
30	Cecil Cooper	.15
31	Jamie Easterly	.06
33	Rollie Fingers	.65
36	Roy Howell	.06
39	Doc Medich	.06
40	Paul Molitor	2.00
41	Don Money	.06
44	Ed Romero	.06
45	Ted Simmons	.20

46	Jim Slaton	.06
47	Don Sutton	.35
48	Gorman Thomas	.15
50	Ned Yost	.06
51	Robin Yount	2.50
54	Al Bumbry	.06
56	*Storm Davis* (FC)	.20
57	Rich Dauer	.06
59	Jim Dwyer	.06
60	Mike Flanagan	.12
67	Eddie Murray	1.75
68	Joe Nolan	.06
69	Jim Palmer	1.00
70	Cal Ripken Jr.	18.00
73	Ken Singleton	.15

75	Tim Stoddard	.06
76	Don Aase	.06
77	Don Baylor	.20
79	● Bob Boone	.15
81	Rod Carew	1.25
82	Bobby Clark	.06
85	Doug DeCinces	.12
86	Brian Downing	.12
88	Tim Foli	.06
89	Ken Forsch	.06
90	Dave Goltz	.10
91	Bobby Grich	.10
93	Reggie Jackson	1.75
94	Ron Jackson	.06
95	Tommy John	.20
96	Bruce Kison	.06
97	Fred Lynn	.20
98	Ed Ott	.06
101	Rob Wilfong	.06
102	Mike Witt	.12
103	Geoff Zahn	.06
104	Willie Aikens	.06
106	Vida Blue	.15
107	*Bud Black* (FC)	.70
108	George Brett	2.50
109	Bill Castro	.06
111	Dave Frost	.06
113	Larry Gura	.06

519 Rickey Henderson

118	Lee May	.12
119	Hal McRae	.20
120	Amos Otis	.12
121	Greg Pryor	.06
122	Dan Quisenberry	.20
123	*Don Slaught* (FC)	.80
126	John Wathan	.12
127	Frank White	.15
128	Willie Wilson	.20
129	Steve Bedrosian (FC)	.35
132	Brett Butler (FC)	.90
133	Rick Camp	.06
134	Chris Chambliss	.12
135	Ken Dayley (FC)	.12
136	Gene Garber	.06
138	Bob Horner	.20
139	Glenn Hubbard	.10
140	Rufino Linares	.06
141	Rick Mahler	.10
142	Dale Murphy	.80
143	Phil Niekro	.40
144	Pascual Perez	.12
149	Bob Walk	.06
151	Bob Watson	.12
155	Steve Carlton	1.25
159	Bob Dernier	.10
160	Bo Diaz	.10
163	Mike Krukow	.10

507 Ryne Sandberg

171 Pete Rose

360 Tony Gwynn

243	Dennis Lamp	.06
245	Vance Law	.06
246	Ron LeFlore	.12
247	Greg Luzinski	.15
250	Mike Squires	.06
251	Steve Trout	.06
252	Jim Barr	.06
253	Dave Bergman	.06
255	Bob Brenly (FC)	.10
256	Jack Clark	.25
257	Chili Davis (FC)	.70
258	Darrell Evans	.15
259	Alan Fowlkes	.06
260	Rich Gale	.06
261	Atlee Hammaker (FC)	.12
262	Al Holland	.06
263	Duane Kuiper	.06
264	Bill Laskey	.06
265	Gary Lavalle	.06
267	Renie Martin	.06
268	Milt May	.06
269	Greg Minton	.06
270	Joe Morgan	.75
272	Reggie Smith	.12
273	Guy Sularz	.06
275	Max Venable	.06
277	Ray Burris	.06
278	Gary Carter	.75

93 Reggie Jackson

280	Andre Dawson	1.75
281	Terry Francona	.06
282	Doug Flynn	.06
283	Woody Fryman	.10
286	Charlie Lea	.06
287	Randy Lerch	.06
290	Al Oliver	.20
292	Tim Raines	.35
293	Jeff Reardon	.80
294	Steve Rogers	.12
297	Bryn Smith	.12
298	Chris Speier	.06
299	Tim Wallach	.20
300	Jerry White	.06
303	Dale Berra	.06
304	John Candelaria	.12
306	Mike Easler	.06
307	Rich Hebner	.06
308	Lee Lacy	.06
309	Bill Madlock	.15
311	John Milner	.06
312	Omar Moreno	.06
314	Steve Nicosia	.06
315	Dave Parker	.35
316	Tony Pena	.15
317	Johnny Ray	.12
318	Rick Rhoden	.10
320	Enrique Romo	.06

280 Andre Dawson

70 Cal Ripken Jr.

625 Frank Viola

426	Jim Clancy	.12
429	Alfredo Griffin	.15
435	Lloyd Moseby	.15
439	*Gene Petralli* (FC)	.15
441	Dave Stieb	.20
442	Willie Upshaw	.12
443	Ernie Whitt	.12
446	Jose Cruz	.15
448	Phil Garner	.15
453	Ray Knight	.20
457	Joe Niekro	.15
463	Nolan Ryan	7.00
466	Dave Smith	.12
471	Floyd Bannister	.12
481	● Dave Henderson (FC)	.40
482	*Mike Moore* (FC)	.80
483	Gaylord Perry	.50
488	*Ed Vande Berg* (FC)	.10
489	Richie Zisk	.12
491	Larry Bowa	.15
492	Bill Buckner	.15
494	Jody Davis	.12
495	Leon Durham	.15
497	Willie Hernandez	.12
498	● Ferguson Jenkins	.50
499	● Jay Johnstone	.12
507	*Ryne Sandberg* (FC)	40.00
508	Lee Smith	2.50

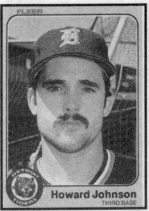

332 Howard Johnson

509	Pat Tabler (FC)	.15
513	Tony Armas	.15
515	Jeff Burroughs	.12
519	Rickey Henderson	3.00
520	Cliff Johnson	.06
521	Matt Keough	.06
522	Brian Kingman	.06
523	Rick Langford	.06
524	Davey Lopes	.06
525	Steve McCatty	.06
526	Dave McKay	.06
527	Dan Meyer	.06
528	Dwayne Murphy	.06
529	Jeff Newman	.06
530	Mike Norris	.06
532	Joe Rudi	.15
539	Hubie Brooks	.15
542	George Foster	.12
543	Ron Gardenhire	.10
544	Brian Giles	.10
545	Ron Hodges	.10
546	Randy Jones	.10
547	Mike Jorgensen	.10
548	Dave Kingman	.20
550	Jesse Orosco (FC)	.20
552	*Charlie Puleo* (FC)	.10
554	● Mike Scott	.15
555	Rusty Staub	.15

15 Willie McGee

67 Eddie Murray

222 Dave Stewart

1983 TOPPS

Topps reached back 20 years for the design of this 726-card set. Like the 1963 set which it resembles, the 1983 edition features a large color photograph of the player with a small round portrait in a lower corner. This design works best when the portrait is contrasted with an action shot. Super Veterans constitute one of the most appealing subsets of the decade. They use a then-and-now theme that displays a contemporary 1983 pose along with a vintage shot from early in the player's career. Rod Carew, Reggie Jackson, Pete Rose, and Carl Yastrzemski highlight this series. In terms of cost, the value given for the complete set is somewhat misleading since a single card, the Ryne Sandberg rookie card (83), by itself accounts for about a third of the price of the entire set. Due to the popularity of the fall Traded sets, Topps omitted all rookie cards from this standard edition.

	MINT
Complete set	**$165.00**
Commons	**.08**

1	Record Breaker (Tony Armas)	$ .20
2	Record Breaker (Rickey Henderson)	2.00
4	Record Breaker (Lance Parrish)	.20
8	Steve Balboni	.08
10	Gorman Thomas	.10
13	Larry Herndon	.08
15	Ron Cey	.10
17	Kent Tekulve	.08
18	Super Vet (Kent Tekulve)	.10
19	Oscar Gamble	.10
20	Carlton Fisk	2.00
21	Orioles Ldrs (Eddie Murray, Jim Palmer)	.45
24	Steve Mura	.08
25	Hal McRae	.20
29	Randy Jones	.10
30	Jim Rice	.35
35	Rollie Fingers	1.00
36	Super Vet (Rollie Fingers)	.50
37	Darrell Johnson	.08
40	Fernando Valenzuela	.35
43	Bob Dernier	.08
44	Don Robinson	.10
45	John Mayberry	.10

83 Ryne Sandberg

46	Richard Dotson	.12
47	Dave McKay	.08
49	*Willie McGee* (FC)	4.00
50	Bob Horner	.20
51	Cubs Ldrs (Leon Durham, Fergie Jenkins)	.15
53	Mike Witt	.30
55	Mookie Wilson	.12
58	Al Holland	.08
60	Johnny Bench	2.00
61	Super Vet (Johnny Bench)	1.00

360 Nolan Ryan

350 Robin Yount

300 Mike Schmidt

163 Cal Ripken

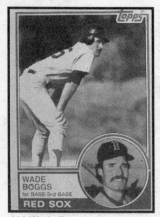

498 Wade Boggs

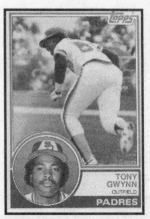

482 Tony Gwynn

600 George Brett

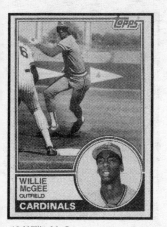

49 Willie McGee

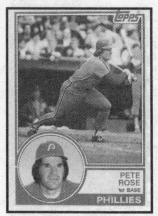

100 Pete Rose

391 Rickey Henderson AS

200 Rod Carew

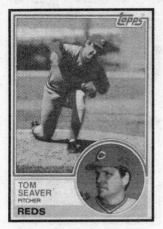

580 Tom Seaver

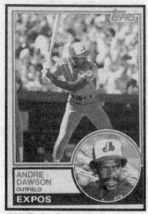

680 Andre Dawson

532	Dave Stewart	.70
540	Ozzie Smith	2.50
543	Ron Gardenhire	.10
544	Brian Giles	.10
545	Floyd Bannister	.10
550	Carl Yastrzemski	2.00
551	Super Vet (Carl Yastrzemski)	1.00
552	Tim Wallach	.20
561	Cardinals Ldrs (Joaquin Andujar, Lonnie Smith)	.15
565	Bucky Dent	.12
568	Willie Hernandez	.10
570	Vida Blue	.15
576	Frank Robinson	.20
580	Tom Seaver	2.00
581	Super Vet (Tom Seaver)	1.00
585	Jose Cruz	.15
586	*Frank Viola* (FC)	6.00
590	Tony Pena	.20
591	White Sox Ldrs (LaMarr Hoyt, Greg Luzinski)	.15
595	Tim Raines	.95
600	George Brett	3.00
603	• Joe Morgan	1.00
604	• Super Vet (Joe Morgan)	.40
610	Steve Garvey	.70
630	Paul Molitor	2.00
635	Graig Nettles	.20
636	Super Vet (Graig Nettles)	.12
640	Andre Thornton	.12
642	Checklist 529-660	.12
645	Bill Madlock	.15
651	Angels Ldrs (Rod Carew, Mike Witt)	.25
666	Sparky Anderson	.10
672	• Jim Kaat	.20
673	Super Vet (Jim Kaat)	.12
679	Mike Scott	.15
680	Andre Dawson	2.50
681	Dodgers Ldrs (Pedro Guerrero, Fernando Valenzuela)	.20
690	Kent Hrbek	.20
693	• Sparky Lyle	.12
699	Lee Smith	3.00
700	Keith Hernandez	.40
701	Batting Ldrs (Al Oliver, Willie Wilson)	.15

586 Frank Viola

702	HR Ldrs (Reggie Jackson, Dave Kingman, Gorman Thomas)	.35
703	RBI Ldrs (Hal McRae, Dale Murphy, Al Oliver)	.25
704	SB Ldrs (Rickey Henderson, Tim Raines)	1.10
705	Victory Ldrs (Steve Carlton, LaMarr Hoyt)	.20
706	SO Ldrs (Floyd Bannister, Steve Carlton)	.20
707	ERA Ldrs (Steve Rogers, Rick Sutcliffe)	.12
708	Leading Firemen (Dan Quisenberry, Bruce Sutter)	.15
710	Willie Wilson	.20
711	Mariners Ldrs (Jim Beattie, Bruce Bochte)	.12
715	Tony Perez	.35
716	Super Vet (Tony Perez)	.20
732	Dave Henderson	.25
735	Tommy John	.25
736	Super Vet (Tommy John)	.15
740	Rusty Staub	.15
742	Padres Ldrs (Terry Kennedy, Tim Lollar)	.12
760	Dale Murphy	1.25
765	● Bob Boone	.15
769	Checklist 661-792	.12
770	Dave Winfield	3.50
771	Twins Ldrs (Bobby Castillo, Kent Hrbek)	.20
781	Rick Rhoden	.12
782	Bobby Murcer	.12

1983 TOPPS TRADED

Don't let the price of the complete set of the 1983 Topps Traded issue fool you. Much of the estimated value is found in one card: the first-card issue of New York Mets superstar Darryl Strawberry, number 108. Other newcomers featured in this late-season series include Julio Franco, Mel Hall, and Ron Kittle. Steve Garvey, now dressed as a Padre, heads the class of veteran players in new uniforms. Because these cards were sold only through hobby dealers, many of whom were skeptical about the set's selling power, fewer sets than usual were distributed to the public.

		MINT
Complete set		**$85.00**
Commons		**.10**

1	Neil Allen	$ .10
2	Bill Almon	.10
3	Joe Altobelli	.10
4	Tony Armas	.20
5	Doug Bair	.10
6	Steve Baker	.10
7	Floyd Bannister	.20
8	Don Baylor	.30
9	Tony Bernazard	.10
10	Larry Biittner	.10
11	Dann Bilardello	.10
12	Doug Bird	.10
14	Greg Brock (FC)	.20

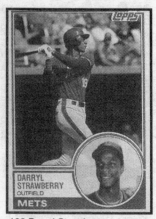

108 Darryl Strawberry

16	Tom Burgmeier	.10
17	Randy Bush (FC)	.15
18	Bert Campaneris	.15
19	Ron Cey	.15
20	Chris Codiroli (FC)	.15
21	Dave Collins	.15
22	Terry Crowley	.10
23	Julio Cruz	.10
24	Mike Davis	.15
25	Frank DiPino	.10
26	Bill Doran (FC)	.80
27	Jerry Dybzinski	.10
28	Jamie Easterly	.10
29	Juan Eichelberger	.10
30	Jim Essian	.10
31	Pete Falcone	.10
33	Terry Forster	.10
34	Julio Franco (FC)	6.00
35	Rich Gale	.10
36	Kiko Garcia	.10
37	Steve Garvey	1.65
39	Mel Hall (FC)	1.50
40	Von Hayes	.20
41	Danny Heep	.10
42	Steve Henderson	.10
43	Keith Hernandez	.50
44	Leo Hernandez	.10
45	Willie Hernandez	.20
46	Al Holland	.10
47	Frank Howard	.15
48	Bobby Johnson	.10
53	Steve Kemp	.15
55	Ron Kittle (FC)	.25
58	Mike Krukow	.15
60	Carney Lansford	.25
66	• Billy Martin	.20
67	Lee Mazzilli	.15
69	Craig McMurtry (FC)	.25
77	• Joe Morgan	2.75
81	Pete O'Brien (FC)	.80
83	Alejandro Pena (FC)	.50
84	Pascual Perez	.20
85	Tony Perez	1.50
87	Tony Phillips (FC)	6.00
90	Jamie Quirk	.10
91	Doug Rader	.15
94	Gary Redus (FC)	.70
95	Steve Renko	.10
96	Leon Roberts	.10
97	Aurelio Rodriguez	.15
100	Mike Scott	.40
101	Tom Seaver	9.00
102	John Shelby (FC)	.20
103	Bob Shirley	.10
104	Joe Simpson	.10
105	Doug Sisk (FC)	.15
106	Mike Smithson (FC)	.20
107	Elias Sosa	.10
108	Darryl Strawberry (FC)	60.00
109	Tom Tellman	.10
110	Gene Tenace	.10
111	Gorman Thomas	.15
112	Dick Tidrow	.10
113	Dave Tobik	.10
114	Wayne Tolleson (FC)	.15
115	Mike Torrez	.15
116	Manny Trillo	.15
117	Steve Trout	.10
118	Lee Tunnell (FC)	.15
119	Mike Vail	.10
120	Ellis Valentine	.10
121	Tom Veryzer	.10
122	George Vukovich	.10
123	Rick Waits	.10
124	Greg Walker (FC)	.15
127	Eddie Whitson	.15
129	Matt Young (FC)	.20

1984 DONRUSS

The combination of a limited print run and the presence of several flashy rookies make the 1984 Donruss set the most expensive regular-season issue of the decade—by far. For starters, nearly one fifth of the current estimated value can be traced to the incredible demand for the first-year card for Don Mattingly. Darryl Strawberry is another very popular rookie. Ironically, neither Mattingly nor Strawberry was included in Rated Rookies, the 20-card subset which highlights outstanding prospects. Two unnumbered cards for Living Legends were distributed only in wax packs: Johnny Bench and Carl Yastrzemski on one; Rollie Fingers and Gaylord Perry on the other.

	MINT
Complete set	**$375.00**
Commons	**.25**

248 Don Mattingly

1	Robin Yount (DK)	$5.00
2	Dave Concepcion (DK)	.30
3	Dwayne Murphy (DK)	.25
5	Leon Durham (DK)	.25
6	Rusty Staub (DK)	.30
7	Jack Clark (DK)	.40
8	Dave Dravecky (DK)	.25
9	Al Oliver (DK)	.35
10	Dave Righetti (DK)	.40
11	Hal McRae (DK)	.30
12	Ray Knight (DK)	.25
13	Bruce Sutter (DK)	.35
14	Bob Horner (DK)	.40
15	Lance Parrish (DK)	.50
16	Matt Young (DK)	.35
17	Fred Lynn (DK)	.35
18	Ron Kittle (DK)	.35
19	Jim Clancy (DK)	.25
20	Bill Madlock (DK)	.30
21	Larry Parrish (DK)	.30
22	Eddie Murray (DK)	2.00
23	Mike Schimdt (DK)	4.00
24	Pedro Guerrero (DK)	.50
25	Andre Thornton (DK)	.30
26	Wade Boggs (DK)	4.50
29	Mike Stenhouse (RR) (number 29 on back)	8.00
29	Mike Stenhouse (RR) (no number on back)	.15
30	*Ron Darling* (RR) (FC) (number 30 on back)	16.00
30	*Ron Darling* (RR) (FC) (no number on back)	3.00
31	*Dion James* (RR) (FC)	.40
32	*Tony Fernandez* (RR) (FC)	6.00
34	*Kevin McReynolds* (RR) (FC)	2.50
35	*Dick Schofield* (RR) (FC)	.45
37	*Tim Teufel* (RR) (FC)	.45
39	*Greg Gagne* (RR) (FC)	1.10
41	*Joe Carter* (RR) (FC)	55.00
44	*Sid Fernandez* (RR) (FC)	5.00
47	Eddie Murray	6.00

68 Darryl Strawberry

48	Robin Yount	10.00
49	Lance Parrish	.50
50	Jim Rice	.55
51	Dave Winfield	9.00
52	Fernando Valenzuela	.40
53	George Brett	10.00
54	Rickey Henderson	13.00
55	Gary Carter	2.00
56	Buddy Bell	.30
57	Reggie Jackson	7.00
58	Harold Baines	1.00
59	Ozzie Smith	6.00
60	Nolan Ryan	28.00
61	Pete Rose	5.00
62	Ron Oester	.15
63	Steve Garvey	1.40
65	Jack Clark	.35
66	Dale Murphy	2.50
67	Leon Durham	.25
68	Darryl Strawberry (FC)	40.00
69	Richie Zisk	.15
70	Kent Hrbek	.75
71	Dave Stieb	.60
72	Ken Schrom	.15
73	George Bell	2.75
74	John Moses	.25
81	Tom Foley	.15
83	Andy Van Slyke (FC)	12.00

84	Bob Lillis	.15
85	Rick Adams	.15
89	Ed Romero	.15
90	John Grubb	.15
93	Candy Maldonado	.25
94	Andre Thornton	.25
96	Don Hill (FC)	.25
97	Andre Dawson	6.00
98	Frank Tanana	.35
100	Larry Gura	.15
103	Dave Righetti	.40
104	Steve Sax	.40
105	Dan Petry	.15
106	Cal Ripken	30.00
107	Paul Molitor	1.35
108	Fred Lynn	.35
109	Neil Allen	.15
110	Joe Niekro	.25
111	Steve Carlton	5.00
113	Bill Madlock	.25
114	Chili Davis	.25
115	Jim Gantner	.15
116	Tom Seaver	7.00
117	Bill Buckner	.25
120	John Castino	.15
121	Dave Concepcion	.30
122	Greg Luzinski	.35
123	Mike Boddicker (FC)	.25

183 Mike Schmidt

116 Tom Seaver

41 Joe Carter

303

60 Nolan Ryan

215	Pat Zachry	.15
216	Julio Franco	2.50
219	Steve Rogers	.30
221	*Mike Smithson* (FC)	.25
222	Frank White	.25
224	Chris Bando	.15
225	Roy Smalley	.15
226	Dusty Baker	.25
227	Lou Whitaker	2.00
229	Ben Oglivie	.30
230	Doug DeCinces	.30
231	Lonnie Smith	.15
232	Ray Knight	.30
233	Gary Matthews	.25
234	Juan Bonilla	.15
237	Mike Caldwell	.15
238	Keith Hernandez	.40
239	Larry Bowa	.25
242	Tom Brunansky	.35
243	Dan Driessen	.15
244	Ron Kittle (FC)	.30
248	*Don Mattingly* (FC)	45.00
250	*Alejandro Pena* (FC)	.60
251	Toby Harrah	.15
263	*Gerald Perry* (FC)	.35
264	Gene Tenace	.15
266	Dickie Noles	.15
268	Jim Gott	.30

274	Lou Piniella	.25
275	Jose Morales	.15
277	Butch Davis	.15
278	*Tony Phillips* (FC)	4.00
279	Jeff Reardon	2.50
281	*Pete O'Brien* (FC)	.60
282	Tom Paciorek	.15
288	Dave Parker	1.15
289	Lee Smith	1.85
291	*John Shelby* (FC)	.25
293	Alan Trammell	2.60
294	Tony Armas	.25
296	Greg Brock	.25
297	Hal McRae	.25
298	Mike Davis	.15
299	Tim Raines	1.60
300	Bucky Dent	.30
301	Tommy John	.40
302	Carlton Fisk	5.00
303	Darrell Porter	.15
304	Dickie Thon	.15
305	Garry Maddox	.15
306	Cesar Cedeno	.25
308	Johnny Ray	.25
311	Ryne Sandberg	30.00
312	George Foster	.35
313	*Spike Owen* (FC)	.60
314	Gary Gaetti	.30

311 Ryne Sandberg

324	Tony Gwynn	15.00
336	*Bob Meacham* (FC)	.25
337	Joe Beckwith	.15
338	Rick Sutcliffe	.40
341	Scott Sanderson	.15
342	Larry Biittner	.15
343	Dave Stewart	1.50
344	Darryl Motley	.15
348	Mike Marshall	.25
350	Rich Dauer	.15
351	Cecil Cooper	.35
352	Rod Carew	5.00
353	Willie McGee	1.10
354	Phil Garner	.15
355	Joe Morgan	1.50
357	John Candelaria	.25
360	Dave Kingman	.25
361	Ron Cey	.25
362	*Matt Young* (FC)	.25
363	Lloyd Moseby	.25
364	Frank Viola	1.75
366	Floyd Bannister	.25
373	*Neal Heaton* (FC)	.30
374	Greg Pryor	.15
375	Wayne Gross	.15
381	*Kevin Gross* (FC)	.60
388	*Craig Lefferts* (FC)	.75
393	*Tom Candiotti* (FC)	1.50

32 Tony Fernandez

395	Dwight Evans	.50
396	Goose Gossage	.40
400	Davey Lopes	.30
406	Eric Show	.30
411	Mel Hall	.60
414	Don Sutton	1.25
415	Jack Morris	2.50
416	John Tudor	.25
417	Willie Randolph	.25
418	Jerry Reuss	.30
421	Tim Wallach	.35
422	Larry Parrish	.25
423	Brian Downing	.25
431	Darrell Evans	.25
435	*Ed Nunez* (FC)	.25
439	Doyle Alexander	.30
446	*Dennis Rasmussen* (FC)	.45
447	Ted Power (FC)	.25
448	*Charlie Hudson* (FC)	.25
449	*Danny Cox* (FC)	.35
450	Kevin Bass (FC)	.30
453	Bryn Smith	.30
457	Dennis "Oil Can" Boyd (FC)	.45
461	*Danny Jackson* (FC)	.65
469	Steve Kemp	.25
473	Ted Simmons	.25

54 Rickey Henderson

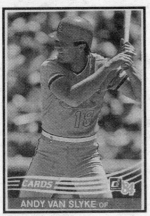

83 Andy Van Slyke

324 Tony Gwynn

1984 FLEER

One of the finest Fleer sets ever offered was the 660-card edition of 1984. The design is simple and clean, with large, unobstructed photos and no glaring errors or variations. Along with the traditional action shots and portraits, some of the zaniest cards of the decade surfaced in 1984. For example, Jay Johnstone posed wearing an umbrella hat (495), while Glenn Hubbard is shown with a boa constrictor draped around his shoulders (182). Card 638 commemorates George Brett's illegal bat coated with pine tar. As usual, the Fleer cards are arranged by team, with players listed alphabetically within each team.

		MINT
Complete set		**$200.00**
Commons		**.12**

1	Mike Boddicker (FC)	$ .35
2	Al Bumbry	.15
5	Storm Davis	.15
6	Rick Dempsey	.15
8	Mike Flanagan	.15
11	Dennis Martinez	.15
13	Scott McGregor	.12
14	Eddie Murray	4.00
16	Jim Palmer	3.00
17	Cal Ripken, Jr.	20.00
20	John Shelby (FC)	.25
21	Ken Singleton	.15
25	Steve Carlton	3.00
26	Ivan DeJesus	.12
29	Bo Diaz	.12
32	Kevin Gross (FC)	.40
33	Von Hayes	.20
34	Willie Hernandez	.12
36	Charles Hudson (FC)	.15
39	Garry Maddox	.15
40	Gary Matthews	.15
42	Tug McGraw	.20
43	Joe Morgan	1.00
44	Tony Perez	.75
45	Ron Reed	.08
46	Pete Rose	3.50
47	Juan Samuel (FC)	1.10
48	Mike Schmidt	9.00
49	Ozzie Virgil	.08
50	Juan Agosto (FC)	.15
51	Harold Baines	.80
52	Floyd Bannister	.12
54	Britt Burns	.08
55	Julio Cruz	.08
56	Richard Dotson	.12
58	Carlton Fisk	3.00
59	Scott Fletcher (FC)	.35
64	Ron Kittle	.15
65	Jerry Koosman	.12
66	Dennis Lamp	.08
67	Rudy Law	.08
68	Vance Law	.12
69	Greg Luzinski	.15
72	Dick Tidrow	.08
73	Greg Walker (FC)	.20
74	Glenn Abbott	.08
78	Tom Brookens	.08
79	Enos Cabell	.08
80	Kirk Gibson	1.00
81	John Grub	.08
82	Larry Herndon	.12
84	Rick Leach	.08
85	Chet Lemon	.15
87	Jack Morris	1.75
88	Lance Parrish	.50
89	Dan Petry	.12
91	Alan Trammell	1.25
92	Lou Whitaker	1.25
93	Milt Wilcox	.08
94	Glenn Wilson	.12
96	Dusty Baker	.20
98	Greg Brock	.12
100	Pedro Guerrero	.35
102	Burt Hooton	.15
103	Steve Howe	.20
105	Mike Marshall	.15
106	Rick Monday	.15
107	Jose Morales	.08
109	Alejandro Pena (FC)	.35

1984 Fleer

131 Don Mattingly

17 Cal Ripken, Jr.

200	Jim Gantner	.20
201	Bob Gibson	.08
202	Moose Haas	.08
207	Paul Molitor	2.75
208	Don Money	.08
210	Ben Oglivie	.15
212	Ed Romero	.08
213	Ted Simmons	.20
214	Jim Slaton	.08
215	Don Sutton	.75
218	Ned Yost	.08
219	Robin Yount	6.00
221	Kevin Bass (FC)	.20
222	Jose Cruz	.12
223	*Bill Dawley* (FC)	.12
225	*Bill Doran* (FC)	.40
226	Phil Garner	.15
229	Ray Knight	.12
231	Mike LaCoss	.08
232	Mike Madden	.08
237	Craig Reynolds	.08
238	Vern Ruhle	.08
239	Nolan Ryan	20.00
240	Mike Scott	.20
241	Tony Scott	.08
242	Dave Smith	.12
243	Dickie Thon	.15
244	Denny Walling	.08

447 Rickey Henderson

245	Dale Berra	.08
246	Jim Bibby	.08
247	John Candelaria	.15
248	*Jose DeLeon* (FC)	.40
249	Mike Easler	.12
250	Cecilio Guante (FC)	.12
251	Richie Hebner	.08
253	Bill Madlock	.12
254	Milt May	.08
255	Lee Mazzilli	.12
258	Dave Parker	.60
259	Tony Pena	.12
260	Johnny Ray	.12
261	Rick Rhoden	.12
262	Don Robinson	.12
264	Rod Scurry	.08
265	Kent Tekulve	.15
266	Gene Tenace	.15
268	*Lee Tunnell* (FC)	.12
269	*Marvell Wynne* (FC)	.15
270	Ray Burris	.08
271	Gary Carter	1.00
273	Andre Dawson	4.00
274	Doug Flynn	.08
276	Bill Gullickson	.08
280	Al Oliver	.20
281	Tim Raines	1.00
282	Bobby Ramos	.08

344 George Brett

504 Ryne Sandberg

283	Jeff Reardon	1.50
284	Steve Rogers	.15
286	Dan Schatzeder	.08
287	Bryn Smith	.08
288	Chris Speier	.08
289	Manny Trillo	.15
290	Mike Vail	.08
291	Tim Wallach	.30
292	Chris Welsh	.08
295	Juan Bonilla	.08
297	Luis DeLeon	.08
298	Dave Dravecky	.25
299	Tim Flannery	.08
300	Steve Garvey	.85
301	Tony Gwynn	10.00
302	*Andy Hawkins* (FC)	.35
304	Terry Kennedy	.12
307	*Kevin McReynolds* (FC)	1.25
312	Eric Show	.12
314	Garry Templeton	.15
315	*Mark Thurmond* (FC)	.12
316	Ed Whitson	.12
322	Bob Forsch	.12
324	George Hendrick	.15
325	Tom Herr	.15
328	Dave LaPoint	.12
329	Willie McGee	.75
331	Darrell Porter	.12

335	Lonnie Smith	.15
336	Ozzie Smith	4.00
338	Bruce Sutter	.25
339	*Andy Van Slyke* (FC)	8.00
343	Bud Black	.15
344	George Brett	6.00
350	Hal McRae	.25
351	Amos Otis	.15
352	Gaylord Perry	.80
354	Dan Quisenberry	.15
357	*Pat Sheridan* (FC)	.15
362	John Wathan	.10
363	Frank White	.15
364	Willie Wilson	.20
369	Jack Clark	.20
370	Chili Davis	.50
371	Mark Davis (FC)	.15
372	Darrell Evans	.15
374	Mike Krukow	.12
379	Jeff Leonard	.15
390	Tony Armas	.15
392	Wade Boggs	10.00
393	*Dennis Boyd* (FC)	.25
396	Dennis Eckersley	.75
397	Dwight Evans	.35
398	Rich Gedman	.12
400	Bruce Hurst	.15
406	Bob Ojeda	.15

307 Kevin McReynolds

339 Andy Van Slyke

599 Darryl Strawberry

148 Jorge Bell

14 Eddie Murray

638	The Pine Tar Incident, 7/24/83 (George Brett, Gaylord Perry) **1.25**		**641**	Going Out in Style (Gaylord Perry) .... .15
639	1983 No-Hitters (Bob Forsch, Dave Righetti, Mike Warren) .... .25		**642**	300 Club & Strikeout Record (Steve Carlton) .... .60
			643	The Managers (Joe Altobelli, Paul Owens) .... .10
640	Retiring Superstars (Johnny Bench, Carl Yastrzemski) **2.50**		**644**	The MVP (Rick Dempsey) .... .55
			645	The Rookie Winner (Mike Boddicker) (FC) .... .12

1984 FLEER UPDATE

After Topps enjoyed free rein over the fall card market for three years with its Traded set, Fleer decided to try for a piece of the action. It duplicated the marketing formula used by Topps in precise detail by designing its own 132-card Update set. Fleer used the same front and back design as the standard 1984 set but added the letter "U" to each card number (it has been omitted from the following list, however). The company published 131 player cards and a checklist, though the checklist seems unnecessary since the cards were sold only as complete boxed sets through hobby dealers. Because Fleer's ability to compete with the Topps Traded set seemed questionable during the first year, some hobby dealers were hesitant to stock the Fleer Update sets. This accounts for the relative scarcity of these cards.

			MINT
	Complete set		**$1000.00**
	Commons		**1.00**
3	Mark Bailey (FC)		$1.00
5	Dusty Baker....................		2.00
6	Steve Balboni (FC)........		1.00
8	Marty Barrett (FC)		2.00
15	Phil Bradley (FC)............		2.00
18	Bill Buckner		2.00
19	Ray Burris		1.00
21	Brett Butler		3.50
22	Enos Cabell....................		1.00
24	Bill Caudill		1.00
27	Roger Clemens (FC) .		450.00
28	Jaime Cocanower		1.00
29	Ron Darling (FC)		8.00
30	Alvin Davis (FC)		1.50
33	Mike Easler		1.00
34	Dennis Eckersley		25.00
36	Darrell Evans.................		1.25
37	Mike Fitzgerald (FC)......		1.00
38	Tim Foli		1.00
39	John Franco (FC)		8.00
41	Rich Gale		1.00
43	Dwight Gooden (FC) ...		85.00
44	• Goose Gossage..........		1.75
46	Mark Gubicza (FC)........		2.50
48	Toby Harrah		1.00
49	Ron Hassey....................		1.00
51	Willie Hernandez		1.00

27 Roger Clemens

52	Ed Hodge	1.00
53	Ricky Horton (FC)	1.00
54	Art Howe	1.25
55	Dane Iorg	1.00
56	Brook Jacoby (FC)	1.50
57	Dion James (FC)	1.50
58	Mike Jeffcoat (FC)	1.25
61	Jimmy Key (FC)	30.00
62	Dave Kingman	1.25
64	Jerry Koosman	1.00
68	Dennis Lamp	1.00
69	Tito Landrum	1.00
70	Mark Langston (FC)	30.00
72	Craig Lefferts (FC)	1.50
75	Carmelo Martinez	1.00
76	Mike Mason (FC)	1.00
77	Gary Matthews	1.10
80	Joe Morgan	10.00
82	Graig Nettles	1.50
83	Phil Niekro	8.00
84	Ken Oberkfell	1.00
85	Al Oliver	2.00
86	Jorge Orta	1.00
87	Amos Otis	1.00
89	Dave Parker	5.00
90	Jack Perconte	1.00
91	Tony Perez	8.00
92	Gerald Perry (FC)	1.50

93	Kirby Puckett (FC)	**400.00**
94	Shane Rawley	1.00
95	Floyd Rayford	1.00
96	Ron Reed	1.00
97	R.J. Reynolds (FC)	1.00
98	Gene Richards	1.00
99	Jose Rijo (FC)	30.00
100	Jeff Robinson (FC)	1.00
101	Ron Romanick (FC)	1.00
102	Pete Rose	25.00
103	Bret Saberhagen	28.00
104	Scott Sanderson	1.50
105	Dick Schofield (FC)	2.00
106	Tom Seaver	24.00
108	Mike Smithson	1.00
111	Jeff Stone (FC)	1.00
113	Jim Sundberg	1.10
114	Rick Sutcliffe	1.50
117	Gorman Thomas	1.10
119	Manny Trillo	1.00
120	John Tudor	1.10
123	Tom Waddell (FC)	1.00
124	Gary Ward	1.00
125	Terry Whitfield	1.00
127	Frank Williams (FC)	1.00
128	Glenn Wilson	1.00
131	Mike Young (FC)	1.00

43 Dwight Gooden

1984 TOPPS

Despite retaining the general format of the 1983 design, the 1984 Topps set was not an immediate hit with collectors. All the single-player cards show a large action photo with a smaller portrait on the front. The first six cards of this 792-card edition highlight events of the previous season, such as Steve Carlton winning his 300th game and becoming the all-time strikeout king; Dave Righetti, Bob Forsch, and Mike Warren pitching no-hitters; and Rickey Henderson stealing 100 bases three seasons in a row. Recognition was also given to Johnny Bench, Gaylord Perry, and Carl Yastrzemski on their retirement. For the second year in a row, no team rookie or Future Stars cards were included.

	MINT
Complete set	**$90.00**
Commons	**.08**

1	1983 Highlight (Steve Carlton)	**$.60**
2	1983 Highlight (Rickey Henderson)	**1.25**
3	1983 Highlight (Dan Quisenberry)	.10
4	1983 Highlight (Steve Carlton, Gaylord Perry, Nolan Ryan)	.80
5	1983 Highlight (Bob Forsch, Dave Righetti, Mike Warren)	.30
6	1983 Highlight (Johnny Bench, Gaylord Perry, Carl Yastrzemski)	.40
7	Gary Lucas	.08
8	*Don Mattingly* (FC)	13.00
9	Jim Gott	.08
10	Robin Yount	2.00
11	Twins Ldrs (Kent Hrbek, Ken Schrom)	.08
12	Billy Sample	.08
14	Tom Brookens	.08
15	Burt Hooton	.08
16	Omar Moreno	.08
18	Dale Berra	.08
19	*Ray Fontenot* (FC)	.10
20	Greg Luzinski	.12
21	Joe Altobelli	.08

182 Darryl Strawberry

22	Bryan Clark	.08
23	Keith Moreland	.08
24	John Martin	.08
25	Glenn Hubbard	.10
27	Daryl Sconiers	.08
28	Frank Viola	.60
29	Danny Heep	.08
30	Wade Boggs	4.50
32	Bobby Ramos	.08
33	Tom Burgmeier	.08
35	Don Sutton	.40
36	Denny Walling	.08
37	Rangers Ldrs (Buddy Bell, Rick Honeycutt)	.12

490 Cal Ripken

48 Julio Franco

100	Reggie Jackson	**1.50**
101	Porfirio Altamirano	.08
102	Ken Oberkfell	.08
105	Tony Armas	.08
106	Tim Stoddard	.08
107	Ned Yost	.08
108	Randy Moffitt	.08
109	Brad Wellman	.08
110	Ron Guidry	.25
111	Bill Virdon	.08
112	Tom Niedenfuer	.08
113	Kelly Paris	.08
114	Checklist 1-132	.12
115	Andre Thornton	.10
116	George Bjorkman	.08
117	Tom Veryzer	.08
118	Charlie Hough	.08
120	Keith Hernandez	.30
121	*Pat Sheridan* (FC)	.15
122	Cecilio Guante (FC)	.10
123	Butch Wynegar	.08
124	Damaso Garcia	.08
125	Britt Burns	.08
126	Braves Ldrs (Craig McMurtry, Dale Murphy)	.20
127	Mike Madden	.08
128	Rick Manning	.08

470 Nolan Ryan

130	Ozzie Smith	**1.25**
131	Batting Ldrs (Wade Boggs, Bill Madlock)	.50
132	HR Ldrs (Jim Rice, Mike Schmidt)	.40
133	RBI Ldrs (Cecil Cooper, Dale Murphy, Jim Rice)	.30
134	SB Ldrs (Rickey Henderson, Tim Raines)	.80
135	Victory Ldrs (John Denny, LaMarr Hoyt)	.10
136	SO Ldrs (Steve Carlton, Jack Morris)	.25
137	ERA Ldrs (Atlee Hammaker, Rick Honeycutt)	.10
138	Leading Firemen (Al Holland, Dan Quisenberry)	.12
139	Bert Campaneris	.12
140	Storm Davis	.12
141	Pat Corrales	.08
143	Jose Morales	.08
145	Gary Lavelle	.08
146	Ed Romero	.08
147	Dan Petry	.08

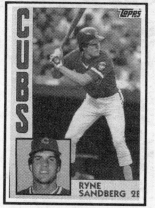

596 Ryne Sandberg

8 Don Mattingly

148	Joe Lefebvre	.08
149	Jon Matlack	.10
150	Dale Murphy	.90
151	Steve Trout	.08
152	Glenn Brummer	.08
153	Dick Tidrow	.08
154	Dave Henderson	.25
155	Frank White	.12
156	Athletics Ldrs (Tim Conroy, Rickey Henderson)	.25
157	Gary Gaetti	.25
158	John Curtis	.08
160	Mario Soto	.10
161	*Junior Ortiz* (FC)	.10
162	Bob Ojeda	.10
164	Scott Sanderson	.08
165	Ken Singleton	.12
166	Jamie Nelson	.08
168	Juan Bonilla	.08
169	Larry Parrish	.12
170	Jerry Reuss	.10
171	Frank Robinson	.12
172	Frank DiPino	.08
173	*Marvell Wynne* (FC)	.20
174	Juan Berenguer	.08
175	Graig Nettles	.20
176	Lee Smith	.80
177	Jerry Hairston	.08
178	Bill Krueger	.20
179	Buck Martinez	.08
180	Manny Trillo	.10
181	Roy Thomas	.08
182	*Darryl Strawberry*	8.00
183	Al Williams	.08
185	Sixto Lezcano	.08
186	Cardinals Ldrs (Lonnie Smith, John Stuper)	.10
187	Luis Aponte	.08
189	*Tim Conroy* (FC)	.12
190	Ben Oglivie	.10
191	Mike Boddicker	.25
192	*Nick Esasky* (FC)	.30
195	Jack Morris	.60
196	Don Slaught (FC)	.12
198	*Bill Doran*	.30
199	Willie Hernandez	.10
200	Andre Dawson	.95
204	*Bobby Meacham* (FC)	.12
206	*Andy Van Slyke* (FC)	3.00
208	*Jose Oquendo* (FC)	.15
210	Joe Morgan	.35
213	Bruce Hurst	.15
215	Tippy Martinez	.15
216	White Sox Ldrs (Richard Dotson, Carlton Fisk)	.15

500 George Brett

220	Fernando Valenzuela	.20
222	Rick Honeycutt	.10
230	Rickey Henderson	3.00
232	Tim Wallach	.15
233	Checklist 133-264	.12
235	*Matt Young*	.12
239	Jay Howell	.10
240	Eddie Murray	1.50
244	Candy Maldonado (FC)	.20
245	Rick Sutcliffe	.15
246	Mets Ldrs (Tom Seaver, Mookie Wilson)	.25
249	Jay Johnstone	.10
250	Bill Madlock	.15
251	Tony Gwynn	4.50
259	Sparky Anderson	.12
260	Scott McGregor	.10
262	*Tom Candiotti* (FC)	.50
265	*Donnie Hill* (FC)	.12
267	*Carmelo Martinez* (FC)	.15
270	*Jeff Russell* (FC)	.40
274	Rick Monday	.10
276	Angels Ldrs (Rod Carew, Geoff Zahn)	.20
278	Jorge Bell	.70
279	Ivan DeJesus	.10
280	Floyd Bannister	.10
290	Dave Dravecky	.10

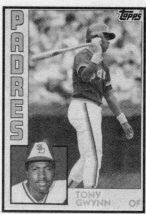

251 Tony Gwynn

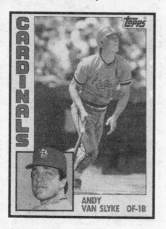

206 Andy Van Slyke

295	Mike Flanagan	.12
300	Pete Rose	1.25
306	Dodgers Ldrs (Pedro Guerrero, Bob Welch)	.15
309	*Tony Phillips*	1.00
310	Willie McGee	.35
311	Jerry Koosman	.12
315	Bob Grich	.10
324	*Alejandro Pena*	.30
330	John Candelaria	.15
331	Bucky Dent	.12
332	*Kevin Gross* (FC)	.25
340	Hal McRae	.15
345	Kent Hrbek	.30
350	George Foster	.15
352	Dave Stewart	.30
357	Ron Cey	.10
359	*Jim Acker* (FC)	.10
360	Willie Randolph	.10
364	Scott Fletcher (FC)	.15
365	Steve Bedrosian	.10
366	Padres Ldrs (Dave Dravecky, Terry Kennedy)	.12
368	Hubie Brooks	.15
370	Tim Raines	.45
376	*Dave Anderson* (FC)	.10
380	Steve Garvey	.40

230 Rickey Henderson

381	Ralph Houk	.10
384	*Lee Tunnell*	.10
385	Tony Perez	.25
386	George Hendrick AS	.10
387	Johnny Ray AS	.10
388	Mike Schmidt AS	.75
389	Ozzie Smith AS	.40
390	Tim Raines AS	.25
391	Dale Murphy AS	.40
392	Andre Dawson AS	.40
393	Gary Carter AS	.30
394	Steve Rogers AS	.30
395	Steve Carlton AS	.30
396	Jesse Orosco AS	.10
397	Eddie Murray AS	.40
398	Lou Whitaker AS	.20
399	George Brett AS	.75
400	Cal Ripken AS	1.75
401	Jim Rice AS	.30
402	Dave Winfield AS	.30
403	Lloyd Moseby AS	.15
404	Ted Simmons AS	.15
405	LaMarr Hoyt AS	.10
406	Ron Guidry AS	.20
407	Dan Quisenberry AS	.15
408	Lou Piniella	.15
409	*Juan Agosto* (FC)	.15
410	Claudell Washington	.10

413	*Spike Owen* (FC)	.25
415	Tommy John	.20
420	Cecil Cooper	.10
422	Jose Cruz	.10
426	Orioles Ldrs (Mike Boddicker, Cal Ripken)	1.00
429	*Randy Bush*	.15
430	Rusty Staub	.12
432	*Charlie Hudson* (FC)	.12
434	Harold Baines	.35
447	Tom Brunansky	.20
450	Gary Carter	.50
456	Cubs Ldrs (Fergie Jenkins, Keith Moreland)	.15
460	Dave Winfield	1.75
465	Mookie Wilson	.12
470	Nolan Ryan	7.00
475	*Gary Redus*	.20
479	Frank Tanana	.10
480	Ron Kittle (FC)	.20
481	*Mark Thurmond* (FC)	.10
483	Fergie Jenkins	.30
485	Rick Rhoden	.10
486	Yankees Ldrs (Don Baylor, Ron Guidry)	.15
488	Jesse Barfield	.15
490	Cal Ripken	7.00

278 Jorge Bell

10 Robin Yount

30 Wade Boggs

740 Tom Seaver

700 Mike Schmidt

560 Carlton Fisk

1984 TOPPS TRADED

During its fourth year, the Topps Traded set reached a new high in popularity. Although the issue was still distributed only through hobby dealers in complete sets, the players are illustrious: Dwight Gooden's debut with Topps came in this series, along with cards for potential legends like Joe Morgan, Pete Rose, and Tom Seaver. However, by the time the set was released in late September, Rose was no longer an Expo, which made his card outdated. Topps continued the practice of adding a "T" suffix to each card number so collectors could easily distinguish between Traded cards and the regular cards issued earlier in the season (though it has been omitted from the following list).

		MINT
Complete set		**$70.00**
Commons		**.20**

1	Willie Aikens	$.20
2	Luis Aponte	.20
3	Mike Armstrong	.20
4	Bob Bailor	.20
5	Dusty Baker	.40
6	Steve Balboni	.25
7	Alan Bannister	.20
8	Dave Beard	.20
9	Joe Beckwith	.20
13	Yogi Berra	.75
15	Phil Bradley (FC)	.50
17	Bill Buckner	.50
20	Brett Butler	1.00
27	Ron Darling (FC)	3.00
28	Alvin Davis (FC)	.60
30	Jeff Dedmon (FC)	.20
33	Mike Easler	.20
34	Dennis Eckersley	6.00
36	Darrell Evans	.30
37	Mike Fitzgerald (FC)	.20
41	Barbaro Garbey	.20
42	Dwight Gooden (FC)	28.00
43	Rich Gossage	.50
45	Mark Gubicza (FC)	1.25
47	Mel Hall	.40
48	Toby Harrah	.20
51	Willie Hernandez	.30
52	Ricky Horton (FC)	.20

104 Bret Saberhagen

55	Brook Jacoby (FC)	.50
56	Mike Jeffcoat (FC)	.20
57	Dave Johnson	.20
59	Ruppert Jones	.20
61	Bob Kearney	.20
62	Jimmy Key (FC)	10.00
63	Dave Kingman	.60
64	Jerry Koosman	.25
65	Wayne Krenchicki	.20
66	Rusty Kuntz	.20
67	Rene Lachemann	.25
68	Frank LaCorte	.20

69	Dennis Lamp	.20
70	Mark Langston (FC)	**11.00**
71	Rick Leach	.20
72	Craig Lefferts	.30
75	Carmelo Martinez	.20
76	Mike Mason (FC)	.20
77	Gary Matthews	.25
78	Andy McGaffigan	.20
79	Larry Milbourne	.20
80	Sid Monge	.20
82	Joe Morgan	**3.00**
83	Graig Nettles	.60
84	Phil Niekro	**2.75**
85	Ken Oberkfell	.20
86	Mike O'Berry	.20
87	Al Oliver	.40
88	Jorge Orta	.20
89	Amos Otis	.20
90	Dave Parker	**2.00**
91	Tony Perez	**3.00**
92	Gerald Perry (FC)	.30
93	Gary Pettis (FC)	.30
94	Rob Picciolo	.20
96	Floyd Rayford	.20
97	Randy Ready (FC)	.25
98	Ron Reed	.20
99	Gene Richards	.20
100	Jose Rijo (FC)	**10.00**

42 Dwight Gooden

101	Jeff Robinson (FC)	.30
102	Ron Romanick (FC)	.20
103	Pete Rose	**9.00**
104	Bret Saberhagen (FC)	**12.00**
105	Juan Samuel (FC)	.70
106	Scott Sanderson	.30
107	Dick Schofield (FC)	.50
108	Tom Seaver	**7.00**
110	Mike Smithson	.20
111	Lary Sorensen	.20
113	Champ Summers	.20
114	Jim Sundberg	.25
115	Rick Sutcliffe	.50
116	Craig Swan	.20
117	Tim Teufel	.50
118	Derrel Thomas	.20
119	Gorman Thomas	.30
120	Alex Trevino	.20
121	Manny Trillo	.25
122	John Tudor	.30
123	Tom Underwood	.20
125	Tom Waddell	.20
127	Curt Wilkerson	.20
128	Frank Williams (FC)	.20
129	Glenn Wilson	.20
130	Johnny Wockenfuss	.20
131	Ned Yost	.20
132	Checklist 1-132	.20

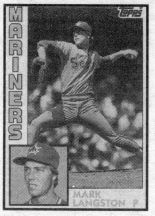

70 Mark Langston

1985 DONRUSS

For the second straight year, a limited print run made Donruss the hottest collectible of 1985. By mid-spring, wax packs were virtually impossible to find on store shelves, and factory-collated sets were ransomed off by lucky dealers. And all this popularity came in spite of two major errors. Card number 424, meant to picture Tom Seaver, wound up with a photo of Floyd Bannister by mistake. The goof was enormous, since Bannister is shown pitching left-handed, while Seaver throws with his right hand. In addition, Terry Pendleton's card front originally gave his name as "Jeff." In both cases the corrections were available only in wax packs. Don Mattingly's card and rookie appearances by Eric Davis and Kirby Puckett highlight the set.

	MINT
Complete set	**$250.00**
Commons	**.08**

1	Ryne Sandberg (DK)...	$4.00
7	Don Mattingly (DK)	3.00
14	Cal Ripken, Jr. (DK)	4.00
15	Jim Rice (DK)	.50
18	Alvin Davis (DK) (FC)	.60
23	Juan Samuel (DK) (FC)...	.40
25	Tony Gwynn (DK)..........	3.00
27	*Danny Tartabull* (RR) (FC)	8.00
36	*Larry Sheets* (RR) (FC) ...	.20
38	*Calvin Schiraldi* (RR) (FC)..............................	.15
39	*Shawon Dunston* (RR) (FC)..............................	1.50
41	*Billy Hatcher* (RR) (FC) ...	.85
45	*Jim Traber* (RR) (FC)	.15
47	Eddie Murray	2.00
48	Robin Yount	4.00
49	Lance Parrish	.15
50	Jim Rice	.20
51	Dave Winfield	4.00
52	Fernando Valenzuela	.35
53	George Brett	4.00
55	Gary Carter	.70
57	Reggie Jackson.............	2.00
59	Ozzie Smith....................	2.00
60	Nolan Ryan	10.00
61	Mike Schmidt.................	5.00
62	Dave Parker	.50
63	Tony Gwynn	5.00

438 Kirby Puckett

66	Dale Murphy	.80
67	Ryne Sandberg	10.00
68	Keith Hernandez	.40
69	*Alvin Davis* (FC)	.30
70	Kent Hrbek	.40
74	Jack Perconte	.10
75	Jesse Orosco	.10
76	Jody Davis.......................	.10
77	Bob Horner......................	.15
79	Joel Youngblood	.08
81	Ron Oester	.08
82	Ozzie Virgil	.08
83	*Ricky Horton* (FC).............	.25
84	Bill Doran........................	.12

222 Bret Saberhagen

27 Danny Tartabull

273 Roger Clemens

312 Darryl Strawberry

241	Dave Collins	.10
242	Gary Gaetti	.30
244	Rudy Law	.08
246	Tom Tellman	.08
247	Howard Johnson	1.75
249	Tony Armas	.12
251	*Mike Jeffcoat* (FC)	.10
252	Dane Iorg	.08
254	Pete Rose	2.00
255	Don Aase	.08
257	Britt Burns	.08
258	Mike Scott	.20
260	Dave Rucker	.08
262	*Jay Tibbs* (FC)	.20
264	Don Robinson	.10
265	Gary Lavelle	.08
267	Matt Young	.10
268	Ernie Whitt	.10
270	*Ken Dixon* (FC)	.10
271	Peter Ladd	.08
273	*Roger Clemens* (FC)	60.00
274	Rick Cerone	.08
275	Dave Anderson	.08
277	Greg Pryor	.08
278	Mike Warren	.08
280	Bobby Grich	.12
281	*Mike Mason* (FC)	.12
282	Ron Reed	.08

190 Dwight Gooden

283	Alan Ashby	.08
285	Joe Lefebvre	.08
286	Ted Power	.08
288	Lee Tunnell	.08
289	Rich Bordi	.08
292	Rollie Fingers	.40
293	Lou Whitaker	.40
294	● Dwight Evans	.15
295	Don Mattingly	8.00
296	Mike Marshall	.15
297	Willie Wilson	.12
298	Mike Heath	.08
299	Tim Raines	.40
300	Larry Parrish	.12
301	Geoff Zahn	.08
302	Rich Dotson	.10
304	Jose Cruz	.12
305	Steve Carlton	1.75
306	Gary Redus	.08
307	Steve Garvey	.50
308	Jose DeLeon	.15
309	Randy Lerch	.08
311	Lee Smith	.15
312	Darryl Strawberry	4.00
313	Jim Beattie	.08
314	John Butcher	.08
316	Mike Smithson	.08
317	Luis Leal	.08

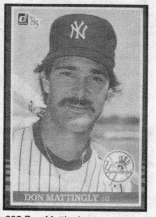

295 Don Mattingly

557 Mark Langston

616 Joe Carter

430	John Candelaria	.12
431	Manny Trillo	.10
433	Rick Sutcliffe	.15
434	Ron Darling	.25
435	Spike Owen	.10
436	Frank Viola	.50
437	Lloyd Moseby	.12
438	*Kirby Puckett* (FC)	50.00
439	Jim Clancy	.10
440	Mike Moore	.15
442	Dennis Eckersley	1.50
443	Gerald Perry	.15
445	Dusty Baker	.10
447	Cesar Cedeno	.12
448	*Rick Schu* (FC)	.15
449	Joaquin Andujar	.10
450	*Mark Bailey* (FC)	.12
451	*Ron Romanick* (FC)	.12
454	Storm Davis	.12
458	Phil Niekro	.50
465	Mickey Rivers	.10
466	John Wathan	.10
468	Andre Thornton	.12
469	Rex Hudler	.10
470	*Sid Bream* (FC)	.80
471	Kirk Gibson	.25
472	John Shelby	.10
475	Willie McGee	.35

581 Orel Hershiser

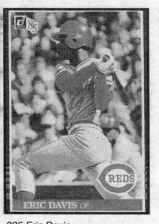

325 Eric Davis

477	Kevin Gross	.12
479	Kent Tekulve	.10
480	Chili Davis	.15
482	Mookie Wilson	.12
487	Jeff Russell	.12
492	*Jose Rijo* (FC)	4.00
493	Bruce Hurst	.15
499	Gary Pettis	.10
518	Dennis Rasmussen	.15
522	*Curt Young* (FC)	.20
528	Andy Hawkins	.12
534	*Jeff Pendleton* (FC) (first name incorrect)	10.00
534	*Terry Pendleton* (FC) (correct name)	30.00
539	*Mike Pagliarulo* (FC)	.40
546	Greg Luzinski	.12
547	Mark Salas (FC)	.15
548	Dave Smith	.10
552	Rick Rhoden	.10
553	Mark Davis	.15
554	*Jeff Dedmon* (FC)	.15
557	*Mark Langston* (FC)	4.00
559	*Jimmy Key* (FC)	4.00
561	Doyle Alexander	.12
563	Sid Fernandez	.50
566	Brian Harper	.50
567	Dan Gladden (FC)	.40

39 Shawon Dunston

176 Rickey Henderson

1985 FLEER

Other than its distinctive numbering system, the 1985 Fleer set of 660 cards has little that is noteworthy when compared to similar offerings from Donruss and Topps. Following Fleer tradition, the set is arranged by team, ranking the clubs by their 1984 results. Thus, the World Champion Detroit Tigers appear first, followed by the San Diego Padres, and then the rest of the teams in order, based on their winning percentages. Players are listed alphabetically within each team. A large, unobstructed color photo highlights the front of all single-player cards, while card backs, despite a small black-and-white portrait, are plain and boring. Rookies are grouped as Major League Prospects, two players to a card. Danny Tartabull tops this group.

		MINT
Complete set		$200.00
Commons		.06

359 Nolan Ryan

1	Doug Bair	$ .06
6	Darrell Evans	.12
8	Kirk Gibson	.20
9	John Grubb	.06
11	Larry Herndon	.06
12	Howard Johnson	1.25
15	Chet Lemon	.08
16	Aurelio Lopez	.06
17	Sid Monge	.06
18	Jack Morris	1.00
19	Lance Parrish	.20
20	Dan Petry	.08
23	Alan Trammell	.35
24	Lou Whitaker	.35
25	Milt Wilcox	.06
27	*Greg Booker* (FC)	.15
28	Bobby Brown	.06
29	Luis DeLeon	.06
32	Steve Garvey	.50
33	Goose Gossage	.20
34	Tony Gwynn	5.00
35	Greg Harris	.06
36	Andy Hawkins	.08
37	Terry Kennedy	.08
38	Craig Lefferts	.08
41	Kevin McReynolds	.30
42	Graig Nettles	.15
44	Eric Show	.08
45	Garry Templeton	.08
47	Ed Whitson	.06
50	Larry Bowa	.12
52	Ron Cey	.20
53	*Henry Cotto* (FC)	.15
54	Jody Davis	.08
56	Leon Durham	.06
57	Dennis Eckersley	.50
60	Dave Lopes	.08
61	Gary Matthews	.10
63	Rick Reuschel	.10
65	Ryne Sandberg	10.00
67	Lee Smith	.15
69	Rick Sutcliffe	.15
70	Steve Trout	.06
74	Hubie Brooks	.10

93 Darryl Strawberry

76	Ron Darling	.35
77	Sid Fernandez (FC)	.50
79	George Foster	.15
82	*Dwight Gooden*	8.00
83	Tom Gorman	.06
84	Danny Heep	.06
85	Keith Hernandez	.30
86	Ray Knight	.10
90	*Rafael Santana* (FC)	.20
91	Doug Sisk	.06
92	Rusty Staub	.12
93	Darryl Strawberry	4.00
94	Walt Terrell	.08
95	Mookie Wilson	.10
97	Willie Aikens	.06
98	Doyle Alexander	.10
99	Jesse Barfield	.25
100	George Bell	.80
101	Jim Clancy	.06
103	Tony Fernandez	.40
104	Damaso Garcia	.06
107	Garth Iorg	.06
110	*Jimmy Key*	4.00
113	Luis Leal	.06
115	Lloyd Moseby	.10
117	Dave Stieb	.15
119	Ernie Whitt	.08
121	Don Baylor	.12

123	Rick Cerone	.06
126	Tim Foli	.06
128	Ken Griffey	.10
129	Ron Guidry	.25
130	Toby Harrah	.08
131	Jay Howell	.08
132	Steve Kemp	.08
133	Don Mattingly	7.50
138	Phil Niekro	.25
139	*Mike Pagliarulo* (FC)	.30
140	Willie Randolph	.15
141	Dennis Rasmussen (FC)	.20
142	Dave Righetti	.25
143	*Jose Rijo*	4.00
146	Dave Winfield	4.00
149	Tony Armas	.10
150	Marty Barrett	.20
151	Wade Boggs	5.00
152	Dennis Boyd	.10
153	Bill Buckner	.12
155	*Roger Clemens*	60.00
157	Mike Easler	.08
158	• Dwight Evans	.15
159	Rich Gedman	.06
161	Bruce Hurst	.15
165	Al Nipper (FC)	.15
166	Bob Ojeda	.10
167	Jerry Remy	.06

187 Cal Ripken, Jr.

168 Jim Rice .... .35
169 Bob Stanley .... .06
170 Mike Boddicker................ .15
171 Al Bumbry......................... .08
172 Todd Cruz .... .06
173 Rich Dauer .... .06
174 Storm Davis..................... .10
176 Jim Dwyer .... .06
179 Wayne Gross .... .06
184 Eddie Murray 2.00
185 Joe Nolan .... .06
187 Cal Ripken, Jr............. 10.00
195 Mike Young .... .08
198 Bud Black .... .06
199 George Brett................. 4.00
201 *Mark Gubicza* .... .50
202 Larry Gura .... .06
204 Dane Iorg .... .06
205 Danny Jackson (FC) .... .50
207 Hal McRae .... .12
209 Jorge Orta .... .06
212 *Bret Saberhagen* 4.00
216 John Wathan .... .08
217 Frank White .... .10
218 Willie Wilson .... .10
219 Neil Allen .... .06
222 Danny Cox (FC) .... .25
223 Bob Forsch .... .08

371 Orel Hershiser

224 David Green .... .06
226 Tom Herr .... .10
227 *Ricky Horton*.................... .20
228 Art Howe .... .06
231 Jeff Lahti.......................... .06
233 Dave LaPoint................... .08
234 Willie McGee .... .30
235 *Tom Nieto* (FC)............... .10
236 *Terry Pendleton* (FC) 8.00
237 Darrell Porter .... .08
238 Dave Rucker .... .06
239 Lonnie Smith .... .08
240 Ozzie Smith.................... 2.00
241 Bruce Sutter .... .12
242 Andy Van Slyke 2.00
245 Bill Campbell .... .06
246 Steve Carlton 1.75
249 John Denny .... .06
250 Bo Diaz............................ .08
251 Greg Gross...................... .06
252 Kevin Gross .... .08
253 Von Hayes....................... .15
259 Garry Maddox .... .10
261 Tug McGraw..................... .12
262 Al Oliver.......................... .12
263 Shane Rawley .... .06
264 Juan Samuel .... .30
265 Mike Schmidt................. 5.00

286 Kirby Puckett

652 Major League Prospect

266	*Jeff Stone*	.12	
268	Glenn Wilson	.08	
271	Tom Brunansky	.12	
272	Randy Bush	.08	
273	John Butcher	.06	
277	Pete Filson	.06	
278	Gary Gaetti	.25	
280	Ed Hodge	.06	
281	Kent Hrbek	.35	
283	Tim Laudner	.06	
285	Dave Meier	.06	
286	*Kirby Puckett*	50.00	
288	Ken Schrom	.06	
290	Tim Teufel	.08	
291	Frank Viola	.50	
293	Don Aase	.06	
295	• Bob Boone	.08	
296	Mike Brown	.06	
297	Rod Carew	1.50	
300	Brian Downing	.10	
301	Ken Forsch	.08	
302	Bobby Grich	.10	
303	Reggie Jackson	2.25	
304	Tommy John	.20	
306	Bruce Kison	.06	
307	Fred Lynn	.20	
311	Dick Schofield	.10	
313	Jim Slaton	.06	
316	Mike Witt	.12	
317	Geoff Zahn	.06	
318	Len Barker	.08	
319	Steve Bedrosian	.12	
321	Rick Camp	.06	
323	*Jeff Dedmon* (FC)	.12	
324	Terry Forster	.08	
325	Gene Garber	.06	
326	*Albert Hall* (FC)	.15	
327	Terry Harper	.06	
328	Bob Horner	.15	
333	Craig McMurtry	.06	
335	Dale Murphy	1.00	
337	Pascual Perez	.10	
338	Gerald Perry	.20	
341	Alex Trevino	.06	
343	Alan Ashby	.06	
344	*Mark Bailey*	.10	
345	Kevin Bass	.10	
346	Enos Cabell	.06	
347	Jose Cruz	.10	
348	Bill Dawley	.06	
350	Bill Doran	.12	
351	Phil Garner	.08	
353	Mike LaCoss	.06	
355	Joe Niekro	.10	
356	Terry Puhl	.06	
358	Vern Ruhle	.06	
359	Nolan Ryan	10.00	
360	Joe Sambito	.06	
361	• Mike Scott	.15	
362	Dave Smith	.08	
364	Dickie Thon	.06	
367	Bob Bailor	.06	
368	Greg Brock	.08	
369	Carlos Diaz	.06	

647 Major League Prospect

370	Pedro Guerrero	.25	414	Bill Almon	.06
371	Orel Hershiser (FC)	3.00	415	Keith Atherton	.06
373	Burt Hooton	.08	416	Bruce Bochte	.06
374	Ken Howell (FC)	.15	417	Tom Burgmeier	.06
376	Candy Maldonado	.12	418	Ray Burris	.06
377	Mike Marshall	.15	420	Chris Codiroli	.06
380	Jerry Reuss	.08	421	Tim Conroy	.06
381	R.J. Reynolds	.15	422	Mike Davis	.08
383	Bill Russell	.08	423	Jim Essian	.06
384	Steve Sax	.25	424	Mike Heath	.06
386	Franklin Stubbs (FC)	.15	425	Rickey Henderson	3.50
387	Fernando Valenzuela	.35	427	Dave Kingman	.15
388	Bob Welch	.15	428	Bill Krueger	.06
390	Steve Yeager	.06	429	Carney Lansford	.10
391	Pat Zachry	.06	430	Steve McCatty	.06
393	Gary Carter	.35	431	• Joe Morgan	.35
394	Andre Dawson	2.50	432	Dwayne Murphy	.08
395	Miguel Dilone	.06	433	Tony Phillips	.40
396	Dan Driessen	.08	436	Curt Young (FC)	.35
397	Doug Flynn	.06	437	Luis Aponte	.06
398	Terry Francona	.06	438	Chris Bando	.06
399	Bill Gullickson	.06	439	Tony Bernazard	.06
403	Gary Lucas	.06	440	Bert Blyleven	.15
404	David Palmer	.06	441	Brett Butler	.10
405	Tim Raines	.35	442	Ernie Camacho	.06
406	Mike Ramsey	.06	443	Joe Carter (FC)	10.00
407	Jeff Reardon	.75	445	Jamie Easterly	.06
408	Steve Rogers	.08	446	Steve Farr (FC)	.30
410	Bryn Smith	.08	447	Mike Fischlin	.06
411	Mike Stenhouse	.06	448	Julio Franco	.15
412	Tim Wallach	.12	449	Mel Hall	.08
413	Jim Wohlford	.06	450	Mike Hargrove	.06

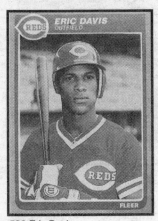

533 Eric Davis

505	Matt Young	.08
507	Harold Baines	.15
508	Floyd Bannister	.10
511	Richard Dotson	.10
513	Carlton Fisk	1.75
514	Scott Fletcher	.08
517	LaMarr Hoyt	.08
518	Ron Kittle	.10
520	Vance Law	.08
521	Greg Luzinski	.10
526	Tom Seaver	1.75
530	Greg Walker	.12
531	Cesar Cedeno	.10
532	Dave Concepcion	.12
533	*Eric Davis* (FC)	6.00
534	Nick Esasky	.15
536	*John Franco*	1.25
544	Dave Parker	.25
546	Tony Perez	.15
549	Gary Redus	.08
550	Pete Rose	2.50
551	Jeff Russell (FC)	.15
552	Mario Soto	.08
553	*Jay Tibbs* (FC)	.15
556	Buddy Bell	.12
558	Charlie Hough	.10
561	*Jeff Kunkel* (FC)	.10
562	*Mike Mason*	.10
563	Pete O'Brien	.12
564	Larry Parrish	.10
565	Mickey Rivers	.08
569	Dave Stewart	.50
570	Frank Tanana	.10
572	Gary Ward	.08
580	Cecil Cooper	.15
581	Rollie Fingers	.50
584	Dion James	.20
588	Paul Molitor	1.50
590	Ben Oglivie	.08
592	*Randy Ready* (FC)	.20
594	Bill Schroeder (FC)	.10
596	Ted Simmons	.20
597	Jim Sundberg	.08
598	Don Sutton	.50
601	Robin Yount	4.00
604	Jack Clark	.20
605	Chili Davis	.15
606	Mark Davis	.10
607	*Dan Gladden* (FC)	.30

452	Brook Jacoby	.15
453	*Mike Jeffcoat* (FC)	.08
454	*Don Schulze* (FC)	.08
455	Roy Smith	.06
456	Pat Tabler	.08
457	Andre Thornton	.10
460	Jerry Willard	.06
461	Dale Berra	.06
462	John Candelaria	.10
463	Jose DeLeon	.12
468	Bill Madlock	.12
469	Lee Mazzilli	.08
472	Tony Pena	.10
473	Johnny Ray	.12
474	Rick Rhoden	.10
475	Don Robinson	.08
477	Kent Tekulve	.08
479	John Tudor	.10
486	*Phil Bradley*	.20
488	*Alvin Davis*	.25
489	Dave Henderson	.20
492	*Mark Langston*	4.00
495	Mike Moore	.15
496	Edwin Nunez (FC)	.08
497	Spike Owen	.08
499	Ken Phelps	.10
500	*Jim Presley* (FC)	.20
503	Gorman Thomas	.08

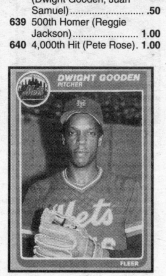

82 Dwight Gooden

155 Roger Clemens

1985 FLEER UPDATE

The realization among hobbyists of the scarcity of the 1984 Fleer Updates generated a massive demand for this 1985 edition. But this 132-card set, issued near the close of the 1985 baseball season, lacked the big names found in the year's earlier edition. That, plus the relative abundance of sets, meant that prices for the boxed update sets have remained low, in stark contrast to the 1984 set. Except for the "U" prefix of the card number on the back (omitted from the following list), there is nothing to distinguish the Updates from the regular 1985 Fleer cards. Many unknown rookies appear in the 1985 Fleer Update because Fleer, unlike Topps, agreed with the Major League Players Association to print cards for all of its members.

28 Vince Coleman

		MINT
Complete set		**$30.00**
Commons		**.15**

1	Don Aase	$.15
3	Dusty Baker	.20
4	Dale Berra	.10
5	Karl Best	.15
6	Tim Birtsas (FC)	.20
7	Vida Blue	.20
8	Rich Bordi	.10
9	Daryl Boston (FC)	.30
10	Hubie Brooks	.20
11	Chris Brown (FC)	.25
12	Tom Browning (FC)	1.00
14	Tim Burke (FC)	.20
15	Ray Burris	.10
16	Jeff Burroughs	.20
17	Ivan Calderon (FC)	1.00
18	Jeff Calhoun	.20
19	Bill Campbell	.10
20	Don Carman (FC)	.25
21	Gary Carter	.85
24	Rick Cerone	.10
25	Jack Clark	.35
26	Pat Clements (FC)	.20
27	Stewart Cliburn (FC)	.15
28	Vince Coleman (FC)	3.00
29	Dave Collins	.15
30	Fritz Connally	.15
31	Henry Cotto (FC)	.20
32	Danny Darwin	.15
33	Darren Daulton (FC)	15.00
34	Jerry Davis	.15
35	Brian Dayett	.15
36	Ken Dixon	.10
38	Mariano Duncan (FC)	1.25
39	Bob Fallon	.15
40	Brian Fisher (FC)	.25
43	Greg Gagne (FC)	.35
44	Oscar Gamble	.15
45	Jim Gott	.15
47	Alfredo Griffin	.15
48	Ozzie Guillen (FC)	1.50

49	Toby Harrah	.15
51	Rickey Henderson	4.00
53	George Hendrick	.15
54	Teddy Higuera (FC)	.25
56	Burt Hooton	.15
57	Jay Howell	.15
58	LaMarr Hoyt	.15
59	Tim Hulett (FC)	.20
62	Howard Johnson	1.50
64	Steve Kemp	.15
66	Mike LaCoss	.15
67	Lee Lacy	.15
68	Dave LaPoint	.15
70	Vance Law	.15
71	Manny Lee (FC)	.50
74	Urbano Lugo (FC)	.15
75	Fred Lynn	.25
76	Steve Lyons (FC)	.15
80	Oddibe McDowell (FC)	.30
81	Roger McDowell (FC)	.50
84	Al Oliver	.25
85	Joe Orsulak (FC)	.20
86	Dan Pasqua (FC)	.50
88	Rick Reuschel	.20
89	Earnie Riles (FC)	.15
94	Mark Salas (FC)	.15
99	Calvin Schiraldi (FC)	.25
100	Rick Schu (FC)	.20

21 Gary Carter

101	Larry Sheets (FC)	.20
102	Ron Sheperd	.15
105	Roy Smalley	.15
106	Lonnie Smith	.15
107	Nate Snell	.10
108	Lary Sorensen	.10
109	Chris Speier	.10
110	Mike Stenhouse	.10
111	Tim Stoddard	.10
112	John Stuper	.10
113	Jim Sundberg	.15
114	Bruce Sutter	.25
116	Bruce Tanner	.10
115	Don Sutton	.70
117	Kent Tekulve	.15
118	Walt Terrell	.15
119	Mickey Tettleton (FC)	7.00
120	Rich Thompson	.10
121	Louis Thornton (FC)	.10
123	John Tudor	.30
124	Jose Uribe (FC)	.25
125	Dave Valle (FC)	.20
126	Dave Von Ohlen	.10
127	Curt Wardle	.10
128	U.L. Washington	.10
129	Ed Whitson	.10
130	Herm Winningham (FC)	.15
131	Rich Yett (FC)	.15

48 Ozzie Guillen

1985 TOPPS

For the first time in its history, Topps added amateur players to its annual edition of baseball cards. The 792-card set features 16 cards showing members of the 1984 U.S. Olympic baseball team. Each player (as well as head coach Rod Dedeaux) appears in his Olympic uniform on what would come to be known as "pre-rookie" cards. Mark McGwire and Cory Snyder are the top names in this group. Another specialty subset presents a dozen "#1 Draft Pick" cards. As for the rest of the set, notable regular rookies include Roger Clemens, Eric Davis, Dwight Gooden, Orel Hershiser, Mark Langston, Kirby Puckett, and Bret Saberhagen.

		MINT
Complete set		**$100.00**
Commons		**.06**

570 Darryl Strawberry

1	Record Breaker (Carlton Fisk)	$ .30
2	Record Breaker (Steve Garvey)	.20
3	Record Breaker (Dwight Gooden)	.70
4	Record Breaker (Cliff Johnson)	.08
5	Record Breaker (Joe Morgan)	.15
6	Record Breaker (Pete Rose)	.60
7	Record Breaker (Nolan Ryan)	1.25
8	Record Breaker (Juan Samuel) (FC)	.20
9	Record Breaker (Bruce Sutter)	.25
10	Record Breaker (Don Sutton)	.20
15	Jerry Koosman	.10
17	Mike Scott	.15
23	*Bret Saberhagen*	2.00
24	Jesse Barfield	.15
25	Steve Bedrosian	.12
30	Cal Ripken	4.00
35	Graig Nettles	.15
40	Phil Niekro	.25
48	Tony Fernandez (FC)	.50
50	John Candelaria	.10
54	Cesar Cedeno	.10
55	Frank Tanana	.10
65	Bill Buckner	.10
67	*Rafael Santana* (FC)	.15
68	Von Hayes	.10
69	*Jim Winn* (FC)	.10
70	Don Baylor	.15
72	Rick Sutcliffe	.12
80	Keith Hernandez	.20
85	Mike Marshall	.15
90	Rich Gossage	.20
93	*Don Schulze* (FC)	.10
95	Jose Cruz	.12
96	Johnny Ray	.10
100	George Brett	1.25
105	Ron Kittle	.10
108	Darnell Coles (FC)	.15
113	Tom Herr	.10

181 Roger Clemens

115 Rickey Henderson

760 Nolan Ryan

219	Gerald Perry	.20
220	Fred Lynn	.20
222	Hubie Brooks	.10
225	Mike Boddicker	.10
228	Dion James (FC)	.20
230	Gary Carter	.35
235	Garry Maddox	.10
237	Julio Franco	.50
238	*Jose Rijo*	1.75
239	Tim Teufel	.10
240	Dave Stieb	.12
243	Barbaro Garbey	.10
245	Chili Davis	.10
249	Harold Baines	.15
253	*Sid Bream* (FC)	.50
260	Dave Righetti	.20
262	*Greg Booker* (FC)	.10
265	Juan Samuel (FC)	.15
266	Frank Viola	.20
267	*Henry Cotto* (FC)	.15
269	*Doug Baker* (FC)	.10
270	Dan Quisenberry	.15
271	Tim Foli (1968 #1 Draft Pick)	.08
272	Jeff Burroughs (1969 #1 Draft Pick)	.08
273	Bill Almon (1974 #1 Draft Pick)	.08

274	Floyd Bannister (1976 #1 Draft Pick)	.08
275	Harold Baines (1977 #1 Draft Pick)	.25
276	Bob Horner (1978 #1 Draft Pick)	.15
277	Al Chambers (1979 #1 Draft Pick)	.08
278	Darryl Strawberry (1980 #1 Draft Pick)	.80
279	Mike Moore (1981 #1 Draft Pick)	.15
280	*Shawon Dunston* (1982 #1 Draft Pick) (FC)	.80
281	Tim Belcher (1983 #1 Draft Pick) (FC)	.75
282	*Shawn Abner* (1984 #1 Draft Pick) (FC)	.20
288	*Jeff Kunkel* (FC)	.10
290	Cecil Cooper	.10
291	Bob Welch	.10
293	*Curt Young* (FC)	.12
294	*Tom Nieto* (FC)	.10
295	Joe Niekro	.06
298	Marty Barrett	.15
300	Rod Carew	.50
303	*Mike Jeffcoat*	.08
304	Gary Gaetti	.15

401 Mark McGwire

305	Dale Berra	.06
306	Rick Reuschel	.10
309	Mike Witt	.10
317	*Jack Lazorko* (FC)	.10
318	Ted Simmons	.10
320	Dale Murphy	.30
321	*Ricky Horton*	.15
326	Kevin Bass	.10
327	Brook Jacoby	.30
333	Willie Hernandez	.15
340	Robin Yount	1.25
342	Ted Power	.06
343	Bill Russell	.08
344	Dave Henderson	.10
346	*Terry Pendleton* (FC)	3.00
347	Rick Langford	.08
348	• Bob Boone	.20
349	Domingo Ramos	.06
350	Wade Boggs	2.00
351	Juan Agosto	.06
352	• Joe Morgan	.25
353	Julio Solano	.06
354	Andre Robertson	.06
355	Bert Blyleven	.12
356	Dave Meier	.08
357	Rich Bordi	.08
358	Tony Pena	.12
359	Pat Sheridan	.08

665 Don Mattingly

360	Steve Carlton	.50
361	Alfredo Griffin	.08
362	Craig McMurtry	.08
363	Ron Hodges	.06
364	Richard Dotson	.10
365	Danny Ozark	.06
366	Todd Cruz	.06
368	Dave Bergman	.06
369	*R.J. Reynolds* (FC)	.15
370	Bruce Sutter	.12
371	Mickey Rivers	.08
372	Roy Howell	.08
373	Mike Moore	.10
374	Brian Downing	.10
375	Jeff Reardon	.12
376	Jeff Newman	.08
379	Charles Hudson	.08
380	Ken Griffey	.10
381	Roy Smith	.06
382	Denny Walling	.06
383	Rick Lysander	.06
384	Jody Davis	.08
385	Jose DeLeon	.15
386	*Dan Gladden* (FC)	.20
387	*Buddy Biancalana* (FC)	.12
388	Bert Roberge	.08
389	1984 US Baseball Team (Rod Dedeaux) (FC)	.15

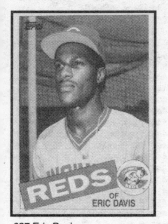

627 Eric Davis

620 Dwight Gooden

390	1984 US Baseball Team (Sid Akins) (FC)	**.10**
391	1984 US Baseball Team (Flavio Alfaro) (FC)	**.06**
392	1984 US Baseball Team (Don August) (FC)	**.20**
393	1984 US Baseball Team (Scott Bankhead) (FC)	**.30**
394	1984 US Baseball Team (Bob Caffrey) (FC)	**.08**
395	1984 US Baseball Team (Mike Dunne) (FC)	**.15**
396	1984 US Baseball Team (Gary Green) (FC)	**.08**
397	1984 US Baseball Team (John Hoover) (FC)	**.06**
398	1984 US Baseball Team (Shane Mack) (FC)	**2.00**
399	1984 US Baseball Team (John Marzano) (FC)	**.25**
400	1984 US Baseball Team (Oddibe McDowell) (FC)	**.50**
401	1984 US Baseball Team (Mark McGwire) (FC)	**28.00**
402	1984 US Baseball Team (Pat Pacillo) (FC)	**.25**
403	1984 US Baseball Team (Cory Snyder) (FC)	**1.50**
404	1984 US Baseball Team (Billy Swift) (FC)	**2.00**
405	Tom Veryzer	**.06**
406	Len Whitehouse	**.06**
407	Bobby Ramos	**.06**
408	Sid Monge	**.06**
409	Brad Wellman	**.06**
410	Bob Horner	**.20**
411	Bobby Cox	**.06**
412	Bud Black	**.06**
413	Vance Law	**.08**
414	Gary Ward	**.08**
415	Ron Darling	**.50**
416	Wayne Gross	**.06**
417	*John Franco* (FC)	**.50**
418	Ken Landreaux	**.08**
419	Mike Caldwell	**.08**
420	Andre Dawson	**.75**
421	Dave Rucker	**.08**
422	Carney Lansford	**.10**
423	Barry Bonnell	**.08**
424	*Al Nipper* (FC)	**.12**
425	Mike Hargrove	**.06**
426	Vern Ruhle	**.06**
429	Rick Cerone	**.06**
430	Ron Davis	**.06**
431	U.L. Washington	**.06**
432	Thad Bosley	**.06**
433	Jim Morrison	**.06**
434	Gene Richards	**.06**
435	Dan Petry	**.06**
436	Willie Aikens	**.08**
437	Al Jones	**.06**
438	Joe Torre	**.08**
439	Junior Ortiz	**.06**
440	Fernando Valenzuela	**.20**
441	Duane Walker	**.06**
442	Ken Forsch	**.06**
443	George Wright	**.06**
444	Tony Phillips	**.25**
445	Tippy Martinez	**.06**
446	Jim Sundberg	**.08**
447	Jeff Lahti	**.06**
448	Derrel Thomas	**.06**
449	*Phil Bradley*	**.20**
450	Steve Garvey	**.35**
451	Bruce Hurst	**.12**
454	Glenn Wilson	**.08**
455	Bob Knepper	**.08**

456	Tim Foli	.06
457	Cecilio Guante	.06
458	Randy Johnson	.06
459	Charlie Leibrandt	.06
460	Ryne Sandberg	**4.00**
461	Marty Castillo	.06
462	Gary Lavelle	.06
463	Dave Collins	.08
464	*Mike Mason* (FC)	.08
465	Bob Grich	.10
466	Tony LaRussa	.10
467	Ed Lynch	.06
468	Wayne Krenchicki	.06
469	Sammy Stewart	.06
470	Steve Sax	.25
471	Pete Ladd	.06
472	Jim Essian	.06
473	Tim Wallach	.12
474	Kurt Kepshire	.06
475	Andre Thornton	.10
476	*Jeff Stone* (FC)	.12
477	Bob Ojeda	.10
478	Kurt Bevacqua	.06
479	Mike Madden	.06
480	Lou Whitaker	.30
481	Dale Murray	.08
482	Harry Spilman	.06
483	Mike Smithson	.06
484	Larry Bowa	.10
485	Matt Young	.06
487	*Frank Williams*	.15
488	Joel Skinner (FC)	.08
489	Bryan Clark	.06
490	Jason Thompson	.06
491	Rick Camp	.06
492	Dave Johnson	.08
493	*Orel Hershiser* (FC)	1.50
494	Rich Dauer	.06
495	Mario Soto	.08
496	Donnie Scott	.06
497	Gary Pettis	.15
498	Ed Romero	.06
499	Danny Cox (FC)	.20
500	Mike Schmidt	1.75
501	Dan Schatzeder	.06
502	Rick Miller	.06
503	Tim Conroy	.06
504	Jerry Willard	.06
505	Jim Beattie	.06

23 Bret Saberhagen

506	*Franklin Stubbs* (FC)	.12
507	Ray Fontenot	.06
508	John Shelby	.08
509	Milt May	.06
510	Kent Hrbek	.25
511	Lee Smith	.15
512	Tom Brookens	.06
515	Dave Concepcion	.12
516	Roy Lee Jackson	.06
517	Jerry Martin	.06
518	Chris Chambliss	.08
519	Doug Rader	.06
520	LaMarr Hoyt	.06
521	Rick Dempsey	.08
522	Paul Molitor	.70
523	Candy Maldonado	.10
524	Rob Wilfong	.06
525	Darrell Porter	.08
526	Dave Palmer	.06
528	Bill Krueger	.06
529	Rich Gedman	.10
530	Dave Dravecky	.15
531	Joe Lefebvre	.06
532	Frank DiPino	.06
533	Tony Bernazard	.06
534	Brian Dayett (FC)	.06
535	Pat Putnam	.06
536	*Kirby Puckett* (FC)	22.00

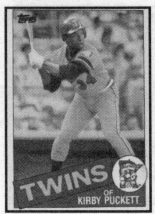

536 Kirby Puckett

537	Don Robinson	.10
538	Keith Moreland	.08
539	Aurelio Lopez	.06
540	Claudell Washington	.10
541	Mark Davis	.08
542	Don Slaught	.06
543	Mike Squires	.06
544	Bruce Kison	.06
545	Lloyd Moseby	.10
546	Brent Gaff	.06
547	Pete Rose	.50
548	Larry Parrish	.08
549	Mike Scioscia	.08
550	Scott McGregor	.08
551	Andy Van Slyke	.40
552	Chris Codiroli	.06
555	Bob Stanley	.06
556	Sixto Lezcano	.06
557	Len Barker	.06
558	Carmelo Martinez	.06
559	Jay Howell	.08
560	Bill Madlock	.12
561	Darryl Motley	.06
562	Houston Jimenez	.06
563	Dick Ruthven	.06
564	Alan Ashby	.06
565	Kirk Gibson	.35
566	Ed Vande Berg	.06

567	Joel Youngblood	.06
568	Cliff Johnson	.06
569	Ken Oberkfell	.06
570	Darryl Strawberry	2.00
571	Charlie Hough	.08
572	Tom Paciorek	.06
573	*Jay Tibbs* (FC)	.15
574	Joe Altobelli	.06
575	Pedro Guerrero	.25
576	Jaime Cocanower	.06
577	Chris Speier	.06
578	Terry Francona	.06
579	*Ron Romanick*	.10
580	• Dwight Evans	.15
581	Mark Wagner	.06
582	Ken Phelps (FC)	.20
583	Bobby Brown	.06
584	Kevin Gross	.10
585	Butch Wynegar	.06
586	Bill Scherrer	.06
587	Doug Frobel	.06
590	Ray Knight	.10
592	*Jeff Robinson*	.15
594	Curt Wilkerson (FC)	.08
598	Jose Oquendo	.08
599	Storm Davis	.12
600	Pete Rose	.70
601	Tom Lasorda	.12

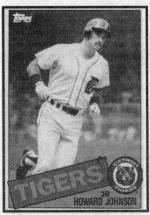

192 Howard Johnson

602	*Jeff Dedmon*	.10
605	Ozzie Smith	.80
608	Craig Lefferts	.08
610	Jack Morris	.35
617	Willie Wilson	.10
619	Jeff Leonard	.10
620	*Dwight Gooden*	4.00
623	Greg Walker	.10
625	*Mark Langston*	2.00
627	*Eric Davis* (FC)	2.75
628	Rene Lachemann	.06
629	Dick Schofield	.12
630	Tim Raines	.35
638	*Mike Pagliarulo* (FC)	.20
649	Sid Fernandez (FC)	.35
660	Tony Gwynn	2.25
665	Don Mattingly	3.00
670	Tom Seaver	.50
690	Alan Trammell	.35

694 Joe Carter

694	Joe Carter (FC)	4.00
698	Jorge Bell	.40
700	Eddie Murray	.80
701	Eddie Murray AS	.30
703	George Brett AS	.70
704	Cal Ripken AS	.30
705	Dave Winfield AS	.50
706	Rickey Henderson AS	.50
707	Tony Armas AS	.08
708	Lance Parrish AS	.15
709	Mike Boddicker AS	.15
710	Frank Viola AS	.12
711	Dan Quisenberry AS	.10
712	Keith Hernandez AS	.20
713	Ryne Sandberg AS	1.25
714	Mike Schmidt AS	.60
715	Ozzie Smith AS	.35
716	Dale Murphy AS	.20
717	Tony Gwynn AS	.60
718	Jeff Leonard AS	.10
719	Gary Carter AS	.20
720	Rick Sutcliffe AS	.12
721	Bob Knepper AS	.08
722	Bruce Sutter AS	.10
723	Dave Stewart	.12
724	Oscar Gamble	.08
725	Floyd Bannister	.10
726	Al Bumbry	.08
729	Don Sutton	.30
730	Dave Kingman	.15
735	Garry Templeton	.08
740	Jack Clark	.25
743	Frank White	.10
745	Buddy Bell	.10
746	Jim Clancy	.06
747	Alex Trevino	.06
748	Lee Mazzilli	.08
750	Rollie Fingers	.25
753	Greg Brock	.08
755	Ken Singleton	.08
756	Rob Picciolo	.06
757	Willie McGee	.25
760	Nolan Ryan	4.00
762	Eddie Whitson	.08
765	Willie Randolph	.10
768	Ron Cey	.10
770	Carlton Fisk	.75
773	Hal McRae	.10
775	Mookie Wilson	.10
778	Mike Davis	.08
779	Nick Esasky	.10
780	Mike Flanagan	.10
781	Jim Gantner	.08
782	Tom Niedenfuer	.08
785	Tony Armas	.08
790	Ron Guidry	.25
791	Ivan DeJesus	.06
792	Darrell Evans	.10

1985 TOPPS TRADED

Collectors began evaluating the Traded sets more on the basis of the specific players included rather than on considerations of scarcity. In 1985, the pickings were slim indeed; the lack of appealing names caused a drastic drop in demand. As for first-card originals, Vince Coleman of the Cardinals and Milwaukee Brewers pitcher Ted Higuera head the list, while Rickey Henderson and Howard Johnson are tops among veteran players. Meanwhile, the hobby debate about the legitimacy of the Traded set continued. Card purists maintained that the 132-card set wasn't a real collectible because it wasn't sold through retail chains and candy stores like standard baseball cards.

	MINT
Complete set	$25.00
Commons	.10

1	Don Aase	$ .10
2	Bill Almon	.10
3	Benny Ayala	.10
4	Dusty Baker	.15
5	George Bamberger	.10
6	Dale Berra	.10
8	Daryl Boston (FC)	.20
9	Hubie Brooks	.25
10	Chris Brown (FC)	.25
11	Tom Browning (FC)	1.00
12	Al Bumbry	.10
13	Ray Burris	.10
14	Jeff Burroughs	.15
15	Bill Campbell	.10
16	Don Carman (FC)	.35
17	Gary Carter	.75
18	Bobby Castillo	.10
19	Bill Caudill	.10
20	Rick Cerone	.10
22	Jack Clark	.35
23	Pat Clements (FC)	.20
24	Vince Coleman (FC)	3.50
25	Dave Collins	.15
26	Danny Darwin	.15
30	Ivan DeJesus	.10
32	Mariano Duncan (FC)	.80
34	Mike Fitzgerald	.10
36	Greg Gagne (FC)	.45
37	Oscar Gamble	.15

49 Rickey Henderson

38	Scott Garrelts	.20
42	Alfredo Griffin	.15
43	Ozzie Guillen (FC)	1.25
46	Toby Harrah	.15
49	Rickey Henderson	4.00
51	George Hendrick	.15
52	Joe Hesketh (FC)	.20
53	Teddy Higuera (FC)	.30
56	Burt Hooton	.15
57	Jay Howell	.15
58	Ken Howell (FC)	.15
60	Tim Hulett (FC)	.15
64	Howard Johnson	2.00

24 Vince Coleman

82	Oddibe McDowell	.20
83	Roger McDowell (FC)	.40
88	Al Oliver	.30
89	Joe Orsulak (FC)	.20
92	Jim Presley (FC)	.20
93	Rick Reuschel	.25
100	Paul Runge (FC)	.15
101	Mark Salas (FC)	.15
104	Rick Schu (FC)	.20
106	Larry Sheets (FC)	.20
108	Roy Smalley	.15
109	Lonnie Smith	.15
110	Nate Snell	.20
112	Mike Stenhouse	.15
114	Jim Sundberg	.15
115	● Bruce Sutter	.25
116	Don Sutton	.75
117	Kent Tekulve	.15
119	Walt Terrell	.15
120	Mickey Tettleton (FC)	7.00
122	Rich Thompson	.15
124	John Tudor	.25
125	Jose Uribe (FC)	.25
129	● Earl Weaver	.15
131	Herm Winningham (FC)	.20

71	Dave LaPoint	.20
73	Vance Law	.15
77	Fred Lynn	.30
78	● Billy Martin	.20
81	Gene Mauch	.15

1986 DONRUSS

The 660-card Donruss set for 1986 kept the Memphis company popular among collectors. This simply designed set offers a unique blend of single-player cards and unusual subsets. Specialty cards include a pair honoring record-breaker Pete Rose, a card of brothers Joe and Phil Niekro, and a shot of the base-stealing tandem of Vince Coleman and Willie McGee. The Rated Rookie cards, however, remain the favorite subset in the issue (they are not to be confused with the similar but separate 1986 Donruss Rookies set). Jose Canseco, Andres Galarraga, Fred McGriff, and Danny Tartabull star in the 20-card run. Note that Canseco's card alone makes up close to one quarter the set's total value.

		MINT
Complete set		**$160.00**
Commons		**.08**
1	Kirk Gibson (DK)	$ .20
4	George Bell (DK)	.25

11	Bret Saberhagen (DK)	.25
18	Orel Hershiser (DK)	.25
19	Johnny Ray (DK)	.12
20	Gary Ward (DK)	.10
25	Andre Dawson (DK)	.50
26	Dwight Gooden (DK)	.40
27	*Kal Daniels* (RR) (FC)	.40

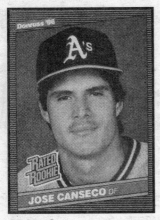

39 Jose Canseco

28 Fred McGriff

87	Andre Dawson	.50
88	Eddie Murray	.60
89	Dion James	.12
90	Chet Lemon	.10
91	Bob Stanley	.06
92	Willie Randolph	.15
93	Mike Scioscia	.10
94	Tom Waddell	.08
95	Danny Jackson	.20
96	Mike Davis	.08
98	Gary Ward	.08
99	Pete O'Brien	.10
100	Bret Saberhagen	.60
101	Alfredo Griffin	.10
102	Brett Butler	.15
103	Ron Guidry	.20
104	Jerry Reuss	.08
105	Jack Morris	.50
106	Rick Dempsey	.08
107	Ray Burris	.08
108	Brian Downing	.10
109	Willie McGee	.15
110	Bill Doran	.10
111	Kent Tekulve	.08
112	Tony Gwynn	3.00
113	Marvell Wynne	.08
115	Jim Gantner	.10
116	George Foster	.15

72 Kirby Puckett

117	Steve Trout	.08
118	Mark Langston	.70
119	Tony Fernandez	.20
120	John Butcher	.08
121	Ron Robinson	.10
122	Dan Spillner	.08
123	Mike Young	.08
124	Paul Molitor	.80
125	Kirk Gibson	.15
126	Ken Griffey	.12
127	Tony Armas	.10
128	*Mariano Duncan* (FC)	.30
129	Pat Tabler	.10
130	Frank White	.15
131	Carney Lansford	.12
132	Vance Law	.08
133	Dick Schofield	.08
134	Wayne Tolleson	.08
135	Greg Walker	.10
136	Denny Walling	.08
137	Ozzie Virgil	.08
138	Ricky Horton	.08
139	LaMarr Hoyt	.08
140	Wayne Krenchicki	.08
142	Cecilio Guante	.08
143	Mike Krukow	.10
144	Lee Smith	.60
145	Edwin Nunez	.08

258 Nolan Ryan

210 Cal Ripken Jr.

146	Dave Stieb	.12
149	Danny Darwin	.08
150	Chris Pittaro	.08
151	Bill Buckner	.12
152	Mike Pagliarulo	.20
153	Bill Russell	.10
154	Brook Jacoby	.15
155	Pat Sheridan	.06
156	*Mike Gallego* (FC)	.25
159	Toby Harrah	.12
160	Richard Dotson	.10
161	Bob Knepper	.10
162	Dave Dravecky	.15
164	Eric Davis	.80
165	Gerald Perry	.10
166	Rick Rhoden	.10
167	Keith Moreland	.10
168	Jack Clark	.12
169	Storm Davis	.15
170	Cecil Cooper	.12
171	Alan Trammell	.35
172	Roger Clemens	12.00
173	Don Mattingly	2.50
174	Pedro Guerrero	.10
175	Willie Wilson	.10
177	Tim Raines	.30
179	Mike Witt	.10
180	Harold Baines	.15

181	*Vince Coleman* (FC)	1.50
182	*Jeff Heathcock* (FC)	.10
183	Steve Carlton	.60
184	Mario Soto	.10
185	Goose Gossage	.10
186	Johnny Ray	.12
187	Dan Gladden	.10
188	Bob Horner	.15
189	Rick Sutcliffe	.12
190	Keith Hernandez	.15
191	Phil Bradley	.20
192	Tom Brunansky	.15
193	Jesse Barfield	.20
194	Frank Viola	.20
195	Willie Upshaw	.08
196	Jim Beattie	.06
197	Darryl Strawberry	2.00
198	Ron Cey	.10
199	Steve Bedrosian	.12
200	Steve Kemp	.10
201	Manny Trillo	.10
202	Garry Templeton	.10
203	Dave Parker	.20
205	Terry Pendleton	1.50
206	Terry Puhl	.08
207	Bobby Grich	.10
208	*Ozzie Guillen* (FC)	.60
209	Jeff Reardon	.50

112 Tony Gwynn

512 Cecil Fielder

37 Paul O'Neill

51 Rickey Henderson

300	Burt Hooton	.10
301	*Stu Cliburn* (FC)	.08
302	Luis Salazar	.08
304	Frank DiPino	.08
305	Von Hayes	.10
306	Gary Redus (1983 2B is 20)	.70
310	Rick Cerone	.08
311	Shawon Dunston	.20
312	Howard Johnson	.50
313	Jim Presley	.10
314	Gary Gaetti	.20
315	Luis Leal	.08
318	Dave Henderson	.15
320	Leon Durham	.12
321	Bruce Sutter	.15
326	Juan Samuel	.15
328	Dave Smith	.10
333	Ben Oglivie	.12
334	Lance Parrish	.15
336	Dennis Rasmussen	.10
342	Charlie Hough	.10
345	*Mickey Tettleton* (FC)	3.00
347	Don Baylor	.12
350	Larry Sheets	.10
351	*Ted Higuera* (FC)	.25
358	Jim Gott	.12
359	*Ernest Riles* (FC)	.20

360	*John Christensen* (FC)	.10
364	Ron Davis (last line in highlights reads "... relievers (9).")	1.00
366	Carlton Fisk	.75
367	Nate Snell	.06
369	Darrell Evans	.15
371	Wade Boggs	3.00
377	Reggie Jackson	.75
380	Glenn Davis (FC)	.75
382	Danny Cox	.10
384	Tom Browning	.15
388	Davey Lopes	.12
390	Doyle Alexander	.10
399	Lonnie Smith	.12
409	Len Barker	.10
412	Andy Van Slyke	.60
417	Dan Pasqua	.15
421	*Tim Burke* (FC)	.15
427	*Don Carman* (FC)	.25
428	Tony Perez	.15
429	Jerry Davis	.08
430	Bob Walk	.08
432	Terry Forster	.10
433	Billy Hatcher	.12
435	*Ivan Calderon* (FC)	1.00
437	Tom Henke	.50
440	Gorman Thomas	.10

61 Mike Schmidt

441 *Rick Aguilera* (FC) **1.50**
444 *Joe Orsulak* (FC) .... .15
447 Buddy Bell .... .10
456 *Bob Melvin* (FC) .... .10
459 Bob Welch .... .12
462 *Tim Birtsas* (FC) .... .10
467 Dusty Baker .... .12
474 *Kirk McCaskill* (FC)........... .15
476 Mike Scott .... .20
477 *Darren Daulton* (FC)...... **4.00**
478 Graig Nettles .... .15
481 *Randy Ready* (FC) .... .10
482 *Lenny Dykstra* (FC) **3.00**
484 • *Harold Reynolds* (FC)... .50
485 Al Oliver .... .12
487 John Franco .... .15
490 *Bill Wegman* (FC) .... .20
491 Frank Tanana .... .10
492 *Brian Fisher* (FC) .... .12
493 Mark Clear .... .08
496 John Wathan .... .08
506 Joe Price .... .08
507 *Milt Thompson* (FC).......... .15
509 Vida Blue .... .10
512 *Cecil Fielder* (FC) **28.00**
514 Tippy Martinez................. .08
515 *Billy Robidoux* (FC) .... .10
517 Bruce Hurst .... .12

181 Vince Coleman

518 Rich Bordi........................ .08
519 Steve Yeager .... .08
521 Hal McRae .... .15
522 Jose Rijo .... .50
523 *Mitch Webster* (FC) .... .15
524 *Jack Howell* (FC) .... .20
526 Ron Kittle........................ .10
527 Phil Garner .... .10
529 Kevin Gross .... .12
530 Bo Diaz........................... .10
532 Rick Reuschel .... .10
540 Steve Sax....................... .25
541 Dan Quisenberry .... .10
543 *Floyd Youmans* (FC) .... .35
544 *Steve Buechele* (FC)........ .70
546 Joe Desa .... .08
548 Kevin Bass .... .10
549 Tom Foley .... .08
551 Bruce Bochy .... .08
553 *Chris Brown* (FC).............. .15
556 Danny Heep .... .08
557 Darnell Coles................... .12
558 Greg Gagne .... .12
559 Ernie Whitt...................... .10
561 Jimmy Key .... .50
562 Billy Swift (FC)................. .80
563 Ron Darling .... .15
565 *Zane Smith* (FC).............. .40

87 Andre Dawson

357

172 Roger Clemens

566	Sid Bream	.10
567	Joel Youngblood ("IF" on front)	1.00
567	Joel Youngblood ("P" on front)	.08
570	Rick Schu	.08
573	Al Holland	.08
576	Mike Flanagan	.10
577	Tim Leary (FC)	.35
580	Phil Niekro	.25
583	Mark Gubicza	.12
584	*Stan Javier* (FC)	.08
586	Jeff Russell	.10
588	Steve Farr	.15
589	*Steve Ontiveros* (FC)	.10
593	Larry Herndon	.08
596	*Pat Perry* (FC)	.12
597	Ray Knight	.10
598	*Steve Lombardozzi* (FC)	.20
600	*Pat Clements* (FC)	.12
601	Joe Niekro	.10
603	*Dwayne Henry* (FC)	.10
604	Mookie Wilson	.10
606	Rance Mulliniks	.06
607	Alan Wiggins	.06
609	Tom Seaver (green stripes around name)	1.00

609	Tom Seaver (yellow stripes around name)	2.00
610	Neil Allen	.08
611	Don Sutton	.20
612	*Fred Toliver* (FC)	.15
617	Bill Madlock	.12
619	Dave Stewart	.12
620	Tim Lollar	.08
621	Gary Lavelle	.08
622	Charlie Hudson	.06
625	Sid Fernandez	.12
629	*Roger McDowell* (FC)	.25
634	*Mike Felder* (FC)	.15
636	Bob Ojeda	.12
642	Mike Brown	.08
644	Ty-Breaking Hit (Pete Rose)	.50
645	• Knuckle Brothers (Joe Niekro, Phil Niekro)	.15
648	Cesar Cedeno	.10
649	Bert Blyleven	.15
651	Fleet Feet (Vince Coleman (FC), Willie McGee)	.35
653	King of Kings (Pete Rose)	1.00

197 Darryl Strawberry

1986 DONRUSS ROOKIES

Donruss followed the leaders in 1986 by creating "The Rookies," a separate set issued in the fall to compete with Topps and Fleer. Unlike the other companies, however, Donruss ignored cards of traded players. This streamlined concept resulted in just 55 cards of the leading rookies of 1986 (along with a rather useless unnumbered checklist). To distinguish the two Donruss sets, border colors switched from the blue of the regular issue to green and "The Rookies" logo is found on the lower left portion of the front of each card. High-powered newcomers include Jose Canseco, Will Clark, Bo Jackson, Barry Bonds, and Ruben Sierra. The value of the set tripled in its first year.

		MINT
Complete set		**$45.00**
Commons		**.10**

1	Wally Joyner (FC)	$1.75
4	Ed Correa (FC)	.15
5	Reggie Williams	.12
6	Charlie Kerfeld	.12
7	Andres Galarraga	2.50
11	Barry Bonds (FC)	15.00
13	Mark Eichhorn (FC)	.15
14	Dan Plesac (FC)	.15
15	Cory Snyder	.35
16	Kelly Gruber	.50
17	Kevin Mitchell (FC)	3.00
18	Steve Lombardozzi	.08
19	Mitch Williams	.30
20	John Cerutti (FC)	.15
21	Todd Worrell	.50
22	Jose Canseco	7.00
23	Pete Incaviglia (FC)	1.25
24	Jose Guzman	.15
25	Scott Bailes (FC)	.15
26	Greg Mathews (FC)	.15
29	Jeff Sellers	.15
30	Bobby Bonilla (FC)	4.00
31	Doug Drabek (FC)	1.50
32	Will Clark (FC)	10.00
33	Leon "Bip" Roberts	1.00
34	Jim Deshaies (FC)	.25
35	Mike Lavalliere (LaValliere) (FC)	.30

32 Will Clark

36	Scott Bankhead	.12
37	Dale Sveum (FC)	.15
38	Bo Jackson (FC)	6.00
39	Rob Thompson (FC)	.80
40	Eric Plunk	.15
41	Bill Bathe	.12
42	John Kruk (FC)	4.00
44	Mark Portugal	.40
45	Danny Tartabull	1.50
48	Rey Quinones	.08
49	Bobby Witt (FC)	.50
52	Ruben Sierra (FC)	8.00

1986 FLEER

Striking photographs and a simple card design make the 1986 Fleer set a winner. Maximum space on each of the 660 cards is devoted to photos, which are surrounded by a dark blue border. Fleer was the only company to provide complete major and minor league stats for all players on card backs, which are otherwise bleak and no longer contain the black-and-white photo of past years. Popular with collectors is a run of 10 Major League Prospect cards, on which two potential rookie sensations, usually teammates, share a card front. Notables in this subset include Jose Canseco, Cecil Fielder, and Benito Santiago. The card that pairs Canseco with Eric Plunk is the most expensive in the set.

	MINT
Complete set	$125.00
Commons	.08

96 Darryl Strawberry

4	Bud Black	$ .06
5	George Brett	2.00
7	Steve Farr	.10
8	Mark Gubicza	.12
9	Dane Iorg	.06
10	Danny Jackson	.20
14	Hal McRae	.15
17	Jorge Orta	.06
19	Bret Saberhagen	.75
23	John Wathan	.10
24	Frank White	.15
25	Willie Wilson	.15
27	Steve Braun	.06
30	Jack Clark	.10
31	*Vince Coleman*	1.75
32	Danny Cox	.10
35	Bob Forsch	.15
37	Tom Herr	.10
40	Jeff Lahti	.06
42	Willie McGee	.20
43	Tom Nieto	.06
44	Terry Pendleton	1.50
46	Ozzie Smith	1.00
47	John Tudor	.10
48	Andy Van Slyke	.25
49	*Todd Worrell* (FC)	.35
50	Jim Acker	.06
52	Jesse Barfield	.20
53	George Bell	.40
56	Jim Clancy	.06
60	Tom Henke	.50
61	Garth Iorg	.06
63	Jimmy Key	.50
64	Dennis Lamp	.06
67	Lloyd Moseby	.10
69	Al Oliver	.10
70	Dave Stieb	.12
72	Willie Upshaw	.10
73	Ernie Whitt	.10
74	*Rick Aguilera* (FC)	1.75
76	Gary Carter	.25
77	Ron Darling	.15
78	*Len Dykstra* (FC)	3.00
79	Sid Fernandez	.12

80	George Foster	.15
81	Dwight Gooden	1.25
83	Danny Heep	.06
84	Keith Hernandez	.15
85	Howard Johnson	.40
86	Ray Knight	.15
87	Terry Leach	.10
89	*Roger McDowell* (FC)	.25
94	Doug Sisk	.06
95	Rusty Staub	.15
96	Darryl Strawberry	1.75
97	Mookie Wilson	.10
98	Neil Allen	.06
99	Don Baylor	.12
100	Dale Berra	.10
104	*Brian Fisher*	.15
105	Ken Griffey	.15
106	Ron Guidry	.20
108	Rickey Henderson	2.00
109	Don Mattingly	2.50
112	Phil Niekro	.15
113	Mike Pagliarulo	.20
114	Dan Pasqua	.12
115	Willie Randolph	.10
116	Dave Righetti	.20
121	Dave Winfield	1.25
124	Bob Bailor	.06
125	Greg Brock	.08

310 Nolan Ryan

109 Don Mattingly

126	Enos Cabell	.06
128	Carlos Diaz	.06
129	*Mariano Duncan*	.40
130	Pedro Guerrero	.10
131	Orel Hershiser	.50
135	Bill Madlock	.12
136	Candy Maldonado	.10
137	Mike Marshall	.15
143	Steve Sax	.20
145	Fernando Valenzuela	.30
146	Bob Welch	.12
149	• Bob Boone	.12
150	John Candelaria	.10
151	Rod Carew	.70
152	*Stewart Cliburn* (FC)	.12
153	Doug DeCinces	.10
155	Ken Forsch	.06
157	Bobby Grich	.12
159	Al Holland	.06
160	Reggie Jackson	1.25
162	*Urbano Lugo*	.08
163	*Kirk McCaskill* (FC)	.15
170	Don Sutton	.15
172	Buddy Bell	.10
173	Tom Browning	.25
174	Dave Concepcion	.15
175	Eric Davis	.80
176	Bo Diaz	.08

1986 Fleer

345 Roger Clemens

284 Cal Ripken, Jr.

649 Major League Prospect

313	Dickie Thon	.12
321	Steve Garvey	.25
322	Goose Gossage	.10
323	Tony Gwynn	3.00
330	*Lance McCullers* (FC)	.15
331	Kevin McReynolds	.15
332	Graig Nettles	.15
334	Eric Show	.10
339	Tony Armas	.10
340	Marty Barrett	.10
341	Wade Boggs	3.00
343	Bill Buckner	.10
345	Roger Clemens	12.00
347	Mike Easler	.10
348	● Dwight Evans	.12
349	Rich Gedman	.10
352	Bruce Hurst	.15
355	Steve Lyons	.08
357	Bob Ojeda	.15
358	Jim Rice	.10
363	Ron Cey	.10
366	Shawon Dunston	.30
367	Leon Durham	.08
368	Dennis Eckersley	.70
371	Bill Hatcher	.15
372	Dave Lopes	.12
373	Gary Matthews	.10
378	Ryne Sandberg	5.00
380	Lee Smith	.60
383	Rick Sutcliffe	.15
386	Bert Blyleven	.10
387	Tom Brunansky	.15

394	Gary Gaetti	.20
395	Greg Gagne	.10
397	Kent Hrbek	.20
401	Kirby Puckett	10.00
408	Frank Viola	.35
411	Dusty Baker	.15
412	*Tim Birtsas*	.10
414	Chris Codiroli	.08
415	Dave Collins	.08
416	Mike Davis	.08
417	Alfredo Griffin	.12
421	Jay Howell	.15
422	Tommy John	.12
423	Dave Kingman	.15
426	Carney Lansford	.10
429	*Steve Ontiveros* (FC)	.10
430	Tony Phillips	.08
431	Jose Rijo	.50
432	*Mickey Tettleton*	3.00
435	Steve Carlton	.80
436	*Don Carman*	.25
438	*Darren Daulton*	4.00
439	John Denny	.08
443	Von Hayes	.12
445	Garry Maddox	.10
449	Juan Samuel	.12
450	Mike Schmidt	2.50
453	● Dave Stewart	.20
455	Kent Tekulve	.10
457	Glenn Wilson	.08
461	Phil Bradley	.15
462	*Ivan Calderon*	.80

378 Ryne Sandberg

31 Vince Coleman

78 Len Dykstra

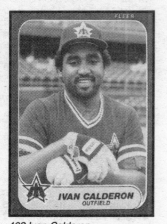

462 Ivan Calderon

646 Major League Prospect
(*Kal Daniels, Paul O'Neill*
(FC)) 3.00
647 Major League Prospect
(*Andres Galarraga, Fred*
Toliver (FC)) 4.00

649 Major League Prospect
(*Jose Canseco, Eric*
Plunk (FC)) 28.00
653 Major League Prospect
(*Cecil Fielder, Cory*
Snyder (FC)) 20.00

1986 FLEER UPDATE

What a difference a year makes. With the inclusion of popular players such as Jose Canseco, Wally Joyner, Kevin Mitchell, and Ruben Sierra, the 1986 Fleer Update set became an immediate hit. In contrast to Topps, the Fleer "extension" set contains a higher percentage of rookies in its 131 cards (and complete set checklist). Although the company skipped Bo Jackson, it scooped Topps by including the phenomenal Ruben Sierra of the Rangers. The Fleer Update cards differ from the standard 1986 cards only by a "U" prefix on the card numbers (omitted from the following list). To satisfy collectors of rookie cards, hobby dealers broke up sets and sold popular cards in lots of 50 or 100.

	MINT
Complete set	**$30.00**
Commons	**.05**

1 Mike Aldrete (FC)	$ .35
2 Andy Allanson (FC)	.20
3 Neil Allen	.08
4 Joaquin Andujar	.08
5 Paul Assenmacher (FC)..	.12
6 Scott Bailes (FC)	.20
7 Jay Baller (FC)	.12
8 Scott Bankhead (FC)........	.15
9 Bill Bathe	.08
10 Don Baylor	.12
11 Billy Beane	.12
12 Steve Bedrosian..............	.15
14 Barry Bonds (FC)	12.00
15 Bobby Bonilla (FC)	3.50
16 Rich Bordi........................	.05
18 Tom Candiotti..................	.20

19 John Cangelosi (FC)	.08
20 Jose Canseco	5.00
21 Chuck Cary (FC)	.08
22 Juan Castillo (FC)	.08
23 Rick Cerone	.08
24 John Cerutti (FC).............	.20
25 Will Clark (FC)...............	8.00
26 Mark Clear.......................	.05
27 Darnell Coles (FC)...........	.15
28 Dave Collins	.12
30 Ed Correa (FC)................	.15
31 Joe Cowley	.08
33 Rob Deer..........................	.45
34 John Denny	.12
35 Jim DeShaies (Deshaies) (FC)	.25
36 Doug Drabek (FC)	1.25
37 Mike Easler	.08
38 Mark Eichhorn (FC).........	.15
41 Scott Fletcher	.12
42 Terry Forster	.08

25 Will Clark

1986 TOPPS

At 792 cards, Topps continued as the largest set of baseball cards on the market. This design was one of Topps' boldest of the decade, with the team name in large letters at the top of each card. Because of the large size of the edition, there was room for a number of specialty subsets. Topps remained the only company to devote a card to each team manager (with a team checklist on the back). Twenty-two All-Star cards are also included, along with a seven-card subset of all-time hit king Pete Rose. On the negative side, Topps included few rookies in the set, opting to save them for the fall Traded set.

	MINT
Complete set	**$40.00**
Commons	**.05**

340 Cal Ripken

1	Pete Rose	$1.00
2	Rose Special 1963-1966.	.35
3	Rose Special 1967-1970.	.35
4	Rose Special 1971-1974.	.35
5	Rose Special 1975-1978.	.35
6	Rose Special 1979-1982.	.35
7	Rose Special 1983-1985.	.35
8	Dwayne Murphy	.07
9	Roy Smith	.05
10	Tony Gwynn	1.10
11	Bob Ojeda	.07
12	*Jose Uribe* (FC)	.10
14	Julio Cruz	.05
15	Eddie Whitson	.05
16	Rick Schu (FC)	.07
17	Mike Stenhouse	.05
18	Brent Gaff	.05
19	Rich Hebner	.07
20	Lou Whitaker	.15
21	George Bamberger	.05
22	Duane Walker	.05
23	*Manny Lee* (FC)	.15
24	Len Barker	.07
25	Willie Wilson	.12
26	Frank DiPino	.05
27	Ray Knight	.07
28	Eric Davis	.40
29	Tony Phillips	.10
30	Eddie Murray	.40
31	Jamie Easterly	.05
32	Steve Yeager	.05
33	Jeff Lahti	.05
34	Ken Phelps (FC)	.07
35	Jeff Reardon	.25
36	Tigers Ldrs (Lance Parrish)	.12
37	Mark Thurmond	.05
40	Ken Griffey	.10
41	Brad Wellman	.05
44	*Lance McCullers* (FC)	.25
45	Damaso Garcia	.05
46	Billy Hatcher (FC)	.10
47	Juan Berenguer	.05
50	Dan Quisenberry	.07
52	Chris Welsh	.05
53	*Len Dykstra* (FC)	1.00
54	John Franco	.12
55	Fred Lynn	.15
56	Tom Niedenfuer	.07
57	Bill Doran	.10

690 Ryne Sandberg

386 Cecil Fielder

80 Darryl Strawberry

123	Greg Walker	.10
124	Luis Sanchez	.05
125	Dave Lopes	.07
126	Mets Ldrs (Mookie Wilson)	.07
127	*Jack Howell* (FC)	.25
128	John Wathan	.07
129	Jeff Dedmon (FC)	.05
130	Alan Trammell	.25
132	Razor Shines	.05
133	Andy McGaffigan	.05
134	Carney Lansford	.10
135	Joe Niekro	.10
136	Mike Hargrove	.05
137	Charlie Moore	.05
138	Mark Davis	.10
139	Daryl Boston	.07
142	Bob Jones	.05
140	John Candelaria	.10
143	Dave Van Gorder	.05
144	Doug Sisk	.05
145	Pedro Guerrero	.10
146	Jack Perconte	.05
147	Larry Sheets	.15
148	Mike Heath	.05
149	Brett Butler	.07
150	Joaquin Andujar	.07
151	Dave Stapleton	.05

152	Mike Morgan	.05
155	Bob Grich	.10
156	White Sox Ldrs (Richard Dotson)	.07
157	Ron Hassey	.05
158	Derrel Thomas	.05
159	Orel Hershiser	.25
160	Chet Lemon	.07
162	Greg Gagne	.07
163	Pete Ladd	.05
164	Steve Balboni	.07
165	Mike Davis	.07
166	Dickie Thon	.07
167	Zane Smith (FC)	.25
168	Jeff Burroughs	.07
169	George Wright	.06
170	Gary Carter	.25
172	Jerry Reed	.05
175	Steve Sax	.15
176	Jay Tibbs	.05
177	Joel Youngblood	.05
178	Ivan DeJesus	.05
179	*Stu Cliburn* (FC)	.10
180	Don Mattingly	1.00
181	Al Nipper	.05
183	Larry Andersen	.05
184	Tim Laudner	.05
185	Rollie Fingers	.12

661 Roger Clemens

1 Pete Rose

300 George Brett

1986 Topps

250 Dwight Gooden

382 Ivan Calderon

329 Kirby Puckett

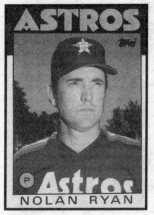

100 Nolan Ryan

500 Rickey Henderson

510 Wade Boggs

536	Jose Rijo	.10
538	Dennis Eckersley	.15
545	Jimmy Key	.10
546	Mariners Ldrs (Dave Henderson)	.07
547	*Roger McDowell*	.12
549	Bob Welch	.07
550	Tom Herr	.10
555	Hubie Brooks	.10
560	Dave Righetti	.12
565	Tom Brunansky	.15
570	Rusty Staub	.10
574	Ron Kittle	.07
575	Mike Boddicker	.07
576	Expos Ldrs (Andre Dawson)	.12
577	Jerry Reuss	.07
580	Willie McGee	.12
581	Bruce Hurst	.15
584	*Brian Fisher* (FC)	.10
589	Sid Bream	.07
592	Frank Tanana	.10
593	Jesse Barfield	.15
595	Dave Parker	.12
598	Jim Presley	.25
599	● *Rick Aguilera* (FC)	.80
600	Dale Murphy	.15
602	*Mariano Duncan*	.25

254 Ozzie Guillen

606	Royals Ldrs (Hal McRae)	.10
610	Ron Guidry	.15
612	Richard Dotson	.10
615	Johnny Ray	.10
620	Bruce Sutter	.15
628	*Kirk McKaskill* (FC)	.12
629	*Mitch Webster* (FC)	.10
630	Fernando Valenzuela	.15
636	Cubs Ldrs (Lee Smith)	.07
640	Jose Cruz	.10
644	Mark Gubicza	.12
647	Mel Hall	.12
648	Steve Bedrosian	.12
650	Dave Stieb	.12
651	Billy Martin	.12
652	Tom Browning	.15
660	Steve Garvey	.20
661	Roger Clemens	4.00
666	Rangers Ldrs (Charlie Hough)	.07
669	Ron Cey	.10
680	George Foster	.15
683	Andy Van Slyke	.30
685	Tim Wallach	.10
689	Dave Stewart	.15
690	Ryne Sandberg	2.00
696	Dodgers Ldrs (Bill Russell)	.07

487 Bret Saberhagen

370 Vince Coleman

290 Carlton Fisk

1986 TOPPS TRADED

After an off year for the regular set in 1986, the Topps Traded set for 1986 delivered the types of big names that rookie-card fans love. Like Fleer and Donruss, Topps provided cards of top rookie stars. Included in the set are Barry Bonds, Bobby Bonilla, Jose Canseco, Will Clark, Bo Jackson, and Kevin Mitchell, while Ruben Sierra was conspicuous by his absence. Collectors buying the set today should find it still in the specially designed box created by Topps. As usual, the complete 132-card sets were distributed only through hobby dealers. For easy handling, the cards are numbered in alphabetical order.

	MINT
Complete set	**$24.00**
Commons	**.06**

1	Andy Allanson (FC)	$ .20
3	Joaquin Andujar	.10
4	Paul Assenmacher (FC)	.20
5	Scott Bailes (FC)	.20
6	Don Baylor	.15
7	Steve Bedrosian	.15
10	Mike Bielecki (FC)	.20
11	Barry Bonds (FC)	7.00
12	Bobby Bonilla (FC)	2.00
16	Rick Burleson	.10
19	John Cangelosi (FC)	.20
20	Jose Canseco (FC)	4.00
23	John Cerutti (FC)	.25
24	Will Clark (FC)	4.00
26	Darnell Coles	.15
27	Dave Collins	.10
30	Joel Davis (FC)	.10
31	Rob Deer	.25
33	Mike Easler	.10
34	Mark Eichhorn (FC)	.20
36	Scott Fletcher	.15
37	Terry Forster	.10
40	Andres Galarraga (FC)	2.00
41	Ken Griffey	.20
43	Jose Guzman (FC)	.35
45	Billy Hatcher	.20
48	Pete Incaviglia (FC)	.70
50	Bo Jackson (FC)	3.50
51	Wally Joyner (FC)	1.00

24 Will Clark

52	Charlie Kerfeld (FC)	.15
53	Eric King (FC)	.12
54	Bob Kipper (FC)	.10
55	Wayne Krenchicki	.08
56	John Kruk (FC)	2.00
57	Mike LaCoss	.08
59	Mike Laga	.08
60	Hal Lanier	.08
61	Dave LaPoint	.12
62	Rudy Law	.08
63	Rick Leach	.08
64	Tim Leary	.08
67	Steve Lyons	.10

69	Candy Maldonado	.15	102 Ted Simmons	.20
70	Roger Mason (FC)	.10	104 Kurt Stillwell (FC)	.25
71	Bob McClure	.08	105 Franklin Stubbs	.20
74	Kevin Mitchell (FC)	1.25	106 Dale Sveum (FC)	.25
77	Phil Niekro	.20	108 Danny Tartabull (FC)	.70
79	Juan Nieves (FC)	.25	109 Tim Teufel	.15
80	Otis Nixon (FC)	.50	110 Bob Tewksbury (FC)	.15
81	Bob Ojeda	.12	111 Andres Thomas (FC)	.15
82	Jose Oquendo	.12	112 Milt Thompson	.12
83	Tom Paciorek	.10	113 Robby Thompson (FC)	.50
86	Lou Piniella	.15	117 Manny Trillo	.10
87	Dan Plesac (FC)	.15	120 Bob Walk	.15
88	Darrell Porter	.10	121 Gene Walter (FC)	.10
89	Rey Quinones (FC)	.10	122 Claudell Washington	.15
91	Bip Roberts	.50	123 Bill Wegman (FC)	.20
92	Billy Jo Robidoux (FC)	.15	125 Mitch Williams (FC)	.35
93	Jeff Robinson	.10	126 Bobby Witt (FC)	.25
101	Tom Seaver	.50	127 Todd Worrell (FC)	.25

1987 DONRUSS

While Topps and Fleer issued relatively conservative cards in 1987, Donruss broke loose with a wacky design. Look closely at the borders of the 1987 cards and you'll discover that each photo covers a wide gold band of tiny baseballs. But the black border surrounding the photos is problematic: As with the 1971 Topps set, scuffing occurs easily and fewer mint cards remain. Top cards in the 1987 set include specially marked Rated Rookie cards for Bo Jackson, Mark McGwire, Benito Santiago, and Greg Swindell. Donruss showed a willingness to scatter other rookies throughout the set, providing lots of buried treasures for rookie-card fanatics.

	MINT
Complete set	**$60.00**
Commons	**.05**

1	Wally Joyner (DK)	$.30
2	Roger Clemens (DK)	.80
3	Dale Murphy (DK)	.25
4	Darryl Strawberry (DK)	.40
5	Ozzie Smith (DK)	.12
6	Jose Canseco (DK)	1.00
7	Charlie Hough (DK)	.07
8	Brook Jacoby (DK)	.10
9	Fred Lynn (DK)	.12
10	Rick Rhoden (DK)	.10
11	Chris Brown (DK)	.10
12	Von Hayes (DK)	.10
13	Jack Morris (DK)	.15
14	Kevin McReynolds (DK) ("Donruss Diamond Kings" in white band on back)	.80
15	George Brett (DK)	.25
16	Ted Higuera (DK)	.20
17	Hubie Brooks (DK)	.10
18	Mike Scott (DK)	.12
19	Kirby Puckett (DK)	.40
20	Dave Winfield (DK)	.25
21	Lloyd Moseby (DK)	.10

22 Eric Davis (DK) ("Donruss
   Diamond Kings" in white
   band on back) .... **.80**
22 Eric Davis (DK) ("Donruss
   Diamond Kings" in yellow
   band on back) .... **.25**
23 Jim Presley (DK) .... **.12**
24 Keith Moreland (DK) .... **.07**
25 Greg Walker (DK) ("Donruss
   Diamond Kings" in white
   band on back) **1.25**
26 Steve Sax (DK) .... **.12**
28 *B.J. Surhoff* (RR) (FC) ..... **.20**
29 *Randy Myers* (RR) (FC) .. **.60**
30 *Ken Gerhart* (RR) (FC) .... **.15**
31 Benito Santiago
   (RR) (FC) .... **.65**
32 *Greg Swindell*
   (RR) (FC) **1.00**
33 *Mike Birkbeck* (RR) (FC) . **.20**
34 *Terry Steinbach*
   (RR) (FC) .... **.50**
35 *Bo Jackson* (RR) **4.00**
36 *Greg Maddux* (RR) (FC) **6.00**
37 *Jim Lindeman* (RR) (FC) . **.12**
38 *Devon White* (RR) (FC) . **1.00**
39 *Eric Bell* (RR) (FC) .... **.12**
40 *Will Fraser* (RR) (FC) ...... **.20**
41 Jerry Browne (RR) (FC) .. **.10**
42 Chris James (RR) (FC) .... **.20**
43 *Rafael Palmeiro*
   (RR) (FC) **4.00**
44 *Pat Dodson* (RR) (FC) ..... **.12**
45 *Duane Ward* (RR) (FC) . **1.00**
46 *Mark McGwire*
   (RR) (FC) **6.00**
47 *Bruce Fields* (RR) (FC)
   (photo is Darnell Coles) ... **.10**
48 Eddie Murray .... **.35**
49 Ted Higuera .... **.20**
50 Kirk Gibson .... **.12**
51 Oil Can Boyd .... **.07**
52 Don Mattingly .... **.80**
53 Pedro Guerrero .... **.15**
54 George Brett .... **.70**
55 Jose Rijo .... **.10**
56 Tim Raines .... **.15**
57 *Ed Correa* .... **.15**
58 Mike Witt .... **.10**

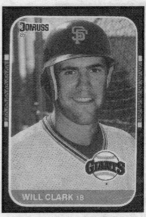

66 Will Clark

59 Greg Walker .... **.10**
60 Ozzie Smith .... **.40**
61 Glenn Davis .... **.25**
62 Glenn Wilson .... **.07**
63 Tom Browning .... **.10**
64 Tony Gwynn .... **.80**
65 R.J. Reynolds .... **.07**
66 *Will Clark* **7.00**
67 Ozzie Virgil .... **.05**
68 Rick Sutcliffe .... **.12**
69 Gary Carter .... **.20**
70 Mike Moore .... **.10**
71 Bert Blyleven .... **.10**
72 Tony Fernandez .... **.20**
73 Kent Hrbek .... **.15**
74 Lloyd Moseby .... **.10**
75 Alvin Davis .... **.12**
76 Keith Hernandez .... **.25**
77 Ryne Sandberg **1.75**
78 Dale Murphy .... **.40**
79 Sid Bream .... **.07**
80 Chris Brown .... **.07**
81 Steve Garvey .... **.25**
82 Mario Soto .... **.07**
84 Willie McGee .... **.12**
85 Jose Cruz .... **.10**
86 Brian Downing .... **.07**
87 Ozzie Guillen .... **.12**

361 Barry Bonds

183	Terry Pendleton	.25
184	*Jim Deshaies*	.15
185	Steve Bedrosian	.12
186	Pete Rose	.50
188	Rick Reuschel	.10
192	Ron Darling	.15
194	Tom Brunansky	.12
195	Dave Stieb	.12
196	Frank Viola	.15
199	Dwight Gooden	.45
208	*Greg Mathews*	.20
209	Charlie Kerfeld	.10
210	Reggie Jackson	.50
211	Floyd Bannister	.10
214	*Dan Plesac*	.10
217	Joe Niekro	.10
224	Pete Incaviglia	.40
227	*Scott Bailes*	.20
228	Rickey Henderson	.85
233	• Bob Boone	.07
241	Roger McDowell	.12
244	Jimmy Key	.12
247	Carlton Fisk	.40
248	Larry Sheets	.08
249	*Juan Castillo* (FC)	.10
250	*Eric King*	.12
251	*Doug Drabek*	1.25
252	Wade Boggs	1.00
255	Frank White	.10
259	Pete O'Brien	.10
262	Darren Daulton	1.25
263	Vince Coleman	.25
265	Eric Davis	.35
266	*Andres Thomas*	.25
267	*Mike Diaz* (FC)	.15
268	Chili Davis	.10
270	Phil Bradley	.12
271	George Bell	.25
273	Storm Davis	.10
274	Rob Deer (FC)	.15
276	Roger Clemens	2.00
278	Steve Sax	.15
286	Bill Doran	.10
289	John Franco	.10
290	*Paul Assenmacher*	.15
292	Lee Smith	.10
298	Mike Pagliarulo	.10
299	Franklin Stubbs	.10
302	*Bill Mooneyham*	.10

46 Mark McGwire

303	Andres Galarraga	.70
306	*Russ Morman* (FC)	.10
307	Todd Worrell	.10
315	*Jamie Moyer* (FC)	.12
321	*Mark Eichhorn*	.15
322	*Lee Guetterman*	.15
323	Sid Fernandez	.10
328	*John Kruk*	2.00
331	*Mike LaValliere*	.20
334	*Ron Karkovice* (FC)	.10
337	*Glenn Braggs* (FC)	.15
339	Don Baylor	.12
341	*Reggie Williams*	.10
346	*Ruben Sierra*	4.00
347	*Mitch Williams*	.25
351	Ron Kittle	.10
361	*Barry Bonds*	10.00
362	Vida Blue	.10
363	Cecil Cooper	.10
365	Dennis Eckersley	.15
368	*Allan Anderson* (FC)	.15
370	*Bobby Thigpen* (FC)	.35
375	Tom Seaver	.40
388	Dave Parker	.20
389	Bob Horner	.12
397	*Bryan Clutterbuck* (FC)	.10
398	Darrell Evans	.12
401	*Phil Lombardi* (FC)	.10

407	*Chuck Finley* (FC)	.60
410	Kevin Bass	.10
413	*Tracy Jones*	.15
417	Andy Van Slyke	.30
422	*Bob Tewksbury*	.12
424	*Mike Kingery* (FC)	.15
425	Dave Kingman	.15
429	Harold Baines	.15
435	Rick Rhoden	.10
439	Jesse Orosco	.10
442	*John Cerutti*	.20
444	Kelly Gruber	.35
446	*Ed Hearn*	.10
450	*Mike Aldrete*	.15
451	Kevin McReynolds	.15
452	*Rob Murphy* (FC)	.15
456	Bobby Grich	.10
457	Jose DeLeon	.10
458	Andre Dawson	.50
460	*Joey Meyer* (FC)	.20
461	*Chuck Cary* (FC)	.10
462	Bill Buckner	.10
464	*Jeff Hamilton* (FC)	.20
465	Phil Niekro	.20
466	Mark Gubicza	.12
468	*Bob Sebra* (FC)	.10
469	Larry Parrish	.10
471	Hal McRae	.10
472	*Dave Leiper* (FC)	.10
474	Dan Pasqua	.10
475	Bob Welch	.10
478	*Chris Bosio* (FC)	.40
483	Rich Gossage	.10
487	Mookie Wilson	.10
488	*Dave Martinez* (FC)	.20
489	• Harold Reynolds	.10
492	*Barry Larkin* (FC)	3.25
502	*David Cone* (FC)	2.75
505	*Ray Chadwick* (FC)	.10
506	*Mike Loynd* (FC)	.15
512	*Terry McGriff* (FC)	.12
513	Ken Griffey	.12
515	*Terry Mulholland* (FC)	1.00
523	Marty Barrett	.10
525	*Jose Gonzalez* (FC)	.15
526	Cory Snyder	.15
529	*Wilfredo Tejeda* (FC)	.10
531	*Dale Mohorcic* (FC)	.20
535	*Mike Maddux* (FC)	.15
537	Ted Simmons	.12
538	*Rafael Belliard* (FC)	.25
542	*Dale Sveum*	.20
544	*Jeff Sellers*	.20
547	*Randy Kutcher* (FC)	.10
549	*Casey Candaele* (FC)	.15
550	Jeff Russell	.10
551	John Candelaria	.10
555	*Bruce Ruffin* (FC)	.20
556	Buddy Bell	.10
557	*Jimmy Jones* (FC)	.20
558	*Bobby Bonilla*	2.50
561	*Glenallen Hill* (FC)	.25
565	*Mike Sharperson* (FC)	.15
566	*Mark Portugal*	.20
567	Rick Leach	.10
568	Mark Langston	.20
573	*Kelly Downs* (FC)	.10
574	*Randy Asadoor* (FC)	.10
575	*Dave Magadan* (FC)	.30
576	*Marvin Freeman* (FC)	.12
585	*Mike Greenwell* (FC)	1.50
587	*Ralph Bryant* (FC)	.12
591	*Jeff Musselman* (FC)	.20
592	*Mike Stanley* (FC)	.50
594	*Drew Hall* (FC)	.20
595	*Rob Nelson* (FC)	.10
597	*Scott Nielsen* (FC)	.10
598	*Brian Holton* (FC)	.20
599	*Kevin Mitchell*	1.50
602	*Barry Jones* (FC)	.10
610	*Dave Valle* (FC)	.12
611	Len Dykstra	.20
617	Steve Carlton	.25
620	Rick Aguilera	.15
621	Fred McGriff	3.00
622	Dave Henderson	.10
623	*Dave Clark* (FC)	.20
627	*Kevin Brown* (FC)	1.75
632	*Ray Hayward* (FC)	.12
635	*Kevin Elster* (FC)	.10
638	*Rey Quinones*	.15
642	*Stan Jefferson* (FC)	.20
646	Howard Johnsn	.30
648	Dave Stewart	.12
651	Bob Brower	.15
654	*Tim Pyznarski* (FC)	.10
655	*Luis Aquino* (FC)	.10
656	Mickey Brantley (FC)	.10

1987 DONRUSS ROOKIES

For the second year in a row, Donruss issued "The Rookies," a 56-card set highlighting players overlooked in the earlier 660-card issue. Donruss hedged its bets by including Bo Jackson and Mark McGwire in this edition, issued in the fall, even though McGwire had been in the larger 1987 set, and Jackson was a member of The Rookies in 1986. Other appealing names in the set include Ellis Burks, Mike Greenwell, David Cone, and Matt Williams. The 55 player cards and one checklist card came in a specially designed box. Although the card numbers hold no special prefixes, Donruss altered these cards slightly in comparison to the regular set by changing the border color from black to green and by stamping "The Rookies" logo on each card front.

		MINT
Complete set		**$20.00**
Commons		**.08**

5 Ellis Burks

1	Mark McGwire	$3.50
4	Mike Greenwell	1.25
5	Ellis Burks (FC)	1.00
6	DeWayne Buice (FC)	.15
8	Devon White	.40
10	Lester Lancaster (FC)	.15
11	Ken Williams (FC)	.15
12	Matt Nokes (FC)	.50
13	Jeff Robinson (FC)	.40
14	Bo Jackson	2.50
15	Kevin Seitzer (FC)	.30
16	Billy Ripken (FC)	.20
17	B.J. Surhoff	.20
21	Les Straker (FC)	.20
22	Mark Davidson (FC)	.15
23	Gene Larkin (FC)	.20
25	Luis Polonia (FC)	.45
26	Terry Steinbach	.15
28	Mike Stanley	.20
30	Todd Benzinger (FC)	.35
31	Fred McGriff	3.00
32	Mike Henneman (FC)	.30
34	Dave Magadan	.25
35	David Cone	2.00
36	Mike Jackson (FC)	.20
37	John Mitchell (FC)	.20
38	Mike Dunne (FC)	.15
39	John Smiley (FC)	.60
40	Joe Magrane (FC)	.25
42	Shane Mack (FC)	1.50
44	Benito Santiago	.40
45	Matt Williams (FC)	5.00
46	Dave Meads (FC)	.20
47	Rafael Palmeiro	3.00
48	Bill Long (FC)	.20
52	Greg Maddux	5.00
55	Chuck Jackson (FC)	.20

1987 FLEER

Fleer produced an attractive and innovative set of baseball cards in 1987. Each of the 660 cards in the annual set features a light blue border fading to white down the sides as it approaches a solid blue bottom. Photos extend into the top border, creating a novel three-dimensional look. The only obstruction on the card fronts are team logos in the lower corners (which seem redundant, since the same logos usually appear on the player's cap or uniform). Fleer produced its last Pete rose card, number 213, labeling him a player-manager. The card of Barry Bonds, number 604, has turned out to be the most valuable rookie card in the bunch.

		MINT
Complete set		**$100.00**
Commons		.06

1	Rick Aguilera	$ .30
3	Wally Backman	.08
4	Gary Carter	.25
5	Ron Darling	.15
6	Len Dykstra	.40
7	*Kevin Elster* (FC)	.20
8	Sid Fernandez	.12
9	Dwight Gooden	.60
10	*Ed Hearn* (FC)	.10
12	Keith Hernandez	.25
13	Howard Johnson	.35
14	Ray Knight	.08
16	Roger McDowell	.12
17	*Kevin Mitchell*	4.00
19	Bob Ojeda	.08
20	Jesse Orosco	.08
23	Darryl Strawberry	.80
25	Mookie Wilson	.10
26	Tony Armas	.08
27	Marty Barrett	.10
28	Don Baylor	.12
29	Wade Boggs	1.75
30	Oil Can Boyd	.08
31	Bill Buckner	.10
32	Roger Clemens	4.00
34	● Dwight Evans	.12
35	Rich Gedman	.08
36	Dave Henderson	.10
37	Bruce Hurst	.10
41	Jim Rice	.10
44	Calvin Schiraldi	.08

45	Tom Seaver	.70
46	*Jeff Sellers* (FC)	.20
51	Kevin Bass	.10
53	Jose Cruz	.12
55	Glenn Davis	.25
56	*Jim Deshaies*	.35
57	Bill Doran	.10
59	Billy Hatcher	.08
62	Dave Lopes	.08
67	Nolan Ryan	4.00
68	Mike Scott	.15
69	Dave Smith	.08
70	Dickie Thon	.08
73	● Bob Boone	.08
75	John Candelaria	.10
78	Brian Downing	.08
79	*Chuck Finley* (FC)	1.25
81	Bobby Grich	.10
83	Jack Howell (FC)	.10
84	Reggie Jackson	1.00
86	Wally Joyner	2.00
88	Kirk McCaskill	.08
93	Don Sutton	.20
94	Rob Wilfong	.06
95	Mike Witt	.10
96	*Doug Drabek*	2.50
97	Mike Easler	.08
99	Brian Fisher	.08
100	Ron Guidry	.15
101	Rickey Henderson	1.50
102	Tommy John	.15
103	Ron Kittle	.10
104	Don Mattingly	1.50
106	Joe Niekro	.10
108	Dan Pasqua	.10
109	Willie Randolph	.10

111	Dave Righetti	.15
117	*Bob Tewksbury*	.12
120	Dave Winfield	1.00
121	Steve Buechele	.08
122	*Ed Correa*	.15
123	Scott Fletcher	.08
124	Jose Guzman	.08
125	Toby Harrah	.08
127	Charlie Hough	.08
128	*Pete Incaviglia*	1.25
130	Oddibe McDowell	.10
131	*Dale Mohorcic* (FC)	.20
132	Pete O'Brien	.10
134	Larry Parrish	.08
136	Darrell Porter	.08
137	Jeff Russell	.10
138	*Ruben Sierra*	10.00
140	Gary Ward	.08
142	*Mitch Williams*	.60
143	*Bobby Witt*	.60
147	*Chuck Cary*	.10
148	Darnell Coles	.08
149	Dave Collins	.08
150	Darrell Evans	.12
151	Kirk Gibson	.20
155	*Eric King*	.20
156	Chet Lemon	.08
158	Jack Morris	.30
160	Lance Parrish	.20
161	Dan Petry	.08
164	Frank Tanana	.08
165	Walt Terrell	.08
167	Alan Trammell	.30
168	Lou Whitaker	.25
170	Steve Bedrosian	.12
171	Don Carman	.10
174	Kevin Gross	.08
175	Von Hayes	.15
179	*Mike Maddux* (FC)	.15
183	*Bruce Ruffin* (FC)	.20
185	Juan Samuel	.12
187	Mike Schmidt	1.50
190	Kent Tekulve	.08
191	Milt Thompson	.08
192	Glenn Wilson	.08
193	Buddy Bell	.10
194	Tom Browning	.10
196	Dave Concepcion	.12
197	Kal Daniels	.25

204 Barry Larkin

198	Eric Davis	.50
200	Bo Diaz	.08
201	Nick Esasky	.15
202	John Franco	.12
204	*Barry Larkin* (FC)	7.00
206	*Rob Murphy* (FC)	.10
208	Dave Parker	.20
209	Tony Perez	.15
213	Pete Rose	.60
214	Mario Soto	.08
215	*Kurt Stillwell*	.25
218	*Carl Willis* (FC)	.10
219	Jesse Barfield	.15
220	George Bell	.25
222	*John Cerutti*	.20
223	Jim Clancy	.08
224	*Mark Eichhorn*	.15
225	Tony Fernandez	.20
227	Kelly Gruber	.25
228	Tom Henke	.08
232	Jimmy Key	.12
236	Lloyd Moseby	.10
238	Dave Stieb	.12
240	Ernie Whitt	.08
241	*Andy Allanson*	.15
242	*Scott Bailes*	.20
246	Brett Butler	.08
249	Joe Carter	1.50

269 Will Clark

251	Julio Franco	.35
252	Mel Hall	.08
253	Brook Jacoby	.10
254	Phil Niekro	.20
260	Cory Snyder	.10
261	Pat Tabler	.08
263	*Rich Yett* (FC)	.12
264	*Mike Aldrete*	.15
266	Vida Blue	.10
269	*Will Clark*	20.00
270	Chili Davis	.08
271	Mark Davis	.12
272	*Kelly Downs* (FC)	.20
278	Jeff Leonard	.08
281	Bob Melvin (FC)	.08
283	Jeff Robinson	.08
285	*Rob Thompson*	1.00
286	Jose Uribe	.08
289	Jack Clark	.15
290	Vince Coleman	.25
292	Danny Cox	.08
295	Bob Forsch	.08
296	Tom Herr	.10
297	Ricky Horton	.08
302	*Mike LaValliere*	.25
303	*Greg Mathews* (FC)	.15
304	Willie McGee	.12
305	Jose Oquendo	.10
306	Terry Pendleton	.10
308	Ozzie Smith	.15
310	John Tudor	.10
311	Andy Van Slyke	.50
312	Todd Worrell	.12
314	Hubie Brooks	.10
315	Tim Burke	.12
316	Andre Dawson	.80
319	Andres Galarraga	.10
323	Vance Law	.08
328	Tim Raines	.25
329	Jeff Reardon	.30
330	*Luis Rivera* (FC)	.10
331	*Bob Sebra* (FC)	.10
332	Bryn Smith	.10
334	Tim Wallach	.12
338	*Chris Bosio* (FC)	.25
339	*Glenn Braggs* (FC)	.20
342	*Bryan Clutterbuck* (FC)	.10
343	Cecil Cooper	.12
344	Rob Deer	.10
346	Ted Higuera	.20
348	*Tim Leary* (FC)	.20
350	Paul Molitor	.50
354	*Dan Plesac*	.20
358	*Dale Sveum*	.20
360	Bill Wegman (FC)	.10
361	Robin Yount	1.25
363	*Scott Bankhead*	.30
366	George Brett	.85
368	Mark Gubicza	.12
369	*Bo Jackson*	8.00
370	Danny Jackson	.15
371	*Mike Kingery*	.15
375	Hal McRae	.10
379	Bret Saberhagen	.35
381	Lonnie Smith	.10
383	Frank White	.10
384	Willie Wilson	.12
389	Jose Canseco	7.00
395	Jay Howell	.10
396	Dave Kingman	.15
397	Carney Lansford	.12
398	*David Leiper* (FC)	.12
399	*Bill Mooneyham*	.10
402	Tony Phillips	.10
404	Jose Rijo	.20
405	*Terry Steinbach* (FC)	.80
406	Dave Stewart	.12

407 Mickey Tettleton .... .10
414 Steve Garvey .... .25
415 Goose Gossage .... .15
416 Tony Gwynn 1.75
420 *John Kruk* 5.00
425 Kevin McReynolds .... .15
427 Bip Roberts 1.00
429 Benito Santiago .... .60
440 Pedro Guerrero .... .15
441 Orel Hershiser .... .30
445 Bill Madlock .... .12
446 Mike Marshall .... .10
453 Steve Sax .... .15
457 Fernando Valenzuela ...... .25
459 Bob Welch .... .10
466 Storm Davis .... .15
474 Fred Lynn .... .15
476 Eddie Murray .... .65
478 Cal Ripken Jr. 3.00
482 Jim Traber (FC) .... .10
485 Harold Baines .... .15
488 Ivan Calderon .... .20
489 *John Cangelosi* .... .12
490 Steve Carlton .... .70
494 Jose DeLeon .... .15
496 Carlton Fisk .... .75
497 Ozzie Guillen .... .10
507 *Bobby Thigpen* (FC) .... .60
508 Greg Walker .... .10
511 *Paul Assenmacher* .... .15
516 Ken Griffey .... .15
518 Bob Horner .... .12
522 Dale Murphy .... .40
528 Ted Simmons .... .12
529 Zane Smith .... .15
530 Bruce Sutter .... .12
531 *Andres Thomas* .... .20
533 • Allan Anderson (FC) ...... .15
536 Bert Blyleven .... .12
537 Tom Brunansky .... .10
540 Gary Gaetti .... .15
544 Kent Hrbek .... .15
549 Kirby Puckett 4.00
554 Frank Viola .... .20
556 Ron Cey .... .10
557 Jody Davis .... .08
558 Ron Davis .... .06
561 Shawon Dunston .... .15
563 Dennis Eckersley .... .15

604 Barry Bonds

566 Guy Hoffman .... .08
570 *Jamie Moyer* (FC) .... .25
572 Ryne Sandberg 3.00
574 Lee Smith .... .35
576 Rick Sutcliffe .... .12
580 Phil Bradley .... .12
584 Alvin Davis .... .12
585 *Lee Guetterman* (FC) .... .15
589 Mark Langston .... .20
590 Mike Moore .... .12
595 *Rey Quinonez*
     (Quinones) .... .10
596 Harold Reynolds .... .15
597 Billy Swift .... .12
598 Danny Tartabull .... .50
602 *Rafael Belliard* (FC) .... .30
604 *Barry Bonds* 30.00
605 *Bobby Bonilla* 4.00
609 *Mike Diaz* (FC) .... .15
611 *Barry Jones* (FC) .... .12
618 Johnny Ray .... .10
619 Rick Reuschel .... .10
621 Rick Rhoden .... .10
625 Youthful Power (Jose
     Canseco, Pete
     Incaviglia) .... .75
628 Rookie All-Stars (Jose
     Canseco, Wally Joyner) .. .80

629 Magic Mets (Gary Carter, Sid Fernandez, Dwight Gooden, Keith Hernandez, Darryl Strawberry) .... **.30**

633 AL Pitcher's Nightmare (Jose Canseco, Kirby Puckett, Jim Rice) **1.00**

634 All-Star Battery (Gary Carter, Roger Clemens) .... **.40**

636 Big Bats at First Sack (Glenn Davis, Eddie Murray)....... **.20**

637 On Base (Wade Boggs, Keith Hernandez) .... **.25**

638 Sluggers from Left Side (Don Mattingly, Darryl Strawberry)....................... **.90**

639 Former MVP's (Dave Parker, Ryne Sandberg) .... **.20**

640 Dr. K and Super K (Roger Clemens, Dwight Gooden) **1.25**

644 Major League Prospects (*Dave Clark, Greg Swindell* (FC))................ **1.75**

646 Major League Prospects (*Willie Fraser, Devon White* (FC))................... **2.00**

647 Major League Prospects (*Jerry Browne, Mike Stanley* (FC)) .... **.70**

648 Major League Prospects (*Phil Lombardi, Dave Magadan* (FC)) .... **.50**

650 Major League Prospects (*Randy Asadoor, Jimmy Jones* (FC)) .... **.25**

651 Major League Prospects (*Marvin Freeman* (FC), *Tracy Jones*) .... **.25**

652 Major League Prospects (*Kevin Seitzer, John Stefero* (FC) .... **.60**

1987 FLEER UPDATE

Following a custom that began in 1984, Fleer continued with its Update series in 1987. A checklist and 131 player cards are included, numbered U-1 through U-132, and arranged alphabetically (the letter "U" has been omitted from the following list) available solely through hobby dealers in a specially designed collector's box. Fleer finally added Mark McGwire to this year's edition. Additional newcomers who make the set appealing are Mike Greenwell, Kevin Mitchell, Fred McGriff, and Matt Williams. A total of 44 cards are included in this edition that are not in the 1987 Topps Traded set.

		MINT
Complete set		**$14.00**
Commons		**.06**

1 Scott Bankhead............ $ **.15**
2 Eric Bell (FC) .... **.15**
5 Mike Birkbeck (FC).......... **.20**
6 Randy Bockus (FC).......... **.10**
7 Rod Booker (FC) .... **.10**
8 Thad Bosley .... **.10**
9 Greg Brock .... **.10**
10 Bob Brower (FC) .... **.15**
11 Chris Brown..................... **.10**
12 Jerry Browne .... **.10**
13 Ralph Bryant .... **.10**
14 DeWayne Buice (FC) ...... **.20**
15 Ellis Burks (FC) **1.00**

16 Casey Candaele (FC) ..... .15
17 Steve Carlton .... .40
19 Chuck Crim (FC) .... .15
20 Mark Davidson (FC) .... .20
21 Mark Davis .... .10
22 Storm Davis..................... .10
24 Andre Dawson................. .40
26 Rick Dempsey .... .10
28 Dave Dravecky .... .10
29 Mike Dunne (FC)............. .20
30 Dennis Eckersley .... .20
31 Cecil Fielder 1.75
32 Brian Fisher .... .10
33 Willie Fraser .... .10
34 Ken Gerhart (FC) .... .15
36 Dan Gladden .... .15
37 Mike Greenwell (FC) 1.25
41 Mickey Hatcher .... .15
44 Mike Henneman (FC)...... .30
45 Guy Hoffman .... .15
47 Chuck Jackson (FC)........ .20
48 Mike Jackson (FC) .... .25
49 Reggie Jackson............... .60
50 Chris James .... .25
51 Dion James .... .15
52 Stan Javier .... .15
53 Stan Jefferson (FC)......... .20
54 Jimmy Jones .... .10
55 Tracy Jones .... .20
56 Terry Kennedy................. .15
57 Mike Kingery .... .15
59 Gene Larkin (FC) .... .20
60 Mike LaValliere............... .10
62 Terry Leach .... .08
63 Rick Leach .... .10
65 Jim Lindeman (FC)........... .10
66 Bill Long (FC) .... .15
67 Mike Loynd (FC)............ .15
68 Greg Maddux (FC) 4.00
69 Bill Madlock .... .20
70 Dave Magadan................. .20
71 Joe Magrane (FC) .... .15
72 Fred Manrique (FC)......... .15
73 Mike Mason .... .06
74 Lloyd McClendon (FC) ..... .15
75 Fred McGriff (FC) 3.00
76 Mark McGwire (FC)...... 3.25
78 Kevin McReynolds .... .15
81 John Mitchell (FC) .... .10

76 Mark McGwire

82 Kevin Mitchell .... .80
84 Jeff Musselman (FC)....... .25
85 Randy Myers (FC)............ .35
87 Joe Niekro .... .10
88 Tom Nieto........................ .06
90 Matt Nokes (FC)............. .45
93 Jose Nunez (FC) .... .25
94 Paul O'Neill .... .30
95 Jim Paciorek .... .15
96 Lance Parrish.................. .20
97 Bill Pecota (FC) .... .15
98 Tony Pena....................... .15
99 Luis Polonia (FC) .... .50
100 Randy Ready .... .15
101 Jeff Reardon................. .15
102 Gary Redus .... .08
103 Rick Rhoden................. .10
104 Wally Ritchie (FC) .... .15
105 Jeff Robinson (FC) .... .15
108 Kevin Seitzer .... .30
110 John Smiley (FC) .... .60
115 B.J. Surhoff (FC) .... .20
116 Greg Swindell................. .50
117 Danny Tartabull.............. .35
121 Andy Van Slyke............... .15
123 Devon White................... .50
129 Matt Williams (FC)......... 5.00
131 Matt Young........................ .06

1987 TOPPS

Topps provided collectors with a blast from the past in its 1987 set. Cards use a simulated wood-grain finish for a border, much like the 1962 Topps or 1955 Bowman sets. Aside from the use of the team logo, a generous photo space is largely unobstructed. For the first time since 1972, player positions did not appear on the card fronts. Although it was first seen in the U.S. Olympic baseball team subset in 1985, Mark McGwire's 1987 Topps card became the hottest "rookie" in this set. Barry Bonds, Will Clark, Mike Greenwell, and Ruben Sierra round out the popular first-timers spotlighted in 1987. Watch for notable but unidentified players on team leader cards.

		MINT
Complete set		$25.00
Commons		.05

1 Record Breaker (Roger Clemens) .... $ .50
2 Record Breaker (Jim Deshaies) .... .07
3 Record Breaker (Dwight Evans) .... .07
4 Record Breaker (Dave Lopes) .... .07
5 Record Breaker (Dave Righetti) .... .07
6 Record Breaker (Ruben Sierra) .... .20
7 Record Breaker (Todd Worrell) .... .07
8 Terry Pendleton .... .20
10 Cecil Cooper .... .10
11 Indian Ldrs (Jack Aker, Chris Bando, Phil Niekro) .07
12 *Jeff Sellers* (FC) .... .10
13 Nick Esasky .... .10
14 Dave Stewart .... .15
15 Claudell Washington .... .07
17 Pete O'Brien .... .10
18 Dick Howser .... .05
20 Gary Carter .... .20
21 Mark Davis .... .10
22 Doug DeCinces .... .07
23 Lee Smith .... .20
25 Bert Blyleven .... .12
26 Greg Brock .... .07
28 Rick Dempsey .... .07

29 Jimmy Key .... .10
30 Tim Raines .... .15
31 Braves Ldrs (Glenn Hubbard, Rafael Ramirez) .... .07
32 Tim Leary .... .07
33 Andy Van Slyke .... .20
34 Jose Rijo .... .15
35 Sid Bream .... .07
36 *Eric King* .... .15
37 Marvell Wynne .... .05
38 Dennis Leonard .... .07
39 Marty Barrett .... .07
40 Dave Righetti................... .12
41 Bo Diaz .... .07
42 Gary Redus .... .05
45 Jim Presley .... .07
46 Danny Gladden .... .05
47 Dennis Powell .... .05
48 Wally Backman .... .05
49 Terry Harper.................... .05
50 Dave Smith...................... .07
51 Mel Hall .... .10
52 Keith Atherton .... .05
53 Ruppert Jones .... .05
54 Bill Dawley...................... .05
55 Tim Wallach .... .10
56 Brewers Ldrs (Jamie Cocanower, Paul Molitor, Charlie Moore, Herm Starrette) .... .07
57 *Scott Nielsen* (FC)............ .10
60 Tony Pena .... .07
61 *Bobby Thigpen* (FC) .... .15
62 Bobby Meacham .... .05
63 Fred Toliver (FC).............. .07

320 Barry Bonds

1987 Topps

420 Will Clark

147	Randy Niemann	.05
148	Dave Collins	.07
149	Ray Searage	.05
150	Wade Boggs	.50
151	Mike LaCoss	.05
152	Toby Harrah	.05
153	*Duane Ward* (FC)	.25
154	Tom O'Malley	.05
155	Eddie Whitson	.07
156	Mariners Ldrs (Bob Kearney, Phil Regan, Matt Young)	.07
158	Tim Teufel	.05
159	Ed Olwine	.05
160	Julio Franco	.15
161	Steve Ontiveros	.05
162	*Mike LaValliere*	.15
165	Jeff Reardon	.15
166	● Bob Boone	.07
167	*Jim Deshaies*	.10
168	Lou Piniella	.10
169	Ron Washington	.05
170	Future Stars (Bo Jackson)	1.25
171	*Chuck Cary* (FC)	.10
172	Ron Oester	.05
173	Alex Trevino	.05
174	Henry Cotto	.07
176	Steve Buechele	.05
177	Keith Moreland	.05
178	Cecil Fielder	1.25
180	Chris Brown	.05
181	Cardinals Ldrs (Mike LaValliere, Ozzie Smith, Ray Soff)	.10
182	Lee Lacy	.05
183	Andy Hawkins	.07
184	*Bobby Bonilla*	.80
185	Roger McDowell	.10
186	Bruce Benedict	.05
187	Mark Huismann	.05
188	Tony Phillips	.07
189	Joe Hesketh	.05
190	Jim Sundberg	.07
191	Charles Hudson	.05
192	Cory Snyder (FC)	.15
193	Roger Craig	.07
194	Kirk McCaskill	.07
195	Mike Pagliarulo	.10
198	Lee Mazzilli	.05
199	Mariano Duncan	.10
200	Pete Rose	.50
201	*John Cangelosi*	.10
203	*Mike Kingery* (FC)	.10
204	Sammy Stewart	.05
205	Graig Nettles	.10
206	Twins Ldrs (Tim Laudner, Frank Viola)	.07
207	George Frazier	.05
208	John Shelby	.07
209	Rick Schu	.05
210	Lloyd Moseby	.07
211	John Morris (FC)	.05
212	Mike Fitzgerald	.05
213	*Randy Myers* (FC)	.30
214	Omar Moreno	.05
215	Mark Langston	.15
216	Future Stars (B.J. Surhoff (FC))	.50
217	Chris Codiroli	.05
218	Sparky Anderson	.07
219	Cecilio Guante	.05
220	Joe Carter	.60
221	Vern Ruhle	.05
222	Denny Walling	.05
223	Charlie Leibrandt	.05
224	Wayne Tolleson	.05
225	Mike Smithson	.05

226	Max Venable	.05
227	Jamie Moyer (FC)	.15
229	Mike Birkbeck (FC)	.15
230	Don Baylor	.10
231	Giants Ldrs (Bob Brenly, Mike Krukow)	.07
232	Reggie Williams	.10
233	Russ Morman (FC)	.10
234	Pat Sheridan	.05
235	Alvin Davis	.12
236	Tommy John	.15
240	Steve Balboni	.07
241	Danny Heep	.05
242	Rick Mahler	.05
243	Whitey Herzog	.07
247	Jeff Reed (FC)	.07
250	Teddy Higuera	.10
252	Denny Martinez	.12
254	*Bob Tewksbury*	.15
255	Juan Samuel	.10
256	Royals Ldrs (George Brett, Frank White)	.15
257	Bob Forsch	.07
259	*Mike Greenwell* (FC)	.70
260	Vida Blue	.07
261	*Ruben Sierra* (FC)	1.50
265	Darrell Evans	.10
266	Jeff Hamilton (FC)	.10
267	Howard Johnson	.25
272	Andres Galarraga	.15
279	*Dan Plesac*	.15
280	Jeffrey Leonard	.10
281	Reds Ldrs (Bo Diaz, Bill Gullickson, Pete Rose)	.10
283	*Doug Drabek* (FC)	.60
291	*Mitch Williams* (FC)	.25
292	Franklin Stubbs	.07
293	Bob Rodgers	.07
295	• Len Dykstra	.15
296	*Andres Thomas*	.07
300	Reggie Jackson	.50
301	*Luis Aquino* (FC)	.07
302	Bill Schroeder	.07
304	Phil Garner	.07
305	John Franco	.10
306	Red Sox Ldrs (Rich Gedman, John McNamara, Tom Seaver)	.07
307	*Lee Guetterman* (FC)	.07
310	Frank Viola	.15
311	Turn Back the Clock (Rickey Henderson)	.25
312	Turn Back the Clock (Reggie Jackson)	.10
313	Turn Back the Clock (Roberto Clemente)	.10
314	Turn Back the Clock (Carl Yastrzemski)	.10
315	Turn Back the Clock (Maury Wills)	.10
318	Jim Fregosi	.07
319	*Greg Swindell* (FC)	.50
320	*Barry Bonds*	3.00
325	Garry Templeton	.07
326	Mark Gubicza	.10
327	*Dale Sveum*	.10
328	Bob Welch	.10
330	Mike Scott	.10
331	Mets Ldrs (Gary Carter, Keith Hernandez, Dave Johnson, Darryl Strawberry)	.10
334	Ed Correa	.10
335	Candy Maldonado	.07
336	• *Allan Anderson* (FC)	.10
340	Roger Clemens	1.25
342	Bob James	.07
343	Hal Lanier	.07
344	Joe Niekro	.10
345	Andre Dawson	.35
346	Shawon Dunston	.12
347	Mickey Brantley (FC)	.07
349	Storm Davis	.07
350	Keith Hernandez	.12
351	Gene Garber	.07
355	Don Carman	07
356	White Sox Ldrs (Ed Brinkman, Julio Cruz)	.07
357	*Steve Fireovid* (FC)	.07
360	Pedro Guerrero	.12
366	*Mark McGwire*	1.75
370	Fred Lynn	.10
371	*Mark Eichhorn*	.10
375	Ron Guidry	.12
380	Rich Gossage	.15
385	Orel Hershiser	.20
393	Pete Rose	.25

400	George Brett	.35
405	Brook Jacoby	.07
406	Yankees Ldrs (Rickey Henderson, Don Mattingly)	.15
409	Milt Thompson	.10
410	Fernando Valenzuela	.12
411	Darnell Coles	.05
412	Eric Davis	.40
415	*Bobby Witt*	.25
417	Pat Perry (FC)	.07
419	*Mark Portugal* (FC)	.10
420	*Will Clark*	2.00
421	Jose DeLeon	.07
422	Jack Howell	.07
425	Tom Seaver	.35
429	*Tim Pyznarski* (FC)	.07
430	Mike Schmidt	.40
431	Dodgers Ldrs (Tom Niedenfuer, Ron Perranoski, Alex Trevino)	.07
433	*Ed Hearn* (FC)	.07
435	Bruce Sutter	.15
436	*Andy Allanson*	.07
438	*Kelly Downs* (FC)	.10
440	Willie McGee	.10
441	*Dave Leiper* (FC)	.07
444	Jeff Russell	.07
445	Dave Lopes	.07
446	*Chuck Finley* (FC)	.40
448	*Chris Bosio* (FC)	.15
449	*Pat Dodson* (FC)	.10
450	Kirby Puckett	1.25
452	Dave Henderson	.10
453	*Scott Terry* (FC)	.07
455	Mike Boddicker	.07
456	A's Ldrs (Carney Lansford, Tony LaRussa, Mickey Tettleton, Dave Von Ohlen)	.07
458	Kelly Gruber (FC)	.15
459	Dennis Eckersley	.15
460	Darryl Strawberry	.30
463	Tom Candiotti	.07
464	Butch Wynegar	.05
465	Todd Worrell	.25
466	Kal Daniels (FC)	.20
469	*Mike Diaz* (FC)	.15

470	Dave Dravecky	.15
472	Bill Doran	.07
476	Danny Tartabull	.75
479	*Bob Sebra* (FC)	.07
480	Jim Rice	.15
481	Phillies Ldrs (Von Hayes, Juan Samuel, Glenn Wilson)	.07
484	Jim Traber (FC)	.07
485	Tony Fernandez	.10
490	Dale Murphy	.15
491	*Ron Karkovice* (FC)	.07
494	*Barry Jones* (FC)	.10
495	Gorman Thomas	.10
497	*Dale Mohorcic* (FC)	.10
499	*Bruce Ruffin* (FC)	.10
500	Don Mattingly	.40
506	Orioles Ldrs (Rich Bordi, Rick Dempsey, Earl Weaver)	.07
508	Scott Bankhead	.10
512	*Dave Magadan* (FC)	.20
516	Ted Simmons	.10
520	Jack Clark	.10
521	Rick Reuschel	.10
525	Phil Bradley	.07
530	Tony Gwynn	.50
531	Astros Ldrs (Yogi Berra, Hal Lanier, Denis Menke, Gene Tenace)	.07
536	*Terry Mulholland* (FC)	.40
541	*Rafael Belliard* (FC)	.10
547	Rob Deer	.15
548	Bill Mooneyham (FC)	.07
550	*Pete Incaviglia*	.30
553	*Mike Maddux* (FC)	.10
555	Dennis Rasmussen	.07
556	Angels Ldrs (Bob Boone, Marcel Lachemann, Mike Witt)	.07
557	*John Cerutti*	.07
559	Lance McCullers	.07
560	Glenn Davis	.15
561	*Rey Quinones*	.07
562	*Bryan Clutterbuck* (FC)	.07
567	*Greg Mathews* (FC)	.10
568	Earl Weaver	.07
569	Wade Rowdon (FC)	.07
570	Sid Fernandez	.10

620 Jose Canseco

1987 TOPPS TRADED

One of the least expensive Topps Traded sets of the past decade, this 132-card issue features more than a few notable first-card appearances. David Cone, Joe Magrane, Fred McGriff, Benny Santiago, and Matt Williams lead the parade of newcomers. One surprising new face in the Traded set is that of veteran outfielder Kevin McReynolds. The Mets outfielder refused to sign baseball card contracts for several years before finally relenting in 1987. Managers Larry Bowa, Tom Trebelhorn, and Cal Ripken, Sr., are also included. These extras had been overlooked by other card companies.

	MINT
Complete set	$10.00
Commons	.06

1	Bill Almon	$ .06
2	Scott Bankhead	.08
3	Eric Bell (FC)	.08
5	Juan Berenguer	.06
7	Thad Bosley	.06
8	Larry Bowa	.10
9	Greg Brock	.10
10	Bob Brower (FC)	.15
11	Jerry Browne (FC)	.30
12	Ralph Bryant (FC)	.10
13	DeWayne Buice (FC)	.15
14	Ellis Burks (FC)	.80
15	Ivan Calderon	.12
17	Casey Candaele (FC)	.10
18	John Cangelosi	.06
19	Steve Carlton	.30
20	Juan Castillo (FC)	.06
21	Rick Cerone	.06
22	Ron Cey	.10
24	Dave Cone (FC)	1.50
25	Chuck Crim (FC)	.15
27	Andre Dawson	.35
28	Rick Dempsey	.10
29	Doug Drabek	.35
30	Mike Dunne	.20
31	Dennis Eckersley	.25
33	Brian Fisher	.10
35	Willie Fraser (FC)	.15
37	Ken Gerhart (FC)	.15

27 Andre Dawson

46	Mike Henneman (FC)	.20
49	Brian Holton (FC)	.15
51	Danny Jackson (FC)	.25
52	Reggie Jackson	.40
53	Chris James (FC)	.10
54	Dion James	.40
55	Stan Jefferson (FC)	.20
56	Joe Johnson (FC)	.08
57	Terry Kennedy	.08
58	Mike Kingery	.08
59	Ray Knight	.10
60	Gene Larkin (FC)	.15
61	Mike LaValliere	.10

65	Jim Lindeman (FC)	.10	96	Luis Polonia (FC)	.50
67	Bill Long (FC)	.20	98	Jeff Reardon	.12
68	Barry Lyons (FC)	.15	99	Gary Redus	.08
69	Shane Mack	.50	101	Rick Rhoden	.10
70	Greg Maddux (FC)	3.00	103	Wally Ritchie (FC)	.10
71	Bill Madlock	.15	104	Jeff Robinson (FC)	.40
72	Joe Magrane (FC)	.15	109	Benny Santiago (FC)	.50
73	Dave Martinez (FC)	.15	110	Dave Schmidt	.08
74	Fred McGriff (FC)	2.50	111	Kevin Seitzer (FC)	.25
75	Mark McLemore (FC)	.10	114	John Smiley (FC)	.40
76	Kevin McReynolds (FC)	.20	116	Mike Stanley (FC)	.20
77	Dave Meads (FC)	.15	117	Terry Steinbach (FC)	.25
80	John Mitchell (FC)	.15	118	Les Straker (FC)	.20
81	Kevin Mitchell	.50	119	Jim Sundberg	.08
83	Jeff Musselman (FC)	.15	120	Danny Tartabull	.35
85	Graig Nettles	.10	121	Tom Trebelhorn	.08
88	Tom Niedenfuer	.08	122	Dave Valle (FC)	.15
89	Joe Niekro	.10	124	Andy Van Slyke	.20
91	Matt Nokes (FC)	.25	127	Bill Wilkinson (FC)	.15
93	Pat Pacillo	.15	128	Frank Williams	.08
94	Lance Parrish	.20	129	Matt Williams (FC)	2.50
95	Tony Pena	.10	131	Matt Young	.10

1988 DONRUSS

Known for gutsy speculation on unknowns while playing down prospective retirees, the 1988 Donruss set includes beginners such as Roberto Alomar, Mark Grace, and Gregg Jefferies. The 660-card set of standard-sized cards features the usual bizarre Donruss design, with off-beat borders of red, black and blue; Diamond Kings artwork; and a series of Rated Rookies. New was a 26-card separately numbered Bonus Card series with stars such as Cal Ripken, Jr. and Darryl Strawberry, but these cards came only in random wax packs. High-numbered cards—600 and up—were scarce early in 1988, causing a permanent price hike. Superstars commanding top dollar here include Wade Boggs, Don Mattingly, and Mark McGwire.

	MINT
Complete set	$20.00
Commons	.05

1	Mark McGwire (DK)	$ .35
2	Tim Raines (DK)	.10
3	Benito Santiago (DK)	.10
4	Alan Trammell (DK)	.10
5	Danny Tartabull (DK)	.15
6	Ron Darling (DK)	.07
7	Paul Molitor (DK)	.12
8	Devon White (DK)	.20
9	Andre Dawson (DK)	.20
10	Julio Franco (DK)	.10
11	Scott Fletcher (DK)	.05

12	Tony Fernandez (DK)	.12
13	Shane Rawley (DK)	.07
14	Kal Daniels (DK)	.10
15	Jack Clark (DK)	.15
16	• Dwight Evans (DK)	.12
17	• Tommy John (DK)	.15
18	Andy Van Slyke (DK)	.15
19	Gary Gaetti (DK)	.10
20	Mark Langston (DK)	.07
21	Will Clark (DK)	.50
22	Glenn Hubbard (DK)	.05
23	Billy Hatcher (DK)	.05
24	Bob Welch (DK)	.10
25	Ivan Calderon (DK)	.10
26	Cal Ripken, Jr. (DK)	.35
27	Checklist 1-27	.07
28	*Mackey Sasser* (RR) (FC)	.20
29	*Jeff Treadway* (RR) (FC)	.20
30	*Mike Campbell* (RR) (FC)	.12
31	*Lance Johnson* (RR) (FC)	.35
32	*Nelson Liriano* (RR) (FC)	.10
33	Shawn Abner (RR) (FC)	.12
34	*Roberto Alomar* (RR) (FC)	4.00
35	*Shawn Hillegas* (RR) (FC)	.10
36	Joey Meyer (RR)	.10
37	Kevin Elster (RR)	.15
38	*Jose Lind* (RR) (FC)	.25
39	Kirt Manwaring (RR) (FC)	.15
40	Mark Grace (RR) (FC)	1.25
41	*Jody Reed* (RR) (FC)	.35
42	*John Farrell* (RR) (FC)	.12
43	*Al Leiter* (RR) (FC)	.12
44	*Gary Thurman* (RR) (FC)	.12
45	*Vicente Palacios* (RR) (FC)	.15
46	*Eddie Williams* (RR) (FC)	.10
47	*Jack McDowell* (RR) (FC)	1.50
51	Roger Clemens	.50
53	Fernando Valenzuela	.10
54	Mark Gubicza	.07
58	*DeWayne Buice*	.07
59	Jose DeLeon	.07
60	Danny Cox	.05
61	Nolan Ryan	.75

62	Steve Bedrosian	.07
63	Tom Browning	.10
64	Mark Davis	.07
66	*Kevin Mitchell*	.25
68	Rick Sutcliffe	.10
69	Dwight Gooden	.25
71	Bert Blyleven	.12
72	Jimmy Key	.10
78	Dale Murphy	.12
79	Doug Drabek	.12
89	Mike Boddicker	.10
90	Ted Higuera	.10
91	Walt Terrell	.07
93	Dave Righetti	.10
94	Orel Hershiser	.15
96	Bret Saberhagen	.15
101	Bobby Witt	.10
102	George Brett	.25
103	Mickey Tettleton	.15
105	Mike Pagliarulo	.10
106	Mike Scioscia	.07
109	Dan Plesac	.10
110	Wally Joyner	.12
114	Benito Santiago	.15
118	Sid Fernandez	.10
122	Jeff Reardon	.10
123	John Franco	.10
127	Jack Morris	.20
137	Ozzie Guillen	.15
139	*Mike Jackson*	.10
140	*Joe Magrane*	.15
144	*Felix Fermin* (FC)	.10
146	Shawon Dunston	.10
148	Dave Stieb	.10
149	Frank Viola	.15
152	*Matt Nokes*	.20
153	Wade Boggs	.30
156	Julio Franco	.10
158	Terry Steinbach	.10
164	Tony Gwynn	.30
171	Cal Ripken	.65
172	*B.J. Surhoff*	.07
173	Lou Whitaker	.15
174	*Ellis Burks*	.30
175	Ron Guidry	.10
176	Steve Sax	.12
177	Danny Tartabull	.15
178	Carney Lansford	.10
182	Ivan Calderon	.10

183	Jack Clark	.10
184	Glenn Davis	.10
193	Alvin Davis	.10
194	Gary Gaetti	.10
195	Fred McGriff	.35
198	Rey Quinones	.05
199	Gary Carter	.12
202	Ken Griffey	.10
203	*Tommy Gregg* (FC)	.20
204	Will Clark	.50
205	John Kruk	.15
211	Harold Baines	.12
215	Chet Lemon	.05
216	Dwight Evans	.12
217	Don Mattingly	.30
218	Franklin Stubbs	.05
220	Bo Jackson	.30
222	Tim Wallach	.07
223	Ruben Sierra	.30
225	Frank White	.07
227	Greg Swindell	.12
228	Willie Randolph	.07
229	Mike Marshall	.07
230	Alan Trammell	.15
231	Eddie Murray	.25
232	Dale Sveum	.07
235	Bill Doran	.07
238	Bobby Bonilla	.25
240	Glenn Braggs	.10
242	Ryne Sandberg	.50
243	Phil Bradley	.07
245	Tom Brunansky	.07
247	Bobby Thigpen	.10
248	Fred Lynn	.15
249	Paul Molitor	.12
250	Darrell Evans	.10
251	Gary Ward	.07
252	Bruce Hurst	.10
253	Bob Welch	.10
254	Joe Carter	.15
255	Willie Wilson	.10
256	Mark McGwire	.50
258	Brian Downing	.07
259	Mike Stanley	.10
260	Carlton Fisk	.25
261	Billy Hatcher	.07
263	Ozzie Smith	.25
265	Kurt Stillwell	.10
269	Andre Dawson	.25

34 Roberto Alomar

275	Kirk Gibson	.12
277	Rickey Henderson	.25
278	Pedro Guerrero	.15
280	Kevin Seitzer	.12
283	Devon White	.15
288	Juan Samuel	.10
289	Kal Daniels	.10
291	Andy Van Slyke	.12
292	Lee Smith	.12
293	Vince Coleman	.12
295	Robin Yount	.25
296	*Jeff Robinson*	.10
297	*Todd Benzinger*	.20
298	Dave Winfield	.20
300	Checklist 240-345	.10
302	Jose Canseco	.40
304	Pete Incaviglia	.10
306	*Bill Long*	.10
307	Willie McGee	.12
308	*Ken Caminiti* (FC)	.25
315	*Paul Noce*	.10
316	Keith Hernandez	.12
317	Mark Langston	.15
319	Tony Fernandez	.12
320	Kent Hrbek	.15
323	Dave Magadan	.12
324	Rafael Palmeiro	.40
326	Barry Bonds	.65

654 Ron Gant

615	*Scott Lusader* (FC) .... .10		**640**	*David Wells* (FC) .... .25
617	Kevin McReynolds .... .15		**643**	*Keith Hughes* (FC) .... .12
625	Ripken Baseball Family (Billy Ripken, Cal Ripken, Jr., Cal Ripken, Sr.) .... .30		**644**	*Tom Glavine* (FC) **2.00**
			653	David Cone .... .40
628	*Matt Williams* **2.00**		**654**	*Ron Gant* (FC) **2.25**
635	*Roberto Kelly* (FC) **1.25**		**656**	George Bell .... .20
637	*Jay Bell* (FC) .... .50		**657**	*Gregg Jefferies* (FC) **2.25**
639	*Damon Berryhill* (FC) .... .12		**658**	*Todd Stottlemyre* (FC)..... .35
			659	*Geronimo Berroa* (FC)..... .15

1988 DONRUSS ROOKIES

Donruss marked its third year of producing "The Rookies" in 1988. Once again, a specially designed box held the set of 55 player cards and an unnumbered checklist. These rookie cards differ in design from the regular set only in border color and "The Rookies" logo in the lower-right portion of each card. But due to a lackluster crop of rookies, this set has just three who are in high demand: Roberto Alomar, Mark Grace, and Jack McDowell. Collectors have overlooked this edition in favor of the larger and more affordable fall issues from Fleer, Score, and Topps.

	MINT
Complete set	**$20.00**
Commons	.10

1 Mark Grace

1	Mark Grace	**$2.50**
3	Todd Frohwirth (FC)	.15
5	Shawn Abner....................	.10
6	Jose Cecena (FC)	.10
7	Dave Gallagher (FC)	.15
8	Mark Parent (FC).............	.15
11	Jay Buhner	.75
12	Pat Borders (FC)	.50
13	Doug Jennings (FC)	.15
14	Brady Anderson (FC)	**1.25**
15	Pete Stanicek	.10
16	Roberto Kelly.................	**1.00**
17	Jeff Treadway...................	.10
18	Walt Weiss (FC)	.25
19	Paul Gibson (FC)	.10
21	Melido Perez	.30
22	Steve Peters (FC)	.10

23	Craig Worthington (FC) ...	.15
27	Al Leiter	.15

28	Tim Belcher	.20	
29	Johnny Paredes (FC)	.10	
30	Chris Sabo (FC)	.80	
31	Damon Berryhill	.15	
32	Randy Milligan (FC)	.25	
33	Gary Thurman	.15	
34	Kevin Elster	.15	
35	Roberto Alomar	12.00	
36	Edgar Martinez	1.25	
37	Todd Stottlemyre	.45	
38	Joey Meyer	.10	
40	Jack McDowell	2.25	

41	Jose Bautista (FC)	.15
42	Sil Campusano (FC)	.10
43	John Dopson (FC)	.12
44	Jody Reed	.40
45	Darrin Jackson (FC)	.40
46	Mike Capel (FC)	.10
47	Ron Gant	2.25
50	Cris Carpenter (FC)	.15
51	Mackey Sasser	.25
52	Luis Alicea (FC)	.25
53	Bryan Harvey (FC)	1.50
55	Mike Macfarlane	.50

1988 FLEER

This 660-card set features backs that carry a wealth of information. Full career statistics and graphs showing performance in various ballparks are complemented by "At Their Best" individualized highlights. Card fronts are white, with a border of busy blue and red diagonals, while player photos feature blended backgrounds. Star combo cards join players by team or position, with Major League Prospects pairing off rookies, Mark Grace among them. Photos featuring surfboards or players with two gloves pleased some purchasers but offended others. As always, however, the greatest complaints concerned spotty distribution.

		MINT
Complete set		$35.00
Commons		.06

2	Don Baylor	$ .10
4	Bert Blyleven	.12
5	Tom Brunansky	.08
8	Mark Davidson (FC)	.08
10	Gary Gaetti	.10
11	Greg Gagne	.08
13	Kent Hrbek	.15
14	Gene Larkin	.20
19	Kirby Puckett	.90
20	Jeff Reardon	.20
21	Dan Schatzader (incorrect spelling)	.40
21	Dan Schatzeder (correct spelling)	.10
24	Les Straker (FC)	.10

25	Frank Viola	.15
26	Jack Clark	.15
27	Vince Coleman	.25
37	Lance Johnson (FC)	.60
40	Joe Magrane	.20
42	Willie McGee	.12
45	Tony Pena	.08
47	Ozzie Smith	.20
48	John Tudor	.10
50	Todd Worrell	.10
54	Darrell Evans	.10
55	Kirk Gibson	.15
57	Mike Henneman	.35
62	Scott Lusader (FC)	.15
63	Bill Madlock	.10
64	Jack Morris	.25
66	Matt Nokes	.35
67	Dan Petry	.08
68	Jeff Robinson (born 12/13/60 on back)	.25

68	*Jeff Robinson* (born 12/14/61 on back) ....**.10**
72	Walt Terrell ....**.08**
74	Alan Trammell ....**.25**
75	Lou Whitaker ....**.25**
78	Will Clark **1.50**
79	Chili Davis ....**.08**
80	Kelly Downs ....**.05**
84	Dave Henderson ....**.15**
88	Jeff Leonard ....**.08**
92	Kevin Mitchell ....**.75**
93	*Jon Perlman* (FC) ....**.08**
94	Rick Reuschel ....**.10**
99	Jose Uribe ....**.08**
100	*Mark Wasinger* (FC) ....**.10**
101	*Matt Williams* **4.00**
102	Jesse Barfield.................**.15**
103	George Bell ....**.25**
107	*Rob Ducey* (FC) ....**.10**
109	Tony Fernandez ....**.12**
110	Cecil Fielder ....**.80**
111	Kelly Gruber ....**.25**
112	Tom Henke......................**.08**
114	Jimmy Key......................**.10**
117	*Nelson Liriano* (FC) ....**.15**
118	Fred McGriff **1.50**
122	*Jose Nunez* ....**.25**
123	Dave Stieb......................**.10**
125	Duane Ward (FC).............**.20**
126	Ernie Whitt......................**.08**
129	*Mark Carreon* (FC) ....**.20**
130	Gary Carter ....**.15**
131	David Cone (FC) ....**.75**
132	Ron Darling ....**.10**
133	Len Dykstra....................**.12**
134	Sid Fernandez ....**.10**
135	Dwight Gooden ....**.25**
136	Keith Hernandez ....**.20**
137	*Gregg Jefferies* (FC) **4.00**
138	Howard Johnson ....**.40**
140	*Barry Lyons* (FC) ....**.10**
141	Dave Magadan ....**.25**
142	Roger McDowell..............**.10**
143	Kevin McReynolds ....**.15**
144	*Keith Miller* (FC) ....**.20**
145	*John Mitchell* (FC) ....**.10**
146	Randy Myers ....**.25**
147	Bob Ojeda ....**.08**
151	Darryl Strawberry ....**.40**

538 Ron Gant

152	Tim Teufel ....**.08**
155	*Jay Aldrich* (FC) ....**.08**
156	Chris Bosio......................**.08**
157	Glenn Braggs..................**.08**
161	Cecil Cooper ....**.10**
162	*Chuck Crim* ....**.10**
163	Rob Deer.........................**.08**
166	Ted Higuera ....**.10**
169	Paul Molitor ....**.15**
170	Juan Nieves ....**.08**
171	Dan Plesac......................**.10**
174	*Steve Stanicek* (FC) ....**.08**
175	B.J. Surhoff ....**.10**
176	Dale Sveum......................**.08**
178	Robin Yount ....**.50**
179	Hubie Brooks....................**.10**
180	Tim Burke ....**.08**
184	Andres Galarraga.............**.10**
187	Vance Law ....**.08**
193	Tim Raines ....**.20**
195	Bob Sebra ....**.08**
196	Bryn Smith ....**.08**
198	Tim Wallach ....**.10**
202	*Brad Arnsberg* (FC) ....**.10**
205	Henry Cotto ....**.08**
206	Mike Easler ....**.08**
207	Ron Guidry ....**.10**
209	Rickey Henderson............**.60**

407 Jack McDowell

340 John Smiley .... .50
341 Andy Van Slyke .... .15
344 Todd Benzinger (FC) .... .30
345 Wade Boggs .... .50
346 Tom Bolton (FC) .... .10
348 Ellis Burks 1.00
349 Roger Clemens 1.10
351 • Dwight Evans .... .15
352 Wes Gardner (FC) .... .10
354 Mike Greenwell .... .35
355 Sam Horn (FC) .... .20
356 Bruce Hurst .... .10
357 John Marzano (FC) .... .08
360 Jody Reed (FC) .... .40
361 Jim Rice .... .20
366 Jeff Sellers .... .08
372 Mike Campbell (FC) .... .10
373 Alvin Davis .... .12
375 Dave Hengel (FC) .... .08
377 Mark Langston .... .17
378 Edgar Martinez (FC) 1.50
379 Mike Moore .... .10
382 Donnell Nixon (FC) .... .10
385 Jim Presley .... .08
388 Harold Reynolds .... .10
390 Bill Wilkinson (FC) .... .08
391 Harold Baines .... .12
394 Ivan Calderon .... .15
395 Jose DeLeon .... .10
397 Carlton Fisk .... .40
398 Ozzie Guillen .... .08
403 Bill Lindsey (FC) .... .08
404 Bill Long (FC) .... .10
406 Fred Manrique .... .08
407 Jack McDowell (FC) 3.50
410 Bobby Thigpen .... .15
411 Greg Walker .... .08
412 Kenny Williams .... .08
415 Andre Dawson .... .35
419 Shawon Dunston .... .20
421 Les Lancaster (FC) .... .10
423 Greg Maddux .... .75
425 Keith Moreland (bunting, photo is Jody Davis) ... 1.50
425 Keith Moreland (standing, correct photo) .... .10
429 Rafael Palmeiro (FC) 1.50
431 Ryne Sandberg 1.00
433 Lee Smith .... .10

539 Tom Glavine

435 Rick Sutcliffe .... .10
440 Kevin Bass .... .08
441 Ken Caminiti (FC) .... .25
442 Rocky Childress (FC) .... .08
443 Jose Cruz .... .10
445 Glenn Davis .... .12
453 Dave Meads .... .10
455 Nolan Ryan 1.50
459 Robbie Wine (FC) .... .10
460 Gerald Young (FC) .... .10
462 Jerry Browne (photo is Bob Brower) 1.50
462 Jerry Browne (correct photo) .... .10
465 Cecil Espy (FC) .... .20
470 Pete Incaviglia .... .15
471 Paul Kilgus (FC) .... .10
475 Pete O'Brien .... .10
478 Jeff Russell .... .10
479 Ruben Sierra 1.00
482 Mitch Williams .... .10
485 Bob Boone .... .15
486 Bill Buckner .... .10
487 DeWayne Buice .... .10
493 Wally Joyner .... .30
502 Johnny Ray .... .10
505 Don Sutton .... .20
506 Devon White .... .20

1988 FLEER UPDATE

This 132-card fall "extension" set, the fifth such release, failed to compete successfully with the Olympian-filled Topps Traded set. Cards for Roberto Alomar, Mark Grace, and John Smoltz are the most precious. And there is one unusual pairing in the set: Card U-113, supposedly of Tommy Gregg, actually depicts Pirates teammate Randy Milligan (Milligan also got his own card, number U-115). Unlike the alphabetical system used by Topps, Fleer Updates are arranged by team. (The "U" that appears on the actual cards has been omitted from the following list.)

	MINT
Complete set	**$18.00**
Commons	**.06**

74 John Smoltz

1	Jose Bautista (FC)	**$ .15**
4	Craig Worthington (FC) ...	**.15**
5	Mike Boddicker................	**.10**
8	Lee Smith	**.20**
10	John Trautwein (FC)	**.10**
11	Sherman Corbett (FC).....	**.08**
12	Chili Davis	**.10**
14	Bryan Harvey (FC)	**1.50**
16	Dave Gallagher (FC)	**.10**
19	Melido Perez	**.20**
20	Jose Segura (FC).............	**.08**
21	Andy Allanson	**.08**
26	Paul Gibson (FC)	**.10**
27	Don Heinkel (FC)	**.08**
30	Luis Salazar	**.08**
31	Mike McFarlane (Macfarlane) (FC).............	**.40**
32	Jeff Montgomery	**.08**
34	Israel Sanchez (FC)	**.06**

35	Kurt Stillwell	.10
37	Don August (FC)	.10
38	Darryl Hamilton (FC)	.30
39	Jeff Leonard	.10
40	Joey Meyer	.15
43	Tom Herr	.06
46	John Candelaria	.10
47	Jack Clark	.15
48	Richard Dotson	.08
49	Al Leiter (FC)	.10
52	Todd Burns (FC)	.10
53	Dave Henderson	.10
55	Dave Parker	.12
56	Walt Weiss	.20
57	Bob Welch	.10
60	Mike Jackson	.12
61	Bill Swift	.20
65	Pat Borders (FC)	.50
66	Sil Campusano (FC)	.10
68	Todd Stottlemyre (FC)	.90
69	David Wells	.20
74	John Smoltz (FC)	5.00
75	Damon Berryhill	.08
76	Goose Gossage	.15
77	Mark Grace	2.50
78	Darrin Jackson	.10
80	Jeff Pico (FC)	.20
81	Gary Varsho (FC)	.10
82	Tim Birtsas	.10
83	Rob Dibble (FC)	.50
84	Danny Jackson	.10
85	Paul O'Neill	.15
86	Jose Rijo	.20
87	Chris Sabo (FC)	.80
88	John Fishel (FC)	.08
89	Craig Biggio (FC)	1.25
92	Louie Meadows (FC)	.08
93	Kirk Gibson	.10
99	John Dopson (FC)	.10
100	Brian Holman (FC)	.25
104	Kevin Elster	.10
105	Jeff Innis (FC)	.10
106	Mackey Sasser (FC)	.15
110	Ricky Jordan (FC)	.35
113	Tommy Gregg (photo is Randy Milligan) (FC)	.15
115	Randy Milligan (FC)	.40
116	Luis Alicea (FC)	.15
122	Roberto Alomar (FC)	10.00
128	Brett Butler	.10

1988 SCORE

Score's 660-card 1988 set was applauded for information-filled backs and color photo insets. Fronts feature a simple bold border in one of six colors. Player names and positions are prominently centered at the bottom with the Score logo at the lower right. The cards were sold in poly-bags that could not be tampered with and resealed (unlike the wax packs from Donruss, Fleer, and Topps). Initially, many cards from the poly-bags were damaged, but they were replaced by the company. Subsets include Rookie Prospects, 1987 Highlights, and a five-card salute to Reggie Jackson. (Rookie Prospects are identified on the following list with the abbreviation RP.)

		MINT
Complete set		$20.00
Commons		.04
1	Don Mattingly	$ .35
2	Wade Boggs	.25

3	Tim Raines	.12
4	Andre Dawson	.15
5	Mark McGwire	.50
6	Kevin Seitzer	.10
7	Wally Joyner	.15
8	Jesse Barfield	.08
9	Pedro Guerrero	.10

10	Eric Davis	.20
11	George Brett	.20
12	Ozzie Smith	.20
13	Rickey Henderson	.35
14	Jim Rice	.10
15	*Matt Nokes*	.25
16	Mike Schmidt	.40
17	Dave Parker	.12
18	Eddie Murray	.15
19	Andres Galarraga	.08
20	Tony Fernandez	.10
21	Kevin McReynolds	.10
22	B.J. Surhoff	.06
23	Pat Tabler	.06
24	Kirby Puckett	.40
25	Benny Santiago	.15
26	Ryne Sandberg	.50
27	Kelly Downs	.06
28	Jose Cruz	.06
29	Pete O'Brien	.06
30	Mark Langston	.12
31	Lee Smith	.10
32	Juan Samuel	.10
33	Kevin Bass	.06
35	Steve Sax	.12
36	John Kruk	.15
37	Alan Trammell	.15
38	Chris Bosio	.06
39	Brook Jacoby	.06
40	Willie McGee	.10
41	Dave Magadan	.10
42	Fred Lynn	.10
43	Kent Hrbek	.12
44	Brian Downing	.08
45	Jose Canseco	.50
46	Jim Presley	.06
47	Mike Stanley	.06
48	Tony Pena	.06
49	David Cone	.35
50	Rick Sutcliffe	.08
51	Doug Drabek	.15
52	Bill Doran	.06
53	Mike Scioscia	.06
54	Candy Maldonado	.04
55	Dave Winfield	.25
56	Lou Whitaker	.15
57	Tom Henke	.08
58	Ken Gerhart	.04
59	Glenn Braggs	.08

78 Will Clark

60	Julio Franco	.15
61	Charlie Leibrandt	.06
62	Gary Gaetti	.10
63	• Bob Boone	.08
64	*Luis Polonia*	.35
65	• Dwight Evans	.10
66	Phil Bradley	.08
67	Mike Boddicker	.08
68	Vince Coleman	.15
69	Howard Johnson	.15
70	Tim Wallach	.08
71	Keith Moreland	.04
72	Barry Larkin	.30
73	Alan Ashby	.04
74	Rick Rhoden	.06
75	Darrell Evans	.08
76	Dave Stieb	.08
77	Dan Plesac	.08
78	Will Clark	.50
79	Frank White	.08
80	Joe Carter	.35
81	Mike Witt	.06
82	Terry Steinbach	.10
83	Alvin Davis	.08
84	Tom Herr	.06
85	Vance Law	.06
86	Kal Daniels	.10
88	Alfredo Griffin	.06

472 Ellis Burks

118 Matt Williams

180	Bo Jackson	.50
181	Carmelo Martinez	.06
185	Mike Krukow	.06
186	Rafael Palmeiro	.40
187	Tim Burke	.06
188	Roger McDowell	.08
189	Garry Templeton	.06
190	Terry Pendleton	.20
191	Larry Parrish	.06
194	Tom Brunansky	.06
196	Dan Pasqua	.08
198	Mark Eichhorn	.06
200	*Bill Ripken*	.15
201	*Sam Horn*	.15
202	Todd Worrell	.08
208	Brian Holton	.08
210	Dave Concepcion	.10
211	Mike Davis	.06
212	Devon White	.15
215	Oddibe McDowell	.06
216	Jimmy Key	.06
219	Larry Sheets	.06
220	Mike Easler	.06
221	Kurt Stillwell	.08
222	*Chuck Jackson*	.08
223	Dave Martinez	.06
224	Tim Leary	.06
225	Steve Garvey	.20
240	Tommy John	.12
248	Jose Oquendo	.08
250	Don Baylor	.08
253	Carney Lansford	.08
261	Tom Neidenfuer (incorrect spelling)	.25
261	Tom Niedenfuer (correct spelling)	.08
265	Barry Bonds	.70
275	John Tudor	.08
276	*Gene Larkin*	.10
277	Harold Reynolds	.08
280	Ted Higuera	.08
285	Ted Simmons	.08
287	*John Smiley*	.45
297	Terry Franconia (incorrect spelling)	.25
297	Terry Francona (correct spelling)	.08
304	Paul O'Neill	.15
305	Hubie Brooks	.08
307	Bobby Thigpen	.10
310	Ron Guidry	.12
325	Gary Carter	.10
331	Goose Gossage	.12
336	Randy Myers	.10
339	Mitch Williams	.08
340	Paul Molitor	.10
350	Dwight Gooden	.25
351	Dave Righetti	.12
358	Tom Pagnazzi	.20
360	Darryl Strawberry	.35
376	*DeWayne Buice*	.08
377	*Bill Pecota*	.15
385	Tony Gwynn	.35
399	Cecil Fielder	.45
400	Keith Hernandez	.08
414	*Shane Mack*	.25
419	John Christansen (incorrect spelling)	.25
419	John Christensen (correct spelling)	.08
422	Kelly Gruber	.15
432	*Mike Dunne*	.08
436	*Donnell Nixon*	.08
442	*Gerald Young*	.08
450	Dale Murphy	.15
460	Glenn Davis	.08
470	Orel Hershiser	.10

647 Ron Gant

472	*Ellis Burks*	.50
481	Kevin Mitchell	.25
485	Pete Incaviglia	.08
496	*Robby Wine Jr.*	.08
497	*Jeff Montgomery*	.25
500	Reggie Jackson (1968-75, Oakland Athletics)	.25
501	Reggie Jackson (1976, Baltimore Orioles)	.25
502	Reggie Jackson (1977-81, New York Yankees)	.25
503	Reggie Jackson (1982-86, California Angels)	.25
504	Reggie Jackson (1987, Oakland Athletics)	.25
508	Jose DeLeon	.08
510	Bob Welch	.08
515	Von Hayes	.08
516	Mark Gubicza	.08
520	*Mike Henneman*	.10
525	Kirk Gibson	.10
526	*Wally Ritchie*	.08
529	Shawon Dunston	.10
535	John Franco	.10
536	*Paul Kilgus*	.08
540	George Bell	.12
542	*Joe Boever*	.08
545	Jack Morris	.12
546	*Todd Benzinger*	.20
549	*Jeff Robinson*	.08
550	Cal Ripken Jr.	.60
555	Phil Niekro	.15
562	*Jeff Blauser*	.15
567	*Tommy Hinzo*	.08
568	*Eric Nolte*	.08
570	*Mark Davidson*	.08
571	*Jim Walewander*	.08
575	Nolan Ryan	.75
583	*Jeff DeWilis*	.08
584	*John Marzano*	.08
585	Bill Gullickson	.10
590	Harold Baines	.10
591	Bill Buckner	.08
592	Carlton Fisk	.20
594	*Doug Jones*	.12
597	*Jose Lind*	.12
598	*Ross Jones*	.08
600	Fernando Valenzuela	.08
602	*Les Lancaster*	.08
603	Ozzie Guillen	.10
605	Chili Davis	.08
615	Sid Fernandez	.08
620	*John Farrell*	.08
623	*Randy Milligan* (RP)	.25
624	Kevin Elster (RP)	.10
625	*Jody Reed* (RP)	.25
626	Shawn Abner (RP)	.12
627	*Kirt Manwaring* (RP)	.10
628	*Pete Stanicek* (RP)	.08
629	*Rob Ducey* (RP)	.08
630	Steve Kiefer	.08
631	*Gary Thurman* (RP)	.10
632	*Darrel Akerfelds* (RP)	.08
633	Dave Clark (RP)	.10
634	*Roberto Kelly* (RP)	.70
635	*Keith Hughes* (RP)	.10
636	*John Davis* (RP)	.10
637	*Mike Devereaux* (RP)	.60
638	Tom Glavine (RP)	2.00
639	*Keith Miller* (RP)	.10
640	Chris Gwynn (RP)	.15
641	*Tim Crews* (RP)	.10
642	*Mackey Sasser* (RP)	.15
643	*Vicente Palacios* (RP)	.12
645	*Gregg Jefferies* (RP)	.75
646	*Jeff Treadway* (RP)	.20
647	Ron Gant (RP)	1.50

648	Rookie Sluggers (Mark McGwire, Matt Nokes) .... .30	653	1987 Highlights (Kirby Puckett) .... .15
649	Speed and Power (Eric Davis, Tim Raines).. .12	654	1987 Highlights (Benito Santiago) .... .10
650	Game Breakers (Jack Clark, Don Mattingly) .... .20	656	1987 Highlights (Steve Bedrosian) .... .06
651	Super Shortstops (Tony Fernandez, Cal Ripken Jr., Alan Trammell)................ .25	657	1987 Highlights (Mike Schmidt) .... .25
		658	1987 Highlights (Don Mattingly) .... .15
		659	1987 Highlights (Mark McGwire)............... .35
652	1987 Highlights (Vince Coleman) .... .08	660	1987 Highlights (Paul Molitor) .... .08

1988 SCORE ROOKIE & TRADED

This modest 110-card offering from Score became the sleeper hit of the year in the hobby world. Although Score's debut set of 660 cards earlier in the year was an immediate success, the cards were taken for granted due to an abundant supply. Hobbyists slow to pick up the regular issue found a smaller supply of the fall extension sets. As with other companies, Score maintained the same card design and marketing formula for the Rookie & Traded set. However, Score grouped all the first-time players in the last half of the set (66 to 110), making things easier for rookie-card specialists. Prominent rookies include Roberto Alomar, Mark Grace, and Jack McDowell. This set is four times more valuable than the company's regular set for 1988.

		MINT			
	Complete set	**$90.00**	8	Tom Herr .... .08
	Commons	**.15**	10	Kirk Gibson...................... .40
			13	Luis Salazar .... .15
1	Jack Clark .... $ .20		14	Goose Gossage .... .25
2	Danny Jackson................ .20		15	Bob Welch .... .20
3	Brett Butler .... .40		18	Dan Quisenberry .... .20
4	Kurt Stillwell................... .20		20	Lee Smith 1.00
5	Tom Brunansky .... .15		22	Pat Tabler........................ .08
7	Jose DeLeon .... .08		23	Larry McWilliams............. .08
			25	Graig Nettles .... .25
			26	Dan Petry .... .15

80 Mark Grace

27	Jose Rijo	.70
28	Chili Davis	.25
29	Dickie Thon	.10
30	Mackey Sasser (FC)	.25
31	Mickey Tettleton	.80
32	Rick Dempsey	.20
33	Ron Hassey	.08
34	Phil Bradley	.08
35	Jay Howell	.20
36	Bill Buckner	.10
37	Alfredo Griffin	.08
38	Gary Pettis	.08
44	Ron Kittle	.20
45	Bob Dernier	.08
46	Steve Balboni	.08
47	Steve Shields	.08
48	Henry Cotto	.08
49	Dave Henderson	.20
50	Dave Parker	.20
51	Mike Young	.06
52	Mark Salas	.06
53	Mike Davis	.10
54	Rafael Santana	.08
55	Don Baylor	.25
56	Dan Pasqua	.20
57	Ernest Riles	.06
58	Glenn Hubbard	.15
59	Mike Smithson	.08
60	Richard Dotson	.08

61	Jerry Reuss	.20
62	Mike Jackson	.25
63	Floyd Bannister	.20
64	Jesse Orosco	.15
65	Larry Parrish	.20
66	Jeff Bittiger (FC)	.15
67	Ray Hayward (FC)	.15
68	Ricky Jordan (FC)	.50
69	Tommy Gregg (FC)	.20
70	Brady Anderson (FC)	6.00
71	Jeff Montgomery (FC)	3.00
72	Darryl Hamilton (FC)	3.00
73	Cecil Espy (FC)	.35
74	Greg Briley (FC)	.25
75	Joey Meyer (FC)	.15
76	Mike Macfarlane (FC)	2.00
77	Oswald Peraza (FC)	.15
78	Jack Armstrong (FC)	1.00
79	Don Heinkel (FC)	.15
80	Mark Grace (FC)	20.00
81	Steve Curry (FC)	.15
82	Damon Berryhill (FC)	.35
83	Steve Ellsworth (FC)	.15
84	Pete Smith (FC)	1.00
85	Jack McDowell (FC)	18.00
86	Rob Dibble (FC)	2.50
87	Brian Harvey (FC)	5.00
88	John Dopson (FC)	.20
89	Dave Gallagher (FC)	.20
90	Todd Stottlemyre (FC)	2.00
91	Mike Schooler (FC)	.25
92	Don Gordon (FC)	.15
93	Sil Campusano (FC)	.15
94	Jeff Pico (FC)	.15
95	Jay Buhner (FC)	5.00
96	Nelson Santovenia (FC)	.15
97	Al Leiter (FC)	.25
98	Luis Alicea (FC)	.35
99	Pat Borders (FC)	2.00
100	Chris Sabo (FC)	3.00
101	Tim Belcher (FC)	.60
102	Walt Weiss (FC)	.50
103	Craig Biggio (FC)	5.00
104	Don August (FC)	.15
105	Roberto Alomar (FC)	60.00
106	Todd Burns (FC)	.15
108	Melido Perez (FC)	2.00
109	Darrin Jackson (FC)	1.50
110	Orestes Destrade (FC)	2.00

1988 TOPPS

The design of the 1988 Topps cards was simple—often compared to a magazine cover—but effective. Sharply focused action photos have soft backgrounds, with bold team names across the top that are partially obscured by the players' heads. Diagonal stripes in the lower right-hand corner display the player name and gray card backs show complete major league stats. Subsets in this 192-card issue include seven Record Breakers (with McGwire and Mattingly, among others), five Future Stars, 26 team leaders with vintage photos, 22 All-Stars, and 10 All-Star rookies honored with special trophy designations (such as second-year player Matt Nokes).

	MINT
Complete set	**$20.00**
Commons	**.04**

1 '87 Record Breakers (Vince Coleman)	$ .12
2 '87 Record Breakers (Don Mattingly)	.15
3 '87 Record Breakers (Mark McGwire)...............	.35
4 '87 Record Breakers (Eddie Murray) (record headline on front)	.40
4 '87 Record Breakers (Eddie Murray) (no headline)	.25
5 '87 Record Breakers (Joe Niekro, Phil Niekro)	.10
6 '87 Record Breakers (Nolan Ryan)	.25
7 '87 Record Breakers (Benito Santiago)	.15
8 Kevin Elster (FC)	.10
10 Ryne Sandberg	.45
18 *Al Leiter* (FC) (photo is Steve George; no "NY" on jersey)	.25
18 *Al Leiter* (FC) (correct photo; "NY" on jersey)	.15
19 *Mark Davidson* (FC)	.12
21 Red Sox Ldrs (Wade Boggs, Spike Owen)	.15
22 Greg Swindell..................	.10
25 Andres Galarraga............	.05
28 *Jose Nunez* (FC)	.12
30 Sid Fernandez.................	.08

35 Harold Baines..................	.10
39 Gerald Perry	.08
40 Orel Hershiser	.15
42 *Bill Landrum* (FC)	.12
45 Kent Hrbek	.12
49 Dave Clark (FC)	.08
50 Hubie Brooks....................	.10
51 Orioles Ldrs (Eddie Murray, Cal Ripken)	.25
55 Phil Bradley....................	.08
57 *Tim Crews* (FC)................	.10
58 Dave Magadan.................	.10
60 Rickey Henderson	.35
61 *Mark Knudson* (FC)..........	.08
62 Jeff Hamilton	.08
63 *Jimmy Jones* (FC)	.08
64 • Ken Caminiti (FC)...........	.20
69 *Mike Hart* (FC)................	.06
70 Roger Clemens	.50
72 Dennis Eckersley	.10
75 Joe Carter	.20
80 Mark Langston	.10
81 Reds Ldrs (John Franco, Ron Robinson)	.06
82 *Darrel Akerfelds* (FC)	.06
85 Howard Johnson	.15
89 *Gary Thurman* (FC)	.12
90 Dale Murphy	.15
91 *Joey Cora* (FC)................	.08
94 *Chuck Jackson* (FC)........	.08
95 Lance Parrish	.08
96 *Todd Benzinger* (FC)	.25
98 *Rene Gonzales* (FC)	.10
100 Jack Clark	.12
102 Barry Larkin.....................	.25
106 *Jim Walewander* (FC).......	.08

269 Ellis Burks

350 Will Clark

520	Dave Smith	.08
522	*Bob Patterson* (FC)	.06
525	Marty Barrett	.06
526	Juan Berenguer	.06
528	Checklist 397-528 (number 455 is Steve Carlton)	.30
528	Checklist 397-528 (number 455 is Shawn Hillegas)	.08
529	Tim Burke	.06
530	Gary Carter	.10
533	*John Farrell* (FC)	.06
534	John Wathan	.06
535	Ron Guidry	.10
539	Mike LaValliere	.06
540	Bret Saberhagen	.15
542	*Paul Noce* (FC)	.06
543	Kent Tekulve	.08
544	Jim Traber	.06
545	Don Baylor	.10
546	John Candelaria	.08
547	*Felix Fermin* (FC)	.08
548	*Shane Mack*	.30
549	Braves Ldrs (Ken Griffey, Dion James, Dale Murphy, Gerald Perry)	.08
550	Pedro Guerrero	.10
551	Terry Steinbach	.10
553	Tracy Jones	.06
555	Brook Jacoby	.06
556	*Stan Clarke* (FC)	.06
558	Bob Ojeda	.08
559	*Ken Williams* (FC)	.08
560	Tim Wallach	.08
563	Jose Guzman	.06
565	Lloyd Moseby	.08
566	*Charlie O'Brien* (FC)	.08
569	Charlie Leibrandt	.08
570	Jeffrey Leonard	.08
571	Mark Williamson (FC)	.06
572	Chris James	.06
574	Graig Nettles	.08
575	Don Sutton	.10
576	*Tommy Hinzo* (FC)	.06
577	Tom Browning	.08
578	Gary Gaetti	.08
579	Mets Ldrs (Gary Carter, Kevin McReynolds)	.08
580	Mark McGwire	.50
582	*Mike Henneman*	.15

463 Fred McGriff

583	Dave Valle (FC)	.06
585	Ozzie Guillen	.08
586	Bob Forsch	.06
588	*Jeff Parrett* (FC)	.06
590	George Bell	.10
591	Doug Drabek	.15
592	Dale Sveum	.06
593	Bob Tewksbury	.06
595	Frank White	.06
596	John Kruk	.15
597	Gene Garber	.06
599	Calvin Schiraldi	.08
600	Mike Schmidt	.30
602	Mike Aldrete	.06
603	Rob Murphy	.06
605	Kirk Gibson	.10
609	Twins Ldrs (Gary Gaetti, Kent Hrbek)	.08
610	Keith Hernandez	.08
611	Tommy John	.12
613	Bobby Thigpen	.10
615	Jody Davis	.06
616	*Jay Aldrich* (FC)	.06
617	Oddibe McDowell	.06
618	Cecil Fielder	.50
619	*Mike Dunne*	.06
620	Cory Snyder	.08
622	Kal Daniels	.08

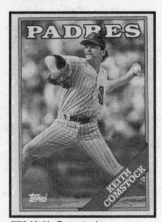

778 Keith Comstock

746	*Gene Larkin*		.10
747	Bobby Witt		.08
750	Bo Jackson		.40
759	A's Ldrs (Jose Canseco, Mark McGwire)		.25
766	Henry Cotto		.06
767	*Jose Lind* (FC)		.15
770	Lou Whitaker		.15
771	Ruben Sierra		.35
774	Gene Mauch		.06
775	Dave Stieb		.08
778	*Keith Comstock* (FC) (team name in white)		1.50
778	*Keith Comstock* (FC) (team name in blue)		.06
779	*Tom Glavine* (FC)		2.00
780	Fernando Valenzuela		.10
781	*Keith Hughes* (FC)		.06
782	*Jeff Ballard* (FC)		.06
785	Alvin Davis		.08
789	Indians Ldrs (Joe Carter, Cory Snyder)		.15
790	Dave Righetti		.08
791	Ted Simmons		.08
792	John Tudor		.08

1988 TOPPS TRADED

Topps pumped up its standard 132-card Traded issue with the addition of a 20-card subset featuring the 1988 U.S. Olympic Baseball Team. The Olympians won the gold medal, and the cards feature big-name rookies who enjoy above-average acclaim, wearing colorful Team USA uniforms. Jim Abbott, Tino Martinez, and Robin Ventura highlight this group. The 1988 edition could be a quality investment as more Olympians achieve fame in the big leagues. Other notables in the set include Ron Gant and Roberto Alomar. This set continues the Topps custom of being sold only through hobby dealers in complete, boxed sets.

		MINT
Complete set		**$30.00**
Commons		**.06**

1	Jim Abbott (FC) (USA)	$7.00
3	Luis Alicea (FC)	.15
4	Roberto Alomar (FC)	8.00
5	Brady Anderson (FC)	1.50
6	Jack Armstrong (FC)	.30
7	Don August	.10
9	Brett Barberie (FC) (USA)	.80
10	Jose Bautista (FC)	.08
11	Don Baylor	.15
12	Tim Belcher	.12
13	Buddy Bell	.10
14	Andy Benes (FC) (USA)	3.50
15	Damon Berryhill (FC)	.12
17	Pat Borders (FC)	.50
18	Phil Bradley	.08
19	Jeff Branson (FC) (USA)	.35
20	Tom Brunansky	.08
21	Jay Buhner (FC)	.80
23	Jim Campanis (FC) (USA)	.20
24	Sil Campusano (FC)	.06
26	Jose Cecena (FC)	.06
28	Jack Clark	.08
29	Kevin Coffman (FC)	.10
30	Pat Combs (FC) (US	
34	Jose DeLeon	

1988 Topps Traded

39 Ron Gant

35	Richard Dotson	.10
36	Cecil Espy (FC)	.15
38	Mike Fiore (FC) (USA)	.20
39	Ron Gant (FC)	1.50
40	Kirk Gibson	.10
41	Rich Gossage	.15
42	Mark Grace (FC)	2.50
44	Ty Griffin (FC) (USA)	.10
45	Bryan Harvey (FC)	1.50
47	Ray Hayward (FC)	.08
48	Dave Henderson	.10
51	Ricky Horton	.08
52	Jay Howell	.10
54	Jeff Innis (FC)	.15
55	Danny Jackson	.08
56	Darrin Jackson (FC)	.35
57	Roberto Kelly (FC)	1.00
58	Ron Kittle	.15
60	Vance Law	.08
62	Mike Macfarlane (FC)	.45
63	Scotti Madison (FC)	.15
64	Kirt Manwaring (FC)	.12
66	Tino Martinez (FC) (USA)	1.75
67	Billy Masse (FC) (USA)	.20
68	Jack McDowell (FC)	2.50
71	Mickey Morandini (FC) (USA)	.75

74	Charles Nagy (FC) (USA)	1.50
75	Al Nipper	.06
77	Jesse Orosco	.06
78	Joe Orsulak	.06
79	Dave Palmer	.06
80	Mark Parent (FC)	.08
81	Dave Parker	.15
82	Dan Pasqua	.08
83	Melido Perez (FC)	.60
84	Steve Peters (FC)	.06
85	Dan Petry	.06
86	Gary Pettis	.06
87	Jeff Pico (FC)	.08
88	Jim Poole (FC) (USA)	.12
92	Jose Rijo	.15
95	Doug Robbins (FC) (USA)	.15
96	• Frank Robinson	.15
98	Chris Sabo (FC)	.80
99	Mark Salas	.06
100	Luis Salazar	.06
101	Rafael Santana	.06
102	Nelson Santovenia	.08
103	Mackey Sasser (FC)	.10
105	Mike Schooler (FC)	.20
106	Scott Servais (FC) (USA)	.25
107	Dave Silvestri (FC) (USA)	.25
109	Joe Slusarski (FC) (USA)	.25
110	Lee Smith	.15
111	Pete Smith (FC)	.10
113	Ed Sprague (FC) (USA)	.40
114	Steve Stanicek (FC)	.06
115	Kurt Stillwell	.10
116	Todd Stottlemyre (FC)	.50
117	Bill Swift	.20
119	Scott Terry (FC)	.10
120	Mickey Tettleton	.15
122	Jeff Treadway (FC)	.15
123	Willie Upshaw	.08
124	Robin Ventura (FC) (USA)	9.00
125	Ron Washington	.06
126	Walt Weiss (FC)	.20
127	Bob Welch	.10
128	David Wells (FC)	.35
129	Glenn Wilson	.10
130	Ted Wood (FC) (USA)	.30

1989 DONRUSS

Once again a Diamond King from each team appears at the beginning of this 660-card, standard-dimension set. These painted portraits display striking background colors and designs. All cards use fading neon colors for the tops and bottoms, with black borders along the sides. Except for the Diamond Kings, player names appear in a simple print style, with the upper right-hand corner reserved for more elaborate team logos or the Rated Rookie subset identification. The white backs, while criticized for having few stats, are packed with full names, team records, specifics of a player's acquisition, and detailed career highlights.

		MINT
Complete set		**$20.00**
Commons		**.04**

1	Mike Greenwell (DK)	$ .10
2	Bobby Bonilla (DK)	.12
3	Pete Incaviglia (DK)	.06
4	Chris Sabo (DK)	.10
5	Robin Yount (DK)	.15
6	Tony Gwynn (DK)	.12
7	Carlton Fisk (DK)	.15
8	Cory Snyder (DK)	.06
9	David Cone (DK)	.10
10	Kevin Seitzer (DK)	.06
11	Rick Reuschel (DK)	.06
12	Johnny Ray (DK)	.06
14	Andres Galarraga (DK)	.06
15	Kirk Gibson (DK)	.08
16	Fred McGriff (DK)	.15
17	Mark Grace (DK)	.10
18	Jeff Robinson (DK)	.12
19	Vince Coleman (DK)	.15
20	Dave Henderson (DK)	.10
22	Gerald Perry (DK)	.06
23	Frank Viola (DK)	.06
24	Steve Bedrosian (DK)	.06
25	Glenn Davis (DK)	.06
26	Don Mattingly (DK)	.10
28	Sandy Alomar Jr. (RR) (FC)	.30
29	Steve Searcy (RR) (FC)	.08
30	Cameron Drew (RR) (FC)	.04
31	Gary Sheffield (RR) (FC)	1.75
32	Erik Hanson (RR) (FC)	.25
33	Ken Griffey Jr. (RR) (FC)	5.00
34	Greg Harris (RR) (FC)	.10
35	Gregg Jefferies (RR)	.40
36	Luis Medina (RR) (FC)	.10
37	Carlos Quintana (RR)	.15
38	Felix Jose (RR) (FC)	.50
39	Cris Carpenter (RR) (FC)	.10
40	Ron Jones (RR) (FC)	.04
41	Dave West (RR) (FC)	.08
42	Randy Johnson (RR) (FC)	.40
43	Mike Harkey (RR) (FC)	.10
44	Pete Harnisch (RR) (FC)	.25
45	Tom Gordon (RR) (FC)	.15
46	Gregg Olson (RR) (FC)	.35
47	Alex Sanchez (RR) (FC)	.06
48	Ruben Sierra	.35
49	Rafael Palmeiro	.20
50	Ron Gant	.35
51	Cal Ripken, Jr.	.50
52	Wally Joyner	.10
53	Gary Carter	.08
54	Andy Van Slyke	.10
55	Robin Yount	.25
56	Pete Incaviglia	.06
57	Greg Brock	.04
58	Melido Perez	.06
60	Gary Pettis	.04
61	Danny Tartabull	.15
63	Ozzie Smith	.15
64	Gary Gaetti	.08
65	Mark Davis	.06
66	Lee Smith	
67	Dennis Eckersley	

1989 Donruss

33 Ken Griffey Jr.

68	Wade Boggs	.25
69	Mike Scott	.05
70	Fred McGriff	.35
73	Mel Hall	.08
74	Don Mattingly	.35
76	Juan Samuel	.08
78	Dave Righetti	.08
80	Eric Davis	.15
82	Todd Worrell	.08
83	Joe Carter	.15
84	Steve Sax	.10
85	Frank White	.06
86	John Kruk	.15
88	Alan Ashby	.04
90	Frank Tanana	.06
91	Jose Canseco	.35
92	Barry Bonds	.50
95	Mark McGwire	.35
96	Eddie Murray	.15
97	Tim Raines	.10
99	Kevin McReynolds	.08
101	Carlton Fisk	.20
104	Dale Murphy	.10
105	Ryne Sandberg	.40
110	Mike Marshall	.06
112	Tom Brunansky	.06
113	Kelly Gruber	.12
115	*Keith Brown* (FC)	.04

116	Matt Nokes	.10
117	Keith Hernandez	.08
118	Bob Forsch	.06
119	Bert Blyleven	.10
122	Jim Rice	.08
124	Danny Jackson	.08
126	Brian Fisher	.06
128	Tony Gwynn	.30
130	Andres Galarraga	.20
132	Kirk Gibson	.08
135	Greg Walker	.06
136	Kirk McCaskill	.06
140	Mike Aldrete	.04
142	Scott Fletcher	.04
143	Steve Balboni	.04
144	Bret Saberhagen	.12
147	Darryl Strawberry	.25
148	Harold Baines	.08
149	George Bell	.10
150	Dave Parker	.12
151	Bobby Bonilla	.15
152	Mookie Wilson	.06
154	Nolan Ryan	.60
155	Jeff Reardon	.10
156	Tim Wallach	.06
158	Rich Gossage	.10
159	Dave Winfield	.25
160	Von Hayes	.06
161	Willie McGee	.10
163	Tony Pena	.06
167	Andre Dawson	.15
168	Joe Boever (FC)	.06
169	Pete Stanicek	.06
170	• Bob Boone	.08
171	Ron Darling	.06
173	Rob Deer	.08
175	Ted Higuera	.06
176	Ozzie Guillen	.10
178	Doyle Alexander	.06
179	Mark Gubicza	.06
180	Alan Trammell	.10
181	Vince Coleman	.10
182	Kirby Puckett	.35
183	Chris Brown	.06
186	Mike Greenwell	.10
187	Billy Hatcher	.06
188	Jimmy Key	.08
189	Nick Esasky	.06
191	Cory Snyder	.08

193	Mike Schmidt	.30
195	John Tudor	.06
232	Greg Swindell	.08
233	John Franco	.10
234	Jack Morris	.15
235	Howard Johnson	.15
236	Glenn Davis	.08
237	Frank Viola	.15
238	Kevin Seitzer	.08
197	Orel Hershiser	.10
198	Kal Daniels	.06
199	Kent Hrbek	.10
201	Joe Magrane	.06
203	Tim Belcher	.10
204	George Brett	.20
205	Benito Santiago	.08
206	Tony Fernandez	.08
208	Bo Jackson	.25
211	Doug Drabek	.08
213	Devon White	.08
214	Dave Stewart	.08
216	Bryn Smith	.06
217	Brett Butler	.06
218	Bob Ojeda	.06
220	Hubie Brooks	.06
221	B.J. Surhoff	.06
223	Rick Sutcliffe	.08
225	Mitch Williams	.08
227	Mark Langston	.08
230	Terry Pendleton	.10
240	● Dwight Evans	.10
242	Bo Diaz	.06
245	Rickey Henderson	.35
246	Roberto Alomar	.75
249	Will Clark	.40
250	Fernando Valenzuela	.08
252	Sid Bream	.06
255	Mark Grace	.35
257	Barry Larkin	.20
259	Billy Ripken	.06
265	Roger McDowell	.08
266	Bobby Thigpen	.08
268	Terry Steinbach	.08
270	Dwight Gooden	.15
275	Damon Berryhill	.06
276	Vance Law	.06
277	Rich Dotson	.06
278	Lance Parrish	.06
280	Roger Clemens	.40

31 Gary Sheffield

281	Greg Mathews	.06
283	Paul Kilgus	.06
284	Jose Guzman	.08
287	Joe Orsulak	.06
290	Jose Lind	.10
291	Paul Molitor	.12
292	Cecil Espy	.08
294	Dan Pasqua	.08
298	Lou Whitaker	.20
303	Ellis Burks	.10
305	Jody Reed	.10
306	Bill Doran	.06
307	David Wells	.08
310	Julio Franco	.10
311	Jack Clark	.10
312	Chris James	.06
315	Al Leiter	.06
316	Mike Davis	.06
317	*Chris Sabo*	.30
318	Greg Gagne	.06
320	John Farrell	.10
322	Kurt Stillwell	.06
323	Shawn Abner	.06
325	Kevin Bass	.06
326	Pat Tabler	.06
329	John Smiley	.10
332	Bob Welch	.08
333	Larry Sheets	.06

246 Roberto Alomar

336	Randy Myers	.10
344	Dan Petry	.06
345	Alvin Davis	.08
348	Danny Cox	.06
349	Dave Stieb	.08
351	Jeff Treadway	.06
355	Gene Larkin	.06
356	Steve Farr	.06
358	Todd Benzinger	.08
360	Paul O'Neill	.10
366	*Nelson Santovenia* (FC)	.08
367	Kelly Downs	.06
369	Phil Bradley	.06
372	Mike Witt	.06
373	Greg Maddux	.15
375	Jose Rijo	.10
381	Tom Glavine	.60
382	Dan Plesac	.06
384	*Dave Gallagher*	.08
385	Tom Henke	.08
386	Luis Polonia	.10
388	David Cone	.20
392	*John Dopson*	.06
395	Willie Randolph	.06
401	Mickey Tettleton	.08
403	Jeff Russell	.08
405	*Jose Alvarez* (FC)	.06
407	*Sherman Corbett* (FC)	.06

408	Dave Magadan	.08
410	Don August	.06
412	Chris Bosio	.06
413	Jerry Reuss	.08
416	*Mike Macfarlane*	.20
418	Pedro Guerrero	.08
419	Alan Anderson	.06
423	Bruce Hurst	.08
425	Jesse Barfield	.06
426	*Rob Dibble* (FC)	.20
428	Ron Kittle	.06
433	Roberto Kelly	.20
437	Jose DeLeon	.08
438	Doug Jones	.08
442	Cecil Fielder	.40
443	*John Fishel* (FC)	.06
445	*Paul Gibson*	.08
446	Walt Weiss	.08
448	Mike Moore	.08
449	Chili Davis	.08
451	*Jose Bautista*	.08
458	Bruce Sutter	.08
461	Bobby Witt	.08
464	● Ramon Martinez (FC)	.50
466	Luis Alicea	.10
471	Sid Fernandez	.08
474	*Israel Sanchez* (FC)	.08
479	Greg Cadaret	.06
480	*Randy Kramer* (FC)	.06
481	*Dave Eiland* (FC)	.08
482	Eric Show	.06
483	Garry Templeton	.06
485	Kevin Mitchell	.15
488	Dave LaPoint	.06
491	*Doug Dascenzo* (FC)	.08
492	Willie Upshaw	.06
493	*Jack Armstrong* (FC)	.10
494	Kirt Manwaring	.08
495	Jeff Ballard	.06
498	Gary Thurman	.06
499	Zane Smith	.08
505	*Doug Jennings*	.06
511	*Brian Holman* (FC)	.10
513	*Jeff Pico* (FC)	.06
517	Jeff Sellers	.06
518	*John Costello* (FC)	.06
519	*Brady Anderson*	.50
522	Drew Hall	.06
523	*Mark Lemke* (FC)	.15

524	Oswald Peraza (FC)	.06
525	Bryan Harvey	.35
527	Tom Prince	.06
529	Jerry Browne	.06
533	Darrell Evans	.08
536	Ken Hill (FC)	.20
538	Shane Mack	.10
541	Wes Gardner	.06
542	Ken Caminiti	.10
543	Duane Ward	.06
544	Norm Charlton (FC)	.20
545	Hal Morris (FC)	.20
547	Hensley Meulens (FC)	.15
552	Tim Leary	.06
555	Tim Jones (FC)	.08
558	Jose DeJesus (FC)	.08
559	Dennis Rasmussen	.06
560	Pat Borders	.12
561	Craig Biggio (FC)	.30
562	Luis de los Santos (FC)	.08
563	Fred Lynn	.06
564	Todd Burns (FC)	.08
569	Craig Worthington	.08
570	Johnny Paredes	.06
575	Juan Nieves	.06
577	Rolando Roomes (FC)	.08
579	Chad Kreuter (FC)	.06
580	Tony Armas	.06
581	Jay Buhner	.10
582	Ricky Horton	.06
583	Andy Hawkins	.06
585	Dave Clark	.06
586	Van Snider (FC)	.06
589	William Brennan (FC)	.06
590	German Gonzalez (FC)	.06
591	Ernie Whitt	.08
592	Jeff Blauser	.08
594	Matt Williams	.25
597	Scott Medvin (FC)	.08
598	Hipolito Pena (FC)	.08
599	Jerald Clark (FC)	.10
603	Mike Devereaux	.10
604	Alex Madrid (FC)	.06
606	Lance Johnson	.06
607	Terry Clark (FC)	.06
609	Scott Jordan (FC)	.06
610	Jay Howell	.06
611	Francisco Melendez (FC)	.06
613	Kevin Brown	.10

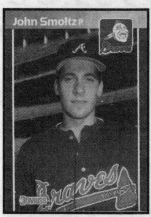

642 John Smoltz

614	Dave Valle	.06
616	Andy Nezelek (FC)	.06
617	Chuck Crim	.06
619	Adam Peterson (FC)	.06
620	Todd Stottlemyre	.12
621	Lance Blankenship (FC)	.11
622	Miguel Garcia (FC)	.06
624	Ricky Jordan (FC)	.10
634	Dante Bichette (FC)	.12
635	Curt Schilling (FC)	.10
636	Scott May (FC)	.08
637	Mike Schooler (FC)	.12
639	Tom Lampkin (FC)	.06
640	Brian Meyer (FC)	.06
642	John Smoltz (FC)	.60
643	40/40 Club (Jose Canseco)	.25
645	Edgar Martinez (FC)	.30
646	Dennis Cook (FC)	.06
648	59 and Counting (Orel Hershiser)	.10
649	Rod Nichols (FC)	.06
651	Bob Milacki (FC)	.18
652	Mike Jackson	.06
653	Derek Lilliquist (FC)	.08
655	Mike Diaz	.06
658	Kevin Blankenship (FC)	.06
660	Eric Hetzel (FC)	.06

1989 DONRUSS ROOKIES

Rookie fever raged on in 1989, as shown by the popularity of the 1989 Donruss set, "The Rookies." The concept was originated by Donruss in 1986, and the company continued in 1989 to feature 55 players and a checklist card in a boxed, complete set. Ironically, more than a third of the 55 "rookies" actually had made prior appearances in Donruss sets, some more than a year before. This hobby-wise company, however, gave leading newcomers encore appearances in this season-ending set. The cards are just like the standard 660-card set from earlier in the year except for "The Rookies" logo in the upper right corner. Ken Griffey's card alone accounts for more than half the set's total value.

	MINT
Complete set	$14.00
Commons	.05

1	Gary Sheffield	$2.25
2	Gregg Jefferies	.35
3	Ken Griffey, Jr.	9.00
4	Tom Gordon	.20
5	Billy Spiers (FC)	.10
6	Deion Sanders (FC)	1.50
8	Steve Carter (FC)	.05
9	Francisco Oliveras (FC)	.05
11	Bob Geren (FC)	.05
12	Tony Castillo	.08
13	Kenny Rogers (FC)	.10
14	Carlos Martinez (FC)	.12
15	Edgar Martinez	.35
16	Jim Abbott	1.50
18	Mark Carreon	.05
20	Luis Medina	.08
21	Sandy Alomar, Jr.	.25
22	Bob Milacki	.10
23	Joe Girardi	.10
25	Craig Worthington	.10
26	Jerome Walton	.25
27	Gary Wayne (FC)	.05
29	Dante Bichette	.10
30	Alexis Infante (FC)	.10
31	Ken Hill	.50
32	Dwight Smith	.10
34	Eric Yelding (FC)	.10
35	Gregg Olson	.45

6 Deion Sanders

37	Ken Patterson	.05
38	Rick Wrona (FC)	.10
41	Jeff Brantley (FC)	.10
42	Ron Jones	.05
44	Kevin Brown	.20
45	Ramon Martinez	.50
46	Greg Harris	.15
47	Steve Finley	.35
49	Erik Hanson	.25
53	Omar Visquel (FC)	.15
54	Derek Lilliquist	.05
55	Junior Felix (FC)	.25

1989 FLEER

Some of Fleer's best photos in the standard-sized 1989 set were not well cropped. The gray pin-striped borders are broad and cut diagonally by poorly edited photos. Bats are often missing, or, even worse, arms are sliced off (as on Chris Sabo, number 170). This tends to disrupt the dynamic concept. Furthermore, print within the pin-striped background is cluttered and hard to read. Gray card backs include "Did You Know" trivia quizzes and charts marking player progress before and after the All-Star break. Informal group cards, star tribute cards, and duo rookie cards are rounded out by a dozen All-Stars with bios on backs.

		MINT
Complete set		**$20.00**
Commons		**.05**

1	Don Baylor	$ .10
2	*Lance Blankenship* (FC)	.10
3	*Todd Burns*	.10
5	Jose Canseco	.30
6	Storm Davis	.05
7	Dennis Eckersley	.12
10	Dave Henderson	.10
14	*Doug Jennings*	.07
15	*Felix Jose* (FC)	.50
17	Mark McGwire	.50
19	Dave Parker	.12
20	Eric Plunk	.07
22	Terry Steinbach	.08
23	Dave Stewart	.08
24	Walt Weiss	.08
25	Bob Welch	.10
26	Curt Young	.05
30	Gary Carter	.08
31	David Cone	.15
32	Ron Darling	.06
33	Len Dykstra	.10
34	Kevin Elster	.06
35	Sid Fernandez	.10
36	Dwight Gooden	.15
37	Keith Hernandez	.08
38	Gregg Jefferies	.35
39	Howard Johnson	.15
41	Dave Magadan	.08
43	Roger McDowell	.06
44	Kevin McReynolds	.08
45	Keith Miller	.10
46	Randy Myers	.10

47	Bob Ojeda	.05
49	Darryl Strawberry	.30
51	*Dave West* (FC)	.10
54	Tim Belcher	.08
56	Mike Devereaux	.08
57	Kirk Gibson	.08
59	Chris Gwynn	.08
61	Danny Heep (home: San Antonio, TX)	.60
62	Orel Hershiser	.08
64	Jay Howell	.06
66	Mike Marshall	.05
67	• *Ramon Martinez* (FC)	.50
70	Steve Sax	.08
75	John Tudor	.06
76	Fernando Valenzuela	.08
77	Tracy Woodson	.05
79	Todd Benzinger	.08
81	Wade Boggs	.25
83	Ellis Burks	.10
85	Roger Clemens	.35
86	*Steve Curry* (FC)	.05
87	• *Dwight Evans*	.10
90	Mike Greenwell	.12
91	Bruce Hurst	.08
93	Spike Owen	.05
95	*Carlos Quintana* (FC)	.15
96	Jody Reed	.12
97	Jim Rice	.08
98	Kevin Romine (photo is Randy Kutcher, batting follow through)	.50
98	Kevin Romine (correct photo, arms crossed on chest)	.60
99	Lee Smith	.10
105	Bert Blyleven	.12
106	*Eric Bullock* (FC)	.05

15 Felix Jose

235	Tom Henke	.10
236	Jimmy Key	.10
240	Fred McGriff	.25
241	Lloyd Moseby	.10
244	Dave Stieb	.10
245	Todd Stottlemyre	.12
247	David Wells	.12
250	Neil Allen (Home: Sarasota, FL)	.60
252	Jack Clark	.15
254	Rickey Henderson	.30
255	Tommy John	.12
256	Roberto Kelly	.25
257	Al Leiter	.08
258	Don Mattingly	.25
260	Hal Morris (FC)	.50
261	Scott Nielsen (FC)	.10
262	Mike Pagliarulo	.10
263	Hipolito Pena (FC)	.08
267	Dave Righetti	.12
274	Dave Winfield	.20

260 Hal Morris

277	George Brett	.30
278	Bill Buckner	.10
279	Nick Capra (FC)	.08
280	Jose DeJesus (FC)	.18
283	Mark Gubicza	.10
284	Tom Gordon (FC)	.15
285	Bo Jackson	.30
287	Mike Macfarlane	.12
291	Bret Saberhagen	.15
292	Kevin Seitzer	.06
294	Pat Tabler	.05
295	Danny Tartabull	.15
296	Gary Thurman	.08
298	Willie Wilson	.10
299	Roberto Alomar	.80
300	Sandy Alomar Jr. (FC)	.20
303	Mark Davis	.10
305	Tony Gwynn	.25
306	Greg Harris (FC)	.10
309	John Kruk	.15
316	Benito Santiago	.12
325	Will Clark	.40
330	Charlie Hayes (FC)	.20
334	Kirt Manwaring	.10
336	Kevin Mitchell	.25
338	Tony Perezchica (FC)	.15
340	Rick Reuschel	.10
346	Matt Williams	.25

347	Trevor Wilson (FC)	.25
353	Craig Biggio	.40
355	Glenn Davis	.20
358	John Fishel	.08
359	Billy Hatcher	.10
361	Louie Meadows	.08
368	Nolan Ryan	.65
371	Hubie Brooks	.10
373	John Dopson	.08
376	Andres Galarraga	.08
379	Brian Holman	.10
381	Randy Johnson (FC)	.40
388	Johnny Paredes (FC)	.10
391	Tim Raines	.10
395	Tim Wallach	.10
397	Rod Allen	.10
400	Joe Carter	.17
402	Dave Clark	.10
403	John Farrell	.10
404	Julio Franco	.10
409	Doug Jones	.20
410	Jeff Kaiser (FC)	.08
411	Luis Medina (FC)	.08
412	Cory Snyder	.08
413	Greg Swindell	.10
414	Ron Tingley (FC)	.06
415	Willie Upshaw	.05
418	Damon Berryhill	.08

602 John Smoltz

420	*Doug Dascenzo* (FC)	.08
422	Andre Dawson	.20
424	Shawon Dunston	.15
425	"Goose" Gossage	.12
426	Mark Grace	.35
427	*Mike Harkey* (FC)	.10
431	Greg Maddux	.12
434	Rafael Palmeiro	.20
437	Ryne Sandberg	.40
439	Rick Sutcliffe	.10
441	*Gary Varsho*	.12
443	*Luis Alicea*	.10
445	Vince Coleman	.15
449	Jose DeLeon	.08
451	Pedro Guerrero	.12
452	Bob Horner	.10
453	*Tim Jones* (FC)	.10
457	Willie McGee	.12
461	Terry Pendleton	.10
463	Ozzie Smith	.15
466	Todd Worrell	.10
468	*Dante Bichette* (FC)	.30
469	● Bob Boone	.07
479	*Bryan Harvey*	.35
481	Wally Joyner	.10
489	Devon White	.10
490	Mike Witt	.07
491	Harold Baines	.12
495	Carlton Fisk	.20
496	*Dave Gallagher*	.08
497	Ozzie Guillen	.15
504	Jack McDowell	.30
505	*Donn Pall*	.12
507	Dan Pasqua	.10
508	*Ken Patterson*	.12
509	Melido Perez	.10
512	Bobby Thigpen	.08
516	*Jose Cecena*	.10
523	Pete Incaviglia	.08
525	Paul Kilgus	.08
532	Ruben Sierra	.30
536	Mitch Williams	.08
537	Bobby Witt	.10
542	Jay Buhner (FC)	.20
546	Alvin Davis	.08
548	*Ken Griffey Jr.* (FC)	6.00
549	*Erik Hanson* (FC)	.25
551	Mark Langston	.12
552	Edgar Martinez	.30
553	*Bill McGuire* (FC)	.10
558	Harold Reynolds	.12
559	*Mike Schooler* (FC)	.12
571	Von Hayes	.10
572	Chris James	.10
575	*Ricky Jordan*	.10
578	Lance Parrish	.08
581	Juan Samuel	.12
582	Mike Schmidt	.35
585	*Jose Alvarez*	.08
588	Jeff Blauser	.10
590	Ron Gant	.35
591	Tom Glavine	.60
592	Tommy Gregg	.10
596	Dale Murphy	.15
599	Ted Simmons	.10
600	Pete Smith	.10
602	*John Smoltz*	.75
603	Bruce Sutter	.10
606	*Brady Anderson* (FC)	.50
607	Jeff Ballard	.07
608	*Jose Bautista*	.10
611	Eddie Murray	.15
612	Carl Nichols (FC)	.20
615	*Oswaldo Peraza* (Oswald) (FC)	.10
616	Bill Ripken (obscenity on bat)	10.00

548 Ken Griffey Jr.

9 FLEER
PDATE

Tradition dictated the production and distribution of another Update set for 1989. Thanks to the fact that some hot rookie names were included, the 132-card 1989 Fleer Update set zoomed in value immediately after its fall release. Rookie card fanatics embraced popular cards of Jim Abbott, Joey Belle, Dwight Smith, Greg Vaughn, Robin Ventura, and Todd Zeile. The complete set price later dropped due to overproduction. Fleer also included a special card commemorating Mike Schmidt's retirement. Unfortunately, the Updates retain the gaudy design of their 1989 Fleer counterparts. Once again cards are arranged by team, and then alphabetically by player within each team. A "U" prefix was added to the card number to distinguish this set from the 660-card set issued earlier in the year (though the letter "U" has been omitted from the following list).

	MINT
Complete set	$10.00
Commons	.04

1 Phil Bradley	$ .04
2 Mike Devereaux	.20
3 Steve Finley	.30
6 Bob Milacki	.12
7 Randy Milligan	.10
8 John Dopson	.10
9 Nick Esasky	.04
11 Jim Abbott (FC)	1.50
12 Bert Blyleven	.15
13 Jeff Manto (FC)	.10
15 Lance Parrish	.10
16 Lee Stevens (FC)	.10
17 Claudell Washington	.08
18 Mark Davis	.06
19 Eric King	.06
21 Matt Merullo (FC)	.08
22 Steve Rosenberg	.06
23 Robin Ventura	2.50
25 Joey Belle (FC)	3.00
29 Pete O'Brien	.06
31 Tracy Jones	.06
32 Mike Schwabe (FC)	.05
35 Kevin Appier	1.00
36 • Bob Boone	.15
37 Luis de los Santos	.06

38 Jim Eisenreich	.08
39 Jamie Navarro (FC)	.30
40 Bill Spiers (FC)	.10
41 Greg Vaughn (FC)	1.50
42 Randy Veres (FC)	.10
46 Jesse Barfield	.08
47 Alvaro Espinoza	.06
48 Bob Geren (FC)	.05
50 Andy Hawkins	.05
51 Hensley Meulens	.15
52 Steve Sax	.10
53 Deion Sanders (FC)	1.50
54 Rickey Henderson	.25
55 Mike Moore	.15
57 Greg Briley	.10
58 Gene Harris (FC)	.05
59 Randy Johnson	.08
60 Jeffrey Leonard	.06
62 Omar Vizquel (FC)	.08
63 Kevin Brown	.10
64 Julio Franco	.12
66 Rafael Palmeiro	.20
67 Nolan Ryan	1.50
68 Francisco Cabrera (FC)	.15
69 Junior Felix (FC)	.20
70 Al Leiter	.08
71 Alex Sanchez	.05
72 Geronimo Berroa	.07
73 Derek Lilliquist	.05
74 Lonnie Smith	.08

75	Jeff Treadway	.08	
77	Lloyd McClendon	.06	
78	Scott Sanderson	.05	
79	Dwight Smith	.10	
80	Jerome Walton	.12	
81	Mitch Williams	.12	
82	Steve Wilson	.08	
83	Todd Benzinger	.08	
84	Ken Griffey	.20	
86	Rolando Roomes	.08	
87	Scott Scudder (FC)	.15	
91	Mike Morgan	.10	
92	Eddie Murray	.15	
93	Willie Randolph	.10	
96	Kevin Gross	.05	
97	Mark Langston	.10	
98	Spike Owen	.05	
101	Barry Lyons	.05	
102	Juan Samuel	.15	
103	Wally Whitehurst	.10	
104	Dennis Cook	.05	
105	Lenny Dykstra	.10	
106	Charlie Hayes	.08	
107	Tommy Herr	.05	
109	John Kruk	.15	
110	Roger McDowell	.08	
111	Terry Mulholland	.06	
112	Jeff Parrett	.06	
114	Jeff King	.08	
115	Randy Kramer	.06	
116	Bill Landrum	.08	
117	Cris Carpenter	.06	
119	Ken Hill	.10	
120	Dan Quisenberry	.08	
121	Milt Thompson	.08	
122	Todd Zeile (FC)	.60	
123	Jack Clark	.10	
124	Bruce Hurst	.10	
125	Mark Parent	.05	
126	Bip Roberts	.08	
127	Jeff Brantley (FC)	.15	
129	Mike LaCoss	.05	
130	Greg Litton (FC)	.10	
131	Mike Schmidt	.50	

1989 SCORE

Card backs had been neglected for years, but Score's second set of 660 cards maintained its reputation for presenting baseball's most appealing cards backs. The company continued to adorn the reverse sides of its card with color photos, stats, and interesting bios. Unfortunately, the company insisted on including action photos on the front of most cards. Several shots are dark or blurred, others show their subjects' faces blocked by helmets, still others catch players with their backs turned to the camera. Score also began to get repetitive in photo selection: Most non-pitchers are shown in their batting stances, while pitchers are seen in their windups. Several valuable cards are found in a specially designated Rookie subset.

		MINT
Complete set		**$20.00**
Commons		**.03**

1	Jose Canseco	$.30
2	Andre Dawson	.15
3	Mark McGwire	.30
4	Benny Santiago	.12
5	Rick Reuschel	.03
6	Fred McGriff	.20
7	Kal Daniels	.10
8	Gary Gaetti	.05
9	Ellis Burks	.08
10	Darryl Strawberry	.15
11	Julio Franco	.10
12	Lloyd Moseby	.06
13	*Jeff Pico*	.03

635 Ramon Martinez

14	Johnny Ray	.06
15	Cal Ripken, Jr.	.50
17	Mel Hall	.06
18	Bill Ripken	.06
19	Brook Jacoby	.05
20	Kirby Puckett	.35
21	Bill Doran	.06
22	Pete O'Brien	.06
23	Matt Nokes	.15
25	Jack Clark	.08
28	Willie Wilson	.08
29	Curt Young	.06
30	Dale Murphy	.10
31	Barry Larkin	.20
32	Dave Stewart	.06
33	Mike LaValliere	.06
35	Ryne Sandberg	.40
36	Tony Pena	.06
37	Greg Walker	.06
38	Von Hayes	.08
39	Kevin Mitchell	.15
40	Tim Raines	.10
41	Keith Hernandez	.08
42	Keith Moreland	.03
43	Ruben Sierra	.30
44	Chet Lemon	.03
45	Willie Randolph	.06
47	Candy Maldonado	.06
50	Dave Winfield	.30
51	Alvin Davis	.06
52	Cory Snyder	.06
53	Hubie Brooks	.08
54	Chili Davis	.06
55	Kevin Seitzer	.08
57	Tony Fernandez	.10
59	Oddibe McDowell	.06
60	Les Lancaster	.06
61	Billy Hatcher	.06
63	Marty Barrett	.06
65	Wally Joyner	.10
66	Mike Greenwell	.10
67	Ken Williams	.06
68	Bob Horner	.08
69	Steve Sax	.15
70	Rickey Henderson	.20
71	Mitch Webster	.06
72	Rob Deer	.06
73	Jim Presley	.06
75	George Brett	.40
76	Brian Downing	.06
77	Dave Martinez	.06
78	Scott Fletcher	.06
79	Phil Bradley	.08
80	Ozzie Smith	.15
83	Darnell Coles	.06
84	Len Dykstra	.15
85	Jim Rice	.10
86	Jeff Treadway	.08
87	Jose Lind	.08
88	Willie McGee	.10
90	Tony Gwynn	.25
92	Milt Thompson	.06
93	Kevin McReynolds	.15
94	Eddie Murray	.25
95	Lance Parrish	.08
96	Ron Kittle	.06
97	Gerald Young	.06
98	Ernie Whitt	.06
100	Don Mattingly	.15
101	Gerald Perry	.08
104	*Chris Sabo*	.25
105	Danny Tartabull	.15
106	Glenn Wilson	.06
108	Dave Parker	.10
109	Eric Davis	.15
110	Alan Trammell	.15
112	Frank Tanana	.06

114 Dennis Martinez .... .10
116 Bob Ojeda .... .06
117 Doug Drabek.................... .10
119 Greg Maddux (FC) .... .10
120 Cecil Fielder (photo on back reversed) .... .30
121 Mike Scioscia .... .06
122 Dan Petry .... .06
124 Kelly Downs .... .08
125 Greg Gross (first name incorrect on back)............ .20
126 Fred Lynn .... .06
127 Barry Bonds .... .20
128 Harold Baines................. .10
132 Teddy Higuera................. .08
135 Ray Knight (photo reversed) .... .25
136 Howard Johnson .... .12
137 Terry Pendleton............... .10
142 *Rich Renteria* (FC) .... .06
143 Jose Guzman .... .08
144 Andres Galarraga .... .06
147 Glenn Braggs .... .06
148 John Kruk .... .10
149 Mike Schmidt................... .25
150 Lee Smith .... .08
151 Robin Yount .... .25
152 Mark Eichhorn .... .06
154 B.J. Surhoff .... .08
155 Vince Coleman................ .08
160 Jesse Barfield................. .08
161 Mark Langston .... .10
162 Kurt Stillwell .... .06
164 Glenn Davis..................... .08
165 Walt Weiss .... .08
166 Dave Concepcion .... .08
171 Darrell Evans.................. .08
174 Andy Van Slyke............... .15
175 Wade Boggs..................... .25
179 Carney Lansford.............. .06
181 Kirk McCaskill .... .06
182 Tony Armas .... .06
184 Tom Brunansky .... .06
185 *Bryan Harvey* .... .35
186 Mike Marshall .... .03
187 Bo Diaz............................ .06
189 Mike Pagliarulo................ .08
193 • Dwight Evans................ .10
195 Bobby Bonilla .... .20

35 Ryne Sandberg

197 Dave Stieb...................... .08
198 *Pat Borders* .... .20
199 Rafael Palmeiro............... .15
200 Doc Gooden .... .12
202 Chris James .... .08
205 Don Baylor .... .08
210 Kirk Gibson .... .10
211 Claudell Washington .... .06
213 Joe Carter .... .15
214 Bill Buckner .... .08
215 Bert Blyleven .... .15
216 Brett Butler .... .06
220 Tim Wallach .... .08
221 David Cone .... .15
222 Don Carman .... .06
223 Rich Gossage.................. .10
225 Dave Righetti................... .10
226 Kevin Bass .... .06
230 Lou Whitaker .... .15
231 *Luis Alicea*...................... .15
232 Roberto Alomar .... .80
233 • Bob Boone .... .06
235 Shawon Dunston............. .08
237 *Craig Biggio*.................... .50
238 Dennis Boyd .... .06
240 Gary Carter .... .15
244 Les Straker .... .06
247 Joe Orsulak .... .06

629 Felix Jose

250	Jack Morris	.15
251	Bret Saberhagen	.10
254	Eric Show	.06
255	Juan Samuel	.10
256	Dale Sveum	.06
260	Steve Bedrosian	.08
261	Jack Howell	.06
265	Todd Worrell	.10
267	Dave Collins	.06
268	Sid Fernandez	.08
270	Shane Mack	.06
276	Dennis Eckersley	.10
277	Graig Nettles	.10
280	Gene Larkin	.08
281	Roger McDowell	.08
282	Greg Swindell	.10
285	Mike Dunne	.08
286	Greg Mathews	.06
287	Kent Tekulve	.06
289	Jack McDowell	.40
290	Frank Viola	.15
291	Mark Gubicza	.10
293	Mike Henneman	.08
295	Charlie Hough	.06
298	Mike Witt	.06
299	Pascual Perez	.06
300	Nolan Ryan	.65
301	Mitch Williams	.08
302	Mookie Wilson	.06
303	Mackey Sasser	.06
305	Jeff Reardon	.12
306	Randy Myers	.08
308	Bob Welch	.08
310	Harold Reynolds	.06
314	Walt Terrell	.06
317	Rick Rhoden	.06
318	Tom Henke	.06
319	*Mike Macfarlane*	.12
320	Dan Plesac	.08
323	Devon White	.10
325	Bruce Hurst	.08
330	Bo Jackson	.25
331	Ivan Calderon	.06
336	Damon Berryhill	.15
338	Dan Pasqua	.08
339	Bill Pecota	.06
342	Ron Guidry	.15
345	Rich Gedman	.06
347	George Bell	.20
350	Roger Clemens	.25
351	Bill Long	.06
352	Jay Bell (FC)	.06
353	Steve Balboni	.06
356	Jesse Orosco	.06
360	Darrin Jackson (FC)	.08
362	Mark Grace	.25
365	Terry Steinbach	.08
367	Jeff Montgomery	.06
369	Chris Brown	.06
370	Orel Hershiser	.10
371	Todd Benzinger	.08
372	Ron Gant	.35
374	Joey Meyer	.08
376	Mike Davis	.06
377	Jeff Parrett (FC)	.08
378	Jay Howell	.06
380	Luis Polonia	.06
382	Kent Hrbek	.15
384	Dave LaPoint	.06
386	Melido Perez	.08
387	Doug Jones	.06
389	Alejandro Pena	.06
390	Frank White	.06
394	Allan Anderson (FC)	.06
398	Mike Jackson	.06
399	Bobby Thigpen	.08
400	Don Sutton	.15

401	Cecil Espy	.06
407	Rick Sutcliffe	.08
409	John Smiley	.15
410	Juan Nieves	.06
412	Wes Gardner (FC)	.06
425	Bruce Sutter	.08
433	Ozzie Guillen	.06
435	Gary Ward	.06
437	Fernando Valenzuela	.06
442	• Tom Glavine	.60
449	Carlton Fisk	.15
450	Will Clark	.35
453	Todd Stottlemyre	.15
455	*Dave Gallagher*	.06
457	Fred Manrique	.06
459	*Doug Jennings* (FC)	.06
460	Joe Magrane	.08
462	*Jack Armstrong*	.10
463	Bobby Witt	.08
465	*Todd Burns*	.10
466	*John Dopson*	.10
475	Mike Flanagan	.06
477	Tommy John	.10
480	Jimmy Key	.08
483	Tom Pagnozzi	.10
486	Jody Reed	.10
487	Roberto Kelly	.25
488	Shawn Hillegas	.06
489	Jerry Reuss	.06
490	Mark Davis	.10
492	Zane Smith	.06
495	Larry Parrish	.06
505	Tim Crews	.06
507	Brian Holton	.15
508	Dennis Lamp	.06
509	Bobby Meacham	.10
520	Dan Quisenberry	.06
525	Bob Forsch	.06
528	*Mike Schooler*	.08
529	Jose Oquendo	.06
530	Jay Buhner	.15
531	Tom Bolton (FC)	.06
533	Dave Henderson	.08
534	*John Costello* (FC)	.06
538	Jim Clancy	.06
548	*Ricky Jordan*	.10
549	Mike Boddicker	.10
550	Mike Scott	.10
551	Jeff Ballard (FC)	.05

237 Craig Biggio

552	Jose Rijo	.20
554	Tom Browning	.08
555	Danny Jackson	.15
556	Rick Dempsey	.06
557	Jeffrey Leonard	.06
558	Jeff Musselman	.06
560	John Tudor	.08
561	Don Slaught	.06
562	Dennis Rasmussen	.08
563	*Brady Anderson*	.50
564	Pedro Guerrero	.15
565	Paul Molitor	.15
570	Jeff Hamilton (FC)	.06
571	*Oswald Peraza*	.08
573	*Jose Bautista* (FC)	.08
575	John Franco	.08
577	Nelson Liriano	.06
580	Al Leiter	.10
581	Dave Stapleton (FC)	.06
582	1988 World Series (Jose Canseco, Kirk Gibson, Orel Hershiser, Dave Stewart)	.12
585	Rene Gonzales (FC)	.06
588	Mario Soto	.06
589	Jeff Blauser	.08
590	Jim Traber	.06

592	Mark Williamson (FC)	.06
595	*Paul Gibson* (FC)	.08
596	Mike Birkbeck	.06
600	Gregg Jefferies	.35
603	Mike Diaz	.06
604	*Gary Varsho* (FC)	.12
607	Jim Eppard (FC)	.08
609	Ken Griffey Sr.	.12
610	Buddy Bell	.06
611	Ted Simmons	.08
612	Matt Williams	.35
613	Danny Cox	.06
616	• John Smoltz (FC)	.60
618	*Rob Dibble*	.20
619	Kirt Manwaring	.10
620	Felix Fermin (1989 Rookie) (FC)	.06
621	*Doug Dascenzo* (1989 Rookie) (FC)	.25
622	*Bill Brennan* (1989 Rookie) (FC)	.08
623	*Carlos Quintana* (1989 Rookie) (FC)	.10
624	*Mike Harkey* (1989 Rookie) (FC)	.10
625	*Gary Sheffield* (1989 Rookie) (FC)	1.50
626	Tom Prince (1989 Rookie) (FC)	.08
627	*Steve Searcy* (1989 Rookie) (FC)	.08
628	*Charlie Hayes* (1989 Rookie) (FC)	.20
629	*Felix Jose* (1989 Rookie) (FC)	.75
630	*Sandy Alomar* (1989 Rookie) (FC)	.30
631	*Derek Lilliquist* (1989 Rookie) (FC)	.08
632	Geronimo Berroa (1989 Rookie) (FC)	.06
633	*Luis Medina* (1989 Rookie) (FC)	.06
634	*Tom Gordon* (1989 Rookie) (FC)	.15
635	*Ramon Martinez* (1989 Rookie) (FC)	.75
636	*Craig Worthington* (1989 Rookie) (FC)	.10
637	Edgar Martinez (1989 Rookie) (FC)	.25
638	*Chad Kreuter* (1989 Rookie) (FC)	.25
639	Ron Jones (1989 Rookie) (FC)	.06
640	*Van Snider* (1989 Rookie) (FC)	.06
641	*Lance Blankenship* (1989 Rookie) (FC)	.10
642	*Dwight Smith* (1989 Rookie) (FC)	.20
643	*Cameron Drew* (1989 Rookie) (FC)	.06
644	*Jerald Clark* (1989 Rookie) (FC)	.10
645	*Randy Johnson* (1989 Rookie) (FC)	.40
646	*Norm Charlton* (1989 Rookie) (FC)	.12
647	Todd Frohwirth (1989 Rookie) (FC)	.08
648	*Luis de los Santos* (1989 Rookie) (FC)	.12
649	*Tim Jones* (1989 Rookie) (FC)	.06
650	*Dave West* (1989 Rookie) (FC)	.10
651	*Bob Milacki* (1989 Rookie) (FC)	.25
652	1988 Highlights (Wrigley Field)	.08
653	1988 Highlights (Orel Hershiser)	.10
654	1988 Highlights (Wade Boggs)	.20
655	1988 Highlights (Jose Canseco)	.20
656	1988 Highlights (Doug Jones)	.06
657	1988 Highlights (Rickey Henderson)	.15
658	1988 Highlights (Tom Browning)	.06
659	1988 Highlights (Mike Greenwell)	.08
660	1988 Highlights (Red Sox winning streak)	.06

1989 SCORE ROOKIE & TRADED

After hobbyists overwhelmed Score with their ceaseless demands for its initial Rookie & Traded set in 1988, the company was prepared for collectors in 1989. Greater availability and fewer hot rookie names kept the second-year set of 110 cards from booming in price immediately. However, it seemed just as popular as the regular Score set. The company even scooped its competition by becoming the only card manufacturer with a photo of Los Angeles Dodgers rookie hurler John Wetteland. Following the lead of rival companies, Score sold its extension offering only through hobby dealers in boxed, complete sets.

	MINT
Complete set	$10.00
Commons	.03

100 Ken Griffey, Jr.

1	Rafael Palmeiro	$ .20
2	Nolan Ryan	1.50
3	Jack Clark	.06
5	Mike Moore	.08
6	Pete O'Brien	.06
7	Jeffrey Leonard	.06
10	Claudell Washington	.06
11	Mike Pagliarulo	.06
14	Andy Hawkins	.04
15	Todd Benzinger	.08
16	Mookie Wilson	.08
17	Bert Blyleven	.10
18	Jeff Treadway	.08
19	Bruce Hurst	.15
20	Steve Sax	.10
21	Juan Samuel	.08
22	Jesse Barfield	.10
23	Carmelo Castillo	.05
25	Mark Langston	.10
26	Eric King	.05
28	Lenny Dykstra	.08
31	Eddie Murray	.10
32	Mitch Williams	.05
33	Jeff Parrett	.05
34	Wally Backman	.05
35	Julio Franco	.12
36	Lance Parrish	.06
38	Luis Polonia	.10
41	Willie Randolph	.06
45	Milt Thompson	.08
48	Kal Daniels	.08
50	Rickey Henderson	.20
52	Tim Leary	.08
53	Roger McDowell	.06
54	Mel Hall	.12
56	Zane Smith	.06

58	Bob McClure	.10
62	Harold Baines	.10
65	Darrell Evans	.15
67	Frank Viola	.15
70	John Kruk	.15
74	• Bob Boone	.10
77	Randy Johnson	.15
81	Cris Carpenter	.10
82	Billy Spiers (FC)	.10
83	Junior Felix (FC)	.20
84	Joe Girardi (FC)	.12
85	Jerome Walton	.20
87	Greg Harris	.10
88	Jim Abbott	1.50
89	Kevin Brown	.20
90	John Wetteland (FC)	.20
91	Gary Wayne (FC)	.25
92	Rich Monteleone (FC)	.15
95	Steve Finley	.30
96	Gregg Olson	.40
97	Ken Patterson	.08
98	Ken Hill	.50
99	Scott Scudder (FC)	.15
100	Ken Griffey, Jr.	5.00
101	Jeff Brantley (FC)	.20
103	Carlos Martinez (FC)	.10
104	Joe Oliver (FC)	.15
106	Joey Belle (FC)	3.50
107	Kenny Rogers (FC)	.08
110	Pete Harnisch	.35

1989 TOPPS

Although Topps maintained the same card size, the company offered several design alterations for 1989. While retaining simple white front borders and crisp, well-cropped photos, bold lettering on the borders sometimes turned overwhelmingly neon (shades of 1972 Topps). Player positions do not appear on card fronts, and player names are dwarfed by team designations. But Topps saved the day by including several appealing subsets. A group of 10 cards, called #1 Draft Picks, consists of promising rookies (mostly former Olympians) in their college uniforms. Jim Abbott, Steve Avery, and Robin Ventura are big names in this category. Top rookies like Sandy Alomar, Jr., Gregg Jefferies, and Gary Sheffield are spotlighted with specially marked Future Star cards.

		MINT
Complete set		**$22.00**
Commons		**.03**

2	Record Breaker (Wade Boggs)	$ .10
3	Record Breaker (Gary Carter)	.05
5	Record Breaker (Orel Hershiser)	.05
6	Record Breaker (Doug Jones)	.05
8	*Dave Eiland* (FC)	.10
9	Tim Teufel	.03
10	Andre Dawson	.15
11	Bruce Sutter	.10
12	Dale Sveum	.03
15	Robby Thompson	.06
16	Ron Robinson	.03
17	Brian Downing	.06
18	Rick Rhoden	.03
19	Greg Gagne	.03
20	Steve Bedrosian	.06
22	Tim Crews	.03
25	Frank White	.06
27	*Orestes Destrade* (FC)	.08
30	Doc Gooden	.15

33	B.J. Surhoff	.08
34	Ken Williams	.03
35	John Tudor	.06
36	Mitch Webster	.03
40	Steve Sax	.15
45	Kal Daniels	.08
48	Tim Burke	.06
49	*Craig Biggio* (FC)	.40
50	George Bell	.10
53	Ruben Sierra	.30
54	Steve Trout	.03
55	Julio Franco	.10
59	Mark Davis	.03
60	Tom Brunansky	.06
63	Mark Clear	.03
65	Rick Reuschel	.06
70	Mark McGwire	.35
73	Pascual Perez	.06
75	Tom Henke	.06
76	*Terry Blocker* (FC)	.10
77	Doyle Alexander	.06
78	Jim Sundberg	.06
80	Cory Snyder	.15
83	*Jeff Blauser* (FC)	.10
84	*Bill Bene* (#1 Draft Pick) (FC)	.10
85	Kevin McReynolds	.15
88	*Darryl Hamilton* (FC)	.15
90	Vince Coleman	.12
95	Gerald Young	.06
97	Greg Mathews	.06
98	Larry Sheets	.06
99	*Sherman Corbett* (FC)	.06
100	Mike Schmidt	.35
105	Ron Darling	.06
107	Jose DeLeon	.10
109	*Hipolito Pena* (FC)	.06
110	Paul Molitor	.15
115	Jody Davis	.06
120	Frank Viola	.15
122	*Lance Johnson* (FC)	.12
126	Sid Bream	.06
129	*Terry Clark* (FC)	.06
130	Gerald Perry	.06
135	Jose Rijo	.08
141	Indians Ldrs (Brook Jacoby)	.06
144	Jay Bell	.06
145	Dave Stewart	.08

764 Robin Ventura

148	Bill Pecota	.06
149	*Doug Dascenzo* (FC)	.08
150	Fernando Valenzuela	.06
156	*Dave Gallagher* (FC)	.10
157	Tom Glavine	.60
161	*Gregg Olson* (#1 Draft Pick) (FC)	.45
163	Bob Forsch	.05
166	*Doug Jennings* (FC)	.06
167	*Steve Searcy* (FS) (FC)	.08
168	Willie Wilson	.08
169	Mike Jackson	.06
170	Tony Fernandez	.10
173	Mel Hall	.06
174	*Todd Burns* (FC)	.08
176	Jeff Parrett	.03
177	*Monty Fariss* (#1 Draft Pick) (FC)	.15
178	Mark Grant	.03
180	Mike Scott	.05
181	*Craig Worthington* (FC)	.08
183	Oddibe McDowell	.06
184	*John Costello*	.06
189	Kevin Mitchell	.15
190	Mike Witt	.08
191	*Sil Campusano*	.03
194	*Greg W. Harris* (FC)	.15
195	Ozzie Guillen	.10

784 Steve Avery

199	*Mike Schooler*	.10
200	George Brett	.25
202	*Brad Moore* (FC)	.05
205	● *Dwight Evans*	.10
206	Roberto Alomar (FC)	.90
209	*Jeff Bittiger* (FC)	.05
210	Dale Murphy	.15
216	Jack Howell	.03
219	Jim Clancy	.03
220	Gary Gaetti	.08
221	Cecil Espy	.06
222	*Mark Lewis* (#1 Draft Pick) (FC)	.25
223	Jay Buhner	.15
224	Tony LaRussa	.06
225	● *Ramon Martinez* (FC)	.50
226	Bill Doran	.06
227	John Farrell	.08
228	*Nelson Santovenia*	.03
229	Jimmy Key	.08
230	Ozzie Smith	.15
232	Ricky Horton	.03
233	Gregg Jefferies (FS) (FC)	.30
234	Tom Browning	.08
235	John Kruk	.15
240	Greg Maddux	.10
241	Brett Butler	.06
243	● *Bob Boone*	.06
245	Jim Rice	.10
249	Tim Leary	.06
250	Cal Ripken	.50
251	*John Dopson* (FC)	.08
252	Billy Hatcher	.06
253	*Jose Alvarez* (FC)	.05
254	Tom Lasorda	.06
255	Ron Guidry	.08
256	Benny Santiago	.15
260	Dave Winfield	.25
262	*Jeff Pico*	.05
264	● *Rob Dibble* (FC)	.20
265	Kent Hrbek	.15
268	Keith Miller	.06
269	Tom Bolton	.03
270	Wally Joyner	.15
273	Jose Lind	.06
275	Danny Tartabull	.15
276	Paul Kilgus	.05
277	Mike Davis	.06
282	*Cris Carpenter* (FC)	.10
286	Darrin Jackson	.10
287	Juan Nieves	.06
289	Ernie Whitt	.06
290	John Franco	.08
291	Mets Ldrs (Darryl Strawberry)	.12
292	*Jim Corsi* (FC)	.08
293	Glenn Wilson	.06
295	Scott Fletcher	.06
296	● *Ron Gant*	.40
297	*Oswald Peraza* (FC)	.10
298	Chris James	.05
300	Darryl Strawberry	.25
302	Gary Ward	.03
303	Felix Fermin	.06
305	Dave Smith	.03
309	Mario Diaz (FC)	.05
310	Rafael Palmeiro	.25
311	Chris Bosio	.03
315	Greg Swindell	.10
316	Walt Weiss	.10
317	*Jack Armstrong*	.10
318	Gene Larkin	.08
320	Lou Whitaker	.15
321	Red Sox Ldrs (Jody Reed)	.06
322	John Smiley	.10
323	Gary Thurman	.10

324	*Bob Milacki* (FC)	.15
326	Dennis Boyd	.06
327	*Mark Lemke* (FC)	.20
330	Eric Davis	.10
332	Tony Armas	.06
333	Bob Ojeda	.06
334	Steve Lyons	.06
335	Dave Righetti	.10
336	Steve Balboni	.06
340	Kirk Gibson	.08
343	*Gary Sheffield* (FS) (FC)	1.50
349	*Ron Jones* (FC)	.10
350	Andy Van Slyke	.15
351	Giants Ldrs (Bob Melvin)	.03
355	Mark Langston	.12
356	Kevin Elster	.05
357	Jerry Reuss	.06
358	*Ricky Jordan* (FC)	.15
359	Tommy John	.10
360	Ryne Sandberg	.35
364	Rob Deer	.06
365	Mike Henneman	.06
367	*Johnny Paredes* (FC)	.05
369	Ken Caminiti	.06
370	Dennis Eckersley	.10
374	John Wathan	.06
375	Terry Pendleton	.10
380	Rickey Henderson	.20
382	*John Smoltz* (FC)	.65
383	Howard Johnson	.10
385	Von Hayes	.08
386	Andres Galarraga AS	.05
387	Ryne Sandberg AS	.20
388	Bobby Bonilla AS	.10
389	Ozzie Smith AS	.10
390	Darryl Strawberry AS	.15
391	Andre Dawson AS	.15
392	Andy Van Slyke AS	.12
393	Gary Carter AS	.10
394	Orel Hershiser AS	.15
395	Danny Jackson AS	.05
396	Kirk Gibson AS	.08
397	Don Mattingly AS	.15
398	Julio Franco AS	.10
399	Wade Boggs AS	.15
400	Alan Trammell AS	.08
401	Jose Canseco AS	.20
402	Mike Greenwell AS	.08

296 Ron Gant

403	Kirby Puckett AS	.15
404	● Bob Boone AS	.06
405	Roger Clemens AS	.15
406	Frank Viola AS	.08
407	Dave Winfield AS	.15
410	Jack Clark	.10
411	Mitch Williams	.08
415	Rich Gossage	.10
416	Fred Lynn	.06
420	Joe Carter	.15
421	Kirk McCaskill	.06
422	Bo Diaz	.03
423	Brian Fisher	.06
424	Luis Polonia	.06
425	Jay Howell	.06
429	Twins Ldrs (Greg Gagne)	.06
430	Mark Gubicza	.05
432	*Chad Kreuter* (FC)	.05
434	*Ken Patterson* (FC)	.05
435	● Len Dykstra	.15
437	*Andy Benes* (#1 Draft Pick)	.70
440	Bobby Bonilla	.25
442	Jose Oquendo	.08
443	*Rod Nichols* (FC)	.05
445	Matt Nokes	.15
450	Roger Clemens	.40
452	*Israel Sanchez*	.05

445

573 Jim Abbott

453	Tom Prince (FC)	.05
455	Johnny Ray	.06
456	Tim Belcher	.06
457	Mackey Sasser	.06
458	*Donn Pall* (FC)	.05
460	Dave Stieb	.08
461	Buddy Bell	.06
462	Jose Guzman	.06
464	Bryn Smith	.06
465	Mark Grace (FC)	.40
469	*Jose Bautista*	.05
470	Lance Parrish	.08
471	*Steve Curry* (FC)	.05
472	Brian Harper	.10
475	Dave Parker	.15
478	Doug Drabek	.06
479	*Mike Macfarlane*	.10
480	Keith Hernandez	.10
482	*Steve Peters*	.05
485	Hubie Brooks	.08
486	Jack McDowell	.40
487	Scott Lusader (FC)	.08
488	Kevin Coffman	.06
489	Phillies Ldrs (Mike Schmidt)	.12
490	*Chris Sabo*	.25
493	Todd Benzinger	.10
494	Shane Rawley	.06

497	Pete Stanicek	.06
499	*Don Heinkel* (FC)	.05
500	Jose Canseco	.30
501	Vance Law	.06
505	● Pete Rose	.25
506	Kirt Manwaring	.10
507	Steve Farr	.05
510	Bob Horner	.08
515	Barry Larkin	.20
516	Eddie Whitson	.06
520	Rick Sutcliffe	.08
521	Mickey Tettleton	.08
522	*Randy Kramer* (FC)	.05
525	Chili Davis	.06
527	Dave Henderson	.10
528	*Luis Medina* (FC)	.05
530	Nolan Ryan	.60
531	Dave Hengel (FC)	.05
535	Todd Worrell	.08
537	Pete Smith	.05
539	Barry Jones	.06
540	Bo Jackson	.20
541	Cecil Fielder	.25
543	Damon Berryhill	.06
545	Mookie Wilson	.06
548	Bobby Witt	.08
550	Orel Hershiser	.10
555	Bert Blyleven	.12
557	*Keith Miller* (FC)	.06
558	Dan Pasqua	.08
560	Rock Raines	.15
565	Jeff Russell	.06
567	David Wells	.08
570	Tony Gwynn	.30
571	Billy Ripken	.06
573	*Jim Abbott* (#1 Draft Pick) (FC)	1.00
574	Dave Clark	.06
575	Juan Samuel	.10
577	Randy Bush	.05
579	Astros Ldrs (Glenn Davis)	.08
580	Harold Reynolds	.08
583	*Paul Gibson* (FC)	.08
584	Randy Velarde (FC)	.05
585	Harold Baines	.10
588	*Luis Alicea*	.15
590	Andres Galarraga	.08
595	Ted Higuera	.06

596	Kurt Stillwell	.06
597	*Terry Taylor* (FC)	.06
600	Wade Boggs	.25
601	Dave Dravecky	.06
602	Devon White	.10
603	Frank Tanana	.06
604	Paul O'Neill	.10
605	Bob Welch	.10
606	Rick Dempsey	.06
607	*Willie Ansley* (#1 Draft Pick) (FC)	.15
608	Phil Bradley	.08
610	Randy Myers	.08
612	Dan Quisenberry	.08
613	*Gary Varsho* (FC)	.10
615	Robin Yount	.25
616	*Steve Rosenberg* (FC)	.05
617	*Mark Parent*	.05
620	Barry Bonds	.30
621	Rick Mahler	.06
622	Stan Javier	.06
625	Eddie Murray	.25
628	Matt Williams	.25
629	Pete O'Brien	.06
630	Mike Greenwell	.08
632	*Bryan Harvey*	.40
634	Marvin Freeman (FC)	.08
635	Willie Randolph	.06
639	Athletics Ldrs (Walt Weiss)	.08
640	Willie McGee	.10
645	Jack Morris	.15
646	Kevin Bass	.06
647	*Randy Johnson* (FC)	.40
648	*Sandy Alomar* (FS) (FC)	.25
650	Kirby Puckett	.35
654	Whitey Herzog	.06
655	Dave Magadan	.08
656	Ivan Calderon	.06
659	Al Leiter	.08
660	Will Clark	.35
661	Turn Back the Clock (Dwight Gooden)	.08
662	Turn Back the Clock (Lou Brock)	.08
663	Turn Back the Clock (Hank Aaron)	.15
664	Turn Back the Clock (Gil Hodges)	.06

530 Nolan Ryan

665	Turn Back the Clock (Tony Oliva)	.06
669	Dodgers Ldrs (Orel Hershiser)	.10
670	Kevin Seitzer	.05
672	Allan Anderson	.06
673	Don Baylor	.08
675	Bruce Hurst	.08
680	Gary Carter	.15
685	Jeff Treadway	.06
686	Scott Terry	.06
687	Alvin Davis	.06
688	Zane Smith	.06
690	Doug Jones	.10
691	Roberto Kelly	.25
693	*Pat Borders*	.15
694	Les Lancaster	.06
695	Carlton Fisk	.20
696	Don August	.06
700	Don Mattingly	.25
701	Storm Davis	.08
704	*Carlos Quintana* (FC)	.15
706	Pete Incaviglia	.06
710	Dave Cone	.15
712	Bill Swift	.10
713	*Ty Griffin* (#1 Draft Pick)	.10
715	Tony Pena	.06
718	Glenn Braggs	.06

720	Tim Wallach	.08
722	Todd Stottlemyre	.15
725	Terry Steinbach	.08
729	Rangers Ldrs (Steve Buechele)	.06
730	Danny Jackson	.06
734	Jody Reed	.10
735	Roger McDowell	.08
737	*Norm Charlton* (FC)	.15
740	Dan Plesac	.08
742	FS (*Mike Harkey*) (FC)	.10
744	Roger Craig	.06
745	Fred McGriff	.25
746	*German Gonzalez* (FC)	.06
750	Bret Saberhagen	.15
757	*Brady Anderson*	.50
760	Lee Smith	.10

761	*Dante Bichette* (FC)	.15
762	Bobby Thigpen	.10
763	Dave Martinez	.06
764	*Robin Ventura* (#1 Draft Pick)	1.00
765	Glenn Davis	.08
770	Alan Trammell	.15
771	Ron Kittle	.06
774	Frank Robinson	.08
775	Jeff Reardon	.10
780	Pedro Guerrero	.10
781	*Greg Briley* (FC)	.10
783	*Trevor Wilson* (FC)	.15
784	*Steve Avery* (#1 Draft Pick) (FC)	1.25
785	Ellis Burks	.12
786	Melido Perez	.10

1989 TOPPS TRADED

Topps stuck with its custom by releasing a ninth annual 132-card Traded set in 1989. The company maintained the same format for the set (which copied the 792-card Topps set from the same year), and packaged the cards in a specially designed box. However, for the first time, the company experimented with selling complete sets in selected retail outlets such as toy stores. This added a new phase to the continuing debate over whether collectors would have to consider Traded cards as official "rookie" cards. Hot cards in the set include Ken Griffey, Jr. and Deion Sanders, while Nolan Ryan made his Topps debut as a Ranger.

		MINT
Complete set		**$8.00**
Commons		**.03**
2	Jim Abbott	$1.00
3	Kent Anderson (FC)	.08
6	Steve Balboni	.03
7	Jesse Barfield	.05
8	Steve Bedrosian	.03
9	Todd Benzinger	.10
11	Bert Blyleven	.15

12	Bob Boone	.08
13	Phil Bradley	.03
14	Jeff Brantley (FC)	.15
15	Kevin Brown	.20
16	Jerry Browne	.03
17	Chuck Cary	.03
20	Jack Clark	.10
23	Mike Devereaux	.08
26	John Dopson	.10
28	Jim Eisenreich	.08
29	Nick Esasky	.03
30	Alvaro Espinoza	.03

31	Darrell Evans	.10
32	Junior Felix (FC)	.20
34	Julio Franco	.20
37	Bob Geren (FC)	.08
38	Tom Gordon (FC)	.15
39	Tommy Gregg	.08
40	Ken Griffey	.10
41	Ken Griffey, Jr. (FC)	5.00
43	Lee Guetterman	.03
44	Mel Hall	.10
45	Erik Hanson	.20
46	Gene Harris (FC)	.03
47	Andy Hawkins	.08
48	Rickey Henderson	.35
49	Tom Herr	.05
50	Ken Hill	.50
51	Brian Holman	.10
55	Bruce Hurst	.10
56	Chris James	.03
57	Randy Johnson	.35
61	Eric King	.03
62	Ron Kittle	.05
63	John Kruk	.15
66	Mark Langston	.15
70	Jim Lefebvre	.10
71	Al Leiter	.05
72	Jeffrey Leonard	.05
73	Derek Lilliquist	.08
75	Tom McCarthy (FC)	.03
76	Lloyd McClendon	.08
79	Roger McDowell	.08
81	Randy Milligan	.10
82	Mike Moore	.08
83	Keith Moreland	.03
84	Mike Morgan	.08
86	Rob Murphy	.03
87	Eddie Murray	.15
88	Pete O'Brien	.05
89	Gregg Olson	.45
90	Steve Ontiveros	.03
91	Jesse Orosco	.03
92	Spike Owen	.03
93	Rafael Palmeiro	.20
94	Clay Parker	.05
95	Jeff Parrett	.05
96	Lance Parrish	.08
99	Doug Rader	.08
100	Willie Randolph	.08
103	Bip Roberts	.10

110 Deion Sanders

104	Kenny Rogers (FC)	.08
105	Ed Romero	.03
106	Nolan Ryan	1.50
107	Luis Salazar	.03
108	Juan Samuel	.10
109	Alex Sanchez	.06
110	Deion Sanders (FC)	1.75
111	Steve Sax	.08
112	Rick Schu	.03
113	Dwight Smith	.10
114	Lonnie Smith	.05
115	Billy Spiers (FC)	.08
116	Kent Tekulve	.10
117	Walt Terrell	.03
118	Milt Thompson	.05
119	Dickie Thon	.03
120	Jeff Torborg	.08
121	Jeff Treadway	.08
122	Omar Vizquel (FC)	.08
123	Jerome Walton (FC)	.20
124	Gary Ward	.05
125	Claudell Washington	.08
126	Curt Wilkerson	.03
127	Eddie Williams	.03
128	Frank Williams	.03
129	Ken Williams	.03
130	Mitch Williams	.10
131	Steve Wilson	.08

1989 UPPER DECK

The biggest hobby event of 1989 in the baseball card world was the arrival of a brand new card company: Upper Deck, a card manufacturer from Anaheim, California, managed to penetrate the market split up among Donruss, Fleer, core and Topps. The Upper Deck cards feature large, crisp color images on both sides and are printed on glossy stock of a heavy weight. The cards came in 15-card foil packs for 89 cents per pack, but within weeks the price shot up to $1.50 a pack. Upper Deck announced that no more than 60,000 to 70,000 foil pack cases were produced in 1989. The set, originally thought to number 700, grew to 800 when the company issued a second series in July, though factory-collated sets contain all 800 cards. Each card includes a small hologram on the back that is said to be counterfeit-proof. (Star Rookies specialty cards are identified with the abbreviation SR.)

	MINT
Complete set (1-700)	**$132.00**
Commons (1-700)	**.08**
Complete set (1-800)	**150.00**
Commons (701-800)	**.10**

1	Ken Griffey Jr. (SR) ...	$60.00
2	Luis Medina (SR)	.10
3	Tony Chance (SR)	.08
5	Sandy Alomar Jr. (SR)	.35
6	Rolando Roomes (SR)	.12
7	David West (SR)	.15
8	Cris Carpenter (SR).........	.20
9	Gregg Jefferies (SR)	1.50
10	Doug Dascenzo (SR)	.10
11	Ron Jones (SR)..............	.10
12	Luis de los Santos (SR) ..	.10
13	Gary Sheffield (SR) (SS designation on front is inverted)	10.00
13	Gary Sheffield (SR) (SS position correct)....	10.00
14	Mike Harkey (SR)	.20
15	Lance Blankenship (SR) ..	.15
16	William Brennan (SR).......	.08
17	John Smoltz (SR)	4.00
18	Ramon Martinez (SR) ...	2.00
19	Mark Lemke (SR)	.30
20	Juan Bell (SR)	.10
21	Rey Palacios (SR)...........	.08
22	Felix Jose (SR)..............	1.00
23	Van Snider (SR).............	.08
24	Dante Bichette (SR)	.35
25	Randy Johnson (SR).....	1.75
26	Carlos Quintana (SR)......	.30
28	Mike Schooler	.30
30	Jerald Clark....................	.30
31	Kevin Gross...................	.08
32	Dan Firova....................	.08
35	Ricky Jordan	.20
37	Bret Saberhagen	.30
39	Dave Dravecky	.15
41	Jeff Musselman	.08
45	Sil Campusano...............	.08
46	Mike Krukow.................	.08
47	Paul Gibson..................	.10
53	Steve Sax	.12
54	Pete O'Brien	.08
56	Rick Rhoden.................	.10
57	John Dopson...................	.10
59	Dave Righetti.................	.10
72	Brian Holton (photo is Shawn Hillegas)	.50
95	Mitch Williams	.10

406 Mike Schmidt

467 Cal Ripken Jr.

243	Melido Perez	.20
244	Willie Wilson	.10
246	Von Hayes	.10
247	Matt Williams	1.25
248	John Candelaria	.10
250	Greg Swindell	.10
253	Vince Coleman	.25
254	Larry Sheets	.10
255	George Bell	.35
256	Terry Steinbach	.12
257	*Jack Armstrong*	.25
259	Ray Knight	.10
260	Darryl Strawberry	.60
263	Jeff Leonard	.10
264	Tom Henke	.10
265	Ozzie Smith	.75
270	Barry Larkin	.75
273	*Craig Biggio*	1.25
275	Eddie Murray	.50
280	John Kruk	.25
281	*Luis Alicea*	.20
283	Billy Ripken	.10
285	Robin Yount	.75
289	Dennis Eckersley	.20
290	Alan Trammell	.25
291	Jimmy Key	.12
296	Roger McDowell	.12
298	Doyle Alexander	.10

300	Mark McGwire	1.50
301	*Darryl Hamilton*	.25
303	Rick Sutcliffe	.12
306	Pedro Guerrero	.10
307	Ron Guidry	.10
312	*Chad Kreuter*	.50
321	*Gary Varsho* (photo is Mike Bielecki on card back, batting right-handed)	1.00
321	*Gary Varsho* (correct photo, batting left-handed)	.25
329	Danny Tartabull	.50
330	Tony Pena	.10
331	Jim Sundberg	.10
334	Jose Lind	.10
336	Juan Samuel	.10
343	B.J. Surhoff	.12
344	Billy Hatcher	.10
346	Jack Clark	.15
347	Gary Thurman	.10
348	*Timmy Jones*	.12
349	Dave Winfield	.75
350	Frank White	.10
351	Dave Collins	.10
352	Jack Morris	.40
356	*Brian Holman*	.25
357	Dale Murphy (front photo reversed, jersey logo backward)	30.00
357	Dale Murphy (correct photo)	.50
360	Tom Glavine	2.50
362	Todd Stottlemyre	.50
364	Cecil Fielder	1.50
366	• Dwight Evans	.12
367	Kevin McReynolds	.10
369	Len Dykstra	.12
370	Jody Reed	.10
371	Jose Canseco	1.25
373	Mike Henneman	.15
374	Walt Weiss	.15
375	*Rob Dibble*	.50
376	Kirby Puckett	1.50
377	Denny Martinez	.15
378	Ron Gant	1.50
383	Dave Stieb	.10
384	Tony Gwynn	1.00
385	Mike Flanagan	.10
387	Bruce Hurst	.10

360 Tom Glavine

1989 Upper Deck

195 Roger Clemens

724 Greg W. Harris (FC) .... .20
725 Craig Worthington (FC) ... .15
726 Tom Howard (FC)............ .50
727 Dale Mohorcic .... .10
728 Rich Yett........................... .10
729 Mel Hall........................... .15
730 Floyd Youmans .... .10
731 Lonnie Smith .... .10
732 Wally Backman .... .10
733 Trevor Wilson (FC).......... .30
734 Jose Alvarez (FC) .... .15
735 Bob Milacki (FC)............. .35
736 Tom Gordon (FC)............ .25
737 Wally Whitehurst (FC) ..... .15
738 Mike Aldrete .... .10
739 Keith Miller (FC) .... .12
740 Randy Milligan................ .20
741 Jeff Parrett..................... .10
742 Steve Finley (FC) .... .75
743 Junior Felix (FC)............. .40
744 Pete Harnisch (FC) .... .60
745 Bill Spiers (FC) .... .15
746 Hensley Meulens (FC) .... .25
747 Juan Bell .... .10
748 Steve Sax .... .25
749 Phil Bradley .... .10
750 Rey Quinones .... .10
751 Tommy Gregg (FC) .... .10
752 Kevin Brown (FC)............ .60
753 Derek Lilliquist (FC)........ .10
754 Todd Zeile (FC) .... .70
755 Jim Abbott (FC) 4.00
756 Ozzie Canseco (FC)........ .25
757 Nick Esasky .... .10
758 Mike Moore .... .25
759 Rob Murphy..................... .10
760 Rick Mahler .... .10
761 Fred Lynn .... .15
762 Kevin Blankenship (FC) .. .15
763 Eddie Murray................... .50
764 Steve Searcy (FC)........... .20
765 Jerome Walton (FC)........ .35
766 Erik Hanson (FC) 1.00
767 • Bob Boone.................... .15
768 Edgar Martinez (FC)...... 1.00
769 Jose DeJesus (FC).......... .15
770 Greg Briley (FC) .... .20
771 Steve Peters (FC) .... .10
772 Rafael Palmeiro............... .90

17 John Smoltz

773 Jack Clark .... .20
774 Nolan Ryan **4.00**
775 Lance Parrish .... .12
776 Joe Girardi (FC).............. .30
777 Willie Randolph .... .20
778 Mitch Williams .... .15
779 Dennis Cook (FC) .... .10
780 Dwight Smith (FC)........... .25
781 Lenny Harris (FC)............ .25
782 Torey Lovullo (FC) .... .12
783 Norm Charlton (FC)......... .60
784 Chris Brown..................... .10
785 Todd Benzinger .... .15
786 Shane Rawley .... .10
787 Omar Vizquel (FC) .... .25
788 LaVel Freeman (FC) .... .10
789 Jeffrey Leonard .... .15
790 Eddie Williams................. .10
791 Jamie Moyer .... .10
792 Bruce Hurst .... .20
793 Julio Franco..................... .35
794 Claudell Washington .... .15
795 Jody Davis....................... .10
796 Oddibe McDowell .... .10
797 Paul Kilgus .... .10
798 Tracy Jones..................... .10
799 Steve Wilson (FC) .... .20
800 Pete O'Brien..................... .12

455

1990 DONRUSS

The nicest part about the 1990 Donruss set is its clean design. While other manufacturers cluttered cards with team logos and other ornamentation, Donruss chose to use large rectangular photos, unblemished by frills. Orange card backs are easy to read, thanks to the placement of player stats in a white box. Following tradition, the 1990 set begins with 26 Diamond Kings (with paintings by Dick Perez), followed by a like number of Rated Rookies. This year's Rookies subset should be an investment winner in future years thanks to the popularity of Eric Anthony, Steve Avery, Juan Gonzalez, Ben McDonald, Greg Vaughn, and Todd Zeile. Donruss closed the set with a commemorative card of late commissioner Bart Giamatti. Flipped negatives, inverted pairs of card backs, and statistical glitches have created numerous error/variation challenges for advanced collectors.

		MINT
Complete set		**$15.00**
Commons		**.03**
1	Bo Jackson (DK)	$ .15
2	Steve Sax (DK)	.08
3	Ruben Sierra (DK) (no line on top border)	.75
3	Ruben Sierra (DK) (correct border)	.15
4	Ken Griffey Jr. (DK)	.50
5	Mickey Tettleton (DK)	.10
6	Dave Stewart (DK)	.15
7	Jim Deshaies (DK)	.07
8	John Smoltz (DK)	.20
9	Mike Bielecki (DK)	.07
10	Brian Downing (DK) (negative reversed)	.80
10	Brian Downing (DK) (correct photo)	.15
11	Kevin Mitchell (DK)	.10
12	Kelly Gruber (DK)	.15
13	Joe Magrane (DK)	.07
14	John Franco (DK)	.10
15	Ozzie Guillen (DK)	.20
16	Lou Whitaker (DK)	.08
17	John Smiley (DK)	.12
18	Howard Johnson (DK)	.40
19	Willie Randolph (DK)	.08
20	Chris Bosio (DK)	.07
21	Tommy Herr (DK)	.07
22	Dan Gladden (DK)	.07
23	Ellis Burks (DK)	.08
24	Pete O'Brien (DK)	.07
25	Bryn Smith (DK)	.07
26	Ed Whitson (DK)	.07
27	Checklist (DK)	.07
28	Robin Ventura (RR) (FC)	.60
29	Todd Zeile (RR) (FC)	.50
30	Sandy Alomar, Jr. (RR)	.10
31	Kent Mercker (RR) (FC)	.10
32	Ben McDonald (RR) (FC)	.50
33	Juan Gonzalez (RR) (FC) (negative reversed)	5.00
33	Juan Gonzalez (RR) (FC) (correct photo)	2.50
34	Eric Anthony (RR) (FC)	.25
35	Mike Fetters (RR) (FC)	.08
36	Marquis Grissom (RR) (FC)	.60
37	Greg Vaughn (RR) (FC)	.50
38	Brian Dubois (RR) (FC)	.08
39	Steve Avery (RR) (FC)	.70
40	Mark Gardner (RR) (FC)	.10
41	Andy Benes (RR) (FC)	.50
42	Delino DeShields (RR) (FC)	.60
43	Scott Coolbaugh (RR) (FC)	.08
44	Pat Combs (RR) (FC)	.08
46	Kelly Mann (RR) (FC)	.08
47	Julio Machado (RR) (FC)	.08
48	Pete Incaviglia	.07
49	Shawon Dunston	.10

36 Marquis Grissom

711 John Olerud

213	Lance Parrish	.07
214	Mike Moore	.06
215	*Steve Finley*	.10
216	Tim Raines	.10
218	Kevin McReynolds	.09
219	Dave Gallagher	.06
220	Tim Wallach	.08
222	Lonnie Smith	.06
223	Andre Dawson	.12
224	Nelson Santovenia	.06
225	Rafael Palmeiro	.15
226	Devon White	.10
227	Harold Reynolds	.07
228	Ellis Burks	.08
230	Will Clark	.30
231	Jimmy Key	.07
233	Eric Davis	.10
234	Johnny Ray	.06
235	Darryl Strawberry	.25
242	Chris Sabo	.10
243	Dave Henderson	.08
244	Andy Van Slyke	.08
249	Brett Butler	.07
250	Willie Randolph	.07
251	Roger McDowell	.07
256	Tom Candiotti	.06
257	Todd Benzinger	.06
262	Frank White	.07

265	David Cone	.10
266	Bobby Thigpen	.10
268	Terry Steinbach	.07
269	Kirby Puckett	.25
270	Gregg Jefferies	.10
272	Cory Snyder	.07
275	Mitch Williams	.08
279	Vince Coleman	.10
280	Mike Boddicker	.07
283	*Kenny Rogers*	.10
284	Jeff Russell	.06
285	*Jerome Walton*	.10
289	Ron Darling	.08
290	Bobby Bonilla	.15
294	Ivan Calderon	.07
296	Mike Henneman	.07
297	Tom Gordon	.07
298	Lou Whitaker	.08
299	Terry Pendleton	.10
304	Rickey Henderson	.15
306	Craig Biggio	.10
308	Tom Browning	.08
310	Greg Swindell	.08
311	Dave Righetti	.07
313	Lenny Dykstra	.10
316	Mike Scioscia	.07
318	*Gary Wayne*	.06
319	Todd Worrell	.06
320	Doug Jones	.07
322	Danny Tartabull	.10
326	Bob Boone	.08
328	Dave Parker	.10
330	Mike Schooler	.06
331	Bert Blyleven	.08
332	Bob Welch	.08
334	Tim Burke	.06
336	Randy Myers	.08
338	Mark Langston	.10
339	Ted Higuera	.07
343	Kevin Brown	.08
344	Chuck Finley	.10
345	Erik Hanson	.08
348	Matt Williams	.10
349	Tom Henke	.07
353	Frank Viola	.12
363	Clay Parker	.06
365	Ken Griffey, Jr.	1.50
368	Kirk Gibson	.08
373	Mike Bielecki	.06

377	Gregg Olson	.08
379	Randy Johnson	.08
380	Jeff Montgomery	.06
382	*Bill Spiers*	.10
383	Dave Magadan	.07
384	*Greg Hibbard* (FC)	.15
387	Dave West	.07
388	Keith Hernandez	.06
390	*Joey Belle* (FC)	.75
391	Rick Aguilera	.08
393	*Dwight Smith*	.10
394	*Steve Wilson*	.12
395	*Bob Geren*	.10
397	Ken Hill	.08
399	Tom Brunansky	.07
402	Harold Baines	.07
404	Joe Girardi	.08
405	*Sergio Valdez* (FC)	.12
408	*Jeff Innis* (FC)	.10
411	Charlie Hough	.06
414	Trevor Wilson (FC)	.10
415	*Kevin Ritz* (FC)	.08
426	Norm Charlton	.06
427	• Deion Sanders	.40
432	Kal Daniels	.08
434	Lenny Harris (FC)	.10
435	*Scott Scudder* (FC)	.15
438	*Steve Olin* (FC)	.10
448	Jay Buhner	.08
449	*Lee Stevens* (FC)	.20
453	*Greg Litton* (FC)	.08
454	Mark Carreon	.06
457	*Tony Fossas* (FC)	.08
463	*Greg Briley* (FC)	.08
465	Benito Santiago	.12
466	*Jeff Brantley*	.08
469	Ken Griffey	.08
473	*Kevin Tapani* (FC)	.25
475	Ron Gant	.35
479	Storm Davis	.03
480	Jeff King (FC)	.10
481	*Kevin Mmahat* (FC)	.08
483	*Omar Vizquel*	.10
487	Ron Jones	.06
489	*Sammy Sosa* (FC)	.50
490	*Kent Anderson* (FC)	.10
499	Pete Smith	.06
501	Gary Sheffield	.15
502	*Terry Bross* (FC)	.08

390 Joey Belle

503	*Jerry Kutzler* (FC)	.08
504	Lloyd Moseby	.06
508	*Mike Stanton* (FC)	.12
510	*Tim Drummond* (FC)	.08
512	*Rick Wrona*	.08
514	Hal Morris	.15
517	Carlos Quintana	.10
519	Randy Milligan	.10
527	*Rick Reed* (FC)	.08
529	*Dean Palmer* (FC)	.20
530	*Jeff Peterek* (FC)	.08
531	*Carlos Martinez*	.10
535	*Doug Strange* (FC)	.12
536	Jose DeLeon	.07
538	Joey Cora (FC)	.10
539	Eric Hetzel	.06
548	Charlie Hayes (FC)	.12
551	Dave Winfield	.12
556	Bud Black	.06
562	*Rick Luecken* (FC)	.06
564	Felix Jose	.25
572	Sid Fernandez	.06
573	Lance Johnson	.08
576	*Tommy Greene* (FC)	.15
577	Mark Grace	.10
578	*Larry Walker* (FC)	.80
582	Greg Harris	.07
586	*Joe Oliver* (FC)	.10

365 Ken Griffey, Jr.

611 Candy Maldonado .... .06
616 Billy Hatcher .... .05
617 Don August .... .05
622 *Mark Guthrie* (FC) .... .08
625 Fernando Valenzuela .... .05
626 *Paul Sorrento* (FC) .... .15
627 Glenallen Hill .... .12
630 Randy Velarde (FC) .... .10
632 *Willie McGee* .... .10
633 Oil Can Boyd .... .06
634 Cris Carpenter .... .08
637 Terry Steinbach AS .... .08
638 Brady Anderson .... .10
639 Jack Morris .... .10
640 *Jaimie Navarro* (FC) .... .15
642 *Mike Dyer* (FC) .... .07
643 Mike Schmidt .... .30
646 *Francisco Cabrera* (FC) .. .10
650 Bo Jackson AS (back reads
    "Recent Major League
    Performance") .... .50
650 Bo Jackson AS (correct
    card-back reads "All-Star
    Game Performance") .... .20
654 Howard Johnson AS .... .10
655 *Mauro Gozzo* (FC) .... .10
656 *Mike Blowers* (FC) .... .10
658 Neal Heaton .... .06

659 5000 K (Nolan Ryan)
    (card number 665
    on back) 3.00
659 5000 K (Nolan Ryan)
    (correct card) .... .50
660 Harold Baines AS
    (back reads "Recent
    Major League
    Performance") 2.00
660 Harold Baines AS (line
    through star on front,
    incorrect back) 4.00
662 *Clint Zavaras* (FC) .... .08
663 Rick Reuschel .... .06
665 King of Kings
    (Nolan Ryan)
    (number 659 on back) ... 2.50
665 King of Kings
    (Nolan Ryan)
    (correct card) .... .50
669 Todd Stottlemyre .... .10
671 *John Wetteland* (FC) .... .10
673 Ruben Sierra AS .... .12
674 Pedro Guerrero AS .... .10
676 Cal Ripken AS .... .25
679 *Gary Mielke* (FC) .... .08
682 *Xavier Hernandez* (FC) ... .10
683 Kirby Puckett AS .... .20
685 ● Ramon Martinez .... .15
689 *Bernie Williams* (FC) ...... .30
691 *Beau Allred* (FC) .... .10
692 Ryne Sandberg AS .... .15
693 Jeff Huson (FC) .... .10
695 Eric Davis AS .... .10
697 Mark McGwire AS .... .15
698 *Steve Cummings* (FC) .... .08
699 *George Canale* (FC) .... .08
701 Julio Franco AS .... .10
703 Dave Stewart AS .... .10
704 *Dave Justice* (FC) 1.25
705 Tony Gwynn AS .... .12
706 Greg Myers .... .06
707 Will Clark AS .... .15
708 Benito Santiago AS .... .10
710 Ozzie Smith AS .... .15
711 *John Olerud* (FC) 1.75
712 Wade Boggs AS .... .10
715 Kevin Mitchell AS .... .08
716 Bart Giamatti .... .25

1990 DONRUSS ROOKIES

Although Donruss was one of the leading card makers of 1990 with its attractive standard set, the company lost steam with "The Rookies," its 56-card extension set. Because of a limited concept, fewer cards, and high cost relative to its competition, collectors were able to restrain their enthusiasm for the set. In fact, "The Rookies" paled in comparison with the larger fall sets from Fleer, Score, Topps, and Upper Deck. Each of these companies produced more cards in their season-ending subsets than Donruss, and each included traded players within its run. In a way, Donruss became a victim of the success of its earlier edition, since so many noted newcomers were featured in the Rated Rookies subset that was part of the standard Donruss edition. The only hot cards in this Rookies set are those of Dave Justice, Carlos Baerga, and John Olerud. Special logos on the card fronts and bright green borders identify the Donruss Rookies, in contrast to the red borders used on the earlier set.

		MINT
Complete set		**$6.00**
Commons		**.04**

1	Sandy Alomar	$ .10
2	John Olerud	2.00
3	Pat Combs	.15
4	Brian Dubois	.03
5	Felix Jose	.25
6	Delino DeShields	.30
7	Mike Stanton	.07
9	Craig Grebeck	.15
10	Joe Kraemer	.07
12	Bill Sampen	.10
13	Brian Bohanon	.07
14	Dave Justice	1.25
15	Robin Ventura	.90
16	Greg Vaughn	.35
17	Wayne Edwards	.08
18	Shawn Boskie	.10
19	Carlos Baerga	1.50
20	Mark Gardner	.10
21	Kevin Appier	.25
22	Mike Harkey	.07
23	Tim Layana	.07
24	Glenallen Hill	.10
26	Mike Blowers	.07
27	Scott Ruskin	.07

14 Dave Justice

28	Dana Kiecker	.07
30	Ben McDonald	.40
31	Todd Zeile	.25
32	Scott Coolbaugh	.07
33	Xavier Hernandez	.07
34	Mike Hartley	.07
35	Kevin Tapani	.25

36	Kevin Wickander	.08
37	Carlos Hernandez	.10
38	Brian Traxler	.07
40	Scott Radinsky	.08
41	Julio Machado	.10
42	Steve Avery	.75
43	Mark Lemke	.10
44	Alan Mills	.07

45	Marquis Grissom	.60
46	Greg Olson	.10
47	Dave Hollins	.80
48	Jerald Clark	.10
49	Eric Anthony	.15
51	John Burkett	.10
54	John Orton	.10
55	Terry Shumpert	.07

1990 FLEER

A modest card design and, at 660 cards, a set smaller in number than some of its competition prevented the 1990 Fleer set from becoming a popular collectible. Card fronts with small photos and large white borders seem unimaginative, while backs, using red-and-blue ink (along with annoying pink-and-white stripes), are hard to read. For cards of younger players with fewer stats, Fleer chose in many cases to leave the remaining space unoccupied. However, the Philadelphia-based company's newest innovation was also it most successful: A "Players of the Decade" subset highlights memorable stars from the 1980s. While Fleer's 1990 set includes many rookies, a number of important names wind up sharing cards. In an outdated practice from previous years, Fleer created a subset for rookie stars using photos of two players. Surprisingly, several of these two-photo cards pair rookies of different teams and unrelated positions.

		MINT
Complete set		**$16.00**
Commons		**.03**

3	Jose Canseco	$.30
6	Dennis Eckersley	.15
9	Dave Henderson	.10
10	Rickey Henderson	.15
12	Stan Javier	.06
13	Felix Jose	.25
14	Carney Lansford	.09
15	Mark McGwire	.25
16	Mike Moore	.10
18	Dave Parker	.12
20	Terry Steinbach	.10
21	Dave Stewart	.15
22	Walt Weiss	.08
23	Bob Welch	.10
29	Andre Dawson	.15

30	Shawon Dunston	.08
31	Joe Girardi	.12
32	Mark Grace	.15
33	Mike Harkey	.08
35	Les Lancaster	.06
37	Greg Maddux	.15
40	Ryne Sandberg	.35
43	Rick Sutcliffe	.08
44	*Jerome Walton*	.10
47	*Dean Wilkins* (FC)	.06
48	Mitch Williams	.10
51	*Mike Benjamin* (FC)	.08
52	*Jeff Brantley*	.10
53	Brett Butler	.07
54	Will Clark	.30
56	Scott Garrelts	.07
61	*Greg Litton*	.08
62	Candy Maldonado	.08
63	Kirt Manwaring	.06
64	*Randy McCament* (FC)	.08

180 Ben McDonald

313 Nolan Ryan

513 Ken Griffey, Jr.

389	Tim Belcher	.10
393	Kirk Gibson	.08
399	Orel Hershiser	.10
402	• Ramon Martinez	.25
404	Eddie Murray	.10
407	Mike Scioscia	.07
409	Fernando Valenzuela	.10
411	*John Wetteland* (FC)	.10
413	Todd Benzinger	.07
415	Tom Browning	.07
417	Eric Davis	.10
418	Rob Dibble	.15
419	John Franco	.07
421	*Chris Hammond* (FC)	.30
423	Barry Larkin	.15
426	*Joe Oliver* (FC)	.10
427	Paul O'Neill	.10
430	Jose Rijo	.07
433	Chris Sabo	.12
434	*Scott Scudder*	.10
437	Jesse Barfield	.07
438	*Mike Blowers* (FC)	.10
441	*Alvaro Espinosa*	.08
442	*Bob Geren*	.08
446	Roberto Kelly	.15
447	Don Mattingly	.20
449	Hensley Muelens	.10
453	Dave Righetti	.07
454	• *Deion Sanders*	.40
455	Steve Sax	.10
458	Dave Winfield	.15
461	Barry Bonds	.20
462	Bobby Bonilla	.20
465	Doug Drabek	.10
467	Billy Hatcher	.07
468	Neal Heaton	.07
469	Jeff King	.10
477	*Rick Reed* (FC)	.10
480	John Smiley	.12
481	Andy Van Slyke	.09
485	*Joey Belle*	.75
488	Tom Candiotti	.07
489	Joe Carter	.15
493	Brook Jacoby	.07
495	Doug Jones	.07
498	Pete O'Brien	.07
499	*Steve Olin* (FC)	.10
503	Greg Swindell	.10
507	Greg Briley	.10

550 Robin Ventura

508	Jay Buhner	.10
513	• Ken Griffey, Jr.	1.25
514	Erik Hanson	.08
516	Brian Holman	.07
518	Randy Johnson	.15
520	Edgar Martinez	.10
524	Harold Reynolds	.07
525	Mike Schooler	.07
528	*Omar Vizquel*	.10
530	Carlton Fisk	.12
533	Ozzie Guillen	.10
534	*Greg Hibbard* (FC)	.20
536	Lance Johnson	.07
538	Ron Kittle	.07
540	Carlos Martinez	.10
541	*Tom McCarthy* (FC)	.10
542	*Matt Merullo*	.08
546	Melido Perez	.07
548	*Sammy Sosa* (FC)	.50
549	Bobby Thigpen	.07
550	Robin Ventura	.60
553	*Pat Combs* (FC)	.10
554	Dennis Cook	.10
556	• Lenny Dykstra	.10
557	Curt Ford	.03
559	Von Hayes	.09
560	Tom Herr	.03
563	Ron Jones	.20

548 Sammy Sosa

1990 FLEER UPDATE

Although this set is Fleer's tenth anniversary edition, there is nothing remarkable about it. The Update cards use exactly the same design used by the larger Fleer set issued earlier in the year. Unfortunately, Fleer (and most other companies) continued the practice of distributing its extension sets only through hobby dealers. Limiting the means available to collectors to obtain them results in all extension sets becoming more expensive. One customer benefit Fleer provided in 1990 was to shrink-wrap individual sets in an effort to deter tampering. This positive move could make it harder for dealers to break open sets and offer individual cards for sale. Notable single cards include a three-image card honoring Nolan Ryan's 300 career victories and 6 no-hitters, along with cards of newcomers Alex Fernandez, John Olerud, and Frank Thomas. Fleer continued as the only major manufacturer to group and number players by team.

		MINT
Complete set		**$8.00**
Commons		**.04**

1	Steve Avery	$ .75
2	Francisco Cabrera	.10
4	Jimmy Kremers	.08
5	Greg Olson	.15
7	Shawn Boskie	.12
8	Joe Kraemer	.08
10	Hector Villanueva	.10
12	Mariano Duncan	.07
13	Billy Hatcher	.08
14	Tim Layana	.08
15	Hal Morris	.15
16	Javier Ortiz	.08
17	Dave Rohde	.08
18	Eric Yelding	.10
20	Kal Daniels	.05
21	Dave Hansen	.15
22	Mike Hartley	.08
24	Jose Offerman	.15
27	Delino DeShields	.50
28	Steve Frey	.10
29	Mark Gardner	.15
30	Chris Nabholz	.20
31	Bill Sampen	.10
34	Chuck Carr	.10

96 Travis Fryman

35	John Franco	.10
36	Todd Hundley	.20
37	Julio Machado	.10
39	Darren Reed	.08
40	Kelvin Torve	.05
41	Darrel Akerfelds	.05
42	Jose DeJesus	.15
43	Dave Hollins	.80

131 Nolan Ryan

1990 SCORE

Score was the surprise hit of the hobby world in 1990. After a mediocre showing in 1989, the 704 cards in the 1990 set surpassed the $40 mark before the All-Star break. Rumors of a short printing drove prices up throughout the summer, but when Score flooded the stores (non-hobby outlets) before Christmas, prices plunged. Still, one of the hottest cards in the set remains number 697, a black-and-white reproduction of Bo Jackson's football/baseball Nike poster. It shows him posing in football shoulder pads and toting a bat across his shoulders. Special subsets include cards of top draft picks from each team, and a 13-card Dream Team with tinted photographs of top stars in a tobacco-card format. Card backs in the Dream Team group include one paragraph profiles by famous sportswriters.

		MINT
Complete set		**$20.00**
Commons		.03

1	Don Mattingly	$ .20
2	Cal Ripken, Jr.	.35
3	Dwight Evans	.08
4	Barry Bonds	.20
5	Kevin McReynolds	.08
6	Ozzie Guillen	.10
9	Alan Trammell	.09
10	Cory Snyder	.05
12	Roberto Alomar	.40
13	Pedro Guerrero	.08
16	Ricky Jordan	.07
17	Joe Magrane	.03
18	Sid Fernandez	.07
20	Jack Clark	.09
23	Lenny Harris (FC)	.12
24	Phil Bradley	.03
25	Andres Galarraga	.12
26	Brian Downing	.06
31	Mike Boddicker	.06
33	Brady Anderson	.10
35	Lance Parrish	.06
36	Von Hayes	.06
37	Lee Smith	.08
40	Mike Scott	.03
45	Dave Smith	.06
46	Dave Magadan	.07
50	Orel Hershiser	.12
51	Bip Roberts (FC)	.10
52	Jerry Browne	.08

560 Ken Griffey, Jr.

54	Fernando Valenzuela	.05
55	Matt Nokes	.07
56	Brook Jacoby	.03
57	Frank Tanana	.06
60	Bob Boone	.08
63	Gregg Olson	.10
65	Todd Benzinger	.07
66	Dale Murphy	.08
69	Cecil Espy	.07
70	Chris Sabo	.10
72	Tom Brunansky	.05
74	B.J. Surhoff	.06
75	Lou Whitaker	.09

606 Kevin Maas

225	Pete Smith	.03
226	Mike Witt	.06
227	Jay Howell	.06
229	*Jerome Walton*	.12
230	Greg Swindell	.10
233	Ken Hill	.12
234	Craig Worthington	.07
235	Scott Terry	.08
236	Brett Butler	.09
240	Dwight Smith	.10
244	Danny Tartabull	.12
245	Wade Boggs	.20
250	Nolan Ryan	.50
252	Randy Milligan	.07
255	Tony Gwynn	.20
257	Greg Harris	.07
258	*Junior Felix*	.10
259	Mark Davis	.03
260	Vince Coleman	.08
262	Mitch Williams	.05
263	Jeff Russell	.06
264	*Omar Vizquel*	.10
265	Andre Dawson	.10
266	Storm Davis	.03
269	Tom Candiotti	.08
270	Bruce Hurst	.09
271	Fred McGriff	.15
272	Glenn Davis	.07
273	John Franco	.10
275	Craig Biggio	.15
277	• Rob Dibble	.15
279	Kevin Bass	.07
280	Bo Jackson	.20
281	Wally Backman	.03
283	Chris Bosio	.07
285	Ozzie Smith	.10
286	George Bell	.10
288	Pat Borders	.10
289	Danny Jackson	.03
290	Carlton Fisk	.12
292	Allan Anderson	.03
293	Johnny Ray	.03
295	Paul O'Neill	.07
296	Carney Lansford	.10
298	Claudell Washington	.03
299	Hubie Brooks	.07
300	Will Clark	.25
301	*Kenny Rogers*	.25
302	Darrell Evans	.07

250 Nolan Ryan

303	Greg Briley	.05
304	Donn Pall	.07
305	Teddy Higuera	.05
306	Dan Pasqua	.07
307	Dave Winfield	.15
309	Jose DeLeon	.05
310	Roger Clemens	.25
311	Melido Perez	.05
312	Devon White	.10
313	Doc Gooden	.10
314	*Carlos Martinez*	.12
315	Dennis Eckersley	.10
316	Clay Parker	.05
317	Rick Honeycutt	.03
319	Joe Carter	.12
320	Robin Yount	.15
321	Felix Jose	.25
322	Mickey Tettleton	.08
324	Edgar Martinez	.12
325	Dave Henderson	.09
326	Chili Davis	.08
330	Jim Abbott	.30
331	John Dopson	.06
334	John Smiley	.10
335	Bobby Thigpen	.09
338	Ken Griffey, Sr. (lists uniform number 25)	1.25

595 Robin Ventura

396	Bill Buckner	.06
397	Robby Thompson	.07
398	Mike Scioscia	.08
400	Kirby Puckett	.25
401	Mark Langston	.12
403	Greg Maddux	.15
404	Lloyd Moseby	.05
405	Rafael Palmeiro	.10
407	Jimmy Key	.09
409	Tim Raines	.10
410	Dave Stewart	.10
411	*Eric Yelding* (FC)	.10
415	Randy Johnson	.10
416	Gary Carter	.07
419	Bryn Smith	.07
420	Ruben Sierra	.20
425	Kelly Gruber	.15
427	• Lenny Dykstra	.12
430	David Cone	.10
440	Andy Van Slyke	.12
443	Kevin Elster	.06
445	Roger McDowell	.06
449	*Bill Spiers* (birthdate reads "19")	**15.00**
449	*Bill Spiers* (birthdate reads "1966")	.25
450	Rick Sutcliffe	.07
454	Benny Santiago	.12
456	Bill Landrum (FC)	.08
460	Paul Molitor	.10
461	• Ramon Martinez (FC)	.20
464	*Bob Geren*	.10
465	Rick Reuschel	.09
467	John Kruk	.10
468	Gregg Jefferies	.15
470	Harold Baines	.08
472	Tom Gordon	.07
481	Tom Glavine	.25
485	Greg Brock	.06
486	Pascual Perez	.06
487	Kirk Gibson	.09
491	David Wells (negative reversed on back)	**2.00**
497	*Greg Litton*	.10
500	Frank Viola	.15
503	Matt Williams	.10
504	Tim Leary	.06
505	Doug Drabek	.12
507	Charlie Hayes	.10

338	Ken Griffey, Sr. (correct card—uniform number 30)	.15
340	Ellis Burks	.10
343	Kevin Mitchell	.10
345	Mike Greenwell	.10
349	Jeff Ballard	.03
351	Randy Myers	.10
352	Shawn Abner	.03
355	Pete Harnisch	.08
360	Rickey Henderson	.25
363	Mark Carreon	.05
364	Ron Jones	.05
365	Jeff Montgomery	.08
369	*Greg Hibbard* (FC)	.20
370	John Smoltz	.20
371	*Jeff Brantley*	.10
372	Frank White	.08
374	Willie McGee	.09
375	Jose Canseco	.30
380	Chuck Finley	.07
381	Kent Hrbek	.12
383	Mel Hall	.06
385	Mark McGwire	.25
388	*John Wetteland*	.25
390	Rob Deer	.07
392	Todd Worrell	.07
395	Willie Randolph	.07

508	*Joey Belle*	.75
511	Jose Rijo	.07
518	*Scott Scudder*	.10
519	Rick Aguilera	.09
521	Jay Buhner	.08
522	Jeff Reardon	.07
527	*Gary Wayne*	.07
528	*Dave Johnson* (FC)	.07
529	Ron Kittle	.08
530	Erik Hanson (FC)	.10
531	Steve Wilson (FC)	.07
535	Joe Girardi	.10
536	Lance Blankenship	.10
539	Mark Knudson (FC)	.08
540	*Jeff Wetherby* (FC)	.10
543	Eric Hetzel (FC)	.10
544	*Rick Reed* (FC)	.10
545	Dennis Cook (FC)	.10
549	Jeff King (FC)	.10
550	• Dave Dravecky (tribute)	.15
551	Randy Kutcher (FC)	.07
553	*Jim Corsi* (FC)	.10
554	Todd Stottlemyre	.15
555	Scott Bankhead	.08
557	*Rick Wrona* (FC)	.10
558	*Sammy Sosa* (FC)	.35
560	Ken Griffey, Jr.	1.50
561	Ryne Sandberg (No Errors) ("3B" on front)	10.00
561	Ryne Sandberg (No Errors) (no position on front)	.20
563	Jay Bell (FC)	.10
564	*Jack Daugherty* (FC)	.12
565	*Rich Monteleone*	.10
566	Bo Jackson (All-Star MVP)	.15
567	Tony Fossas (FC)	.10
569	*Jaime Navarro* (FC)	.10
570	Lance Johnson (FC)	.10
571	*Mike Dyer* (FC)	.12
572	*Kevin Ritz* (FC)	.10
575	Scott Lusader (FC)	.07
576	*Joe Oliver*	.10
577	Sandy Alomar Jr.	.10
578	Andy Benes (FC)	.30
580	*Randy McCament* (FC)	.10
581	Curt Schilling (FC)	.15
582	*John Orton* (FC)	.10

663 Frank Thomas

583	*Milt Cuyler* (FC) (back reads "pitched in 989 games")	1.00
583	*Milt Cuyler* (FC) (back reads "pitched in 98 games")	.30
584	Eric Anthony (FC)	.40
585	*Greg Vaughn* (FC)	.30
586	• Deion Sanders (FC)	.40
587	Jose DeJesus (FC)	.15
588	*Chip Hale* (FC)	.10
589	*John Olerud* (FC)	1.75
590	Steve Olin (FC)	.10
591	Marquis Grissom (FC)	.60
592	*Moises Alou* (FC)	.30
593	Mark Lemke (FC)	.08
594	Dean Palmer (FC)	.75
595	Robin Ventura (FC)	.60
596	*Tino Martinez* (FC)	.35
597	*Mike Huff* (FC)	.10
598	Scott Hemond (FC)	.10
599	*Wally Whitehurst* (FC)	.10
600	*Todd Zeile* (FC)	.35
601	Glenallen Hill (FC)	.10
602	Hal Morris (FC)	.35
603	Juan Bell (FC)	.10
604	*Bobby Rose* (FC)	.10
605	*Matt Merullo* (FC)	.10
606	*Kevin Maas* (FC)	.20

650 Dave Justice

609	*Mike Stanton* (FC)	.10
611	*Charles Nagy* (FC)	.35
615	*Jeff Huson* (FC)	.10
616	*Mickey Weston* (FC)	.10
619	*Bernie Williams* (FC)	.35
620	*Shawn Holman* (FC)	.10
621	*Gary Eave* (FC)	.05
622	*Darrin Fletcher* (FC)	.10
623	*Pat Combs* (FC)	.10
624	*Mike Blowers* (FC)	.10
625	*Kevin Appier* (FC)	.20
629	*Scott Hammond* (FC)	.35
630	*Dean Wilkins* (FC)	.10
631	*Larry Walker* (FC)	.80
634	*Stan Belinda* (FC)	.15
636	*Hensley Meulens* (FC)	.10
637	*Juan Gonzalez* (FC)	2.50
639	*Mark Gardner* (FC)	.10
640	*Tommy Greene* (FC)	.50
641	*Mike Hartley* (FC)	.10
642	*Phil Stephenson* (FC)	.10
645	*Delino DeShields* (FC)	.60
646	Kevin Blankenship (FC)	.10
647	*Paul Sorrento* (FC)	.15
650	*Dave Justice* (FC)	1.25
651	*Scott Cooper* (FC)	.30
658	Carlos Quintana	.12
660	Jerald Clark	.08
661	*Donald Harris* (1st Round Pick) (FC)	.10
662	*Paul Coleman* (1st Round Pick) (FC)	.10
663	*Frank Thomas* (1st Round Pick) (FC)	6.00
664	*Brent Mayne* (1st Round Pick) (FC)	.15
665	*Eddie Zosky* (1st Round Pick) (FC)	.30
666	*Steve Hosey* (1st Round Pick) (FC)	.50
667	*Scott Bryant* (1st Round Pick) (FC)	.10
668	*Tom Goodwin* (1st Round Pick) (FC)	.15
669	*Cal Eldred* (1st Round Pick) (FC)	.60
670	*Earl Cunningham* (1st Round Pick) (FC)	.10
671	*Alan Zinter* (1st Round Pick) (FC)	.10
672	*Chuck Knoblauch* (1st Round Pick) (FC)	.80
673	*Kyle Abbott* (1st Round Pick) (FC)	.25
674	*Roger Salkeld* (1st Round Pick) (FC)	.15
675	*Maurice Vaughn* (1st Round Pick) (FC)	1.00
676	*Keith "Kiki" Jones* (1st Round Pick) (FC)	.15
677	*Tyler Houston* (1st Round Pick) (FC)	.10
678	*Jeff Jackson* (1st Round Pick) (FC)	.10
679	*Greg Gohr* (1st Round Pick) (FC)	.10
680	*Ben McDonald* (1st Round Pick) (FC)	.35
681	*Greg Blosser* (1st Round Pick) (FC)	.15
682	*Willie Green* (1st Round Pick) (FC)	.20
683	Wade Boggs (Dream Team)	.10
684	Will Clark (Dream Team)	.15
685	Tony Gwynn (Dream Team)	.10

686	Rickey Henderson (Dream Team) .10	**694**	Bobby Thigpen (Dream Team) .10
687	Bo Jackson (Dream Team) .15	**695**	Mitch Williams (Dream Team) .10
688	Mark Langston (Dream Team) .10	**696**	Nolan Ryan (5000 K) .35
689	Barry Larkin (Dream Team) .10	**697**	Bo Jackson (NIKE poster photo) 1.50
690	Kirby Puckett (Dream Team) .10	**698**	Rickey Henderson (ALCS MVP) .15
691	Ryne Sandberg (Dream Team) .15	**699**	Will Clark (NLCS MVP) .15
692	Mike Scott (Dream Team) .10	**700**	World Series Games 1 and 2 .20
693	Terry Steinbach (Dream Team) .10	**702**	World Series Game 3 .20
		703	World Series Game 4 .20
		704	Wade Boggs (200 hits) .10

1990 SCORE ROOKIE & TRADED

Score's popularity continued with its 110-card Rookie & Traded set. Unlike other companies, Score divided its updated set into two parts. Cards numbered 1 through 66 portray traded players in their new uniforms, while numbers 67 to 110 depict rookies and newcomers. This second group, though no more difficult to find than the first, is generally more valuable. Top names among rookies include Steve Avery, Bernard Gilkey, Ray Lankford, and Frank Thomas. Surprisingly, the most talked about cards feature two of the least-known players. Card number 97 features D.J. Dozier, a football star attempting to start a second career with the Mets. And card number 100 shows Blue Jays prospect Eric Lindros, another two-sport man, who will also pop up in current cards for hockey players. The cards of Thomas and Lindros will help drive the value of this update set, Score's third, which is available mainly from hobby dealers.

	MINT			
		7	Tony Pena	.05
Complete set	**$13.00**	**8**	Candy Maldonado	.05
Commons	**.04**	**9**	Cecil Fielder	.25
		11	Mark Langston	.08
1	Dave Winfield $ .15	**12**	Dave Parker	.12
2	Kevin Bass .05	**14**	Tony Phillips	.05
		15	John Franco	.10

109 Steve Avery

57	Keith Hernandez	.10
67	Francisco Cabrera	.07
68	*Gary DiSarcina*	.10
69	Greg Olson	.15
70	Beau Allred	.10
71	Oscar Azocar	.10
72	Kent Mercker	.10
73	John Burkett	.40
74	Carlos Baerga	2.00
75	Dave Hollins	1.00
76	Todd Hundley	.35
77	Rick Parker	.08
78	Steve Cummings	.08
79	Bill Sampen	.08
81	Derek Bell	1.50
82	Kevin Tapani	.35
83	Jim Leyritz	.10
84	Ray Lankford	1.00
85	Wayne Edwards	.10
86	Frank Thomas	6.00
87	Tim Naehring	.25
88	Willie Blair	.05
89	Alan Mills	.10
90	Scott Radinsky	.10
91	Howard Farmer	.05
92	Julio Machado	.05
93	Rafael Valdez	.05
94	Shawn Boskie	.10

16	Randy Myers	.10
17	Jeff Reardon	.10
18	Sandy Alomar, Jr.	.10
19	Joe Carter	.15
20	Fred Lynn	.07
21	Storm Davis	.03
22	Craig Lefferts	.03
23	Pete O'Brien	.05
25	Lloyd Moseby	.05
27	Tim Leary	.07
28	Gerald Perry	.07
31	Dale Murphy	.10
32	Alejandro Pena	.07
33	Juan Samuel	.07
34	Hubie Brooks	.07
35	Gary Carter	.10
38	Matt Nokes	.07
41	Jeff Huson	.05
42	Billy Hatcher	.10
46	Luis Polonia	.10
48	Lee Smith	.12
49	Tom Brunansky	.05
50	Mike Witt	.05
51	Willie Randolph	.07
52	Stan Javier	.05
54	John Candelaria	.07
55	Bryn Smith	.07
56	Glenn Braggs	.07

86 Frank Thomas

95	David Segui	.10	
96	Chris Hoiles	.50	
97	D.J. Dozier	.20	
98	Hector Villanueva	.10	
99	Eric Gunderson	.10	
100	Eric Lindros	6.00	
101	Dave Otto	.12	
102	Dana Kiecker	.05	
103	Tim Drummond	.05	
104	Mickey Pina	.05	
105	Craig Grebeck	.15	
106	Bernard Gilkey	.50	
107	Tim Layana	.05	
108	Scott Chiamparino	.05	
109	Steve Avery	1.50	
110	Terry Shumpert	.10	

1990 TOPPS

Topps unveiled an eye-popping card design for one of its wildest-looking sets in nearly two decades. Not since 1972 had the usually conservative company dabbled with such a gaudy array of multi-colored borders. Surprisingly, the two-tone, partially speckled borders are contrasted with traditional plain backs of yellow-and-black ink on gray card stock. One of the most popular features of the 1990 set is the return of #1 Draft Pick cards, which show pre-rookies in collegiate uniforms. An All-Star subset also resurfaced. In a new twist, future Hall-of-Famer Nolan Ryan is honored on the first five cards of the set. Due to what seemed like a higher-than-normal public distribution of cards and the abundance of prepackaged factory sets in retail stores, Topps prices have risen at a slower rate than most other 1990 sets.

		MINT
Complete set		**$20.00**
Commons		**.03**
1	Nolan Ryan	$ .65
2	Nolan Ryan (The Mets Years)	.25
3	Nolan Ryan (The Angels Years)	.25
4	Nolan Ryan (The Astros Years)	.25
5	Nolan Ryan (The Rangers)	.25
6	1989 Record Breaker (Vince Coleman)	.10
7	1989 Record Breaker (Rickey Henderson)	.10
8	1989 Record Breaker (Cal Ripken)	.15
10	Barry Larkin	.10
11	Paul Gibson	.04
12	Joe Girardi (FC)	.15
14	*Mike Fetters* (FC)	.07
15	Teddy Higerua	.08
16	*Kent Anderson*	.10
17	Kelly Downs	.03
18	Carlos Quintana	.09
20	Mark Gubicza	.05
23	Randy Velarde	.07
25	Willie Randolph	.08
28	Duane Ward	.04
30	David Cone	.10
32	John Farrell	.03
33	Greg Walker	.05
34	*Tony Fossas* (FC)	.07
35	Benito Santiago	.12
40	Jay Howell	.06
41	Matt Williams	.25
42	Jeff Robinson	.03
43	Dante Bichette	.07
44	*Roger Salkeld* (#1 Draft Pick) (FC)	.20
45	Dave Parker	.08

477

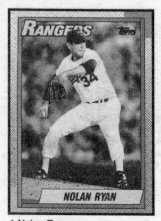

1 Nolan Ryan

164	*Jeff Juden* (#1 Draft Pick) (FC)	.25
165	Walt Weiss	.08
167	*Kevin Appier* (FC)	.20
168	Jose Lind	.04
170	George Bell	.12
172	Tom Lampkin (FC)	.03
173	Tim Belcher	.08
175	Mike Moore	.07
177	Mike Henneman	.07
178	Chris James	.05
180	Rock Raines	.10
185	Ruben Sierra	.20
187	*Rick Wrona* (FC)	.10
190	Rick Reuschel	.03
191	Pat Borders	.07
193	Andy Benes	.20
194	Glenallen Hill (FC)	.15
195	Tim Burke	.07
197	Doug Drabek	.07
198	Mike Marshall	.03
199	*Sergio Valdez* (FC)	.10
200	Don Mattingly	.20
201	Cito Gaston	.03
203	*Mike Roesler* (FC)	.08
205	Mark Davis	.07
206	Nick Esasky	.05
207	Bob Ojeda	.04
208	Brook Jacoby	.06
210	Ryne Sandberg	.30
213	Scott Bankhead	.05
216	Ricky Jordan	.10
220	Barry Bonds	.35
221	*Gary Mielke* (FC)	.12
222	Kurt Stillwell	.05
223	Tommy Gregg	.06
224	*Delino DeShields* (FC)	.60
227	*Kevin Tapani* (FC)	.25
230	Keith Hernandez	.05
236	Hal Morris (FC)	.30
237	*Kevin Ritz* (FC)	.20
238	Felix Jose (FC)	.20
239	Eric Show	.04
240	Mark Grace	.25
245	Roger Clemens	.30
249	*Mike Smith* (FC)	.05
250	Jose Canseco	.30
252	Otis Nixon	.03
255	Bobby Thigpen	.06

714 Marquis Grissom

257	Jose DeLeon	.07
260	Eric Davis	.10
261	Whitey Herzog	.05
263	*Mel Stottlemyre Jr.* (FC)	.12
265	Pete O'Brien	.06
270	Dave Stewart	.09
271	Chet Lemon	.04
273	Bobby Bonilla	.15
274	*Goose Gozzo* (FC)	.05
275	Mickey Tettleton	.06
277	Lenny Harris (FC)	.10
278	Pascual Perez	.06
280	Lou Whitaker	.07
281	Kevin Bass	.03
282	Derek Lilliquist	.05
283	*Joey Belle* (FC)	.60
284	*Mark Gardner* (FC)	.10
285	Willie McGee	.06
287	Vance Law	.05
288	Greg Briley	.10
289	Norm Charlton	.10
290	Robin Yount	.20
292	Jim Gott	.04
295	Fred McGriff	.15
296	Jeff Ballard	.04
297	Tom Herr	.05
299	Adam Peterson (FC)	.09
300	Bo Jackson	.15

283 Joey Belle

412	Jamie Moyer	.04
413	*Brian DuBois* (FC)	.08
414	*Frank Thomas* (#1 Draft Pick) (FC)	3.50
416	*Dave Johnson* (FC)	.05
417	Jim Gantner	.06
418	Tom Browning	.08
419	*Beau Allred* (FC)	.10
420	Carlton Fisk	.10
423	Fred Toliver	.03
424	Jerry Reuss	.04
425	Bill Landrum	.06
428	*Steve Davis* (FC)	.05
429	Tom Kelly	.03
430	Pete Incaviglia	.06
431	Randy Johnson	.12
433	*Steve Olin* (FC)	.12
434	Mark Carreon (FC)	.05
435	Kevin Seitzer	.08
436	Mel Hall	.05
438	Greg Myers (FC)	.10
439	Jeff Parrett	.06
440	Alan Trammell	.09
442	Jerry Browne	.07
443	Cris Carpenter	.05
444	*Kyle Abbott* (#1 Draft Pick) (FC)	.15
446	Dan Pasqua	.06
448	Greg Gagne	.03
450	Rickey Henderson	.15
451	Mark Lemke (FC)	.10
454	Jeff King (FC)	.10
455	Jeffrey Leonard	.06
456	Chris Gwynn (FC)	.09
457	Gregg Jefferies	.10
460	Mike Scott	.09
461	*Carlos Martinez* (FC)	.15
464	*Jerome Walton*	.10
465	Kevin Gross	.05
468	Billy Ripken	.03
469	John Kruk	.10
470	Frank Viola	.15
472	Jose Uribe	.05
475	Bob Welch	.08
479	Frank White	.06
480	Sid Fernandez	.08
482	*Steve Carter* (FC)	.05
486	Jeff Treadway	.05
490	Dan Plesac	.07

414 Frank Thomas

491	*Dave Cochrane* (FC)	.12
493	*Jason Grimsley* (FC)	.07
495	Lee Smith	.06
496	Cecil Espy	.04
500	Kevin Mitchell	.10
505	Kelly Gruber	.10
506	Tom Glavine	.25
510	Doc Gooden	.10
511	Clay Parker	.06
515	• Len Dykstra	.12
516	Tim Leary	.05
517	Roberto Alomar	.40
519	Bucky Dent	.03
520	Mitch Williams	.09
521	Craig Worthington	.05
525	Wally Joyner	.15
528	*Kevin Wickander* (FC)	.07
529	Greg Harris	.05
530	Mark Langston	.10
531	Ken Caminiti	.06
533	Tim Jones (FC)	.05
535	John Smoltz	.20
536	*Bob Geren*	.10
537	Mark Grant	.03
538	*Billy Spiers*	.12
539	Neal Heaton	.06
540	Danny Tartabull	.15
544	Dennis Boyd	.05

44 Roger Salkeld

545	Kevin McReynolds	.09
546	Kevin Hickey	.04
547	Jack Howell	.05
550	Julio Franco	.10
552	*Mike Smith* (FC)	.05
553	*Scott Scudder* (FC)	.15
554	Jay Buhner	.08
555	Jack Morris	.10
557	*Jeff Innis*	.12
560	Steve Sax	.12
562	Chad Kreuter	.03
563	Alex Sanchez	.03
564	*Tyler Houston* (#1 Draft Pick) (FC)	.10
567	Ron Gant	.25
568	John Smiley	.10
569	Ivan Calderon	.06
570	Cal Ripken	.15
571	Brett Butler	.06
572	Greg Harris	.09
574	Bill Swift	.10
575	Lance Parrish	.07
576	*Mike Dyer* (FC)	.08
577	Charlie Hayes (FC)	.10
578	Joe Magrane	.07
580	Joe Carter	.15
581	Ken Griffey, Sr.	.10
584	*Phil Stephenson* (FC)	.09
585	Kal Daniels	.05
587	Lance Johnson	.10
588	Rick Rhoden	.04
589	Mike Aldrete	.05
590	Ozzie Smith	.12
591	Todd Stottlemyre	.08
593	Scott Bradley	.04
594	*Luis Sojo* (FC)	.10
595	Greg Swindell	.10
596	Jose DeJesus (FC)	.10
597	Chris Bosio	.07
598	Brady Anderson	.05
599	Frank Williams	.04
600	Darryl Strawberry	.35
601	Luis Rivera	.05
602	Scott Garrelts	.07
605	Mike Scioscia	.06
606	Storm Davis	.07
608	*Eric Anthony* (FC)	.35
609	Sparky Anderson	.03
610	Pedro Guerrero	.10
612	Dave Gallagher	.05
613	Jeff Pico	.04
614	Nelson Santovenia	.03
615	Rob Deer	.07
616	Brian Holman	.10
617	Geronimo Berroa	.05
618	Eddie Whitson	.05
619	Rob Ducey	.08
620	*Tony Castillo* (FC)	.10
621	Melido Perez	.08
622	Sid Bream	.05
623	Jim Corsi	.04
624	Darrin Jackson	.08
625	Roger McDowell	.07
626	Bob Melvin	.04
627	Jose Rijo	.07
628	Candy Maldonado	.08
629	Eric Hetzel (FC)	.10
630	Gary Gaetti	.05
631	*John Wetteland* (FC)	.12
632	Scott Lusader	.05
633	Dennis Cook (FC)	.10
634	Luis Polonia	.06
635	Brian Downing	.05
638	Jeff Montgomery	.07
639	Tony LaRussa	.03
640	Rick Sutcliffe	.06
641	*Doug Strange* (FC)	.12

1990 TOPPS TRADED

Topps wasn't the first company to issue an updated set, but its yearly fall issue continues as one of the most popular. Card fronts duplicate the gaudy, multi-colored borders found in the 792-card set issued earlier in the year. The company scooped the competition with its annual practice of creating manager cards. World Championship manager Lou Piniella made his first appearance in a Reds uniform, and yet another card was issued for Hall-of-Famer Red Schoendienst (because of his brief interim service as a Cardinals manager). Once again, rookie newcomers remain the most popular traded-set entries with collectors. In terms of value, cards of Travis Fryman and John Olerud are tops with hobbyists. The Traded sets were issued in specially-designed boxes, available mainly through hobby dealers. Gray-backed cards were circulated in test-issue wax packs.

	MINT
Complete set	**$7.00**
Commons	**.04**

1	Darrel Akerfelds	$ .06
2	Sandy Alomar	.10
3	Brad Arnsberg	.10
4	Steve Avery	.80
5	Wally Backman	.03
6	Carlos Baerga	1.50
7	Kevin Bass	.06
8	Willie Blair	.06
9	Mike Blowers	.15
10	Shawn Boskie	.10
16	John Burkett	.35
17	Casey Candaele	.08
19	Gary Carter	.10
20	Joe Carter	.20
22	Scott Coolbaugh	.10
26	Edgar Diaz	.08
27	Wayne Edwards	.08
29	Scott Erickson	.50
31	Cecil Fielder	.35
32	John Franco	.10
33	Travis Fryman	1.50
35	Darryl Hamilton	.08
36	Mike Harkey	.10
38	Billy Hatcher	.10

29 Scott Erickson

41	Dave Hollins	.90
43	Steve Howard	.05
44	Todd Hundley	.15
45	Jeff Huson	.12
48	Dave Justice	1.25
49	Jeff Kaiser	.10
50	Dana Kiecker	.10
51	Joe Klink	.10

52 Brent Knackert .... .10
54 Mark Langston .... .10
55 Tim Layana .... .15
56 Rick Leach .... .03
57 Terry Leach .... .03
58 Tim Leary .... .03
59 Craig Lefferts .... .03
60 Charlie Leibrandt.............. .03
61 Jim Leyritz .... .10
63 Kevin Maas .... .20
65 Candy Maldonado .... .10
66 Fred Manrique................. .03
67 Mike Marshall .... .03
68 Camelo Martinez .... .03
69 John Marzano .... .08
70 Ben McDonald................. .35
71 Jack McDowell .... .25
73 Orlando Mercado .... .06
74 Stump Merrill .... .06
75 Alan Mills......................... .10
76 Hal Morris........................ .20
77 Lloyd Moseby .... .08
78 Randy Myers .... .10
79 Tim Naehring................... .20
80 Junior Noboa .... .06
81 Matt Nokes .... .06
82 Pete O'Brien .... .06
83 John Olerud.................. 1.75
84 Greg Olson .... .20
85 Junior Ortiz .... .06
86 Dave Parker .... .12
87 Rick Parker...................... .12
88 Bob Patterson .... .06
89 Alejandro Pena................ .08
90 Tony Pena........................ .10
91 Pascual Perez .... .08
92 Gerald Perry .... .06
93 Dan Petry .... .06
94 Gary Pettis .... .06
95 Tony Phillips .... .08
96 Lou Piniella...................... .10
97 Luis Polonia..................... .06
98 Jim Presley...................... .12
99 Scott Radinsky .... .10
100 Willie Randolph .... .08
101 Jeff Reardon .... .12
102 Greg Riddoch .... .06
103 Jeff Robinson .... .03
104 Ron Robinson .... .03

48 Dave Justice

105 Kevin Romine .... .03
106 Scott Ruskin .... .20
107 John Russell................... .06
108 Bill Sampen .... .20
109 Juan Samuel .... .12
110 Scott Sanderson............. .08
111 Jack Savage................... .06
112 Dave Schmidt................. .06
113 Red Schoendienst........... .20
114 Terry Shumpert............... .20
115 Matt Sinatro .... .06
116 Don Slaught .... .06
117 Bryn Smith .... .06
118 Lee Smith .... .15
119 Paul Sorrento .... .35
120 Franklin Stubbs .... .10
121 Russ Swan .... .08
122 Bob Tewksbury .... .10
123 Wayne Tolleson .... .03
124 John Tudor .... .06
125 Randy Veres .... .03
126 Hector Villanueva .... .10
127 Mitch Webster .... .03
128 Ernie Whitt..................... .06
129 Frank Wills .... .06
130 Dave Winfield .... .12
131 Matt Young..................... .03
132 Checklist........................ .06

1990 UPPER DECK

After the impressive debut of the 1989 set, only a few changes were made to the 1990 Upper Decks. The color photos are larger due to the elimination of some ornamentation, and the Upper Deck logo was moved from the lower left corner to the upper right. But apart from the presence of the team logo, this design is closer than any other to the simple beauty of the stunning 1953 Bowman Color edition. Although the initial printing contained a few notable errors, they were quickly corrected. For example, Ben McDonald's card first appeared with an Orioles rather than a Rookies logo; Mickey Weston was incorrectly identified as "Jamie," both on his card and on the Orioles' checklist; and incorrect photos were used for both Scott Garrelts and Jim Gott. As in 1989, team checklist cards display star portraits by artist Vernon Wells, who also created cards honoring Mike Schmidt's retirement and Nolan Ryan's 5,000th strikeout. The final 100 cards of the 1990 set were issued in a popular mid-season, high-number series, 701-800. This final series came both in foil packs and in a factory-collated complete "set." In the following list, Star Rookies are identified with the abbreviation SR.

	MINT
Complete set (1-700)	**$30.00**
Commons (1-700)	.04
Complete set (1-800)	45.00
Commons (701-800)	.05

2 *Randy Nosek* (FC)	$ .10
3 *Tom Drees* (SR) (FC)	.10
9 *Marquis Grissom* (SR) (FC)	1.50
11 Rick Aguilera	.10
13 *Deion Sanders* (SR) (FC)	1.50
15 David West	.10
17 *Sammy Sosa* (SR) (FC)	1.00
19 Jack Howell	.05
20 Mike Schmidt (special card)	.50
21 Robin Ventura (SR) (FC)	1.75
22 Brian Meyer (FC)	.10
23 *Blaine Beatty* (FC)	.10

25 *Greg Vaughn* (SR) (FC)	.70
26 *Xavier Hernandez* (FC)	.15
27 *Jason Grimsley* (FC)	.15
28 *Eric Anthony* (SR) (FC)	.80
30 David Wells	.08
31 Hal Morris (FC)	.35
33 *Kelly Mann* (SR) (FC)	.15
34 Nolan Ryan (special card)	1.00
35 *Scott Service* (FC)	.15
37 *Tino Martinez* (SR) (FC)	.50
38 Chili Davis	.10
42 *Scott Coolbaugh* (SR) (FC)	.10
43 *Jose Cano* (FC)	.05
44 *Jose Vizcaino* (FC)	.20
45 *Bob Hamelin* (SR) (FC)	.10
46 *Jose Offerman* (SR) (FC)	.35
47 Kevin Blankenship	.10
49 *Tommy Greene* (SR) (FC)	1.00
50 Will Clark (special card)	.30
51 Rob Nelson (FC)	.09
52 *Chris Hammond* (SR) (FC)	.15

156 Ken Griffey Jr.

Robin Ventura

21 Robin Ventura

169	Robby Thompson	.09
170	Rolando Roomes	.15
171	Mark McGwire	.55
172	Steve Sax	.15
174	Mitch Williams	.10
176	Rob Deer	.08
177	Tim Raines	.15
179	Harold Reynolds	.10
181	Chris Sabo	.15
182	Darryl Strawberry	.30
183	Willie Randolph	.09
186	Todd Benzinger	.09
187	Kevin Elster	.07
189	Tom Browning	.10
190	Keith Miller	.09
191	Don Mattingly	.40
192	Dave Parker	.12
193	Roberto Kelly	.12
197	Hubie Brooks	.08
198	Bill Doran	.08
204	Bob Ojeda	.07
206	Dave Henderson	.10
213	Greg Maddux	.20
214	Mike Schooler	.09
215	Lonnie Smith	.08
216	Jose Rijo	.09
218	Jim Gantner	.08
219	Allan Anderson	.09
220	Rick Mahler	.08
221	Jim Deshaies	.09
222	Keith Hernandez	.10
223	Vince Coleman	.12
224	David Cone	.15
225	Ozzie Smith	.15
226	Matt Nokes	.09
227	Barry Bonds	.80
228	Felix Jose	.35
231	Shawon Dunston	.10
232	Ron Gant	.50
233	*Omar Vizquel*	.10
235	Erik Hanson	.15
236	Kirby Puckett	.60
237	*Bill Spiers*	.15
242	Joe Magrane	.08
243	Dave Magadan	.09
244	Pedro Guerrero	.12
245	Glenn Davis	.10
246	Terry Steinbach	.12
247	Fred Lynn	.09
250	Sid Bream	.08
251	Bob Welch	.12
253	Carney Lansford	.09
254	Paul Molitor	.12
255	Jose DeJesus	.15
256	Orel Hershiser	.15
257	Tom Brunansky	.10
258	Mike Davis	.08
260	Scott Terry	.09
261	Sid Fernandez	.10
262	Mike Marshall	.08
263	Howard Johnson	.15
264	Kirk Gibson	.09
265	Kevin McReynolds	.15
266	Cal Ripken Jr.	1.00
267	Ozzie Guillen	.10
269	Bobby Thigpen	.10
271	Bob Boone	.09
272	Dave Stewart	.10
273	Tim Wallach	.09
275	Mike Moore	.10
276	Tony Pena	.09
277	Eddie Murray	.20
278	Milt Thompson	.08
282	Tom Henke	.09
286	Dan Pasqua	.08
287	Larry Sheets	.07
291	Spike Owen	.08

293	Chris Bosio	.09
295	Don August	.09
297	Mickey Tettleton	.09
298	Mike Scioscia	.10
302	Kevin Bass	.08
303	Bip Roberts (FC)	.10
304	Joe Girardi	.10
308	Ed Whitson	.09
313	Bill Swift	.15
314	Charlie Hough	.08
316	Luis Polonia	.08
323	Roger Clemens	.75
324	Ryne Sandberg	.80
325	Benito Santiago	.15
326	Bret Saberhagen	.15
327	Lou Whitaker	.10
328	Dave Gallagher	.10
331	Jeffrey Leonard	.09
332	Torey Lovullo	.15
333	Pete Incaviglia	.09
334	Rickey Henderson	.50
335	Rafael Palmeiro	.12
336	Ken Hill	.12
337	Dave Winfield	.15
338	Alfredo Griffin	.08
341	Steve Wilson	.10
342	Jack Clark	.10
343	Ellis Burks	.25
344	Tony Gwynn	.20
345	*Jerome Walton*	.10
346	Roberto Alomar	1.25
347	*Carlos Martinez* (FC)	.15
353	Harold Baines	.09
354	Mike Greenwell	.10
355	Ruben Sierra	.20
357	Andre Dawson	.20
358	*Jeff Brantley* (FC)	.15
359	Mike Bielecki	.09
361	Kurt Stillwell	.09
362	Brian Holman	.10
363	Kevin Seitzer	.10
365	Tom Gordon	.10
366	Bobby Bonilla	.35
367	Carlton Fisk	.20
372	*Gary Wayne* (FC)	.10
374	*Mike Dyer* (FC)	.15
375	Joe Carter	.25
376	Dwight Smith	.10
377	*John Wetteland* (FC)	.20

382	Frank White	.09
386	Donn Pall (FC)	.09
387	John Smiley	.09
388	Tom Candiotti	.10
393	Lee Smith	.09
396	John Tudor	.09
416	Roger McDowell	.09
417	Jeff Reardon	.10
421	Lloyd Moseby	.09
422	Doug Drabek	.09
423	Lenny Harris	.12
425	*Dave Johnson* (FC)	.10
426	Jerry Browne	.09
427	*Eric Yelding* (FC)	.12
430	Mariano Duncan (FC)	.15
433	Bruce Hurst	.10
434	*Jeff Huson* (FC)	.10
436	*Mark Guthrie* (FC)	.10
437	Charlie Hayes (FC)	.10
442	Bill Landrum	.09
445	Fernando Valenzuela	.10
446	*Joey Belle* (FC)	2.50
447	*Ed Whited* (FC)	.10
452	Kent Hrbek	.15
453	Von Hayes	.10
462	Jimmy Key	.10
464	Rob Ducey	.09
465	Carlos Quintana	.09
466	*Larry Walker* (FC)	1.75
467	Todd Worrell	.10
469	Terry Pendleton	.15
472	• Len Dykstra	.12
474	Terry Mulholland (FC)	.10
478	Scott Garrelts (photo is Bill Bathe)	3.50
478	Scott Garrelts (correct photo)	.25
479	Dave Righetti	.10
505	Willie McGee	.10
513	Dennis Eckersley	.12
515	Tim Burke	.09
523	Cris Carpenter	.10
524	*Matt Winters* (FC)	.10
527	Bert Blyleven	.09
532	Edgar Martinez	.30
533	Dale Murphy	.15
534	Jay Buhner	.09
535	John Smoltz	.50
536	Andy Van Slyke	.12

537	Mike Henneman	.09
542	Walt Weiss	.10
543	*Greg Hibbard* (FC)	.35
544	Nolan Ryan	1.25
545	*Todd Zeile* (FC)	.30
546	Hensley Meulens	.10
547	Tim Belcher	.09
551	*Tony Castillo* (FC)	.12
552	Jeff Robinson	.08
553	*Steve Olin* (FC)	.25
554	Alan Trammell	.12
555	Wade Boggs	.40
556	Will Clark	.40
557	Jeff King (FC)	.15
561	Scott Bankhead	.09
562	*Jeff Innis* (FC)	.12
563	Randy Johnson	.15
564	*Wally Whitehurst*	.10
566	Norm Charlton	.09
567	Robin Yount	.30
568	*Joe Oliver* (FC)	.12
571	Tom Glavine	.50
572	Rod Nichols (FC)	.10
573	Jack Morris	.15
574	Greg Swindell	.12
575	Steve Searey	.09
576	Ricky Jordan	.15
577	Matt Williams	.30
581	Randy Myers	.10
582	*Rick Wrona* (FC)	.15
583	Juan Samuel	.09
586	• Rob Dibble	.15
593	Luis Quinones (FC)	.09
598	Billy Hatcher	.08
601	Joey Cora (FC)	.10
602	*Steve Finley*	.15
603	Kal Daniels	.10
604	Gregg Olson	.15
605	Dave Stieb	.10
606	*Kenny Rogers* (FC)	.25
613	Pete Smith	.09
621	*Rick Luecken* (FC)	.10
622	Greg W. Harris	.09
623	Pete Harnisch	.10
624	Jerald Clark	.10
626	Frank Viola	.20
627	Ted Higuera	.10
645	Jim Abbott	.40
646	*Jaime Navarro* (FC)	.25

647	Mark Langston	.10
652	Mike Boddicker	.09
655	Sandy Alomar Jr.	.55
656	Danny Tartabull	.10
671	John Dopson	.09
672	*John Orton* (FC)	.15
673	Eric Hetzel (FC)	.10
674	Lance Parrish	.10
675	• Ramon Martinez	.25
676	Mark Gubioza	.09
677	Greg Litton	.10
683	*Jamie Weston* (first name incorrect) (FC)	2.50
683	*Mickey Weston* (correct name) (FC)	.30
685	Steve Buechele	.09
688	Dante Bichette	.09
689	Todd Burns	.09
690	Dan Petry	.09
691	*Kent Anderson* (FC)	.10
692	Todd Stottlemyre	.12
693	Wally Joyner	.15
694	Mike Rochford (FC)	.10
700	Checklist 601-700 (lists "Jamie Weston")	3.00
700	Checklist 601-700 (correct card—lists "Mickey Weston")	.25
701	Jim Gott	.10
702	Rookie Threats (Delino DeShields, Marquis Grissom, Larry Walker)	.35
704	Willie Randolph	.10
705	Tim Leary	.10
706	*Chuck McElroy* (FC)	.25
707	Gerald Perry	.10
709	John Franco	.15
711	Dave Justice	3.00
713	Scott Ruskin (FC)	.10
714	Glenn Braggs	.10
715	*Kevin Bearse* (FC)	.10
716	Jose Nunez	.10
717	*Tim Layana* (FC)	.10
718	Greg Myers (FC)	.12
719	Pete O'Brien	.10
720	John Candelaria	.10

721 Craig Grebeck (FC) .... .30
722 Shawn Boskie (FC) .... .10
723 Jim Leyritz (FC) .... .10
724 Bill Sampen (FC) .... .10
725 Scott Radinsky .... .12
726 Todd Hundley (FC) .... .25
727 Scott Hemond (FC) .... .10
728 Lenny Webster (FC) .... .10
729 Jeff Reardon.................... .12
731 Brian Bohanon (FC) .... .10
733 Terry Shumpert (FC) .... .10
734 Nolan Ryan's Sixth
     No-Hitter (with "300th
     WIN!" stripe on
     front) 1.00
734 Nolan Ryan's Sixth
     No-Hitter (w/o
     "300th WIN" stripe on
     front) 6.00
735 John Burkett (FC) .... .50
736 Derrick May (FC) 1.10
737 Carlos Baerga 2.50
738 Greg Smith...................... .10
739 Scott Sanderson.............. .10
740 Joe Kraemer.................... .10
741 Hector Villanueva (FC) .... .20
742 Mike Fetters .... .15
743 Mark Gardner .... .25
744 Matt Nokes .... .10
745 Dave Winfield .... .15
746 Delino DeShields (FC) .. 1.50
747 Dann Howitt (FC) .... .10
748 Tony Pena....................... .15
749 Oil Can Boyd .... .10
750 Mike Benjamin (FC)......... .10
751 Alex Cole (FC).................. .35
753 Howard Farmer .... .10
754 Joe Carter .... .20
755 Ray Lankford (FC) 1.50
756 Sandy Alomar Jr.............. .15
758 Nick Esasky..................... .05
759 Stan Belinda.................... .20
761 Gary DiSarcina (FC)........ .35
762 Wayne Edwards (FC) .... .10
763 Pat Combs .... .15
764 Mickey Pina (FC)............. .15
765 Wilson Alvarez (FC) .... .80
766 Dave Parker .... .15
767 Mike Blowers (FC)........... .10

755 Ray Lankford

768 Tony Phillips.................... .10
769 Pascual Perez .... .10
771 Fred Lynn........................ .10
772 Mel Rojas (FC) .... .12
773 David Segui (FC).............. .20
774 Gary Carter .... .15
775 Rafael Valdez .... .12
776 Glenallen Hill .... .15
777 Keith Hernandez .... .12
778 Billy Hatcher .... .10
780 Candy Maldonado .... .10
781 Mike Marshall .... .10
783 Mark Langston .... .12
784 Paul Sorrento (FC) .... .50
785 Dave Hollins (FC) 1.50
786 Cecil Fielder .... .50
787 Matt Young .... .10
788 Jeff Huson .... .10
789 Lloyd Moseby .... .10
791 Hubie Brooks................... .10
792 Craig Lefferts .... .10
793 Kevin Bass .... .10
794 Bryn Smith...................... .12
795 Juan Samuel .... .12
796 Sam Horn .... .10
797 Randy Myers .... .15
799 Bill Gullickson................. .10
800 Checklist 701-800 .... .10

1991 DONRUSS

For the first time in its history, Donruss decided to issue its regular set in two individual series. Blue borders distinguish the first-series cards, which number 1 through 386; the second-series cards, issued in February, run from 387 through 770 and have green borders. These late-series cards have current photos so Darryl Strawberry, for example, is shown wearing the cap of his new team, the Dodgers. In factory-collated complete sets, Donruss included sample cards from the Leaf set that the company had issued in late summer. However, dealers removed the specially-marked Leaf "preview" cards from the Donruss sets, sold them for $5 to $10 each, and then discounted the standard set from $5 to $15. Donruss Elite or mini cards were also added at random in wax packs as surprise bonuses, but they are not considered part of the regular set.

	MINT
Complete set	$15.00
Commons	.04

1	Dave Stieb (DK)	$ .05
2	Craig Biggio (DK)	.05
3	Cecil Fielder (DK)	.10
4	Barry Bonds (DK)	.12
5	Barry Larkin (DK)	.10
6	Dave Parker (DK)	.05
7	Len Dykstra (DK)	.08
8	Bobby Thigpen (DK)	.08
9	Roger Clemens (DK)	.12
10	Ron Gant (DK)	.12
11	Delino DeShields (DK)	.12
12	Roberto Alomar (DK)	.08
13	Sandy Alomar (DK)	.10
14	Ryne Sandberg (DK)	.12
15	Ramon Martinez (DK)	.10
16	Edgar Martinez (DK)	.06
17	Dave Magadan (DK)	.05
18	Matt Williams (DK)	.08
19	Rafael Palmeiro (DK)	.10
20	Bob Welch (DK)	.06
21	Dave Righetti (DK)	.08
22	Brian Harper (DK)	.06
23	Gregg Olson (DK)	.08
24	Kurt Stillwell (DK)	.05
25	Pedro Guerrero (DK)	.08
26	Chuck Finley (DK)	.08
27	Checklist (DK)	.05
28	Tino Martinez (RR)	.12
29	Mark Lewis (RR) (FC)	.12
30	*Bernard Gilkey* (RR) (FC)	.15
31	Hensley Meulens (RR)	.10
32	*Derek Bell* (RR)	.30
33	Jose Offerman (RR) (FC)	.15
34	Terry Bross (RR)	.05
35	*Leo Gomez* (RR) (FC)	.15
36	Derrick May (RR) (FC)	.25
37	*Kevin Morton* (RR) (FC)	.15
38	Moises Alou (RR) (FC)	.25
39	Julio Valera (RR) (FC)	.10
40	Milt Cuyler (RR) (FC)	.20
41	*Phil Plantier* (RR) (FC)	.50
42	*Scott Chiamparino* (RR) (FC)	.05
43	*Ray Lankford* (RR) (FC)	.45
44	*Mickey Morandini* (RR) (FC)	.12
45	Dave Hansen (RR) (FC)	.12
46	*Kevin Belcher* (RR) (FC)	.05
47	Darrin Fletcher (RR) (FC)	.05
48	Steve Sax (AS)	.10
49	Ken Griffey, Jr. (AS)	.25
50	Jose Canseco (AS)	.15
51	Sandy Alomar (AS)	.05
52	Cal Ripken (AS)	.15
53	Rickey Henderson (AS)	.12
54	Bob Welch (AS)	.08
55	Wade Boggs (AS)	.12
56	Mark McGwire (AS)	.15
57	Jack McDowell	.12
59	*Alex Fernandez* (FC)	.30
60	Pat Combs	.04

61 *Mike Walker* (FC) .... .10
62 Juan Samuel .... .06
63 Mike Blowers .... .05
64 Mark Guthrie .... .04
65 Mark Salas .... .04
67 Tim Leary .... .04
68 Andres Galarraga .... .06
69 Bob Milacki .... .04
70 Tim Belcher .... .04
71 Todd Zeile .... .10
72 Jerome Walton .... .05
73 Kevin Seitzer .... .06
74 Jerald Clark .... .05
75 John Smoltz .... .04
77 Ken Griffey, Jr. .... .60
78 Jim Abbott .... .10
79 Gregg Jefferies .... .08
80 Kevin Reimer (FC) .... .10
81 Roger Clemens .... .15
83 Bruce Hurst .... .06
84 Eric Davis .... .10
85 Paul Molitor .... .08
86 Will Clark .... .20
87 Mike Bielecki .... .04
88 Bret Saberhagen .... .08
89 Nolan Ryan .... .40
90 Bobby Thigpen .... .08
91 Dickie Thon .... .04
93 Luis Polonia .... .04
94 Terry Kennedy .... .04
95 Kent Hrbek .... .10
96 Danny Jackson .... .04
97 Sid Fernandez .... .05
98 Jimmy Key .... .05
99 Franklin Stubbs .... .05
100 Checklist .... .06
101 R.J Reynolds .... .04
102 Dave Stewart .... .08
103 Dan Pasqua .... .06
104 Dan Pleasac .... .04
105 Mark McGwire .... .15
107 Don Mattingly .... .12
108 Carlton Fisk .... .12
109 Ken Oberkfell .... .04
110 Darrel Akerfelds .... .04
111 Gregg Olson .... .08
112 Mike Scioscia .... .06
113 Bryn Smith .... .05
114 Bob Geren .... .04

41 Phil Plantier

115 Tom Candiotti .... .05
116 Kevin Tapani .... .10
117 Jeff Treadway .... .04
118 Alan Trammell .... .08
120 Joel Skinner .... .04
121 Mike LaValliere .... .04
122 • Dwight Evans .... .08
123 Jody Reed .... .05
125 Tim Burke .... .06
126 Dave Johnson .... .04
127 Fernando Valenzuela .... .06
128 Jose DeLeon .... .04
129 Andre Dawson .... .15
131 Greg Harris .... .04
132 Tom Glavine .... .20
133 Lance McCullers .... .04
134 Randy Johnson .... .06
135 Lance Parrish .... .04
136 Mackey Sasser .... .04
137 Geno Petralli .... .04
138 Dennis Lamp .... .04
139 Dennis Martinez .... .06
140 Mike Pagliarulo .... .04
141 Hal Morris .... .15
142 Dave Parker .... .12
143 Brett Butler .... .08
144 Paul Assenmacher .... .04
145 Mark Gubicza .... .05

536 Jose Canseco

146	Charlie Hough	.04
147	Sammy Sosa	.20
148	Randy Ready	.05
149	Kelly Gruber	.08
150	Devon White	.08
151	Gary Carter	.08
153	Chris Sabo	.12
154	David Cone	.12
155	Todd Stottlemyre	.05
157	Bob Walk	.04
158	Mike Gallego	.04
159	Greg Hibbard	.08
160	Chris Bosio	.04
161	Mike Moore	.06
163	Steve Sax	.08
164	Melido Perez	.05
165	Danny Darwin	.04
166	Roger McDowell	.05
167	Bill Ripken	.06
168	Mike Sharperson	.04
169	Lee Smith	.10
170	Matt Nokes	.04
171	Jesse Orosco	.04
172	Rick Aguilera	.05
173	Jim Presley	.04
174	Lou Whitaker	.08
175	Harold Reynolds	.06
176	Brook Jacoby	.04
177	Wally Backman	.04
178	Wade Boggs	.10
181	Pete Harnisch	.04
182	Mike Morgan	.04
183	Bob Tewksbury	.04
184	Joe Girardi	.04
185	Storm Davis	.04
186	Ed Whitson	.04
187	Steve Avery	.25
188	Lloyd Moseby	.04
189	Scott Bankhead	.04
190	Mark Langston	.10
191	Kevin McReynolds	.06
192	Julio Franco	.10
193	John Dopson	.04
194	Oil Can Boyd	.04
195	Bip Roberts	.04
196	Billy Hatcher	.04
197	Edgar Diaz	.04
198	Greg Litton	.04
199	Mark Grace	.10
200	Checklist	.06
201	George Brett	.15
202	Jeff Russell	.04
203	Ivan Calderon	.06
205	Tom Henke	.08
206	Bryan Harvey	.10
207	Steve Bedrosian	.05
208	Al Newman	.04
209	Randy Myers	.06
211	Manny Lee	.04
212	Dave Smith	.04
213	Don Slaught	.04
214	Walt Weiss	.05
215	Donn Pall	.04
216	Jaime Navarro	.04
218	Rudy Seanez (FC)	.08
219	*Jim Leyritz* (FC)	.10
220	Ron Karkovice	.04
221	Ken Caminiti	.06
222	Von Hayes	.08
223	Cal Ripken	.35
224	Lenny Harris	.04
225	Milt Thompson	.04
228	Dan Gladden	.04
229	Jeff Blauser	.04
230	Mike Heath	.04
231	Omar Vizquel	.04
232	Doug Jones	.04

233	Jeff King	.04
234	Luis Rivera	.04
235	Ellis Burks	.10
236	Greg Cadaret	.04
237	Dave Martinez	.04
239	Stan Javier	.04
240	Ozzie Smith	.08
241	*Shawn Boskie*	.08
242	Tom Gordon	.05
243	Tony Gywnn	.15
244	Tommy Gregg	.04
246	Keith Comstock	.04
247	Jack Howell	.04
248	Keith Miller	.04
249	Bobby Witt	.06
250	Rob Murphy	.04
251	Spike Owen	.04
252	Garry Templeton	.04
253	Glenn Braggs	.04
255	Kevin Mitchell	.08
256	Les Lancaster	.04
257	*Mel Stottlemyre* (FC)	.10
258	Kenny Rogers	.04
259	Lance Johnson	.04
260	John Kruk	.12
261	Fred McGriff	.12
262	Dick Schofield	.04
263	Trevor Wilson	.04
265	Scott Scudder	.04
266	Dwight Gooden	.12
267	*Willie Blair* (FC)	.05
268	Mark Portugal	.04
269	Doug Drabek	.08
270	Dennis Eckersley	.08
271	Eric King	.04
272	Robin Yount	.15
273	Carney Lansford	.05
274	Carlos Baerga	.15
275	Dave Righetti	.08
277	Eric Yelding	.04
278	Charles Hayes	.04
279	Jeff Ballard	.04
280	Orel Hershiser	.08
281	Jose Oquendo	.04
283	Mitch Webster	.04
284	Greg Gagne	.04
285	*Greg Olson*	.10
286	Tony Phillips	.04
292	Steve Frey	.08

548 Dave Justice

295	Joe Magrane	.05
296	*Hector Villaneuva* (FC)	.10
298	Joe Carter	.12
300	Checklist	.06
306	Greg Harris	.10
307	Marquis Grissom	.10
315	Robin Ventura	.20
321	Rob Dibble	.10
325	Bobby Bonilla	.12
326	Dave Henderson	.10
330	*Colby Ward* (FC)	.12
331	*Oscar Azocar* (FC)	.10
333	Eric Anthony	.10
336	Kal Daniels	.08
338	*Alan Mills*	.10
351	*Bill Sampen*	.10
356	• Bob Boone	.04
358	*Chris Hoiles* (FC)	.20
359	Larry Walker	.20
367	*Tim Naehring* (FC)	.10
371	Juan Gonzalez	.40
383	Alex Cole (FC)	.08
387	Rickey Henderson MVP	.15
389	Fred McGriff MVP	.10
390	Dave Parker MVP	.08
392	Ken Griffey, Jr. MVP	.25
393	Gregg Olson MVP	.08
394	Rafael Palmeiro MVP	.08

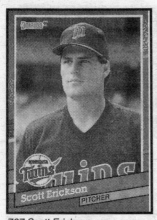

767 Scott Erickson

477 Frank Thomas

43 Ray Lankford

1991 DONRUSS ROOKIES

A cash-crop of successful newcomers points to a bright future for the 1991 Donruss Rookies. The set caught on quickly because it became available in mid-September of 1991, before the comparable extension sets were distributed by Fleer, Score, and Topps. Cards of Jeff Bagwell, Ivan Rodriguez, and Todd Van Poppel also boosted its popularity. In appearance, the cards closely resemble their standard-set counterparts except that these have a red border with a neon-green back. Available through hobby dealers, each set comes shrink wrapped in a collector's box, complete with a miniature puzzle of Hall-of-Famer Willie Stargell. One unusual card, number 50, shows Reds Rookie Chris Jones in a vestlike jersey reminiscent of the 1950s. It was worn during a nostalgia promotion game against the Phillies.

		MINT
Complete set		**$5.00**
Commons		**.04**

1	Pat Kelly (FC)	$ .20
3	Wes Chamberlain	.20
4	Scott Leius (FC)	.10
5	Darryl Kile (FC)	.25
7	Todd Van Poppel (FC)	.50
8	Ray Lankford	.30
9	Brian Hunter (FC)	.25
11	Ced Landrum (FC)	.10
12	Dave Burba (FC)	.08
15	Warren Newson (FC)	.10
17	Luis Gonzalez	.25
18	Charles Nagy	.15
20	Frank Castillo (FC)	.08
21	Pedro Munoz	.20
22	Orlando Merced (FC)	.20
24	Kirk Dressendorfer (FC)	.08
25	Heathcliffe Slocumb (FC)	.08
29	Mark Leiter (FC)	.10
30	Jeff Bagwell (FC)	1.50
31	Brian McRae	.20
32	Mark Whiten	.15
33	Ivan Rodriguez (FC)	1.25
34	Wade Taylor (FC)	.10
35	Darren Lewis (FC)	.15
36	Mo Vaughn	.45
37	Mike Remlinger (FC)	.12

39 Chuck Knoblauch

38	Rick Wilkins (FC)	.10
39	Chuck Knoblauch	.30
42	Mark Lewis	.15
44	Chris Haney (FC)	.08
47	Jeff Johnson (FC)	.08
48	Dean Palmer	.30
52	Al Osuna (FC)	.07
53	Rusty Meacham (FC)	.07
54	Chito Martinez (FC)	.10
55	Reggie Jefferson (FC)	.15

1991 FLEER

Although Fleer's 720-card set was the smallest among the big five in 1991, the company pioneered two upgrades. First and most impressive was the color portrait on each card back. Second, instead of leaving white space on the back of the card when stats didn't fill the space, Fleer added text to create a more finished and consistent look. But the company abandoned its past practice of pairing two popular rookies on a single card, and the set has been criticized by collectors because it uses outdated photos of relocated players wearing their old team uniforms. One of the most popular novelty cards is number 710, aptly called Second Generation Stars, which pictures Ken Griffey, Jr. and Barry Bonds.

		MINT
Complete set		**$15.00**
Commons		.04

107 Phil Plantier

1	Troy Afenir (FC)	$ .10
2	Harold Baines	.07
5	Jose Canseco	.20
6	Dennis Eckersley	.10
7	Mike Gallego	.05
8	Ron Hassey	.05
9	Dave Henderson	.10
10	Rickey Henderson	.12
14	Carney Lansford	.08
15	Darren Lewis (FC)	.25
16	Willie McGee	.10
17	Mark McGwire	.15
18	Mike Moore	.06
20	Dave Otto	.06
21	Jamie Quirk	.05
22	Willie Randolph	.07
24	Terry Steinbach	.08
25	Dave Stewart	.07
26	Walt Weiss	.08
27	Bob Welch	.08
29	Wally Backman	.05
30	Stan Belinda	.07
31	Jay Bell	.07
33	Barry Bonds	.25
34	Bobby Bonilla	.15
35	Sid Bream	.07
36	Doug Drabek	.10
37	Carlos Garcia (FC)	.10
39	Jeff King	.07
40	Bob Kipper	.07
41	Bill Landrum	.07
43	Jose Lind	.05
44	Carmelo Martinez	.05
48	R.J. Reynolds	.05
50	John Smiley	.10
51	Zane Smith	.07
52	Randy Tomlin (FC)	.15
53	Andy Van Slyke	.10
54	Bob Walk	.05
55	Jack Armstrong	.05
59	Tom Browning	.10
60	Norm Charlton	.08
61	Eric Davis	.10
62	Rob Dibble	.10

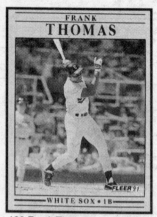

138 Frank Thomas

64	Mariano Duncan	.05
65	Chris Hammond	.05
66	Billy Hatcher	.05
68	Barry Larkin	.10
69	*Tim Layana*	.12
70	*Terry Lee* (FC)	.07
72	Hal Morris	.15
73	Randy Myers	.08
75	Joe Oliver	.05
76	Paul O'Neill	.10
79	Jose Rijo	.10
80	Chris Sabo	.12
81	Scott Scudder	.07
82	Herm Winningham	.03
85	Mike Boddicker	.08
86	Wade Boggs	.20
88	Tom Brunansky	.05
89	Ellis Burks	.15
90	Roger Clemens	.25
91	Scott Cooper (FC)	.25
92	John Dopson	.05
93	Dwight Evans	.08
95	*Jeff Gray* (FC)	.10
96	Mike Greenwell	.08
98	*Daryl Irvine* (FC)	.10
99	Dana Kiecker	.05
103	John Marzano	.05
105	*Tim Naehring*	.10

106	Tony Pena	.07
107	*Phil Plantier* (FC)	.40
108	Carlos Quintana	.08
109	Jeff Reardon	.08
111	Jody Reed	.05
113	Kevin Romine	.05
115	Ivan Calderon	.08
117	*Alex Fernandez*	.25
118	Carlton Fisk	.12
119	Scott Fletcher	.05
120	*Craig Grebeck*	.12
121	Ozzie Guillen	.07
123	Lance Johnson	.08
125	Ron Karkovice	.05
128	Carlos Martinez	.08
129	Jack McDowell	.08
130	Donn Pall	.05
131	Dan Pasqua	.07
133	Melido Perez	.06
135	*Scott Radinsky*	.12
136	Sammy Sosa	.20
137	Bobby Thigpen	.10
138	Frank Thomas	1.10
139	Robin Ventura	.25
141	*Chuck Carr*	.05
142	Mark Carreon	.05
143	David Cone	.08
145	Kevin Elster	.07
147	John Franco	.08
148	Dwight Gooden	.15
149	Tom Herr	.05
150	*Todd Hundley*	.20
151	Gregg Jefferies	.10
152	Howard Johnson	.15
153	Dave Madagan	.08
154	Kevin McReynolds	.08
158	Alejandro Pena	.05
159	*Darren Reed*	.08
160	Mackey Sasser	.05
161	Darryl Strawberry	.20
164	Julio Valera	.12
165	Frank Viola	.15
168	*Derek Bell* (FC)	.30
169	George Bell	.15
170	*Willie Blair*	.08
171	Pat Borders	.05
173	Junior Felix	.08
174	Tony Fernandez	.08
175	Kelly Gruber	.10

176	Tom Henke	.08
177	Glenallen Hill	.15
178	Jimmy Key	.06
180	Fred McGriff	.15
181	Rance Mulliniks	.05
182	Greg Myers	.05
183	John Olerud	.60
184	Luis Sojo	.08
185	Dave Stieb	.10
186	Todd Stottlemyre	.08
189	*Mark Whiten*	.20
192	Mookie Wilson	.05
195	Hubie Brooks	.05
198	Kal Daniels	.08
199	Kirk Gibson	.10
200	Jim Gott.	.05
203	Dave Hansen	.15
204	Lenny Harris	.05
205	Mike Hartley	.10
207	*Carlos Hernandez* (FC)	.10
208	Orel Hershiser	.10
209	Jay Howell	.08
210	Mike Huff	.08
211	Stan Javier	.05
212	Ramon Martinez	.12
214	Eddie Murray	.15
215	*Jim Neidlinger* (FC)	.10
216	Jose Offerman	.15
217	*Jim Poole* (FC)	.10
218	Juan Samuel	.08
221	Mike Sharperson	.05
222	Fernando Valenzuela	.08
225	*Scott Anderson* (FC)	.08
226	Dennis Boyd	.05
228	Delino DeShields	.15
230	Tom Foley	.05
231	Steve Frey	.05
232	Andres Galarraga	.08
233	Mark Gardner	.10
234	Marquis Grissom (FC)	.20
238	Dennis Martinez	.08
240	*Chris Nabholz*	.10
241	Otis Nixon	.05
244	Tim Raines	.12
245	*Mel Rojas* (FC)	.12
246	*Scott Ruskin* (FC)	.15
247	*Bill Sampen*	.15
248	Nelson Santovenia	.05
249	Dave Schmidt	.05

391 Wes Chamberlain

250	Larry Walker	.12
251	Tim Wallach	.05
255	Jeff Brantley	.05
256	John Burkett	.10
257	Brett Butler	.08
258	Gary Carter	.08
259	Will Clark	.20
260	*Steve Decker* (FC)	.15
262	Scott Garrelts	.05
264	Mike Lacoss	.05
265	*Mark Leonard* (FC)	.10
267	Kevin Mitchell	.10
269	*Rich Parker*	.07
270	Rick Reuschel	.05
273	Robby Thompson	.05
275	Jose Uribe	.05
276	Matt Williams	.15
277	Trevor Wilson	.07
278	*Gerald Alexander* (FC)	.10
279	Brad Arnsberg	.05
280	*Kevin Belcher* (FC)	.20
281	*Joe Bitker* (FC)	.08
285	Julio Franco	.10
286	Juan Gonzalez	.50
287	*Bill Hasleman* (FC)	.06
288	Charlie Hough	.06
290	Pete Incaviglia	.05
291	Mike Jeffcoat	.05

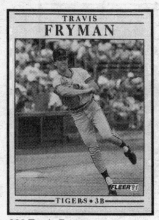

336 Travis Fryman

432	Dwight Smith	.08
434	Rick Sutcliffe	.06
436	*Hector Villaneuva*	.15
437	Jerome Walton	.08
446	Jay Buhner	.10
447	*Dave Burba* (FC)	.15
450	Ken Griffey, Jr.	.50
451	Erik Hanson	.08
453	Brian Holman	.06
455	Randy Johnson	.07
457	Edgar Martinez	.10
458	Tino Martinez	.10
460	Harold Reynolds	.07
461	Mike Schooler	.06
468	Juan Bell (FC)	.10
470	Steve Finley	.08
472	*Leo Gomez* (FC)	.20
476	*Chris Hoiles*	.25
481	Ben McDonald	.15
484	Randy Milligan	.06
485	*John Mitchell* (FC)	.08
486	Gregg Olson	.08
489	Bill Ripken	.08
490	Cal Ripken, Jr.	30
491	Curt Schilling	.06
492	*David Segui*	.20
493	*Anthony Telford* (FC)	.20
494	Mickey Tettleton	.06
498	Eric Anthony	.10
499	Craig Biggio	.08
500	Ken Caminiti	.06
501	Casey Candaele	.06
502	*Andujar Cedeno* (FC)	.20
505	Glenn Davis	.12
507	*Luis Gonzalez* (FC)	.35
508	Bill Gullickson	.10
514	*Karl Rhodes* (FC)	.20
515	Mike Scott	.06
516	*Mike Simms* (FC)	.10
521	Gerald Young	.06
523	Roberto Alomar	.15
524	Andy Benes	.15
525	Joe Carter	.15
526	Jack Clark	.06
528	Paul Faries (FC)	.06
529	Tony Gwynn	.20
532	*Thomas Howard*	.20
533	Bruce Hurst	.08
541	*Richard Rodriguez* (FC)	.10

561 Bo Jackson

542	Benito Santiago	.08
549	Kevin Appier	.10
551	Bob Boone	.06
552	George Brett	.15
553	*Jeff Conine* (FC)	.40
555	Mark Davis	.06
559	Tom Gordon	.08
560	Mark Gubicza.	06
561	Bo Jackson	.15
563	*Brian McRae* (FC)	.25
567	Bret Saberhagen	.08
568	*Jeff Schultz* (FC)	.08
569	Kevin Seitzer	.08
570	*Terry Shumpert*	.10
572	Danny Tartabull	.08
574	Frank White	.06
575	Willie Wilson	.06
577	Greg Brock	.06
578	George Canale	.07
580	Rob Deer	.06
586	Ted Higuera	.07
589	*Tim McIntosh* (FC)	.08
591	Paul Molitor	.15
593	Dave Parker	.10
596	Gary Sheffield	.12
597	Bill Spiers	.10
599	Greg Vaughn	.15
601	Robin Yount	.15

450 Ken Griffey, Jr.

1991 FLEER UPDATE

The 1991 Fleer Update won little applause from the hobby community. Why? Due to the company's unimpressive card choices earlier in the year, the updated subset was filled with names common to other 1991 issues. Fleer was one of the last companies to offer cards of rookies Jeff Bagwell and Chuck Knoblauch. On the other hand, the company atoned for one of its worst mistakes of the summer—omitting Tommy Greene, Philadelphia's no-hit hurler. Fleer did manage to include cards of major stars like Darryl Strawberry on their current teams. As usual, each Fleer card resembles the larger 1991 set and is numbered U-1 through U-132 (though the "U" has been omitted from the following list). The set was issued in a specially designed collector's box and was originally distributed only in complete-set form through hobby dealers. But don't expect any quick price climbs from this 132-card offering, one of Fleer's most forgettable post-season products in years.

		MINT
Complete set		**$6.00**
Commons		**.04**

1	Glenn Davis	$ .05
2	Dwight Evans	.08
3	Jose Mesa	.05
4	Jack Clark	.10
7	Mo Vaughn (FC)	.25
10	Dave Parker	.10
11	Joey Cora	.05
12	Charlie Hough	.05
13	Matt Merullo	.08
14	Warren Newson	.08
15	Tim Raines	.15
16	Albert Belle	.15
17	Glenallen Hill	.08
19	Mark Lewis	.12
20	Charles Nagy	.20
21	Mark Whiten	.08
23	Rob Deer	.05
24	Mickey Tettleton	.05
26	Kirk Gibson	.10
27	David Howard	.08
28	Brent Mayne (FC)	.10
30	Mark Lee	.08
31	Julio Machado	.05
33	Willie Randolph	.08
36	Chili Davis	.08
37	Chuck Knoblauch (FC)	.30
38	Scott Leius	.15
39	Jack Morris	.10
40	Mike Pagliarulo	.05
41	Lenny Webster (FC)	.10
44	Jeff Johnson	.05
45	Scott Kamieniecki	.10
46	Pat Kelly	.10
47	Hensley Meulens	.08
48	Wade Taylor	.10
49	Bernie Williams (FC)	.20
50	Kirk Dressendorfer	.10
52	Rich DeLucia	.12
59	Rich Gossage	.07
60	Jose Guzman	.05
61	Dean Palmer (FC)	.35
62	Ivan Rodriguez	1.00
63	Roberto Alomar	.20
64	Tom Candiotti	.07
65	Joe Carter	.10
66	Ed Sprague	.10
67	Pat Tabler	.05
68	Mike Timlin	.10
69	Devon White	.07
70	Rafael Belliard	.05
76	Terry Pendleton	.10

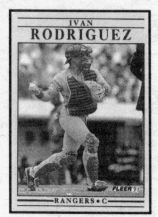

62 Ivan Rodriguez

77	George Bell	.10
79	Chuck McElroy	.07
80	Gary Scott	.12

81	Heathcliff Slocumb	.10
83	Rick Wilkins	.10
84	Freddie Benavides	.10
86	Mo Sanford	.10
87	Jeff Bagwell	1.25
89	Pete Harnisch	.06
90	Darryl Kile (FC)	.10
91	Brett Butler	.07
96	Darryl Strawberry	.15
102	Vince Coleman	.10
103	Jeff Innis	.10
104	Pete Schourek	.10
105	Andy Ashby	.10
108	Tommy Greene	.07
110	Mitch Williams	.07
112	Orlando Merced	.10
115	John Wehner	.10
118	Geronimo Pena	.15
123	Tony Fernandez	.07
124	Darrin Jackson	.05
125	Fred McGriff	.12
126	Jose Mota	.10
130	Willie McGee	.10
131	Dave Righetti	.08

1991 SCORE

With large doses of rookie cards and innovative subsets, Score's 900-card set for 1991 outdistances its competitors in both size and value. Specialty cards in the set include caricatures of All-Stars, artistic poses for the "Dream Team," and a subset of black-and-white poses called The Franchise that honors a top player from every team. Among the creative photos found in the set is an extreme close-up of Bob Welch's hand, showing the proper grip for launching a forkball. There is also a Cooperstown series of seven players that is found only in factory-collated sets. (Rookie Prospects are identified on the following list with the abbreviation "RP.") The pre-Christmas sales of factory sets in retail stores lessened this set's value.

	MINT
Complete set	$20.00
Commons	.04

1	Jose Canseco	$ .15
2	Ken Griffey, Jr.	.50

3	Ryne Sandberg	.20
4	Nolan Ryan	.40
5	Bo Jackson	.15
6	Bret Saberhagen	.08
7	Will Clark	.15
8	Ellis Burks	.10
9	Joe Carter	.08

10	Rickey Henderson	.15
11	Ozzie Guillen	.08
12	Wade Boggs	.12
13	Jerome Walton	.03
14	John Franco	.07
15	Ricky Jordan	.05
17	Ron Dibble	.10
19	Cory Snyder	.05
20	Kal Daniels	.08
21	Mark Langston	.10
23	Don Mattingly	.12
24	Dave Righetti	.08
25	Roberto Alomar	.08
26	Robby Thompson	.07
27	Jack McDowell	.07
28	Bip Roberts	.07
29	Jay Howell	.06
30	Dave Stieb	.10
32	Steve Sax	.12
34	Lee Guetterman	.05
35	Tim Raines	.08
37	Lance Parrish	.07
38	Tony Phillips	.06
39	Todd Stottlemyre	.06
40	Alan Trammell	.06
42	Mookie Wilson	.05
44	Jeffrey Leonard	.05
45	Doug Jones	.06
48	Harold Reynolds	.07
49	Paul Molitor	.10
51	Danny Darwin	.05
55	Dave Justice	.35
56	Greg Olson	.08
57	Willie Blair	.05
59	Shawn Boskie	.08
60	Kevin Tapani	.08
61	Dave Hollins	.08
62	Scott Radinsky	.05
63	Francisco Cabrera	.03
65	Jim Leyritz	.08
67	*Lee Stevens*	.08
68	Bill Sampen	.05
69	Craig Grebeck	.06
71	Hector Villanueva	.08
72	Oscar Azocar	.05
74	Carlos Baerga	.25
75	Charles Nagy	.15
76	Tim Drummond	.05
77	Dana Kiecker	.05

815 Ryne Sandberg

78	*Tom Edens*	.05
79	Kent Mercker	.07
80	Steve Avery	.25
81	Lee Smith	.10
83	Dave Winfield	.15
84	Bill Spiers	.08
85	Dan Pasqua	.06
89	Keith Hernandez	.06
90	Todd Benzinger	.05
93	Candy Maldonado	.05
94	John Kruk	.08
95	Cal Ripken, Jr.	.25
97	Mike Felder	.04
98	Bill Landrum	.06
100	Chuck Finley	.10
101	Kirt Manwaring	.05
102	Jaime Navarro	.06
105	Jim Abbott	.10
106	Tom Brookens	.03
107	Darryl Hamilton	.05
110	Greg Swindell	.09
111	Juan Berenguer	.05
114	Jack Morris	.10
117	Garry Templeton	.05
119	Roberto Kelly	.12
120	George Brett	.15
121	Oddibe McDowell	.05
125	Jay Buhner	.12

55 Dave Justice

4 Nolan Ryan

221	Jose DeLeon	.05
223	Darrel Akerfelds	.03
225	Dwight Evans	.08
227	Paul O'Neill	.10
228	Marty Barrett	.03
229	Tom Browning	.08
230	Terry Pendleton	.10
232	Mike Boddicker	.08
234	Marquis Grissom	.12
235	Bert Blyleven	.08
236	Curt Young	.05
240	Todd Zeile	.10
241	Larry Walker	.20
243	Jeff Ballard	.03
244	Jeff King	.03
245	Tom Brunansky	.03
248	Rob Deer	.05
250	Lenny Dykstra	.07
252	Mike Hartley	.08
253	Joey Cora	.05
254	Ivan Calderon	.07
256	Sammy Sosa	.07
257	Steve Buechele	.05
260	Teddy Higuera	.05
264	Edgar Martinez	.08
265	Carlton Fisk	.10
266	Chuck Finley	.06
267	John Wetteland	.05
268	Kevin Appier	.10
270	Mickey Tettleton	.06
272	Steve Jeltz	.05
273	R.J. Reynolds	.05
276	Mike Morgan	.07
277	Jeff Russell	.07
278	Pete Incaviglia	.05
279	Kevin Seitzer	.05
280	Bobby Thigpen	.06
281	Stan Javier	.05
284	Shane Mack	.07
285	Brian Holman	.05
290	Randy Johnson	.08
291	Harold Baines	.10
292	Kent Hrbek	.10
295	Kurt Stillwell	.05
296	Stan Belinda	.05
297	Lou Whitaker	.10
300	Ramon Martinez	.10
301	Dwight Smith	.07
304	Sid Bream	.05

331 Brian McRae

307	Mackey Sasser	.05
308	Franklin Stubbs	.07
309	Jack Daugherty	.05
310	Eddie Murray	.10
311	Bob Welch	.07
312	Brian Harper	.07
315	Bobby Bonilla	.10
317	Greg Maddux	.12
319	Mark Portugal	.05
320	Robin Ventura	.15
321	Bob Ojeda	.05
322	Mike Harkey	.08
323	Jay Bell	.06
324	Mark McGwire	.20
325	Gary Gaetti	.10
327	Kevin McReynolds	.08
328	Frank Tanana	.05
329	Eric Yelding	.05
330	Barry Bonds	.25
331	*Brian McRae* (FC)	.25
332	*Pedro Munoz* (RP) (FC)	.20
333	*Daryl Irvine* (FC)	.06
335	*Thomas Howard* (FC)	.08
336	*Jeff Schultz* (FC)	.06
337	Jeff Manto (FC)	.06
338	Beau Allred	.06
339	*Mike Bordick* (FC)	.25
340	*Todd Hundley*	.15

1991 Score

332 Pedro Munoz

428	Eric Plunk	.05
432	Tony Fernandez	.08
433	Rance Mulliniks	.05
436	*Steve Frey*	.08
437	Jamie Moyer	.05
438	Junior Ortiz	.05
441	Jose Canseco (Dream Team)	1.00
443	Andres Galarraga	.07
444	Bryn Smith	.05
445	Andre Dawson	.15
446	Juan Samuel	.08
448	Ron Gant	.12
449	Fernando Valenzuela	.07
450	Vince Coleman	.10
451	Kevin Mitchell	.10
452	Spike Owen	.03
453	Mike Bielecki	.03
454	Dennis Martinez	.07
455	Brett Butler	.08
456	Ron Darling	.05
457	Dennis Rasmussen	.03
459	Steve Bedrosian	.06
460	Frank Viola	.10
462	Chris Sabo	.10
463	Dante Bichette	.03
464	Rick Mahler	.05
465	John Smiley	.10
466	Devon White	.07
469	Billy Hatcher	.05
470	Wally Joyner	.15
471	Gene Larkin	.05
472	Doug Drabek	.08
473	Gary Sheffield	.25
475	Andy Van Slyke	.10
476	Mike Gallego	.05
477	B.J. Surhoff	.05
479	Mariano Duncan	.05
480	Fred McGriff	.15
482	Alvin Davis	.07
484	Dave Parker	.10
485	Dennis Eckersley	.12
486	Erik Hanson	.06
487	Bill Ripken	.06
488	Tom Candiotti	.06
490	Gregg Olson	.10
492	Pete Harnisch	.07
493	Julio Franco	.05
495	Ruben Sierra	.15

1 Jose Canseco

497	Mike Fetters	.03
500	Tony Gwynn	.15
501	Randy Myers	.06
503	Craig Worthington	.03
505	Barry Larkin	.06
507	Bobby Witt	.08
511	Storm Davis	.03
512	Bob Milacki	.03
513	Bill Pecota	.08
514	Glenallen Hill	.08
515	Danny Tartabull	.08
516	Mike Moore	.06
520	Mike Scioscia	.03
523	Jack Clark	.08
524	Bruce Ruffin	.05
525	Robin Yount	.10
528	Greg Vaughn	.10
531	Marvell Wynne	.03
532	Jim Gantner	.03
533	Greg Litton	.03
537	Roger McDowell	.06
538	Andy Benes	.10
540	Doc Gooden	.10
541	Scott Garrelts	.05
545	Delino DeShields	.10
546	Mike Sharperson	.03
549	David Cone	.08
550	Orel Hershiser	.08

2 Ken Griffey, Jr.

485 Dennis Eckersley

570 Travis Fryman

874 Frank Thomas

1991 SCORE ROOKIE & TRADED

The primary outward difference between this late-season update edition and the regular set issued earlier in the year is in the borders: On the Rookie & Traded set they have a metallic-maroon color. Although Score's enormous 900-card two-series set provides more than its fair share of newcomers making rookie-card appearances, this 110-card addition has an abundance of fresh faces as well. Specifically, cards numbered 81-110 depict rookies; the remainder show traded players. As usual, cards were available primarily from hobby-related sources in boxed, complete-set form, instead of being sold through department stores and other standard outlets. While this R & T offering was more widely available than in previous years, expect a gradual carryover effect in popularity (and price appreciation) from the principal set.

		MINT
Complete set		**$7.00**
Commons		**.04**

1	Bo Jackson	$ .20
4	Jack Clark	.07
6	Ivan Calderon	.09
7	Glenn Davis	.07
10	Tim Raines	.10
11	Joe Carter	.15
12	Sid Bream	.07
13	George Bell	.10
16	Darryl Strawberry	.15
19	Willie McGee	.10
31	Dave Parker	.07
34	Deion Sanders	.25
36	Pete Harnisch	.08
44	Roberto Alomar	.20
48	Devon White	.09
50	Terry Pendleton	.10
56	Bill Gullickson	.07
57	Vince Coleman	.12
58	Fred McGriff	.20
62	• Dwight Evans	.08
66	Tony Fernandez	.09
70	Chili Davis	.12

1 Bo Jackson

74	Jack Morris	.12
80	Curt Schilling	.08
81	Brian Drahman (FC)	.07
82	Ivan Rodriguez (FC)	**1.00**
85	Mike Timlin (FC)	.07
86	Darryl Kile (FC)	.12

88	Bruce Walton (FC)	.07
90	Gary Scott (FC)	.12
93	Chuck Knoblauch (FC)	.60
94	Dana Allison (FC)	.12
95	Erik Pappas (FC)	.12
96	Jeff Bagwell (FC)	1.50
97	Kirk Dressendorfer (FC)	.12
98	Freddie Benavides (FC)	.08
99	Luis Gonzalez (FC)	.30
100	Wade Taylor (FC)	.08
101	Ed Sprague (FC)	.10
102	Bob Scanlan (FC)	.15
103	Rick Wilkins (FC)	.15
104	Chris Donnels (FC)	.15
105	Joe Slusarski (FC)	.12
106	Mark Lewis (FC)	.12
107	Pat Kelly (FC)	.20
108	John Briscoe (FC)	.08
109	Luis Lopez (FC)	.10
110	Jeff Johnson (FC)	.10

1991 TOPPS

To celebrate 40 seasons of card making, Topps organized a season-long promotion to tout its 1991 set and highlighted each card with a baseball logo overwritten with "Topps 40 Years of Baseball." The Brooklyn-based company also gave away previously published Topps cards by inserting them in assorted wax packs. Because of the anniversary connection, Topps went to considerable trouble to correct a number of statistical errors in an early printing, some of which approach the $.50 to $1.50 range. The 792-card set provided Topps debuts for 118 players, and the company continues to be the only one willing to print individual cards of team managers. Due to the easy availability of this set, however, gains in value will come slowly.

		MINT
Complete set		**$20.00**
Commons		**.04**
1	Nolan Ryan	$ .50
2	Record Breaker (George Brett)	.08
3	Record Breaker (Carlton Fisk)	.08
4	Record Breaker (Kevin Mass)	.08
5	Record Breaker (Cal Ripken)	.08
6	Record Breaker (Nolan Ryan)	.25
7	Record Breaker (Ryne Sandberg)	.08
8	Bob Thigpen	.08
9	Darrin Fletcher (FC)	.06
10	Gregg Olson	.10
11	Roberto Kelly	.10
13	Mariano Duncan	.05
15	Von Hayes	.08
16	Mike Heath	.05
17	Jeff Brantley	.05
20	Pedro Guerrero	.08
21	Joe Morgan	.03
22	Storm Davis	.03
23	Jim Gantner	.05
24	Dave Martinez	.05
25	Tim Belcher	.08
27	Bobby Witt	.08
29	Bob Walk	.05
30	Gregg Jefferies	.08
31	*Colby Ward* (FC)	.05
32	*Mike Simms* (FC)	.05
33	Barry Jones	.05
35	Greg Maddux	.08
39	*Jim Neidlinger* (FC)	.05
40	Kevin Mitchell	.08
42	*Chris Hoiles* (FC)	.15
43	Roger McDowell	.06
44	Mike Felder	.05

45 Chris Sabo .... .06
47 Brook Jacoby .... .03
49 Pat Borders .... .06
50 Bob Welch...................... .07
51 Art Howe .... .03
52 *Francisco Oliveras* (FC) .. .06
53 Mike Sharperson .... .05
55 Jeffrey Leonard .... .03
56 Jeff Parrett..................... .03
58 Mel Stottlemyre .... .05
59 Eric Yelding .... .05
60 Frank Viola .... .07
65 Bruce Hurst .... .08
67 Rick Honeycutt .... .05
68 Gary Sheffield .... .12
70 Ellis Burks .... .08
71 Jim Acker .... .05
72 Junior Ortiz.................... .05
73 Craig Worthington .... .03
74 *Shane Andrews* (#1 Draft
   Pick) (FC) .... .15
75 Jack Morris .... .07
77 Drew Hall .... .05
78 Geno Petralli .... .05
79 Frank Thomas 1.25
80 Fernando Valenzuela ...... .05
81 Cito Gaston .... .06
82 Tom Glavine .... .20
84 Bob McClure .... .03
85 Jesse Barfield................ .05
87 Tracy Jones.................... .03
88 Bob Tewksbury .... .05
89 Darren Daulton............... .05
90 Danny Tartabull .... .08
91 *Greg Colbrunn* (FS) (FC). .20
92 Danny Jackson................ .03
93 Ivan Calderon .... .08
95 Paul Molitor .... .10
96 Trevor Wilson .... .06
99 Chris Gwynn .... .05
100 Don Mattingly .... .15
101 Rob Ducey .... .05
102 Gene Larkin .... .05
103 *Tim Costo* (#1 Draft Pick) .20
105 Kevin McReynolds .... .05
106 Ed Nunez .... .03
110 Tom Henke...................... .08
111 Andres Thomas............... .03
112 Frank DiPino .... .03

227 Steve Avery

113 *Carl Everett* (#1 Draft Pick)
    (FC) .... .25
114 *Lance Dickson* (FC) .... .20
115 Hubie Brooks................... .05
117 Dion James .... .05
118 *Tom Edens* (FC)............... .06
120 Joe Carter .... .15
121 Eric King....................... .03
122 Paul O'Neill .... .15
124 Randy Bush.................... .05
126 *Bernard Gilkey* (FC) .... .15
128 *Travis Fryman* .... .50
130 Ozzie Smith .... .10
131 Checklist....................... .08
133 Greg Briley .... .05
134 Kevin Elster .... .03
135 Jerome Walton .... .05
139 Jeff Treadway................. .05
140 Fred McGriff .... .10
144 Dave Henderson .... .08
145 Lou Whitaker................... .08
146 Dan Plesac .... .05
147 *Carlos Baerga* .... .25
149 *Al Osuna* (FC) .... .10
150 Cal Ripken...................... .35
152 Mickey Hatcher .... .05
155 Dwight Evans .... .08
157 John Smoltz .... .10

790 Ken Griffey, Jr.

158	Jose Uribe	.05
160	Vince Coleman	.08
162	*Ozzie Canseco* (FC)	.08
165	Sandy Alomar	.08
166	Harold Baines	.08
167	*Randy Tomlin*	.20
168	John Olerud	.30
170	Carlton Fisk	.10
171	Tony LaRussa	.03
174	Ken Caminiti	.07
175	Jack Armstrong	.05
176	John Orton	.08
177	*Reggie Harris* (FC)	.08
180	Tony Gwynn	.15
183	Clay Parker	.03
185	Joe Magrane	.03
189	*Daryl Irvine* (FC)	.06
190	Matt Williams	.15
191	*Willie Blair*	.05
192	Rob Deer	.06
194	Xavier Hernandez (FC)	.08
195	Wally Joyner	.10
196	*Jim Vatcher* (FC)	.08
197	*Chris Nabholz* (FC)	.10
199	Mike Hartley (FC)	.08
200	Darryl Strawberry	.15
201	Jim Kelly	.06
202	*Jim Leyritz*	.08

204	Herm Winningham	.03
205	*Mike Perez* (FC)	.15
206	Carlos Quintana	.08
207	Gary Wayne	.05
208	Willie Wilson	.05
210	Lance Parrish	.08
211	*Brian Barnes* (FC)	.10
212	Steve Finley	.10
213	Frank Willis	.05
214	Joe Giraldi	.05
215	Dave Smith	.03
217	Chris Bosio	.05
219	Jack McDowell	.15
220	Tim Wallach	.08
222	*Brian McRae* (FC)	.30
224	*Juan Gonzalez*	.50
225	Randy Johnson	.10
227	Steve Avery	.25
228	Rex Hudler	.05
229	Rance Mulliniks	.05
230	Sid Fernandez	.05
232	Len Dykstra	.08
234	*Scott Erickson*	.15
235	Dave Parker	.20
237	Rick Cerone	.03
239	*Darren Lewis* (FC)	.15
240	Mike Scott	.05
242	Mike LaCoss	.05

79 Frank Thomas

243 Lance Johnson 12
244 Mike Jeffcoast 05
245 Kal Daniels 05
247 Jody Reed 08
248 Tom Gordon 05
250 Dennis Eckersley 10
251 Mark Lemke 07
252 *Mel Rojas* (FC) 08
254 Shawn Boskie 05
255 Brian Downing 08
258 Chris Hammond 15
259 Hensley Meulens 08
260 Harold Reynolds.............08
261 Bud Harrelson 05
263 Checklist........................06
264 Dave Hollins 20
265 Mark Gubicza 05
267 Mark Knudson 03
269 Joe Hesketh 03
270 Mark McGwire 15
271 *Omar Olivares* 10
272 Jeff King 05
273 Jim Key 05
275 Alan Trammell 10
277 Scott Coolbaugh (FC) 06
278 *Alex Fernandez* (FC).....30
280 Bret Saberhagen 06
281 Larry Sheets 03
283 Marquis Grissom 10
284 Bill Spiers 05
285 Jim Abbott 10
286 Ken Oberkfell 05
288 Derrick May (FC) 25
289 Tim Birtsas 05
290 Steve Sax......................12
291 John Wathan 05
293 Jay Bell 06
294 Mike Moore 08
295 Rafael Palmeiro 10
297 Manny Lee 05
298 Omar Vizquel 05
299 Scott Radinsky 05
300 Kirby Puckett 15
301 Steve Farr 05
303 Mike Boddicker.............05
304 Kevin Reimer (FC)...........10
305 Mike Scioscia 05
306 Lee Smith 08
307 Andy Benes.....................10

600 Bo Jackson

308 Tom Pagnozzi 05
309 Norm Charlton.................07
310 Gary Carter 06
312 Charlie Hayes.................07
315 Roberto Alomar 20
318 Rick Aguilera 07
319 Jeff McKnight (FC) 10
320 Tony Fernandez 10
322 Terry Shumpert (FC) 10
323 Cory Snyder 05
324 Ron Kittle......................05
325 Brett Butler....................08
329 Dave Justice...................30
330 Doc Gooden 10
333 *Chipper Jones* (#1 Draft
     Pick) (FC) 1.00
335 Mitch Williams 07
336 Matt Nokes.....................07
337 Keith Comstock (Cubs) .1.00
337 Keith Comstock
     (Mariners).........................03
339 Larry Walker 10
340 Ramon Martinez 15
342 *Mickey Morandini* 15
345 Len Dykstra 12
347 Greg Vaughn 15
348 Todd Stottlelmyre 08
350 Glenn Davis....................05

529 Marc Newfield

502	Carney Lansford	.07
504	*Julio Valera* (FC)	.10
505	Chuck Finley	.08
509	Glenallen Hill	.08
510	John Franco	.10
513	*Jerald Clark*	.08
516	Karl Rhodes (FC)	.08
519	• Sparky Anderson	.06
520	Mark Grace	.07
523	*Rodney McCray* (FC)	.07
526	Moises Alou (FC)	.30
528	Dennis Martinez	.06
529	*Marc Newfield* (#1 Draft Pick) (FC)	.60
530	Roger Clemens	.20
531	*Dave Rohde* (FC)	.08
535	Ruben Sierra	.20
538	Bip Roberts	.06
540	George Brett	.15
545	Dale Murphy	.10
548	Jaime Navarro	.07
550	Eric Davis	.10
554	Brian Harper	.08
555	*Turner Ward* (FC)	.07
561	Tim McIntosh (FC)	.10
563	*Brent Knackert*	.08
565	Craig Biggio	.08
566	*Craig Wilson* (FC)	.10
570	Barry Bonds	.25
573	*Rich Rodriguez* (FC)	.08
575	Robin Yount	.15
576	Jeff Kaiser (FC)	.08
580	Dave Stewart	.08
586	Fred Lynn	.06
587	Jose Offerman (FC)	.10
588	Mark Whiten (FC)	.25
590	Eddie Murray	.15
596	*Ronnie Walden* (#1 Draft Pick) (FC)	.10
600	Bo Jackson	.20
603	*Wes Chamberlain* (FC) (photo is Louie Meadows)	.50
603	*Wes Chamberlain* (FC) (correct photo)	.20
605	Jeff Reardon	.08
607	Edgar Martinez	.07
610	Andres Galarraga	.08
615	Bert Blyleven	.08

603 Wes Chamberlain

616	Todd Zeile	.10
620	Ozzie Guillen	.08
627	*Tim Layana*	.08
630	Dave Winfield	.12
631	Mike Morgan	.06
633	Kevin Tapani	.12
636	*Geronimo Pena* (FC)	.10
639	• Frank Robinson	.10
640	Andre Dawson	.10
642	Hal Morris	.10
646	*Andujar Cedeno* (FC)	.25
648	Lee Stevens (FC)	.15
649	*Bill Sampen*	.08
653	*Anthony Teleford* (FC)	.08
654	Paul Sorrento (FC)	.15
655	Erik Hanson	.06
658	*Scott Aldred* (FC)	.10
659	*Oscar Azocar* (FC)	.10
660	Lee Smith	.10
662	Rob Dibble	.08
670	Rickey Henderson	.20
672	Shane Mack	.07
673	*Greg Olson*	.15
677	Bill Ripken	.08
680	David Cone	.08
682	*Ray Lankford* (FC)	.35
684	Milt Cuyler (FC)	.15
685	Doug Drabek	.08

688	Rosario Rodriguez	.06
690	Orel Hershiser	.06
692	*Efrain Valdez* (FC)	.06
700	Jose Canseco	.20
702	*Tim Naehring*	.10
710	Kent Hrbek	.08
720	Cecil Fielder	.15
724	*David Segui* (FC)	.10
725	Ron Gant	.15
730	Barry Larkin	.12
740	Ryne Sandberg	.20
750	Bobby Bonilla	.12
751	*Wayne Edwards*	.10
753	*Paul Marak* (FC)	.07

755	Mark Langston	.10
760	Benny Santiago	.08
763	*Dana Kiecker*	.06
765	Shawon Dunston	.08
767	*Dan Wilson* (#1 Draft Pick)	.15
769	*Tim Sherrill* (FC)	.10
772	Kent Mercker (FC)	.10
775	Julio Franco	.10
776	Brent Mayne (FC)	.15
780	Randy Myers	.08
790	Ken Griffey, Jr.	.50
791	Mike Benjamin (FC)	.08
792	Mike Greenwell	.06

1991 TOPPS TRADED

Topps had boasted for months that its 1990 Traded set would include cards for members of the U.S. Olympic baseball team. But the company backed out at the last minute with the claim that using cards of underclassmen would endanger their amateur standing. This 1991 edition, however, is loaded with Olympians (identified on the following lists with USA after their names). It has recaptured much of the appeal of the 1988 Traded set, when phenoms like Mark McGwire and Jim Abbott were pictured in their Team USA finery. Another feature of the 1991 Topps Traded set is the addition of newly hired baseball managers: Jim Essian of the Chicago Cubs, Montreal's Tom Runnels, Cleveland's Mike Hargrove, Philadelphia's Jim Fregosi, Kansas City's Hal McRae, and Baltimore's Johnny Oates make exclusive appearances. This issue is likely to repeat the experience of the 1988 Topps Traded set, which enjoyed large price gains as the many featured Olympians began to achieve recognition in the majors.

	MINT
Complete set	**$12.00**
Commons	**.04**

1	Juan Agosto	$ .03
4	Jeff Bagwell (FC)	1.25
7	Derek Bell (FC)	.30
8	George Bell	.07
10	Dante Bichette	.03
12	Mike Boddicker	.03

13	Sid Bream	.05
14	Hubie Brooks	.03
15	Brett Butler	.05
16	Ivan Calderon	.05
18	Tom Candiotti	.03
19	Gary Carter	.05
20	Joe Carter	.15
22	Jack Clark	.05
23	Vince Coleman	.08
24	Scott Coolbaugh	.03
25	Danny Cox	.03

26	Danny Darwin	.03
27	Chili Davis	.08
28	Glenn Davis	.05
29	Steve Decker (FC)	.10
30	Rob Deer	.03
31	Rich DeLucia (FC)	.10
32	John Dettmer (USA) (FC)	.20
33	Brian Downing	.03
34	Darren Dreifort (USA) (FC)	1.00
35	Kirk Dressendorfer (FC)	.12
36	Jim Essian	.03
37	• Dwight Evans	.09
39	Jeff Fassero (FC)	.05
41	Tony Fernandez	.10
42	Steve Finley	.09
44	Gary Gaetti	.03
45	Jason Giambi (USA) (FC)	.45
47	Leo Gomez (FC)	.15
48	Luis Gonzalez (FC)	.25
49	Jeff Granger (USA) (FC)	.80
50	Todd Greene (USA) (FC)	.30
51	Jeffrey Hammonds (USA) (FC)	2.50
53	Pete Harnish	.07
54	Rick Helling (USA) (FC)	.60
55	Glenallen Hill	.07
58	Bo Jackson	.15
60	Reggie Jefferson (FC)	.15
61	Charles Johnson (USA) (FC)	1.00
62	Jeff Johnson (FC)	.08
63	Todd Johnson (USA) (FC)	.25
65	Chris Jones (FC)	.07
66	Scott Kamieniecki (FC)	.10
67	Pat Kelly (FC)	.20
68	Darryl Kile (FC)	.25
69	Chuck Knoblauch (FC)	.35
71	Scott Leius (FC)	.10
72	Donnie Leshnock (USA) (FC)	.30
73	Mark Lewis (FC)	.10
75	Jason McDonald (USA) (FC)	.15
76	Willie McGee	.08

4 Jeff Bagwell

77	Fred McGriff	.12
78	Billy McMillon (USA) (FC)	.25
79	• Hal McRae	.10
80	Dan Melendez (USA) (FC)	.30
81	Orlando Merced (FC)	.25
82	Jack Morris	.12
83	Phil Nevin (USA) (FC)	1.10
88	Dean Palmer	.30
89	Dave Parker	.10
90	Terry Pendleton	.10
92	Doug Piatt (USA) (FC)	.10
93	Ron Polk (USA) (FC)	.10
94	Rock Raines	.06
98	Chris Roberts (USA) (FC)	.60
101	Ivan Rodriguez (FC)	1.00
102	Steve Rodriguez (FC)	.25
105	Bob Scanlan (FC)	.10
106	Pete Schourek (FC)	.10
107	Gary Scott (FC)	.12
108	Paul Shuey (USA) (FC)	.45
109	Doug Simons (FC)	.08
110	Dave Smith	.03
113	Kennie Steenstra (USA) (FC)	.30
114	Darryl Strawberry	.15

116	Todd Taylor (USA) (FC) ..	.12	124 Jeff Ware (USA) (FC) ...... .25
117	Wade Taylor (FC)	.07	126 Mark Whiten .... .12
121	Mike Timlin (FC)	.10	130 Chris Wimmer
122	David Tuttle (USA) (FC) ..	.20	(USA) (FC) .... .25
123	Mo Vaughn (FC)	.35	131 Ivan Zweig (USA) (FC) .... .20

1991 UPPER DECK

While Upper Deck's main set displayed few obvious changes, collectors pursued the 800 cards for another reason: Throughout the season, individual packs chosen at random contained specially produced, limited-edition cards signed by Nolan Ryan and Hank Aaron (the latter only in the high-number series, 701-800). Another pack premium was a card of basketball star Michael Jordan wearing a White Sox uniform. Two of the more unusual cards in the regular set feature minor stars with famous companions: Ozzie Canseco's photo includes his brother, Jose, while Ken Griffey shares his card with his superstar son. Investment started at a moderate level in 1991 sets because of an abundance of 1990 complete sets flooding department stores and other retail, non-hobby markets. Several abbreviations are used in the following list to identify subsets: SR for Star Rookies, TC for Team Checklist, and TP for Top Prospect.

	MINT			
			3	D.J. Dozier (SR) (FC) ...... .10
Complete set			4	Dave Hansen (SR) (FC) .. .20
(1-700)	**$25.00**		5	Maurice Vaughn
Commons (1-700)	.04			(SR) (FC) .... .75
Commons (701-800)	.05		6	Leo Gomez (SR) (FC) ..... .35
Complete set			7	Scott Aldred (SR) (FC) .... .15
(1-800)	35.00		8	Scott Chiamparino (SR)
Autographed				(FC) .... .10
Aaron card	400.00		9	Lance Dickson (SR) (FC) .20
Autographed			10	Sean Berry (SR) (FC) ...... .20
Ryan card	600.00		11	Bernie Williams
Michael Jordan				(SR) (FC) .... .45
insert	10.00		12	Brian Barnes (SR) (FC) .... .10
			13	Narciso Elvira (SR) (FC).. .07
			15	Greg Colbrunn (SR) (FC) .10
1	Star Rookie checklist.... $ .05		16	Bernard Gilkey (SR) (FC) .25
2	Phil Plantier (SR) (FC)...... .60		17	Mark Lewis (SR) (FC) .... .15
			18	Mickey Morandini
				(SR) (FC) .... .20
			19	Charles Nagy (SR) (FC) .. .40

20 *Geronimo Pena*
(SR) (FC).......................12
21 *Henry Rodriguez*
(SR) (FC).......................30
22 Scott Cooper (SR) (FC)....50
23 *Andujar Cedeno*
(SR) (FC).......................35
24 *Eric Karros* (SR) (FC)....**1.25**
25 *Steve Decker* (SR) (FC)...12
26 *Kevin Belcher* (SR) (FC)..12
27 *Jeff Conine* (SR) (FC).......70
28 Dave Stewart (TC)...........08
29 Carlton Fisk (TC)............08
30 Rafael Palmeiro (TC).......08
31 Chuck Finley (TC)...........08
33 Bret Saberhagen (TC).....08
35 *Scott Leius* (FC)..............15
37 *Terry Lee* (FC).................10
40 Chuck Knoblauch (FC)..**1.00**
43 Mike Greenwell (TC)........10
44 Kelly Gruber (TC)............08
46 Sandy Alomar Jr. (TC).....08
47 Gregg Olson (TC)............08
48 Dave Parker (TC)............08
49 Roberto Kelly (TC)...........08
51 Kyle Abbott (TP) (FC).......15
52 Jeff Juden (TP) (FC).......20
53 *Todd Van Poppel*
(TP) (FC).......................80
54 *Steve Karsay*
(TP) (FC).......................30
55 *Chipper Jones*
(TP) (FC)....................**1.50**
56 *Chris Johnson* (TP) (FC)..10
57 *John Ericks* (TP) (FC)......15
58 *Gary Scott* (TP) (FC)........15
59 Kiki Jones (TP) (FC).........10
60 *Wilfredo Cordero*
(TP) (FC)....................**1.00**
61 *Royce Clayton* (TP) (FC)..70
62 Tim Costo (TP) (FC).........30
63 Roger Salkeld (TP) (FC)...20
64 *Brook Fordyce* (TP) (FC)..15
65 *Mike Mussina* (TP) (FC)**2.50**
66 *Dave Staton* (TP) (FC)....35
67 *Mike Lieberthal* (TP) (FC).30
68 *Kurt Miller* (TP) (FC)........35
69 *Dan Peltier* (TP) (FC).......20
70 Greg Blosser (TP) (FC)....20

71 Reggie Sanders

71 *Reggie Sanders*
(TP) (FC)....................**1.50**
72 Brent Mayne (TP) (FC)....10
73 *Rico Brogna* (TP) (FC).....15
74 *Willie Banks* (TP) (FC).....30
75 *Len Brutcher* (TP) (FC)....10
76 *Pat Kelly* (TP) (FC)...........30
77 Chris Sabo (TC)..............10
78 Ramon Martinez (TC).......10
79 Matt Williams (TC)............08
80 Roberto Alomar (TC).......12
81 Glenn Davis (TC).............08
82 Ron Gant (TC).................15
83 Fielder's Feat (Cecil
Fielder)...........................25
84 *Orlando Merced* (FC).......60
87 *Andres Santana* (FC)......25
88 John Dopson...................06
92 Carmelo Martinez............03
94 Barry Bonds (TC)............10
95 Gregg Jefferies (TC)........10
99 Mark Grace (TC)..............08
100 Checklist 1-100..............08
101 Kevin Elster....................03
103 Mackey Sasser...............03
105 Kevin McReynolds...........06
106 Dave Stieb......................12
107 Jeffrey Leonard...............03

2 Phil Plantier

226	Joe Carter	.20
227	Julio Franco	.12
228	Craig Lefferts	.03
232	Carlos Quintana	.10
233	Gary Gaetti	.03
234	Mark Langston	.10
236	Greg Swindell	.10
237	Eddie Murray	.20
238	Jeff Manto (FC)	.07
239	Lenny Harris	.05
240	Jesse Orosco	.03
243	*Jim Leyritz*	.07
244	Cecil Fielder	.25
245	Darryl Strawberry	.20
246	Frank Thomas (FC)	3.50
247	Kevin Mitchell	.10
248	Lance Johnson	.08
249	Rick Reuschel	.03
252	Brian Holman	.05
254	B.J. Surhoff	.06
255	Tony Gwynn	.30
256	Andy Van Slyke	.10
257	Todd Stottlemyre	.08
261	Bobby Thigpen	.08
262	*Jimmy Kremers* (FC)	.08
263	Robin Ventura	.40
264	John Smoltz	.20
265	Sammy Sosa	.10
266	Gary Sheffield	.15
267	Lenny Dykstra	.10
268	Bill Spiers	.05
270	Brett Butler	.10
271	Bip Roberts	.08
272	Rob Deer	.08
273	Fred Lynn	.06
274	Dave Parker	.15
275	Andy Benes	.15
276	Glenallen Hill	.15
277	*Steve Howard*	.08
278	Doug Drabek	.12
279	Joe Oliver	.06
280	Todd Benzinger	.06
284	Jack Daugherty	.06
285	Ivan Calderon	.10
287	Kevin Bass	.07
290	John Franco	.08
293	Eric Show	.03
296	Mickey Tettleton	.08
298	Jose Rijo	.10

65 Mike Mussina

300	Checklist 201-300	.07
302	Pete Harnisch	.08
303	Greg Olson	.10
304	*Anthony Telford* (FC)	.10
306	*Chris Hoiles* (FC)	.25
307	Bryn Smith	.08
308	Mike Devereaux	.08
315	*Eric Gunderson*	.05
317	Dante Bichette	.05
319	Damon Berryhill	.06
320	Walt Terrell	.03
323	Jack McDowell	.20
324	Paul Molitor	.15
325	Ozzie Guillen	.12
326	Gregg Olson	.08
327	Pedro Guerrero	.08
331	Jack Clark	.08
332	Jerome Walton	.05
334	Derrick May	.25
335	Roberto Alomar	.50
337	Dave Winfield	.15
339	Chili Davis	.10
341	Ted Higuera	.06
342	*David Segui*	.10
344	Robin Yount	.15
345	Nolan Ryan	.75
346	*Ray Lankford*	.50
347	Cal Ripken Jr.	.50

1991 Upper Deck

225 Travis Fryman

348	Lee Smith	.10
351	Hal Morris	.12
352	• Deion Sanders	.30
353	Barry Larkin	.20
354	Don Mattingly	.25
355	Eric Davis	.20
356	Jose Offerman	.07
357	*Mel Rojas*	.10
361	Ron Gant	.20
362	*Howard Farmer*	.05
363	Dave Justice	.50
364	Delino DeShields	.25
365	Steve Avery	.75
366	David Cone	.12
367	Lou Whitaker	.10
368	Von Hayes	.05
370	Tim Teufel	.03
372	Roberto Kelly	.20
374	Kelly Gruber	.10
375	Kevin Maas	.20
376	Randy Johnson	.10
378	*Brent Knackert* (FC)	.05
383	*Scott Ruskin*	.15
385	Dennis Martinez	.10
387	Felix Jose	.20
388	Alejandro Pena	.06
389	Chet Lemon	.06
390	*Craig Wilson* (FC)	.20

396	*Tim Layana*	.10
400	Checklist 301-400	.07
406	Roger McDowell	.08
411	Juan Berenguer	.06
418	Jeff Reardon	.10
421	Willie Randolph	.05
422	Steve Bedrosian	.03
423	Mike Moore	.08
424	Jeff Brantley	.07
425	Bob Welch	.10
426	Terry Mulholland	.07
427	*Willie Blair* (FC)	.05
428	Darrin Fletcher	.05
431	Tom Gordon	.05
432	*Pedro Munoz* (FC)	.35
433	Kevin Seitzer	.07
434	Kevin Tapani	.15
435	Bret Saberhagen	.10
436	Ellis Burks	.10
437	Chuck Finley	.12
438	Mike Boddicker	.05
439	Francisco Cabrera	.03
440	*Todd Hundley*	.15
442	*Dann Howitt* (FC)	.10
443	Scott Garrelts	.03
444	Rickey Henderson	.20
445	Will Clark	.30
446	Ben McDonald	.25
447	Dale Murphy	.12
448	Dave Righetti	.08
452	Dwight Smith	.05
453	Pete Incaviglia	.05
454	Andre Dawson	.15
455	Ruben Sierra	.15
456	Andres Galarraga	.06
457	Alvin Davis	.05
461	Vince Coleman	.15
462	Steve Sax	.12
463	*Omar Olivares* (FC)	.10
464	*Oscar Azocar* (FC)	.05
465	Joe Magrane	.05
466	*Karl Rhodes* (FC)	.10
471	*Shawn Boskie*	.10
473	Rick Sutcliffe	.06
474	Rafael Palmeiro	.15
475	Mike Harkey	.10
476	Jaime Navarro	.07
477	Marquis Grissom	.25
480	Tom Glavine	.30

484 Terry Pendleton................ .10
485 Jesse Barfield.................. .07
486 Jose DeJesus.................. .08
487 *Paul Abbott* (FC) .... .10
494 Kevin Reimer (FC).......... .15
500 Checklist 401-500 .... .07
507 *Dana Kiecker* (FC) .... .05
513 Dave Smith...................... .03
514 *Chuck Carr* (FC) .... .10
517 Devon White.................... .10
521 Terry Shumpert .... .05
522 *Scott Erickson* (FC) .... .30
524 Orel Hershiser .... .10
525 George Brett.................... .20
526 Greg Vaughn.................... .15
527 *Tim Naehring* (FC) .... .12
530 Sam Horn .... .07
532 George Bell .... .10
533 Eric Anthony .... .05
534 *Julio Valera* (FC) .... .15
535 Glenn Davis .... .05
536 Larry Walker .... .12
538 *Chris Nabholz* (FC).......... .20
543 *Brian McRae* (FC) .... .40
544 Kirby Puckett .... .40
545 Bo Jackson...................... .20
546 Wade Boggs .... .20
547 Tim McIntosh (FC)........... .10
549 Dwight Evans .... .08
550 Billy Ripken .... .07
551 Erik Hanson..................... .07
553 Tino Martinez .... .20
554 Jim Abbott .... .25
555 Ken Griffey Jr. 1.00
556 Milt Cuyler (FC) .... .35
557 *Mark Leonard* (FC) .... .20
561 *Mark Whiten* (FC) .... .60
563 Junior Felix .... .08
564 *Darren Lewis* (FC) .... .30
565 Fred McGriff .... .15
566 Kevin Appier.................... .10
567 *Luis Gonzalez* (FC) .... .65
573 Lee Stevens (FC) .... .12
574 Edgar Martinez .... .10
584 Willie McGee .... .10
594 *Scott Lewis* (FC)............. .15
600 Checklist 501-600 .... .07
602 Bruce Hurst .... .09
604 *Jim Vatcher* (FC) .... .10

246 Frank Thomas

605 Dan Pasqua .... .07
606 Kenny Rogers .... .07
607 *Jeff Schulz* (FC) .... .10
614 Bill Landrum .... .08
615 Scott Scudder.................. .10
617 1917 Revisited (White Sox
 Team)........................... .15
621 *Scott Radinsky* (FC).... .10
624 Jerald Clark .... .07
625 Carlos Martinez .... .08
626 *Wes Chamberlain* (FC).... .35
632 *Jim Neidlinger* (FC) .... .10
633 Tom Browning .... .08
634 Kirk Gibson...................... .10
635 Rob Dibble .... .12
636 Stolen Base Leaders
 (Lou Brock,
 Rickey Henderson).... .25
637 Jeff Montgomery .... .10
638 Mike Schooler .... .08
640 *Rich Rodriguez* (FC)........ .15
642 Kent Mercker.................... .10
643 Carlton Fisk.................... .15
644 *Mike Bell* (FC)................. .10
645 *Alex Fernandez* (FC)....... .50
646 Juan Gonzalez 1.10
648 Jeff Russell..................... .07
649 *Chuck Malone* (FC) .... .12

53 Todd Van Poppel

365 Steve Avery

755 Jeff Bagwell

263 Robin Ventura

767	*Heathcliff Slocumb* (FC)	.07	784	Beau Allred (FC)	.10
768	Vince Coleman	.07	785	*Mike Timlin* (FC)	.10
769	Mitch Williams	.05	786	Ivan Calderon	.05
770	Brian Downing	.05	787	Hubie Brooks	.03
771	*Dana Allison* (FC)	.07	788	Juan Agosto	.03
772	Pete Harnisch	.10	789	Barry Jones	.03
773	Tim Raines	.08	790	Wally Backman	.03
774	*Darryl Kile* (FC)	.40	791	Jim Presley	.03
775	Fred McGriff	.25	792	Charlie Hough	.03
776	Dwight Evans	.10	793	Larry Andersen	.03
777	*Joe Slusarski* (FC)	.20	794	Steve Finley	.05
778	Dave Righetti	.08	795	Shawn Abner	.03
779	Jeff Hamilton	.03	796	Jeff M. Robinson	.03
780	Ernest Riles	.03	797	*Joe Bitker* (FC)	.10
781	Ken Dayley	.03	798	Eric Show	.03
782	Eric King	.03	799	Bud Black	.03
783	Devon White	.10	800	Checklist	.07

1991 UPPER DECK FINAL EDITION

The Upper Deck Company gave in to temptation after two years and decided to produce a season-ending set to compete with its rivals. However, their 100-card Final Edition shows more creativity than the usual traded or update sets by including several notable minor leaguers. Together with *Baseball America,* Upper Deck salutes 10 American League and 10 National League Prospects to begin the set. Boston's Frankie Rodriguez and Cincinnati's Reggie Sanders are cited as examples of "Most Exciting Players." Other players are recognized in "Diamond Skills" categories such as "best throwing arm," "best power," and so on, while the last 20 cards honor the 1991 All-Stars. Technically, the Final Edition isn't considered an extension of the 800-card set because these cards were not available in foil packs. The cards are also numbered separately from the principal set 1F through 100F (the letter "F" has been omitted from the following list).

		MINT
Complete set		**$12.00**
Commons		**.04**

1	Diamond Skills Checklist (Reggie Sanders, Ryan Klesko)	$ .50
2	Pedros Martinez (FC)	.70
4	Royce Clayton	.35
6	Dan Wilson (FC)	.30
7	Dmitri Young (FC)	1.25
8	Ryan Klesko (FC)	1.25
10	Rondell White (FC)	1.00
11	Reggie Sanders	.50

46 Rick Wilkins

26 Derek Bell

1992 DONRUSS

With a complete overhaul of its 784-card edition, Donruss staged a major comeback in 1992. A counterfeit-resistant UV coating was added to the card backs so that a company logo appears when the card is tilted. And color photos appear on the backs for the first time. But the 26-card Diamond King series, a Donruss feature since 1982, is now a limited-edition insert, not part of the regular set. For the second straight year, the set was distributed in two series, and foil wrappers replaced wax packs as suggested retail prices climbed to 99 cents (a reasonable increase considering the improvements). Factory-collated sets include four preview cards from the 1992 Leaf Studio set that add between $7 and $15 to the cost of the entire package. Among the eight bonus cards (not considered part of the regular set but included in random packs) are those displaying logos of the expansion teams, the Colorado Rockies and the Florida Marlins; these fetch prices of 25 to 50 cents each.

	MINT
Complete set	**$20.00**
Commons	**.04**

13 Ryan Klesko

1	*Mark Wohlers* (RR) (FC)	$ .15
2	Wil Cordero (RR) (FC)	.25
3	Kyle Abbott (RR) (FC)	.07
4	*Dave Nilsson* (RR) (FC)	.15
5	*Kenny Lofton* (RR) (FC)	.40
6	*Luis Mercedes* (RR) (FC)	.15
7	Roger Salkeld (RR) (FC)	.15
8	Eddie Zosky (RR)	.07
9	Todd Van Poppel (RR)	.20
10	*Frank Seminara* (RR)	.10
11	*Andy Ashby* (RR) (FC)	.10
12	Reggie Jefferson (RR)	.10
13	Ryan Klesko (RR)	.60
14	*Carlos Garcia* (RR) (FC)	.30
15	John Ramos (RR) (FC)	.20
16	Eric Karros (RR) (FC)	.50
17	*Pat Lennon* (RR) (FC)	.10
18	*Eddie Taubensee* (RR) (FC)	.12
19	*Roberto Hernandez* (RR) (FC)	.12
20	D.J. Dozier (RR)	.08
21	Dave Henderson AS	.05
22	Cal Ripken AS	.10
23	Wade Boggs AS	.07
24	Ken Griffey, Jr. AS	.10
25	Jack Morris AS	.05
26	Danny Tartabull AS	.05
27	Cecil Fielder AS	.07
28	Roberto Alomar AS	.07
29	Sandy Alomar AS	.05
30	Rickey Henderson AS	.05
31	Ken Hill	.07

33 Otis Nixon (Highlights) .... .05
34 Tim Wallach .... .05
35 Cal Ripken........................ .20
36 • Gary Carter .... .05
39 Kirk Gibson .... .05
40 Benito Santiago .... .07
43 Brian Holman .... .05
45 Dave Magadan .... .05
46 Rafael Palmeiro .... .07
47 Jody Reed .... .05
49 Greg Harris .... .05
50 Chris Sabo .... .10
51 Paul Molitor .... .10
53 Dave Smith...................... .05
54 Mark Davis .... .05
56 Donn Pall .... .05
57 Lenny Dykstra .... .07
58 Roberto Alomar .... .15
60 Willie McGee .... .07
61 Jay Buhner .... .07
63 Paul O'Neill .... .07
64 Hubie Brooks .... .05
65 Kelly Gruber .... .07
66 Ken Caminiti .... .07
67 Gary Redus .... .05
68 Harold Baines .... .07
69 Charlie Hough .... .05
70 B.J. Surhoff .... .05
71 Walt Weiss .... .05
73 Roberto Kelly................... .07
74 Jeff Ballard .... .05
75 Craig Biggio .... .07
76 Pat Combs .... .05
77 Jeff Robinson .... .05
78 Tim Belcher .... .05
79 Cris Carpenter .... .05
81 Steve Avery .... .35
83 Brian Harper .... .05
85 Mickey Tettleton .... .05
88 Bob Walk .... .05
89 • Jeff Reardon................. .07
91 Danny Jackson................. .05
95 Rick Aguilera .... .05
97 David Cone .... .07
98 John Olerud .... .35
100 Jay Bell........................... .05
101 Bob Milacki...................... .05
104 Terry Steinbach .... .05
105 Juan Samuel .... .05

289 Ivan Rodguez

106 Steve Howe .... .05
108 Joey Cora .... .05
110 Gregg Olson .... .07
111 Frank Tanana .... .05
112 Lee Smith......................... .07
115 Chili Davis .... .05
116 Kent Mercker .... .05
119 Andre Dawson................... .15
120 Carlos Baerga .... .10
123 Bruce Hurst .... .05
126 Matt Nokes .... .05
127 George Bell .... .07
128 Bret Saberhagen .... .07
129 Jeff Russell .... .05
130 Jim Abbott .... .12
132 Todd Zeile........................ .08
133 • Dave Winfield .... .10
135 Matt Williams .... .10
137 Marquis Grissom .... .10
138 Erik Hanson .... .05
139 Rob Dibble .... .05
140 Don August .... .05
143 George Brett...................... .15
144 Jerald Clark .... .05
145 Robin Ventura .... .15
146 • Dale Murphy.................. .05
147 Dennis Eckersley .... .07
149 Mario Diaz .... .05

16 Eric Karros

150	Casey Candaele	.05
153	Kevin Maas	.15
154	Nolan Ryan (Highlights)	.30
156	Chris Hoiles	.12
158	Pedro Guerrero	.05
163	*Brian Hunter*	.15
164	Alan Trammell	.05
165	Ken Griffey, Jr.	.60
167	Brian Downing	.05
169	Jack Clark	.05
171	Tim Teufel	.05
173	• Robin Yount	.15
176	Mike Boddicker	.05
177	Dean Palmer	.15
179	Randy Ready	.05
180	Devon White	.05
182	Mike Felder	.05
185	Barry Larkin	.15
186	John Franco	.05
187	*Ed Sprague*	.15
189	Jose Lind	.05
190	Bob Welch	.05
191	Alex Fernandez	.20
192	Gary Sheffield	.20
193	Rickey Henderson	.15
195	*Scott Kamieniecki*	.15
199	Leo Gomez	.10
200	Mike Morgan	.05
202	Sid Bream	.05
203	Sandy Alomar	.10
204	Greg Gagne	.05
206	Cecil Fielder	.25
210	Wade Boggs	.15
211	Bryan Harvey	.05
213	*Alonzo Powell* (FC)	.10
214	Will Clark	.20
215	Rickey Henderson (Highlights)	.15
216	Jack Morris	.10
217	Junior Felix	.05
218	Vince Coleman	.05
220	Alex Cole	.05
222	Randy Milligan	.05
223	Jose Rijo	.07
225	Dave Stewart	.05
226	Lenny Harris	.05
228	Jeff Blauser	.05
229	Ozzie Guillen	.05
230	John Kruk	.07
232	Milt Cuyler	.08
233	Felix Jose	.08
234	Ellis Burks	.05
235	Pete Harnisch	.05
236	Kevin Tapani	.05
237	Terry Pendleton	.10
239	Harold Reynolds	.05
242	Felix Fermin	.05
243	Barry Bonds	.15
244	Roger Clemens	.25
245	Dennis Rasmussen	.05
247	Orel Hershiser	.05
248	Mel Hall	.05
249	*Rick Wilkins*	.20
250	Tom Gordon	.05
254	Tom Pagnozzi	.05
255	Chuck Finley	.05
258	Hal Morris	.15
260	Billy Swift	.05
261	Joe Oliver	.05
263	Todd Stottlemyre	.05
264	Matt Merullo	.05
267	Lance Johnson	.05
270	Luis Gonzalez	.15
271	Jose Guzman	.05
273	Mark Lewis	.15
275	*Jeff Johnson*	.10
277	Delino DeShields	.10

281	Mark Grace	.12
283	Fred McGriff	.12
284	Ron Gant	.15
285	Lou Whitaker	.07
286	Edgar Martinez	.08
289	*Ivan Rodriguez*	.40
291	*Chris Haney*	.20
292	Darrin Jackson	.05
294	Ted Higuera	.05
295	Jeff Brantley	.05
297	Jim Eisenreich	.05
298	Ruben Sierra	.15
300	Jose DeJesus	.05
301	*Mike Timlin*	.10
302	Luis Sojo	.05
303	Kelly Downs	.05
304	Scott Bankhead	.05
305	Pedro Munoz	.20
306	Scott Scudder	.05
307	Kevin Elster	.05
308	Duane Ward	.05
309	*Darryl Kile*	.25
310	Orlando Merced	.10
311	Dave Henderson	.07
312	Tim Raines	.07
314	Mike Gallego	.05
315	Charles Nagy	.12
316	Jesse Barfield	.05
318	Al Osuna	.05
319	Darrin Fletcher	.05
321	David Segui	.08
324	Jeff Treadway	.05
325	Mark Whiten	.08
326	Kent Hrbek	.05
327	Dave Justice	.20
330	Kevin Morton	.05
331	John Smiley	.05
333	Wally Joyner	.10
334	*Heathcliff Slocumb*	.12
336	*Mike Remlinger* (FC)	.10
337	Mike Moore	.05
339	Al Newman	.05
340	Kirk McKaskill	.05
341	Howard Johnson	.10
342	Greg Myers	.05
343	Kal Daniels	.05
344	Bernie Williams	.15
345	Shane Mack	.05
346	Gary Thurman	.05

5 Kenny Lofton

347	Dante Bichette	.05
348	Mark McGwire	.15
349	Travis Fryman	.20
350	Ray Lankford	.15
352	Jack McDowell	.07
353	Mitch Williams	.05
354	Mike Devereaux	.05
355	Andres Galarraga	.05
356	Henry Cotto	.05
358	*Jeff Bagwell*	.40
359	Scott Leius	.05
360	Zane Smith	.05
362	Tony Fernandez	.05
369	Brett Butler	.07
370	Pat Kelly	.12
372	Gregg Jefferies	.10
376	Bernard Gilkey	.07
383	Andy Van Slyke	.07
384	Wes Chamberlain	.12
387	Brian McRae	.10
389	Steve Decker	.10
390	Chuck Knoblauch	.12
392	● Eddie Murray	.08
393	Juan Gonzalez	.60
397	Royce Clayton (RR)	.20
398	*John Jaha* (RR) (FC)	.35
399	Dan Wilson (RR)	.10
400	*Archie Corbin* (RR) (FC)	.15

165 Ken Griffey, Jr.

401	*Barry Manuel* (RR) (FC) ..	**.12**
402	Kim Batiste (RR)	**.10**
403	*Pat Mahomes* (RR) (FC) .	**.20**
404	Dave Fleming (RR)	**.25**
405	Jeff Juden (RR)	**.10**
406	*Jim Thome* (RR) (FC)	**.25**
407	Sam Militello (RR)	**.15**
408	*Jeff Nelson* (RR) (FC)	**.12**
409	Anthony Young (RR)	**.15**
410	Tino Martinez (RR)	**.12**
411	*Jeff Mutis* (RR) (FC)	**.12**
412	*Rey Sanchez* (RR) (FC)	**.12**
413	*Chris Gardner* (RR) (FC) .	**.08**
414	*John VanderWal* (RR) (FC)	**.12**
415	Reggie Sanders (RR)	**.25**
416	*Brian Williams* (RR) (FC) .	**.12**
417	Mo Sanford (RR)	**.10**
418	*David Weathers* (RR) (FC)	**.12**
419	*Hector Fajardo* (RR) (FC)	**.12**
420	*Steve Foster* (RR) (FC)	**.12**
421	Lance Dickson (RR)	**.10**
432	• Ozzie Smith	**.08**
436	Ben McDonald	**.08**
441	Tony Gwynn	**.10**
442	John Smoltz	**.10**
449	Bret Barberie	**.07**

461	*Rod Beck* (FC)	**.10**
463	Scott Erickson	**.10**
470	Bo Jackson	**.10**
488	Phil Plantier	**.20**
492	Frank Castillo	**.08**
500	Albert Belle	**.10**
504	Darren Holmes	**.07**
505	Mike Bordick	**.07**
508	Keith Mitchell	**.07**
514	Mo Vaughn	**.15**
520	Greg Maddux	**.08**
523	Mike Greenwell	**.07**
524	Andy Benes	**.07**
530	*Jose Hernandez* (FC)	**.15**
534	Juan Guzman	**.25**
543	• Carlton Fisk	**.10**
545	Ricky Bones	**.10**
548	Jose Canseco	**.15**
549	Andujar Cedeno	**.10**
555	Gossage/Ryan (Highlights)	**.10**
558	*Chito Martinez* (FC)	**.08**
559	Darryl Strawberry	**.12**
564	Deion Sanders	**.10**
568	Todd Hundley	**.10**
572	Jose Melendez	**.07**
576	Ryne Sandberg	**.20**
581	Derek Bell	**.15**
583	Kevin Mitchell	**.07**
589	*Jose Tolentino*	**.08**
591	*Scott Brosius* (FC)	**.10**
592	Frank Thomas	**1.00**
596	Don Mattingly	**.12**
598	Andy Mota	**.07**
602	Stan Royer	**.07**
605	Denny Neagle	**.07**
610	Bobby Bonilla	**.10**
615	Darren Lewis	**.08**
617	Kirby Puckett	**.15**
626	Joe Slusarski	**.07**
629	Tom Glavine	**.15**
632	Mike Mussina	**.50**
633	Mark Leiter	**.07**
640	Doug Piatt	**.07**
647	*Jim Campanis* (FC)	**.10**
651	Sean Berry	**.07**
656	Ramon Martinez	**.07**
658	Ramon Garcia	**.07**
659	*Milt Hill* (FC)	**.10**

662	Ced Landrum	.07
663	*Doug Henry*	.15
667	*Craig Shipley*	.08
668	Warren Newson	.05
669	Mickey Morandini	.07
671	Ryan Bowen	.10
672	Bill Krueger	.05
675	Scott Livingstone	.10
677	Joe Carter (Highlights)	.10
681	*Ted Wood* (FC)	.08
683	Eric Bullock	.05
685	Dave Hollins	.05
686	Dennis Martinez	.07
688	Doug Simons	.05
689	Tim Spehr	.08
690	Calvin Jones (FC)	.08
693	Joe Carter	.12
695	Pascual Perez	.05
697	Gerald Williams	.08
698	*Chris Cron* (FC)	.10
700	Paul McClellan	.07
703	*Rob Maurer* (FC)	.10
704	Pat Hentgen	.10
707	Nolan Ryan	.30
712	*Rheal Cormier* (FC)	.15
717	Jeff Fassero	.07
718	Cal Eldred	.15
720	*Bob Zupcic* (FC)	.25

534 Juan Guzman

722	*Cliff Brantley* (FC)	.10
726	Mlke Hartley	.05
727	Arthur Rhodes	.10
729	Steve Sax	.05
731	John Wehner	.10
733	Ruben Amaro	.10
737	Gil Heredia	.12
745	*Darrin Chapin* (FC)	.10
749	Skeeter Barnes	.05
750	Roger McDowell	.05
751	Dann Howitt	.05
752	Paul Sorrento	.07
753	*Braulio Castillo* (FC)	.15
756	*Jeremy Hernandez* (FC)	.10
757	Curt Schilling	.05
760	Willie Banks	.07
763	Scott Servais	.07
764	Ray Stephens	.07
766	*Jim Olander*	.07
768	Lance Blankenship	.05
769	Mike Humphreys	.07
770	*Jarvis Brown* (FC)	.08
774	*Gary Cooper* (FC)	.10
775	Carney Lansford	.07
781	Reggie Harris	.05
782	Xavier Hernandez	.07
783	*Bryan Hickerson*	.15

488 Phil Plantier

1992 DONRUSS ROOKIES

After six years of factory-collated, 56-card sets, Donruss sharply reduced production of "The Rookies," increased the number of cards to 132, and sold them the old-fashioned way, one foil pack at a time. These cards also qualify for official rookie card status; thus most names are shown below in italics. A subset consisting of 20 foil-stamped cards called Phenoms was also offered, the first 12 of which were included only in random foil packs, with the remainder available in assorted jumbo packs. Prices range from $2 to $15 for individual members of this subset, which is not considered part of the regular set. Based on the limited popularity of past Donruss extension sets, few investors would hazard a prediction as to the financial future of these revamped Rookies, but prices could skyrocket.

	MINT
Complete set	**$12.00**
Commons	**.05**

42 Brent Gates

3	*Rich Amaral* (FC)	$ .15
4	*Ruben Amaro* (FC)	.15
5	*Billy Ashley* (FC)	.60
6	*Pedro Astacio* (FC)	.25
7	*Jim Austin* (FC)	.07
11	*Brian Bohanon* (FC)	.10
13	*Jeff Branson* (FC)	.10
15	*John Briscoe* (FC)	.07
16	*Doug Brocail* (FC)	.07
17	*Rico Brogna* (FC)	.10
18	*J.T. Bruett* (FC)	.15
19	*Jacob Brumfield* (FC)	.10
20	*Jim Bullinger* (FC)	.10
21	Kevin Campbell	.10
22	*Pedro Castellano* (FC)	.10
25	*Mark Clark* (FC)	.10
26	*Craig Colbert* (FC)	.15
27	*Victor Cole* (FC)	.10
29	Tim Costo	.10
30	*Chad Curtis* (FC)	.50
33	*John Doherty* (FC)	.20
34	*Mike Draper* (FC)	.10
35	*Monty Fariss* (FC)	.10
37	*John Flaherty* (FC)	.10
39	*Eric Fox* (FC)	.12
40	*Jeff Frye* (FC)	.10
41	*Ramon Garcia* (FC)	.10
42	• *Brent Gates* (FC)	.45
43	*Tom Goodwin*	.10
44	*Buddy Groom* (FC)	.10
45	*Jeff Grotewold* (FC)	.10
47	*Johnny Guzman* (FC)	.10
48	*Shawn Hare* (FC)	.10
49	*Ryan Hawblitzel* (FC)	.10
50	*Bert Heffernan* (FC)	.10
51	*Butch Henry* (FC)	.10

52	*Cesar Hernandez* (FC)	.10
53	*Vince Horsman* (FC)	.10
54	*Steve Hosey*	.10
55	*Pat Howell* (FC)	.15
59	*Shawn Jeter* (FC)	.10
60	*Joel Johnston* (FC)	.10
61	*Jeff Kent* (FC)	.15
64	*Danny Leon* (FC)	.10
68	*Al Martin* (FC)	.50
69	*Pedro Martinez* (FC)	.25
70	*Derrick May* (FC)	.30
71	*Matt Maysey* (FC)	.10
75	*Jeff McNeely* (FC)	.10
80	*Joe Millette* (FC)	.15
81	*Blas Minor* (FC)	.10
82	*Dennis Moeller* (FC)	.10
83	*Raul Mondesi* (FC)	.10
84	*Rob Natal* (FC)	.10
85	*Troy Neel* (FC)	.15
86	*David Nied* (FC)	.10
87	*Jerry Nielsen* (FC)	.10
88	*Donovan Osborne* (FC)	.15
89	*John Patterson* (FC)	.10
90	*Roger Pavlik* (FC)	.20
91	*Dan Peltier* (FC)	.10
92	*Jim Pena* (FC)	.10
94	*Mike Perez* (FC)	.12
97	*Harvey Pulliam* (FC)	.07
101	*Darren Reed* (FC)	.12
102	*Shane Reynolds* (FC)	.10
107	*Johnny Ruffin* (FC)	.10
111	*Dave Silvestri* (FC)	.07
112	*Matt Stairs* (FC)	.10
113	*William Suero* (FC)	.10
114	*Jeff Tackett* (FC)	.10
117	*Scooter Tucker* (FC)	.12
118	*Shane Turner* (FC)	.10
120	*Paul Wagner* (FC)	.15
121	• *Tim Wakefield* (FC)	.35
125	*Bob Wickman* (FC)	.50
128	*Eric Young* (FC)	.10
129	*Kevin Young* (FC)	.10

1992 FLEER

Matching the Donruss make-over, Fleer updated its own traditional look with some snappy improvements highlighted by color photos on card backs and the use of thicker, glossier cardboard. The factory-collated 732-card sets includes three of the 12 commemorative cards featuring Roger Clemens, along with a special nine-card subset dubbed The Lumber Co. The Clemens cards earned $1 to $2 apiece, while the Lumber Co. subset brought $10 to $15. A few dealers stripped sets of these "special" cards for a quick profit, which devalued "regular" complete sets. Fleer also distributed a 24-card insert set in wax packs, with 20 Team Leader inserts in rack packs. The 20 Rookie Sensations insert cards (available in cello packs) sold for $150 to $200 during the 1992 season. Several abbreviations are used to identify subsets: "P" for Prospects, "RS" for Record Setters, "LL" for League Leaders, and "PV" for Pro Visions.

		MINT
Complete set		**$20.00**
Commons		**.04**
1	Brady Anderson	$ .05
2	Jose Bautista	.04
3	Juan Bell	.04
5	Mike Devereaux	.04
6	• Dwight Evans	.06
8	Leo Gomez	.08
9	Chris Hoiles	.10
13	*Chito Martinez* (FC)	.10
14	Ben McDonald	.08

269 Todd Van Poppel

655 Kenny Lofton

425 Jeff Bagwell

709 Ken Griffey, Jr.

1992 FLEER UPDATE

Fleer limited production of its 132-card Update set. Continuing the marketing pattern begun in 1984, the set was initially available only in boxed, complete-set form through hobby dealers. To simplify sorting, the set is arranged by team and then alphabetically by player within each team. World Champions Jack Morris and Dave Winfield are shown as Toronto Blue Jays for the first time in a Fleer edition. And the traditional Update mix was enhanced by including a number rookies such as Damion Easley, Albert Martin, Mike Piazza, Ryan Thompson, and Bob Wickman.

		MINT
Complete set		**$140.00**
Commons		**.30**

4	John Valentin (FC)	$1.10
6	Bob Zupcic (FC)	1.00
7	Mike Butcher (FC)	.40
8	Chad Curtis (FC)	7.00
9	Damion Easley (FC)	5.00
10	Tim Salmon (FC).........	25.00
13	Roberto Hernandez (FC)	1.00
14	Shawn Jeter (FC)	.40
17	Kenny Lofton	7.00
18	Paul Sorrento	.35
19	Rico Brogna	.40
20	John Doherty (FC).........	2.00
22	Buddy Groom (FC)	.40
23	Shawn Hare (FC)	.40
24	John Kiely (FC)	.40
25	Kurt Knudsen (FC)	.40
26	Gregg Jefferies.............	.80
27	Wally Joyner...................	.40
32	Hipolito Pichardo (FC) ...	1.00
33	James Austin (FC)	.40
35	John Jaha (FC)	1.50
36	Pat Listach (FC)	3.00
37	Dave Nilsson (FC)	.60
40	Pat Mahomes (FC)..........	1.00
43	Sam Militello (FC)..........	1.75
44	Andy Stankiewicz (FC)	.40
45	Danny Tartabull..............	.50
46	Bob Wickman (FC).........	5.00

117 Tim Wakefield

49	Vince Horsman (FC)........	.40
50	Troy Neel (FC)...............	2.00
51	Ruben Sierra	1.10
54	• Bret Boone (FC)	2.25
55	Dave Fleming (FC)	3.50
57	Jeff Nelson (FC)	.60
59	Jose Canseco	2.50
60	Jeff Frye (FC)	.40
61	Danilo Leon (FC).............	.40
62	Roger Pavlik (FC)	1.25
63	David Cone	.50
64	Pat Hentgen (FC)	5.00
65	Randy Knorr (FC)............	.40

66	• Jack Morris	.50	
67	• Dave Winfield	2.00	
68	David Nied (FC)	10.00	
72	Alex Arias (FC)	1.00	
73	Jim Bullinger (FC)	.40	
75	Rey Sanchez (FC)	1.25	
77	Sammy Sosa	1.00	
80	Steve Foster (FC)	.40	
81	Wilie Greene (FC)	1.50	
85	Juan Guerrero (FC)	.40	
88	Brian Williams (FC)	.50	
92	Mike Piazza (FC)	60.00	
94	Eric Young (FC)	2.50	
95	Moises Alou	1.50	
96	Greg Colbrunn (FC)	1.00	
97	Wil Cordero (FC)	3.00	
99	John Vander Wal (FC)	.70	
101	Bobby Bonilla	1.00	
102	Eric Hillman (FC)	.70	
103	Pat Howell (FC)	.40	
104	Jeff Kent (FC)	1.10	
106	Ryan Thompson (FC)	1.00	
110	Jeff Grotewold (FC)	.40	
113	Victor Cole (FC)	.40	
114	Albert Martin (FC)	6.00	
116	Blas Minor (FC)	.40	
117	• Tim Wakefield (FC)	2.00	
118	Mark Clark (FC)	.40	
119	Rheal Cormier (FC)	.70	
120	Donovan Osborne (FC)	2.00	
122	Jeremy Hernandez (FC)	.50	
124	Frank Seminara (FC)	.50	
125	Gary Sheffield	3.00	
126	Dan Walters (FC)	.40	
127	Steve Hosey	1.00	
129	Jim Pena (FC)	.40	

1992 SCORE

Score's fifth anniversary was celebrated with one of the hobby's most diverse designs. The company maintained its tradition of including all-action shots (excluding draft picks), but the cards offer one of the smallest photo spaces of any company product. Happily, Score continued to be among the industry leaders in creating quirky subsets, including the artistic Dream Team, with black-and-white posed cards, and All-Star cards, with cartoon caricatures. Despite the innovative look, however, set prices seemed slow to rise. Because of the abundant supply of unsold 1991 factory-collated sets in non-hobby retail outlets, along with individual retail prices under 60 cents a pack, the availability of sets delighted budget-conscious collectors but worried investors. Rookie Prospects are identified on the following list with the abbreviation "RP."

		MINT
Complete set		**$20.00**
Commons		**.04**

1	Ken Griffey, Jr.	$ .50
2	Nolan Ryan	.50
3	Will Clark	.20
4	Dave Justice	.20
5	Dave Henderson	.06
6	Bret Saberhagen	.06
7	Fred McGriff	.10
8	Erik Hanson	.05
9	Darryl Strawberry	.15
10	Doc Gooden	.10
11	Juan Gonzalez	.60
12	Mark Langston	.06
13	Lonnie Smith	.04
14	Jeff Montgomery	.05
15	Roberto Alomar	.20
16	Delino DeShields	.08
17	Steve Bedrosian	.04

424 Juan Guzman

18	Terry Pendleton	.10
19	Mark Carreon	.04
20	Mark McGwire	.12
21	Roger Clemens	.15
23	Don Mattingly	.20
24	Dickie Thon	.04
25	Ron Gant	.20
26	Milt Cuyler	.08
28	Dan Gladden	.04
29	Melido Perez	.04
30	Willie Randolph	.04
31	Albert Belle	.20
32	• Dave Winfield	.10
34	Kevin Gross	.04
35	Andres Galarraga	.04
36	Mike Devereaux	.04
37	Chris Bosio	.04
38	Mike LaValliere	.04
39	Gary Gaetti	.04
40	Felix Jose	.10
42	Rick Aguilera	.05
43	Mike Gallego	.04
44	Eric Davis	.08
45	George Bell	.08
46	Tom Brunansky	.04
49	David Wells	.04
50	Cecil Fielder	.25
51	Walt Weiss	.04
52	Todd Zeile	.06
53	Doug Jones	.05
54	Bob Walk	.04
55	Rafael Palmeiro	.12
56	Rob Deer	.05
57	Paul O'Neill	.08
58	• Jeff Reardon	.08
60	Scott Erickson	.12
61	Paul Molitor	.08
62	Jack McDowell	.06
63	Jim Acker	.04
64	Jay Buhner	.06
65	Travis Fryman	.35
66	Marquis Grissom	.06
67	Mike Harkey	.08
69	Ken Caminiti	.06
70	Chris Sabo	.12
71	Gregg Olson	.07
72	• Carlton Fisk	.12
73	Juan Samuel	.04
74	Todd Stottlemyre	.04
75	Andre Dawson	.15
76	Alvin Davis	.04
78	B.J. Surhoff	.04
79	Kirk McCaskill	.04
80	• Dale Murphy	.10
81	Jose DeLeon	.04
82	Alex Fernandez	.10
83	Ivan Calderon	.05
84	Brent Mayne	.08
86	Randy Tomlin	.05
87	Randy Milligan	.05
89	Hensley Meulens	.05
90	Joe Carter	.15
92	Ozzie Guillen	.10
94	Chili Davis	.06
95	Vince Coleman	.05
100	Barry Larkin	.12
104	Ken Hill	.06
108	Julio Franco	.06
110	Kal Daniels	.05
111	Bruce Hurst	.05
112	Willie McGee	.07
115	Doug Drabek	.10
122	Robin Ventura	.15
125	Hal Morris	.12
128	Carlos Baerga	.20
133	Andy Benes	.10
137	Harold Baines	.06

140	Chris Nabholz	.08
145	Danny Tartabull	.10
146	Lance Johnson	.06
149	Rich Rodriguez	.08
150	• Dwight Evans	.06
152	Kevin Reimer	.06
153	Orlando Merced	.25
154	Mel Hall	.07
163	Gerald Alexander	.06
168	Kevin McReyonlds	.06
185	Pat Kelly	.10
189	Carlos Quintana	.05
190	Dennis Eckersley	.08
192	Gregg Jefferies	.10
195	• Eddie Murray	.08
196	Bill Landrum	.08
199	• Larry Walker	.10
200	Ryne Sandberg	.20
201	Dave Magadan	.05
210	Luis Gonzalez	.08
212	*Chris Donnels*	.06
214	Mike Timlin	.10
220	Frank Viola	.05
223	Ray Lankford	.15
224	Pete Harnisch	.05
225	Bobby Bonilla	.12
230	Matt Williams	.10
231	Jaime Navarro	.05
232	Jose Rijo	.07
235	John Kruk	.12
240	Leo Gomez	.12
241	Steve Avery	.25
242	Bill Gullickson	.05
245	Benny Santiago	.06
249	*Mike Bell* (FC)	.08
250	Harold Reynolds	.05
255	Lou Whitaker	.07
258	Sammy Sosa	.07
259	Tim Naehring	.08
260	Dave Righetti	.05
267	Norm Charlton	.05
269	Greg Maddux	.07
270	Ellis Burks	.10
278	*Jose Segura* (FC)	.08
285	Bob Scanlan	.15
287	John Smoltz	.15
288	Pat Borders	.05
298	Lance Parrish	.05
300	Bob Welch	.05

442 Ryne Sandberg

302	Charlie Hough	.05
309	Joe Slusarski	.08
310	Kevin Seitzer	.05
315	Eric Anthony	.05
317	Steve Decker	.10
318	Jack Clark	.05
322	Bryan Harvey	.05
324	Roberto Kelly	.10
330	Charles Nagy	.08
332	*Pete Schourek*	.15
334	Omar Olivares	.10
345	John Olerud	.30
361	Bo Jackson	.10
365	Brady Anderson	.08
372	Lee Stevens	.07
376	Pedro Guerrero	.05
384	Wes Chamberlain	.08
392	Dean Palmer	.15
395	*Rusty Meacham* (FC)	.08
396	*Andy Ashby* (FC)	.08
397	*Jose Melendez* (FC)	.08
398	*Warren Newson* (FC)	.08
399	*Frank Castillo* (FC)	.12
400	*Chito Martinez* (FC)	.10
401	Bernie Williams (RP)	.25
402	Derek Bell (RP) (FC)	.25
403	*Javier Ortiz* (RP) (FC)	.08
404	*Tim Sherill* (RP) (FC)	.08

700 Ivan Rodriguez

405	*Rob MacDonald* (RP) (FC)	.08
406	Phil Plantier (RP)	.20
407	Troy Afenir (RP)	.06
408	Gino Mutelli (RP)	.08
409	*Reggie Jefferson* (RP) (FC)	.20
410	Mike Remlinger (RP)	.06
411	*Carlos Rodriguez* (RP) (FC)	.12
412	*Joe Redfield* (RP) (FC)	.15
413	Alonzo Powell (RP)	.06
414	*Scott Livingstone* (RP) (FC)	.25
415	*Scott Kamieniecki* (RP) (FC)	.15
416	*Tim Spehr* (RP) (FC)	.08
417	*Brian Hunter* (RP) (FC)	.15
418	*Ced Landrum* (RP) (FC)	.12
419	*Bret Barberie* (RP) (FC)	.20
420	Kevin Morton (RP) (FC)	.10
421	*Doug Henry* (RP) (FC)	.08
422	*Doug Piatt* (RP) (FC)	.12
423	*Pat Rice* (RP) (FC)	.15
424	*Juan Guzman* (RP) (FC)	.25
425	Nolan Ryan (No-Hit Club)	.30
426	Tommy Greene (No-Hit Club)	.08
430	Rickey Henderson (Highlight)	.15
431	Cecil Fielder AS	.10
432	Julio Franco AS	.05
433	Cal Ripken, Jr. AS	.10
434	Wade Boggs AS	.10
435	Joe Carter AS	.10
436	Ken Griffey, Jr. AS	.35
437	Ruben Sierra AS	.10
438	Scott Erickson AS	.08
439	Tom Henke AS	.08
440	Terry Steinbach AS	.05
441	Rickey Henderson (Dream Team)	.25
442	Ryne Sandberg (Dream Team)	.35
443	Otis Nixon	.05
445	Mark Grace	.08
448	Glenallen Hill	.05
450	Tom Glavine	.15
452	Al Osuna	.05
455	Rob Dibble	.06
460	Craig Biggio	.06
470	Dennis Martinez	.06
475	Steve Sax	.06
478	Brian McRae	.10
480	Rickey Henderson	.12
485	Edgar Martinez	.06
489	• Gary Carter	.06
490	Ruben Sierra	.12
493	Zane Smith	.05
494	Darryl Kile	.08
495	Kelly Gruber	.06
500	Jose Canseco	.20
504	Ed Sprague	.07
505	Frank Thomas	1.00
510	Sandy Alomar, Jr.	.05
514	Pedro Munoz	.12
525	• Robin Yount	.10
528	Mark Lewis	.10
530	Kent Hrbek	.08
535	Wally Joyner	.06
540	Cal Ripken	.25
544	Bernard Gilkey	.08
545	Mike Greenwell	.05
550	Howard Johnson	.08
554	David Segui	.05
555	Barry Bonds	.15
556	Mo Vaughn	.15

562	Darren Lewis	.08
572	Chuck Knoblauch	.15
576	Jeff Bagwell	.30
580	Dave Stewart	.06
587	Mark Whiten	.08
589	Gary Sheffield	.12
590	Ozzie Smith	.10
596	Tino Martinez	.08
599	Andujar Cedeno	.08
600	Kirby Puckett	.20
602	Todd Hundley	.08
605	John Franco	.05
610	Ramon Martinez	.10
613	Kevin Maas	.08
615	Glenn Davis	.05
620	Jim Abbott	.10
625	Tony Gwynn	.15
630	Lee Smith	.08
632	Mike Simms	.05
633	Terry Steinbach	.05
634	Shawon Dunston	.05
635	Tim Raines	.05
640	Kevin Mitchell	.05
645	Tony Fernandez	.08
648	Carney Lansford	.07
650	• George Brett	.10
652	Jack Morris	.08
653	Orel Hershiser	.05
655	Andy Van Slyke	.07
658	Ben McDonald	.08
660	Wade Boggs	.10
680	David Cone	.10
681	Mike Bordick	.05
700	*Ivan Rodriguez*	.35
736	Arthur Lee Rhodes (RP)	.10
737	*Terry Mathews* (RP)	.10
738	Jeff Fassero (RP)	.08
739	*Mike Magnante* (RP)	.08
740	*Kip Gross* (RP)	.10
741	*Jim Hunter* (RP)	.10
742	Jose Mota (RP)	.08
744	*Tim Mauser* (RP)	.10
745	Ramon Garcia (RP)	.08
746	*Rod Beck* (RP)	.25
748	Keith Mitchell (RP)	.10
749	*Wayne Rosenthal* (RP)	.10
750	*Bryan Hickerson* (RP)	.10
751	Bruce Egloff (RP)	.08
752	John Wehner (RP)	.10

809 Aaron Sele

755	Mike Mussina (RP)	.60
756	Anthony Young (RP)	.12
758	Ricky Bones (RP)	.12
759	*Mark Wohlers* (RP) (FC)	.15
762	Ryan Bowen (RP)	.10
765	*Terry McDaniel* (RP)	.10
766	*Esteban Beltre* (RP)	.10
767	*Rob Maurer* (RP) (FC)	.15
768	*Ted Wood* (RP)	.10
771	*Gil Heredia* (RP)	.10
772	Monty Farriss (RP)	.10
773	Will Clark AS	.10
774	Ryne Sandberg AS	.10
775	Barry Larkin AS	.10
776	Howard Johnson AS	.10
777	Barry Bonds AS	.15
778	Brett Butler AS	.08
779	Tony Gwynn AS	.10
780	Ramon Martinez AS	.08
781	Lee Smith AS	.10
792	Chuck Knoblauch (Rookie of Year)	.10
793	Jeff Bagwell (Rookie of Year)	.15
794	Cal Ripken (Man of Year)	.10
795	David Cone (Highlight)	.10
799	*Allen Watson* (1st Round Pick) (FC)	.20

800 Manny Ramirez

800	*Manny Ramirez* (1st Round Pick) (FC)	**1.00**
801	*Cliff Floyd* (1st Round Pick)	**2.00**
802	*Al Shirley* (1st Round Pick)	.25
805	*Brent Gates* (1st Round Pick)	.45
808	*Benji Gil* (1st Round Pick)	.25
809	*Aaron Sele* (1st Round Pick)	**1.25**
810	*Tyler Green* (1st Round Pick) (FC)	.20
814	*Don Wakamatsu* (RP)	.08
815	Mike Humphreys (RP)	.08
818	John Ramos (RP)	.08
820	*Milt Hill* (RP)	.10
821	Carlos Garcia (RP)	.10
822	Stan Royer (RP)	.08
823	*Jeff Plympton* (RP)	.10
825	David Haas (RP)	.08
827	Eric Karros (RP)	.25
828	*Shawn Hare* (RP)	.08
829	Reggie Sanders (RP)	.20
830	Tom Goodwin (RP)	.10
831	Dan Gakeler (RP)	.08
834	Cal Eldred (RP)	.25
835	Chris George (RP)	.08
839	*Jim Olander* (RP)	.08
840	*Gary Cooper* (RP)	.10
841	Royce Clayton (RP)	.15
842	*Hector Fajardo* (RP)	.10
845	Kenny Lofton (RP)	.30
846	*Scott Brosius* (RP)	.10
850	*Bob Zupcic* (RP)	.15
851	Rheal Cormier (RP)	.08
855	*Kevin Campbell* (RP)	.08
856	*Craig Shipley* (RP)	.08
859	Jim Thome (RP)	.20
862	*Kevin Ward* (RP)	.08
863	Steve Wapnick (RP)	.06
865	Todd Van Poppel (RP)	.25
871	*Eddie Taubensee* (RP)	.15
877	*Armando Reynoso* (RP) (FC)	.08
878	Ty Cobb (Memorabilia)	.35
879	Babe Ruth (Memorabilia)	.50
880	Honus Wagner (Memorabilia)	.15
881	Lou Gehrig (Memorabilia)	.35
882	Satchel Paige (Memorabilia)	.20
883	Will Clark (Dream Team)	.15
884	Cal Ripken (Dream Team)	.35
885	Wade Boggs (Dream Team)	.15
886	Tony Gwynn (Dream Team)	.15
887	Kirby Puckett (Dream Team)	.20
888	Craig Biggio (Dream Team)	.10
889	Scott Erickson (Dream Team)	.12
890	Tom Glavine (Dream Team)	.15
891	Rob Dibble (Dream Team)	.12
892	Mitch Williams (Dream Team)	.08
893	Frank Thomas (Dream Team)	.75

1992 SCORE ROOKIE & TRADED

Score limited production of its 1992 extension set. Keeping with the company tradition, the cards reflect the same design seen in the regular 1992 edition. As for content, the set's title is strongly reflected in the selection of players, with a nearly even distribution of traded players—those late acquisitions not represented in the pre-season Score set—and rookies. Score was guilty of being the only company not to produce a 1992 card of Cleveland Indians sensation Kenny Lofton, but that error was corrected in this 110-card issue. Noted rookies such as Chad Curtis, Dave Fleming, and Pat Listach are also included. As in past years, dealers enjoyed breaking up the boxed, factory-collated complete sets (distributed only through dealers) in order to sell off the rookies for top dollar, then dumping commons of veteran players.

	MINT
Complete set	**$60.00**
Commons	**.25**

1 Gary Sheffield

1	Gary Sheffield	$ 2.50
2	Kevin Seitzer	.25
3	Danny Tartabull	.10
4	Steve Sax	.40
5	Bobby Bonilla	.60
6	Frank Viola	.40
7	• Dave Winfield	1.50
8	Rick Sutcliffe	.40
9	Jose Canseco	1.75
10	Greg Swindell	.40
11	Eddie Murray	.70
13	Wally Joyner	.40
14	Kenny Lofton (FC)	5.00
15	• Jack Morris	.40
17	Pete Incaviglia	.40
18	Kevin Mitchell	.50
19	Kurt Stillwell	.25
20	Bret Saberhagen	.30
21	Steve Buechele	.25
23	Sammy Sosa	.90
24	George Bell	.40
26	Dick Schofield	.25
27	David Cone	.40
28	Dan Gladden	.25
29	Kirk McKaskill	.25
32	Bill Swift	.25
33	Dave Martinez	.25
35	Willie Randolph	.30

92 Tim Wakefield

82	Sam Militello (FC)	1.25
83	Brian Jordan (FC)	1.75
84	Jeff Kent (FC)	.80
85	Dave Fleming (FC)	2.50
86	Jeff Tackett (FC)	.25
87	Chad Curtis (FC)	5.00
88	Eric Fox (FC)	.30
89	Denny Neagle (FC)	.25
90	Donovan Osborne (FC)	2.00
91	Carlos Hernandez (FC)	.25
92	• Tim Wakefield (FC)	2.00
93	Tim Salmon (FC)	18.00
94	Dave Nilsson (FC)	.50
95	Mike Perez (FC)	.30
96	Pat Hentgen (FC)	4.00
97	Frank Seminara (FC)	.30
98	Ruben Amaro Jr.	.25
99	Archi Cianfrocco (FC)	.40
100	Andy Stankiewicz (FC)	.30
101	Jim Bullinger (FC)	.30
102	Pat Mahomes (FC)	.70
103	Hipolito Pichardo (FC)	.70
104	• Bret Boone (FC)	1.50
105	John Vander Wal (FC)	.40
106	Vince Horsman (FC)	.30
108	Brian Williams (FC)	.70
109	Dan Walters (FC)	.30
110	Wil Cordero (FC)	2.00

36	Melido Perez	.30
38	Doug Jones	.30
39	Gregg Jefferies	.60
41	Dickie Thon	.25
46	• Jeff Reardon	.40
48	Cory Snyder	.25
51	Dave Burba	.25
52	Bill Pecota	.25
53	Chuck Crim	.25
54	Mariano Duncan	.30
59	• Gary Carter	.50
60	Andres Galarraga	.70
61	Ken Hill	1.00
62	Eric Davis	.40
63	Ruben Sierra	1.00
68	Tom Candiotti	.25
69	Hubie Brooks	.25
70	Kal Daniels	.25
71	Bruce Ruffin	.25
72	Billy Hatcher	.25
73	Bob Melvin	.25
74	Lee Guetterman	.25
75	Rene Gonzales	.25
76	Kevin Bass	.25
78	John Wetteland	.30
79	Bip Roberts	.30
80	Pat Listach (FC)	2.50
81	John Doherty (FC)	1.50

5 Bobby Bonilla

1992 TOPPS

Once again, Topps remained a dependable supplier to the hobby market in 1992. Individual packs (now without gum and wax wrappers) as well as factory-collated complete sets were easy to find. In fact, this unlimited access—at less than 60 cents per pack initially—confounded investors but delighted collectors. Among the improvements for 1992 is the bright white card stock, which makes it much easier to read the stats on the card backs. Also on the backs of many cards are color photos of the player's home stadium. Promising rookies are shown four to a card, grouped by position rather than by team. Rookie cards of Ryan Klesko and Brien Taylor are two of the most desirable choices in the 792-card edition. The Topps custom of printing cards for team managers and league All Stars from the previous season continued in 1992.

		MINT
Complete set		**$20.00**
Commons		**.03**

78 Ivan Rodriguez

1	Nolan Ryan	$ .50
2	Record Breaker (Rickey Henderson)	.08
3	Record Breaker (Jeff Reardon)	.08
4	Record Breaker (Nolan Ryan)	.30
5	Record Breaker (Dave Winfield)	.10
6	*Brien Taylor* (Draft Pick) (FC)	2.00
7	*Jim Olander* (FC)	.08
8	*Bryan Hickerson* (FC)	.15
9	*Jon Farrell* (FC)	.08
10	Wade Boggs	.15
11	Jack McDowell	.05
12	Luis Gonzalez	.12
13	Mike Scioscia	.03
14	Wes Chamberlain	.12
15	Denny Martinez	.05
16	Jeff Montgomery	.05
18	Greg Cadaret	.03
22	Bill Wegman	.03
23	Chuck Knoblauch	.15
24	Randy Myers	.04
25	Ron Gant	.10
26	Mike Bielecki	.03
27	Juan Gonzalez	.15
29	Mickey Tettleton	.03
30	John Kruk	.08
32	Chris Nabholz	.03
33	Carlos Baerga	.05
34	Jeff Juden	.12
35	Dave Righetti	.04
36	*Scott Ruffcorn* (Draft Pick) (FC)	.10
38	Tom Candiotti	.03
40	Cal Ripken	.20
41	Craig Lefferts	.03
44	Rick Aguilera	.03

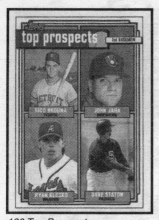

126 Top Prospects

6 *Brien Taylor*

676 Top Prospects, Pitchers

618 Top Prospects, Outfielders

520 Jeff Bagwell

156 Manny Ramirez

703 *Mark Wohlers* (FC) .... .15	**750** Travis Fryman .... .15
705 • Dwight Evans .... .06	**755** Alex Fernandez .... .10
707 Gregg Jefferies................ .12	**759** Jeff Torborg..................... .05
710 Kevin Maas .... .10	**760** Ozzie Smith..................... .10
711 Ricky Bones .... .10	**764** *Tyler Green*
714 *Calvin Reese*	(Draft Pick) (FC) .... .20
(Draft Pick) (FC) .... .20	**768** *Jim Thome* (FC) .... .20
716 *Kirk Dressendorfer* .... .12	**771** *Arthur Rhodes* (FC)......... .15
724 Kevin Morton .... .07	**773** Hal Morris...................... .10
725 Doc Gooden .... .15	**776** *Doug Henry* (FC)............. .15
730 Ramon Martinez .... .10	**777** John Olerud.................... .10
734 *Scott Hatteberg*	**780** • Eddie Murray................ .10
(Draft Pick) (FC) .... .15	**782** Phil Plantier .... .10
738 Dennis Eckersley .... .08	**785** Albert Belle.................... .15
743 Darren Lewis .... .10	**786** Royce Clayton (FC)......... .12
746 Bernard Gilkey .... .08	**790** Joe Carter .... .10
747 Willie Banks (FC)............. .12	**792** • Dave Winfield............... .15

1992 TOPPS TRADED

Duplicating a successful concept from the past, the 1992 Topps Traded set features more than a dozen members of the U.S. Olympic Baseball Team (indicated below with "USA"). But don't be surprised these cards look familiar: Earlier in 1992, Topps produced a 33-card set of Team USA stars that was distributed at Dairy Queen stores. And despite the numerous managerial turnovers, Felipe Alou of the Expos, Boston's Butch Hobson, Gene Lamont of the White Sox, and Jim Lefebvre of the Cubs were the only non-players in the set (other than Olympic coach Ron Fraser). Continuing the format developed in 1981, complete boxed sets were available only from hobby dealers. Unfortunately, Topps clung to the outdated practice of issuing a checklist card, losing the chance to add one more player to this small set. Still, with the exciting mix of rookies and Olympic stars, the 1992 Topps Traded has outstanding investment potential.

	MINT
Complete set	**$20.00**
Commons	**.06**

1 Willie Adams (USA) (FC) .... $ .25	**2** Jeff Alkire (USA) (FC)...... .70
	4 Moises Alou..................... .20
	5 Ruben Amaro .... .10
	9 George Bell .... .10
	10 Freddie Benavides (FC) .. .10
	13 Ricky Bones .... .10
	14 Bobby Bonilla .... .15

1992 Topps Traded

82 Phil Nevin

17	Jim Bullinger (FC)	.10
19	Kevin Campbell (FC)	.10
22	• Gary Carter	.15
23	Archi Cianfrocco (FC)	.15
25	Chad Curtis (FC)	1.10
26	Eric Davis	.15
27	Tim Davis (USA) (FC)	.50
29	Darren Dreifort (USA)	1.00
39	Nomar Garciaparra (USA) (FC)	.40
43	Jeff Granger (USA)	.70
44	Rick Greene (USA) (FC)	.30
45	Jeffrey Hammonds (USA)	3.00
48	Rick Helling (USA) (FC)	.60
49	Butch Henry (FC)	.10
51	Ken Hill	.25
53	Vince Horsman (FC)	.10
56	Charles Johnson (USA)	1.00
58	Brian Jordan (FC)	.40
60	Daron Kirkreit (USA)	.50
64	Danny Leon (FC)	.10
65	Pat Listach (FC)	.80
66	Kenny Lofton	1.25
68	Derrick May (FC)	.20
70	Chad McConnell (USA) (FC)	.70

74	Kevin Mitchell	.12
75	Jason Moler (USA) (FC)	.40
78	Calvin Murray (USA) (FC)	1.00
79	• Eddie Murray	.20
82	Phil Nevin (USA)	1.50
85	Donovan Osborne (FC)	.60
89	Hipolito Pichardo (FC)	.20
91	Darren Reed (FC)	.10
93	Chris Roberts (USA)	.70
94	Steve Rodriguez (USA)	.20
98	Rey Sanchez (FC)	.20
100	Curt Schilling	.15
104	Frank Seminara (FC)	.15
105	Gary Sheffield	.50
108	Paul Sorrento	.15
109	Sammy Sosa	.15
119	Michael Tucker (USA) (FC)	1.75
121	Marc Valdes (USA) (FC)	.30
123	Jason Varitek (USA) (FC)	1.50
124	Rick Villone (USA)	.40
126	B.J. Wallace (USA) (FC)	1.00
128	Craig Wilson (USA) (FC)	.20
129	Chris Wimmer (USA)	.25
130	• Dave Winfield	.20

119 Michael Tucker

1992 UPPER DECK

Upper Deck unveiled a number of subsets and an array of specialty cards in this 800-card set. Bloodlines cards saluting ball-playing relatives and Diamond Skills cards picking players with the best individual skills (indicated below with "DS") were among the most innovative subsets of the year. Other subsets are identified as follows: "DD" for Diamond Debuts, "SR" for Star Rookies, "TC" for Team checklist, and "TP" for Top Prospect. Continuing a past practice, unusual triple-exposure photography was used on cards of Ken Griffey, Jr. and Jose Canseco. The California company's high-number addition (701-800) included many mid-season newcomers. The Upper Deck cards are available in individual packs and scooped update sets from Fleer, Topps, and Score. In fact, some collectors saw the Fleer and Donruss design changes merely as attempts to match the quality of Upper Deck. Following a slump in popularity from the easy-to-find and inexpensive 1991 set, Upper Deck collectors are optimistic about the investment potential of the 1992 edition.

		MINT
Complete set (1-700)		
		$22.00
Commons (1-700)		.04
Commons (701-800)		.05
Complete set (1-800)		40.00

2	Royce Clayton (SR)	$ .25
3	Brian Jordan (SR)	.50
4	Dave Fleming (SR) (FC)	.35
5	Jim Thome (SR)	.25
6	Jeff Juden (SR)	.12
7	Roberto Hernandez (SR) (FC)	.20
8	Kyle Abbott (SR)	.08
9	Chris George (SR) (FC)	.15
10	Rob Mauer (SR) (FC)	.20
11	Donald Harris (SR)	.12
12	Ted Wood (SR) (FC)	.12
13	Patrick Lennon (SR)	.15
14	Willie Banks (SR)	.12
15	Roger Salkeld (SR)	.15
16	Wilfredo Cordero (SR)	.25
17	Arthur Rhodes (SR)	.15
18	Pedro Martinez (SR)	.25
19	Andy Ashby (SR)	.15
20	Tom Goodwin (SR)	.15
21	Braulio Castillo (SR) (FC)	.20
22	Todd Van Poppel (SR)	.20
23	Brian Williams (SR) (FC)	.10
24	Ryan Klesko (SR)	.80
25	Kenny Lofton (SR)	.45
26	Derek Bell (SR)	.25
27	Reggie Sanders (SR)	.35
28	Winfield's 400 HR	.08
29	Dave Justice (TC)	.10
32	• Eddie Murray (TC)	.08
33	Fred McGriff (TC)	.10
41	Steve Avery/NLCS	.12
42	Jeremy Hernandez (FC)	.15
43	Doug Henry (FC)	.15
44	Chris Donnels	.10
45	Mo Sanford (FC)	.15
46	Scott Kamieniecki	.15
47	Mark Lemke	.05
49	Francisco Oliveras	.04
50	Ced Landrum	.08
52	Eduardo Perez (TP) (FC)	.80
53	Tom Nevers (TP) (FC)	.15
54	David Zancanaro (TP (FC)	.20
55	Shawn Green (TP) (FC)	.20

24 Ryan Klesko

75 David McCarty

166 Frank Thomas

276 Jeff Bagwell

52 Eduardo Perez

18 Pedro Martinez

1993 DONRUSS

For the third consecutive year Donruss implemented a two-series format with its regular-issue set. The two-series format is designed to allow for transactions and expansion, but it has been moderately received by hobbyists. The 1993 Donruss release, once again, features a series of randomly inserted subsets. Diamond Kings, featuring the artwork of Dick Perez were once again very popular among collectors. The number of Diamond Kings was increased to 31 cards due to expansion. Spirit of the Game cards made their debut in 1993. The 20-card subset was designed to showcase outstanding action photos of the games greatest players. Spirit of the Game cards sold in the $2-$10 range compared to Diamond Kings which sold in the $2-$7 range. The regular cards in the set featured white borders surrounding full-color glossy player photos. At the bottom of the photo, the team logo appears in a diamond with a banner showcasing the player's name. The backs feature a second player photo and statistics.

	MINT
Complete set	**$30.00**
Commons	**.05**

1	Craig Lefferts	$ .05
2	Kent Mercker	.06
3	Phil Plantier	.10
4	*Alex Arias* (FC)	.15
5	Julio Valera	.08
6	Dan Wilson (FC)	.12
7	Frank Thomas	.70
8	Eric Anthony	.08
9	Derek Lilliquist	.05
10	*Rafael Bournigal* (FC)	.15
11	*Manny Alexander* (FC)	.15
12	Bret Barbarie	.08
13	Mickey Tettleton	.08
14	Anthony Young (FC)	.08
15	Tim Spehr (FC)	.08
16	*Bob Ayrault*	.10
17	Bill Wegman	.06
18	Jay Bell	.08
19	Rick Aguilera	.08
20	Todd Zeile	.08
21	Steve Farr	.06
22	Andy Benes	.08
24	Ted Wood	.08
26	Steve Avery	.08
27	Brian Bohanon	.08

7 Frank Thomas

28	Rick Wilkins	.08
29	Devon White	.08
30	*Bobby Ayala* (FC)	.12
31	Leo Gomez	.08
32	Mike Simms	.08
33	Ellis Burks	.08
35	Jim Abbott	.08
36	Tim Wallach	.06
37	Wilson Alvarez	.06

110 J.T. Snow

176 Tim Salmon

1993 Donruss

209 Mike Piazza

393 Phil Hiatt

737 Nigel Wilson

405	Carlos Baerga	.15
406	Carlos Hernandez	.08
407	*Pedro Astacio*	.15
408	Mel Rojas	.08
409	Scott Livingstone	.10
411	Brian McRae	.06
412	Ben Rivera	.07
413	Ricky Bones	.07
414	Andy Van Slyke	.10
415	Chuck Knoblauch	.10
417	Bob Wickman	.20
418	*Doug Brocail* (FC)	.10
419	Scott Brosius	.07
420	Rod Beck	.12
421	Edgar Martinez	.12
422	Ryan Klesko	.25
423	Nolan Ryan	.50
424	Rey Sanchez	.08
425	Roberto Alomar	.20
426	Barry Larkin	.10
427	Mike Mussina	.25
428	Jeff Bagwell	.20
429	Mo Vaughn	.08
430	Eric Karros	.25
432	Wil Cordero (FC)	.10
433	Jack McDowell	.08
434	Howard Johnson	.07
435	Albert Belle	.15
436	John Kruk	.20
437	Skeeter Barnes	.07
440	Tim Laker (FC)	.12
441	Robin Yount	.12
442	Brian Jordan	.10
443	Kevin Tapani	.08
444	Gary Sheffield	.15
446	Will Clark	.20
450	Mike Harkey	.07
451	Julio Franco	.08
452	*Kevin Young*	.20
453	Kelly Gruber	.06
454	Jose Rijo	.08
455	Mike Devereaux	.08
456	Andujar Cedeno	.10
457	*Damion Easley* (FC)	.20
462	Dwight Gooden	.10
463	Warren Newson	.05
464	Jose DeLeon	.05
465	Jose Mesa	.05
466	Danny Cox	.05
467	Dan Gladden	.05
470	Jeff Gardner	.07
473	Dan Peltier	.08
474	Mike Stanton	.08
475	John Smiley	.08
476	Dwight Smith	.08
479	Mark McGwire	.12
480	Pete Incaviglia	.08
482	Eric Davis	.10
483	John Olerud	.25
484	Kent Bottenfield	.08
485	Mark McLemore	.06
486	Dave Magadan	.06
487	John Marzano	.05
488	Ruben Amaro	.05
489	Rob Ducey	.05
490	Stan Belinda	.06
491	Dan Pasqua	.05
492	Joe Magrane	.05
493	Brook Jacoby	.05
494	Gene Harris	.08
496	Bryan Hickerson	.08
503	Pat Kelly	.07
505	Terry Steinbach	.08
506	*Butch Huskey* (FC)	.15
510	Moises Alou	.10
514	Ricky Jordan	.07
519	Carlton Fisk	.10

792 David Nied

423 Nolan Ryan

657 Chris Gwynn .... .05
658 Lonnie Smith .... .05
659 Jim Austin .... .05
660 Checklist............................. .05
661 Tim Hulett .... .05
662 Marvin Freeman .... .05
663 Greg Harris .... .05
664 Heathcliff Slocumb .... .05
665 Mike Butcher .... .08
666 Steve Foster...................... .07
668 Darryl Kile......................... .08
669 Jesse Levis .... .10
671 *Mark Hutton*...................... .20
672 Brian Drahman .... .10
673 Chad Kreuter..................... .08
674 Tony Fernandez .... .07
675 Jose Lind........................... .06
676 Kyle Abbott........................ .06
677 Dan Plesac........................ .05
678 Barry Bonds .... .25
679 Chili Davis .... .07
680 Stan Royer .... .05
681 Scott Kamieniecki............. .05
682 Carlos Martinez .... .05
683 Mike Moore........................ .06
684 Candy Maldonado .... .06
685 Jeff Nelson........................ .07
686 Lou Whitaker..................... .08

687 Jose Guzman .... .06
688 Manuel Lee .... .05
689 Bob MacDonald................ .05
690 Scott Bankhead................ .05
691 Alan Mills........................... .05
692 Brian Williams................... .05
693 Tom Brunansky .... .05
694 Lenny Webster.................. .05
695 Greg Briley .... .05
696 Paul O'Neill .... .08
697 Joey Cora.......................... .06
698 Charlie O'Brien................. .05
699 Junior Ortiz....................... .05
700 Ron Darling .... .05
701 Tony Phillips...................... .08
702 William Pennyfeather .... .10
704 Steve Hosey...................... .06
706 *David Hulse* (FC) .... .20
707 Mike Pagliarulo................. .06
708 Dave Stieb........................ .05
709 Melido Perez .... .05
710 Jimmy Key......................... .08
712 David Cone........................ .08
713 Russ Swan .... .05
714 Mark Guthrie .... .05
715 Checklist............................. .05
716 *Al Martin*........................... .20
717 Randy Knorr...................... .07
718 Mike Stanley...................... .07
719 Rick Sutcliffe .... .07
721 Chipper Jones .... .30
723 Tom Henke........................ .08
725 Harold Baines.................... .07
726 Scott Sanderson .... .06
728 Bryan Harvey .... .08
730 *Eric Young*....................... .20
731 Dave Weathers (FC) .... .12
737 *Nigel Wilson* .... .80
739 Jeff Reardon..................... .07
740 Willie Blair .... .05
744 Rob Natal .... .08
750 Gary Scott .... .08
752 Armando Reynoso .... .10
761 Pedro Castellano (FC) .... .12
762 Chuck Carr .... .08
764 Andres Galarraga............. .10
765 Jeff Conine .... .10
766 Ted Power......................... .05
767 Butch Henry .... .05

768	Steve Decker	.05
769	Storm Davis	.05
770	Vinny Castilla	.05
771	Junior Felix	.05
772	Walt Terrell	.05
773	*Brad Ausmus*	.15
776	Charlie Hayes	.08
777	Jack Armstrong	.06
778	Dennis Rasmussen	.05
779	Darren Holmes	.05

780	*Alex Arias*	.10
782	Javy Lopez (FC)	.35
783	Dante Bichette	.07
784	John Johnstone (FC)	.20
787	Jeromy Burnitz	.15
788	Michael Huff	.05
789	Anthony Telford	.05
790	Jerald Clark	.05
791	Joel Johnston	.05
792	*David Nied*	.75

1993 FLEER

Fleer released its 720-card 1993 set in two 360-card series. Many random insert cards can be found in packs including Golden Moments, All-Stars, Prospects, and Pro-Visions. Inserts commonly sold in the $1-$4 range. Rookie Sensations were once again randomly inserted in cello packs. Kenny Lofton and Chad Curtis were among the rookies featured and among the highest priced in the $8-$10 range. Team Leaders cards were inserted in Rack Packs. Tom Glavine was the subject of a special 15-card insert set. The regular issue cards feature silver borders and team color-coded stripes on the front. The flip sides are horizontal and feature an additional player photo and statistics. The cards are checklisted alphabetically and according to teams.

		MINT
Complete set		**$30.00**
Commons		**.04**

1	Steve Avery	$ .07
2	Sid Bream	.04
3	Ron Gant	.08
4	Tom Glavine	.12
5	Brian Hunter	.08
6	Ryan Klesko (FC)	.25
7	Charlie Leibrandt	.04
8	Kent Mercker	.04
9	*David Nied* (FC)	.80
10	Otis Nixon	.06
11	Greg Olson	.04
12	Terry Pendleton	.08
13	Deion Sanders	.15
14	John Smoltz	.08
15	Mike Stanton	.04

16	Mike Wohlers	.08
17	Paul Assenmacher	.04
18	Steve Buechele	.04
19	Shawon Dunston	.06
20	Mark Grace	.08
21	Derrick May	.10
22	Chuck McElroy	.04
23	Mike Morgan	.06
24	Rey Sanchez	.10
25	Ryne Sandberg	.20
26	Bob Scanlan	.04
27	Sammy Sosa	.06
28	Rick Wilkins	.06
29	*Bobby Ayala* (FC)	.15
30	Tim Belcher	.06
31	*Jeff Branson* (FC)	.12
32	Norm Charlton	.08
33	*Steve Foster* (FC)	.12
34	Willie Greene (FC)	.12
35	Chris Hammond	.06

1993 Fleer

197 Tim Salmon

138	Tony Gwynn	.12
143	Fred McGriff	.10
144	Jose Melendez	.08
146	Frank Seminara	.08
147	Gary Sheffield	.12
149	*Dan Walters*	.10
150	Rod Beck	.06
154	Will Clark	.15
155	Royce Clayton	.08
157	Darren Lewis	.08
159	Willie McGee	.06
160	Cory Snyder	.06
161	Bill Swift	.06
163	Brady Anderson	.10
164	Glenn Davis	.06
165	Mike Devereaux	.08
167	Leo Gomez	.06
168	Chris Hoiles	.08
169	Ben McDonald	.08
172	Mike Mussina	.25
173	Gregg Olson	.08
174	Arthur Rhodes	.10
176	Ellis Burks	.08
177	Roger Clemens	.25
178	Scott Cooper	.08
181	*Paul Quantrill* (FC)	.12
182	Jody Reed	.05
183	*John Valentin*	.12
184	Mo Vaughn	.08
185	Frank Viola	.08
186	Bob Zupcic	.08
187	Jim Abbott	.08
189	*Damion Easley*	.15
190	Junior Felix	.06
191	Chuck Finley	.06
192	Joe Grahe	.06
193	Bryan Harvey	.06
194	Mark Langston	.08
197	*Tim Salmon*	1.00
200	George Bell	.08
201	Alex Fernandez	.08
203	Ozzie Guillen	.06
204	Lance Johnson	.06
206	Kirk McCaskill	.05
207	Jack McDowell	.10
209	Tim Raines	.08
210	Frank Thomas	.70
211	Robin Ventura	.12
212	Sandy Alomar, Jr.	.10

210 Frank Thomas

213	Carlos Baerga	.12
215	Thomas Howard	.06
216	Mark Lewis	.08
218	Kenny Lofton	.20
219	Charles Nagy	.15
220	Steve Olin	.06
221	Paul Sorrento	.06
222	Jim Thome	.10
223	Mark Whiten	.10
224	Milt Cuyler	.06
225	Rob Deer	.06
226	*John Doherty*	.12
227	Cecil Fielder	.12
228	Travis Fryman	.15
229	Mike Henneman	.06
230	*John Kiely*	.12
231	*Kurt Knudsen*	.12
232	Scott Livingstone	.10
233	Tony Phillips	.08
234	Mickey Tettleton	.08
235	Kevin Appier	.08
236	George Brett	.12
238	Gregg Jeffries	.10
239	Wally Joyner	.10
240	*Kevin Koslofski*	.12
242	Brian McRae	.08
243	Rusty Meacham	.08
244	Keith Miller	.06

709 Juan Gonzalez

431 Nigel Wilson

551 Cal Ripken, Jr.

571 Chad Curtis

690 Nolan Ryan

1993 FLEER FINAL EDITION

Fleer ended its update set tradition in 1993 with the release of a 300-card Final Edition set. The set features traded players, free agents, rookies, and the expansion team players. Cards were sold only as complete boxed sets—available through hobby dealers. The cards are designed very much like the regular 1993 Fleer cards, but are numbered with an "F" designation. Cliff Floyd, Aaron Sele, and Darrell Whitmore are among the top players featured in the set. A 10-card "Diamond Tribute" set is included with the Final Edition set. Wade Boggs, George Brett, Andre Dawson, Carlton Fisk, Paul Molitor, Nolan Ryan, Lee Smith, Ozzie Smith, Dave Winfield, and Robin Yount are the veterans to look for in this set.

		MINT
Complete set		**$25.00**
Commons		**.07**

92 Cliff Floyd

3	Greg Maddux	$ .15
4	Greg McMichael (FC)	.35
5	Tony Tarasco (FC)	.35
11	Matt Walbeck (FC)	.25
12	Turk Wendell (FC)	.25
15	Roberto Kelly	.15
17	Kevin Mitchell	.12
18	Jeff Reardon	.12
19	John Roper (FC)	.20
24	Pedro Castellano (FC)	.20
28	Scott Fredrickson (FC)	.25
29	Jay Gainer (FC)	.15
30	Andres Galarraga	.15
32	Ryan Hawblitzel	.15
33	Charlie Hayes	.15
36	David Nied	.50
37	J. Owens (FC)	.25
38	Lance Painter (FC)	.20
39	Jeff Parrett	.07
40	Steve Reed	.07
41	Armondo Reynoso	.12
43	Danny Sheaffer (FC)	.20
44	Keith Shepherd (FC)	.15
47	Eric Young	.25
49	Alex Arias	.15
56	Chuck Carr	.20
57	Jeff Conine	.25
59	Orestes Destrade	.20
66	Mitch Lyden (FC)	.20
67	Bob Natal (FC)	.25
68	Scott Pose	.20
71	Gary Sheffield	.25
72	Matt Turner (FC)	.20
74	Darrell Whitmore (FC)	.70
75	Nigel Wilson (FC)	.60
81	Omar Daal	.25
82	Raul Mondesi	.20
88	Tavo Alvarez (FC)	.20

150 Barry Bonds

204 Manny Ramirez

238	David McCarty (FC)	.60	**256**	Scott Lydy (FC)	.25
239	Pat Meares (FC)	.25	**257**	Henry Mercedes	.20
240	George Tsamis (FC)	.25	**258**	Mike Mohler (FC)	.25
241	Dave Winfield	.20	**259**	Troy Neel	.30
242	Jim Abbott	.20	**268**	John Cummings (FC)	.25
243	Wade Boggs	.20	**270**	Mike Hampton (FC)	.20
244	Andy Cook (FC)	.20	**277**	Jeff Bronkey (FC)	.20
245	Russ Davis (FC)	.25	**278**	Benji Gil	.25
246	Mike Humphreys (FC)	.20	**283**	Jon Shave (FC)	.25
249	Bobby Munoz (FC)	.20	**286**	Scott Brow (FC)	.30
252	Dave Silvestri (FC)	.20	**287**	Willie Canate (FC)	.30
253	Marcos Armas (FC)	.40	**289**	Domingo Cedeno (FC)	.30
254	Brent Gates (FC)	.30	**297**	Woody Williams (FC)	.25

1993 SCORE

Due to the earlier arrival of its "Select" and "Pinnacle" editions, Score saved its lower-priced regular 1993 set for last. Score whittled the set down to 660 cards, but kept the offering filled with its traditionally popular subsets. These included the 20 All-Star caricature "big head cards," the 12-card "Dream Team," the six "award winners," and five "season and World Series highlights." Although card fronts contained much larger photos, Score maintained the same text-laden back design introduced in 1988. Blending two different product lines, each 16-card pack (suggested retail of 69 cents) contained one of 90 special "Score Select Stat Leaders" not found in the regular Select set. Additionally, a 28-card "Franchise" subset (not considered part of the regular set) saluted one star from each team. Odds of finding a "Franchise" card averaged one in every 24 packs. Super Packs, containing 35 cards and averaging $1.69, had a 30-card "Boys of Summer" premium subset, with cards appearing in at least one of every four Super Packs. No factory-collated "collector" sets were issued.

		MINT			
Complete set		**$30.00**	**8**	Bobby Bonilla	.10
Commons		**.04**	**9**	Carlos Baerga	.20
			10	Darren Daulton	.10
1	Ken Griffey, Jr.	$ .50	**11**	Travis Fryman	.25
2	Gary Sheffield	.15	**12**	Andy Van Slyke	.08
3	Frank Thomas	.80	**13**	Jose Canseco	.15
4	Ryne Sandberg	.20	**14**	Roberto Alomar	.20
5	Larry Walker	.15	**15**	Tom Glavine	.15
6	Cal Ripken, Jr.	.25	**16**	Barry Larkin	.10
7	Roger Clemens	.25	**17**	Gregg Jeffries	.10
			18	Craig Biggio	.08
			19	Shane Mack	.06

20	Brett Butler	.05
21	Dennis Eckersley	.10
22	Will Clark	.15
23	Don Mattingly	.15
24	Tony Gwynn	.10
25	Ivan Rodriguez	.20
26	Shawon Dunston	.05
27	Mike Mussina	.20
28	Marquis Grissom	.10
29	Charles Nagy	.06
30	Lenny Dykstra	.08
31	Cecil Fielder	.10
32	Jay Bell	.06
33	B.J. Surhoff	.05
34	Bob Tewksbury	.05
35	Danny Tartabull	.06
36	Terry Pendleton	.06
37	Jack Morris	.06
38	Hal Morris	.06
39	Luis Polonia	.05
40	Ken Caminiti	.05
41	Robin Ventura	.15
42	Darryl Strawberry	.10
43	Wally Joyner	.08
44	Fred McGriff	.10
45	Kevin Tapani	.05
46	Matt Williams	.10
47	Robin Yount	.10

1 Ken Griffey, Jr.

3 Frank Thomas

48	Ken Hill	.06
49	Edgar Martinez	.06
50	Mark Grace	.08
51	Juan Gonzalez	.50
52	Curt Schilling	.08
53	Doc Gooden	.08
54	Chris Hoiles	.08
55	Frank Viola	.06
56	Ray Lankford	.10
57	George Brett	.12
58	Kenny Lofton	.20
59	Nolan Ryan	.40
60	Mickey Tettleton	.08
61	John Smoltz	.08
62	Howard Johnson	.05
63	Eric Karros	.20
64	Rick Aguilera	.05
65	Steve Finley	.05
66	Mark Langston	.06
67	Bill Swift	.06
68	John Olerud	.25
69	Kevin McReynolds	.04
70	Jack McDowell	.08
71	Rickey Henderson	.10
72	Brian Harper	.06
73	Mike Morgan	.04
74	Rafael Palmeiro	.08
75	Dennis Martinez	.05

51 Juan Gonzalez

153 Jeff Brantley .... .04
154 Kevin Appier.................... .07
155 Darrin Jackson .... .05
156 Kelly Gruber .... .05
157 Royce Clayton................. .10
158 Chuck Finley .... .06
159 Jeff King .... .05
160 Greg Vaughn.................... .08
161 Geronimo Pena .... .04
162 Steve Farr .... .04
163 Jose Oquendo.................. .04
164 Mark Lewis .... .04
165 John Wetteland .... .06
166 Mike Henneman .... .05
167 Todd Hundley .... .04
168 Wes Chamberlain............. .05
169 Steve Avery..................... .12
170 Mike Devereaux .... .06
171 Reggie Sanders .... .12
172 Jay Buhner .... .08
173 Eric Anthony.................... .05
174 John Burkett .... .06
175 Tom Candiotti................... .04
176 Phil Plantier..................... .10
177 Doug Henry .... .04
178 Scott Leius .... .04
179 Kirt Manwaring .... .04
180 Jeff Parrett....................... .04
181 Don Slaught .... .04
182 Scott Radinsky .... .04
183 Luis Alicea .... .04
184 Tom Gordon .... .04
185 Rick Wilkins .... .06
186 Todd Stottlemyre............. .04
187 Moises Alou...................... .08
188 Joe Grahe .... .04
189 Jeff Kent .... .05
190 Bill Wegman .... .04
191 Kim Batiste .... .04
192 Matt Nokes .... .04
193 Mark Wohlers .... .06
194 Paul Sorrento .... .06
195 Chris Hammond .... .05
196 Scott Livingstone............. .04
197 Doug Jones .... .05
198 Scott Cooper .... .08
199 Ramon Martinez.............. .06
200 Dave Valle....................... .04
201 Mariano Duncan.............. .04

260 J.T. Snow

202 Ben McDonald................. .08
203 Darren Lewis .... .06
204 Kenny Rogers .... .05
205 Manuel Lee .... .04
206 Scott Erickson .... .04
207 Dan Gladden .... .04
208 Bob Welch .... .04
209 Greg Olson...................... .04
210 Dan Pasqua .... .04
211 Tim Wallach .... .05
212 Jeff Montgomery .... .05
213 Derrick May .... .08
214 Ed Sprague .... .06
215 David Haas .... .06
216 Darrin Fletcher .... .04
217 Brian Jordan .... .10
218 Jaime Navarro .... .05
219 Randy Velarde .... .04
220 Ron Gant.......................... .08
221 *Paul Quantrill*................... .10
222 *Damion Easley* .... .25
223 Charlie Hough .... .05
224 *Brad Brink* .... .04
225 *Barry Manuel*................... .08
226 *Kevin Koslofski*............... .07
227 *Ryan Thompson*............... .12
228 *Mike Munoz*..................... .05
229 *Dan Wilson*...................... .08

286 Mike Piazza

346 Tim Salmon

286	Mike Piazza	2.50
287	Mike Trombley	.10
288	Jim Pena	.08
289	Bob Ayrault	.06
290	Henry Mercedes	.10
291	Bob Wickman	.20
292	Jacob Brumfield	.06
293	David Hulse	.15
294	Ryan Klesko	.25
295	Doug Linton	.06
296	Steve Cooke	.15
297	Eddie Zosky	.05
298	Gerald Williams	.06
299	Jonathan Hurst	.10
300	Larry Carter	.10
301	William Pennyfeather	.08
302	Cesar Hernandez	.06
303	Steve Hosey	.10
304	Blas Minor	.07
305	Jeff Grotewald	.05
306	Bernardo Brito	.05
307	Rafael Bournigal	.20
308	Jeff Branson	.06
309	Tom Quinlan	.15
310	Pat Gomez	.12
311	Sterling Hitchcock	.25
312	Kent Bottenfield	.10
313	Alan Trammell	.06

553 David Nied

488 B.J. Wallace

314	Cris Colon	.08
315	Paul Wagner	.08
316	Matt Maysey	.05
317	Mike Stanton	.05
318	Rick Trlicek	.07
319	Kevin Rogers	.10
320	Mark Clark	.05
321	Pedro Martinez	.10
322	Al Martin	.20
323	Mike Macfarlane	.05
324	Rey Sanchez	.05
325	Roger Pavlik	.08
326	Troy Neel	.10
327	Kerry Woodson	.05
328	Wayne Kirby	.08
329	Ken Ryan	.15
330	Jesse Levis	.08
331	James Austin	.04
332	Dan Walters	.04
333	Brian Williams	.04
334	Wil Cordero	.10
335	Bret Boone	.25
336	Hipolito Pichardo	.04
337	Pat Mahomes	.10
338	Andy Stankiewicz	.04
339	Jim Bullinger	.04
340	Archi Cianfrocco	.06
343	Pat Hentgen	.08

1993 Score

586 Eric Young

344	Dave Nilsson	.10
345	Mike Perez	.05
346	Tim Salmon	1.00
347	Tim Wakefield	.15
349	Donovan Osborne	.10
351	Sam Militello	.15
354	Chad Curtis	.20
356	Dave Fleming	.10
357	Pat Listach	.15
359	John Vander Wal	.05
360	Arthur Rhodes	.05
362	Bob Zupcic	.06
363	Mel Rojas	.05
364	Jim Thome	.10
367	Mitch Williams	.07
368	Cal Eldred	.15
369	Stan Belinda	.05
370	Pat Kelly	.05
371	Rheal Cormier	.05
372	Juan Guzman	.15
373	Damon Berryhill	.05
375	Norm Charlton	.05
376	Roberto Hernandez	.07
377	Scott Kamieniecki	.05
378	Rusty Meacham	.04
379	Kurt Stillwell	.04
380	Lloyd McClendon	.04
381	Mark Leonard	.04

382	Jerry Browne	.04
383	Glenn Davis	.05
384	Randy Johnson	.08
385	Mike Greenwell	.06
387	George Bell	.06
388	Steve Olin	.06
390	Mark Gardner	.05
391	Rod Beck	.08
394	Julio Franco	.06
395	Pete Harnisch	.05
396	Sid Bream	.05
402	Jeff Conine	.08
405	Jerald Clark	.05
406	Vince Horsman	.05
407	Kevin Mitchell	.08
411	Charlie Hayes	.07
412	Alex Fernandez	.06
413	Jeff Russell	.05
414	Jody Reed	.05
415	Mickey Morandini	.05
416	Darnell Coles	.04
417	Xavier Hernandez	.05
418	Steve Sax	.04
419	Joe Girardi	.04
420	Mike Fetters	.04
421	Danny Jackson	.05
423	Tim Belcher	.05
425	Junior Felix	.05

11 Travis Fryman

428	Dante Bichette	.06
430	Darryl Kile	.06
431	Lonnie Smith	.05
433	Reggie Jefferson	.06
436	Duane Ward	.06
438	Roberto Kelly	.08
439	Paul O'Neill	.08
440	Alan Mills	.04
441	Roger Mason	.04
442	Gary Pettis	.04
443	Steve Lake	.04
444	Gene Larkin	.04
445	Larry Anderson	.04
446	Doug Dascenzo	.04
447	Daryl Boston	.04
448	John Candelaria	.04
452	Tim Naehring	.05
454	Joey Cora	.05
458	Terry Jorgensen	.06
464	Tommy Greene	.06
468	Greg Myers	.05
469	Kirk McCaskill	.05
471	Lenny Webster	.05
472	Francisco Cabrera	.04
473	Turner Ward	.04
475	Al Osuna	.04
474	Dwayne Henry	.04
476	Craig Wilson	.04
477	Chris Nabholz	.04
478	Rafael Belliard	.04
479	Terry Leach	.04
480	Tim Teufel	.04
481	Dennis Eckersley	.06
482	Barry Bonds	.15
483	Dennis Eckersley	.06
484	Greg Maddux	.08
485	Pat Listach	.10
486	Eric Karros	.15
487	Jamie Arnold	.15
488	B.J. Wallace	.40
489	Derek Jeter	.35
490	Jason Kendall	.25
491	Rick Helling	.15
492	Derek Wallace	.20
493	Sean Lowe	.12
494	Shannon Stewart	.25
495	Benji Grigsby	.20
496	Todd Steverson	.20
497	Dan Serafini	.15

494 Shannon Stewart

498	Michael Tucker	.60
499	Chris Roberts	.20
500	Pete Janicki	.20
501	Jeff Schmidt	.10
502	Edgar Martinez	.08
504	Ken Griffey, Jr.	.30
505	Kirby Puckett	.12
506	Joe Carter	.10
507	Ivan Rodriguez	.10
508	Jack Morris	.05
509	Dennis Eckersley	.06
510	Frank Thomas	.40
511	Roberto Alomar	.10
512	Mickey Morandini	.06
513	Dennis Eckersley	.06
514	Jeff Reardon	.05
515	Danny Tartabull	.05
516	Bip Roberts	.05
517	George Brett	.10
518	Robin Yount	.10
520	Ed Sprague	.10
521	Dave Winfield	.10
522	Ozzie Smith	.10
523	Barry Bonds	.12
524	Andy Van Slyke	.06
525	Tony Gwynn	.10
526	Darren Daulton	.10
527	Greg Maddux	.10

6 Cal Ripken, Jr.

528	Fred McGriff	.10
529	Lee Smith	.05
530	Ryne Sandberg	.12
531	Gary Sheffield	.10
532	Ozzie Smith	.06
533	Kirby Puckett	.12
534	Gary Sheffield	.12
535	Andy Van Slyke	.06
536	Ken Griffey, Jr.	.25
537	Ivan Rodriguez	.15
538	Charles Nagy	.05
539	Tom Glavine	.12
540	Dennis Eckersley	.06
541	Frank Thomas	.75
542	Roberto Alomar	.12
543	Sean Berry	.05
545	Chuck Carr	.08
547	Gary Scott	.05
550	Kirby Puckett	.15
552	Andre Dawson	.10
553	David Nied	.70
556	Sid Fernandez	.05
557	Mark McGwire	.15
558	Bryan Harvey	.06
559	Harold Reynolds	.05
560	Barry Bonds	.25
561	Eric Wedge	.15
562	Ozzie Smith	.10

563	Rick Sutcliffe	.05
564	Jeff Reardon	.05
565	Alex Arias	.12
566	Greg Swindell	.05
568	Pete Incaviglia	.05
570	Eric Davis	.06
572	Tony Fernandez	.05
573	Steve Reed	.10
574	Cory Snyder	.05
575	Joe Carter	.12
576	Greg Maddux	.10
577	Bert Blyleven	.05
579	Carlton Fisk	.10
580	Doug Drabek	.05
583	Chili Davis	.05
585	Harold Baines	.05
586	Eric Young	.20
587	Lance Parrish	.04
588	Juan Bell	.04
589	Bob Ojeda	.04
590	Joe Orsulak	.04
591	Benito Santiago	.06
592	Wade Boggs	.10
593	Robby Thompson	.06
595	Hensley Meulens	.05
596	Lou Whitaker	.06
597	Dale Murphy	.05
598	Paul Molitor	.05
599	Greg W. Harris	.04
600	Darren Holmes	.04
602	Tom Henke	.06
606	Kirby Puckett	.20
607	Randy Myers	.06
608	Ruben Sierra	.10
609	Wilson Alvarez	.08
612	Tom Brunansky	.05
613	Willie Randolph	.05
614	Tony Phillips	.06
615	Candy Maldonado	.05
616	Chris Bosio	.05
617	Bret Barbarie	.05
618	Scott Sanderson	.05
619	Ron Darling	.05
620	Dave Winfield	.10
622	Greg Hibbard	.05
626	Terry Steinbach	.06
631	Dave Magadan	.05
632	Scott Fletcher	.05
633	Cris Carpenter	.05

634	Kevin Maas	.06	**649** Andres Galarraga	.08
635	Todd Worrell	.05	**650** Vince Coleman	.05
636	Rob Deer	.05	**651** Rob Dibble	.05
637	Dwight Smith	.05	**654** David Cone	.06
639	Jimmy Key	.08	**655** Jack Armstrong	.05
641	Mike Moore	.05	**656** Dave Stewart	.06
642	Pat Borders	.05	**658** Tim Raines	.08
646	Jim Abbott	.10	**659** Walt Weiss	.05
648	David Wells	.05	**660** Jose Lind	.04

1993 TOPPS

Topps inserted a gold card in every 15-card pack and Black Gold cards were randomly inserted. A full set of gold cards was issued, but checklist cards were replaced in the gold set by additional player cards. The two inserts helped the popularity of the 1993 Topps set. This 825-card set was released in two series. Series I featured cards 1-396 and Series II included cards 397-825. The cards feature white borders surrounding full-color action photos. The backs feature a player close-up photo, statistics, and career highlights. Pre-production samples and sheets promoting the cards were released. The pre-production cards sold in the 50-cent-$3 range. The Black Gold cards sold in the $3-$10 range. Barry Bonds and Ryne Sandberg are among the superstars featured in the 22-card Black Gold insert set. Like in past years, Topps is using the same card style for all its major sports cards.

		MINT		
Complete set		$30.00		
Commons (1-792)		.03		

			30	Fred McGriff	.10
			32	Don Mattingly	.12
			33	B.J. Wallace	.12
			34	Juan Gonzalez	.50
			35	John Smoltz	.08
			36	Scott Servais	.08
1	● Robin Yount	$ .10	**37**	Lenny Webster	.08
2	Barry Bonds	.25	**40**	Ozzie Smith	.10
3	Ryne Sandberg	.25	**41**	Alex Fernandez	.08
4	Roger Clemens	.25	**45**	Dave Fleming	.10
5	Tony Gwynn	.12	**46**	*Eric Fox*	.12
6	*Jeff Tackett*	.12	**50**	Roberto Alomar	.20
10	Will Clark	.15	**52**	Bobby Bonilla	.10
11	Eric Karros	.25	**56**	*Chad Mottola* (FC)	1.00
15	Marquis Grissom	.08	**58**	Jose Melendez	.08
17	Dave Hollins	.08	**60**	Roberto Kelly	.08
20	*Tim Salmon*	1.00	**67**	Felix Jose	.08
27	*Carlos Garcia*	.15	**69**	*John Vander Wal*	.12

20 Tim Salmon

70	Roberto Hernandez	.08
72	*Jeff Grotewold*	.12
75	Juan Guzman	.10
76	Kevin Appier	.08
80	Cecil Fielder	.10
83	Reggie Sanders	.15
85	Sandy Alomar	.08
90	Scott Erickson	.08
93	*Pedro Astacio* (FC)	.15
95	Larry Walker	.10
98	*Derek Jeter* (FC)	.30
99	*Mike Williams* (FC)	.15
100	Mark McGwire	.15
101	*Jim Bullinger*	.12
102	Brian Hunter	.08
104	*Mike Butcher* (FC)	.15
105	Gregg Jefferies	.08
106	Howard Johnson	.08
107	*John Kiely*	.12
110	Barry Larkin	.08
117	Eddie Taubensee	.08
118	David Justice	.10
119	Pedro Munoz	.10
120	Ramon Martinez	.08
123	Moises Alou	.08
126	*Bob Ayrault* (FC)	.12
131	Dave Winfield	.10
132	*Preston Wilson* (FC)	.50

135	Mickey Tettleton	.08
140	Gary Sheffield	.10
145	*Eric Young* (FC)	.15
149	Rheal Cormier	.08
150	Frank Thomas	.70
151	*Archi Cianfrocco*	.15
155	Dennis Eckersley	.08
158	*Kevin Koslofski* (FC)	.12
159	*Doug Linton* (FC)	.12
161	Chad McDonnell	.30
163	*Tim Wakefield*	.15
166	*Tim Scott* (FC)	.12
170	David Justice	.20
172	*Jeff Reboulet* (FC)	.12
179	Ken Griffey, Jr.	.50
180	Darren Daulton	.08
181	John Jaha	.12
183	Greg Maddux	.08
184	*Damion Easley* (FC)	.20
185	Jack Morris	.08
188	Sid Fernandez	.08
189	Tony Phillips	.08
190	Doug Drabek	.08
191	Sean Lowe	.15
193	*Steve Foster* (FC)	.15
196	Pat Kelly	.08
197	*Jeff Frye* (FC)	.12
200	Kirby Puckett	.20
205	Gary Carter	.08
207	Paul Molitor	.08
210	Mark Langston	.08
215	*Pat Howell* (FC)	.12
217	Kevin Mitchell	.08
218	Ben McDonald	.08
219	Bip Roberts	.08
220	Benny Santiago	.08
221	Carlos Baerga	.20
222	Bernie Williams	.10
223	*Roger Pavlik* (FC)	.20
225	Matt Williams	.08
226	Willie Banks	.08
227	Jeff Bagwell	.12
228	Tom Goodwin	.08
229	Mike Perez	.08
230	Carlton Fisk	.08
231	John Wetteland	.08
232	Tino Martinez	.08
233	*Rick Greene* (FC)	.12
236	*Kevin Campbell*	.10

34 Juan Gonzalez

56 Chad Mottola

132 Preston Wilson

750	Rickey Henderson	.10	795	Deion Sanders .10
752	Pat Hentgen	.12	797	Brad Pennington .10
754	Brian Jordan	.10	799	*Jim Edmonds* (FC) .20
767	*Rich Ireland* (FC)	.12	800	*Shawn Jeter* (FC) .10
770	Robin Ventura	.12	803	*Ed Pierce* (FC) .12
774	*Curtis Leskanic* (FC)	.12	804	Jose Valentin .20
780	Jim Abbott	.10	806	*Mark Hutton* .15
782	*Reynal Mendoza/Dan Roman* (FC)	.20	807	Troy Neel .12
			808	Bret Boone .15
786	1993 Prospects *(Mike Christopher, Ken Ryan, Aaron Taylor, Gus Gandarillas* (FC)	.20	809	*Cris Colon* (FC) .10
			810	*Domingo Martinez* (FC) .15
			811	Javy Lopez .30
			812	*Matt Walbeck* (FC) .12
787	*Mike Matthews* (FC)	.20	815	*Billy Ashley* .30
789	Jeff Conine	.10	819	William Pennyfeather .10
791	Pat Rapp	.10	822	Kevin Rogers .10

1993 TOPPS TRADED

For the thirteenth consecutive year Topps released a 132-card Traded set. Traded players, free agents, rookies, Team U.S.A., and the expansion teams are featured. The cards are styled like the regular 1993 Topps release. National League Rookie of the Year Mike Piazza, Barry Bonds, and Aaron Sele are the top players included in the set. The cards are numbered on the back and include a "T" designation along with the number. The set was available as a complete boxed set only and was distributed through hobby shops and dealers. Many of the rookies featured in the set were included in prospect cards in the regular 1993 Topps issue.

		MINT
Complete set		**$15.00**
Commons		.05

1	Barry Bonds	$ .80	9	Tony Fernandez	.06
2	Rich Renteria	.05	10	Jay Gainer (FC)	.20
3	Aaron Sele (FC)	1.00	11	Orestes Destrade	.10
4	Carlton Loewer (FC)	.25	12	A.J. Hinch (FC)	.25
5	Erik Pappas (FC)	.15	13	Bobby Munoz	.20
6	Greg McMichael (FC)	.25	14	Tom Henke	.06
7	Freddie Benavides	.05	15	Rob Butler (FC)	.10
8	Kirk Gibson	.08	16	Gary Wayne	.05
			17	David McCarty (FC)	.50
			19	Todd Helton (FC)	.20
			20	Mark Whiten	.08
			21	Ricky Gutierrez (FC)	.15
			22	Dustin Hermanson (FC)	.20

3 Aaron Sele

24 Mike Piazza

92	Andre Dawson	.15	113 Scott Pose (FC)	.15
93	Andy Barkett (FC)	.15	114 Dave Stewart	.10
94	Doug Drabek	.08	115 Russ Johnson (FC)	.20
97	Danny Graves (FC)	.20	116 Armando Reynoso	.08
98	Pat Meares (FC)	.15	118 Woody Williams (FC)	.10
99	Mike Lansing (FC)	.25	119 Tim Bogar (FC)	.20
100	Marcos Armas (FC)	.25	120 Bob Scafa (FC)	.20
101	Darren Grass (FC)	.20	122 Gregg Jefferies	.15
102	Chris Jones	.08	123 Norm Charlton	.06
103	Ken Ryan	.15	124 Bret Wagner (FC)	.20
104	Ellis Burks	.10	125 David Cone	.10
105	Bobby Kelly	.12	126 Daryl Boston	.05
107	Paul Wilson	.20	127 Tim Wallach	.06
108	Rob Natal (FC)	.10	128 Mike Martin (FC)	.15
109	Paul Wagner	.10	129 John Cummings (FC)	.15
110	Jeromy Burnitz	.45	130 Ryan Bowen	.06
112	Kevin Mitchell	.10	131 John Powell (FC)	.15

1993 UPPER DECK

Upper Deck introduced a new look in 1993 and released its 840-card set in two series. Keeping up with its tradition of subsets, Upper Deck inserted Future Heroes, Home Run Heroes, Clutch Performers, On Deck, Willy Mays Heroes, Then and Now, and Triple Crown cards in its products. Triple Crown inserts proved to be the most popular and valuable, selling in the $4-$12 range. These cards were available only in hobby foil packs. A special commemorative card honoring the 3,000th hit of George Brett and Robin Yount was also randomly inserted into packs. The card style still featured the white borders, but eliminated the baseline design and displayed the player's name in script. The backs are printed vertically and feature a close-up photo.

	MINT			
Complete set	$45.00	7	Dan Smith (FC)	.20
Commons (1-420)	.05	8	Kevin Rogers (FC)	.20
		9	Nigel Wilson (FC)	1.00
		10	Joe Vitko (FC)	.15
2	Mike Piazza (FC)	$ 4.00	11 Tim Costo	.15
3	Rene Arocha (FC)	.60	12 Alan Embree (FC)	.15
4	Willie Greene (FC)	.15	13 Jim Tatum (FC)	.25
5	Manny Alexander (FC)	.25	14 Cris Colon (FC)	.15
6	Dan Wilson	.12	15 Steve Hosey (FC)	.12
			16 Sterling Hitchcock (FC)	.30

2 Mike Piazza

27 Dave Nied

25 Tim Salmon

81	Harold Baines	.08
82	Lee Smith	.08
85	Mark Gubicza	.06
86	Mickey Tettleton	.08
87	Bobby Witt	.06
88	Mark Lewis	.06
89	Kevin Appier	.08
91	Rafael Belliard	.05
92	Kenny Rogers	.05
93	Randy Velarde	.05
94	Luis Sojo	.05
95	Mark Leiter	.05
96	Jody Reed	.06
97	Pete Harnisch	.06
98	Tom Candiotti	.06
99	Mark Portugal	.05
100	Dave Valle	.05
101	Shawon Dunston	.08
102	B.J. Surhoff	.08
103	Jay Bell	.08
104	Sid Bream	.05
105	Checklist 1-105	.05
106	Mike Morgan	.05
107	Bill Doran	.05
108	Lance Blankenship	.05
109	Mark Lemke	.05
110	Brian Harper	.06
111	Brady Anderson	.08
112	Bip Roberts	.08
113	Mitch Williams	.08
114	Craig Biggio	.08
115	Eddie Murray	.08
121	Hal Morris	.08
123	Ivan Rodriguez	.20
124	Andy Van Slyke	.08
125	Roberto Alomar	.30
126	Robby Thompson	.06
127	Sammy Sosa	.06
128	Mark Langston	.06
129	Jerry Browne	.05
131	Frank Viola	.08
132	Leo Gomez	.08
133	Ramon Martinez	.10
134	Don Mattingly	.20
135	Roger Clemens	.30
136	Rickey Henderson	.15
137	Darren Daulton	.12
138	Ken Hill	.08
139	Ozzie Guillen	.08
140	Jerald Clark	.08
141	Dave Fleming	.15
142	Delino DeShields	.12
143	Matt Williams	.10
144	Larry Walker	.20
145	Ruben Sierra	.12
146	Ozzie Smith	.12
147	Chris Sabo	.08
148	*Carlos Hernandez* (FC)	.12
149	Pat Borders	.08
150	Orlando Merced	.08
151	Royce Clayton	.08
153	Dave Hollins	.10
154	Mike Greenwell	.08
155	Nolan Ryan	.70
156	Felix Jose	.08
158	Derek Bell	.10
161	*Pat Howell* (FC)	.15
163	Terry Pendleton	.10
164	Jack Morris	.10
165	Tony Gwynn	.15
166	Deion Sanders	.15
167	Mike Devereaux	.08
168	Ron Darling	.08
169	Orel Hershiser	.08
172	*Dan Walters* (FC)	.12
173	Darren Lewis	.08
174	Carlos Baerga	.12

23 J.T. Snow

9 Nigel Wilson

266 Juan Guzman

1993 Upper Deck

375 Cal Eldred